# ROAD Atlas

## Conte[nts]

### MAP LEGEN[D]

**ROADS/HIGHWAYS**
- INTERSTATE
- CONTROLLED ACCESS
- CONTROLLED ACCESS TOLL
- TOLL ROAD
- PRIMARY DIVIDED
- PRIMARY UNDIVIDED
- SECONDARY DIVIDED
- SECONDARY UNDIVIDED
- LOCAL DIVIDED
- LOCAL UNDIVIDED
- UNPAVED ROAD
- UNDER CONSTRUCTION
- TUNNEL
- PEDESTRIAN ONLY
- AUTO FERRY
- PASSENGER FERRY
- SCENIC BYWAY
- 10 DISTANCE BETWEEN MARKERS
- EXIT NUMBER-FREE/TOLL
- INTERCHANGE FULL/PARTIAL
- WELCOME/INFORMATION CENTER
- REST AREA/ SERVICE CENTER

**BOUNDARIES**
- INTERNATIONAL
- STATE
- COUNTY
- TIME ZONE
- CONTINENTAL DIVIDE

**ROAD SHIELDS**
- 95 95 INTERSTATE/BUSINESS
- 22 22 22 U.S./STATE/COUNTY
- 22 22 FOREST/INDIAN
- TRANS- CANADA
- 1 PROVINCIAL AUTOROUTE/ KING'S HIGHWAY
- 1 MEXICO
- 66 HISTORIC ROUTE 66
- VT 41 REFERENCE PAGE INDICATOR

**AREAS OF INTEREST**
- INDIAN
- MILITARY
- PARK
- FOREST
- GRASSLANDS
- HISTORIC
- INT'L/REGIONAL AIRPORT
- INCORPORATED CITY

**POINTS OF INTEREST**
- TOWN
- NATIONAL CAPITAL
- STATE/PROVINCIAL CAPITAL
- AAA/CAA CLUB LOCATION
- FEATURE OF INTEREST
- COLLEGE/UNIVERSITY
- CUSTOMS STATION
- HISTORIC
- LIGHTHOUSE
- MONUMENT/MEMORIAL
- STATE/PROVINCIAL PARK
- NATIONAL WILDLIFE REFUGE
- SKI AREA
- SPORTS COMPLEX
- DAM

**CITIES/TOWNS** are color-coded by size, showing where to find AAA Approved and Diamond rated lodgings or restaurants listed in the AAA TourBook guides and on AAA.com:
- ● Red - major destinations and capitals; many listings
- ● Black - destinations; some listings
- ● Grey - no listings

COPYRIGHT 2016 HERE

United States population figures - U.S. Census Bureau; Census 2010
Canadian population figures - Statistics Canada's 2011 GeoSuite, by permission of Canadian Minister of Industry.

**Printed in the United States**
Library of Congress 85-117512
*This atlas was printed on third-party certified sustainably forested paper.*

# Mileage Table

**The routes used to determine these mileages are not necessarily the shortest distance between cities, but represent the route considered the easiest drive for general travel.** Distances are shown in miles.

| City (rows) |
|---|
| Albany, NY |
| Albuquerque, NM |
| Atlanta, GA |
| Baltimore, MD |
| Billings, MT |
| Birmingham, AL |
| Boise, ID |
| Boston, MA |
| Buffalo, NY |
| Charleston, WV |
| Charlotte, NC |
| Cheyenne, WY |
| Chicago, IL |
| Cincinnati, OH |
| Cleveland, OH |
| Columbus, OH |
| Dallas, TX |
| Denver, CO |
| Des Moines, IA |
| Detroit, MI |
| El Paso, TX |
| Hartford, CT |
| Houston, TX |
| Indianapolis, IN |
| Jackson, MS |
| Kansas City, MO |
| Las Vegas, NV |
| Little Rock, AR |
| Los Angeles, CA |
| Louisville, KY |
| Memphis, TN |
| Miami, FL |
| Milwaukee, WI |
| Minneapolis, MN |
| Mobile, AL |
| Montgomery, AL |
| Nashville, TN |
| New Orleans, LA |
| New York City, NY |
| Norfolk, VA |
| Oklahoma City, OK |
| Omaha, NE |
| Orlando, FL |
| Philadelphia, PA |
| Phoenix, AZ |
| Pittsburgh, PA |
| Portland, ME |
| Portland, OR |
| Raleigh, NC |
| Reno, NV |
| Richmond, VA |
| Salt Lake City, UT |
| San Antonio, TX |
| San Diego, CA |
| San Francisco, CA |
| Seattle, WA |
| St. Louis, MO |
| Tampa, FL |
| Washington, DC |
| Wichita, KS |

Columns: Albany, NY; Albuquerque, NM; Anchorage, AK; Atlanta, GA; Atlantic City, NJ; Baltimore, MD; Billings, MT; Birmingham, AL; Bismarck, ND; Boise, ID; Boston, MA; Buffalo, NY; Calgary, AB; Charleston, SC; Charleston, WV; Charlotte, NC; Charlottetown, PE; Cheyenne, WY; Chicago, IL; Cincinnati, OH; Cleveland, OH; Columbus, OH; Concord, NH; Dallas, TX; Denver, CO; Des Moines, IA; Detroit, MI; Dover, DE; El Paso, TX; Halifax, NS; Hartford, CT; Houston, TX; Indianapolis, IN; Jackson, MS; Kansas City, MO; Las Vegas, NV; Little Rock, AR; Los Angeles, CA; Louisville, KY; Memphis, TN; Mexico City, DF; Miami, FL; Milwaukee, WI; Minneapolis, MN; Mobile, AL; Montgomery, AL; Montpelier, VT; Montréal, QC; Myrtle Beach, SC; Nashville, TN; New Orleans, LA; New York City, NY; Norfolk, VA; Oklahoma City, OK; Omaha, NE; Orlando, FL; Ottawa, ON; Philadelphia, PA; Phoenix, AZ; Pierre, SD; Pittsburgh, PA; Portland, ME; Portland, OR; Providence, RI; Raleigh, NC; Regina, SK; Reno, NV; Richmond, VA; Salt Lake City, UT; San Antonio, TX; San Diego, CA; San Francisco, CA; Savannah, GA; Seattle, WA; St. John, NB; St. Louis, MO; Tampa, FL; Toronto, ON; Vancouver, BC; Washington, DC; Whitehorse, YT; Wichita, KS; Winnipeg, MB; Yellowknife, NT

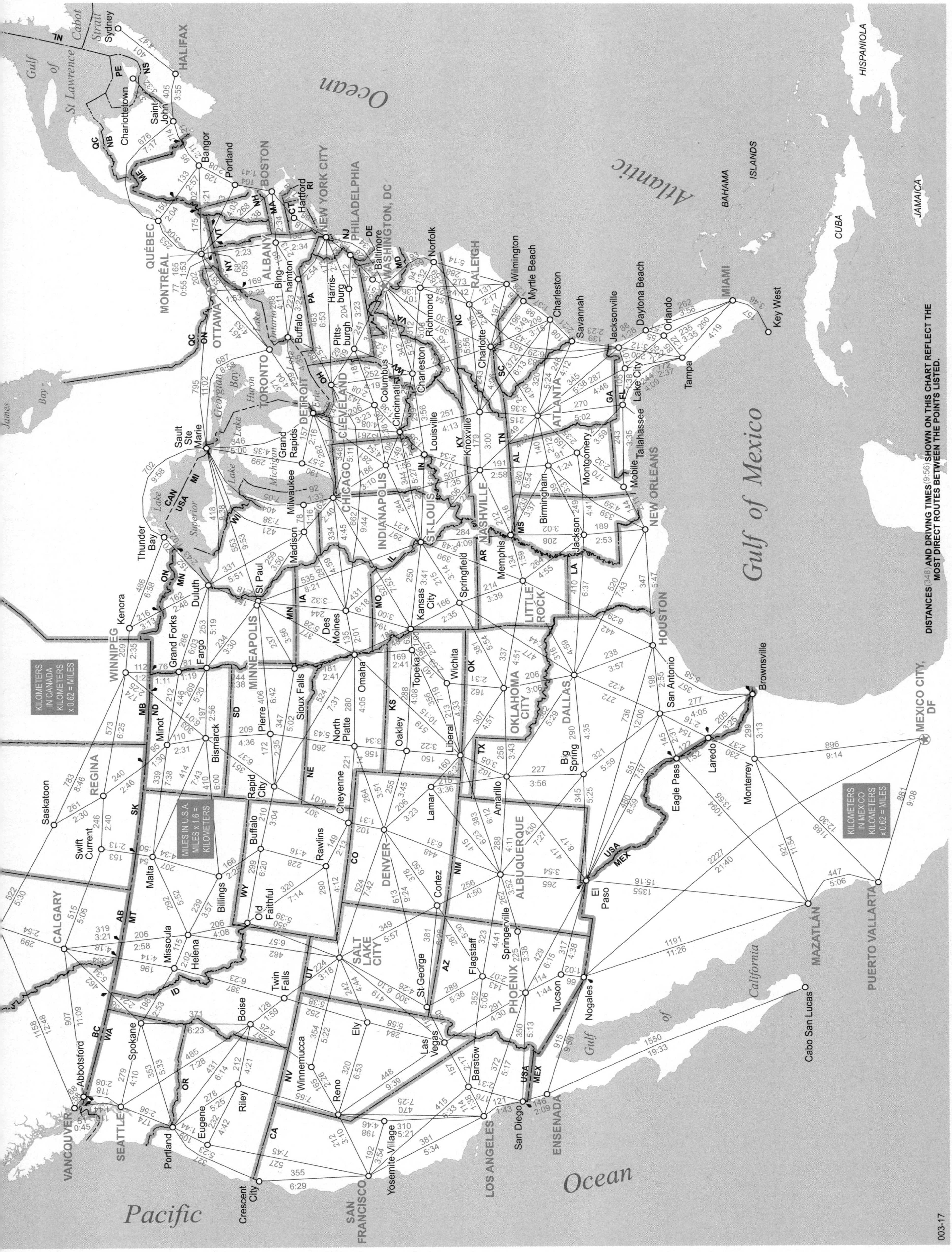
DISTANCES (348) AND DRIVING TIMES (9:56) SHOWN ON THIS CHART REFLECT THE MOST DIRECT ROUTES BETWEEN THE POINTS LISTED.
KILOMETERS IN CANADA KILOMETERS x 0.62 = MILES
MILES IN U.S.A. MILES x 1.6 = KILOMETERS
KILOMETERS IN MEXICO KILOMETERS x 0.62 = MILES
Pacific Ocean
Atlantic Ocean
Gulf of Mexico
Gulf of St Lawrence
Cabot Strait
Gulf of California
BAHAMA ISLANDS
CUBA
JAMAICA
HISPANIOLA
VANCOUVER
SEATTLE
Portland
Eugene
Crescent City
SAN FRANCISCO
Yosemite Village
LOS ANGELES
San Diego
ENSENADA
CALGARY
REGINA
WINNIPEG
Saskatoon
Swift Current
Kenora
Thunder Bay
Sault Ste Marie
TORONTO
OTTAWA
MONTRÉAL
QUÉBEC
HALIFAX
Saint John
Charlottetown
Sydney
BOSTON
NEW YORK CITY
PHILADELPHIA
WASHINGTON, DC
CHICAGO
DETROIT
CLEVELAND
INDIANAPOLIS
ST LOUIS
MINNEAPOLIS
DENVER
SALT LAKE CITY
ALBUQUERQUE
PHOENIX
DALLAS
HOUSTON
OKLAHOMA CITY
LITTLE ROCK
NASHVILLE
ATLANTA
RALEIGH
NEW ORLEANS
MIAMI
Key West
MEXICO CITY, DF
PUERTO VALLARTA
MAZATLÁN
Cabo San Lucas
003-17

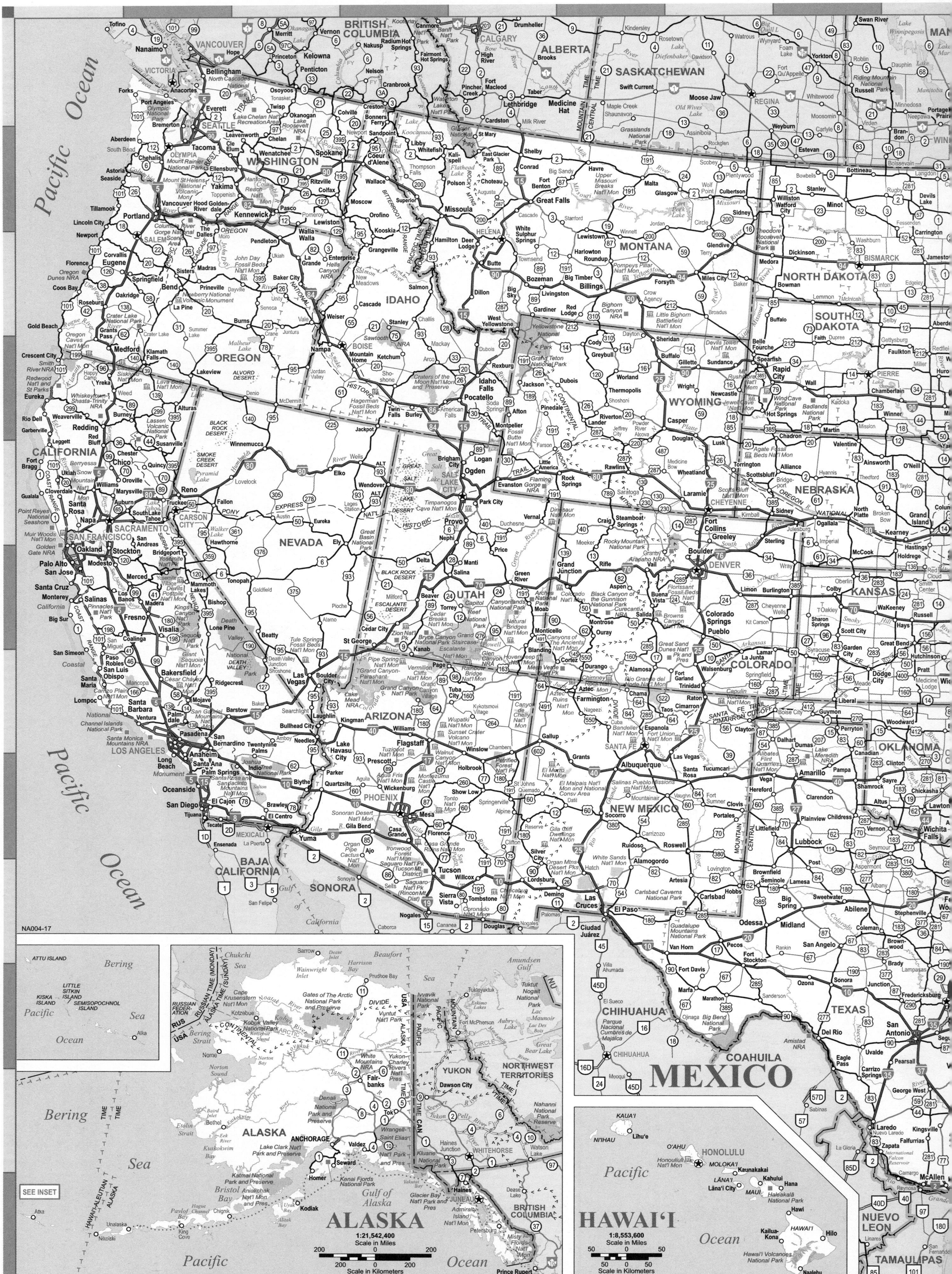
BRITISH COLUMBIA
ALBERTA
SASKATCHEWAN
WASHINGTON
OREGON
CALIFORNIA
NEVADA
IDAHO
MONTANA
WYOMING
UTAH
ARIZONA
COLORADO
NEW MEXICO
NORTH DAKOTA
SOUTH DAKOTA
NEBRASKA
KANSAS
OKLAHOMA
TEXAS
BAJA CALIFORNIA
SONORA
CHIHUAHUA
COAHUILA
NUEVO LEON
TAMAULIPAS
MEXICO
Pacific Ocean
Gulf of California
NA004-17
ALASKA
1:21,542,400
Scale in Miles
Scale in Kilometers
YUKON
NORTHWEST TERRITORIES
Bering Sea
Gulf of Alaska
SEE INSET
HAWAI'I
1:8,553,600
Scale in Miles
Scale in Kilometers
HONOLULU

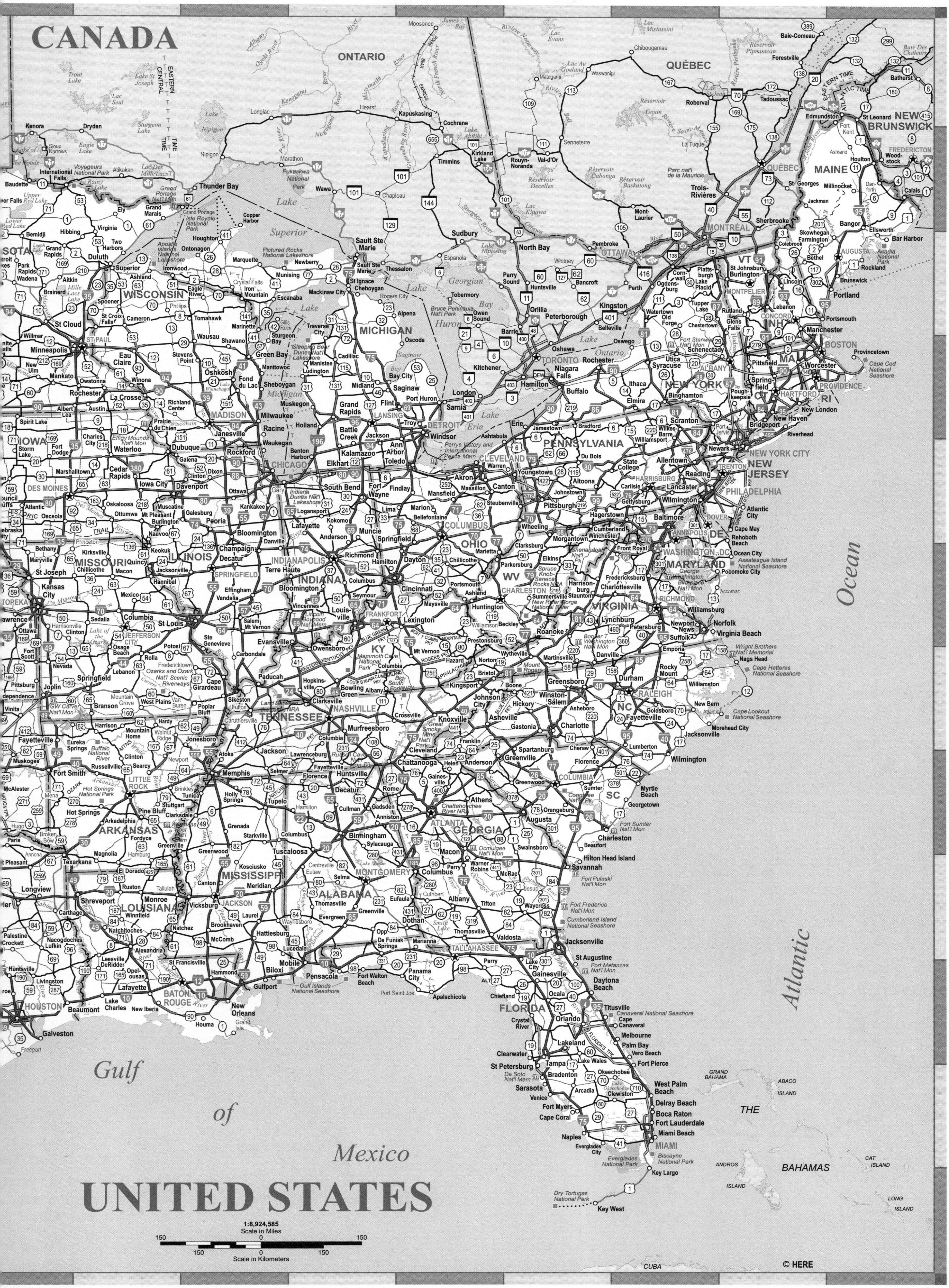

CANADA

UNITED STATES

Gulf

of

Mexico

1:8,924,585
Scale in Miles
150    0    150

150    0    150
Scale in Kilometers

© HERE

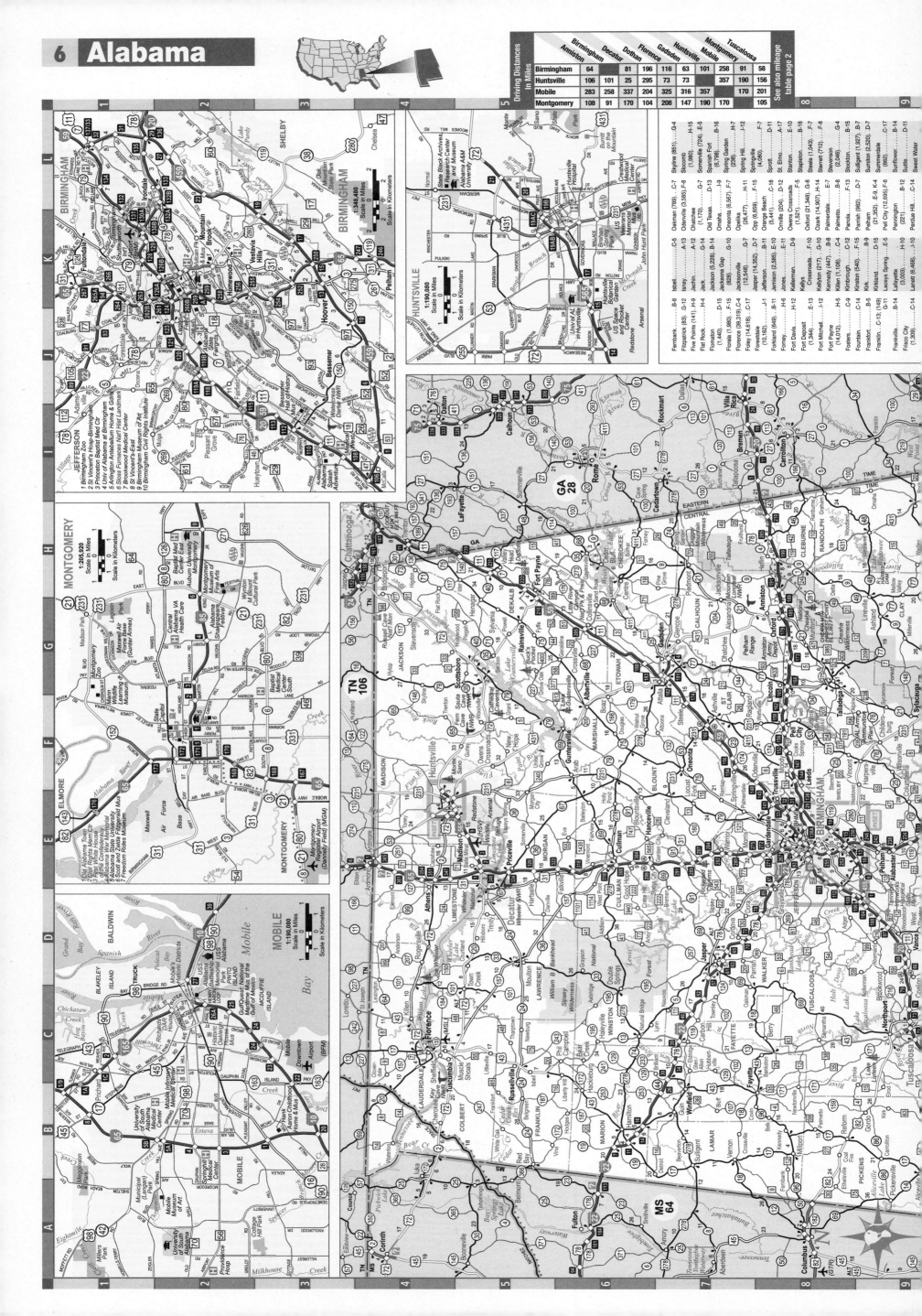

| Driving Distances In Miles | Anniston | Birmingham | Decatur | Dothan | Florence | Gadsden | Huntsville | Mobile | Montgomery | Tuscaloosa |
|---|---|---|---|---|---|---|---|---|---|---|
| Birmingham | 64 | | 81 | 196 | 116 | 63 | 101 | 258 | 91 | 58 |
| Huntsville | 106 | 101 | 25 | 295 | 73 | 73 | | 357 | 190 | 156 |
| Mobile | 283 | 258 | 337 | 204 | 325 | 316 | 357 | | 170 | 201 |
| Montgomery | 108 | 91 | 170 | 104 | 208 | 147 | 190 | 170 | | 105 |

See also mileage table page 2

Fernbank....B-8
Fitzpatrick (83)..G-12
Five Points (141)..H-9
Flat Rock....H-4
Flomaton (1,440)....D-15
Florala (1,980)...F-15
Florence (39,319)..C-4
Foley (14,618)...C-17
Forestdale (10,162)....J-1
Forkland (649)...B-11
Forney....H-6
Fort Davis....H-12
Fort Deposit (1,344)....E-13
Fort Mitchell....I-12
Fort Payne (14,012)....H-5
Fosters....C-9
Fountain....C-14
Frankfort....B-5
Franklin...C-13; (149) G-11
Frankville....B-14
Frisco City (1,309)....C-14
Isbell....C-5
Isney....A-13
Jachin....A-12
Jack....G-14
Jackson (5,228)..B-14
Jacksons Gap (828)....G-10
Jacksonville (12,548)....G-7
Jasper (14,352)...D-7
Jefferson....B-11
Jemison (2,585)..E-10
Jones....E-11
Kellerman....D-9
Kellys Crossroads....F-10
Kellyton (217)...G-10
Kennedy (447)....B-8
Killen (1,108)....C-4
Kimbrough....C-12
Kinston (540)....F-15
Kirk....B-9
Kirkland....D-15
Laceys Spring....E-5
Lafayette (3,003)....H-10
Lanett (6,468)....I-10
Oakman (789)...C-7
Odenville (3,585).F-8
Ohatchee (1,170)....G-7
Old Texas....D-13
Omaha....I-9
Oneonta (6,567)..F-7
Opelika (26,477)....H-11
Opp (6,659)....F-15
Orange Beach (5,441)....C-18
Orrville (204)...D-12
Owens Crossroads (1,521)....F-5
Oxford (21,348)..G-8
Ozark (14,907)..H-14
Palmerdale....E-7
Palmetto....B-8
Panola....F-13
Parrish (982)....D-7
Pelham (21,352)..E-9, K-4
Pell City (12,695).F-8
Pennington (221)....B-12
Perdue Hill....C-14
Skyline (851)....G-4
Slocomb (1,980)....H-15
Somerville (724)..E-5
Spanish Fort (6,798)....B-16
Spring Garden (238)....H-7
Spring Hill....I-12
Springville (4,080)....F-7
Sprott....D-11
St. Elmo....A-17
Stanton....E-10
Stapleton....B-16
Steele (1,043)...F-7
Sterrett (712)....F-8
Stevenson (2,046)....G-4
Stockton....B-15
Sulligent (1,927)..B-7
Sumiton (2,520)..D-7
Summerdale (862)....C-17
Sunflower....B-14
Suttle....D-11
Sweet Water

LEGEND
Interstate Highway (95)
Controlled Access Hwy
Controlled Access Hwy Toll
Wildlife Refuge
Nat'l/State Park
National Forest

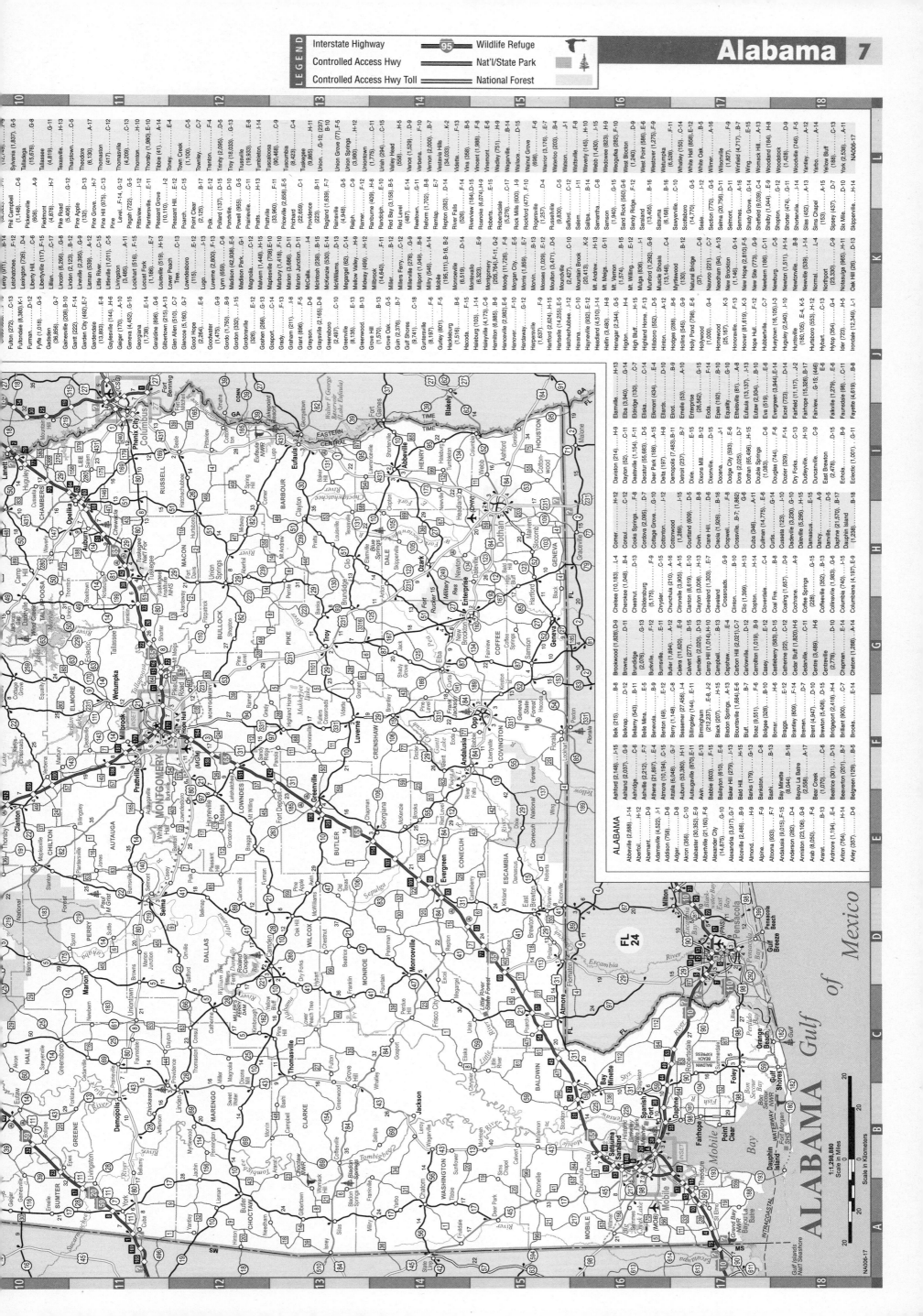

ALABAMA

NA006-17

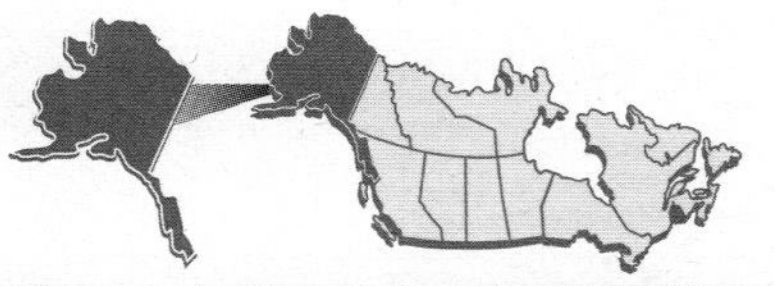

# ALASKA & Northwestern CANADA

1:6,019,200
Scale in Miles
100    0    100

Scale in Kilometers
100    0    100

## ALEUTIAN ISLANDS

1:11,088,000
Scale in Miles
100    0    100

Scale in Kilometers
100    0    100

### WHITEHORSE YT

1:95,040
Scale in Kilometers
0.3   0   0.3

0.3   0   0.3

MILES IN U.S
MILES x 1.6
KILOMETER

FOR ADJOINING AREA
SEE INSET MAP

NA008-17

PIPELINE ROAD CLOSED TO PUBLIC AT THIS POINT

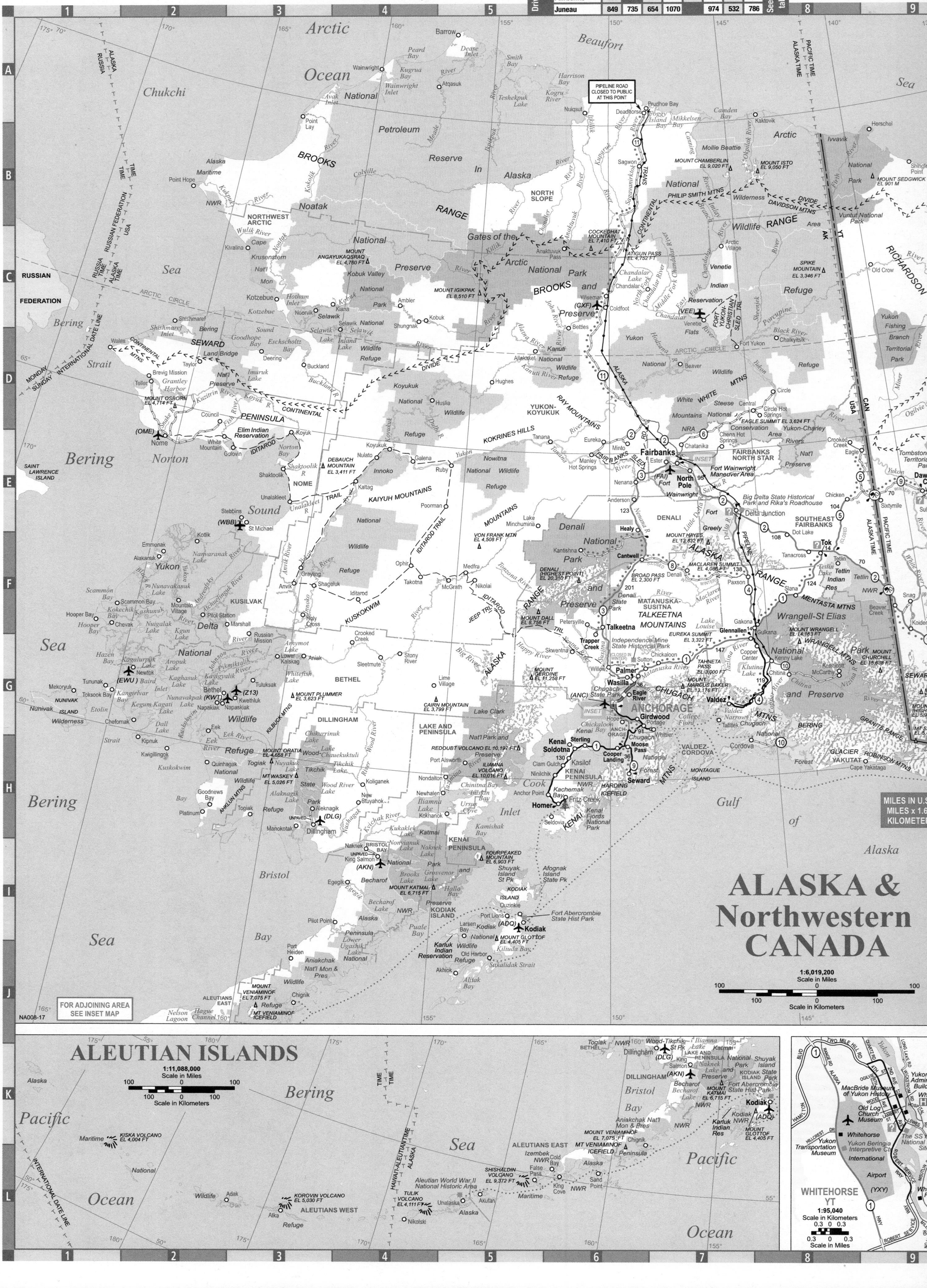

**Driving Distances In Kilometers**

| | Dawson City,YT | Fort Liard,NT | Fort Simpson,NT | Haines Jct.,YT | Inuvik,NT | Watson Lake,YT | Whitehorse,YT | Yellowknife,NT |
|---|---|---|---|---|---|---|---|---|
| Dawson City,YT | | 1633 | 1187 | 659 | 774 | 969 | 533 | 2413 |
| Whitehorse,YT | 533 | 1103 | 1379 | 155 | 1227 | 438 | | 1895 |
| Yellowknife,NT | 2413 | 795 | 632 | 2035 | 3112 | 1449 | 1895 | |

See also mileage table page 2

NA008-17

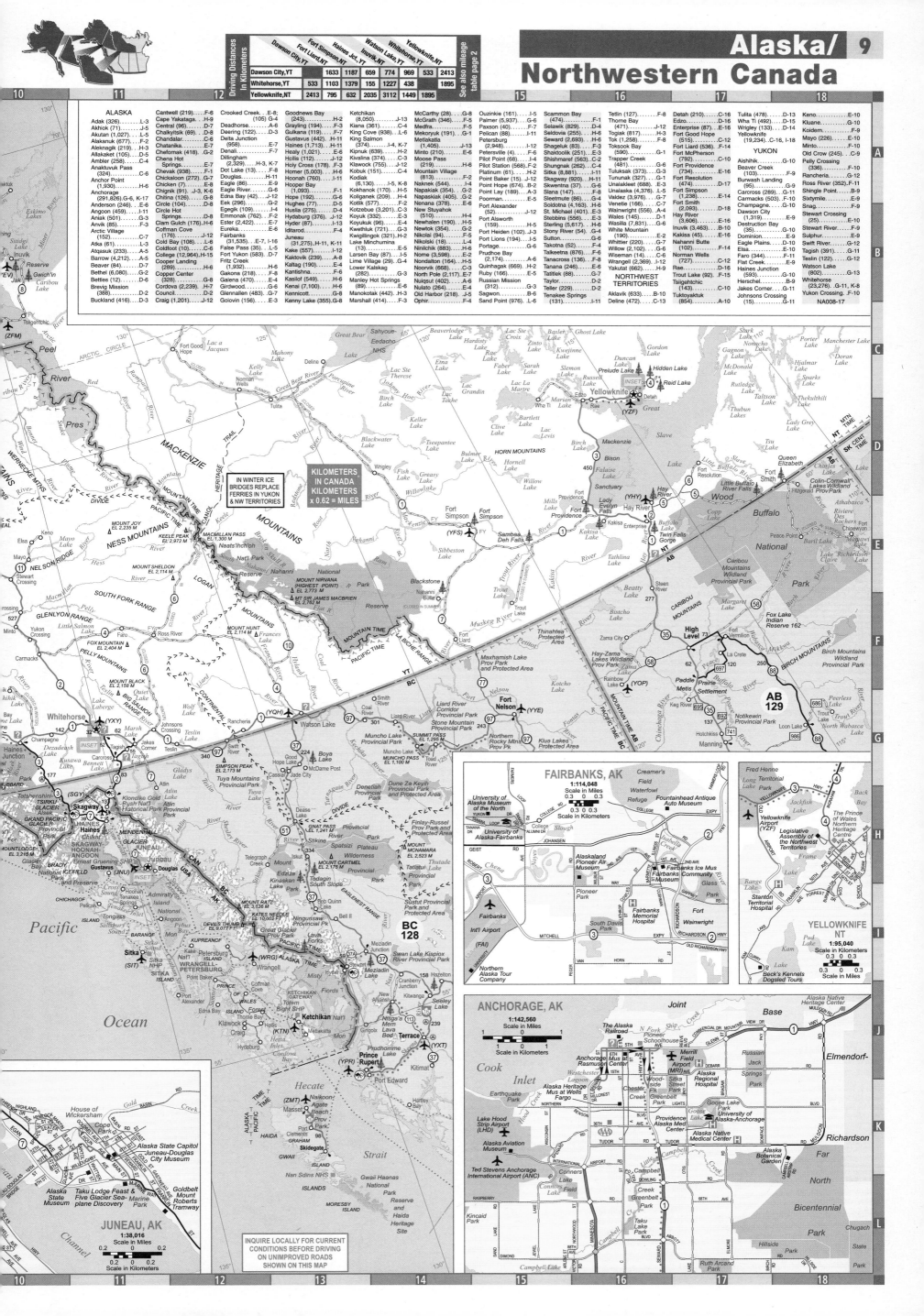

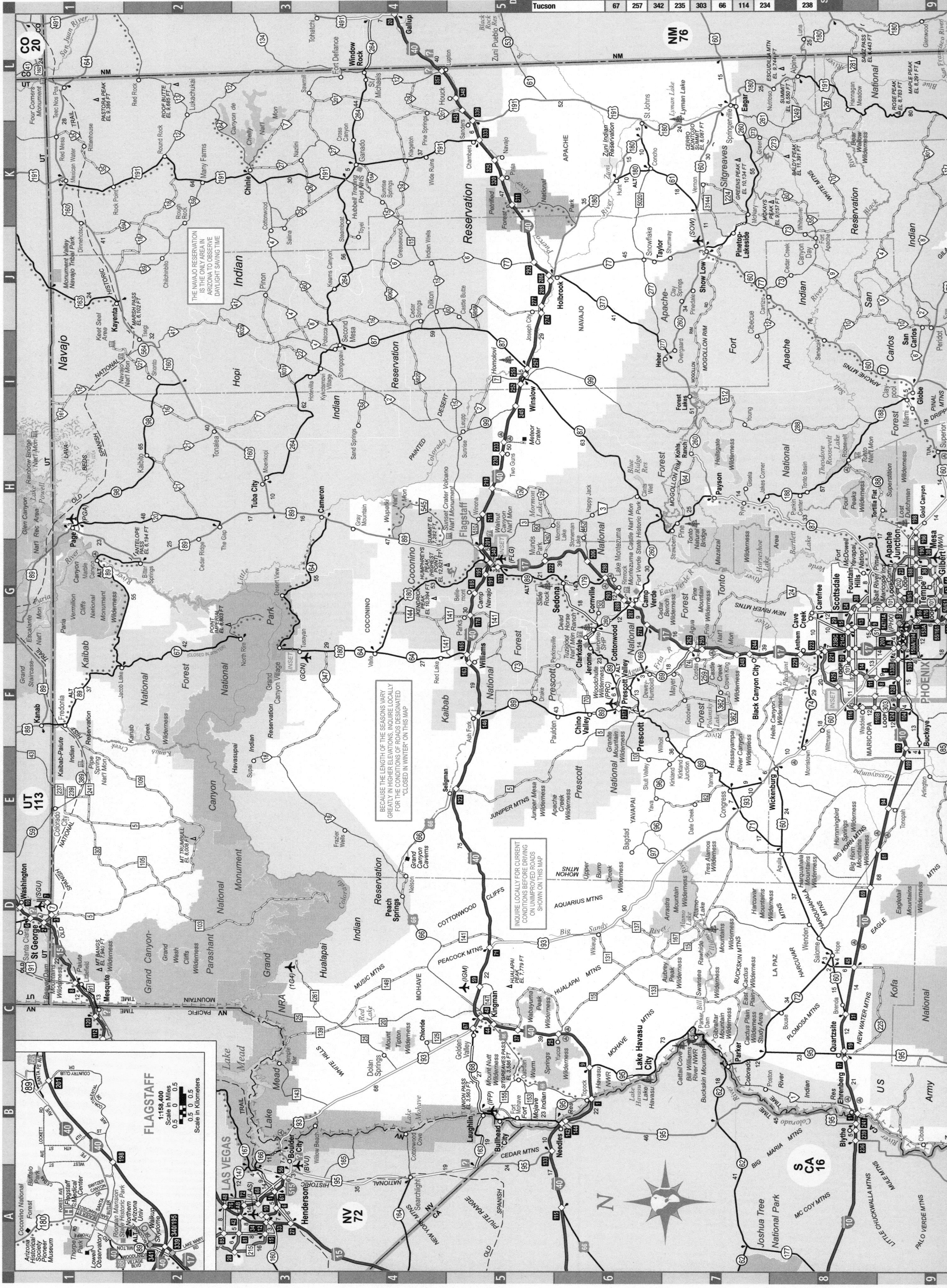

| Driving Distances in Miles | Casa Grande | Grand Canyon Village | Flagstaff | Holbrook | Kingman | Nogales | Phoenix | Springerville | Tucson | Yuma |
|---|---|---|---|---|---|---|---|---|---|---|
| Flagstaff | 192 | 87 | | 90 | 148 | 321 | 143 | 182 | 257 | 321 |
| Grand Canyon Village | 277 | | 87 | 178 | 174 | 406 | 228 | 270 | 342 | 405 |
| Phoenix | 49 | 143 | 228 | 186 | 190 | 178 | | 225 | 114 | 184 |
| Tucson | 67 | 257 | 342 | 235 | 303 | 66 | 114 | 234 | | 238 |

See also mileage table page 2

THE NAVAJO RESERVATION IS THE ONLY AREA IN ARIZONA TO OBSERVE DAYLIGHT SAVING TIME

BECAUSE THE LENGTH OF THE SEASONS VARY GREATLY IN HIGHER ELEVATIONS INQUIRE LOCALLY FOR THE CONDITIONS OF ROADS DESIGNATED "CLOSED IN WINTER" ON THIS MAP

INQUIRE LOCALLY FOR CURRENT CONDITIONS BEFORE DRIVING ON UNIMPROVED ROADS SHOWN ON THIS MAP

FLAGSTAFF
1:158,400
Scale in Miles
Scale in Kilometers

LEGEND

- Interstate Highway
- Controlled Access Hwy
- Controlled Access Hwy Toll
- Wildlife Refuge
- Nat'l/State Park
- National Forest

## ARIZONA

NA010-17

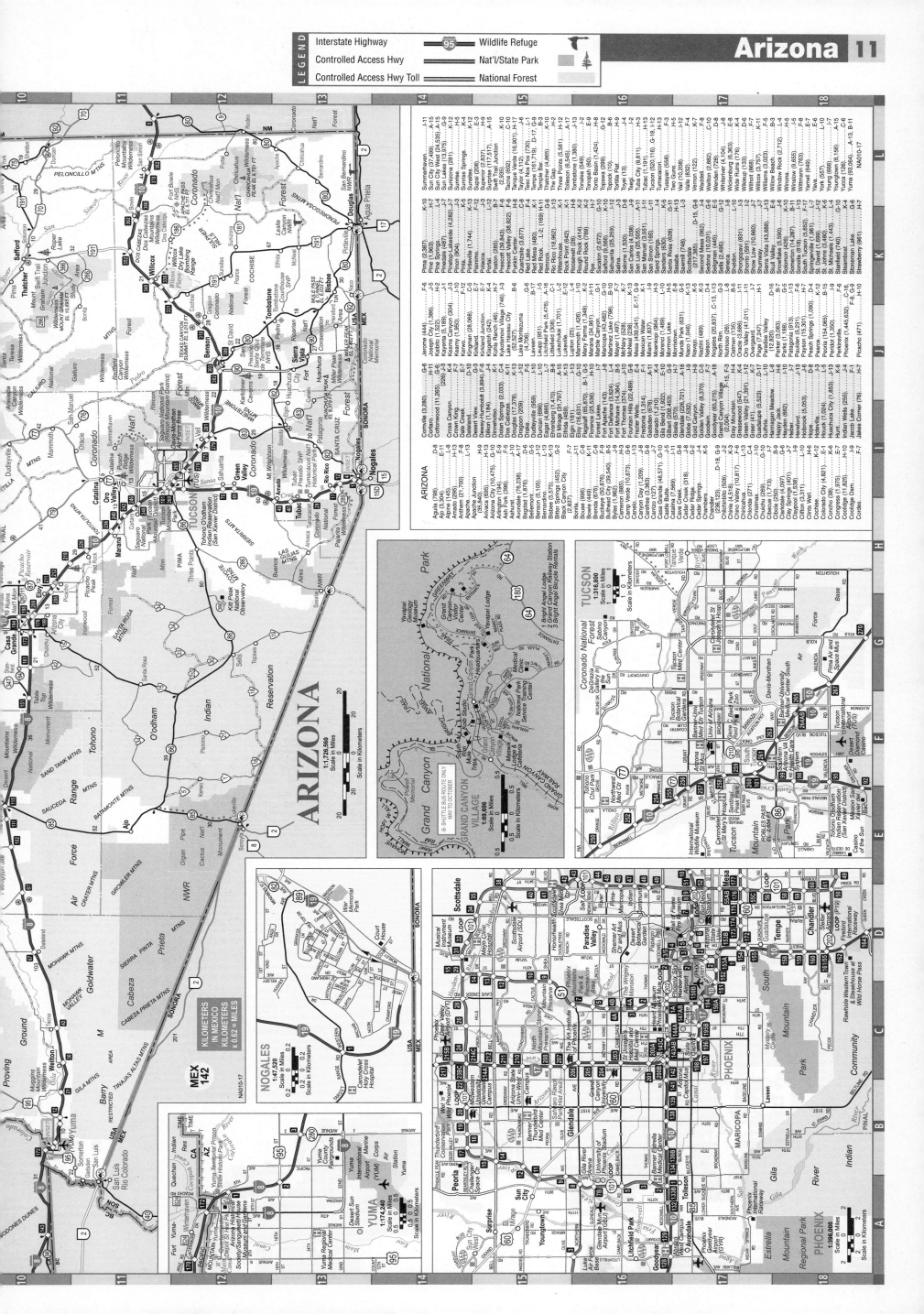

| Driving Distances In Miles | Branson,MO | El Dorado | Fayetteville | Fort Smith | Hot Springs | Jonesboro | Little Rock | Memphis,TN | Pine Bluff | Texarkana |
|---|---|---|---|---|---|---|---|---|---|---|
| Fort Smith | 158 | 259 | 58 | | 131 | 257 | 158 | 287 | 200 | 181 |
| Little Rock | 170 | 117 | 188 | 158 | 56 | 130 | | 134 | 44 | 143 |
| Memphis,TN | 273 | 251 | 318 | 287 | 191 | 70 | 134 | | 177 | 276 |
| Texarkana | 305 | 87 | 237 | 181 | 114 | 271 | 143 | 276 | 153 | |

See also mileage table page 2

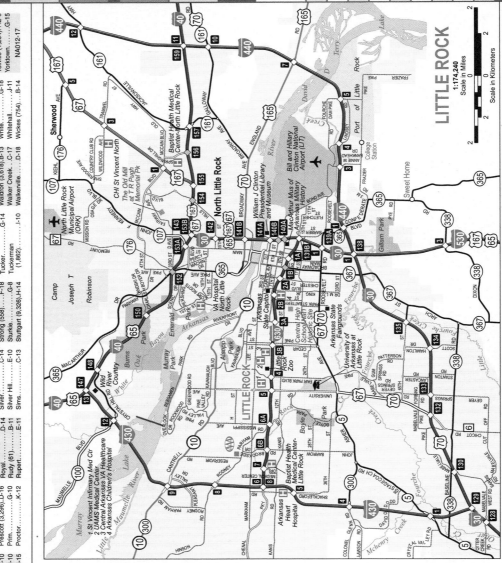

LITTLE ROCK
1:174,240

1 St Vincent Infirmary Med Ctr
2 UAMS / Central Arkansas Healthcare
3 CHI St Vincent North
4 Arkansas Children's Hospital

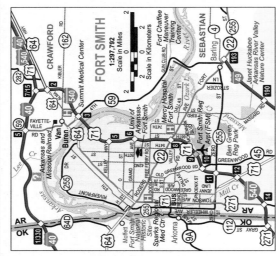

FORT SMITH
1:297,792

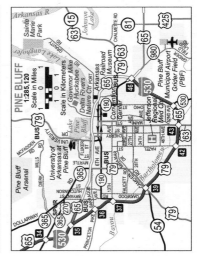

PINE BLUFF
1:285,120

LEGEND

| | | |
|---|---|---|
| Interstate Highway | 95 | Wildlife Refuge |
| Controlled Access Hwy | | Nat'l/State Park |
| Controlled Access Hwy Toll | | National Forest |

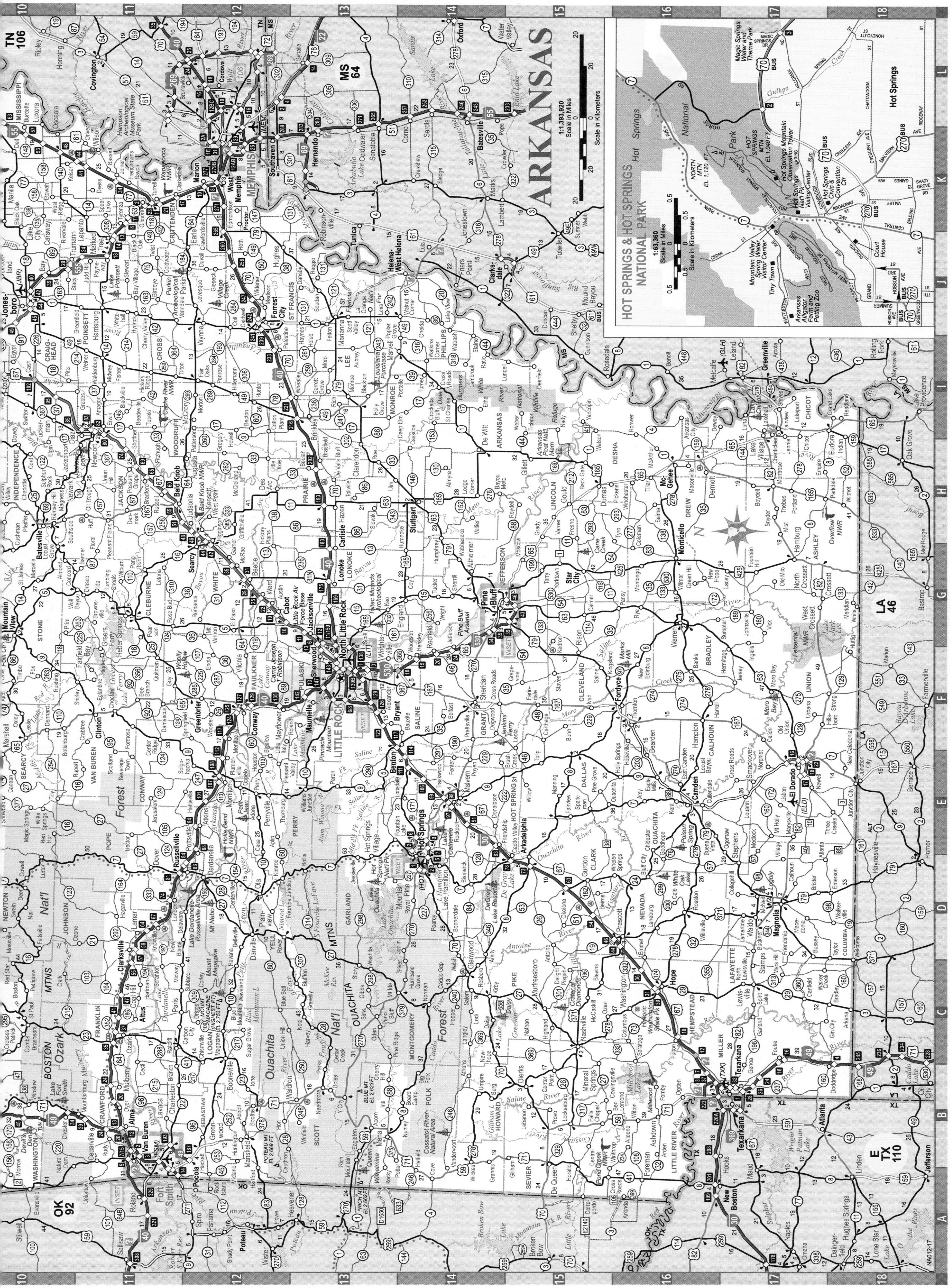

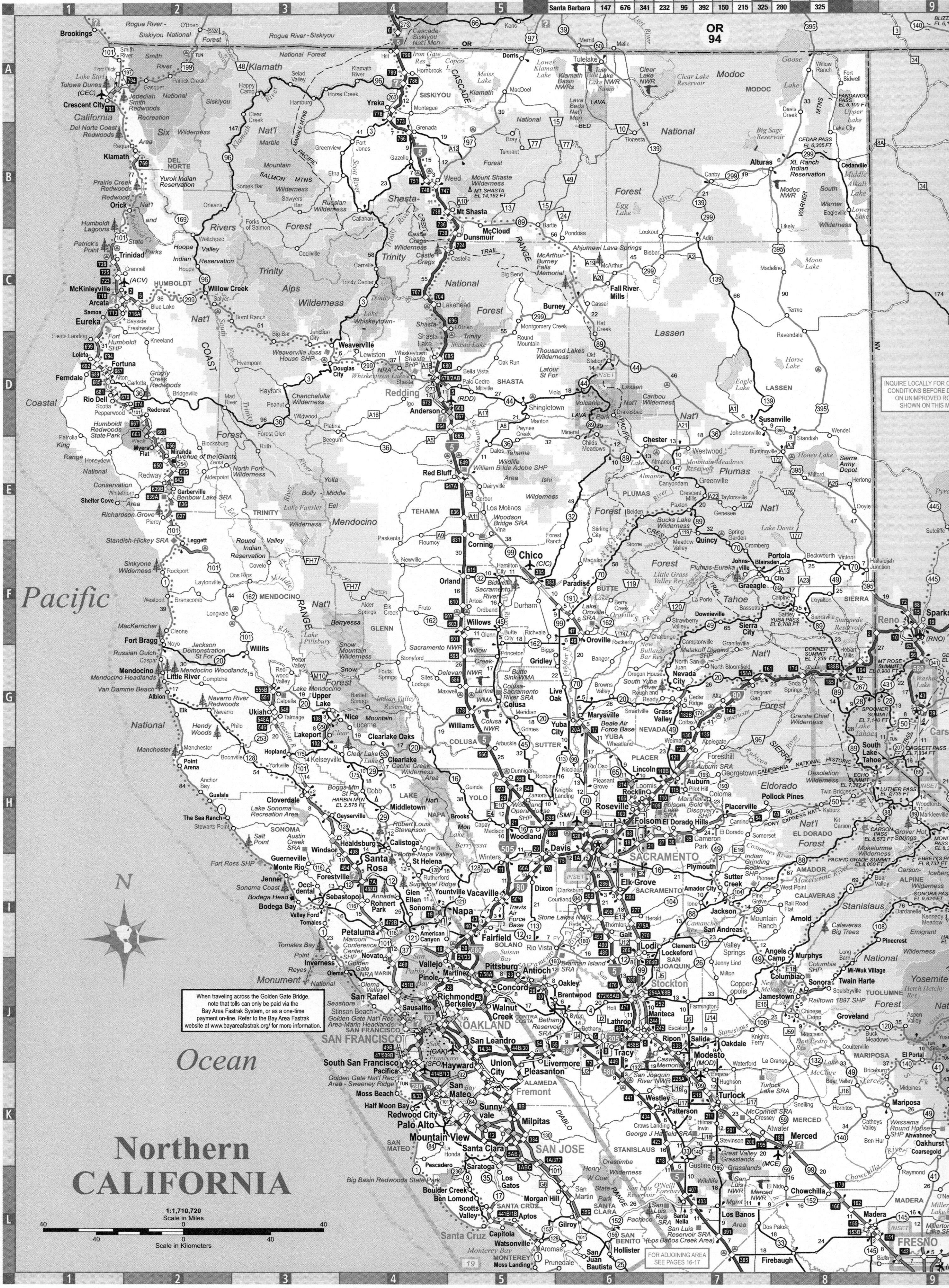

Northern **CALIFORNIA**

See also mileage table page 2

FOR ADJOINING AREA
SEE PAGES 16-17

| Driving Distances In Miles | Bakersfield | Crescent City | Furnace Creek | Fresno | Los Angeles | Sacramento | San Bernardino | San Diego | San Francisco | San Jose | Santa Barbara | Yosemite Village |
|---|---|---|---|---|---|---|---|---|---|---|---|---|
| Los Angeles | 111 | 755 | 286 | 219 | | 385 | 60 | 121 | 381 | 341 | 95 | 310 |
| Sacramento | 277 | 374 | 440 | 169 | 385 | | 438 | 505 | 87 | 115 | 392 | 173 |
| San Diego | 232 | 870 | 355 | 338 | 121 | 505 | 107 | | 502 | 461 | 215 | 431 |
| San Francisco | 283 | 355 | 530 | 186 | 381 | 87 | 434 | 502 | | 47 | 325 | 192 |
| Santa Barbara | 147 | 676 | 341 | 232 | 95 | 392 | 150 | 215 | 325 | 280 | | 325 |

When traveling across the Golden Gate Bridge, note that tolls can only be paid via the Bay Area Fastrak System, or as a one-time payment on-line. Refer to the Bay Area Fastrak website at www.bayareafastrak.org/ for more information.

INQUIRE LOCALLY FOR C CONDITIONS BEFORE DI ON UNIMPROVED RO SHOWN ON THIS

Pacific Ocean

1:1,710,720
Scale in Miles
Scale in Kilometers

LEGEND

| | |
|---|---|
| Interstate Highway | Wildlife Refuge |
| Controlled Access Hwy | Nat'l/State Park |
| Controlled Access Hwy Toll | National Forest |

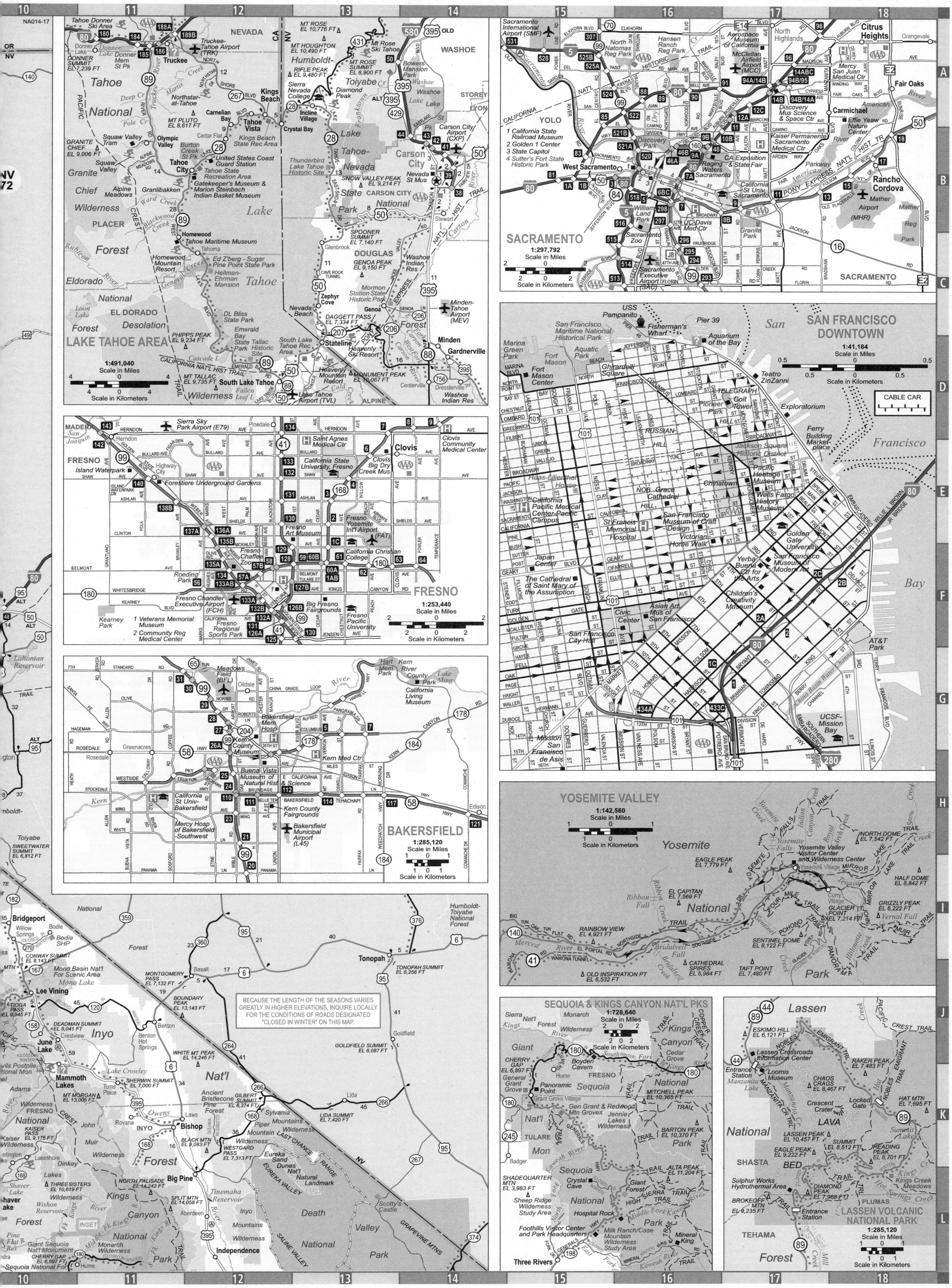

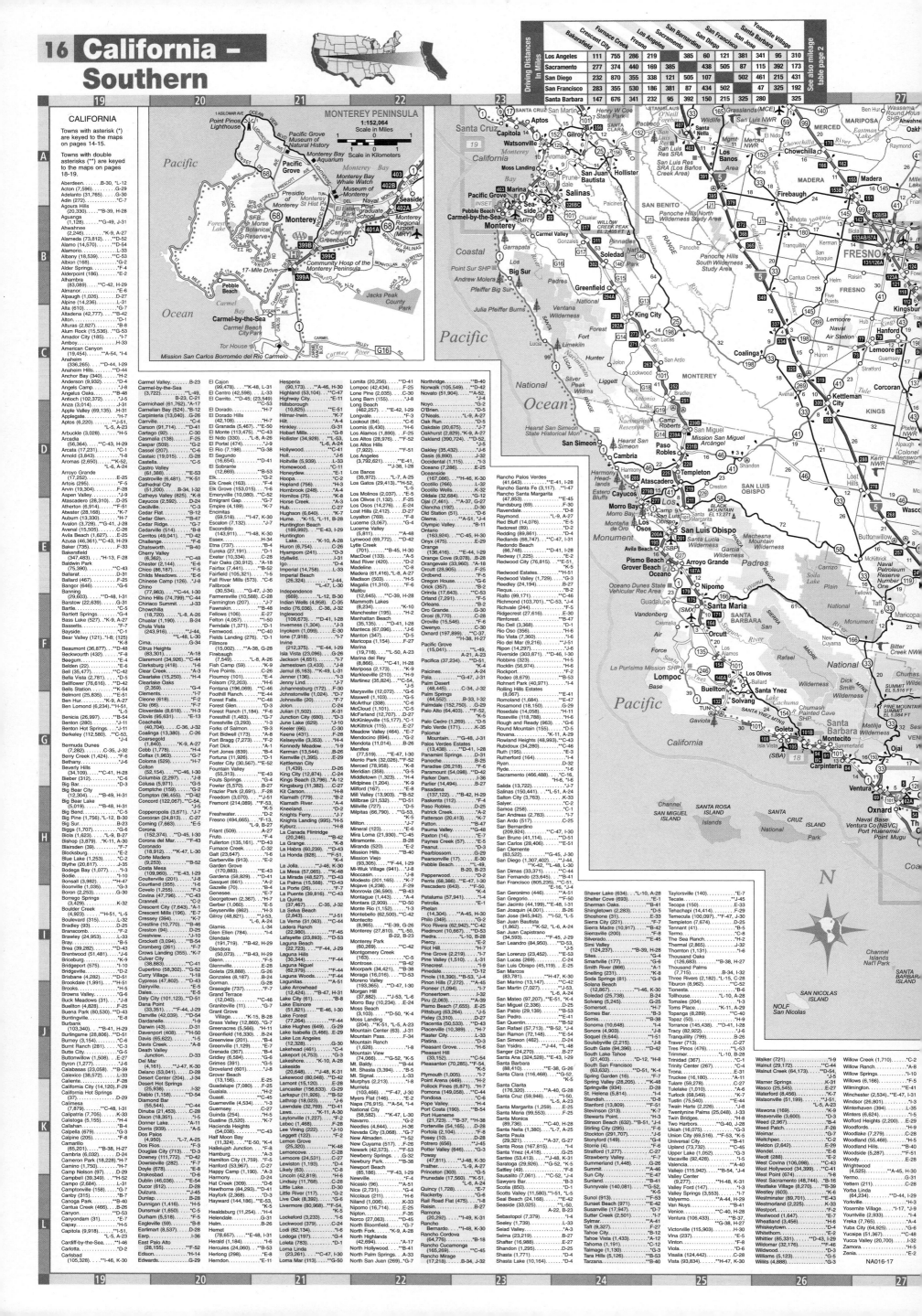

Driving Distances In Miles

| | Bakersfield | Crescent City | Furnace Creek | Fresno | Los Angeles | Sacramento | San Bernardino | San Diego | San Francisco | San Jose | Santa Barbara | Yosemite Village |
|---|---|---|---|---|---|---|---|---|---|---|---|---|
| Los Angeles | 111 | 755 | 286 | 219 | | 385 | 60 | 121 | 381 | 341 | 95 | 310 |
| Sacramento | 277 | 374 | 440 | 169 | 385 | | 434 | 505 | 87 | 115 | 392 | 173 |
| San Diego | 232 | 870 | 355 | 338 | 121 | 505 | 107 | | 502 | 461 | 215 | 431 |
| San Francisco | 283 | 355 | 530 | 186 | 381 | 87 | 434 | 502 | | 47 | 325 | 192 |
| Santa Barbara | 147 | 676 | 341 | 237 | 95 | 392 | 150 | 215 | 325 | 280 | | 325 |

See also mileage table page 2

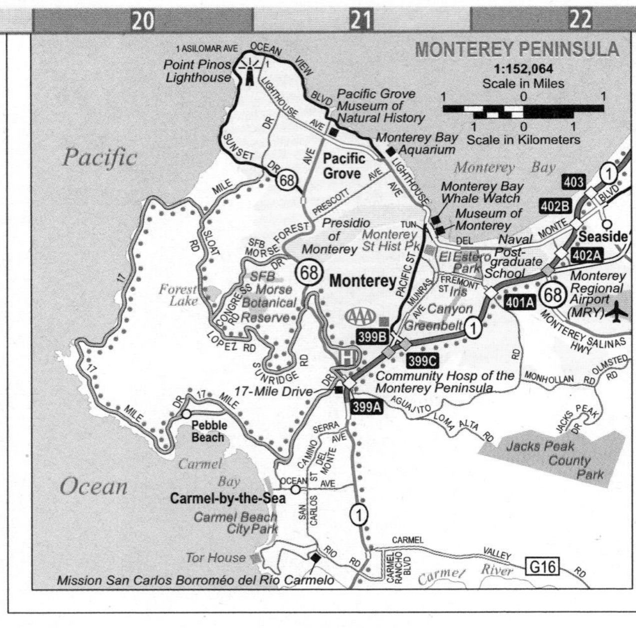

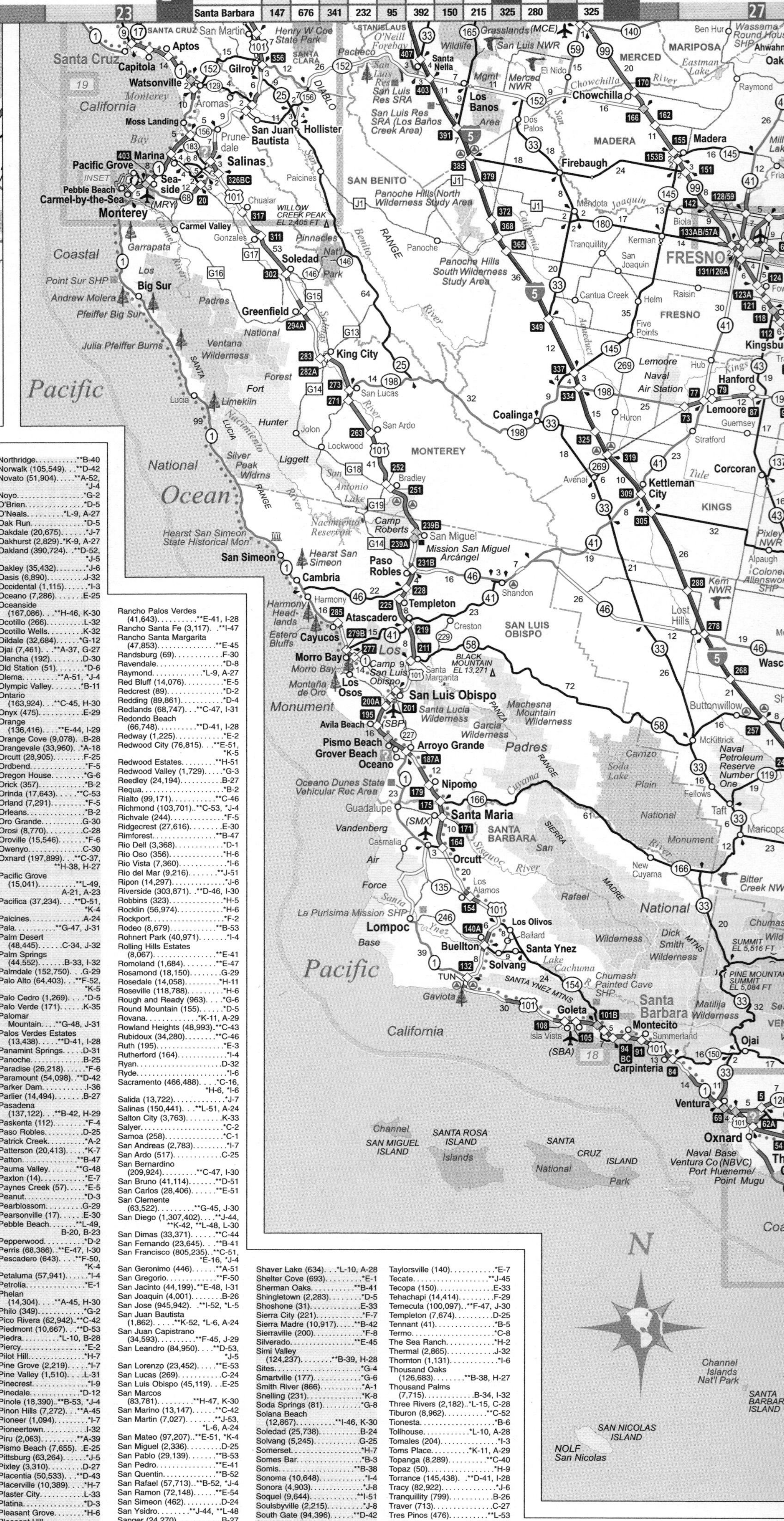

**CALIFORNIA**

Towns with asterisk (*) are keyed to the maps on pages 14-15.

Towns with double asterisks (**) are keyed to the maps on pages 18-19.

LEGEND

Interstate Highway — 95
Controlled Access Hwy
Controlled Access Hwy Toll
Wildlife Refuge
Nat'l/State Park
National Forest

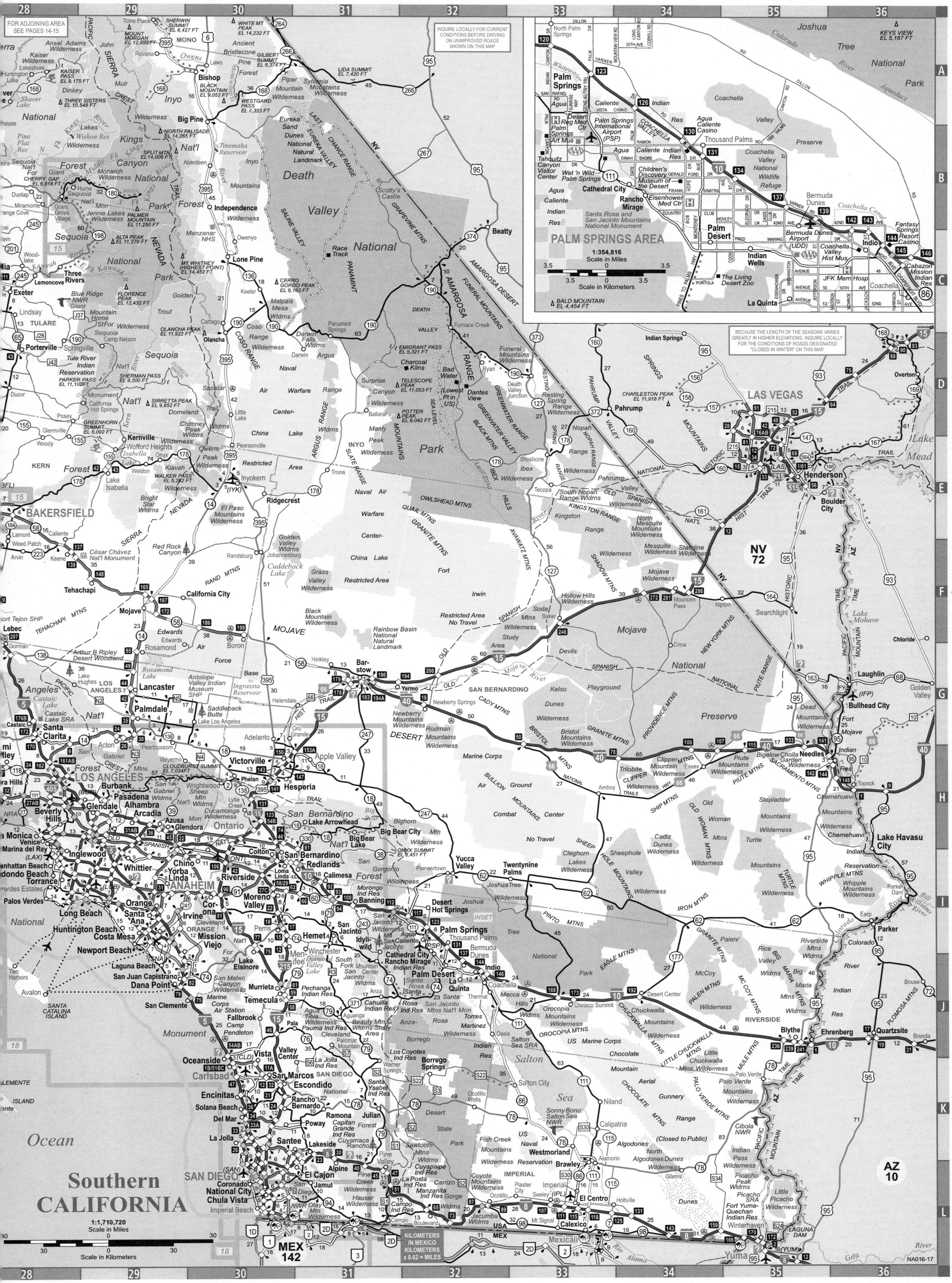

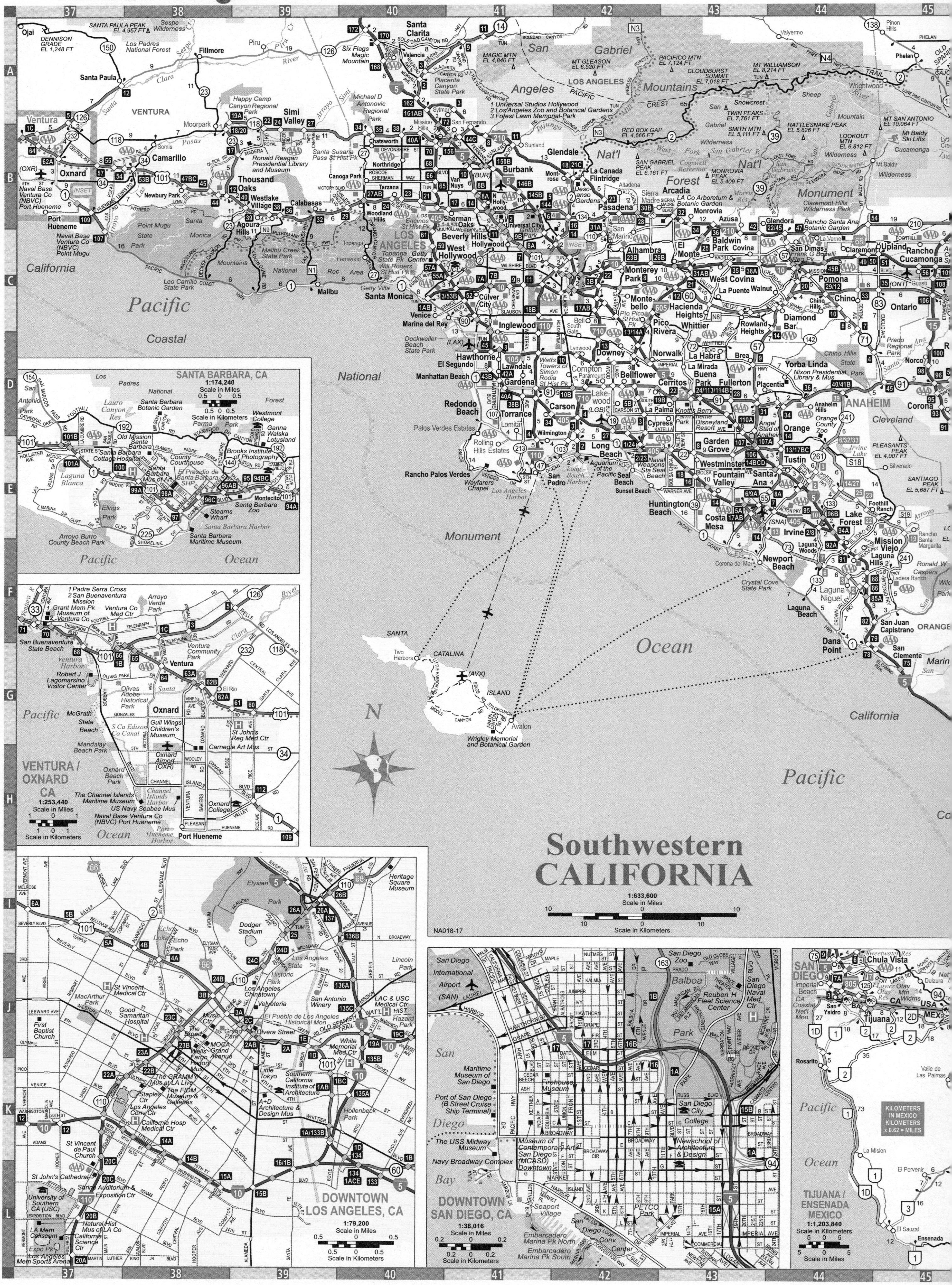

# Southwestern CALIFORNIA

1:633,600
Scale in Miles
10          10
Scale in Kilometers
10          10

NA018-17

## SANTA BARBARA, CA
1:174,240
Scale in Miles
0.5    0    0.5
Scale in Kilometers
0.5    0    0.5

## VENTURA / OXNARD CA
1:253,440
Scale in Miles
1    0    1
Scale in Kilometers
1    0    1

## DOWNTOWN LOS ANGELES, CA
1:79,200
Scale in Miles
0.5    0    0.5
Scale in Kilometers
0.5    0    0.5

## DOWNTOWN SAN DIEGO, CA
1:38,016
Scale in Miles
0.2    0    0.2
Scale in Kilometers
0.2    0    0.2

## TIJUANA / ENSENADA MEXICO
1:1,203,840
Scale in Kilometers
5    0    5

KILOMETERS IN MEXICO
KILOMETERS x 0.62 = MILES

Pacific Ocean

Pacific Coastal

National Monument

LEGEND
Interstate Highway — 95 — Wildlife Refuge
Controlled Access Hwy — Nat'l/State Park
Controlled Access Hwy Toll — National Forest

## SAN FRANCISCO CA BAY AREA

1:544,896
Scale in Miles

Scale in Kilometers

When traveling across the Golden Gate Bridge, note that tolls can only be paid via the Bay Area Fastrak System, or as a one-time payment on-line. Refer to the Bay Area Fastrak website at www.bayareafastrak.org/ for more information.

1 Mission Santa Clara de Asis
2 Winchester Mystery House
3 Rosicrucian Egyptian Museum
4 Overfelt Gardens
5 SAP Center at San Jose
6 Avaya Stadium

MEX 142

KILOMETERS IN MEXICO
Kilometers x 0.62 = MILES

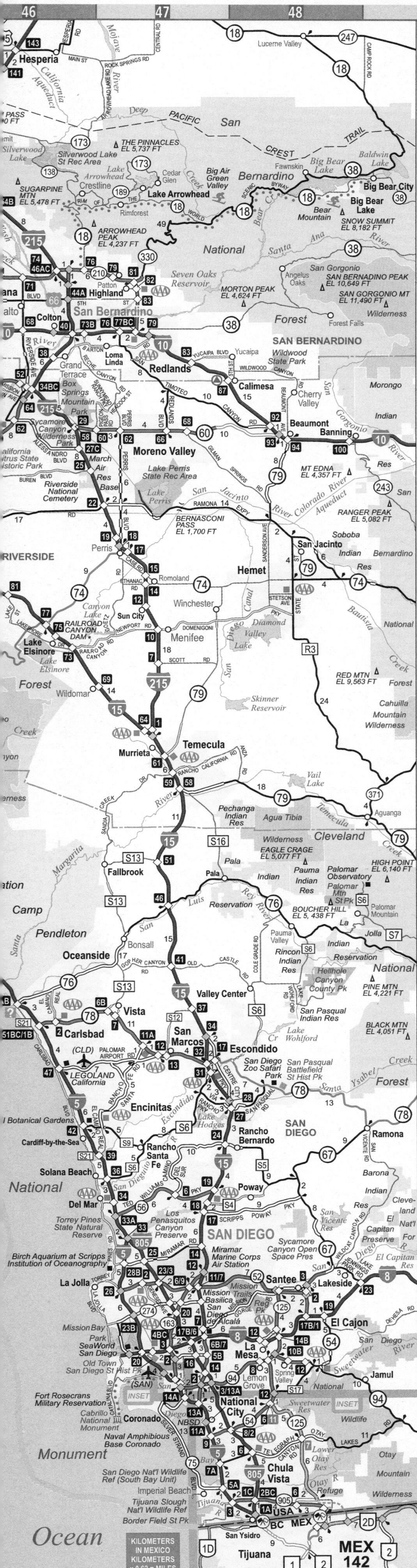

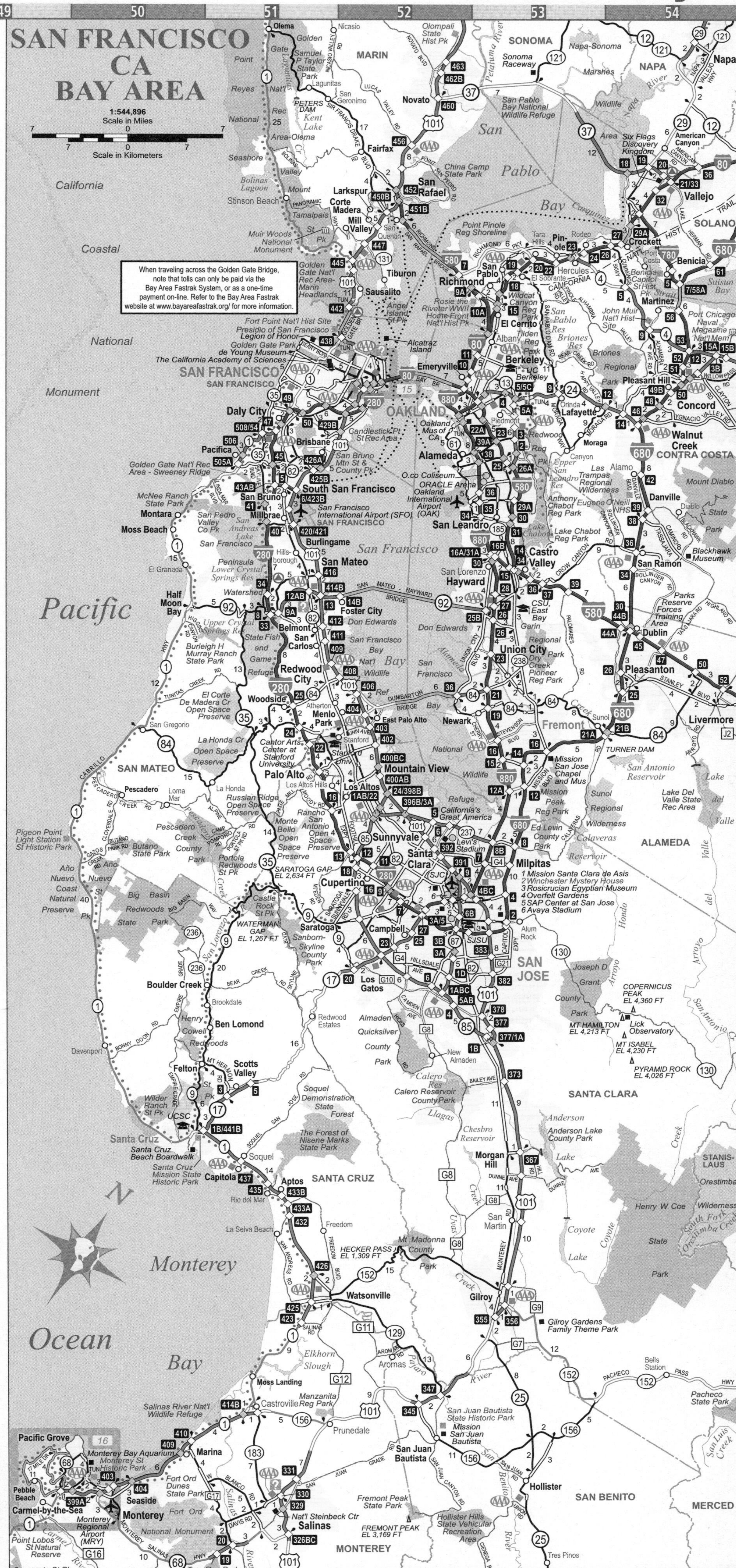

| Driving Distances In Miles | Alamosa | Colorado Springs | Cortez | Denver | Durango | Grand Junction | Greeley | Lamar | Poncha Springs | Pueblo |
|---|---|---|---|---|---|---|---|---|---|---|
| Colorado Springs | 164 | | 355 | 70 | 313 | 310 | 123 | 161 | 106 | 44 |
| Denver | 218 | 70 | 378 | | 336 | 244 | 55 | 206 | 141 | 115 |
| Durango | 149 | 313 | 44 | 336 | | 168 | 387 | 351 | 195 | 271 |
| Pueblo | 122 | 44 | 314 | 115 | 271 | 285 | 168 | 122 | 100 | |

See also mileage table page 2

## COLORADO

Agate. . . . . G-10
Aguilar (538). . . . . K-9
Akron (1,702). . . . . E-11
Alamosa (8,780). . . . K-7
Allenspark (528). . . B-15
Alma (270). . . . . G-6
Almont. . . . . H-5
Amherst (58). . . . . D-13
Antero Junction. . . . . H-6
Anton. . . . . F-11
Antonito (781). . . . . L-6
Arapahoe. . . . . H-13
Arboles (280). . . . . L-4
Arlington. . . . . I-11
Aroya. . . . . H-11
Arriba (193). . . . . G-11
Arvada (106,433). . . F-16
Aspen (6,658). . . . . G-5
Atwood (133). . . . . D-11
Ault (1,519). . . . . D-9
Aurora (325,078). . D-18, F-9, G-18
Avon (6,447). . . . . F-5
Avondale (674). . . . . I-9
Axial. . . . . E-3
Bailey. . . . . G-7
Bartlett. . . . . K-13
Basalt (3,857). . . . . G-5
Battlement Mesa (4,471). . . . . G-3
Bayfield (2,333). . . . L-4
Bedrock. . . . . I-1
Bennett (2,308). . . . . F-9
Berthoud (5,105). . . A-17
Bethune (237). . . . . G-13
Beulah. . . . . J-8
Black Forest (13,116). . . . . H-9
Black Hawk (118). . D-16
Blanca (385). . . . . K-7
Bond. . . . . F-5
Boone (339). . . . . I-9
Boulder (97,385). . . C-17, E-8
Bowie. . . . . H-4
Brandon (21). . . . . I-13
Branson (74). . . . . L-10
Breckenridge (4,540). . . . . G-6
Breen. . . . . L-3
Briggsdale. . . . . D-9
Brighton (33,352). . . C-18, E-8
Bristol. . . . . I-13
Broomfield (55,889). . . . . C-17
Brush (5,463). . . . . E-10
Buena Vista (2,617). . H-6
Buffalo Creek. . . . . G-8
Buford. . . . . E-4
Burlington (4,254). . G-13
Cahone. . . . . K-1
Calhan (780). . . . . H-9
Campo (109). . . . . L-13
Canon City (16,400). . I-8
Capulin (200). . . . . K-6
Carbondale (6,427). . G-4
Carr. . . . . C-8
Cascade. . . . . H-8
Castle Rock (48,231). . . . . G-8
Cedaredge (2,253). . H-3
Centennial (100,377). . . . . I-18
Center (2,230). . . . . J-6
Central City (663). . . . . D-16, F-7
Cheraw (252). . . . . J-11
Cherry Hills Village (5,987). . . . . H-17
Cheyenne Wells (846). . . . . H-13
Chimney Rock. . . . . L-4
Chivington. . . . . I-12
Chromo. . . . . L-5
Cimarron. . . . . I-4
Clark. . . . . D-5
Clifton (19,889). . . . . G-2
Coaldale (255). . . . . I-7
Collbran (708). . . . . G-3
Colona (30). . . . . I-3
Colorado Springs (416,427). . . H-9, K-16
Columbine. . . . . D-5
Commerce City (45,913). . . . . F-17
Como. . . . . G-7
Conejos (58). . . . . L-6
Conifer. . . . . G-8
Cope. . . . . F-12
Copper Mountain (385). . . . . G-6
Cortez (8,482). . . . . K-2
Cotopaxi (47). . . . . I-7
Cowdrey. . . . . D-6
Craig (9,464). . . . . D-4
Crawford (431). . . . . H-4
Creede. . . . . J-5
Crested Butte (1,487). . . . . H-5
Crestone (127). . . . . J-7
Cripple Creek (1,189). . . . . H-8
Crook (110). . . . . C-12
Crowley (176). . . . . I-10
Cuchara. . . . . K-8
Dacono (4,152). . . . B-18
De Beque (504). . . . . G-3
Deckers. . . . . G-8
Deer Trail (546). . . . F-10
Del Norte (1,686). . . . K-6
Delhi. . . . . K-10
Delta (8,915). . . . . H-3
Denver (600,158). . D-17, D-18, F-8, G-17
Dillon (904). . . . . F-6
Dinosaur (339). . . . . E-1
Divide (127). . . . . H-8
Dolores (936). . . . . K-2
Dove Creek (735). . . . J-1
Doyleville. . . . . I-5
Dunton. . . . . J-3
Durango (16,887). . . K-3
Eads (609). . . . . I-12
Eagle (6,508). . . . . F-5
Eaton (4,365). . . . . D-9
Echo Lake. . . . . D-15
Eckley (257). . . . . E-12
Edwards (10,266). . . F-5
Egnar. . . . . J-1
El Jebel (3,801). . . . . G-4
Elbert (230). . . . . G-9
Eldorado Springs (585). . . . . C-16
Elizabeth (1,358). . . . G-9
Elk Springs. . . . . E-2
Empire (282). . . . . D-15
Englewood (30,255). . . D-17, H-17
Erie (18,135). . . . . B-17
Estes Park (5,858). . E-7
Evans (18,537). . . . A-18
Evergreen (9,038). . D-16
Fairplay (679). . . . . G-6
Farisita. . . . . J-8
Federal Heights (11,467). . . . . E-16
Firestone (10,147). . B-18
Flagler (561). . . . . G-11
Fleming (408). . . . . D-12
Florence (3,881). . . . . I-8
Fort Carson (13,813). . . . H-8, L-16
Fort Collins (143,986). . . . . D-8
Fort Garland (433). . K-7
Fort Lupton (7,377). . . . . B-18
Fort Morgan (11,315). . . . . E-10
Fountain (25,846). . . H-9
Fowler (1,182). . . . . J-10
Fraser (1,224). . . . . C-14
Frisco (2,683). . . . . F-6
Fruita (12,646). . . . . G-2
Fruitvale (7,675). . . . G-2
Galatea. . . . . I-12
Gardner. . . . . J-8
Genoa (139). . . . . G-11
Georgetown (1,034). . . . D-15, F-7
Gilcrest (1,034). . . . A-18
Gill. . . . . D-9
Glendale (4,184). . . G-17
Glenwood Springs (9,614). . . . . F-4
Golden (18,867). . . D-17, F-8, G-14
Gould. . . . . D-6
Granada (517). . . . . J-13
Granby (1,864). . . . . E-6
Grand Junction (58,566). . . . . G-2
Grand Lake (471). . A-14
Granite. . . . . H-6
Grant. . . . . G-7
Greeley (92,889). . . . D-9
Greenwood Village (13,925). . . . . H-17
Grover (137). . . . . C-9
Guffey (98). . . . . H-7
Gunnison (5,854). . . . I-5
Gypsum (6,477). . . . . F-5
Hamilton. . . . . E-4
Hartman (81). . . . . I-13
Hartsel. . . . . H-7
Hasty (144). . . . . J-12
Haswell (68). . . . . I-11
Hawley. . . . . J-10
Haxtun (946). . . . . D-12
Hayden (1,810). . . . . D-4
Hebron. . . . . D-6
Hereford. . . . . C-9
Hermosa. . . . . K-3
Hesperus. . . . . K-3
Highlands Ranch. . . . I-16
Hillrose (264). . . . . E-11
Holly (802). . . . . J-13
Holyoke (2,313). . . . D-13
Hooper (103). . . . . J-7
Hot Sulphur Springs (663). . . . . E-6
Hotchkiss (944). . . . . H-3
Howard (723). . . . . I-7
Hoyt. . . . . E-10
Hudson (2,356). . . . . E-9
Hugo (730). . . . . G-11
Hygiene. . . . . B-17
Idaho Springs (1,717). . . . . D-15
Idalia (88). . . . . F-13
Ignacio (697). . . . . L-3
Iliff (266). . . . . D-11
Jefferson. . . . . G-7
Joes (80). . . . . F-12
Johnstown (9,887). . A-18
Julesburg (1,225). . C-13
Karval. . . . . H-11
Keenesburg (1,127). . E-9
Ken Caryl (32,438). . I-15
Kersey (1,454). . . . . E-9
Keystone (1,079). . . . F-6
Kim (74). . . . . K-11
Kiowa (723). . . . . G-9
Kirk (59). . . . . F-12
Kit Carson (233). . . H-12
Kremmling (1,444). . . E-6
La Garita. . . . . J-6
La Jara (818). . . . . K-6
La Junta (7,077). . . . J-11
La Veta (800). . . . . K-8
Lafayette (24,453). . C-17
Laird (47). . . . . E-13
Lake City (408). . . . . J-4
Lake George. . . . . H-8
Lakewood (142,980). . . . . D-17, F-8, H-15
Lamar (7,804). . . . . J-12
Laporte (2,450). . . . . D-8
Larkspur (183). . . . . G-8
Las Animas (2,410). . J-11
Last Chance. . . . . F-11
Lay. . . . . D-3
Leadville (2,602). . . . G-6
Lewis (302). . . . . K-2
Limon (1,880). . . . . G-10
Lincoln Park (3,546). . I-8
Lindon. . . . . F-11
Littleton (41,737). . E-17, F-8, I-16
Livermore. . . . . D-8
Log Lane Village (873). . . . . E-10
Loma (1,293). . . . . G-1
Lone Tree (10,218). . I-18
Longmont (86,270). B-17
Louisville (18,376). . C-17
Loveland (66,859). . . . A-17, E-8
Lyons (2,033). . . . . B-16
Manassa (991). . . . . L-6
Mancos (1,336). . . . K-2
Manitou Springs (4,992). . . . . K-14
Marble (131). . . . . G-4
Masonville. . . . . D-8
Matheson. . . . . G-10
Maybell (72). . . . . D-3
McClave. . . . . I-12
McCoy (24). . . . . F-5
Mead (3,405). . . . . B-17
Meeker (2,475). . .
Merino (284). . . .
Mesa. . . . .
Milner. . . . .
Mineral Hot Spring
Minturn (1,027). . .
Model. . . . .
Moffat (116). . . .
Mogote. . . . .
Monarch. . . . .
Monte Vista (4,44
Montrose (19,132
Monument (5,530
Monument Park. .
Morrison (428). . .
Mosca. . . . .
Mt. Crested Butte (801). . . .
Nathrop. . . . .
Naturita (546). . . .
Nederland (1,445)
New Castle (4,518
Niwot (4,006). . . .

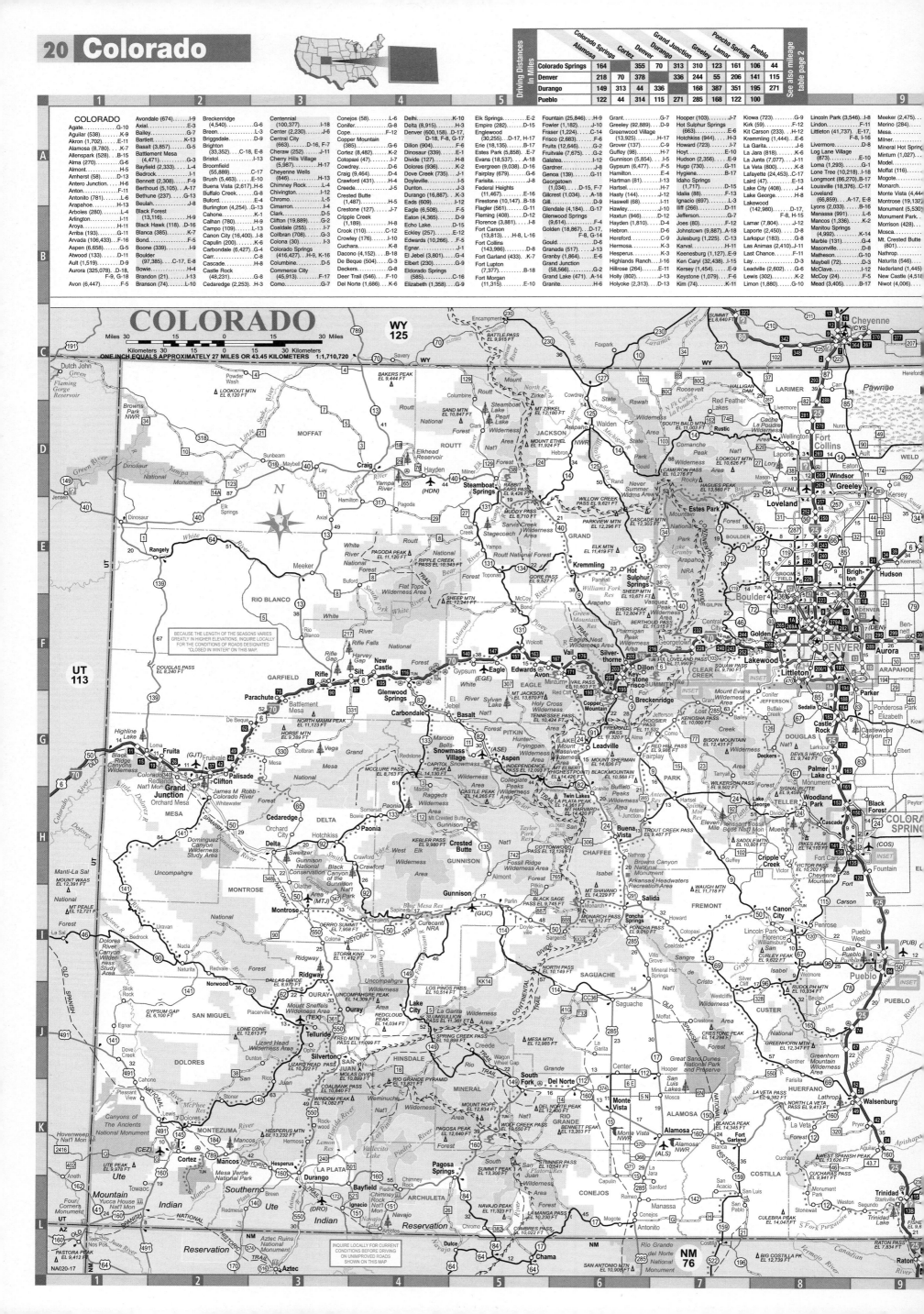

LEGEND
Interstate Highway
Controlled Access Hwy
Controlled Access Hwy Toll
Wildlife Refuge
Nat'l/State Park
National Forest

NA020-17

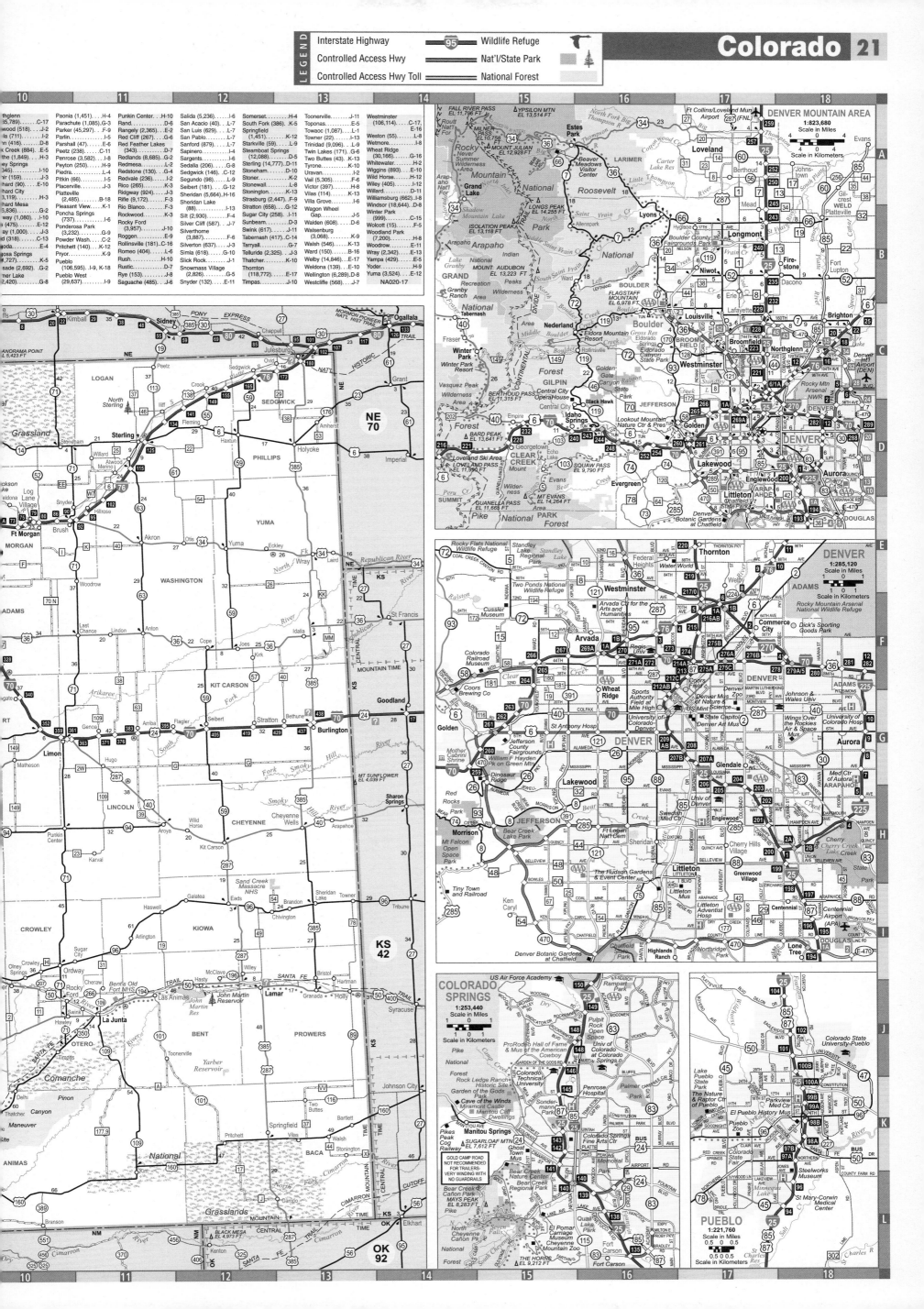

**Driving Distances In Miles**

| | Bridgeport | Canaan | Danbury | Hartford | New Haven | New London | Norwalk | Norwich | Stamford | Waterbury |
|---|---|---|---|---|---|---|---|---|---|---|
| Bridgeport | | 72 | 31 | 54 | 21 | 66 | 14 | 73 | 23 | 30 |
| Hartford | 54 | 43 | 59 | | 38 | 46 | 70 | 40 | 79 | 30 |
| New Haven | 21 | 65 | 37 | 38 | | 48 | 33 | 56 | 42 | 23 |
| New London | 66 | 88 | 91 | 46 | 48 | | 78 | 14 | 87 | 63 |

See also mileage table page 2

## CONNECTICUT

Driving Distances In Miles

| | Dover | Georgetown | Lewes | Newark | Philadelphia, PA | Rehoboth Beach | Smyrna | Wilmington |
|---|---|---|---|---|---|---|---|---|
| Dover | | 36 | 42 | 47 | 79 | 44 | 12 | 48 |
| Lewes | 42 | 17 | | 86 | 119 | 8 | 54 | 88 |
| Wilmington | 48 | 82 | 88 | 15 | 30 | 90 | 35 | |

See also mileage table page 2

DELAWARE

NA023-17

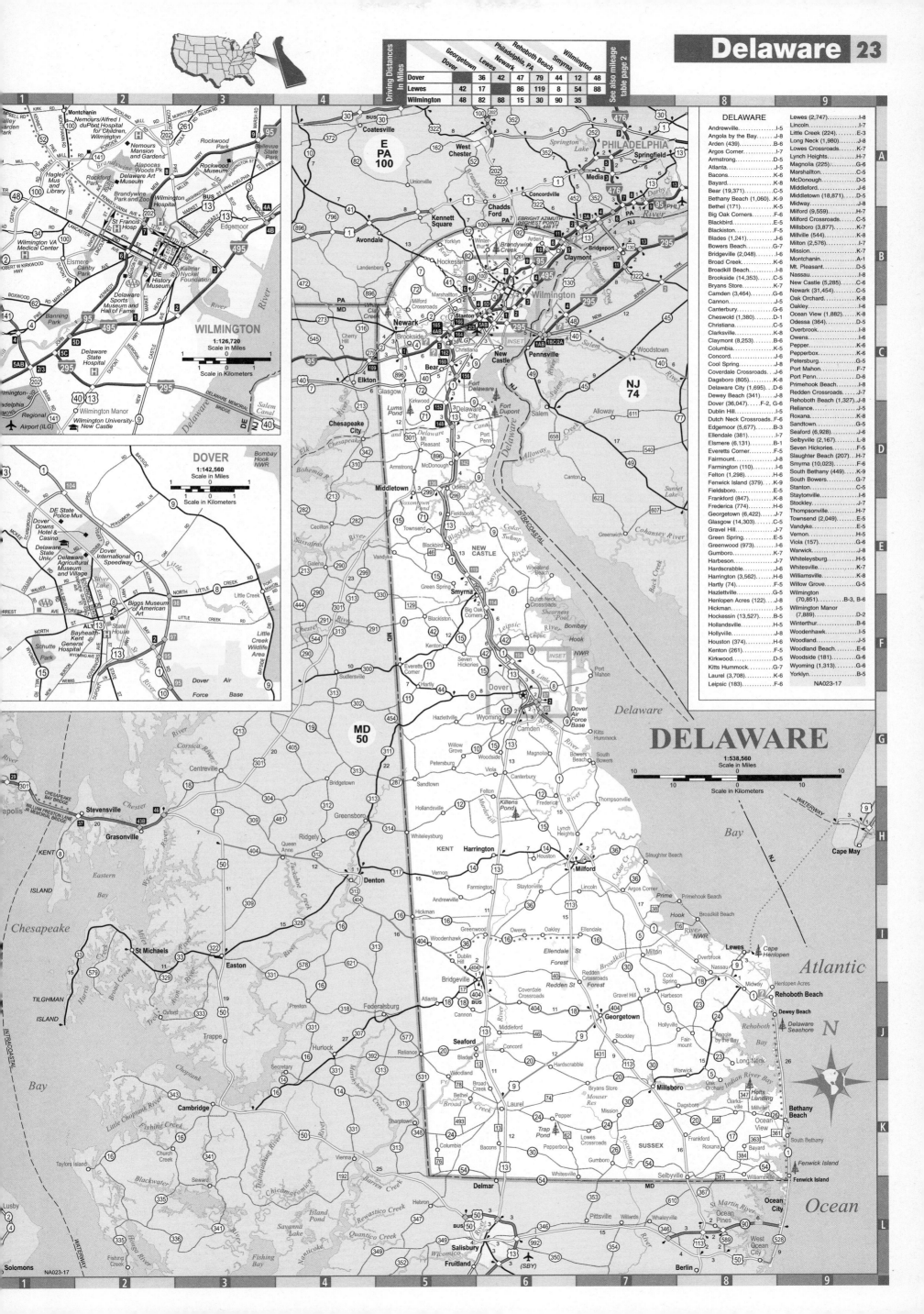

| Driving Distances In Miles | Daytona Beach | Fort Myers | Gainesville | Jacksonville | Key West | Miami | Orlando | Pensacola | St. Petersburg | Tallahassee | Tampa | West Palm Beach |
|---|---|---|---|---|---|---|---|---|---|---|---|---|
| Jacksonville | 88 | 302 | 71 | | 503 | 347 | 140 | 357 | 221 | 164 | 200 | 283 |
| Miami | 262 | 160 | 341 | 347 | 157 | | 235 | 677 | 269 | 472 | 260 | 75 |
| Orlando | 55 | 163 | 114 | 140 | 391 | 235 | | 450 | 106 | 245 | 85 | 168 |
| Tallahassee | 253 | 367 | 148 | 164 | 613 | 472 | 245 | 197 | 252 | | 244 | 405 |
| Tampa | 139 | 126 | 132 | 200 | 399 | 260 | 85 | 444 | 24 | 244 | | 202 |

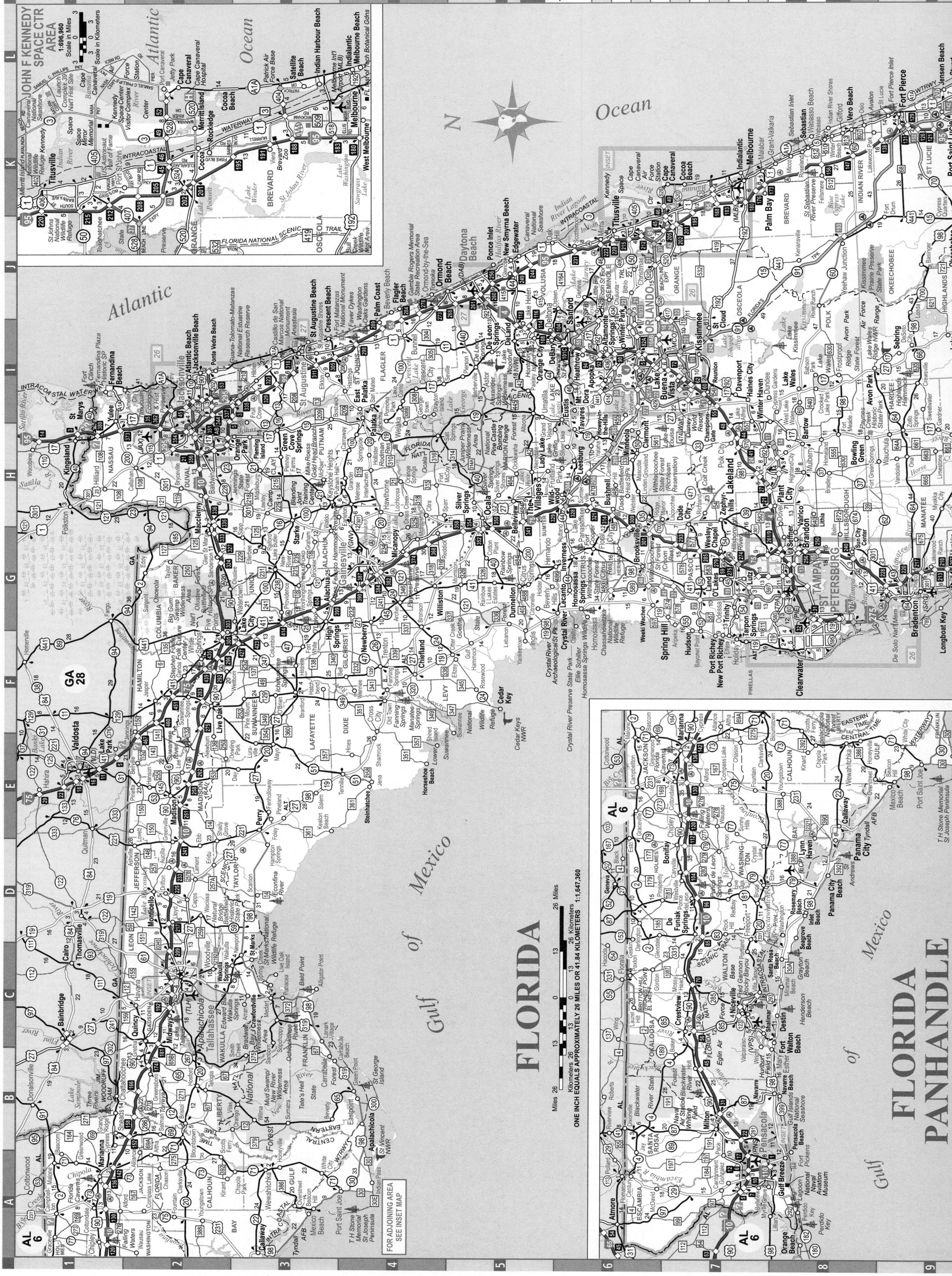

## FLORIDA

## FLORIDA PANHANDLE

LEGEND
Interstate Highway
Controlled Access Hwy
Controlled Access Hwy Toll
Wildlife Refuge
Nat'l/State Park
National Forest

When traveling along Florida's toll roads, note that many tolls are being converted to cashless collection and can only be paid via SunPass, E-Pass, or Toll-By-Plate. Refer to the authority websites below for more information.
Florida's Turnpike at www.floridasturnpike.com
Tampa Hillsborough County Expressway Authority at www.tampa-xway.com
Miami Dade Expressway Authority at www.mdxort.com
Orlando-Orange County Expressway Authority at www.oocea.com

## FLORIDA

Towns with asterisk (*) are keyed to the maps on pages 26-27.

NA024-17

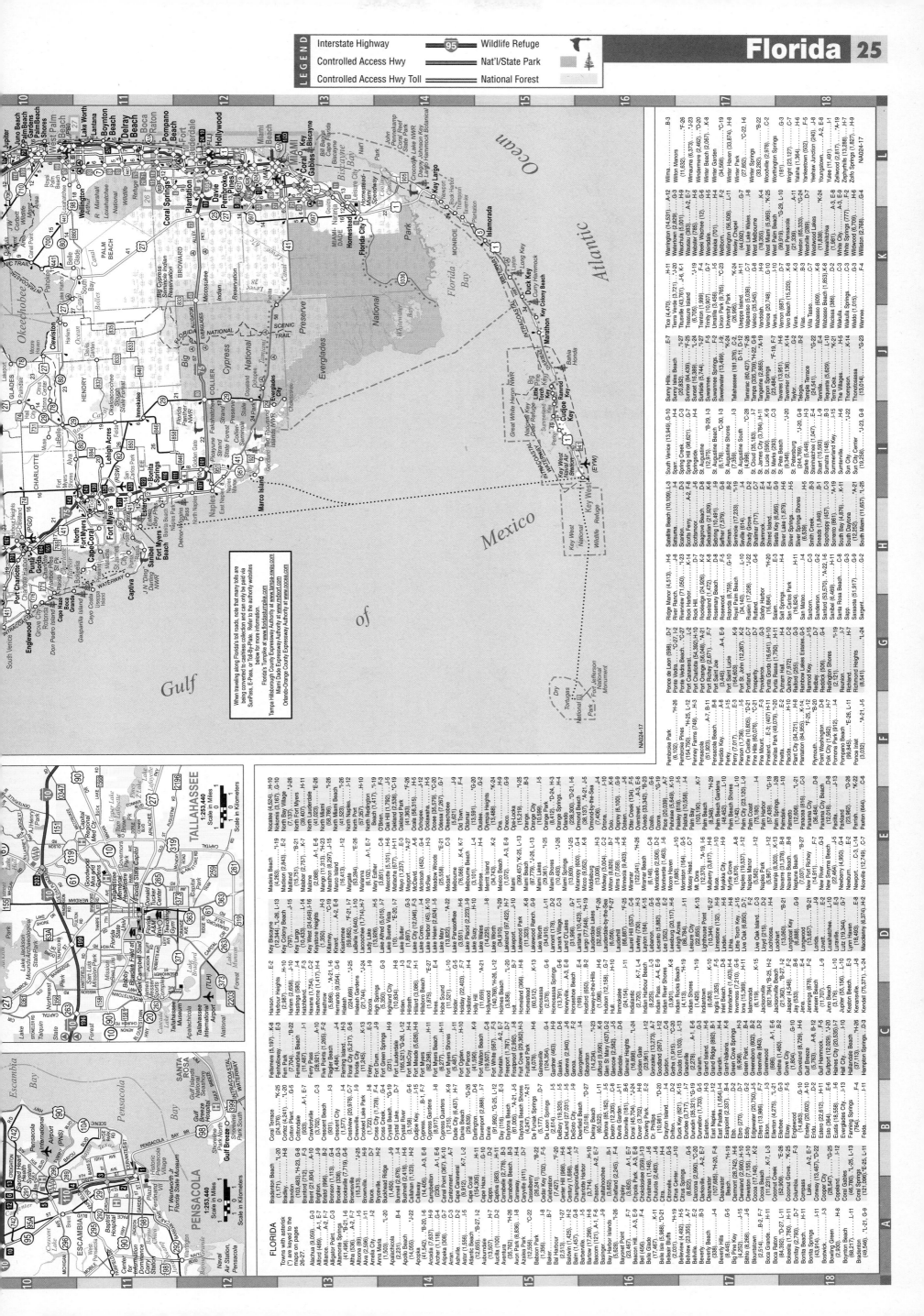

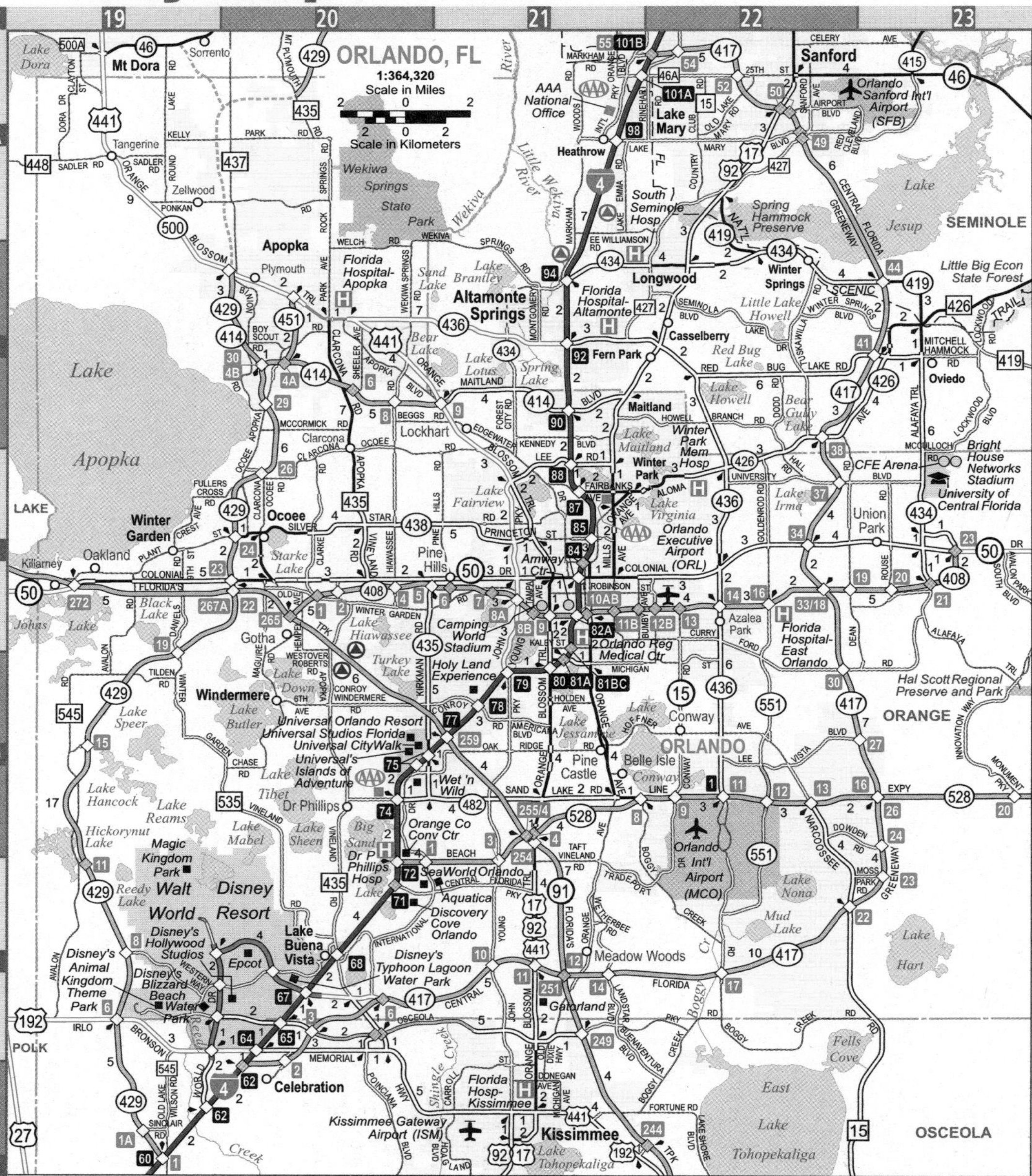

**ORLANDO, FL**
1:364,320
Scale in Miles
Scale in Kilometers

AAA National Office

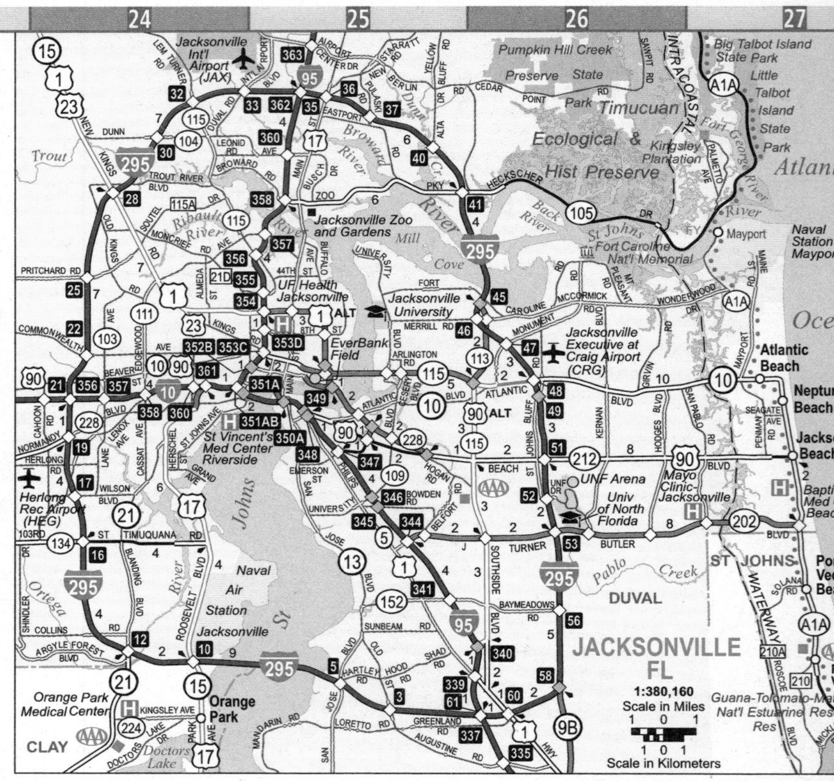

**JACKSONVILLE FL**
1:380,160
Scale in Miles
Scale in Kilometers

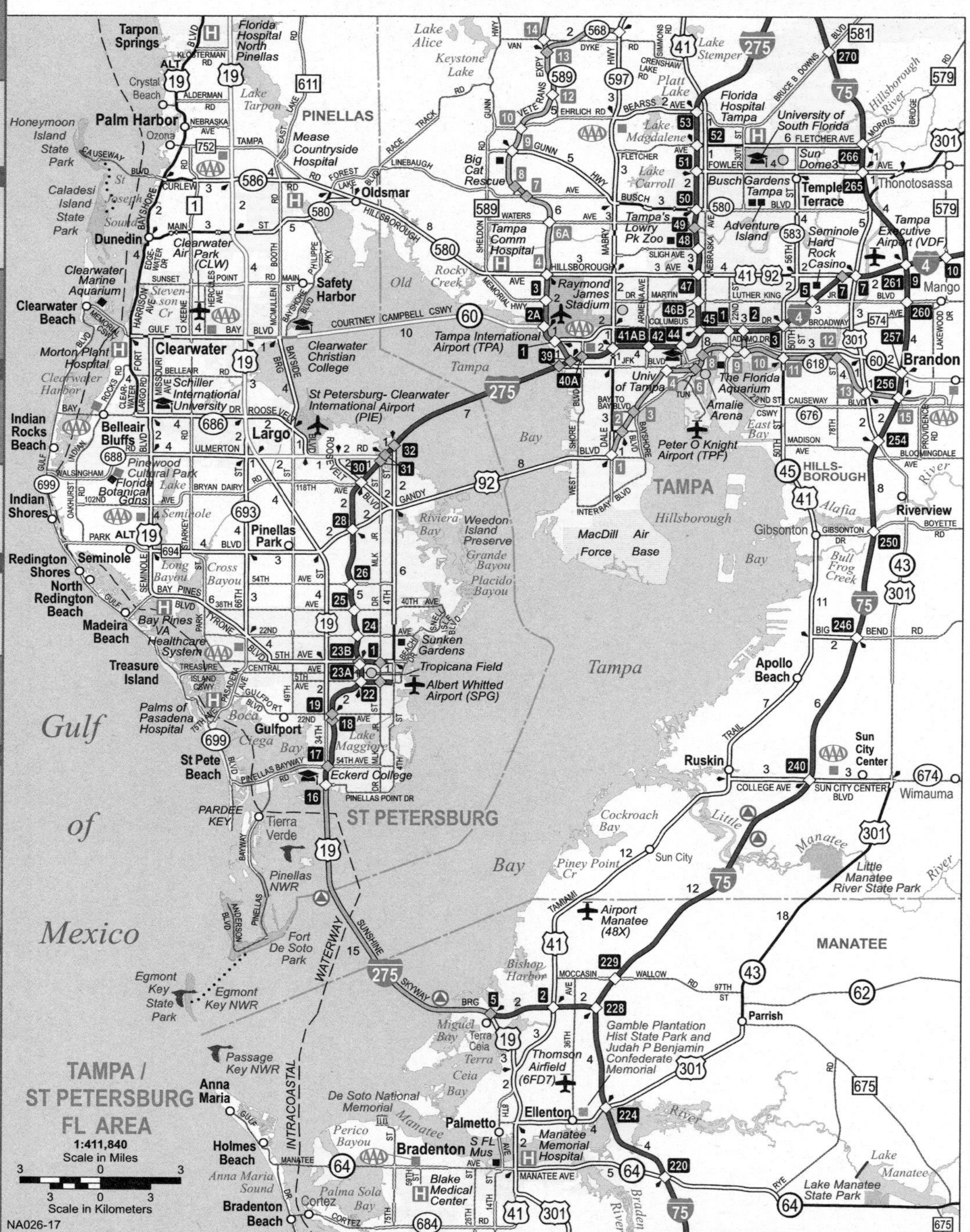

**TAMPA / ST PETERSBURG FL AREA**
1:411,840
Scale in Miles
Scale in Kilometers

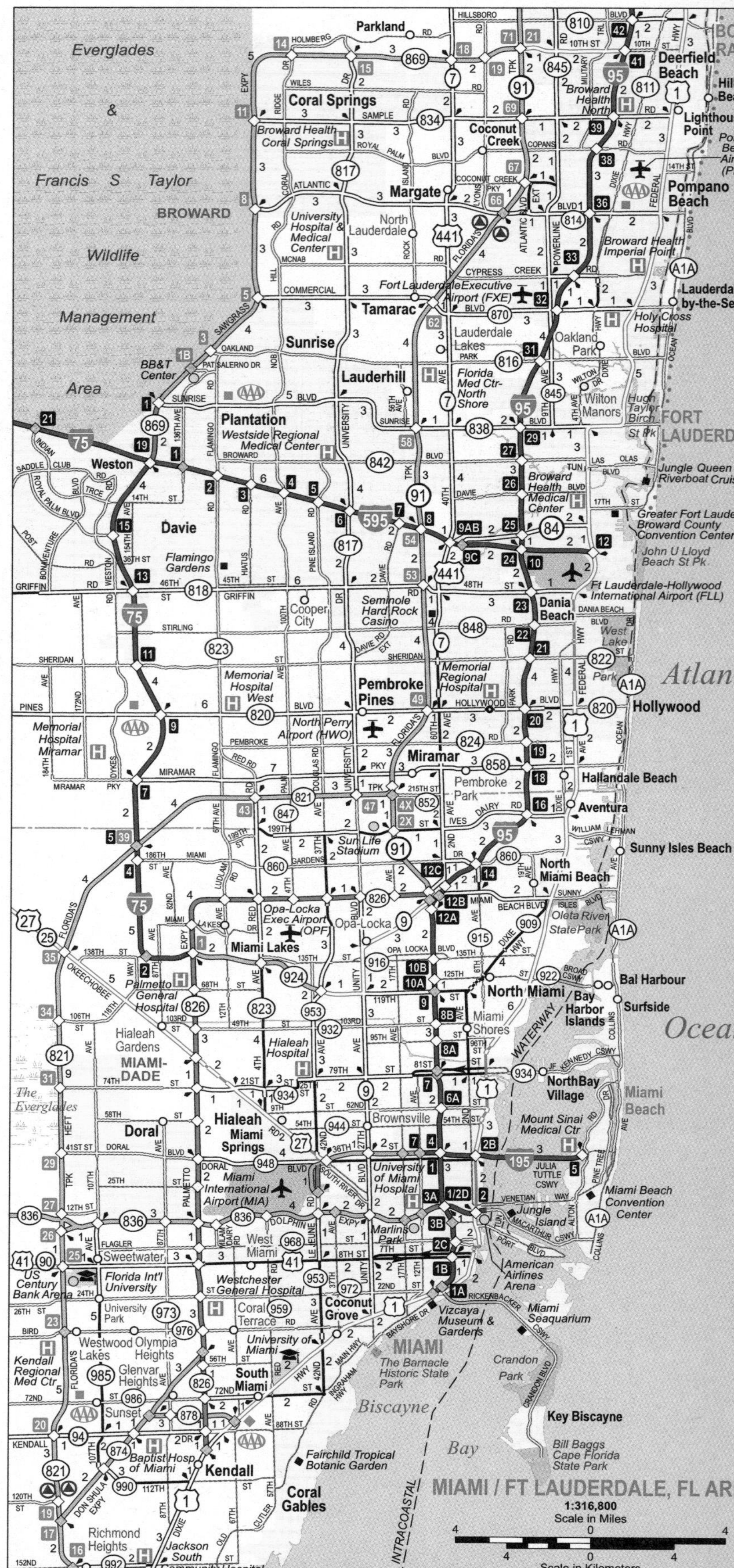

**MIAMI / FT LAUDERDALE, FL AREA**
1:316,800
Scale in Miles
Scale in Kilometers

Gulf of Mexico

Atlantic Ocean

Everglades & Francis S Taylor Wildlife Management Area

NA026-17

ST AUGUSTINE, FL
1:126,720
Scale in Miles
Scale in Kilometers

DAYTONA BEACH FL
1:253,440
Scale in Miles
Scale in Kilometers

WEST PALM BEACH FL
1:158,400
Scale in Miles
Scale in Kilometers

COLUMBUS, GA
1:221,760
Scale in Miles
Scale in Kilometers

ATLANTA, GA & VICINITY
1:253,440
Scale in Miles
Scale in Kilometers

MACON, GA
1:190,080
Scale in Miles
Scale in Kilometers

DOWNTOWN ATLANTA, GA
1:57,024
Scale in Miles
Scale in Kilometers

SAVANNAH GA
1:190,080
Scale in Miles
Scale in Kilometers

BRUNSWICK GA
1:348,480
Scale in Miles
Scale in Kilometers

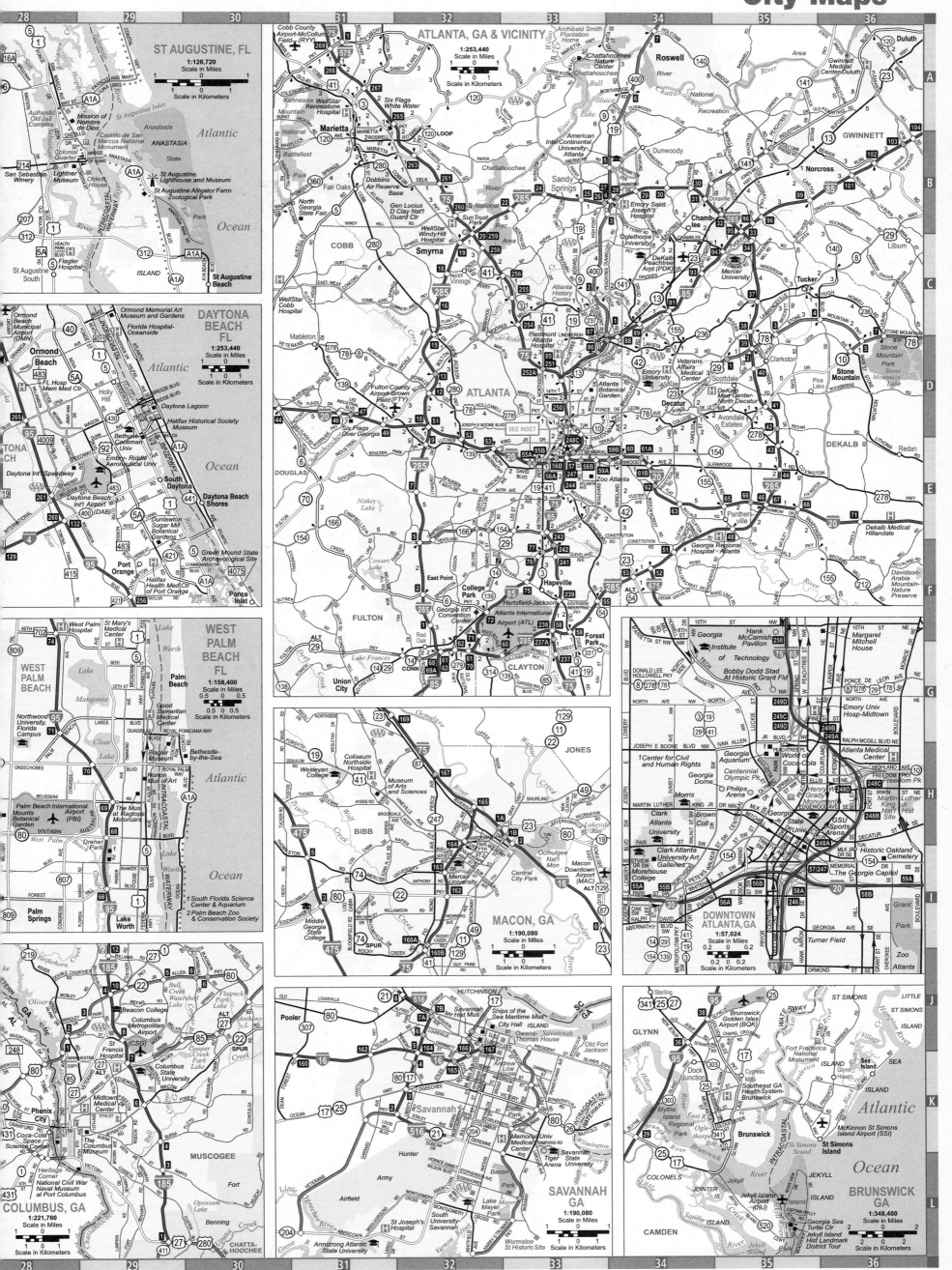

See also mileage table page 2

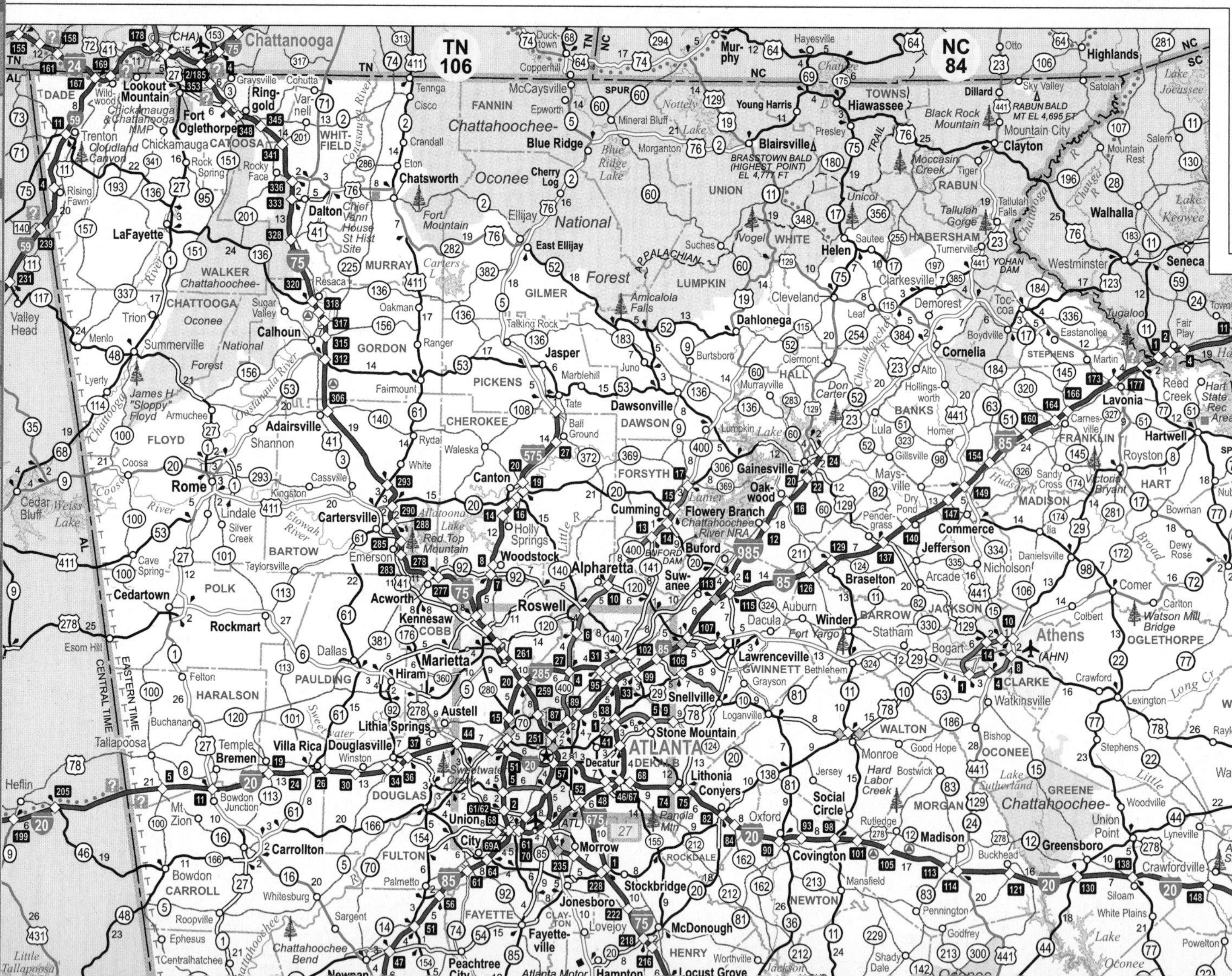

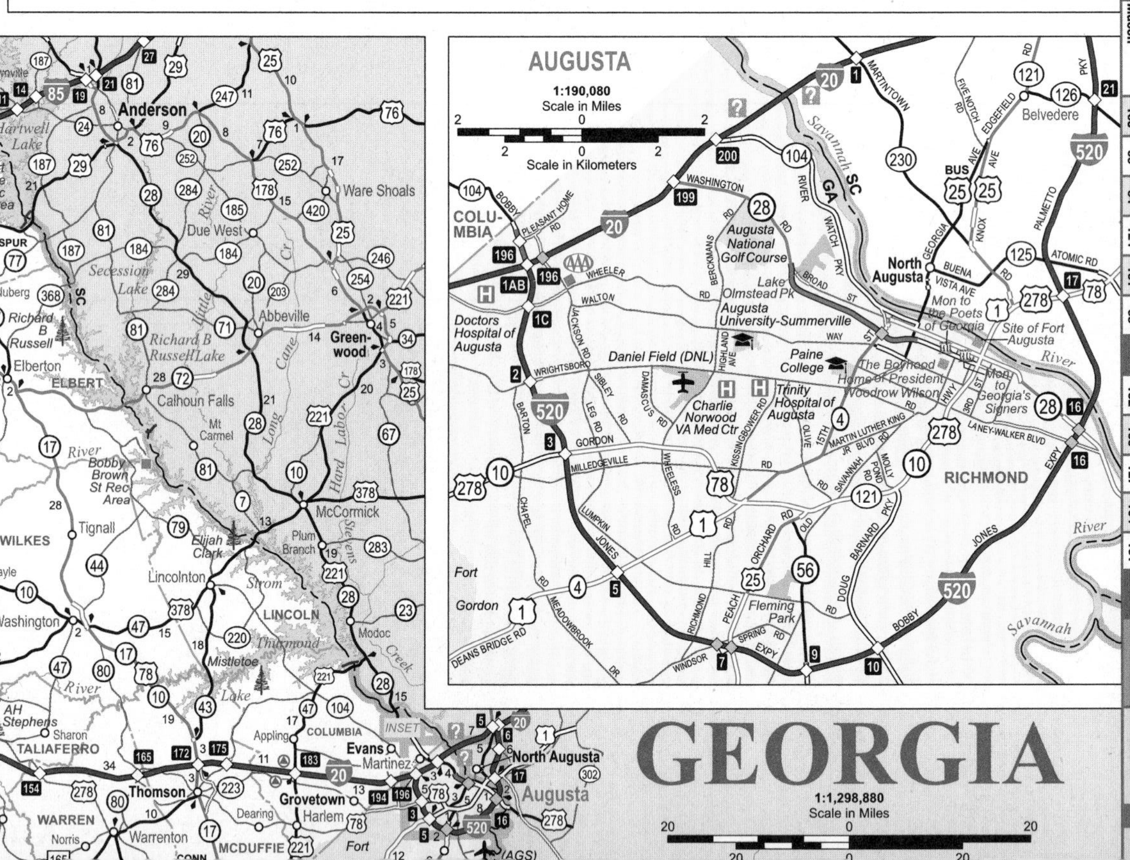

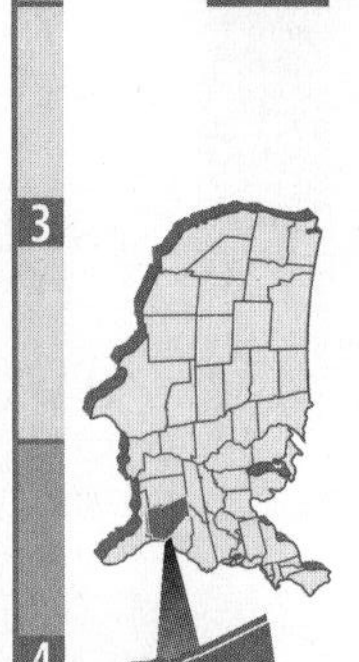

## Driving Distances in Miles

| | Albany | Athens | Atlanta | Augusta | Brunswick | Columbus | Macon | Rome | Savannah | Statesboro | Tifton | Valdosta |
|---|---|---|---|---|---|---|---|---|---|---|---|---|
| **Albany** | | 198 | 182 | 229 | 174 | 86 | 105 | 232 | 251 | 212 | 42 | 80 |
| **Atlanta** | 182 | 71 | | 148 | 273 | 107 | 84 | 90 | 248 | 209 | 181 | 228 |
| **Augusta** | 229 | 97 | 148 | | 200 | 249 | 124 | 217 | 126 | 83 | 228 | 238 |
| **Columbus** | 86 | 180 | 107 | 249 | 258 | | 99 | 142 | 250 | 210 | 126 | 174 |
| **Macon** | 105 | 93 | 84 | 124 | 191 | 99 | | 152 | 166 | 127 | 104 | 151 |

GEORGIA
1:1,298,880
Scale in Miles

AUGUSTA
1:190,080
Scale in Miles
Scale in Kilometers

---

**GEORGIA**

Towns with asterisk (*) are keyed to the maps on page 27.

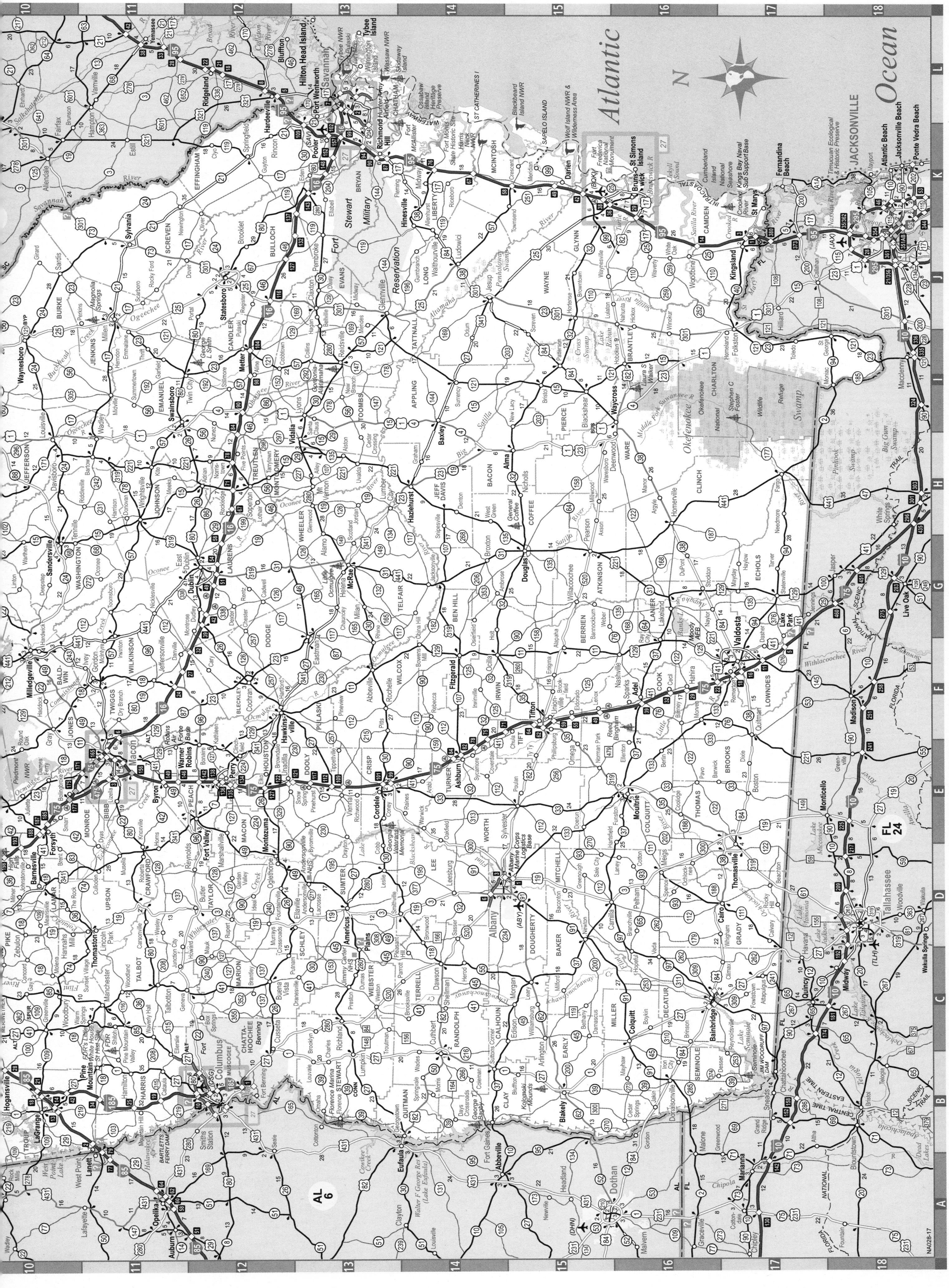

LEGEND
Interstate Highway
Controlled Access Hwy
Controlled Access Hwy Toll
Wildlife Refuge
Nat'l/State Park
National Forest

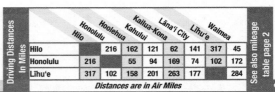

| Driving Distances In Miles | Hilo | Honolulu | Hoolehua | Kahului | Kailua-Kona | Lāna'i City | Līhu'e | Waimea |
|---|---|---|---|---|---|---|---|---|
| Hilo | | 216 | 162 | 121 | 62 | 141 | 317 | 45 |
| Honolulu | 216 | | 55 | 94 | 169 | 74 | 102 | 172 |
| Līhu'e | 317 | 102 | 158 | 201 | 263 | 177 | | 284 |

See also mileage table page 2

Distances are in Air Miles

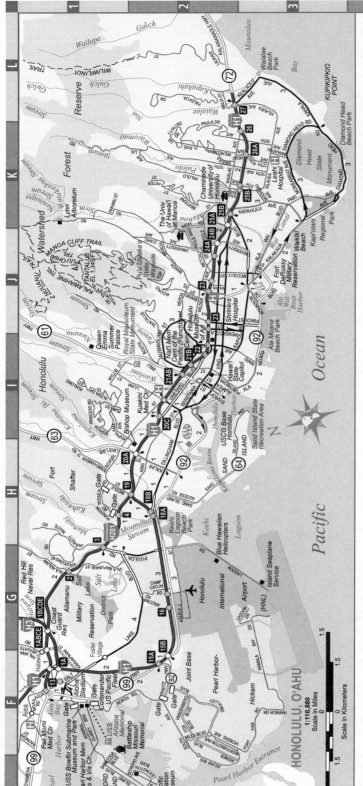

HONOLULU, O'AHU
1:110,880

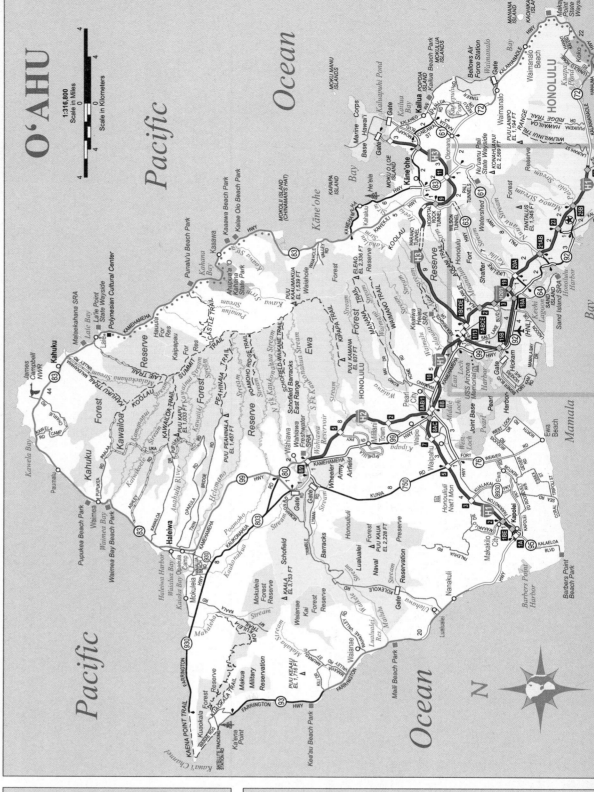

O'AHU
1:316,800

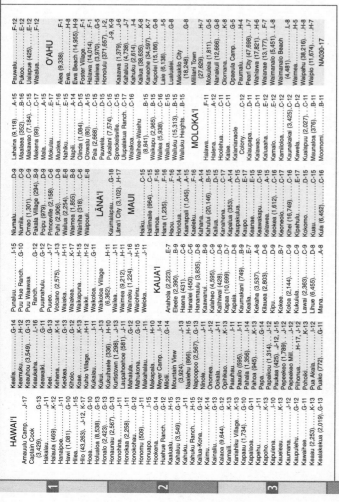

STATE OF HAWAI'I
1:6,336,000

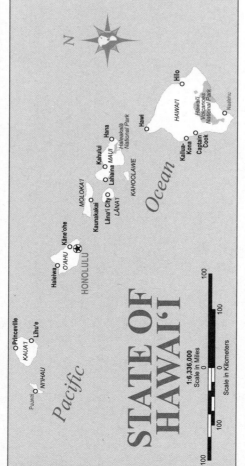

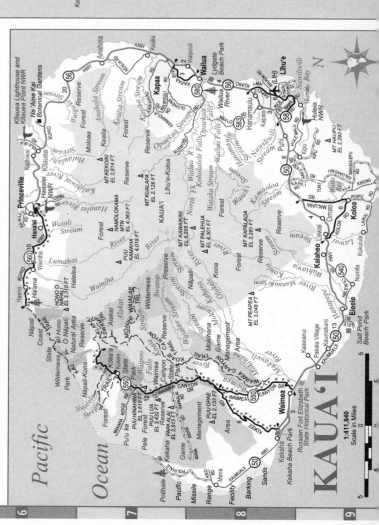

KAUA'I
1:411,840

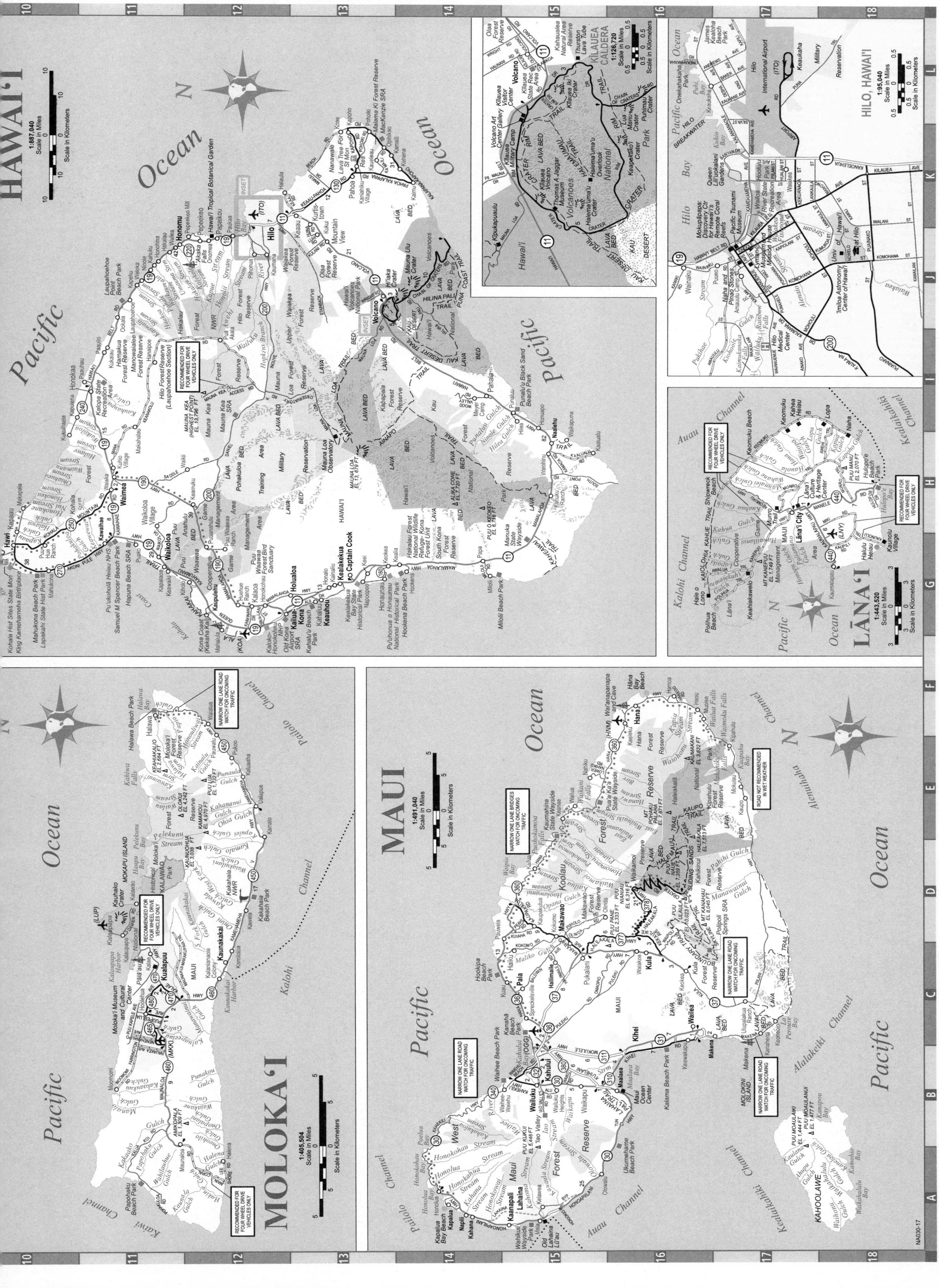

LEGEND
Interstate Highway — 95 — Wildlife Refuge
Controlled Access Hwy — Nat'l/State Park
Controlled Access Hwy Toll — National Forest

HAWAI'I
1:1,887,040
Scale in Miles
Scale in Kilometers

KILAUEA CALDERA
1:126,720
Scale in Miles
Scale in Kilometers

HILO, HAWAI'I
1:95,040
Scale in Miles
Scale in Kilometers

LĀNA'I
1:443,520
Scale in Miles
Scale in Kilometers

MOLOKA'I
1:405,504
Scale in Miles
Scale in Kilometers

MAUI
1:491,040
Scale in Miles
Scale in Kilometers

NA030-17

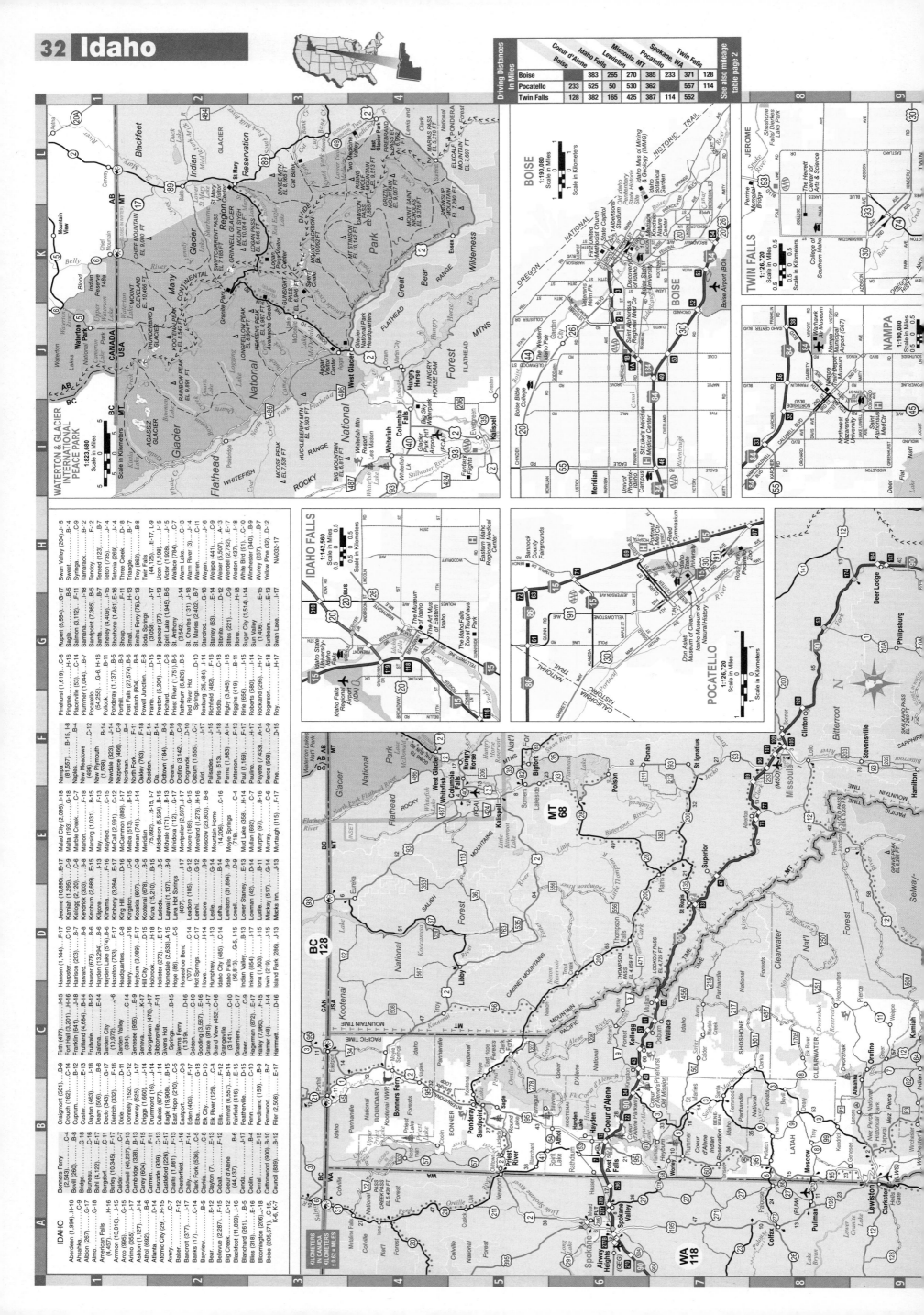

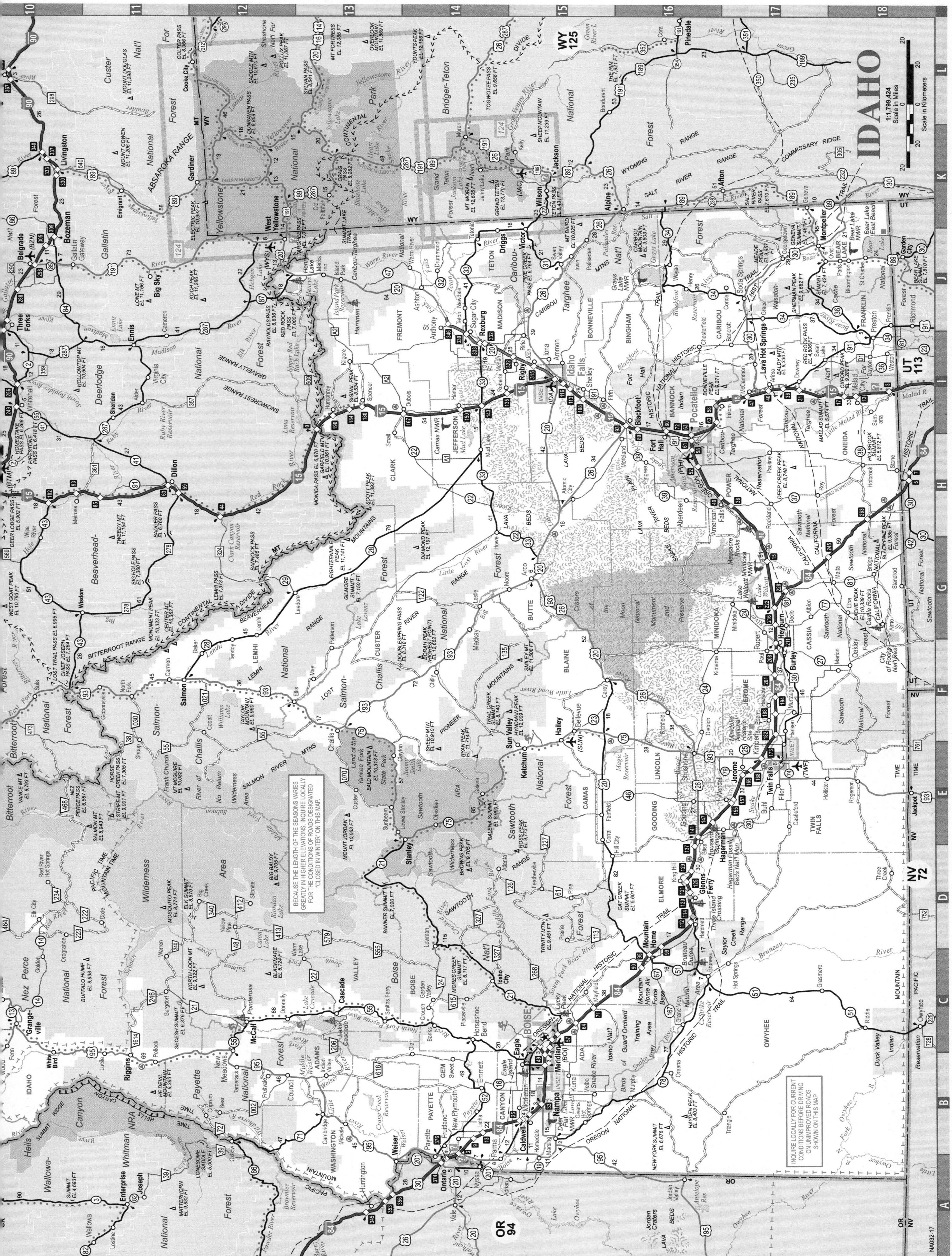

LEGEND

| | |
|---|---|
| Interstate Highway | Wildlife Refuge |
| Controlled Access Hwy | Nat'l/State Park |
| Controlled Access Hwy Toll | National Forest |

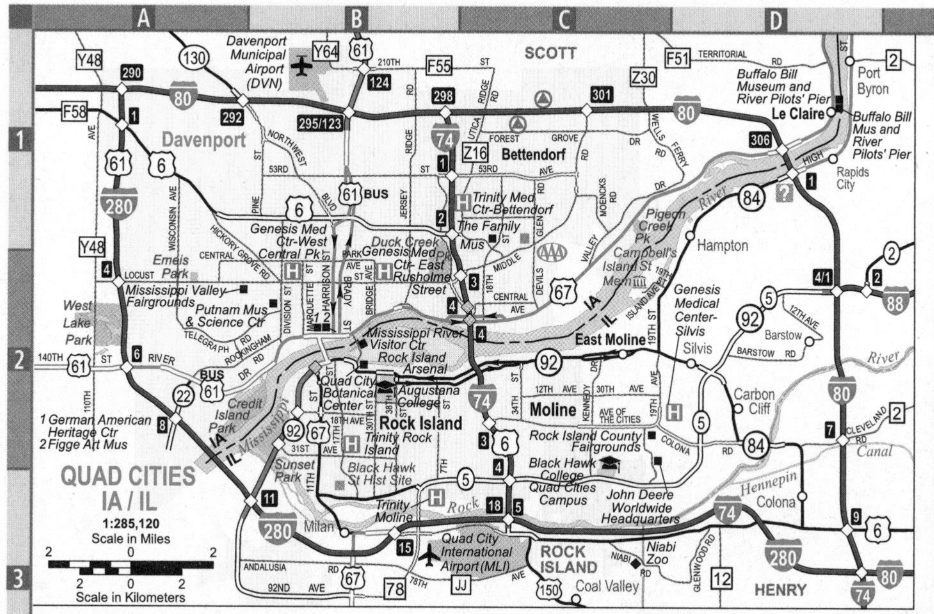

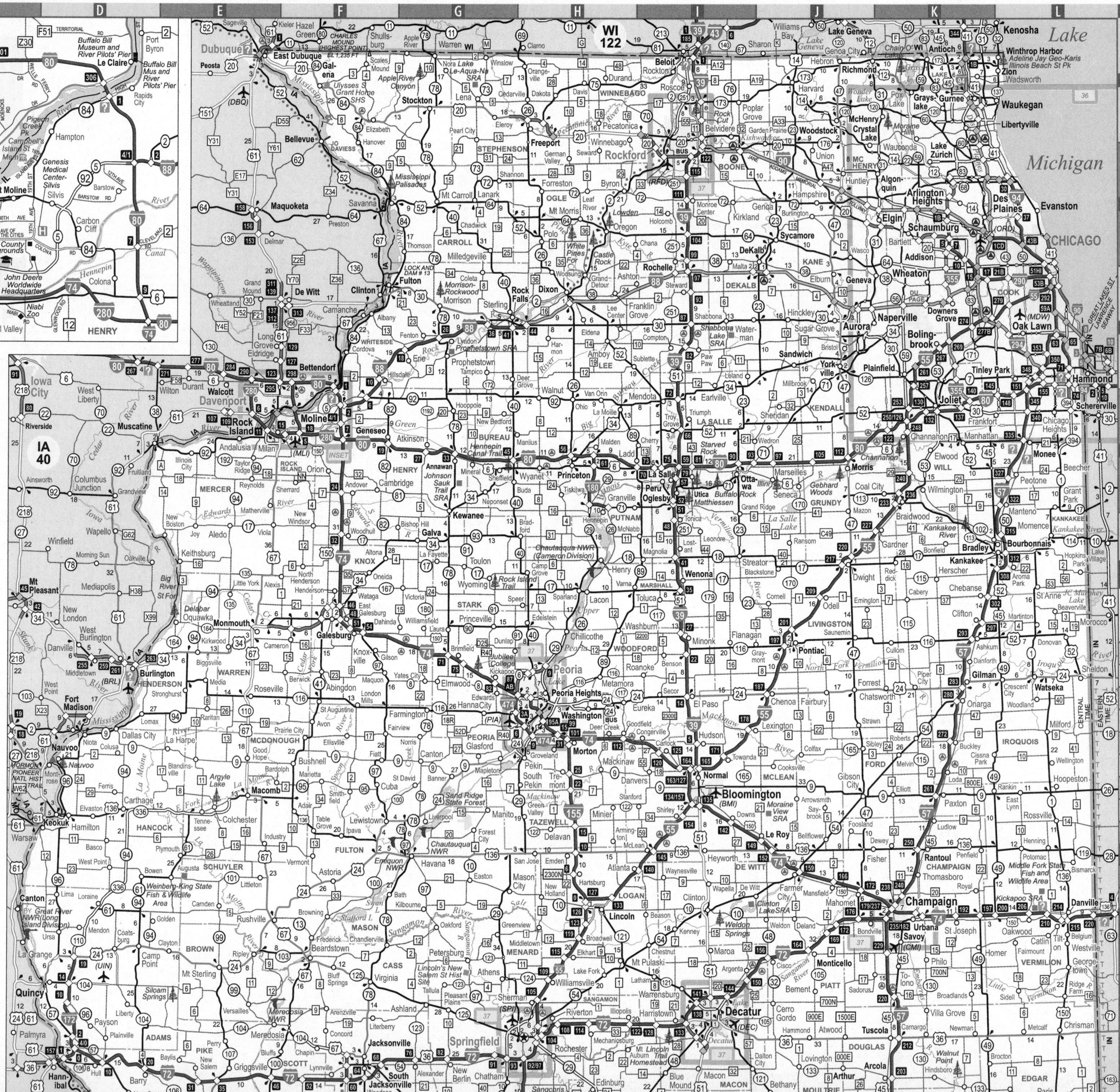

| Driving Distances In Miles | Bloomington | Champaign | Chicago | Davenport, IA | Decatur | Joliet | Mt. Vernon | Peoria | Quincy | Rockford | Springfield | St. Louis, MO |
|---|---|---|---|---|---|---|---|---|---|---|---|---|
| Bloomington | | 51 | 138 | 136 | 46 | 97 | 192 | 38 | 181 | 133 | 67 | 163 |
| Champaign | 51 | | 136 | 188 | 48 | 114 | 142 | 90 | 199 | 183 | 85 | 175 |
| Chicago | 138 | 136 | | 174 | 180 | 40 | 279 | 167 | 314 | 84 | 201 | 297 |
| Peoria | 38 | 90 | 167 | 98 | 85 | 129 | 232 | | 129 | 135 | 72 | 168 |
| Rockford | 133 | 183 | 84 | 126 | 178 | 94 | 325 | 135 | 269 | | 195 | 291 |

See also mileage table page 2

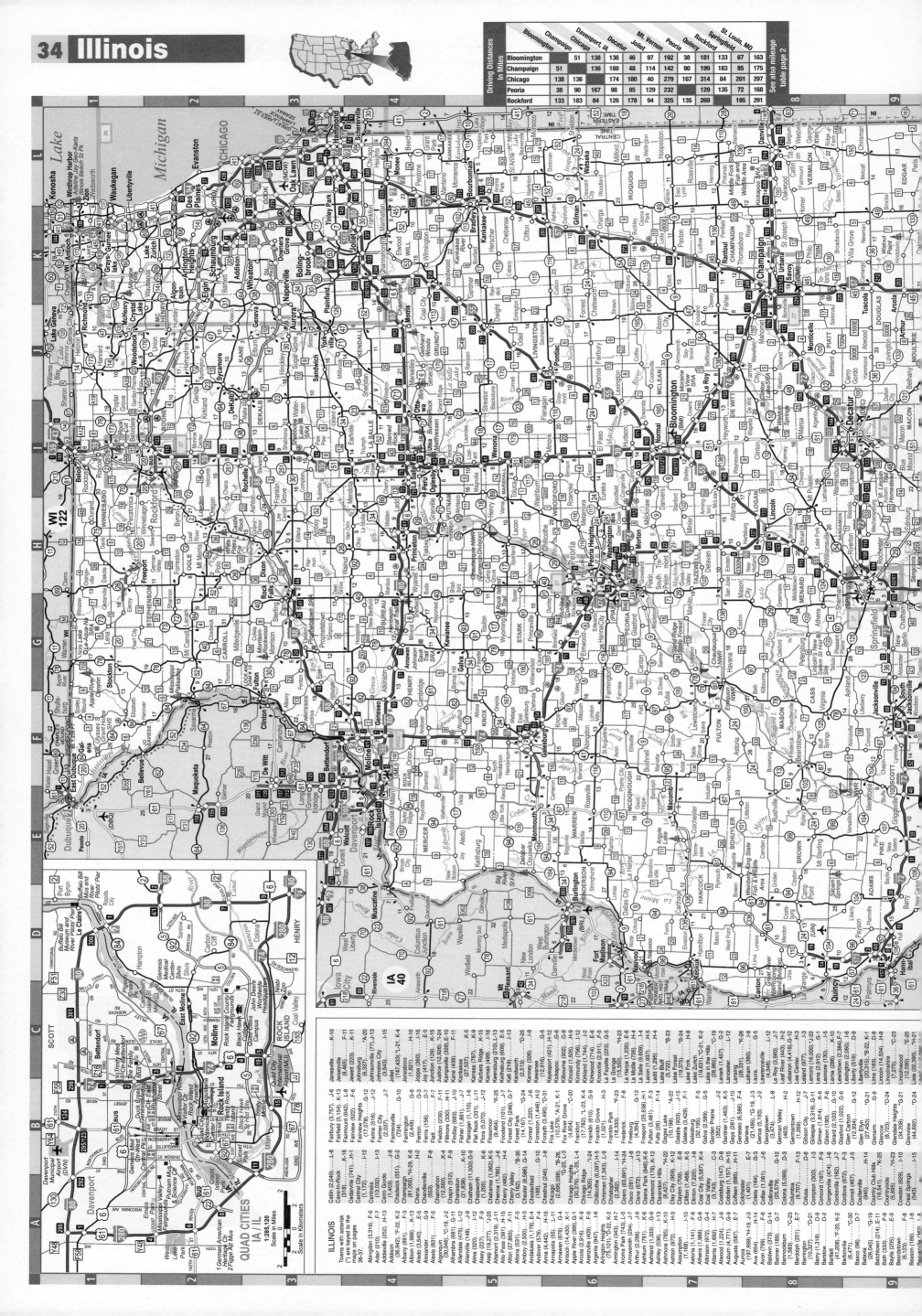

**LEGEND**

| | | |
|---|---|---|
| Interstate Highway | —95— | Wildlife Refuge |
| Controlled Access Hwy | | Nat'l/State Park |
| Controlled Access Hwy Toll | | National Forest |

# ILLINOIS

**1:1,298,880**

Scale in Miles

Scale in Kilometers

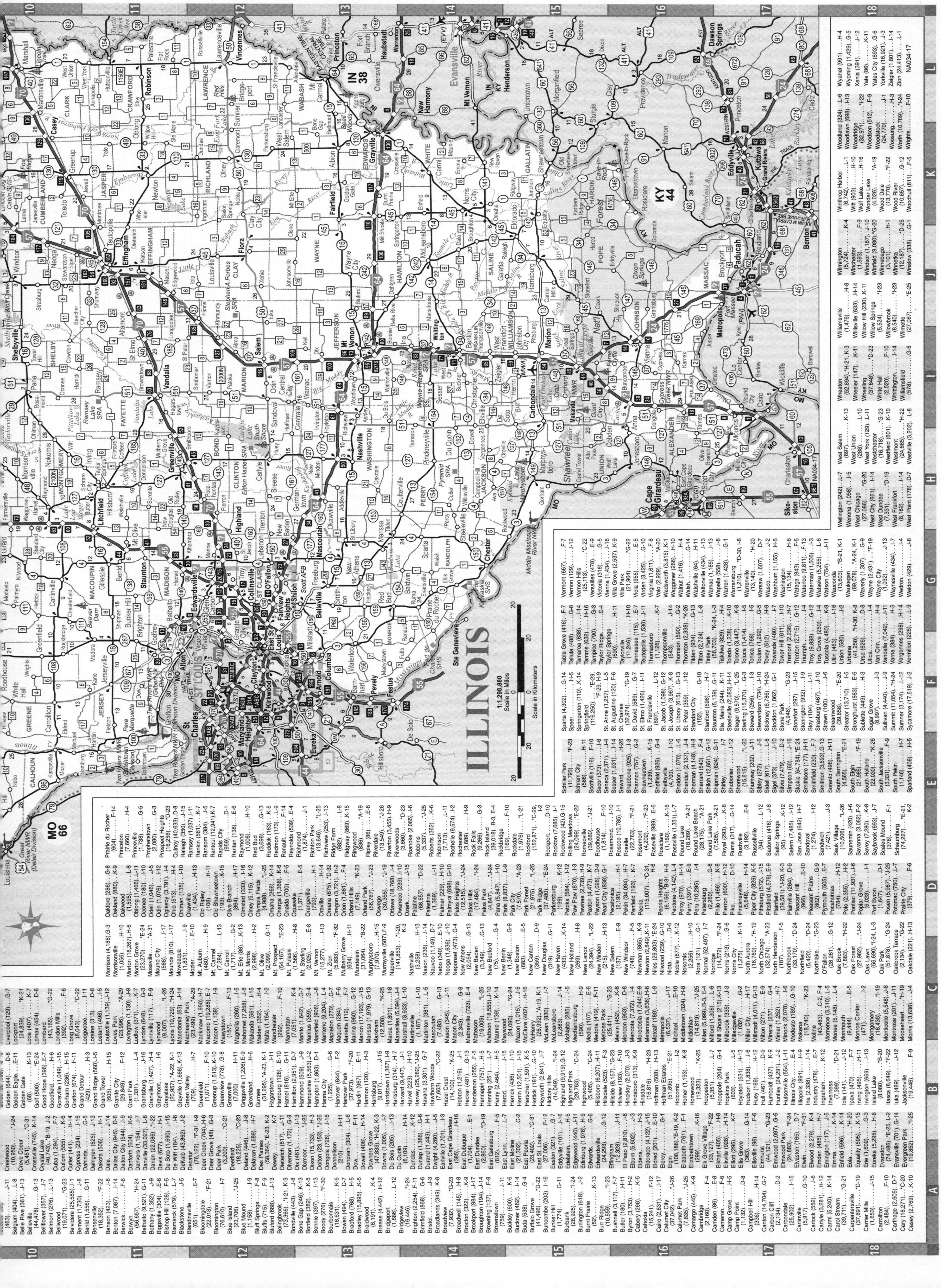

19
20
21
22
23
24
25
26
27
A
B
C
D
E
F
G
H
I
J
K
L
Lake Michigan
N
1:57,000
Scale in mi.
Scale in Km.
SEE INSET
NA036-17
McHENRY
LAKE
COOK
KANE
DUPAGE
KENDALL
WILL
GRUNDY
Waukegan
Gurnee
Grayslake
McHenry
Crystal Lake
Mundelein
Libertyville
Lake Forest
Highland Park
Highwood
Lake Zurich
Vernon Hills
Lincolnshire
Bannockburn
Deerfield
Algonquin
Lake in the Hills
Barrington
Buffalo Grove
Wheeling
Northbrook
Glencoe
Winnetka
Kenilworth
Wilmette
Evanston
Palatine
Arlington Heights
Rolling Meadows
Mt Prospect
Prospect Heights
Glenview
Skokie
Niles
Morton Grove
Des Plaines
Park Ridge
Rosemont
West Dundee
East Dundee
Carpentersville
South Barrington
Hoffman Estates
Schaumburg
Elgin
South Elgin
Streamwood
Hanover Park
Roselle
Elk Grove Village
Bensenville
Wood Dale
Itasca
Schiller Park
Franklin Park
Bartlett
Wayne
St Charles
Geneva
Batavia
West Chicago
Carol Stream
Bloomingdale
Glendale Heights
Addison
Northlake
Stone Park
Melrose Park
Elmhurst
Villa Park
Lombard
Glen Ellyn
Wheaton
Oak Park
Forest Park
Hillside
Westchester
Berwyn
Cicero
Oakbrook Terrace
Oak Brook
Brookfield
Lyons
Stickney
Chicago
Warrenville
Aurora
North Aurora
Naperville
Lisle
Downers Grove
Westmont
Clarendon Hills
Hinsdale
La Grange
Countryside
Bedford Park
Summit
Bridgeview
Burbank
Woodridge
Darien
Willowbrook
Burr Ridge
Willow Springs
Justice
Oak Lawn
Evergreen Park
Chicago Ridge
Hickory Hills
Palos Hills
Worth
Alsip
Blue Island
Palos Park
Palos Heights
Crestwood
Robbins
Posen
Riverdale
Dolton
Bolingbrook
Romeoville
Lemont
Montgomery
Oswego
Plainfield
Orland Park
Orland Hills
Oak Forest
Midlothian
Harvey
Dixmoor
Markham
Tinley Park
South Holland
Hazel Crest
Homewood
Country Club Hills
Thornton
Lansing
Glenwood
Flossmoor
Calumet City
Hammond
East Chicago
Munster
Highland
Lockport
Crest Hill
Joliet
Shorewood
Rockdale
New Lenox
Mokena
Frankfort
Matteson
Richton Park
Park Forest
Chicago Heights
Steger
Sauk Village
Lynwood
Dyer
Schererville
Whiting
GREAT LAKES ST LAWRENCE SEAWAY
Chicago O'Hare International Airport (ORD)
Chicago Midway International Airport (MDW)
Fermi National Accelerator Laboratory (Fermilab)
Argonne National Laboratory
The Newberry Library
Loyola University Chicago
Museum of Contemporary Art
Lurie Children's Hospital
Northwestern Mem Hospital
Willis Tower
Art Institute of Chicago
Millennium Park
Grant Park
Buckingham Memorial Fountain
The Field Museum
Soldier Field
Burnham Park
Glessner House
Mercy Hospital and Medical Center
Chicago River
DOWNTOWN CHICAGO

LEGEND

| | | | |
|---|---|---|---|
| Interstate Highway | 95 | Wildlife Refuge | |
| Controlled Access Hwy | | Nat'l/State Park | |
| Controlled Access Hwy Toll | | National Forest | |

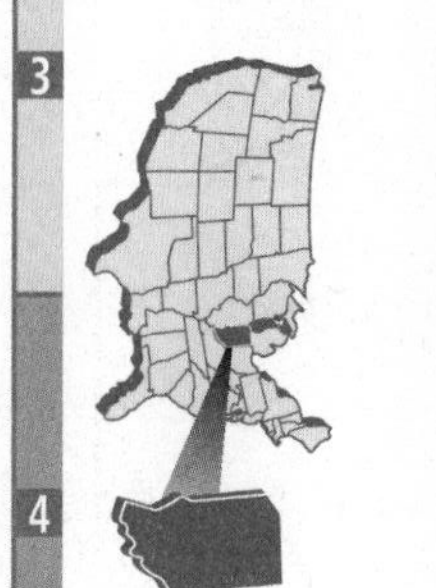

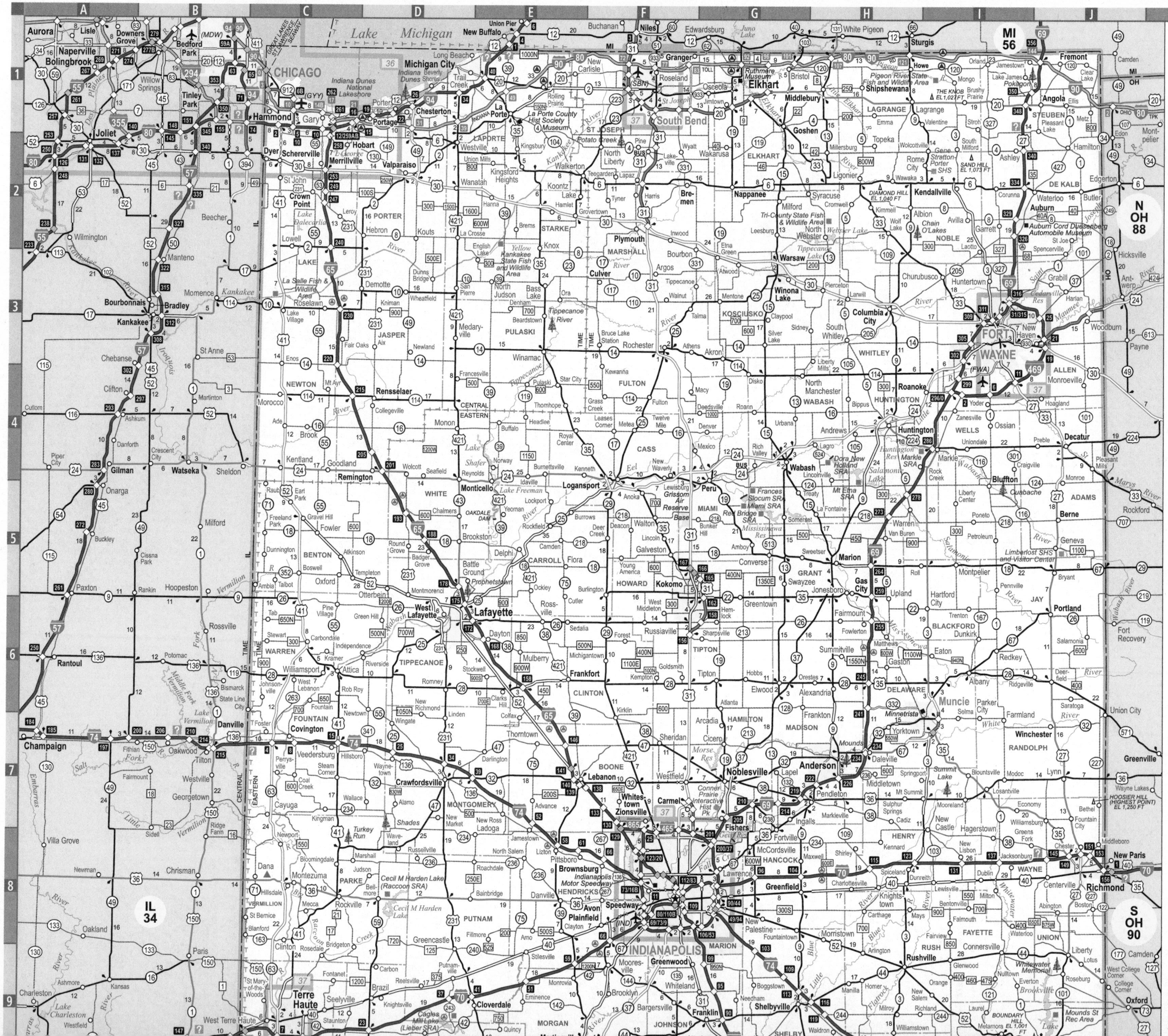




## Driving Distances in Miles

| | Bloomington | Chicago, IL | Columbus | Evansville | Fort Wayne | Indianapolis | Lafayette | Louisville, KY | Michigan City | Richmond | South Bend | Terre Haute |
|---|---|---|---|---|---|---|---|---|---|---|---|---|
| Fort Wayne | 176 | 166 | 168 | 311 | | 122 | 115 | 236 | 118 | 96 | 93 | 206 |
| Indianapolis | 60 | 186 | 46 | 182 | 122 | | 63 | 114 | 152 | 72 | 138 | 77 |
| Michigan City | 200 | 58 | 197 | 304 | 118 | 152 | 92 | 265 | | 222 | 35 | 195 |
| Richmond | 122 | 256 | 89 | 254 | 96 | 72 | 134 | 159 | 222 | | 205 | 150 |
| Terre Haute | 59 | 177 | 103 | 110 | 206 | 77 | 87 | 173 | 195 | 150 | 216 | |

See also mileage table page 2

LEGEND

Interstate Highway (95)
Controlled Access Hwy
Controlled Access Hwy Toll
Wildlife Refuge
Nat'l/State Park
National Forest

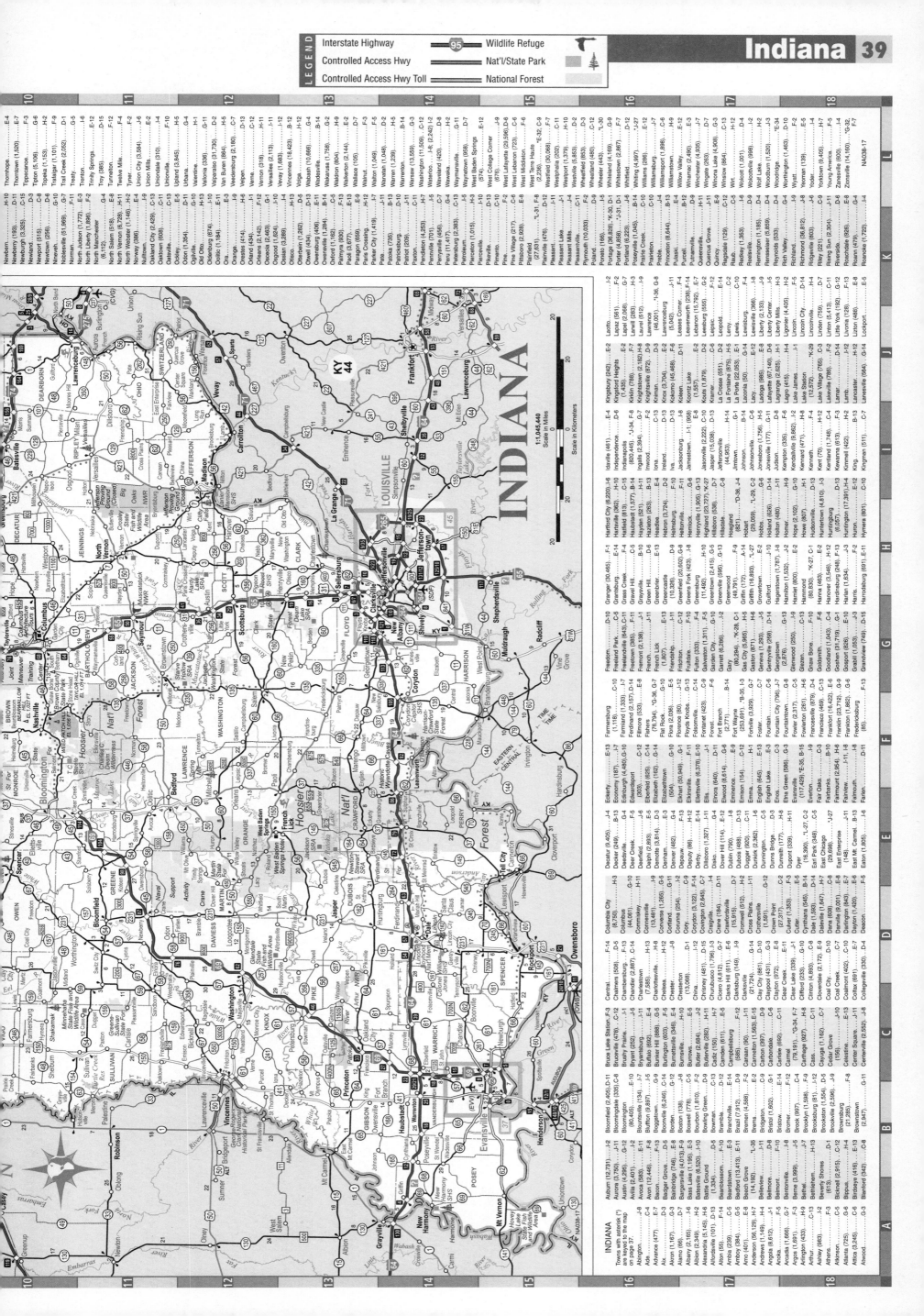

INDIANA

Towns with asterisk (*) are keyed to the map on page 37.

NA038-17

| Driving Distances In Miles | Cedar Rapids | Davenport | Des Moines | Dubuque | Iowa City | Keokuk | Mason City | Omaha NE | Sioux City | Waterloo |
|---|---|---|---|---|---|---|---|---|---|---|
| Davenport | 81 | | 167 | 70 | 54 | 118 | 218 | 302 | 367 | 136 |
| Des Moines | 127 | 167 | | 201 | 115 | 182 | 121 | 135 | 200 | 111 |
| Sioux City | 270 | 367 | 200 | 306 | 314 | 381 | 201 | 98 | | 218 |
| Waterloo | 55 | 136 | 111 | 92 | 83 | 173 | 83 | 247 | 218 | |

See also mileage table page 2

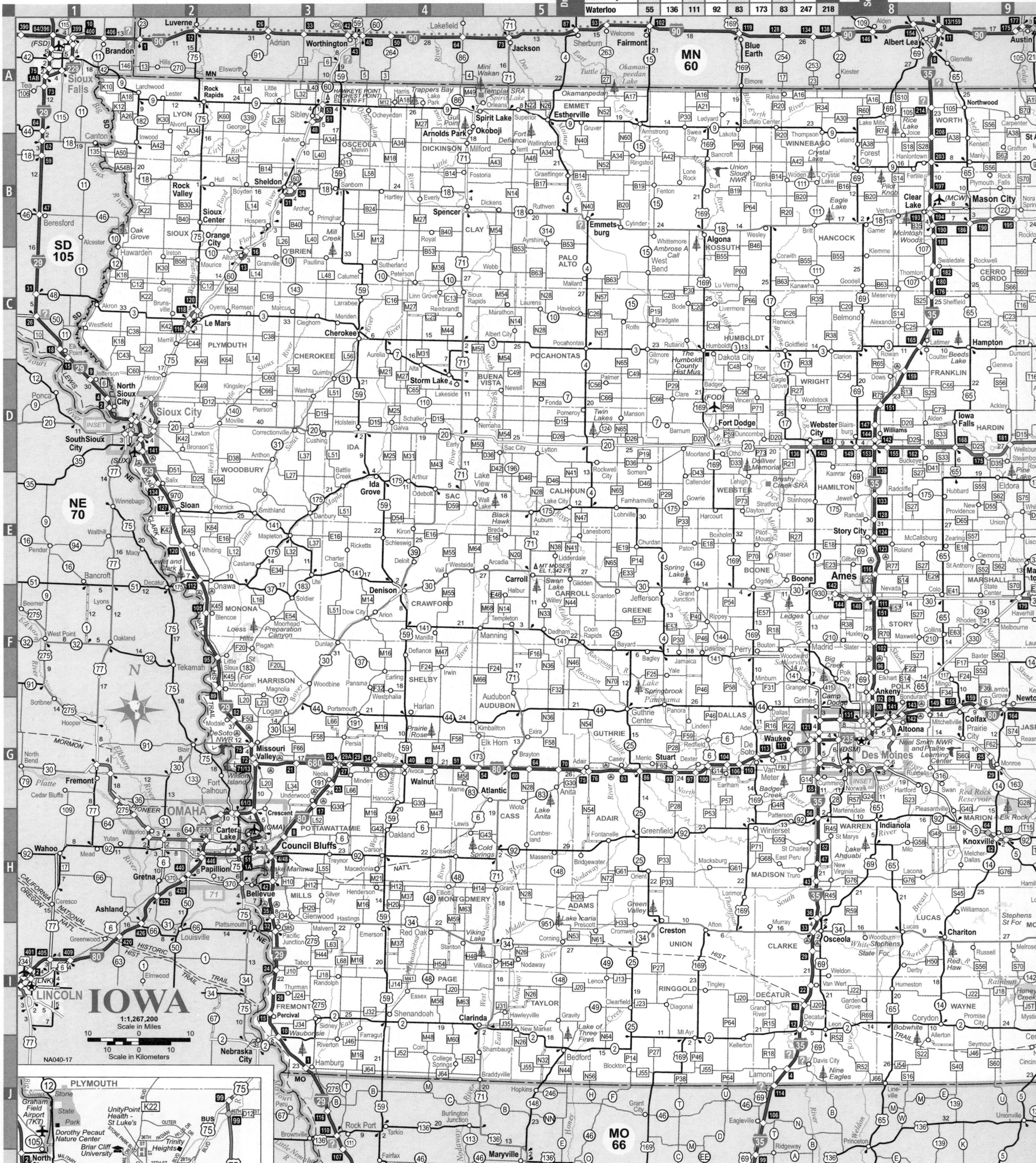

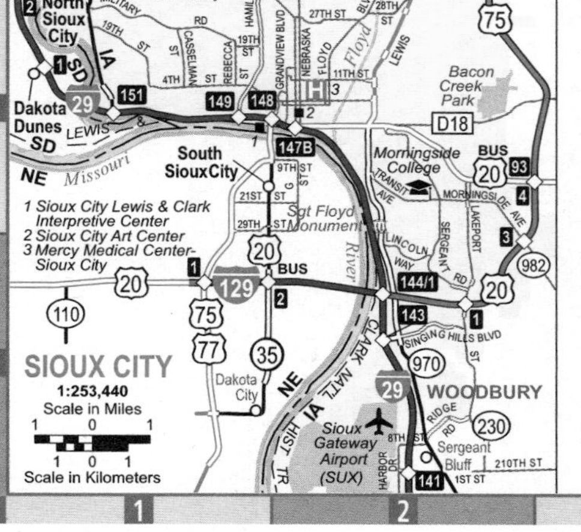

LEGEND
Interstate Highway
Controlled Access Hwy
Controlled Access Hwy Toll
Wildlife Refuge
Nat'l/State Park
National Forest

NA040-17

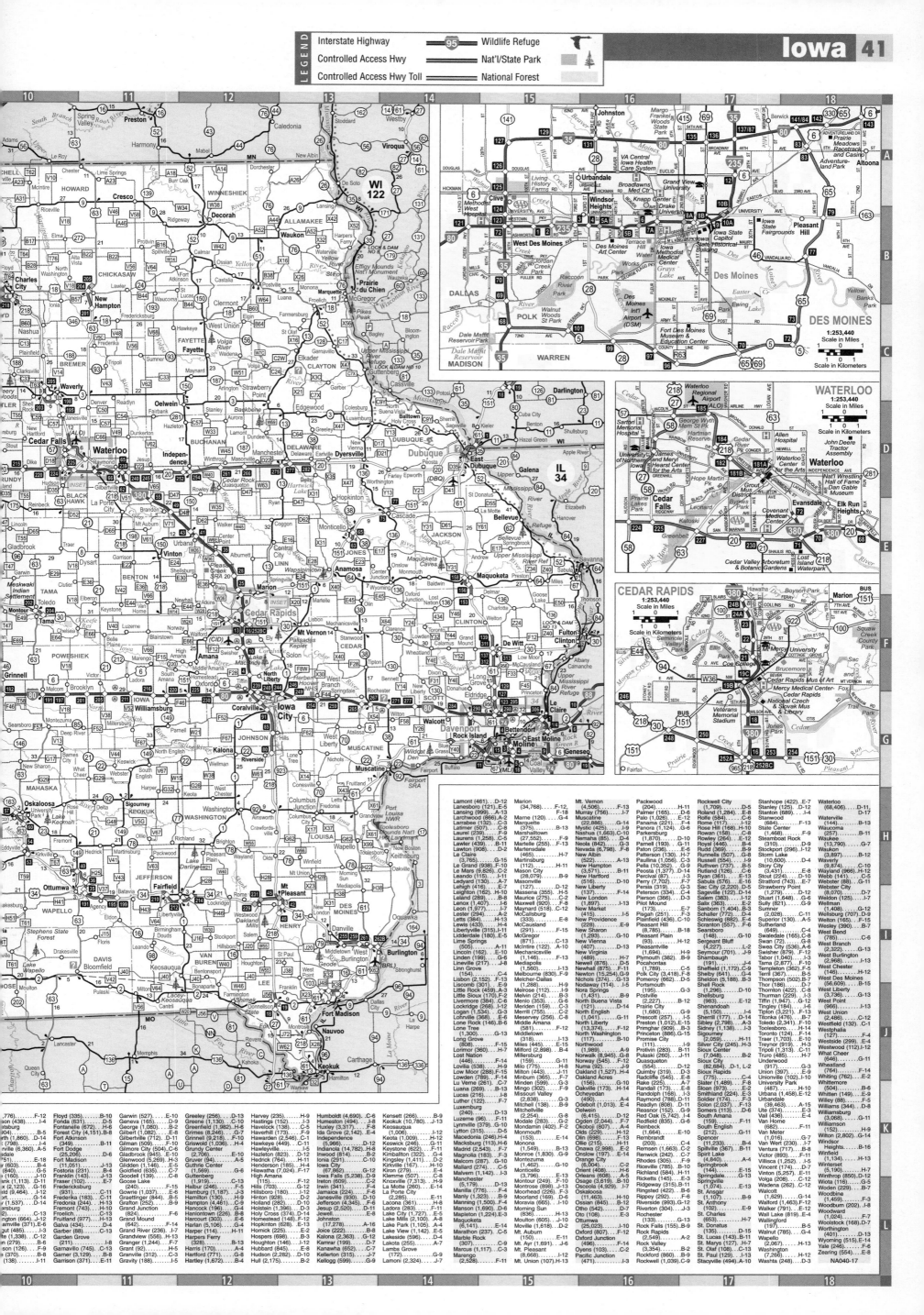

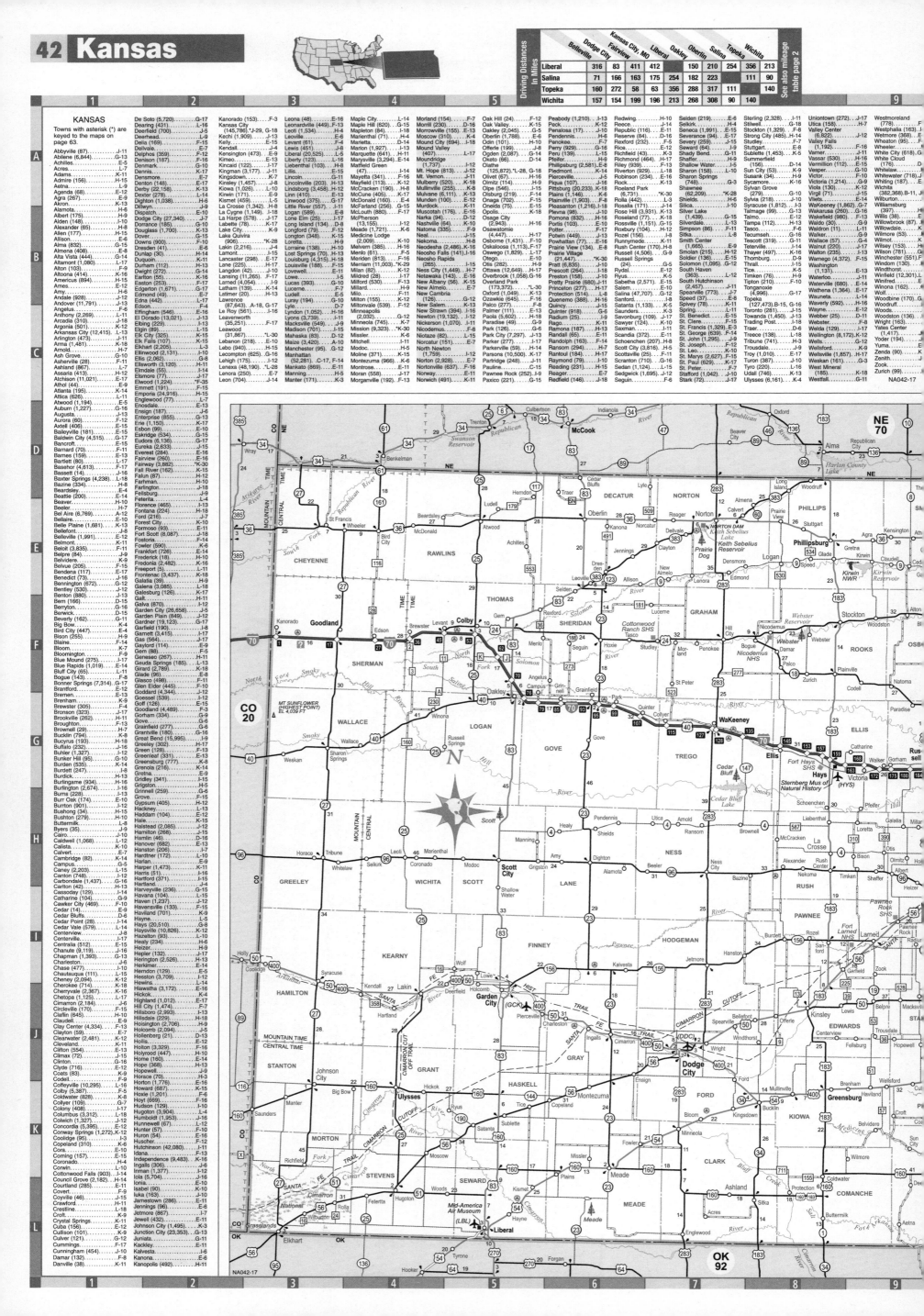

| Driving Distances In Miles | Belleville | Dodge City | Fairview | Kansas City, MO | Liberal | Oakley | Oberlin | Salina | Topeka | Wichita |
|---|---|---|---|---|---|---|---|---|---|---|
| Liberal | 316 | 83 | 411 | 412 | | 150 | 210 | 254 | 356 | 213 |
| Salina | 71 | 166 | 163 | 175 | 254 | 182 | 223 | | 111 | 90 |
| Topeka | 160 | 272 | 58 | 63 | 356 | 288 | 317 | 111 | | 140 |
| Wichita | 157 | 154 | 199 | 196 | 213 | 268 | 308 | 90 | 140 | |

See also mileage table page 2

## KANSAS

Towns with asterisk (*) are keyed to the maps on page 63.

Abbyville (87)....J-11
Abilene (6,844)....G-13
Achilles....E-5
Acres....L-7
Adams....K-11
Admire (156)....H-15
Aetna....L-9
Agenda (68)....E-12
Agra (267)....E-9
Akron....K-13
Alamota....H-6
Albert (175)....H-9
Alden (148)....I-10
Alexander (65)....H-8
Allen (177)....H-15
Allison....E-6
Alma (832)....G-15
Almena (408)....E-8
Alta Vista (444)....G-14
Altamont (1,080)....L-17
Alton (103)....F-9
Altoona (414)....K-16
Americus (894)....H-15
Ames....E-12
Amy....H-6
Andale (928)....J-12
Andover (11,791)....J-13
Angelus....F-6
Anthony (2,269)....L-11
Arcadia (310)....J-18
Argonia (501)....K-12
Arkansas City (12,415)....L-13
Arlington (473)....J-11
Arma (1,481)....K-18
Arnold....H-7
Ash Grove....G-10
Asherville (28)....F-11
Ashland (867)....L-7
Assaria (413)....H-12
Atchison (11,021)....E-17
Athol (44)....E-9
Atlanta (195)....K-14
Attica (626)....L-11
Atwood (1,194)....E-5
Auburn (1,227)....G-16
Augusta....J-13
Aurora (60)....F-12
Axtell (406)....E-15
Baileyville (181)....E-15
Baldwin City (4,515)....G-17
Bancroft....E-15
Barnard (70)....F-11
Barnes (159)....E-13
Bartlett (80)....L-17
Basehor (4,613)....F-17
Bassett (14)....J-16
Baxter Springs (4,238)....L-18
Bazine (334)....H-8
Beardsley....E-4
Beattie (200)....E-14
Beaver....H-10
Beeler....H-7
Bel Aire (6,769)....A-12
Bellaire....E-10
Belle Plaine (1,681)....K-13
Bellefont....J-8
Belleville (1,991)....E-12
Belmont....K-11
Beloit (3,835)....F-11
Belpre (84)....J-9
Belvidere....K-9
Belvue (205)....F-15
Bendena (117)....E-17
Benedict (73)....J-16
Bennington (672)....G-12
Bentley (530)....J-12
Benton (880)....J-13
Bern (166)....D-15
Berryton....G-16
Berwick....D-15
Beverly (162)....G-11
Big Bow....K-4
Bird City (447)....E-4
Bison (255)....H-9
Blaine....F-14
Bloom....K-7
Bloomington....F-9
Blue Mound (275)....I-17
Blue Rapids (1,019)....E-14
Bluff City (65)....L-11
Bogue (143)....F-8
Bonner Springs (7,314)....G-17
Brantford....E-12
Bremen....E-13
Brenham....K-9
Brewster (305)....F-4
Bronson (323)....J-17
Brookville (262)....H-11
Broughton....F-13
Brownell (29)....H-7
Bucklin (794)....K-8
Bucyrus (193)....H-18
Buffalo (232)....J-16
Buhler (1,327)....I-12
Bunker Hill (95)....G-10
Burden (535)....K-14
Burdett (247)....I-8
Burdick....H-13
Burlingame (934)....H-16
Burlington (2,674)....I-16
Burns (228)....I-13
Burr Oak (174)....E-10
Burrton (901)....I-12
Bushong (34)....H-15
Bushton (279)....H-10
Buttermilk....L-8
Byers (35)....J-9
Cairo....J-10
Caldwell (1,068)....L-12
Calista....K-10
Calvert....E-7
Cambridge (82)....K-14
Campus....G-5
Caney (2,203)....L-15
Canton (748)....I-12
Carbondale (1,437)....G-16
Carlton (42)....H-13
Cassoday (129)....I-14
Catharine (104)....G-9
Cawker City (469)....F-10
Cedar (14)....E-9
Cedar Bluffs....D-6
Cedar Point (28)....I-14
Cedar Vale (579)....L-14
Centerview....J-8
Centerville....I-17
Centralia (512)....E-15
Chanute (9,119)....J-16
Chapman (1,393)....G-13
Charleston....J-6
Chase (477)....I-10
Chautauqua (111)....L-15
Cheney (2,094)....K-12
Cherokee (714)....K-18
Cherryvale (2,367)....K-16
Chetopa (1,125)....L-17
Cimarron (2,184)....J-6
Circleville (170)....F-15
Claflin (645)....H-10
Claudell....E-9
Clay Center (4,334)....F-13
Clayton (59)....E-7
Clearwater (2,481)....K-12
Cleveland....K-11
Clifton (554)....E-13
Climax (72)....J-15
Clinton....G-16
Clyde (716)....E-12
Coats (83)....K-9
Codell....F-9
Coffeyville (10,295)....L-16
Colby (5,387)....F-5
Coldwater (828)....K-8
Collyer (109)....G-7
Colony (408)....I-17
Columbus (3,312)....L-18
Colwich (1,327)....J-12
Concordia (5,395)....E-12
Conway Springs (1,272)..K-12
Coolidge (95)....I-3
Copeland (310)....K-6
Cora....E-10
Corning (157)....E-15
Coronado....H-4
Corwin....L-10
Cottonwood Falls (903)....I-14
Council Grove (2,182)....H-14
Courtland (285)....E-11
Covert....F-9
Coyville (46)....J-15
Crawford....H-11
Crestline....L-18
Croft....K-9
Crystal Springs....K-11
Cuba (156)....E-12
Cullison (101)....K-9
Culver (121)....G-12
Cummings....F-17
Cunningham (454)....J-10
Damar (132)....F-8
Danville (38)....K-11
De Soto (5,720)....G-17
Dearing (431)....L-16
Deerfield (700)....J-5
Deerhead....L-9
Delia (169)....F-15
Dellvale....E-7
Delphos (359)....F-12
Denison (187)....F-16
Denmark....G-10
Dennis....K-17
Densmore....E-7
Denton (148)....E-17
Derby (22,158)....K-13
Dexter (278)....L-14
Dighton (1,038)....H-6
Dillwyn....J-9
Dispatch....E-10
Dodge City (27,340)....J-7
Dorrance (185)....G-10
Douglass (1,700)....K-13
Dover....G-15
Downs (900)....F-10
Dresden (41)....E-6
Dunlap (30)....H-14
Duquoin....K-11
Durham (112)....H-13
Dwight (272)....G-14
Earlton (55)....K-16
Easton (253)....F-17
Edgerton (1,671)....G-17
Edmond (49)....E-7
Edna (442)....L-17
Edson....F-4
Effingham (546)....E-16
El Dorado (13,021)....J-13
Elbing (229)....I-13
Elgin (89)....L-15
Elk City (325)....K-15
Elk Falls (107)....K-15
Elkhart (2,205)....L-3
Ellinwood (2,131)....I-10
Ellis (2,062)....G-8
Ellsworth (3,120)....H-11
Elmdale (55)....I-14
Elsmore (77)....J-17
Elwood (1,224)....*F-35
Emmett (191)....F-15
Emporia (24,916)....H-15
Englewood (77)....L-7
Enosdale....E-13
Ensign (187)....J-6
Enterprise (855)....G-13
Erie (1,150)....K-17
Esbon (99)....E-10
Eskridge (534)....G-15
Eudora (6,136)....G-17
Eureka (2,633)....J-15
Everest (284)....E-16
Fairview (260)....E-16
Fairway (3,882)....*K-30
Fall River (162)....K-15
Falun (87)....H-12
Farhman....H-10
Farlington....J-18
Fellsburg....J-9
Feterita....L-4
Florence (465)....I-13
Fontana (224)....H-18
Ford (216)....J-7
Forest City....K-10
Formoso (93)....E-11
Fort Scott (8,087)....J-18
Fostoria....F-14
Fowler (590)....K-6
Frankfort (726)....E-14
Frederick (18)....H-10
Fredonia (2,482)....K-16
Freeport (5)....L-11
Frontenac (3,437)....K-18
Galatia (39)....H-9
Galena (3,085)....L-18
Galesburg (126)....K-17
Galt....H-11
Galva (870)....I-12
Garden City (26,658)....J-5
Garden Plain (849)....J-12
Gardner (19,123)....G-17
Garfield (190)....I-8
Garnett (3,415)....I-17
Gas (564)....J-17
Gaylord (114)....E-9
Gem (88)....F-5
Geneseo (267)....H-11
Geuda Springs (185)....L-13
Girard (2,789)....K-18
Glade (96)....E-8
Glasco (498)....F-11
Glen Elder (445)....F-10
Goddard (4,344)....J-12
Goessel (539)....I-12
Goff (126)....E-15
Goodland (4,489)....F-3
Gorham (334)....G-9
Gove....G-6
Grainfield (277)....G-6
Grantville (180)....G-16
Great Bend (15,995)....I-9
Greeley (302)....H-17
Green (128)....F-13
Greenleaf (331)....E-13
Greensburg (777)....K-8
Grenola (216)....K-14
Gretna....E-9
Gridley (341)....I-15
Grigston....H-5
Grinnell (259)....G-6
Grove....F-15
Gypsum (405)....H-12
Hackney....L-13
Haddam (104)....E-12
Hale....K-15
Halstead (2,085)....J-12
Hamilton (268)....J-15
Hamlin (46)....D-16
Hanover (682)....E-13
Hanston (206)....I-7
Hardtner (172)....L-10
Harlan....E-9
Harper (1,473)....K-11
Harris (51)....I-16
Hartford (371)....I-15
Hartland....J-4
Harveyville (236)....G-15
Havana (104)....L-15
Haven (1,237)....J-12
Havensville (133)....F-15
Haviland (701)....K-9
Hayne....L-5
Hays (20,510)....G-8
Haysville (10,826)....K-12
Hazelton (93)....L-10
Healy (234)....H-6
Heizer....H-9
Hepler (132)....J-17
Herington (2,526)....H-13
Herkimer....E-14
Herndon (129)....E-5
Hesston (3,709)....I-12
Hewins....L-14
Hiawatha (3,172)....E-16
Hickok....K-4
Highland (1,012)....E-17
Hill City (1,474)....F-7
Hillsboro (2,993)....I-13
Hillsdale (229)....H-18
Hoisington (2,706)....H-9
Holcomb (2,094)....J-5
Hollenberg (21)....D-13
Hollis....E-12
Holton (3,329)....F-16
Holyrood (447)....H-10
Home (160)....E-14
Hope (368)....H-13
Hopewell....J-9
Horace (70)....H-3
Horton (1,776)....E-16
Howard (687)....K-15
Hoxie (1,201)....F-6
Hoyt (669)....F-16
Hudson (129)....I-10
Hugoton (3,904)....L-4
Humboldt (1,953)....J-16
Hunnewell (67)....L-12
Hunter (57)....F-10
Huron (54)....E-16
Huscher....F-12
Hutchinson (42,080)....I-11
Idana....F-13
Independence (9,483)....K-16
Ingalls (306)....J-6
Inman (1,377)....I-12
Iola (5,704)....J-16
Ionia....E-10
Isabel (90)....K-10
Iuka (163)....J-10
Jamestown (286)....E-11
Jennings (96)....E-6
Jetmore (867)....I-7
Jewell (432)....E-11
Johnson City (1,495)....K-3
Junction City (23,353)....G-13
Juniata....G-11
Kackley....E-11
Kalvesta....I-6
Kanona....E-6
Kanopolis (492)....H-11
Kanorado (153)....F-3
Kansas City (145,786).*J-29, G-18
Kechi (1,909)....J-13
Kelly....E-15
Kendall....J-4
Kensington (473)....E-9
Kimeo....E-13
Kincaid (122)....I-17
Kingman (3,177)....J-11
Kingsdown....K-7
Kinsley (1,457)....J-8
Kiowa (1,026)....L-10
Kirwin (171)....E-9
Kismet (459)....L-5
La Crosse (1,342)....H-8
La Cygne (1,149)....I-18
La Harpe (578)....J-17
Labette (78)....K-17
Lake City....K-9
Lake Quivira (906)....*K-28
Lakin (2,216)....J-4
Lamont....I-15
Lancaster (298)....E-17
Lane (225)....H-17
Langdon (42)....J-10
Lansing (11,265)....F-17
Larned (4,054)....I-9
Latham (139)....K-14
Latimer (20)....H-13
Lawrence (87,643)....A-18, G-17
Le Roy (561)....I-16
Leavenworth (35,251)....F-17
Leawood (31,867)....*L-30
Lebanon (218)....E-10
Lebo (940)....H-15
Lecompton (625)....G-16
Lehigh (175)....I-12
Lenexa (48,190)....*L-28
Lenora (250)....E-7
Leon (704)....J-14
Leona (48)....E-16
Leonardville (449)....F-13
Leoti (1,534)....H-4
Leoville....E-6
Levant (61)....F-4
Lewis (451)....J-8
Liberal (20,525)....L-5
Liberty (123)....L-16
Liebenthal (103)....H-8
Lillis....E-15
Lincoln....G-11
Lincolnville (203)....H-13
Lindsborg (3,458)....H-12
Linn (410)....E-13
Linwood (375)....G-17
Little River (557)....I-11
Logan (589)....E-8
Lone Elm (25)....I-17
Long Island (134)....D-8
Longford (79)....F-12
Longton (348)....K-15
Loretta....H-9
Lorraine (138)....H-10
Lost Springs (70)....H-13
Louisburg (4,315)....H-18
Louisville (188)....F-15
Lovewell....E-11
Lowe....I-5
Lucas (393)....G-10
Lucerne....F-7
Ludell....E-5
Luray (194)....G-10
Lyle....D-7
Lyndon (1,052)....H-16
Lyons (3,739)....I-11
Macksville (549)....J-9
Madison (701)....I-15
Mahaska (83)....D-12
Maize (3,420)....A-10
Manchester (95)....G-12
Manhattan (52,281)....C-17, F-14
Mankato (869)....E-11
Manning....H-5
Manter (171)....K-3
Maple City....L-14
Maple Hill (620)....G-15
Mapleton (84)....I-18
Marienthal (71)....H-4
Marietta....D-14
Marion (1,927)....I-13
Marquette (641)....H-11
Marysville (3,294)....E-14
Matfield Green (47)....I-14
Mayetta (341)....F-16
Mayfield (113)....K-12
McCracken (190)....H-8
McCune (405)....K-17
McDonald (160)....E-4
McFarland (256)....G-15
McLouth (880)....F-17
McPherson (13,155)....I-12
Meade (1,721)....K-6
Medicine Lodge (2,009)....K-10
Melvern (385)....H-16
Menlo (61)....F-5
Meriden (813)....F-16
Merriam (11,003)....*K-29
Milan (82)....K-12
Mildred (28)....I-17
Milford (530)....F-13
Millard....H-9
Milo....F-11
Milton (155)....K-12
Miltonvale (539)....F-12
Minneapolis (2,032)....G-12
Minneola (745)....K-7
Mission (9,323)....*K-30
Missler....K-6
Mitchell....I-11
Modoc....H-5
Moline (371)....K-15
Montezuma (966)....K-6
Montrose....E-11
Moran (558)....J-17
Morganville (192)....F-13
Morland (154)....F-7
Morrill (230)....D-16
Morrowville (155)....E-13
Moscow (310)....K-4
Mound City (694)....I-18
Mound Valley (407)....L-17
Moundridge (1,737)....I-12
Mt. Hope (813)....J-12
Mt. Vernon....J-11
Mulberry (520)....K-18
Mullinville (255)....K-8
Mulvane (6,111)....K-13
Munden (100)....E-12
Murdock....K-11
Muscotah (176)....E-16
Narka (94)....D-12
Nashville (64)....K-10
Natoma (335)....F-9
Neal....J-15
Nekoma....H-8
Neodesha (2,486)....K-16
Neosho Falls (141)....I-16
Neosho Rapids (265)....I-15
Ness City (1,449)....H-7
Netawaka (143)....E-16
New Albany (56)....K-15
New Almelo....E-7
New Cambria (126)....G-12
New Salem....K-13
New Strawn (394)....I-16
Newton (19,132)....I-12
Nickerson (1,070)....I-11
Nicodemus....F-8
Niotaze (82)....L-15
Norcatur (151)....E-7
North Newton (1,759)....I-12
Norton (2,928)....E-7
Nortonville (637)....F-16
Norway....E-11
Norwich (491)....K-11
Oak Hill (24)....F-12
Oak Valley....K-15
Oakley (2,045)....G-5
Oberlin (1,788)....E-6
Odin (101)....H-10
Offerle (199)....J-8
Ogden (2,087)....G-14
Oketo (66)....D-14
Olathe (125,872).*L-28, G-18
Olivet (67)....H-16
Olmitz (114)....H-9
Olpe (546)....I-15
Olsburg (219)....F-14
Onaga (702)....F-15
Oneida (75)....E-15
Opolis....K-18
Osage City (2,943)....H-16
Osawatomie (4,447)....H-17
Osborne (1,431)....F-10
Oskaloosa (1,113)....F-17
Oswego (1,829)....L-17
Otego....E-10
Otis (282)....H-9
Ottawa (12,649)....H-17
Overbrook (1,058)....G-16
Overland Park (173,372)....*L-30
Oxford (1,049)....K-13
Ozawkie (645)....F-16
Palco (277)....F-8
Palmer (111)....E-13
Paola (5,602)....H-18
Paradise (49)....G-9
Park (126)....G-6
Park City (7,297)....J-13
Parker (277)....I-17
Parkerville (59)....H-14
Parsons (10,500)....K-17
Partridge (248)....J-11
Pauline....C-15
Pawnee Rock (252)....I-9
Paxico (221)....G-15
Peabody (1,210)....I-13
Peck....K-12
Penalosa (17)....J-10
Pendennis....H-6
Penokee....F-7
Perry (929)....G-16
Peru (139)....L-15
Pfeifer....H-9
Phillipsburg (2,581)....E-8
Piedmont....K-14
Pierceville....J-5
Piqua (107)....J-16
Pittsburg (20,233)....K-18
Plains (1,146)....K-6
Plainville (1,903)....F-8
Pleasanton (1,216)....I-18
Plevna (98)....J-10
Pomona (832)....H-16
Portis (103)....E-10
Potter....F-17
Potwin (449)....J-13
Powhattan (77)....E-16
Prairie View (134)....E-8
Prairie Village (21,447)....*K-30
Pratt (6,835)....J-10
Prescott (264)....I-18
Preston (158)....J-10
Pretty Prairie (680)....J-11
Princeton (277)....H-17
Protection (514)....L-8
Quenemo (388)....H-16
Quincy....J-15
Quinter (918)....G-6
Radium (25)....I-9
Rago....K-11
Ramona (187)....H-13
Randall (65)....E-11
Randolph (163)....F-14
Ransom (294)....H-7
Rantoul (184)....H-17
Raymond (79)....I-10
Reading (231)....H-15
Reager....E-7
Redfield (146)....J-18
Redwing....H-10
Reece....J-14
Republic (116)....E-11
Reserve (84)....D-16
Rexford (232)....F-5
Rice....E-12
Richfield (43)....K-3
Richmond (464)....H-17
Riley (939)....F-13
Riverton (929)....L-18
Robinson (234)....E-16
Rock....K-13
Roeland Park (6,731)....*K-30
Rolla (442)....L-3
Rosalia (171)....J-14
Rose Hill (3,931)....K-13
Roseland (77)....K-18
Rossville (1,151)....G-15
Roxbury (104)....H-12
Rozel (156)....I-8
Runnymede....K-11
Rush Center (170)....H-8
Russell (4,506)....G-9
Russell Springs (24)....G-5
Rydal....E-12
Ryus....K-5
Sabetha (2,571)....E-15
Salem....E-10
Salina (47,707)....G-12
Sanford....I-8
Satanta (1,133)....K-5
Saunders....K-3
Savonburg (109)....J-17
Sawyer (124)....K-10
Saxman....I-11
Scandia (372)....E-11
Schoenchen (207)....H-8
Scott City (3,816)....H-5
Scottsville (25)....F-11
Scranton (710)....G-16
Sedan (1,124)....L-15
Sedgwick (1,695)....J-12
Seguin....F-6
Selden (219)....E-6
Selkirk....H-4
Seneca (1,991)....E-15
Severance (94)....E-17
Severy (259)....J-15
Seward (64)....I-9
Shady Bend....G-11
Shaffer....H-9
Shallow Water....I-5
Sharon (158)....L-10
Sharon Springs (748)....G-3
Shawnee (62,209)....*K-28
Shields....H-6
Silica....I-10
Silver Lake (1,439)....G-15
Silverdale....L-13
Simpson (86)....F-11
Sitka....L-8
Smith Center (1,665)....E-9
Smolan (215)....H-12
Soldier (136)....E-15
Solomon (1,095)....G-12
South Haven (363)....L-12
South Hutchinson (2,457)....J-11
Spearville (773)....J-7
Speed (37)....E-8
Spivey (78)....K-11
Spring....L-11
St. Benedict....E-15
St. Clere....F-15
St. Francis (1,329)....E-3
St. George (639)....F-14
St. John (1,295)....J-9
St. Joseph....F-12
St. Leo....K-10
St. Marys (2,627)....F-15
St. Paul (629)....K-17
St. Peter....F-7
Stafford (1,042)....J-10
Stark (72)....J-17
Sterling (2,328)....I-11
Stilwell....G-18
Stockton (1,329)....F-8
Strong City (485)....H-14
Studley....F-7
Stuttgart....E-8
Sublette (1,453)....K-5
Summerfield (156)....D-14
Sun City (53)....K-9
Susank (34)....H-9
Sycamore....K-16
Sylvan Grove (279)....G-10
Sylvia (218)....J-10
Syracuse (1,812)....I-3
Talmage (99)....G-13
Talmo....E-12
Tampa (112)....H-13
Tasco....F-6
Tecumseh....G-16
Tescott (319)....G-11
Teterville....I-14
Thayer (497)....K-16
Thornburg....D-9
Thrall....I-15
Tice....K-5
Timken (76)....H-9
Tipton (210)....F-10
Tonganoxie (4,996)....G-17
Topeka (127,473)....B-15, G-16
Toronto (281)....J-15
Towanda (1,450)....J-13
Trading Post....I-18
Traer....D-6
Treece (138)....L-18
Tribune (741)....H-3
Trousdale....J-9
Troy (1,010)....E-17
Turon (387)....J-10
Tyro (220)....L-16
Udall (746)....K-13
Ulysses (6,161)....K-4
Uniontown (272)....J-17
Utica (158)....H-7
Valley Center (6,822)....J-12
Valley Falls (1,192)....F-16
Varner....J-11
Vassar (530)....H-16
Vermillion (112)....E-15
Vesper....G-10
Victor....F-10
Victoria (1,214)....G-9
Viola (130)....K-12
Virgil (71)....J-15
Vliets....E-14
WaKeeney (1,862)....G-7
Wakarusa (260)....G-16
Wakefield (980)....F-13
Waldo (30)....G-9
Waldron (11)....L-11
Walker....G-9
Wallace (57)....G-4
Walnut (220)....J-17
Walton (235)....I-13
Wamego (4,372)....F-15
Washington (1,131)....E-13
Waterloo....J-11
Waterville (680)....E-14
Wathena (1,364)....E-17
Wauneta....L-14
Waverly (592)....H-16
Wayne....E-12
Webber (25)....D-11
Webster....F-8
Welda (129)....I-17
Wellington (8,172)....K-12
Wells....G-12
Wellsford....K-9
Wellsville (1,857)....H-17
Weskan (161)....G-3
West Mineral (185)....K-18
Westfall....G-11
Westmoreland (778)....F
Westphalia (163)....I
Wetmore (368)....E
Wheaton (95)....F
Wheeler....
White City (618)....G
White Cloud (176)....D
Whitelaw....
Whitewater (718)....J
Whiting (187)....E
Wichita (382,368)....B-11, J
Wilburton....
Williamsburg (397)....H
Willis (38)....E
Willowbrook (87)....
Willowdale....K
Wilmore (53)....
Wilmot....K
Wilsey (153)....H
Wilson (781)....G
Winchester (551)....F
Windom (130)....
Windthorst....
Winfield (12,301)....L
Winifred....E
Winona (162)....
Wolf....
Woodbine (170)....G
Woodruff....
Woods....
Woodston (136)....
Wright (163)....
Yates Center (1,417)....J
Yoder (194)....J
Yuma....E
Zenda (90)....K
Zenith....J
Zook....
Zurich (99)....

NA042-17

LEGEND

| | | | |
|---|---|---|---|
| Interstate Highway | 95 | Wildlife Refuge | |
| Controlled Access Hwy | | Nat'l/State Park | |
| Controlled Access Hwy Toll | | National Forest | |

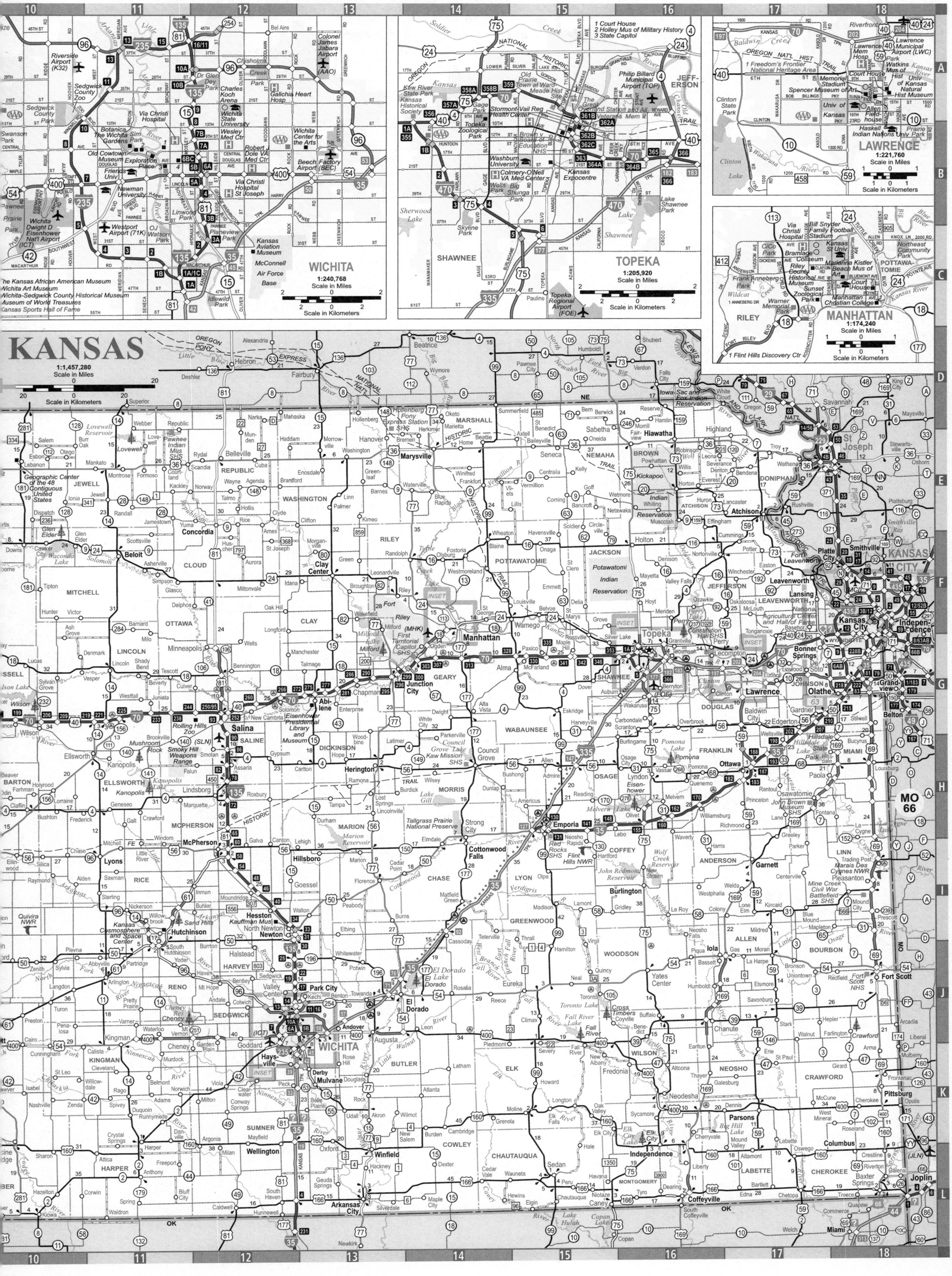

| Driving Distances In Miles | Ashland | Bowling Green | Cincinnati, OH | Corbin | Evansville, IN | Frankfort | Lexington | Louisville | Madisonville | Middlesboro | Owensboro | Paducah |
|---|---|---|---|---|---|---|---|---|---|---|---|---|
| Cincinnati, OH | 135 | 211 | | 169 | 220 | 80 | 83 | 100 | 251 | 211 | 213 | 314 |
| Evansville, IN | 304 | 111 | 220 | 269 | | 174 | 189 | 114 | 48 | 316 | 41 | 109 |
| Frankfort | 141 | 146 | 80 | 114 | 174 | | 28 | 53 | 187 | 156 | 158 | 250 |
| Lexington | 118 | 152 | 83 | 87 | 189 | 28 | | 74 | 192 | 129 | 178 | 255 |
| Louisville | 190 | 151 | 100 | 163 | 114 | 53 | 74 | | 154 | 205 | 106 | 217 |

See also mileage table page 2

KENTUCKY

Aberdeen.........G-7
Adairville (852)...H-7
Adolphus.........H-8
Akersville.........H-9
Albany (2,033). .H-11
Alexandria (8,477)........B-12
Allegre...........G-6
Allen (193)......E-16
Allen Springs.....H-8
Allendale........F-10
Allensville (157). .H-6
Almo..............K-1
Alvaton...........H-8
Amandaville.....H-11
Ammons..........E-8
Amos.............H-9
Anchorage (2,348)........J-14
Andyville.........D-8
Annville (1,095). .F-13
Argillite..........C-16
Argyle...........G-12
Arjay............H-14
Arlington (324). . .H-2
Arnett...........F-14
Ary..............F-15
Ashcamp........F-17
Asher...........G-15
Ashland (21,684)......C-16
Athens..........L-18
Athol............F-14
Auburn (1,340). . .H-7
Augusta (1,190)..B-13
Aurora............K-2
Austin............H-9
Badger..........F-10
Bagdad..........D-11
Bandana (203). . .G-2
Barbourville (3,165)........H-14
Bardstown (11,700).......E-10
Bardwell (723)....H-2
Barlow (675).....G-2
Barrier..........H-12
Barthell..........H-12
Baskett...........E-6
Battletown........D-8
Bayou............G-3
Beattyville (1,307)........F-14
Beaver Dam (3,409).........F-7
Becks Store.....H-10
Bedford (599). . .C-10
Bee Spring.......F-8
Beech Grove (243)..........F-6
Belcher..........F-17
Belton............G-7
Benham (500)...G-16
Benton (4,349)....H-4, J-1
Berea (13,561). .F-13
Berkeley..........H-2
Berlin............C-13
Berry (264)......C-12
Bethlehem.......C-11
Beulah Heights. .H-12
Big Clifty..........F-9
Big Creek........G-14
Big Laurel.......G-15
Big Spring.........E-9
Bighill............F-13
Bimble...........H-14
Birdsville..........G-3
Black Hawk........J-3
Blackey (120)....G-16
Bladeston........B-13
Blaine (47).......D-16
Bledsoe.........G-15
Bloomfield (838)..E-10
Blue Lick Springs........C-13
Boaz.............H-3
Bonnieville (255). .F-9
Bonnyman.......F-15
Boonesboro......E-13
Booneville (81)...F-14
Boston (266).....E-10
Bow.............H-10
Bowling Green (58,067). . .G-8, J-8
Bradford.........B-13
Bradfordsville (294)..........F-11
Brandenburg (2,643)..........E-9
Breeding.........G-10
Bremen (197).....F-6
Briensburg.........J-1
Brodhead (1,211).........F-12
Bronston.........G-12
Brooks (2,401)...D-10
Brooksville (642).C-13
Browder..........G-7
Brownsville (836)......G-8, L-6
Bryantsville......E-12
Buckeye.........E-12
Buckhorn (162). .F-15
Buckner (5,837)..C-10
Buena Vista......E-12
Buffalo (498).....F-10
Bulan............F-15
Burgin (965).....E-12
Burkesville (1,521)........H-10
Burlington (15,926).......B-12
Burna (257).......G-4
Burnside (611)...G-12
Bush............G-14
Butler (612)......B-13
Cadiz (2,558).H-5, J-3
Calhoun (763).....F-6
California (90). . .B-13
Calvert City (2,566).....G-4, I-1
Calvin...........H-14
Camargo (1,081)........D-14
Campbellsburg (813)..........C-11
Campbellsville (9,108)........F-10
Campton (441)...E-14
Caneyville (608)...F-8
Canmer...........F-9
Canton............K-2
Carlisle (2,010). .D-13
Carrie............F-16
Carrollton (3,938).........C-11
Carrsville (50).....F-4
Carter...........C-15
Catlettsburg (1,856)........C-16
Cave City (2,240).....G-9, L-9
Cave Spring......H-7
Cawood (731). . .H-15
Cecilia (572)......E-9
Cedar Bluff.........I-3
Cedar Springs. . . .H-9
Center...........G-10
Centertown (423)..F-7
Central City (5,978)..........F-6
Chaplin (418)....E-11
Charters.........C-15
Chatham.........B-13
Chavies..........F-15
Cherry.............L-1
Clarksburg.......C-15
Clarkson (875)....F-8
Clay (1,181).......F-5
Clay City (1,077).E-14
Claymour.........H-6
Clearfield........D-15
Clementsville.....F-11
Clermont.........E-10
Clifty.............G-6
Climax...........F-13
Clinton (1,388)....H-2
Clover Bottom. . .F-13
Cloverport (1,152).E-7
Coal Run.........F-17
Cobb..............J-3
Coldwater.........H-3
Columbia (4,452)........G-10
Columbus..K-18; (170) H-2
Concord (35)....C-14
Confederate.......J-2
Conkling.........F-14
Cooper..........H-11
Corbin (7,304)...G-13
Corinth.....H-7; (232) C-12
Cornettsville.....G-15
Corydon (720)....E-5
Covington (40,640).......B-12
Coxs Creek......E-10
Crab Orchard (841)..........F-12
Crayne (173)......F-4
Creston..........G-11
Crittenden (3,815)........B-12
Crockett.........D-15
Crofton (749).....G-6
Cromwell..........F-7
Cub Run...........F-9
Cumberland (2,237)........G-16
Cunningham......G-2
Curdsville.........E-6
Custer............E-8
Cynthiana (6,402)........C-13
Danville (16,218).E-12
David............F-16
Dawson Springs (2,764).........G-5
Daysville..........H-6
DeMossville......B-12
Deane...........G-16
Debord...........E-17
Deer Lick.........G-7
Delphia..........G-15
Denniston........E-14
Dewitt...........H-14
Dexter (277)......K-1
Dixon (786).......F-5
Dog Walk........F-12
Donaldson.........K-3
Dorton...........F-17
Dot...............H-7
Dover (252)......B-14
Draffenville........J-1
Drakesboro (515)..G-7
Drip Rock........F-13
Dry Ridge (2,191)........C-12
Dukes.............E-7
Dulaney............I-2
Dunbar...........G-7
Dundee...........F-7
Dunmor...........G-7
Dunnville........G-11
Dwarf............F-15
Dycusburg (26). . .G-4
Dyer..............E-8
Eagle Station....C-11
Earlington (1,413).G-5
East Bernstadt (716)..........G-13
East Point.......E-16
Eastern..........F-16
Eastview..........F-9
Eastwood........D-10
Eddyville (2,554).....G-4, I-2
Edmonton (1,595)........G-10
Egypt............F-14
Ekron (135).......E-9
Elias............F-14
Elizabethtown (28,531)........E-9
Elkhorn City (982)..........F-17
Elkton (2,062).....H-6
Elliottville........D-15
Ellisburg.........F-11
Emerson.........C-15
Eminence (2,498)........C-11
Epleys...........G-7
Eubank (319). . .G-12
Evarts (962).....H-15
Ewing (264).....C-14
Exie.............G-10
Ezel (235).......E-15
Fairdealing........J-1
Fairfield (113). . .E-10
Fairview. .C-13; (286) H-6
Falcon...........E-16
Fall Rock........G-14
Falls of Rough....F-8
Falmouth (2,169)........C-13
Fancy Farm (458)...........H-3
Farmers (284)...D-14
Farmington (245)..H-3
Faywood.........J-15
Fenton............K-2
Ferguson (924)..G-12
Finchville........D-10
Flaherty..........E-9
Flat Lick (960)...H-14
Flat Rock........H-12
Fleming-Neon (770).........G-16
Flemingsburg (2,658)........C-14
Flippin...........H-9
Florence (29,951)......B-12
Fordsville (524)...F-7
Fountain Run (217)...........H-9
Fourmile.........H-14
Frakes..........H-14
Frances..........G-4
Frankfort (25,527).D-11, H-17
Franklin (8,408). .H-8
Frazer..........G-12
Fredonia (401). . .G-4
Freeburn (399). .F-18
Frenchburg (486)..........E-14
Frogue..........H-10
Fulton (2,445).....I-2
Furnace.........E-14
Gamaliel (376). . .H-9
Garfield..........E-8
Garrard.........G-14
Garrett.....E-9, F-16
Garrison (866). .C-15
Gasper...........G-7
Georgetown (29,098)......D-12
Germantown (154).........C-13
Ghent (323).....B-11
Gilbertsville (458)......G-4, I-1
Gilpin...........G-11
Girdler..........G-14
Glasgow (14,028).......G-9
Glencoe (360)...C-12
Glendale..........F-9
Glenview (531). .J-12
Goddard.......C-14
Golden Pond......H-4, K-2
Goose Rock....G-14
Goshen (909). . .C-10
Gracey (138).....H-5
Graham..........G-6
Grand Rivers (382)......G-4, J-1
Gratz (78).......C-11
Gravel Switch. . .F-11
Gray............G-13
Gray Hawk......F-14
Grayson (4,217).D-16
Greensburg (2,163).......G-10
Greenup (1,188)........C-16
Greenville (4,312).........G-6
Greenwood.....H-12
Gregory.........H-12
Grider...........H-10
Guston...........E-8
Guthrie (1,419). . .H-6
Halfway..........H-8
Halls Gap.......F-12
Hamlin............L-2
Hanson (742).....F-6
Hardin (615).H-4, K-1
Hardinsburg (2,343).........E-8
Hardyville (156). .G-9
Hargett..........E-13
Harlan (1,745)...H-15
Harned...........E-8
Harrods Creek. . .I-13
Harrodsburg (8,340)........E-11
Hartford (2,672)...F-7
Hawesville (945). .E-7
Hazard (4,456). .G-15
Hazel Green (228)..........E-15
Head of Grassy..C-15
Hebron (5,929). .B-12
Hedgeville.......F-12
Henderson (28,757)........E-5
Henshaw.........F-4
Hensley..........E-8
Herndon..........H-5
Hickman (2,395). .H-2
Hickory..........H-3
Hico.............K-1
Hillsboro........D-14
Hillview (8,172)..D-10
Hindman (777). .F-16
Hiseville (240)....G-9
Hitchins.........D-16
Hobson..........F-10
Hodgenville (3,206).........F-9
Hollyhill.........H-13
Holmes Mill.....H-16
Holt..............E-8
Holy Cross......E-10
Honeybee.......H-13
Hooktown.......C-13
Hope...........D-14
Hopkinsville (31,577)........H-6
Hopson...........J-3
Horse Branch.....F-7
Horse Cave (2,311).........G-9
Huddy...........E-17
Hudson...........E-8
Hurley..........F-13
Hurstbourne (4,216).......J-13
Hustonville (405).........F-12
Hutchison........I-18
Hyden (365)....G-15
Ida..............H-11
Idamay.........F-14
Independence (24,757)......B-12
Inez (717).......E-17
Ingram..........H-14
Irvine (2,715)....E-13
Irvington (1,181). .E-8
Island (458).......F-6
Isom............G-16
Isonville.........D-15
Iuka..............I-1
Ivel.............F-16
Jackson (2,231)..F-15
Jacktown........F-11
Jamestown (1,794)........G-11
Jeff (323).........G-15
Jeffersontown (26,595). .D-10, K-13
Jeffersonville (1,506).........E-14
Jenkins (2,203)...G-16
Jeriel............D-16
Joy...............F-4
Junction City (2,241).........F-12
Keavy............G-13
Kentontown.......C-13
Kevil (376).........G-2
Keysburg..........H-7
Kidder............H-12
Kidds Crossing. . .H-12
Kidds Store.......F-11
Kimper...........F-17
Kinniconick.......C-15
Kirkmansville......G-6
Kite...............F-16
Knob Lick.........G-10
Kuttawa (649). .G-4, I-2
La Center (1,009). .G-2
La Fayette (165). . .H-5
La Grange (8,082).........C-10
Lake City......G-4, I-1
Lamasco...........J-2
Lancaster (3,442)..F-12
Lawrenceburg (10,505)........D-11
Lebanon (5,539). .F-11
Lebanon Junction (1,813)..........E-9
Ledbetter (1,683). .G-3
Leitchfield (6,699). .F-8
Lenoxburg........B-13
Levi..............F-14
Lewisburg (810). . .G-7
Lewisport (1,670). .E-7
Lexington (295,803).D-12, K-17
Liberty (2,168)....F-11
Lily..............G-13
Linton.............K-2
Livermore (1,365). .F-6
Livingston (226)...F-13
Lloyd............C-16
Lola...............F-4
London (7,993). . .G-13
Lone Oak.........G-3
Lookout..........F-17
Loretto (713).....F-10
Lost Creek........F-15
Louisa (2,467)....D-16
Louisville (597,337).D-10, L-12
Lovelaceville (148).G-3
Lowes (98)........H-3
Lowmansville....E-16
Loyall (1,461).....H-15
Lucas.............H-9
Lynch (747)......G-16
Lynn Grove........H-3
Lynnville..........H-3
Maceo (413).......E-7
Mackville (222)....E-11
Madisonville (19,591).........F-6
Madrid............F-8
Magnolia (524).....F-9
Malone...........E-15
Mammoth Cave.......G-9, L-8
Manchester (1,255).........G-14
Manitou (181)......F-5
Mannsville........F-11
Marcellus.........E-12
Marion (3,039).....F-4
Marrowbone (217)..........H-10
Martha...........D-16
Martin (634).......F-16
Massac (4,505)....G-3
Mattoon...........F-4
Mayfield (10,024). .H-3
Mayking (487)....G-16
Mays Lick (242). .C-14
Maysville (9,011). .C-14
McCarr (164).....E-17
McCreary.........E-12
McDaniels.........F-8
McHenry (388).....F-7
McKee (800)......F-13
Meally...........E-16
Means...........E-14
Melber............G-3
Meshack.........H-10
Middlefork.........F-13
Middlesboro......H-14
Middletown (7,218).........J-14
Midway (1,641). . .D-12
Milburn............H-2
Mill Springs.......G-12
Millersburg (792). .D-13
Millwood..........F-8
Milton (574).......B-10
Minerva..........C-14
Mintonville.......G-12
Mize.............E-15
Monterey (138). . .C-11
Monticello (6,188).H-11
Mooleyville.........D-8
Moorefield........D-13
Morehead (6,845).........D-15
Moreland.........F-12
Morganfield (3,285)...........E-5
Morgantown (2,394)..........G-7
Mortons Gap (863)............G-6
Mouthcard........F-17
Mt. Aerial..........H-8
Mt. Carmel........C-14
Mt. Eden...............D-11
Mt. Olive..............F-14
Mt. Olivet (299)........C-13
Mt. Pisgah.............H-12
Mt. Sherman...........F-10
Mt. Sterling (6,895).....D-13
Mt. Vernon (2,477)......F-13
Mt. Washington (9,117)..D-10
Mud Lick...............H-9
Muldraugh (947)........E-9
Munfordville (1,615)......G-9
Murray (17,741).....H-4, L-1
Myers.................D-13
Nancy.................G-12
Nazareth...............E-10
Nebo (236)..............F-5
New Castle (912).......C-11
New Concord............L-1
New Haven (855).......E-10
New Hope (129)........F-10
New Liberty............C-11
New Market............F-10
New Roe................H-8
New Zion..............F-14
Newport (15,273).......A-12
Nicholasville (28,015). . .E-12
North Middletown (643).D-13
Nortonville (1,204).......G-6
Oak Grove (7,489).......H-6
Oakland (225)...........G-8
Olive....................K-1
Olive Hill (1,599).......D-15
Olympia................D-14
Oneida (410)..........G-14
Owensboro (57,265).E-6, J-5
Owenton (1,327)........C-11
Owingsville (1,530).....D-14
Paducah (25,024). . .G-3, L-5
Paint Lick..............F-12
Paintsville (3,459).......E-16
Palma...................J-1
Paris (8,553)............D-13
Park City (537)..........G-9
Parksville..............F-11
Patesville...............E-7
Payneville...............E-8
Pellville.................E-7
Pembroke (869).........H-6
Pendleton..............C-10
Perry Park.............C-11
Perryville (751).........E-11
Petersburg.............A-16
Petroleum...............H-8
Pewee Valley (1,456). . .J-14
Peytonsburg............H-10
Phelps (893)...........F-18
Philpot..................E-7
Pierce..................G-10
Pikeville (6,903)........F-17
Pinckneyville............G-4
Pine Knot (1,621)......H-12
Pineville (1,732)........H-14
Pippa Passes (533).....F-16
Piqua...................C-13
Pisgah..................K-15
Pittsburg...............G-13

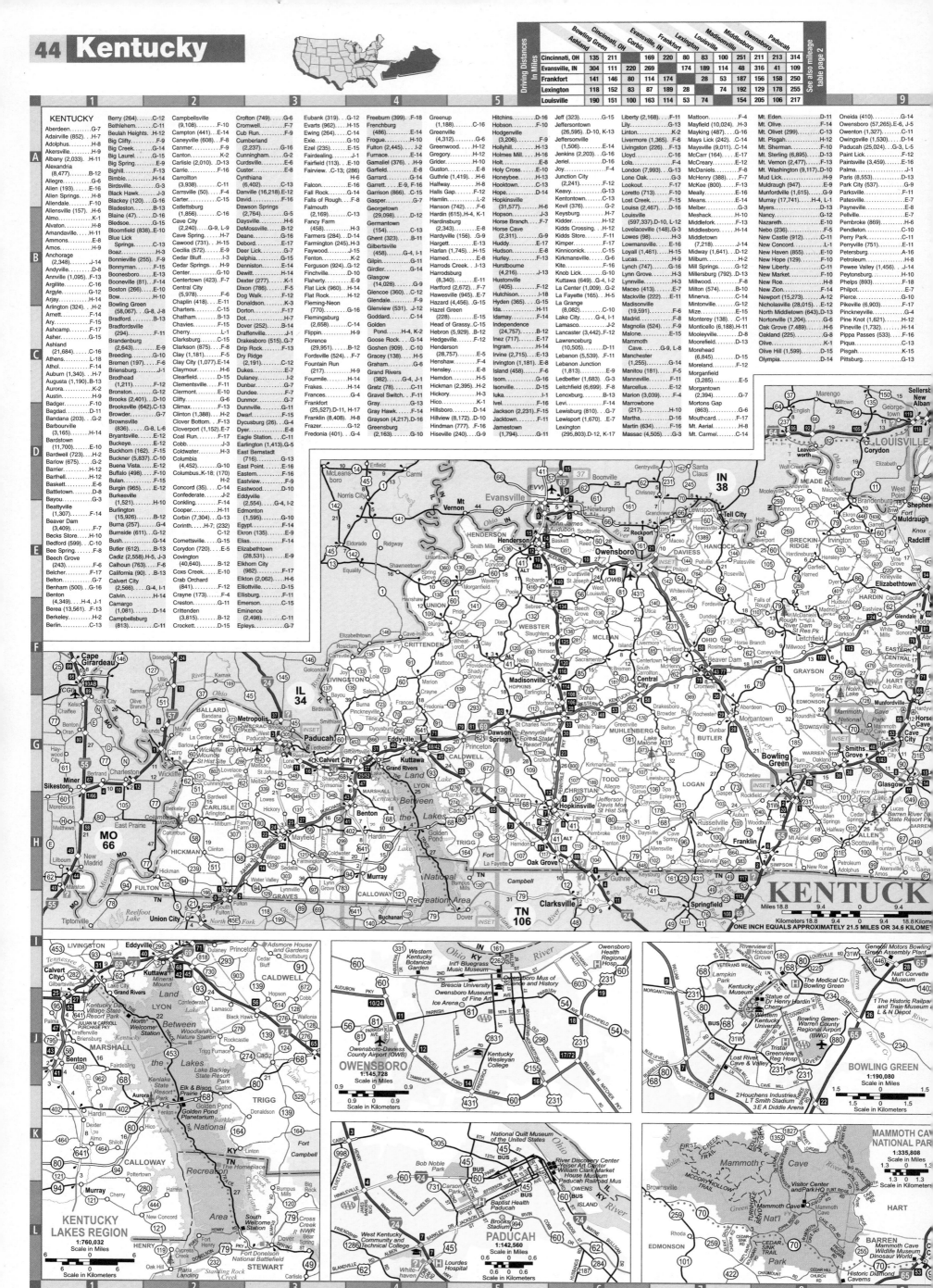

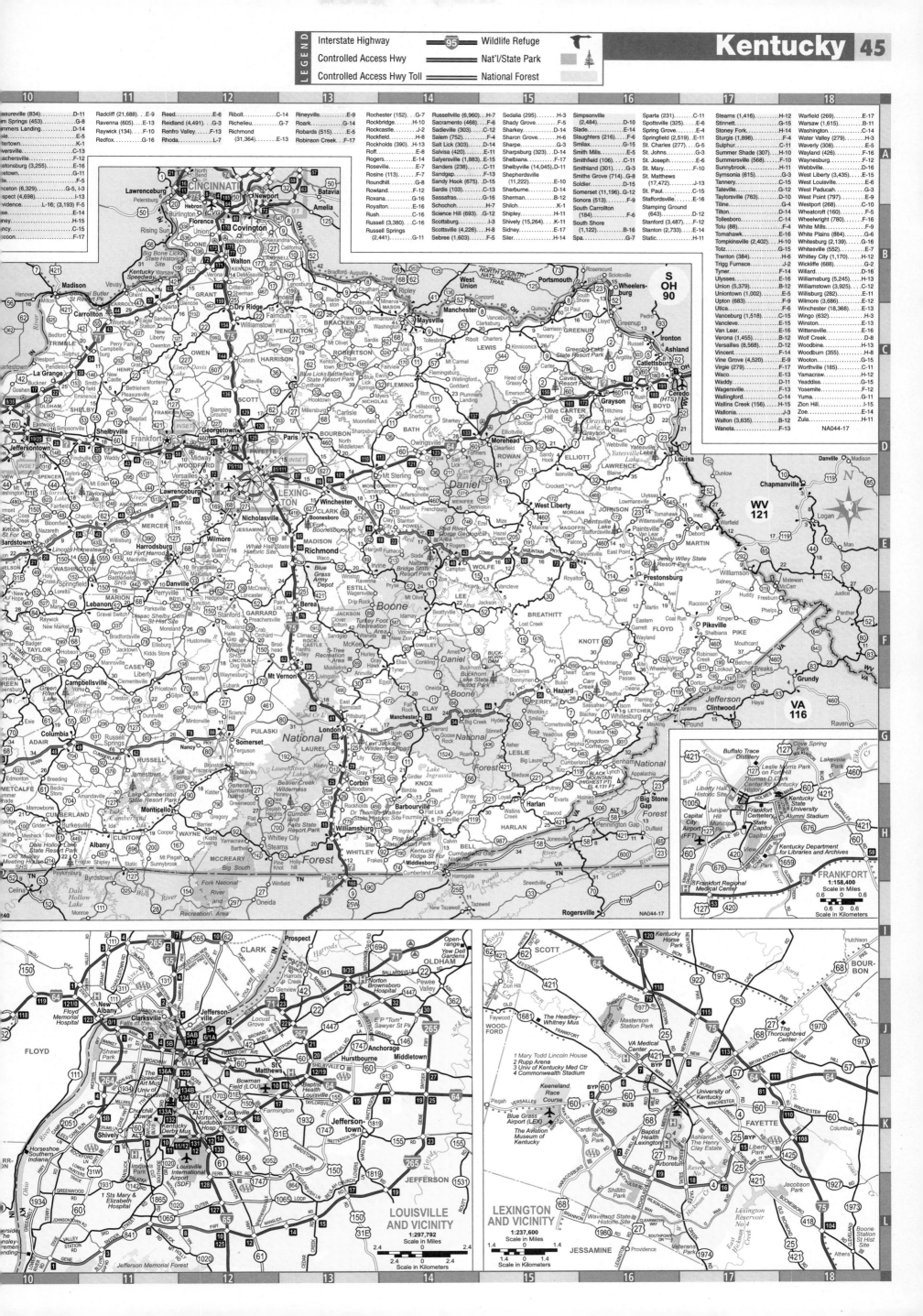

LEGEND
| | | | |
|---|---|---|---|
| Interstate Highway | 95 | Wildlife Refuge | |
| Controlled Access Hwy | | Nat'l/State Park | |
| Controlled Access Hwy Toll | | National Forest | |

LOUISVILLE AND VICINITY
1:297,792
Scale in Miles
Scale in Kilometers

LEXINGTON AND VICINITY
1:237,600
Scale in Miles
Scale in Kilometers

1 Mary Todd Lincoln House
2 Rupp Arena
3 Univ of Kentucky Med Ctr
4 Commonwealth Stadium

FRANKFORT
1:158,400
Scale in Miles
Scale in Kilometers

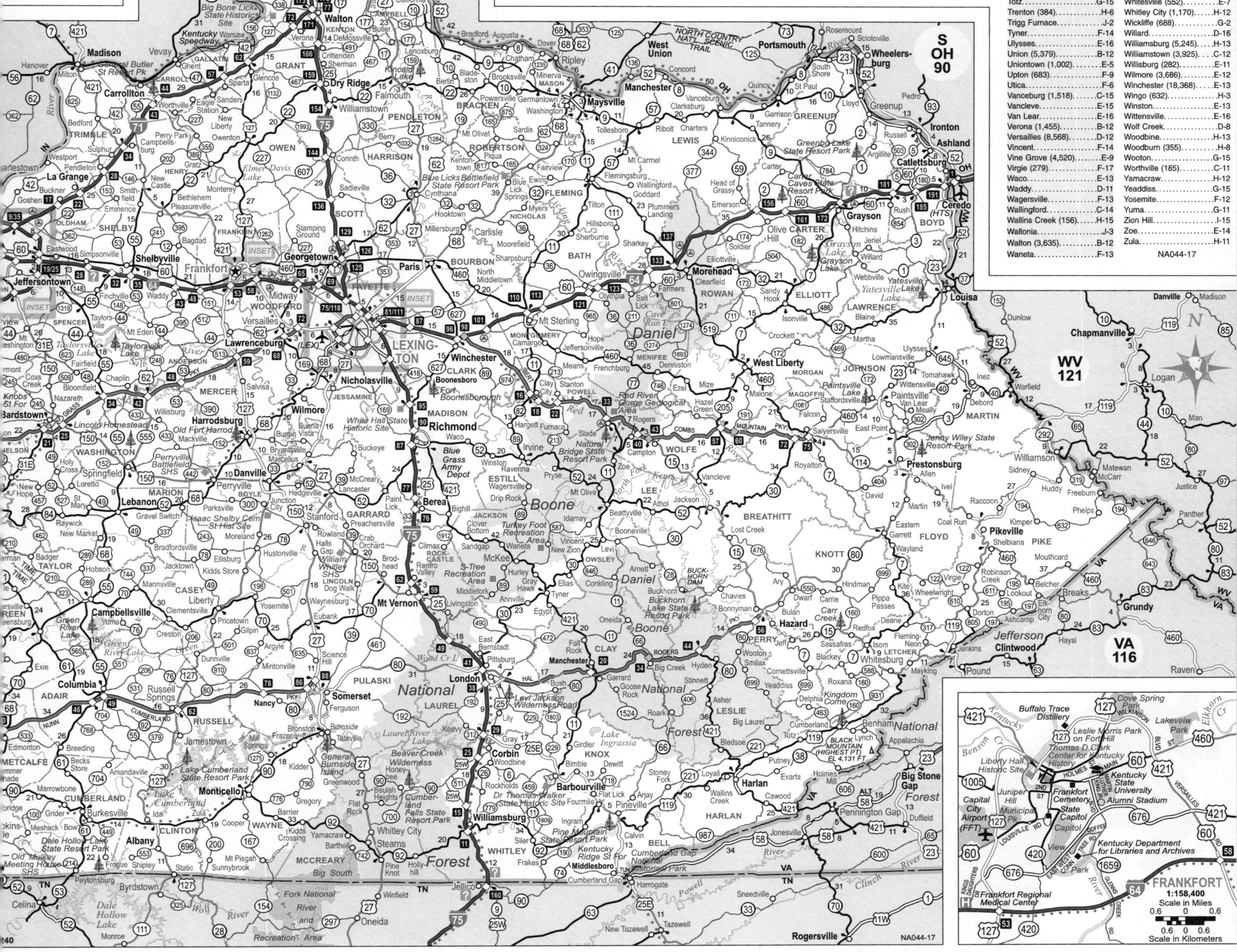

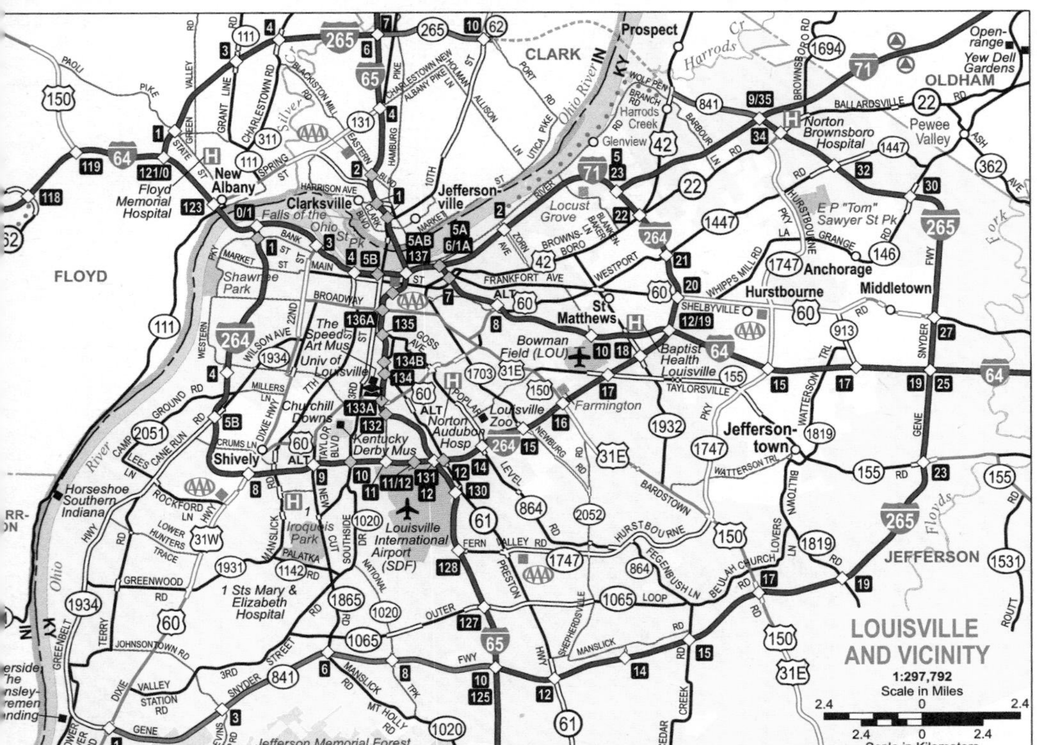

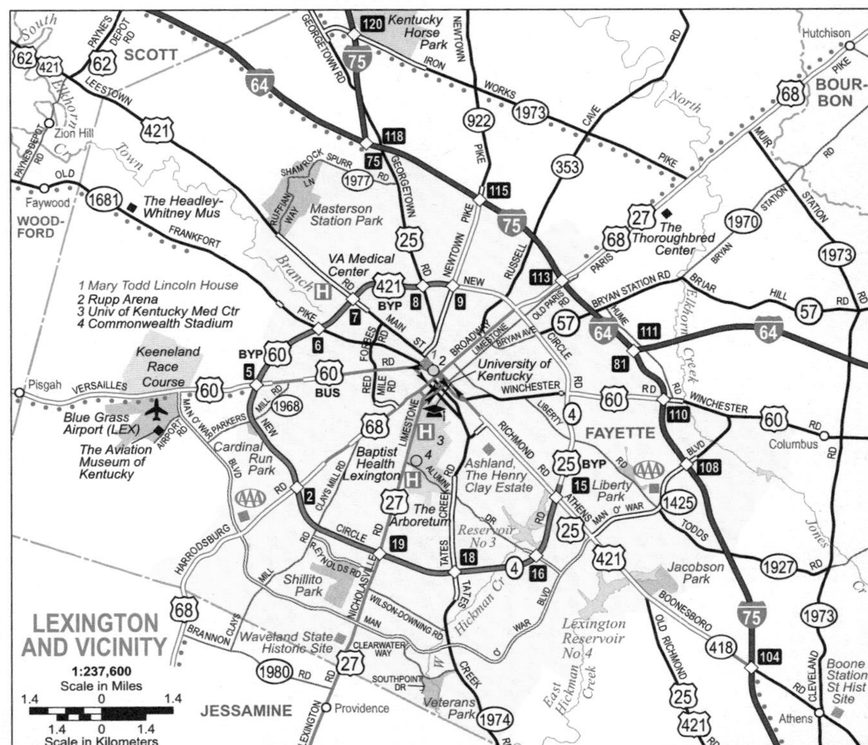

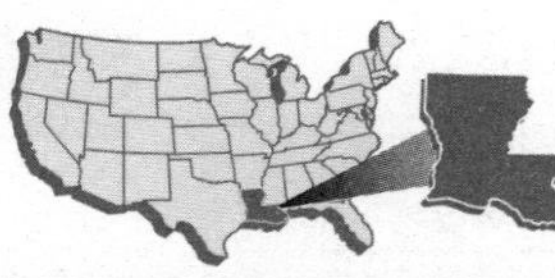

See also mileage table page 2

| Driving Distances In Miles | Alexandria | Baton Rouge | Hammond | Lafayette | Lake Charles | Monroe | New Orleans | Shreveport | Tallulah | Winnfield |
|---|---|---|---|---|---|---|---|---|---|---|
| Baton Rouge | 115 | | 47 | 56 | 126 | 185 | 81 | 233 | 164 | 171 |
| Lake Charles | 97 | 126 | 172 | 75 | | 192 | 206 | 221 | 221 | 145 |
| New Orleans | 218 | 81 | 57 | 135 | 206 | 264 | | 341 | 246 | 265 |
| Shreveport | 124 | 233 | 289 | 212 | 221 | 98 | 341 | | 154 | 94 |

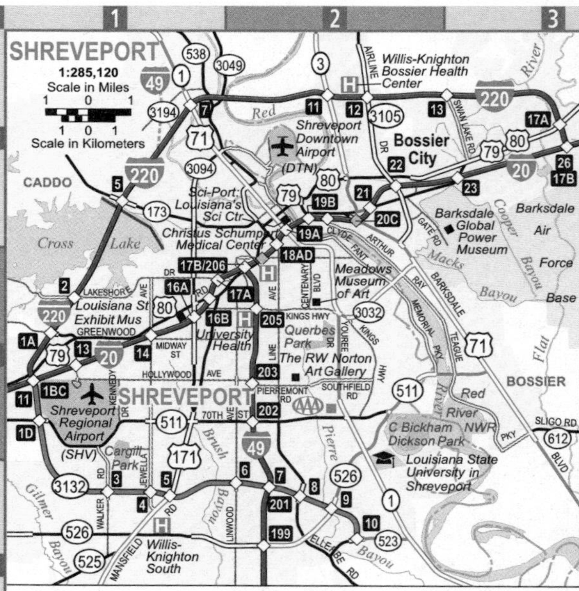

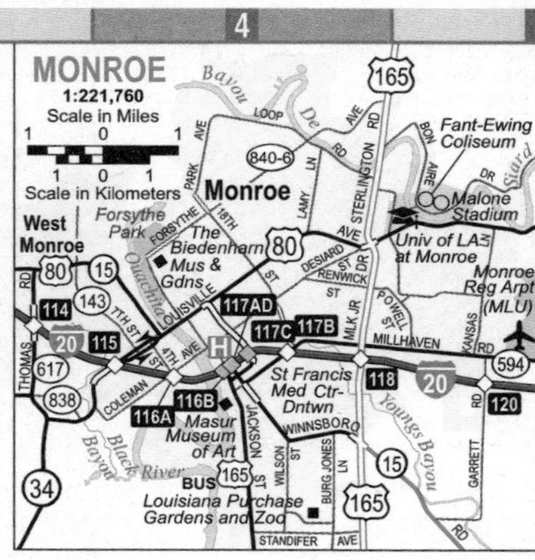

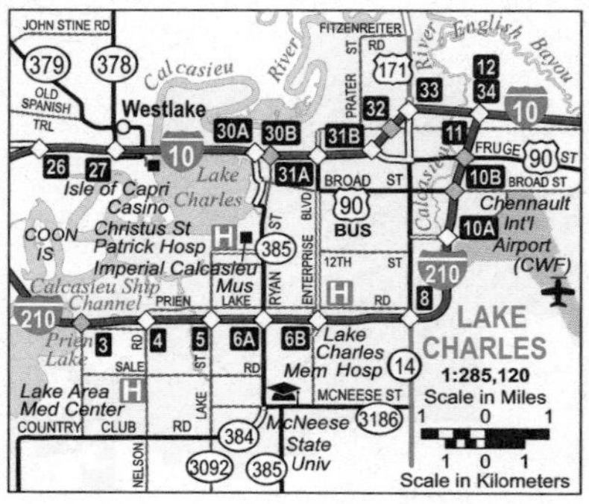

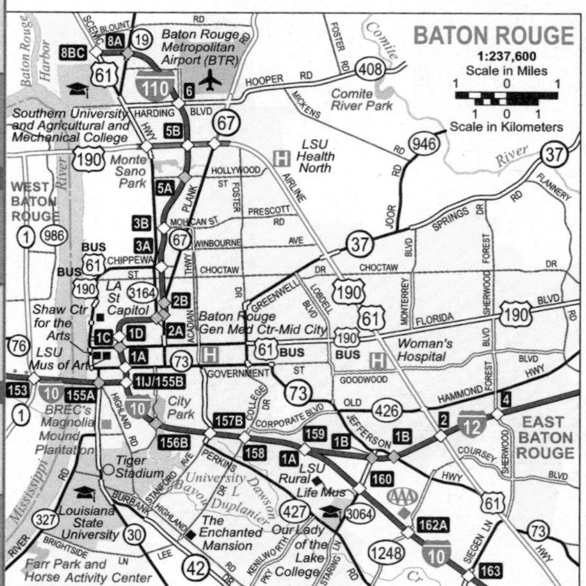

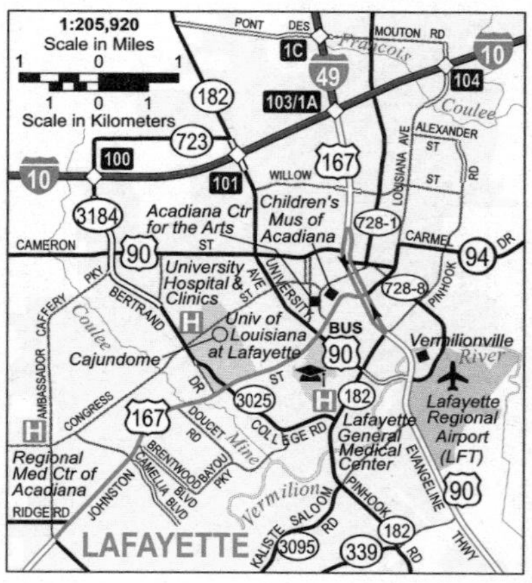

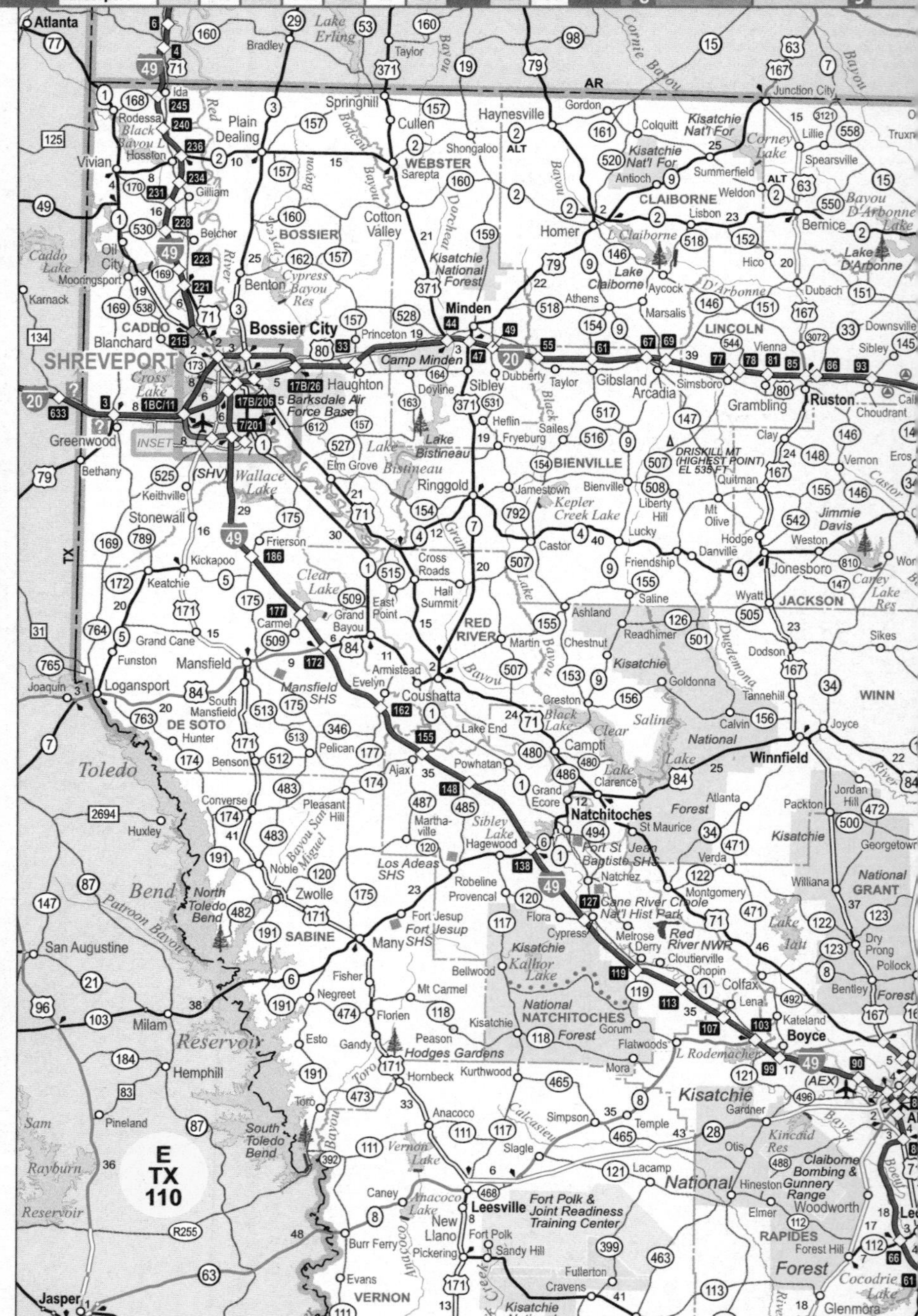

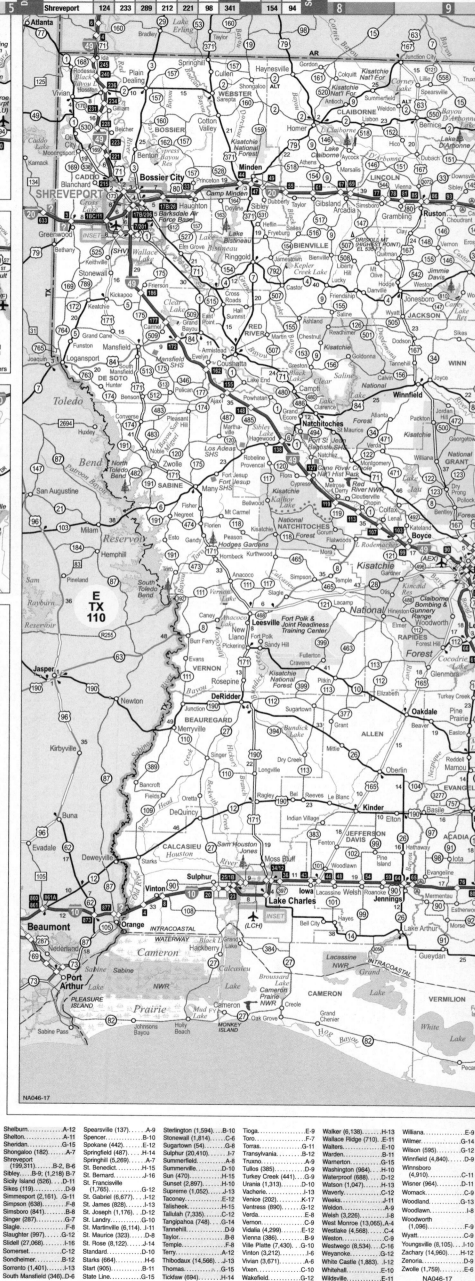

## LOUISIANA

NA046-17

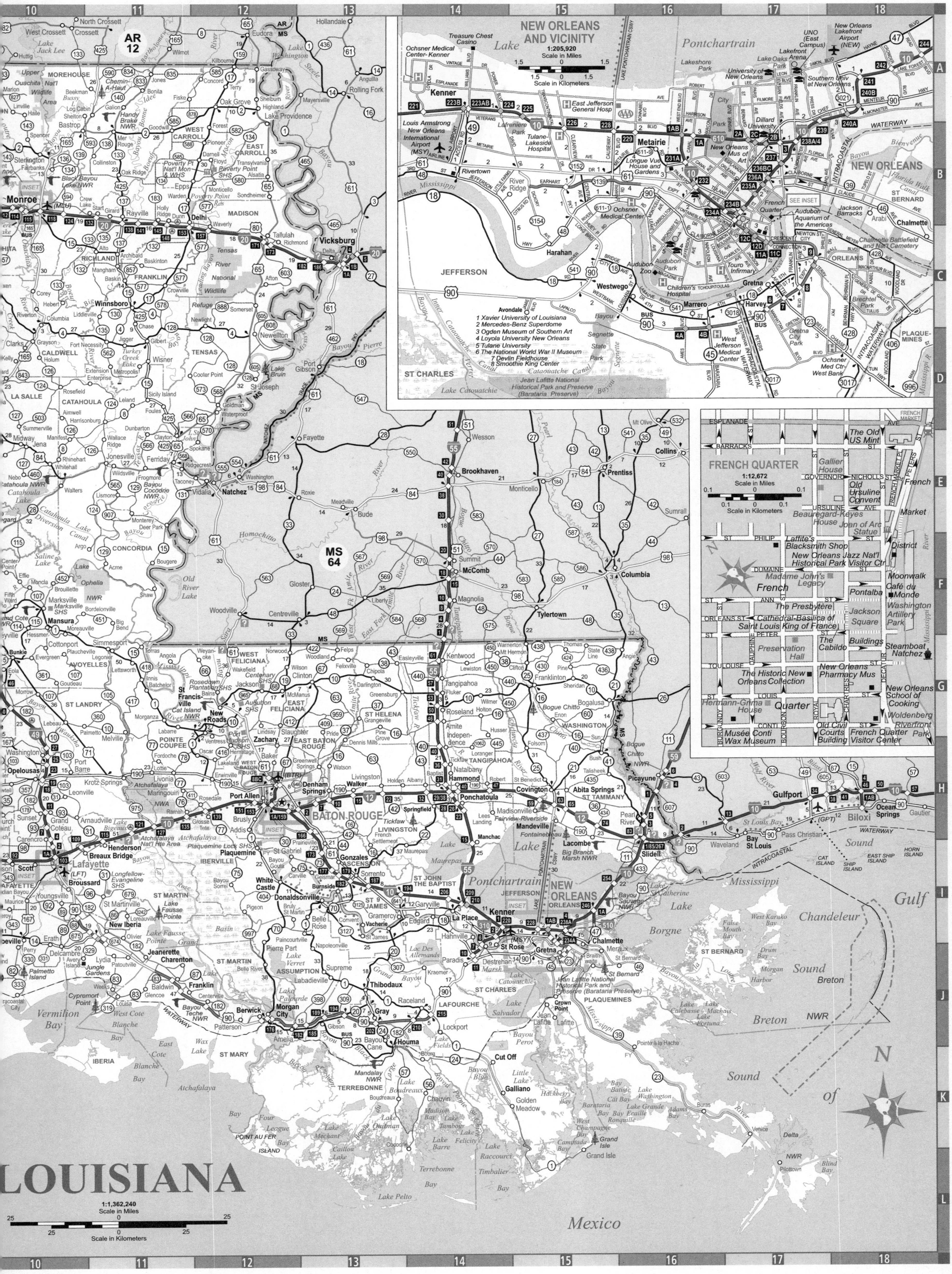

LEGEND

| | | |
|---|---|---|
| Interstate Highway | Wildlife Refuge | |
| Controlled Access Hwy | Nat'l/State Park | |
| Controlled Access Hwy Toll | National Forest | |

**NEW ORLEANS AND VICINITY**
1:205,920
Scale in Miles
Scale in Kilometers

1 Xavier University of Louisiana
2 Mercedes-Benz Superdome
3 Ogden Museum of Southern Art
4 Loyola University New Orleans
5 Tulane University
6 The National World War II Museum
7 Devlin Fieldhouse
8 Smoothie King Center

**FRENCH QUARTER**
1:12,672
Scale in Miles
Scale in Kilometers

**LOUISIANA**
1:1,362,240
Scale in Miles
Scale in Kilometers

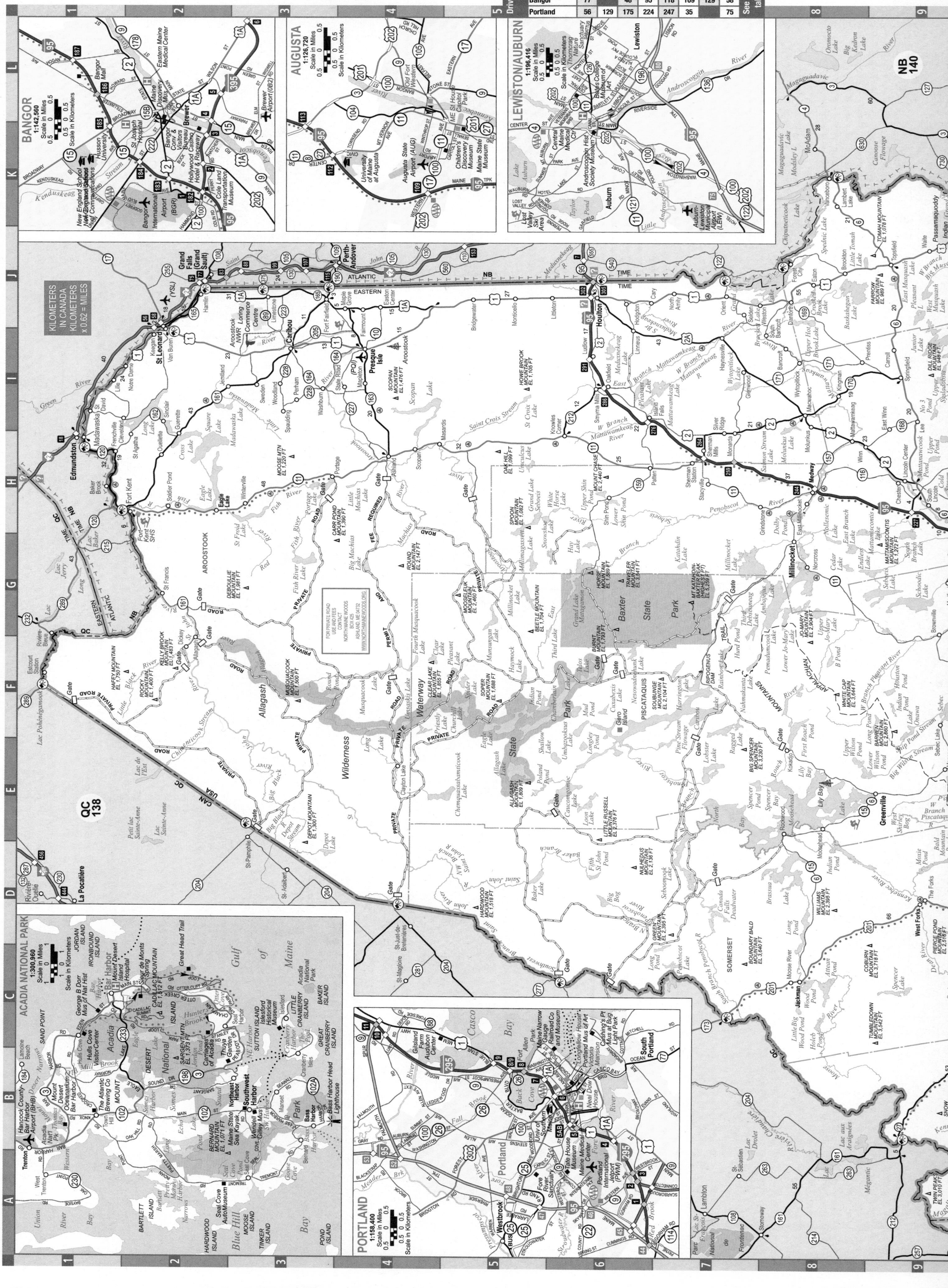

See also page 2

| Driving Distances In Miles | Augusta | Bangor | Bar Harbor | Calais | Houlton | Lewiston | Portland | Waterville |
|---|---|---|---|---|---|---|---|---|
| Augusta | | 77 | 103 | 170 | 193 | 34 | 56 | 21 |
| Bangor | 77 | | 48 | 95 | 118 | 109 | 129 | 58 |
| Portland | 56 | 129 | 175 | 224 | 247 | 35 | | 75 |

See also mileage table page 2

LEGEND

- Interstate Highway
- Controlled Access Hwy
- Controlled Access Hwy Toll
- Wildlife Refuge
- Nat'l/State Park
- National Forest

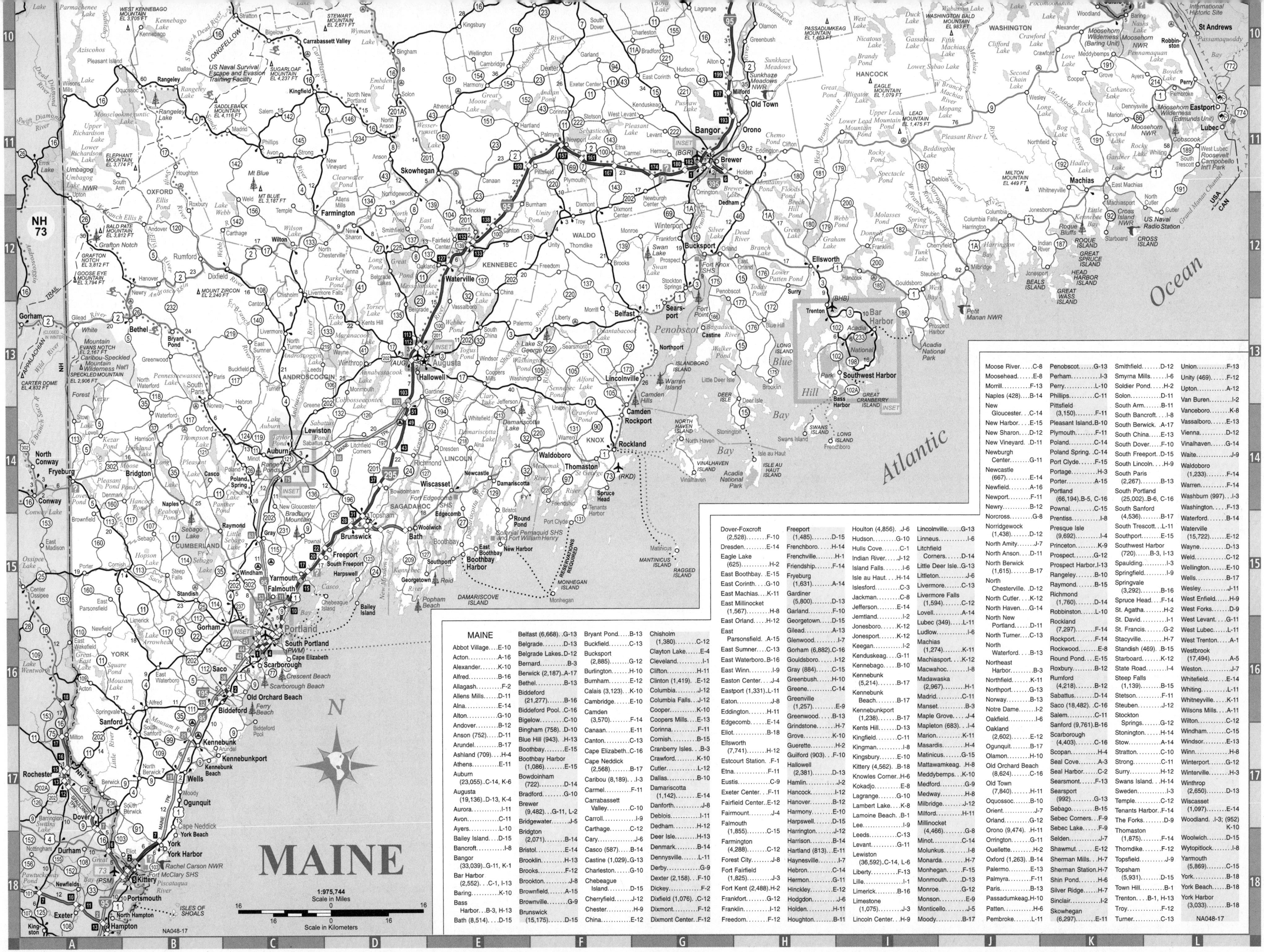

MAINE

NA048-17

| Driving Distances in Miles | Annapolis | Baltimore | Cumberland | Frederick | Hagerstown | Ocean City | Salisbury | Washington, DC |
|---|---|---|---|---|---|---|---|---|
| Annapolis | | 31 | 161 | 71 | 96 | 118 | 89 | 33 |
| Baltimore | 31 | | 139 | 49 | 75 | 138 | 110 | 39 |
| Washington, DC | 33 | 39 | 133 | 44 | 70 | 147 | 117 | |

See also mileage table page 2

## MARYLAND

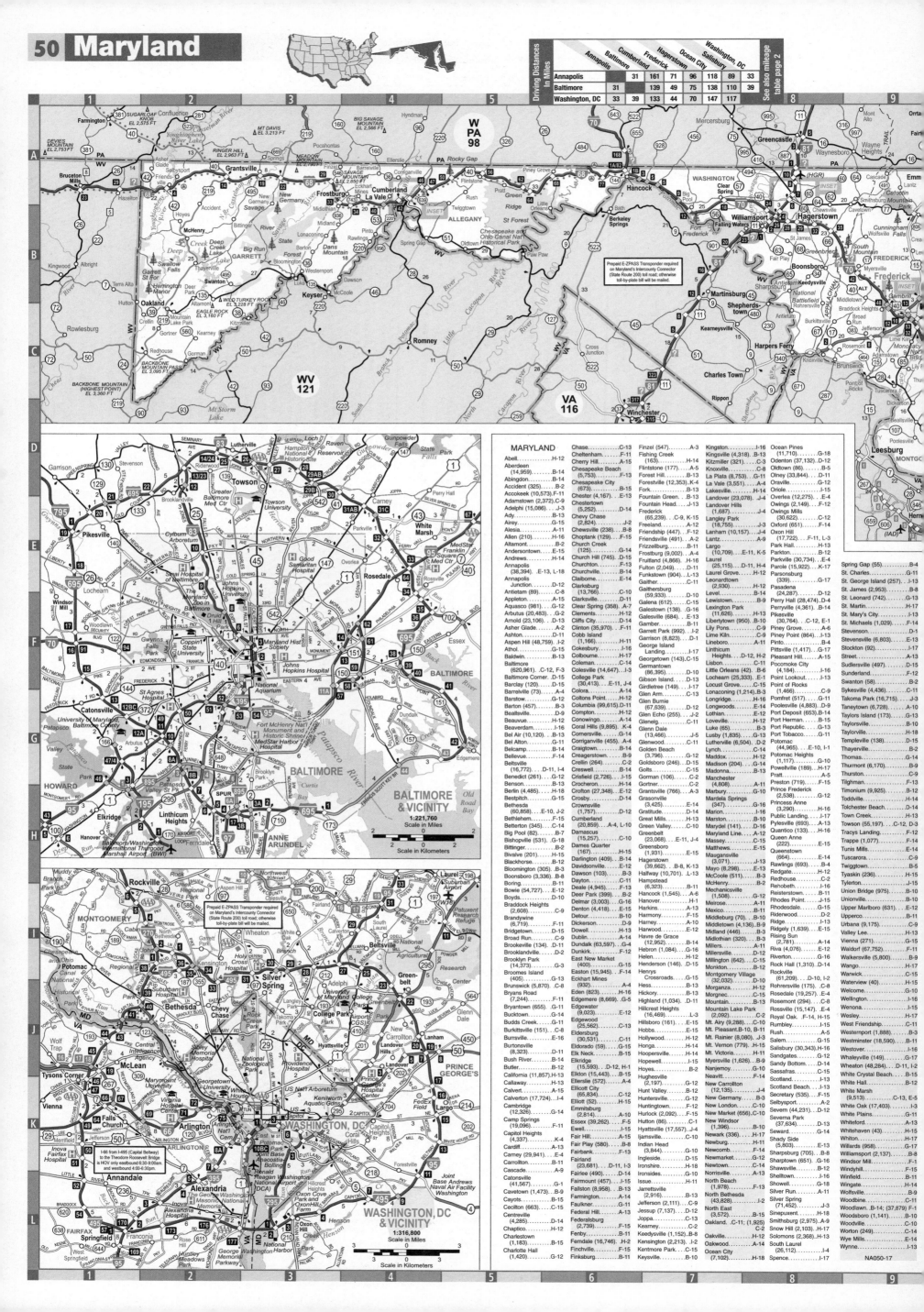

**LEGEND**

| | |
|---|---|
| Interstate Highway | 95 Wildlife Refuge |
| Controlled Access Hwy | Nat'l/State Park |
| Controlled Access Hwy Toll | National Forest |

# MARYLAND DISTRICT OF COLUMBIA

1:792,000
Scale in Miles
15 0 15
Scale in Kilometers
15 0 15

**CUMBERLAND**
1:126,560
Scale in Miles
1 0 1
Scale in Kilometers

**HAGERSTOWN**
1:174,240
Scale in Miles
1 0 1
Scale in Kilometers

**FREDERICK**
1:190,080
Scale in Miles
1 0 1
Scale in Kilometers

**ANNAPOLIS**
1:126,720
Scale in Miles
1 0 1
Scale in Kilometers

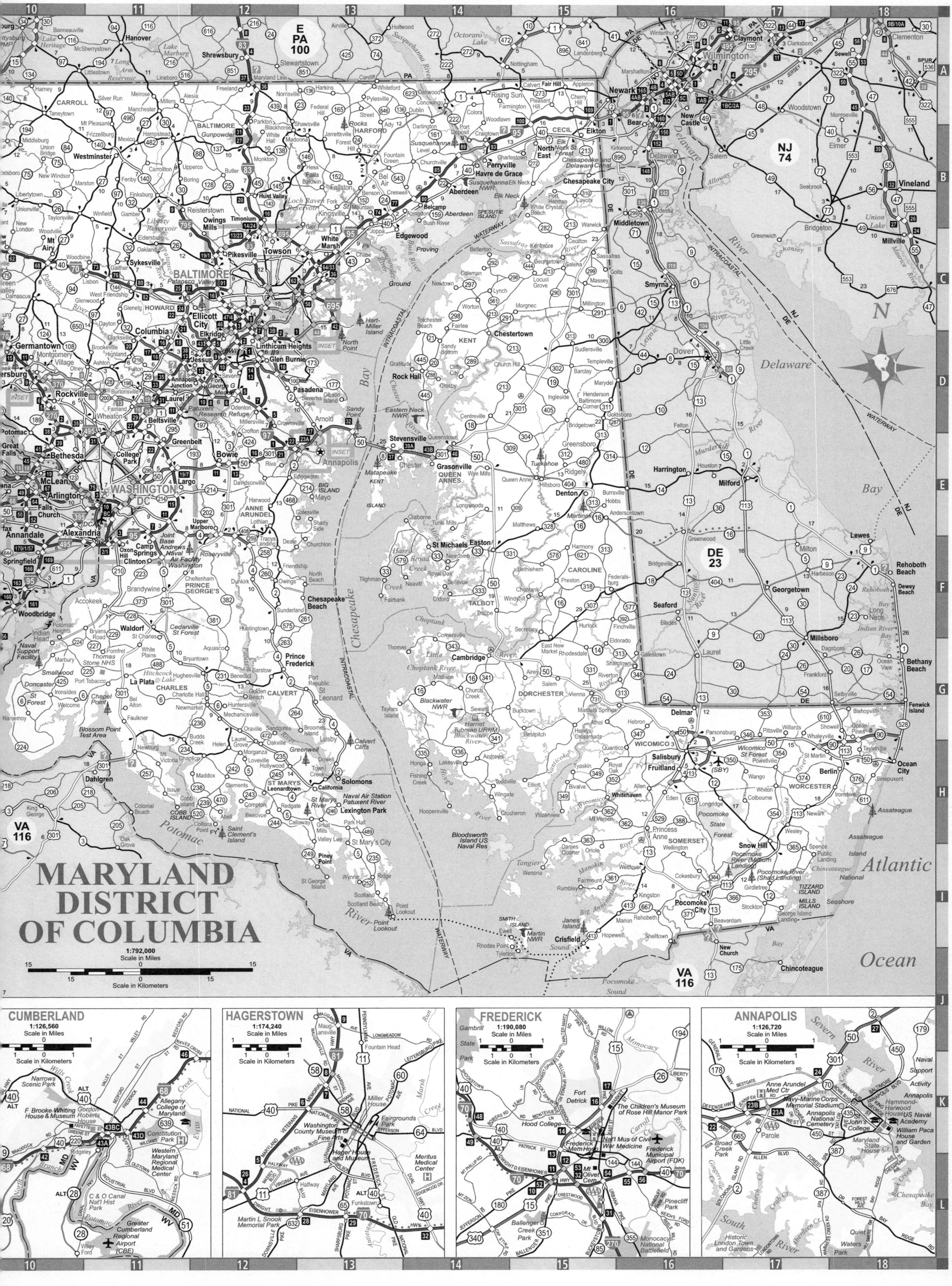

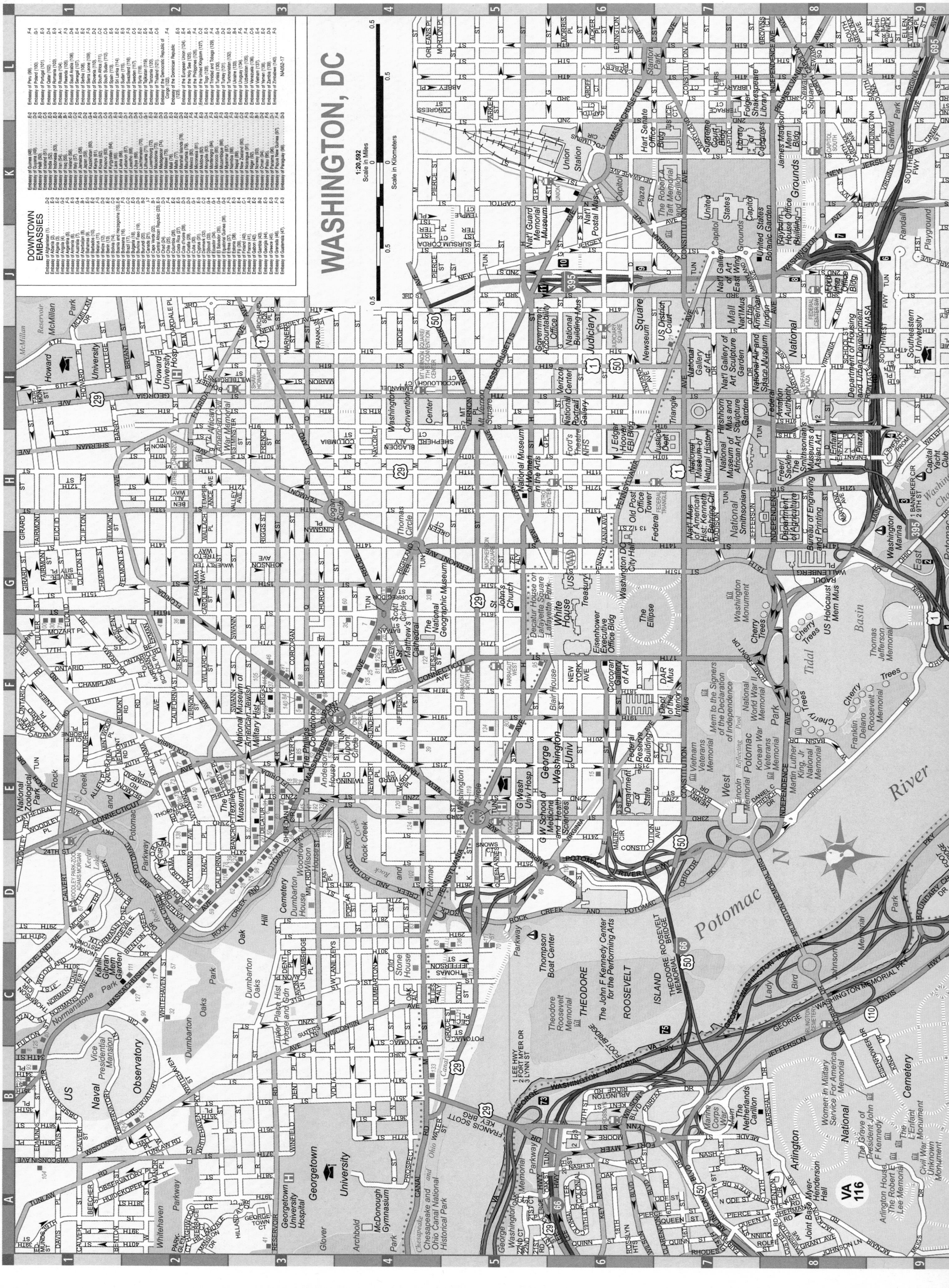

## WASHINGTON, DC

1:20,592

Scale in Miles

Scale in Kilometers

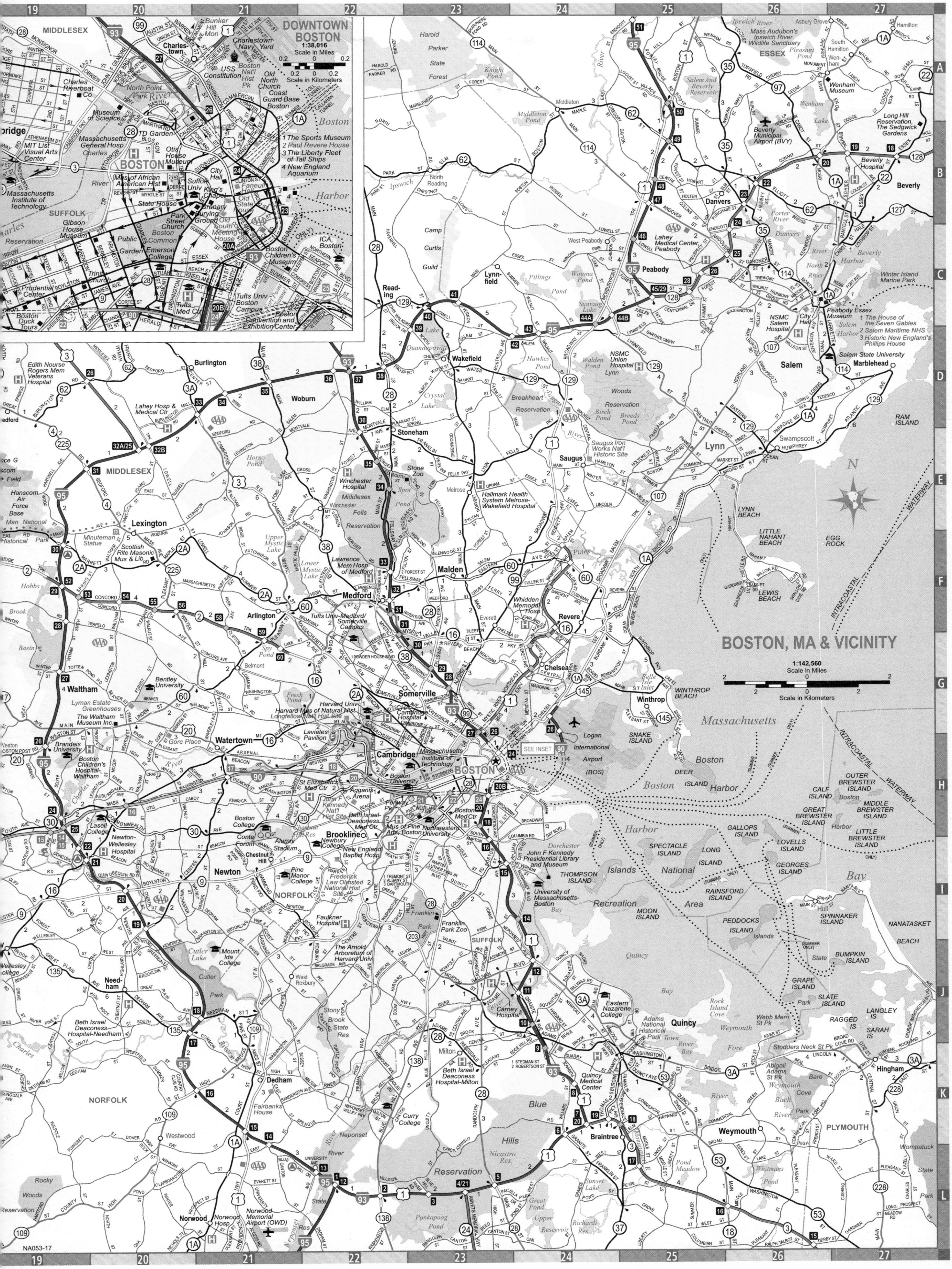

DOWNTOWN BOSTON
1:38,016
Scale in Miles

1 The Sports Museum
2 Paul Revere House
3 The Liberty Fleet of Tall Ships
4 New England Aquarium

BOSTON, MA & VICINITY
1:142,560
Scale in Miles

Massachusetts

Boston Harbor

Islands National Recreation Area

Quincy Bay

Boston
Bay

See also mileage table page 2

**Driving Distances In Miles**

| | Boston | Great Barrington | New Bedford | Newburyport | Plymouth | Provincetown | Sagamore | Springfield | Williamstown | Worcester |
|---|---|---|---|---|---|---|---|---|---|---|
| Boston | | 137 | 58 | 37 | 40 | 116 | 55 | 90 | 141 | 44 |
| New Bedford | 58 | 162 | | 95 | 34 | 93 | 31 | 116 | 182 | 70 |
| Springfield | 90 | 55 | 116 | 128 | 124 | 196 | 134 | | 75 | 52 |
| Worcester | 44 | 99 | 70 | 74 | 77 | 149 | 87 | 52 | 119 | |

**MASSACHUSETTS**

Towns with asterisk (*) are keyed to the maps on page 53.

Abington (15,985)..G-13
Acton...............C-11
Adams (5,515)......C-3
Agawam (28,438)...L-1
Alford............F-1
Amesbury
  (16,283).......B-13
Amherst...........E-6
Andover (8,762)...C-12
Aquinnah..........*F-21
Arlington
  (42,844)........*F-21
Asbury Grove....*A-27
Ashburnham.......C-9
Ashby.............C-9
Ashfield..........D-4
Ashland...........F-11
Ashley Falls......G-2
Assonet...........I-13
Athol (8,265).....D-7
Attleboro (43,593)..H-12

Auburn............L-5
Avon..............G-13
Ayer (2,868)......D-10
Baldwinville
  (2,028).........D-8
Barnstable
  (45,193)........I-16
Barre (1,009).....E-8
Becket............F-3
Becket Center.....F-3
Bedford...........D-19
Belchertown
  (2,899).........E-6
Bellingham
  (4,854).........G-11
Berlin............E-10
Bernardston......C-5
Beverly
  (39,502)......*B-27, D-14
Billerica.........D-12
Blackinton........C-2
Blackstone........C-10
Blandford (393)...F-4

Bliss Corner
  (5,280).........J-14
Bolton............E-10
Bondsville........F-6
Bourne (1,418)....I-15
Boxborough......D-10
Boxford (2,339)...C-13
Boylston..........E-9
Braintree
  (33,744)....*K-25, F-13
Brant Rock........G-14
Brewster (2,000)...I-18
Bridgewater
  (7,841).........H-13
Briggsville.......C-3
Brimfield.........F-6
Brockfield (833)...F-8
Brookline
  (58,732)......*H-22
Bryantville.......H-14
Buckland..........D-4

Burlington
  (24,498).......*D-20
Buzzards Bay......I-15
Byfield...........C-13
Cambridge
  (105,162)......*B-19
Canton (5,169)....F-12
Carlisle..........D-11
Carver............H-14
Cataumet..........J-15
Centerville.......J-16
Charlemont........C-4
Charleston......*A-21
Charlton..........G-8
Charlton City.....G-8
Charlton Depot....F-8
Chartley..........H-13
Chatham (1,421)...J-18
Chelmsford
  (35,177)......*G-24
Chelsea
  (35,177)......*G-24
Cheshire (514)....D-2
Chester (527).....F-4
Chesterfield......E-4

Chestnut Hill.....*I-21
Chicopee (55,298)..J-1
Chilmark..........L-14
Clarksburg........C-3
Clayton...........G-2
Clinton (7,389)...E-10
Cochituate
  (6,569).........E-11
Cohasset (7,261)..F-14
Cold Spring......F-3
Colrain...........C-5
Concord...........E-11
Conway............D-5
Cordaville (2,650)..F-10
Cotuit............J-16
Cummington........E-4
Dalton............D-2
Danvers (26,493)..B-14
Dartmouth.........J-13
Dedham
  (24,729)......*K-21, F-12
Deerfield (643)...D-5
Dell..............D-2
Dennis (2,407)....I-17
Dennis Port
  (3,162).........J-17

Dighton...........I-12
Douglas...........G-9
Dracut............B-11
Drury.............C-3
Dunstable.........C-11
Duxbury (1,802)...G-14
East Bridgewater..H-13
East Brookfield
  (1,323).........F-8
East Douglas......G-9
East Falmouth
  (6,038).........J-15
East Freetown.....I-13
East Harwich
  (4,872).........I-18
East Leverett.....E-6
East Longmeadow...L-3
East Orleans......I-18
East Otis.........F-3
East Sandwich.....I-16
East Templeton....D-8
East Walpole......G-12
East Wareham......I-15
East Windsor......D-3

Eastham...........I-18
Easthampton.......F-5
Easton............G-12
Edgartown.........K-15
Elmwood...........G-6
Erving............D-6
Essex (1,471).....C-14
Everett (41,667)..*F-23
Fairhaven
  (2,231).........J-14
Fall River
  (88,857)....I-8, J-12
Falmouth (3,799)..J-15
Falmouth Heights..J-15
Farley............D-6
Feeding Hills.....G-5
Fiskdale (2,083)..G-8
Fitchburg (40,318)..D-9
Florida...........C-3
Forestdale (4,099)..J-15
Foxboro (5,625)...G-12
Framingham
  (68,318)........F-11
Franklin (31,635)..G-10
Harwich...........I-18
Harwich Port
  (1,643).........J-17

Glendale..........F-2
Gloucester
  (28,789).......C-14
Goshen............E-4
Grafton...........F-10
Great Barrington
  (5,650)......*K-27, F-14
Green Harbor......G-15
Greenfield (17,456)..D-5
Griswoldville.....D-5
Groton (1,124)....D-10
Hadley............E-6
Halifax...........H-14
Hamilton..........C-13
Hampden...........G-6
Hancock...........C-2
Hanover (936).....F-14
Hanson (2,118)....G-14
Hardwick..........E-7
Hartsville........F-2
Harvard...........D-10
Hatchville........J-15

Hatfield (1,318)..E-5
Haverhill (60,879)..C-12
Hawley............D-4
Haydenville.......E-5
Heath.............C-4
Hingham
  (5,650)......*K-27, F-14
Hinsdale..........D-3
Hixville..........J-13
Holbrook (10,791)..G-13
Holden............E-9
Holland (1,464)...G-7
Holliston.........F-11
Holyoke
  (39,880)......F-5, J-1
Hoosac Tunnel.....C-3
Hopedale (3,753)..G-10
Hopkinton (2,550)..F-11
Housatonic (1,109)..F-1
Hubbardston.......D-8
Hudson (14,907)...E-10
Hull (10,293).....I-26
Humarock..........G-14
Huntington (936)..F-4
Hyannis
  (15,784).......J-16
Mattapoisett......J-14

Jefferson.........E-9
Konkapot..........G-2
Lake Pleasant.....D-6
Lanesborough......D-2
Lawrence
  (76,377).......C-12
Lee (2,061).......E-2
Leeds.............E-5
Leicester.........F-9
Lenox (1,675).....E-2
Lenox Dale........E-2
Leominster
  (40,759).......E-9
Leverett..........E-6
Lexington.........*D-27
Leyden............C-5
Lincoln...........E-11
Linwood...........G-9
Lithia............E-4
Littleton.........D-10
Locks Village.....D-6
Longmeadow
  (15,784).......L-2

Lowell
  (106,519)...C-11, E-17
Ludlow............J-3
Lunenburg (1,760)..D-9
Lynn
  (90,329)....*E-26, D-13
Lynnfield
  (11,596)......*C-23
Lyonsville........C-5
Madaket (236).....*L-7
Malden (56,450)...*F-23
Manchester........C-5
Manchester.......D-14
Manomet...........H-15
Mansfield.........G-12
Marblehead
  (19,808)......*D-27
Marion............J-14
Marlborough
  (38,499)........E-10
Marshfield
  (4,335).........G-14
Marshfield Hills..G-14
Mashpee...........J-15
Maynard (10,106)..E-11

Medfield
  (106,519)...C-11, E-17
Medford (56,173)..*F-22
Medway............F-11
Menauhant.........J-15
Menemsha..........L-13
Merrimac..........B-13
Methuen (47,255)..C-12
Middleboro (10,791)..H-13
Middlefield.......E-4
Milford (25,055)..G-10
Mill River........G-2
Millers Falls.....D-6
Millis
  (1,139)........F-11
Milton (27,003)...*K-23
Monponsett........G-14
Monroe Bridge.....C-4
Monson............F-7
Montague..........D-6
Monterey..........F-2
Montville.........E-2

Montville.........E-2
Monument Beach....J-15
Mt. Hermon
  (2,790).........C-5
Mt. Washington....F-1
Nantucket (7,446)..L-9
Natick
  (28,886).......F-11
Needham
  (28,886).......F-11
New Ashford.......C-2
New Bedford (13,708)...J-13, K-15
New Bedford.......J-13
New Boston........F-3
New Braintree.....E-7
New Marlborough...G-2
New Salem.........D-6
Newbury...........C-13
Newburyport
  (17,416).......B-13
Newton (85,146)...*H-21
Nichewaug.........E-7
Norfolk...........G-11
North Adams
  (13,708).......C-3
North Amherst
  (6,819).........E-6

---

**SPRINGFIELD** 1:190,080
**WORCESTER** 1:142,560
**FALL RIVER** 1:190,080
**NEW BEDFORD** 1:158,400

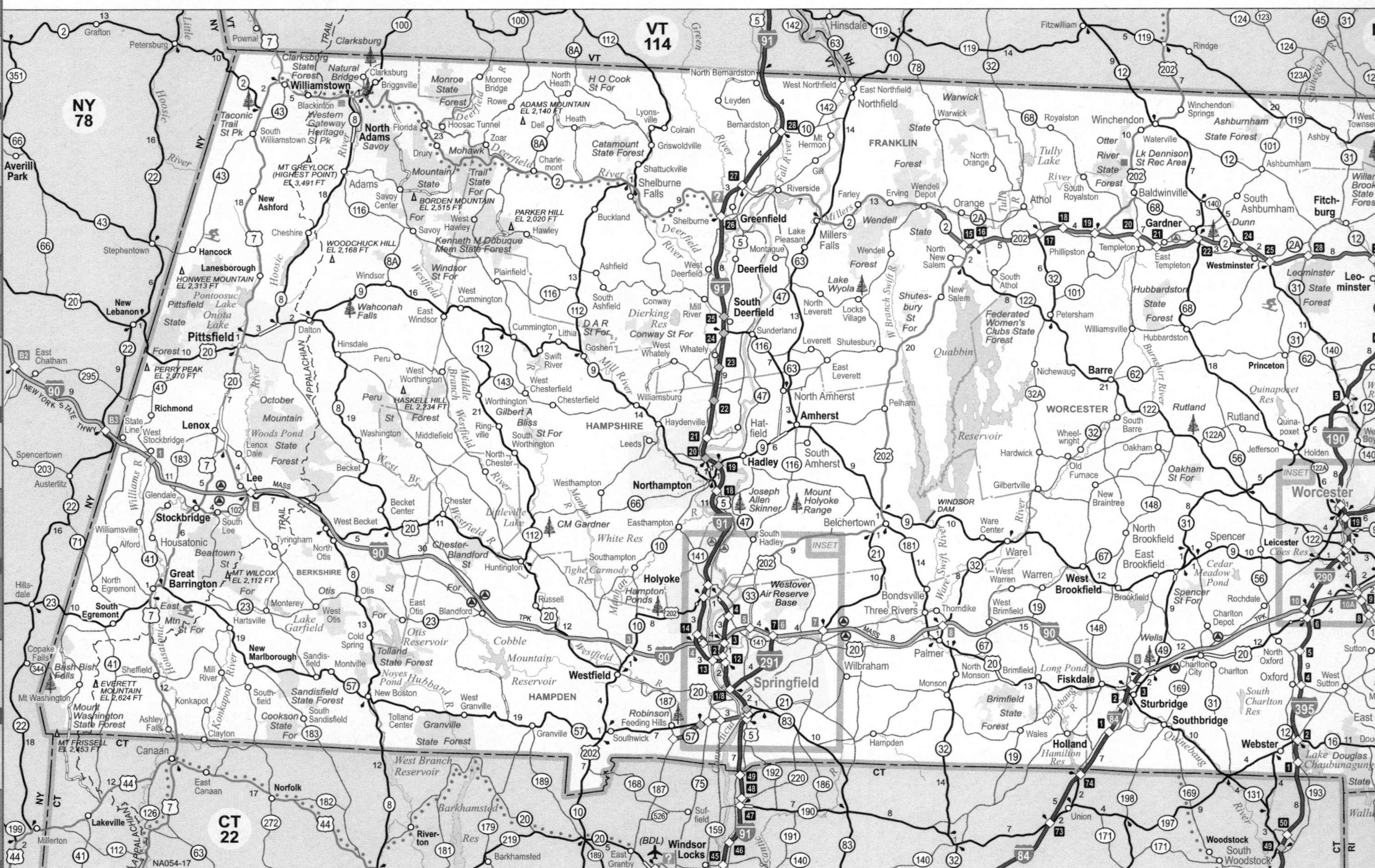

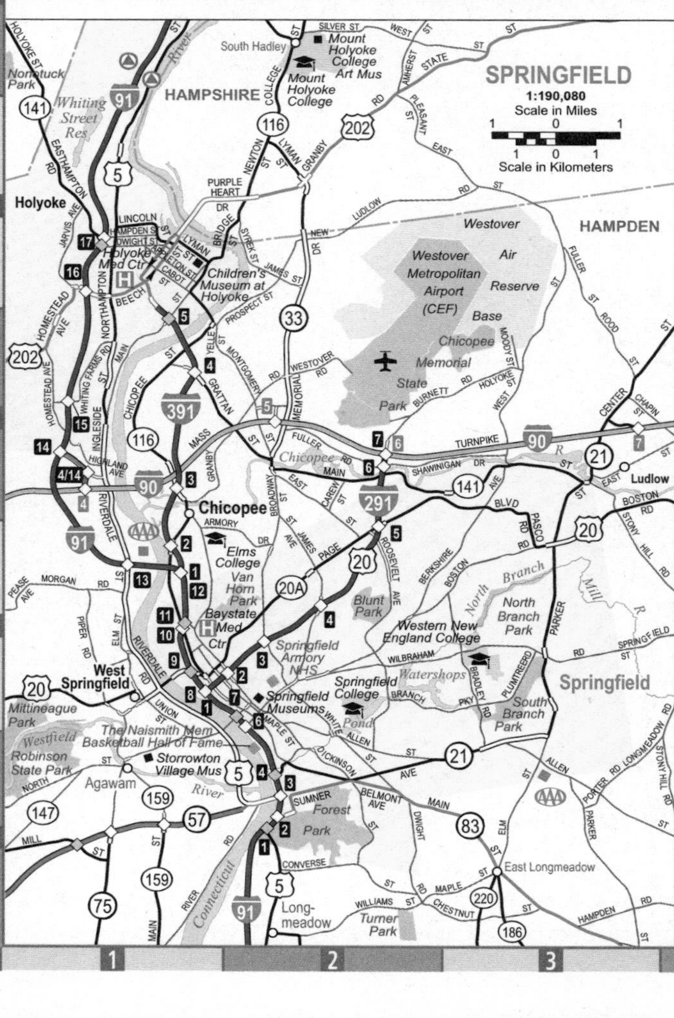

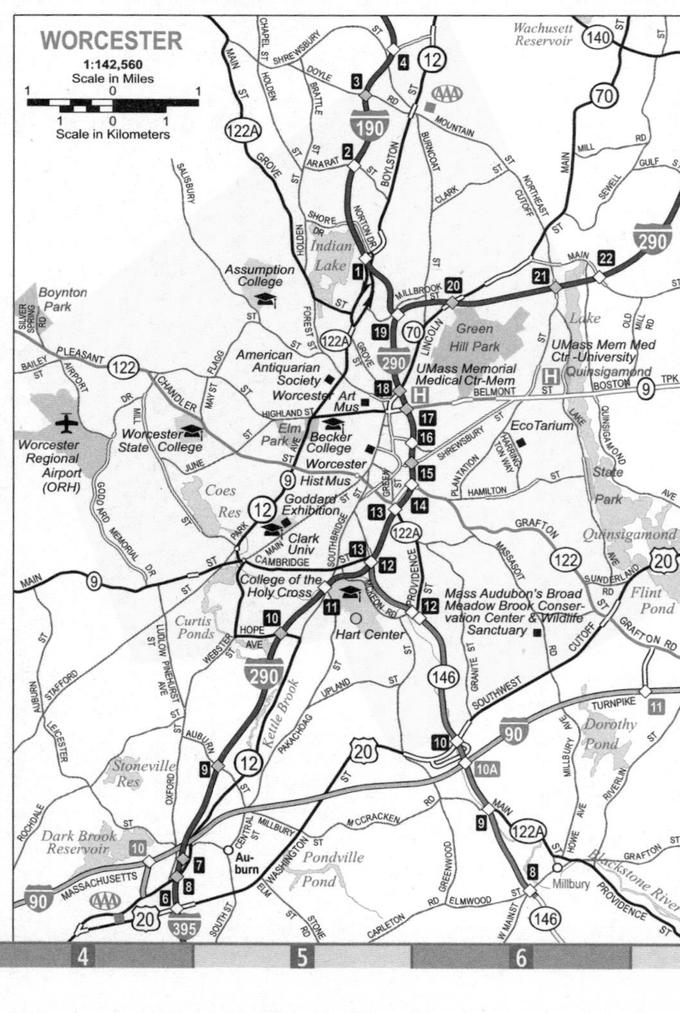

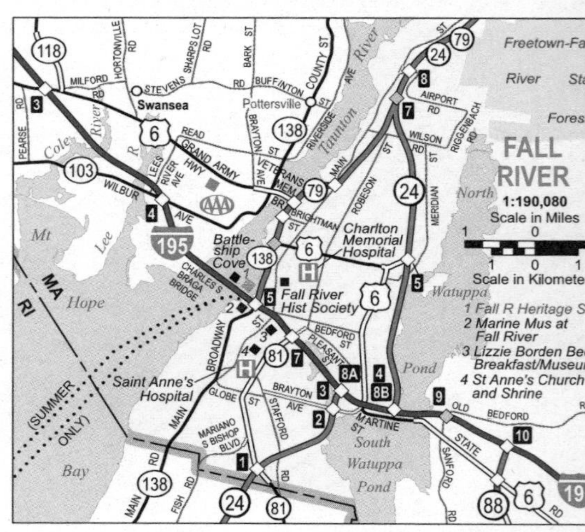

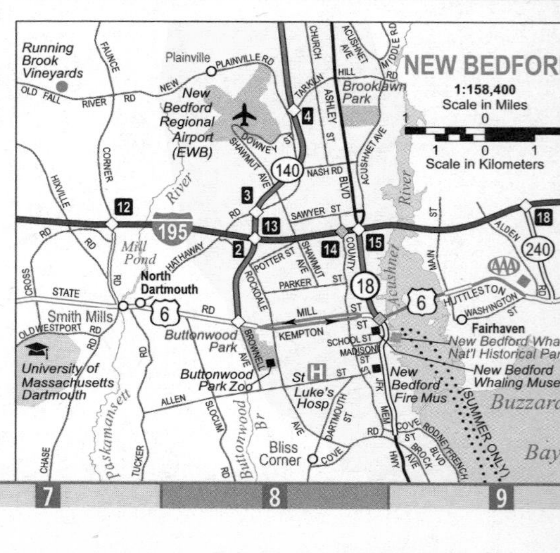

LEGEND
Interstate Highway — Wildlife Refuge
Controlled Access Hwy — Nat'l/State Park
Controlled Access Hwy Toll — National Forest

NA054-17

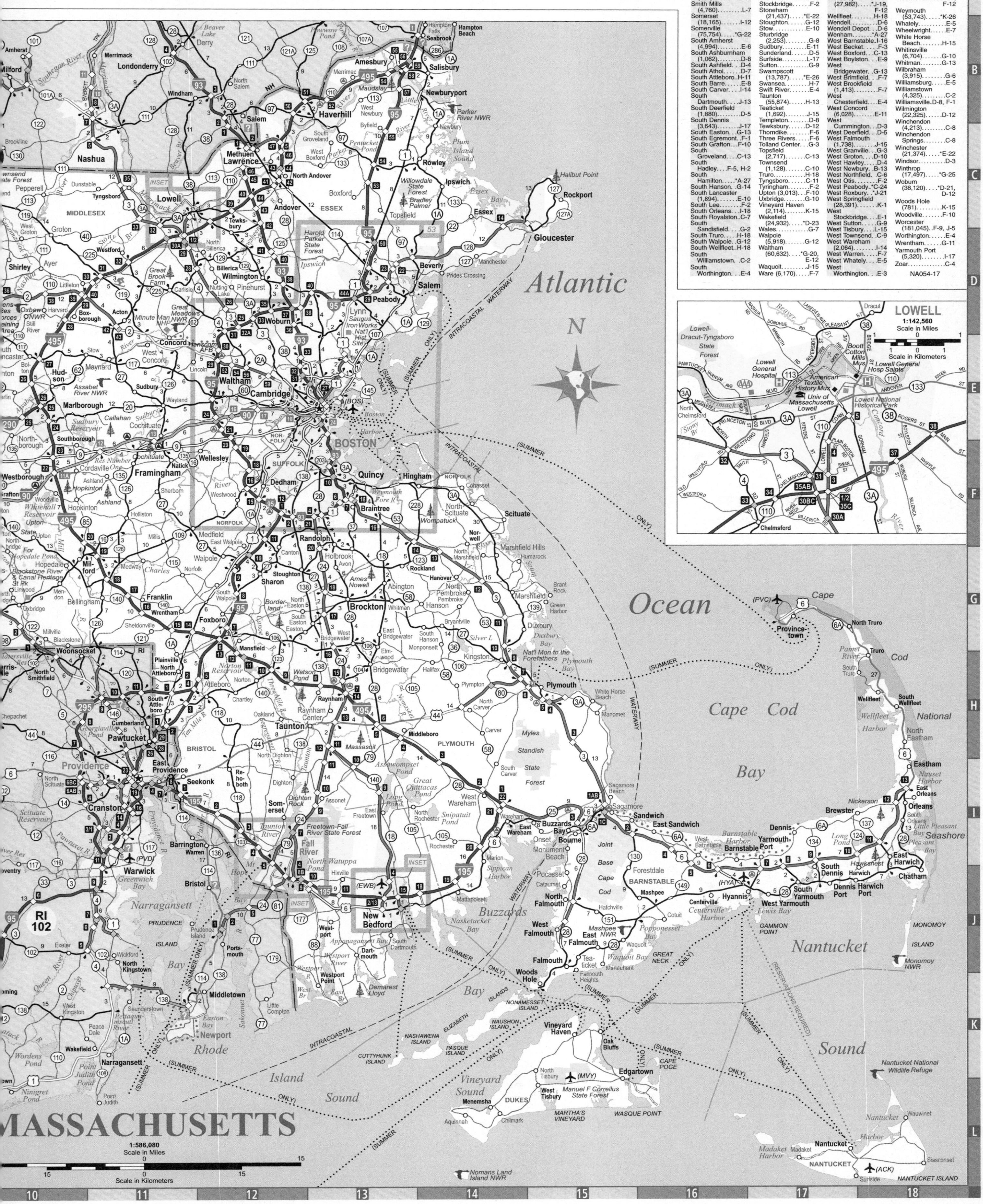

See also mileage table page 2

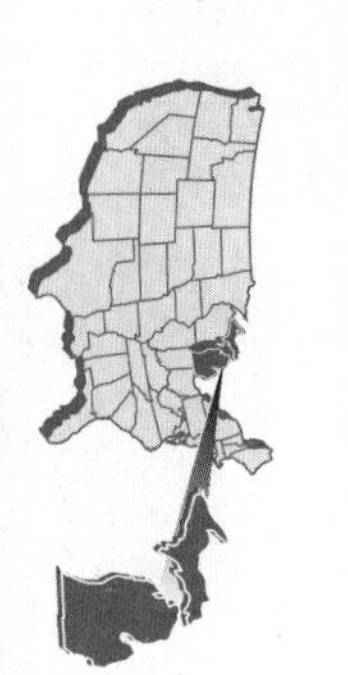

**Driving Distances In Miles**

| | Battle Creek | Bay City | Detroit | Escanaba | Flint | Grand Rapids | Ironwood | Lansing | Marquette | Muskegon | Port Huron | Sault Ste Marie |
|---|---|---|---|---|---|---|---|---|---|---|---|---|
| Detroit | 120 | 115 | | 434 | 68 | 157 | 599 | 90 | 455 | 197 | 63 | 346 |
| Flint | 110 | 51 | 68 | 369 | | 113 | 534 | 54 | 391 | 153 | 67 | 282 |
| Grand Rapids | 65 | 130 | 157 | 387 | 113 | | 464 | 58 | 408 | 41 | 180 | 299 |
| Lansing | 54 | 96 | 90 | 374 | 54 | 68 | 539 | | 396 | 107 | 118 | 287 |
| Muskegon | 106 | 146 | 197 | 402 | 153 | 41 | 567 | 107 | 424 | | 220 | 315 |

# MICHIGAN

Scale 1:1,077,120

FOR ADJOINING AREA SEE PAGES 58-59

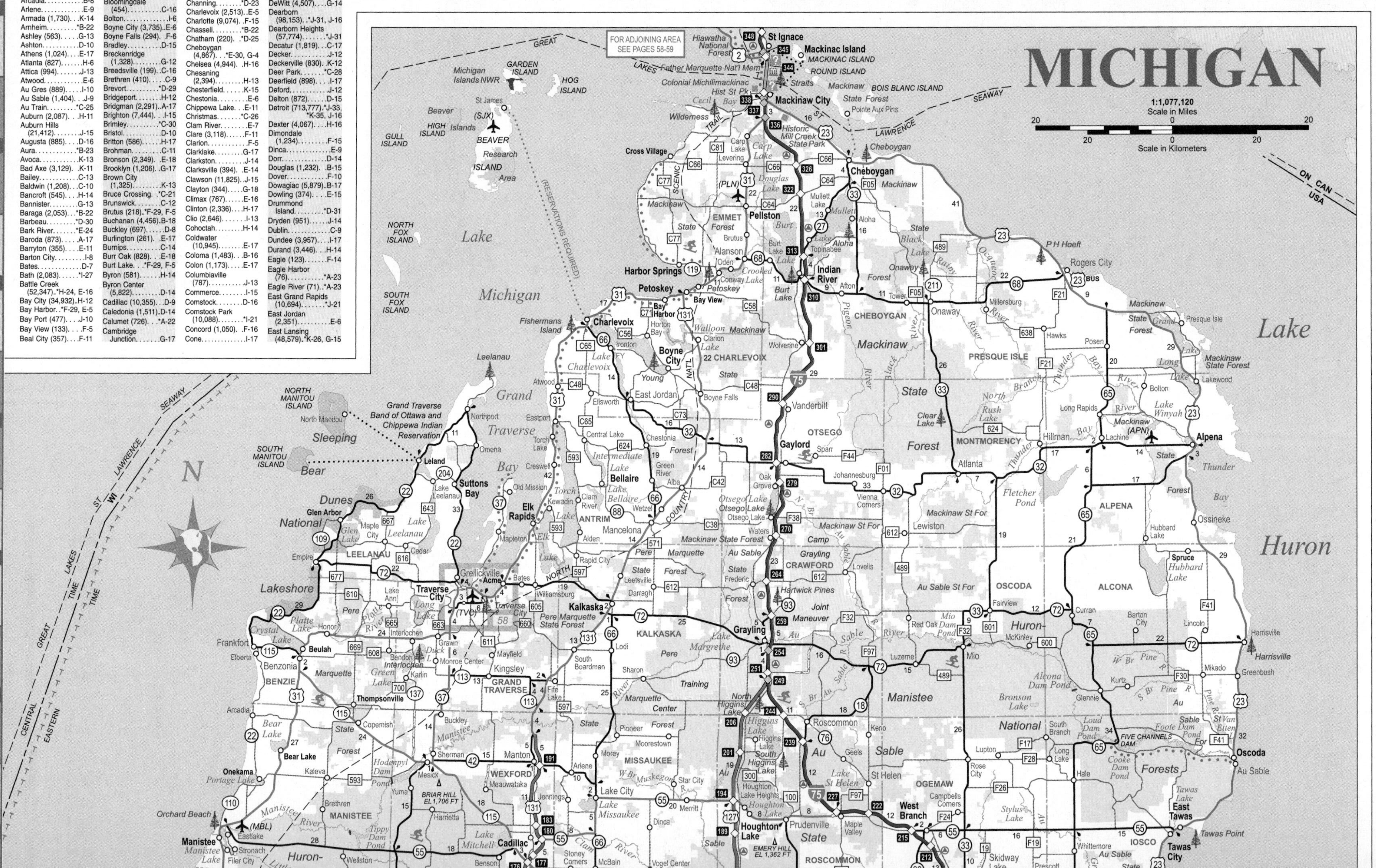

LEGEND

Interstate Highway — 95
Controlled Access Hwy
Controlled Access Hwy Toll
Wildlife Refuge
Nat'l/State Park
National Forest

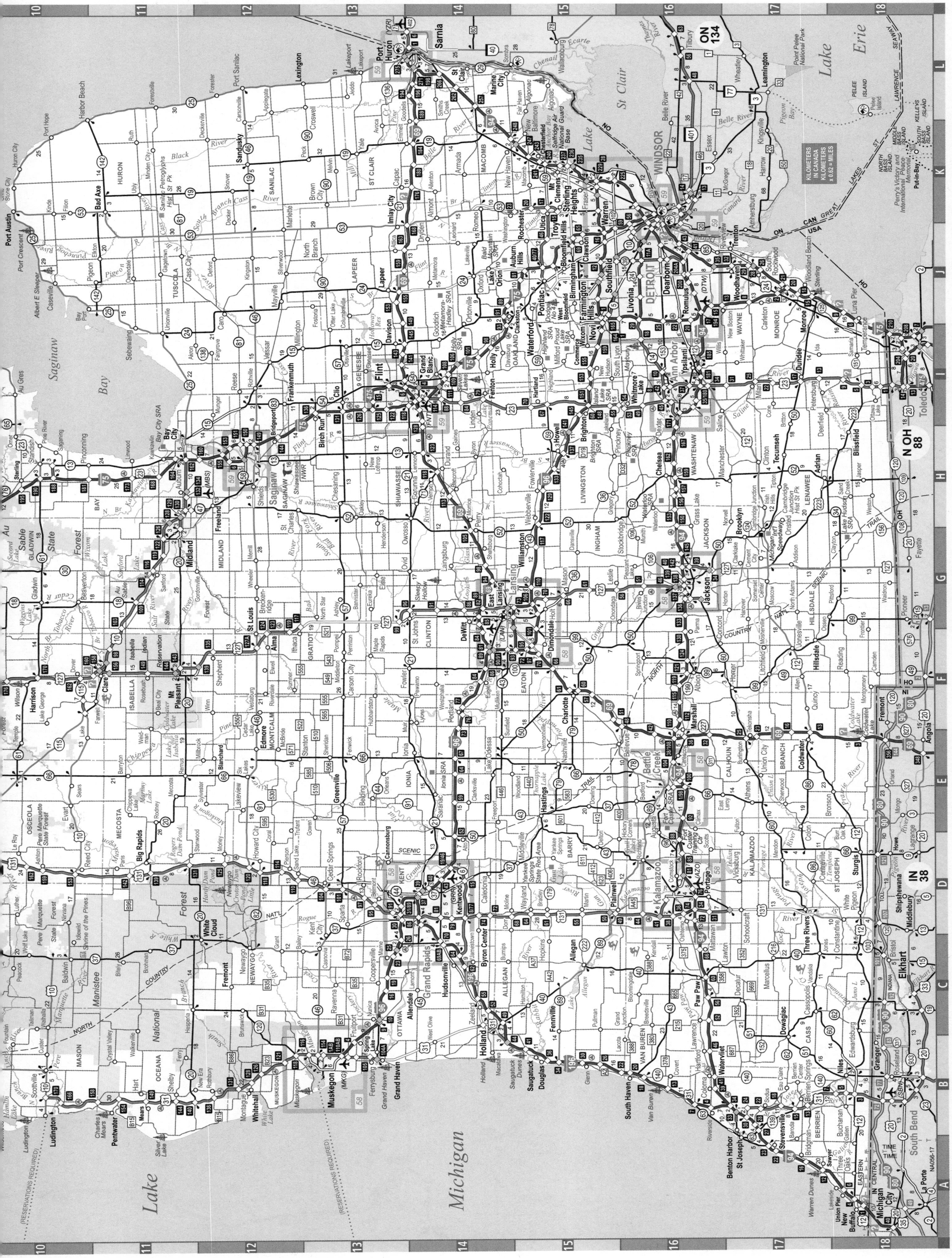

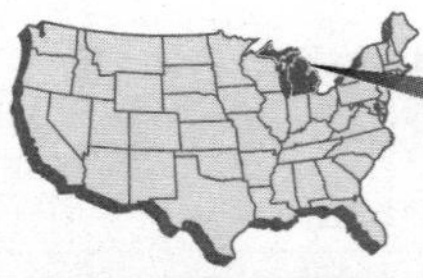

**Driving Distances In Miles** — See also mileage table page 2

|          | Battle Creek | Bay City | Detroit | Escanaba | Flint | Grand Rapids | Ironwood | Lansing | Marquette | Muskegon | Sault Ste Marie | Port Huron |
|----------|----|----|----|----|----|----|----|----|----|----|----|----|
| Detroit      | 120 | 115 |     | 434 | 68  | 157 | 599 | 90  | 455 | 197 | 63  | 346 |
| Flint        | 110 | 51  | 68  | 369 |     | 113 | 534 | 54  | 391 | 153 | 67  | 282 |
| Grand Rapids | 65  | 130 | 157 | 387 | 113 |     | 464 | 68  | 408 | 41  | 180 | 299 |
| Lansing      | 54  | 96  | 90  | 374 | 54  | 68  | 539 |     | 396 | 107 | 118 | 287 |
| Muskegon     | 106 | 146 | 197 | 402 | 153 | 41  | 567 | 107 | 424 |     | 220 | 315 |

## Upper Peninsula of MICHIGAN
1:1,425,600 — Scale in Miles

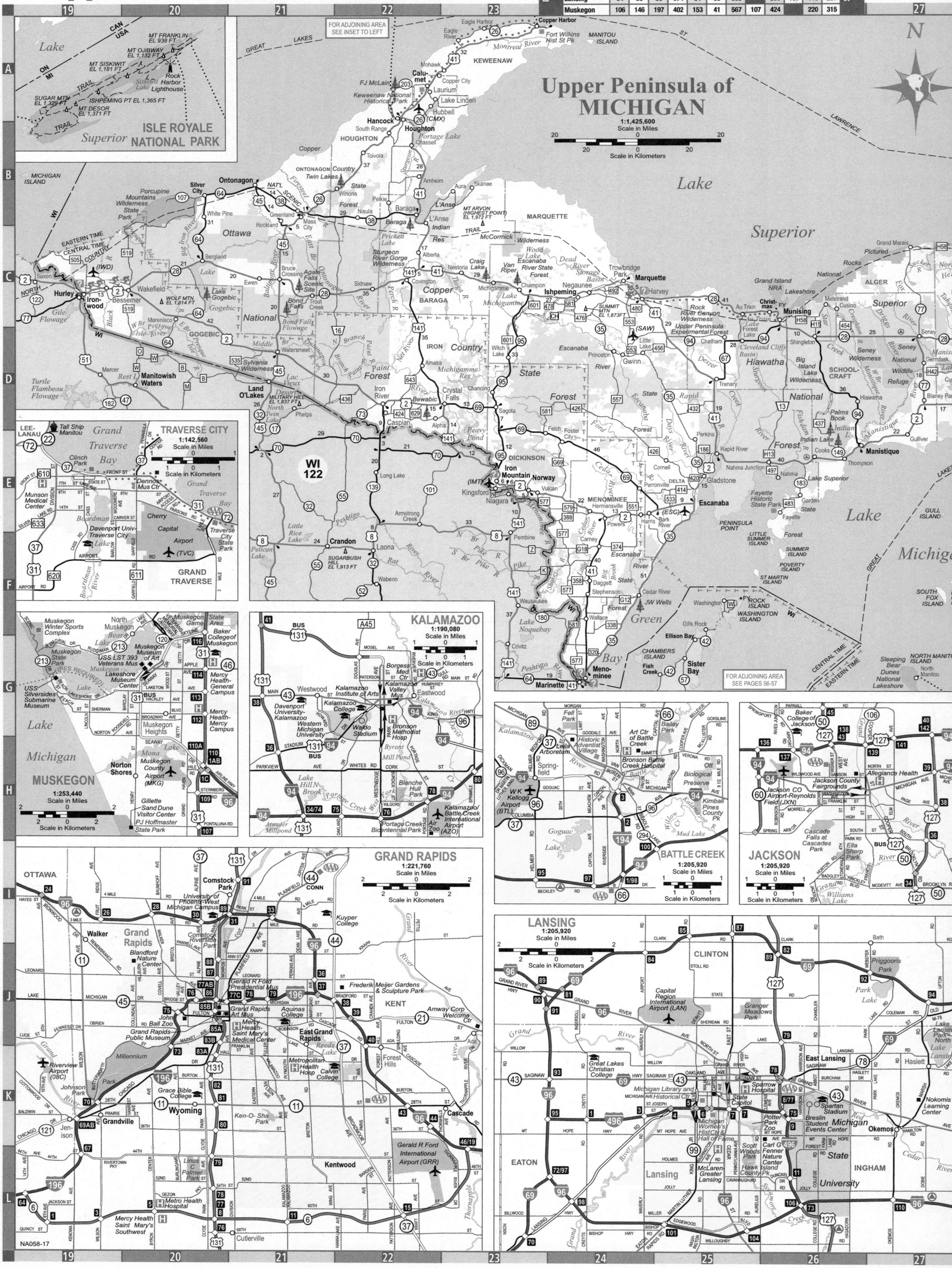

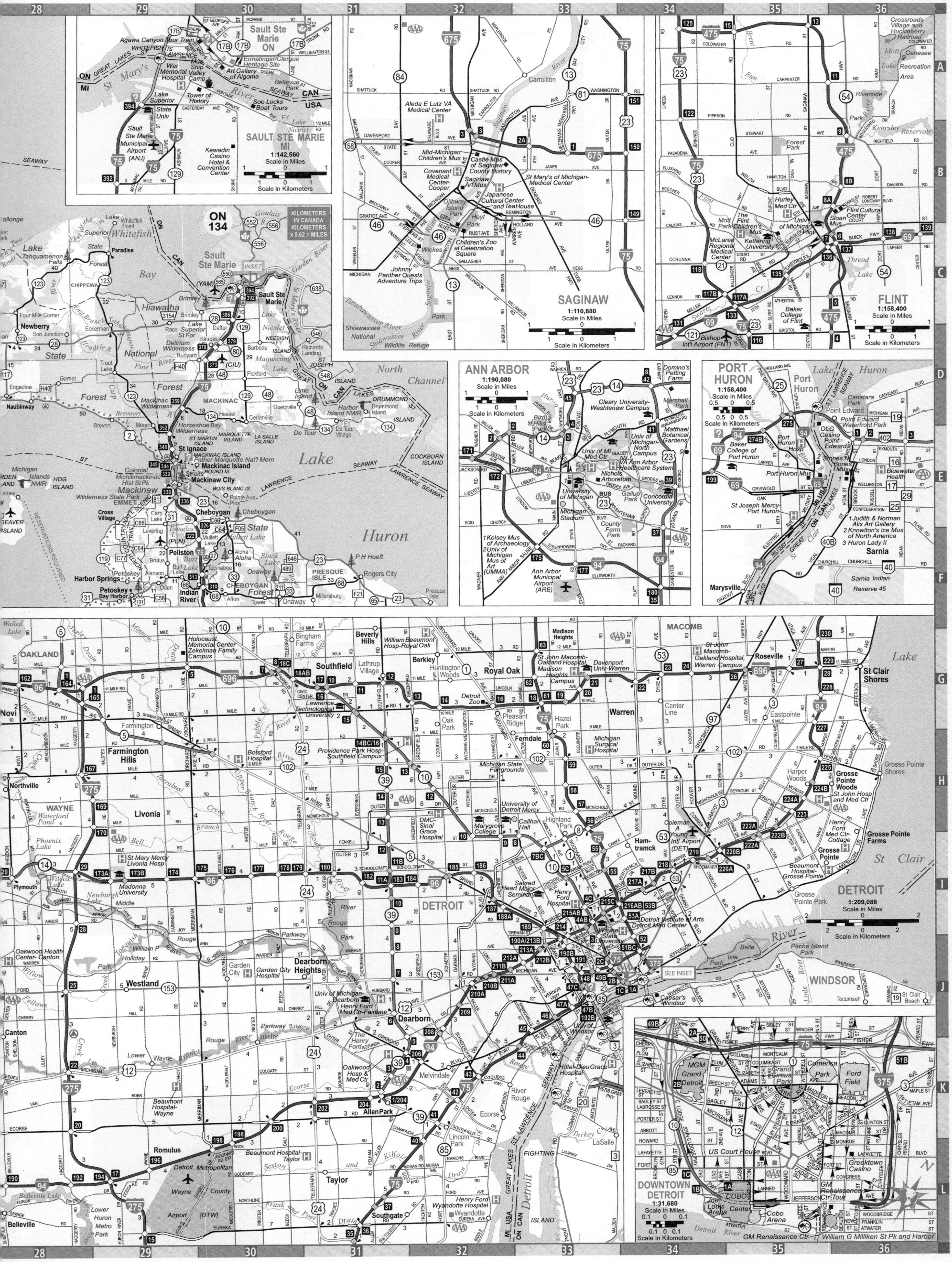

**LEGEND**

| | |
|---|---|
| Interstate Highway | Wildlife Refuge |
| Controlled Access Hwy | Nat'l/State Park |
| Controlled Access Hwy Toll | National Forest |

**SAULT STE MARIE MI**
1:142,560
Scale in Miles
Scale in Kilometers

**SAGINAW**
1:110,880
Scale in Miles
Scale in Kilometers

**FLINT**
1:158,400
Scale in Miles
Scale in Kilometers

**ANN ARBOR**
1:190,080
Scale in Miles
Scale in Kilometers

**PORT HURON**
1:158,400
Scale in Miles
Scale in Kilometers

**DETROIT**
1:209,088
Scale in Miles
Scale in Kilometers

**DOWNTOWN DETROIT**
1:31,680
Scale in Miles
Scale in Kilometers

KILOMETERS IN CANADA
KILOMETERS x 0.62 = MILES

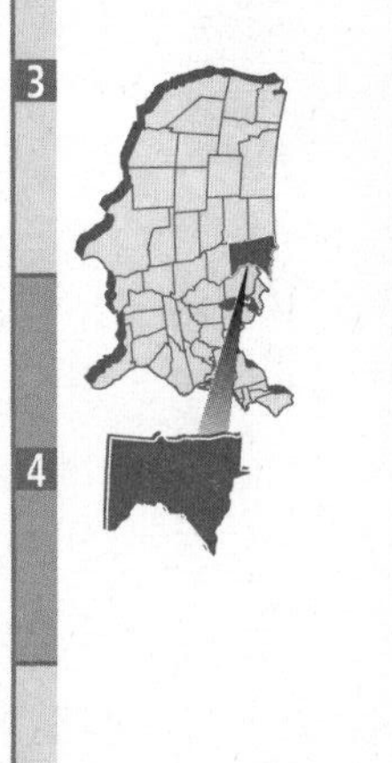

## Driving Distances (In Miles)

| | Albert Lea | Bemidji | Duluth | Fargo, ND | International Falls | Minneapolis | Rochester | St. Cloud | Sioux Falls, SD | St. Paul |
|---|---|---|---|---|---|---|---|---|---|---|
| Duluth | 249 | 153 | | 253 | 162 | 155 | 234 | 147 | 391 | 151 |
| International Falls | 387 | 112 | 162 | 250 | | 294 | 372 | 270 | 512 | 290 |
| Minneapolis | 97 | 224 | 155 | 234 | 294 | | 87 | 70 | 237 | 10 |
| Rochester | 62 | 311 | 234 | 323 | 372 | 87 | | 159 | 237 | 77 |

See also mileage table page 2

## MINNESOTA

Scale 1:1,552,320

Scale in Miles / Scale in Kilometers

KILOMETERS IN CANADA
KILOMETERS x 0.62 = MILES

FOR ADJOINING AREA SEE INSET MAP

---

### MINNESOTA index

Towns with asterisks (*) are keyed to the map on page 62.

*(Extensive alphabetical index of Minnesota towns with populations and map grid references, arranged in columns A through L, accompanied by the detailed state road map and inset maps.)*

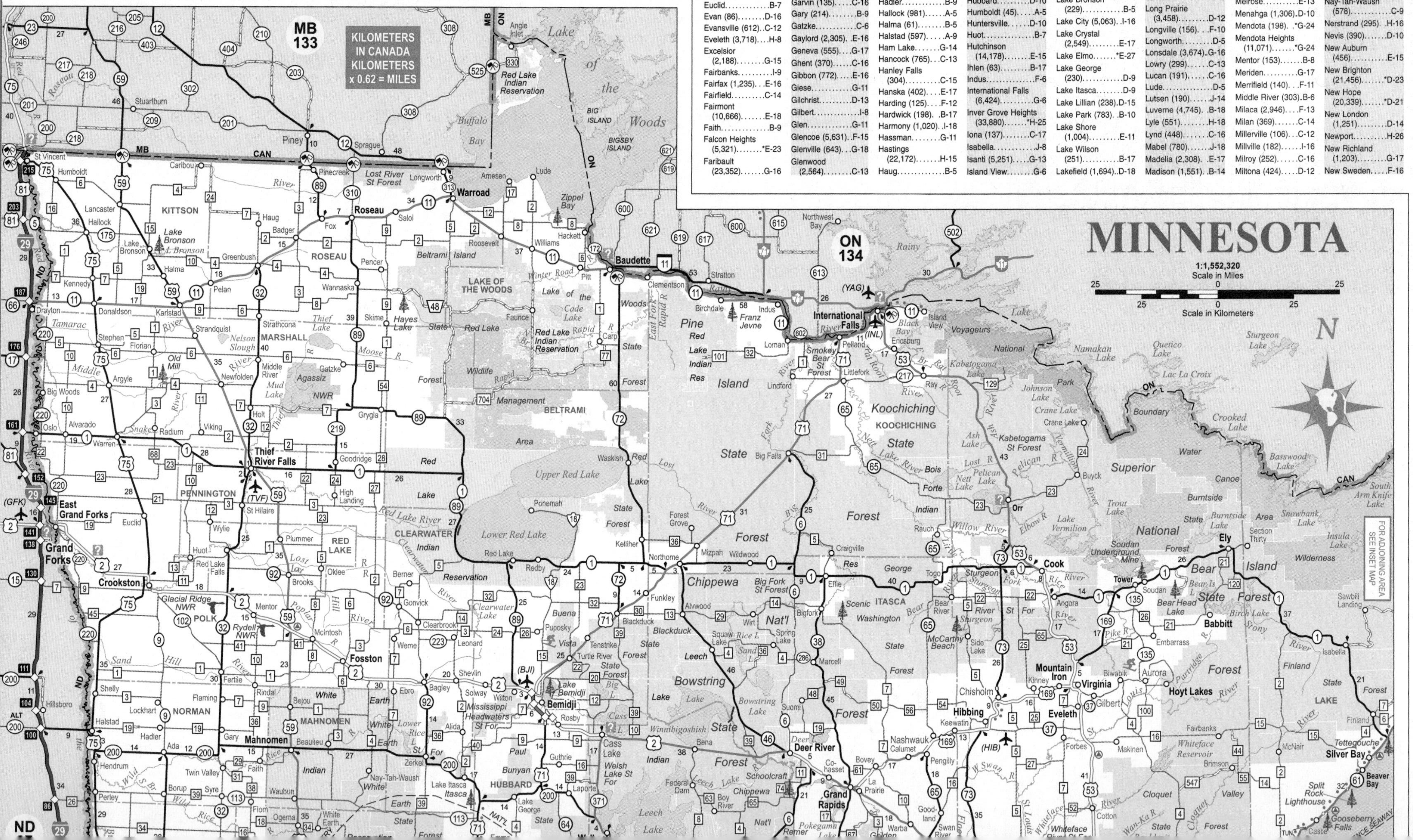

LEGEND

| | |
|---|---|
| Interstate Highway | Wildlife Refuge |
| Controlled Access Hwy | Nat'l/State Park |
| Controlled Access Hwy Toll | National Forest |

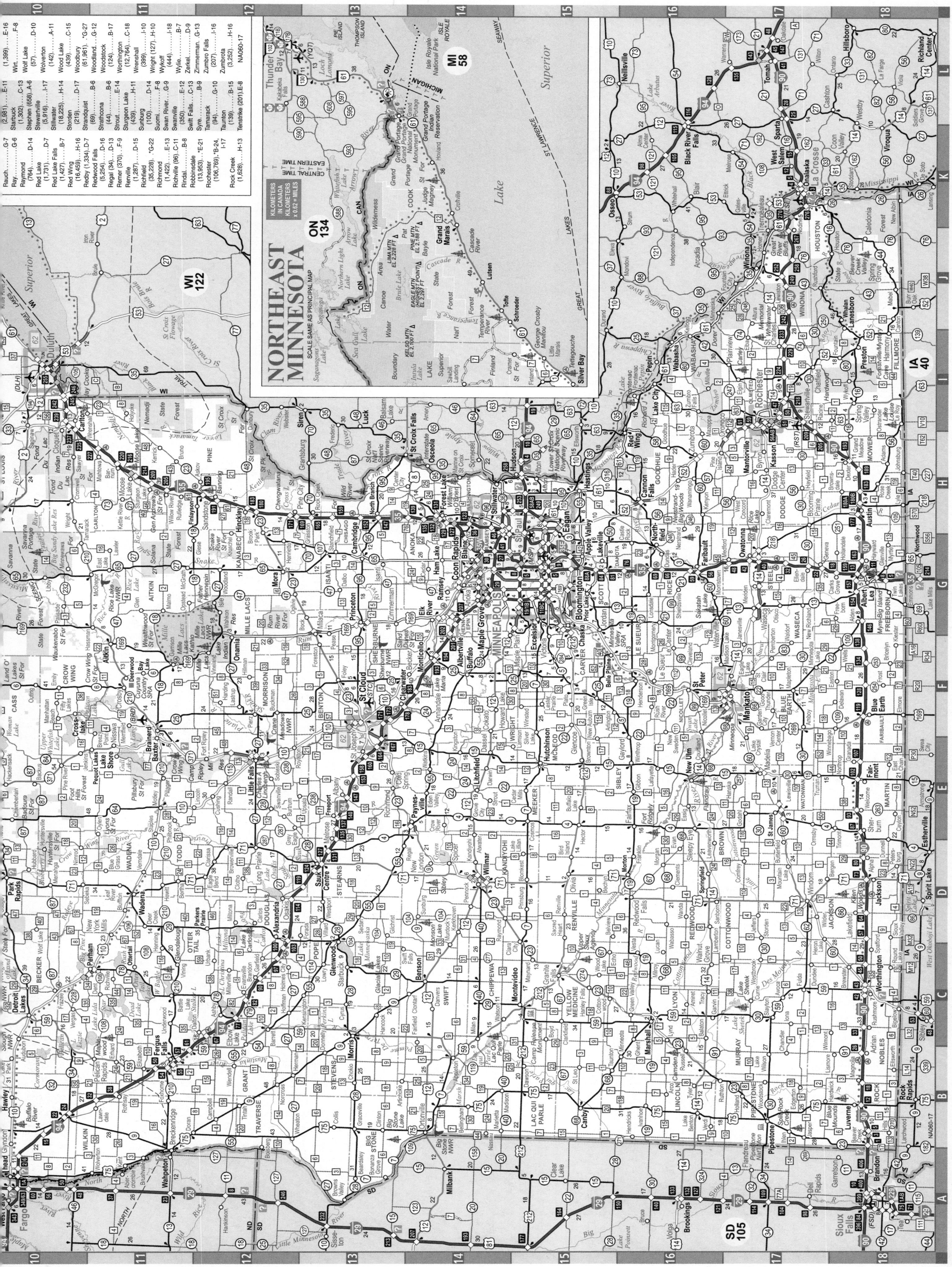

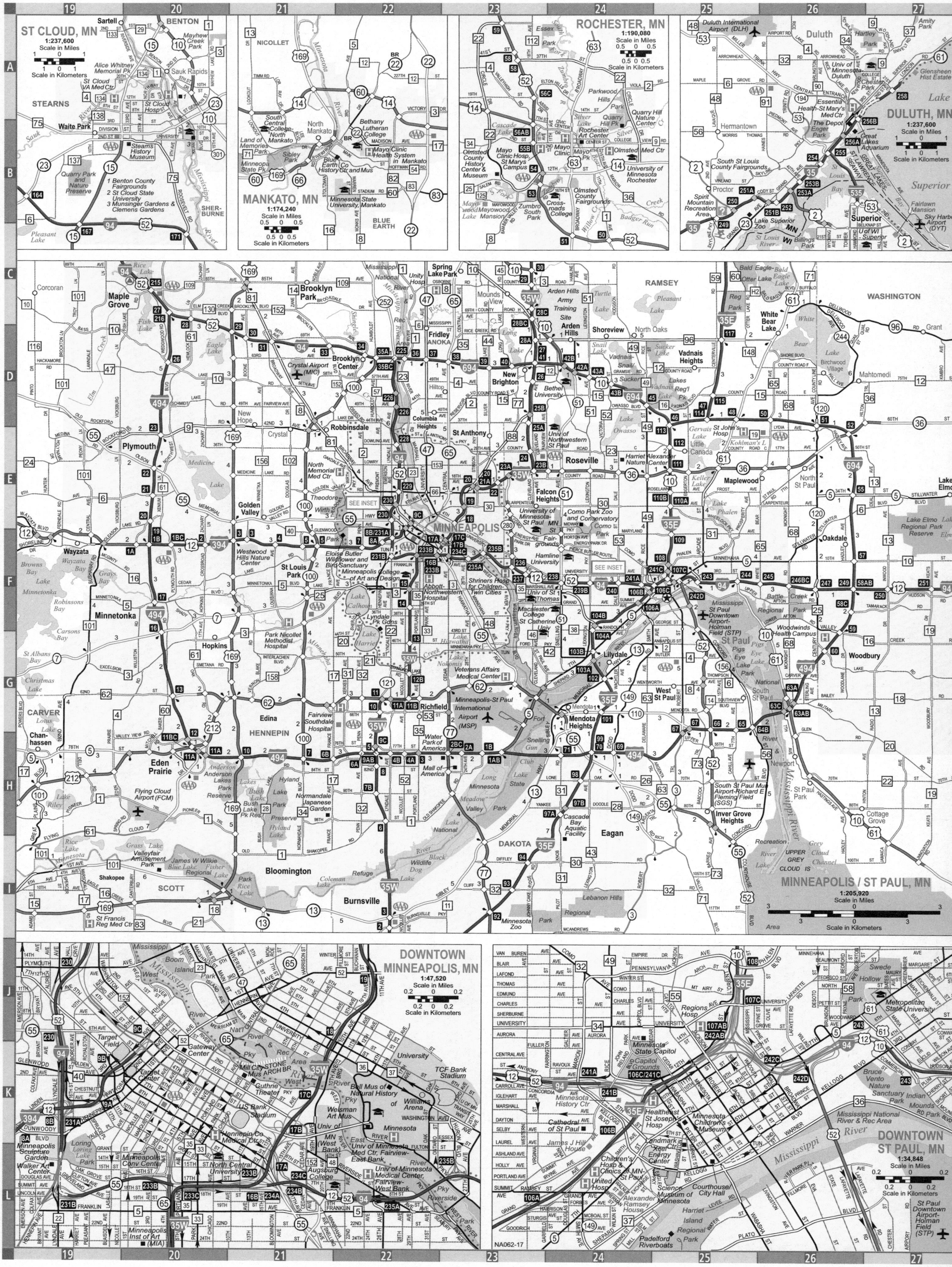
ST CLOUD, MN
1:237,600
Scale in Miles
Scale in Kilometers
MANKATO, MN
1:174,240
Scale in Miles
Scale in Kilometers
ROCHESTER, MN
1:190,080
Scale in Miles
Scale in Kilometers
DULUTH, MN
1:237,600
Scale in Miles
Scale in Kilometers
MINNEAPOLIS / ST PAUL, MN
1:205,920
Scale in Miles
Scale in Kilometers
DOWNTOWN MINNEAPOLIS, MN
1:47,520
Scale in Miles
Scale in Kilometers
DOWNTOWN ST PAUL, MN
1:34,848
Scale in Miles
Scale in Kilometers
NA062-17

ST LOUIS, MO
1:259,776
Scale in Miles
Scale in Kilometers
St Charles
St Peters
Florissant
Hazelwood
Bridgeton
Chesterfield
Clayton
University City
Kirkwood
Webster Groves
Maplewood
Brentwood
Richmond Heights
Ladue
Creve Coeur
Maryland Heights
Ballwin
Manchester
Eureka
Fenton
Sunset Hills
Mehlville
Lemay
Oakville
East St Louis
Cahokia
Collinsville
Edwardsville
Granite City
Fairview Heights
O'Fallon
Pontoon Beach
ST CHARLES
JEFFERSON
Lambert St Louis Int'l Airport (STL)
St Louis Downtown Parks Airport (CPS)

ST JOSEPH, MO
1:190,080
Scale in Miles
Scale in Kilometers
ANDREW
BUCHANAN
Rosecrans Memorial Airport (STJ)
Elwood
Missouri Western State University

KANSAS CITY, MO/KS
1:253,440
Scale in Miles
Scale in Kilometers
Kansas City International Airport (MCI)
KANSAS CITY
CLAY
PLATTE
Liberty
Gladstone
Parkville
Riverside
North Kansas City
Kansas City
Independence
Raytown
Merriam
Overland Park
Prairie Village
Leawood
Lenexa
Olathe
Shawnee
WYANDOTTE
JOHNSON
JACKSON
LEAVENWORTH
Lee's Summit Municipal Airport (LXT)

JOPLIN, MO
1:190,080
Scale in Miles
Scale in Kilometers
JASPER
NEWTON
Missouri Southern State University
Saginaw

SPRINGFIELD, MO
1:253,440
Scale in Miles
Scale in Kilometers
Springfield-Branson National Airport (SGF)
Downtown Airport (3DW)
Missouri State University

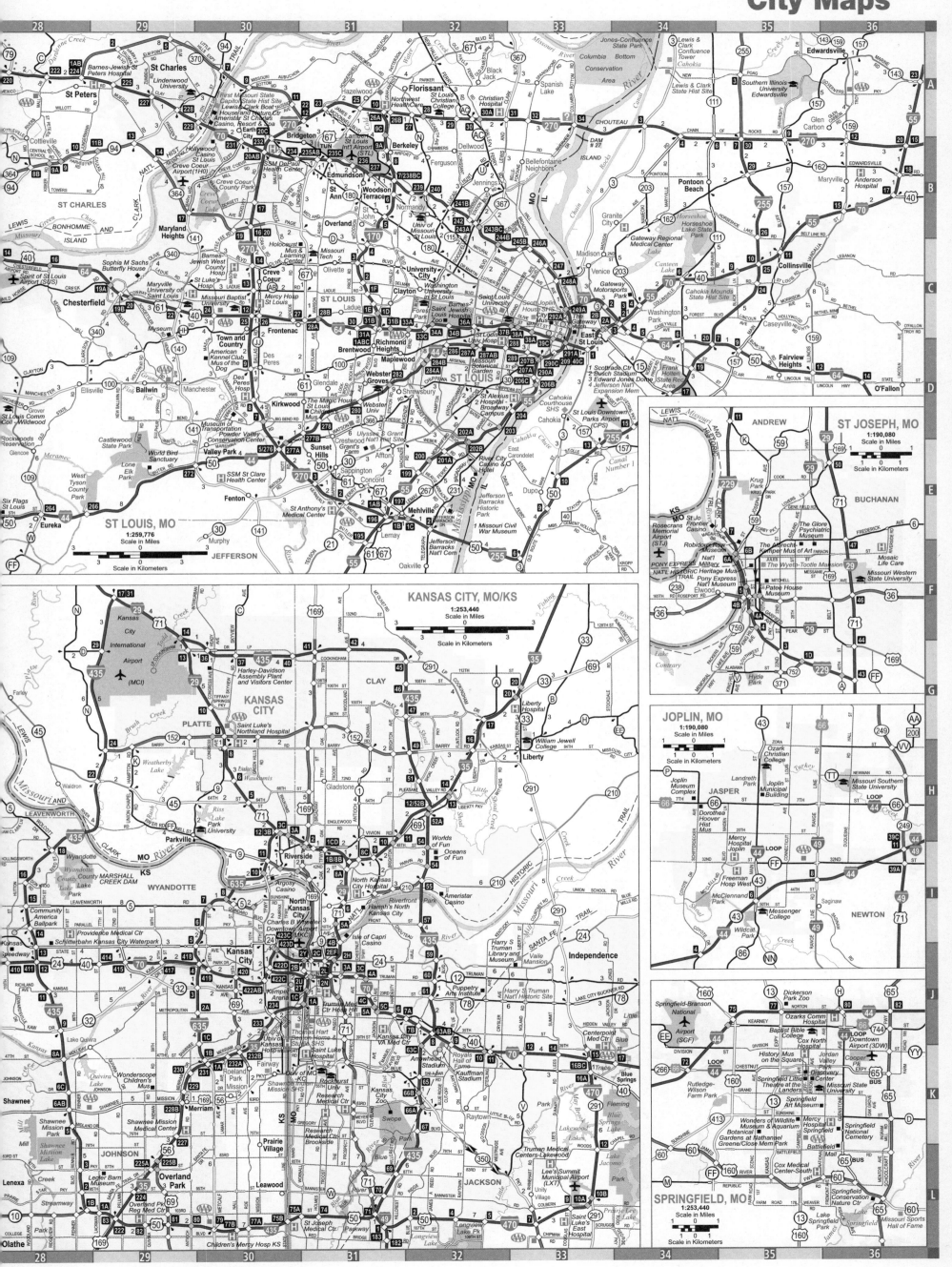

| Driving Distances In Miles | Biloxi | Clarksdale | Columbus | Gulfport | Hattiesburg | Jackson | Meridian | Natchez | Tupelo | Vicksburg |
|---|---|---|---|---|---|---|---|---|---|---|
| Biloxi | | 318 | 256 | 9 | 75 | 169 | 165 | 221 | 308 | 207 |
| Jackson | 169 | 148 | 172 | 163 | 93 | | 95 | 120 | 191 | 49 |
| Meridian | 165 | 238 | 90 | 159 | 90 | 95 | | 204 | 143 | 134 |
| Tupelo | 308 | 112 | 69 | 302 | 232 | 191 | 143 | 307 | | 255 |

See also mileage table page 2

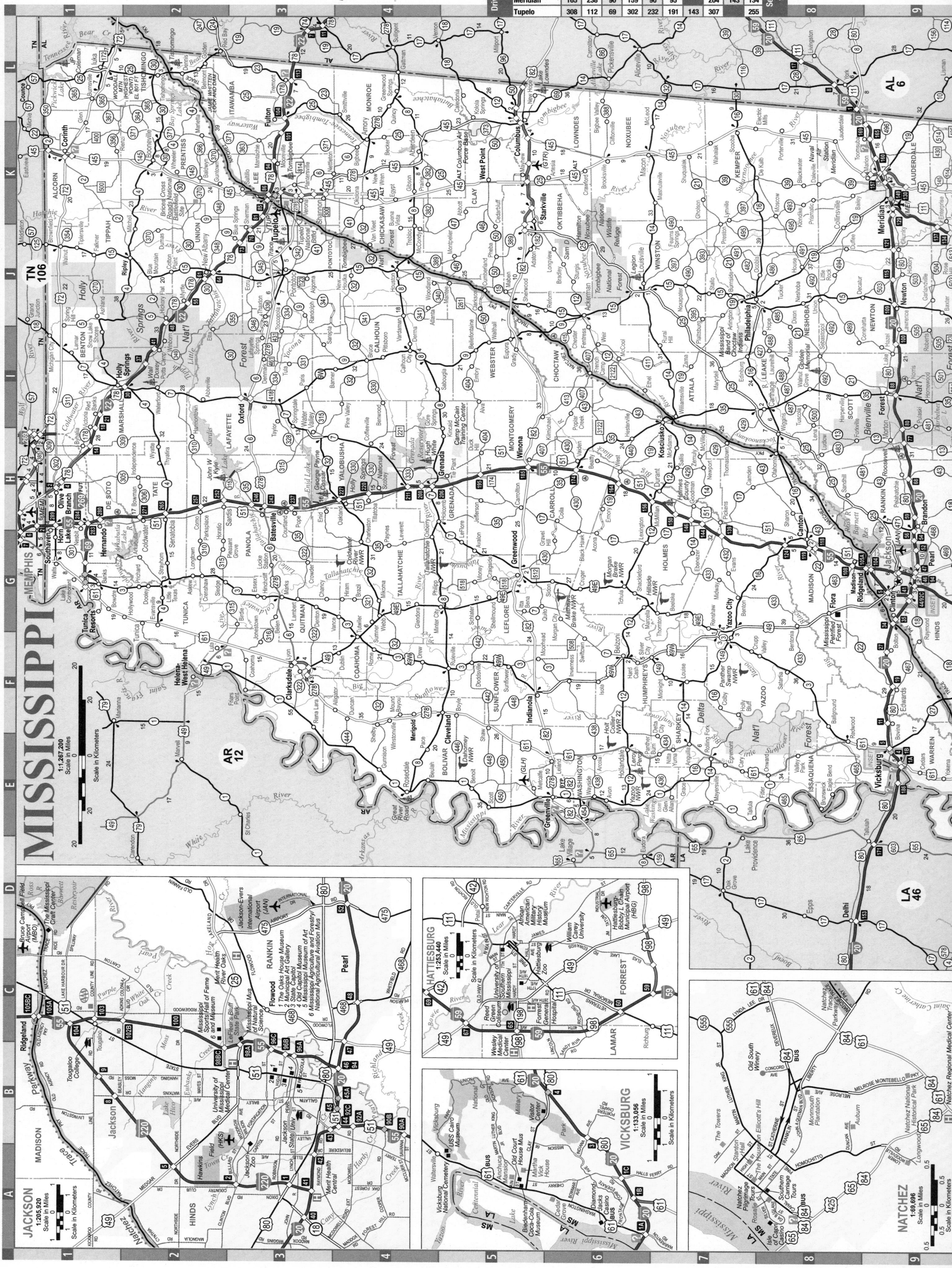

**LEGEND**

| | | |
|---|---|---|
| Interstate Highway | 95 | Wildlife Refuge |
| Controlled Access Hwy | | Nat'l/State Park |
| Controlled Access Hwy Toll | | National Forest |

GULFPORT / BILOXI

1:190,080
Scale in Miles
Scale in Kilometers

Gulf of Mexico

Mississippi Sound

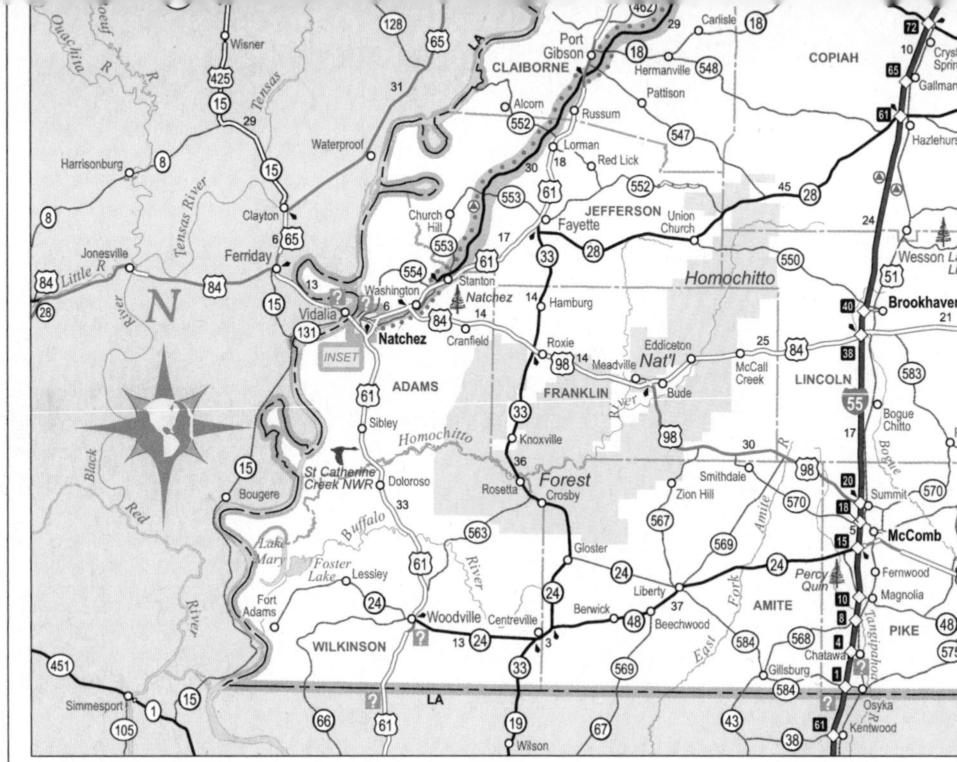

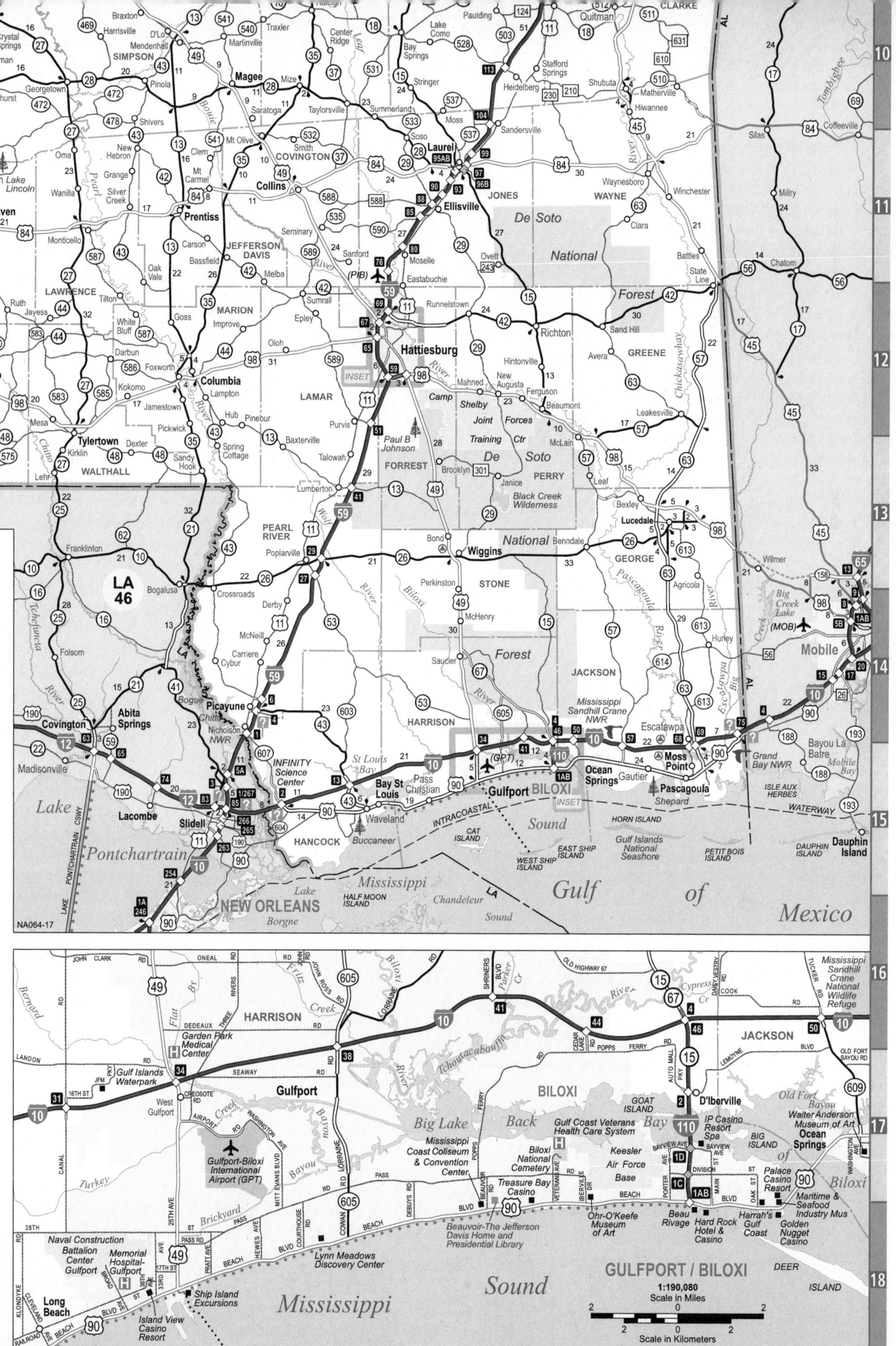

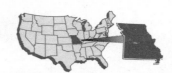

| Driving Distances In Miles | Branson | Columbia | Jefferson City | Joplin | Kansas City | Poplar Bluff | Sikeston | Springfield | St. Joseph | St. Louis |
|---|---|---|---|---|---|---|---|---|---|---|
| Kansas City | 210 | 126 | 150 | 157 | | 357 | 381 | 166 | 53 | 250 |
| Sikeston | 262 | 257 | 252 | 303 | 381 | 48 | | 236 | 435 | 147 |
| Springfield | 44 | 167 | 133 | 71 | 166 | 190 | 236 | | 223 | 215 |
| St. Louis | 252 | 126 | 134 | 284 | 250 | 153 | 147 | 215 | 302 | |

See also mileage table page 2

## MISSOURI

Towns with asterisk (*) are keyed to the map on page 63.

Adrian (1,677)........F-8
Advance (1,347)....J-17
Affton (20,307)....*E-31
Agency (684)..........C-7
Alba (555)................I-8
Albany (1,730)........B-8
Aldrich (80)...........H-10
Alexandria (159)...B-14
Allendale (53).........A-8
Alma (402)............E-10
Altamont (204)........C-9
Altenburg (352).....H-17
Alton (871)............K-14
Amazonia (312)......C-7
Amity (54)..............C-8
Amoret (190)..........G-8
Amsterdam (242)....F-8
Anderson (1,961)....K-8
Annada (29)..........D-15
Annapolis (345)......I-15
Anniston (232).......J-18
Appleton City (1,127)................G-9
Arbela (41)...........A-13
Arbyrd (509)..........L-16
Arcadia (608)........H-15
Archie (1,170).........F-8
Arcola (55).............H-9
Argyle (162)..........G-13
Arkoe (68)...............B-7
Armstrong (284)....D-11
Arnold (20,808).....F-16
Arrow Rock (56)....E-11
Asbury (207)............I-8
Ash Grove (1,472)................I-10
Ashburn (52).........D-14
Ashland (3,707)....E-12
Atlanta (385).........C-12
Augusta (253).......F-15
Aurora (7,508).........J-9
Auxvasse (983)....E-13
Ava (2,993)............J-11
Avilla (125)...............I-9
Baker (3)...............J-17
Bakersfield (246)..K-12
Ballwin (30,404)..*D-29
Baring (132)..........B-12
Barnard (221).........B-7
Barnett (203).........F-11
Bates City (219)......E-9
Beaufort................F-14
Belgrade..............H-15
Bell City (448).......J-17
Belle (1,545).........G-13
Bellefontaine Neighbors (10,860)...........*B-33
Belleview.............H-15
Bellflower (393).....E-14
Belton (23,116).......E-8
Benton (863)..........I-18
Benton City (104).................E-13
Berger (221)..........F-14
Berkeley (8,978).*B-31
Bernie (1,958).......K-17
Bethany (3,292)......B-9
Bethel (122)..........C-13
Bevier (718)..........C-12
Biehle (48)............H-17
Bigelow (27)...........B-6
Billings (1,035).......J-10
Birch Tree (679)....J-14
Bismarck (1,546)..H-15
Bixby....................H-14
Black....................H-15
Black Jack (6,929).............*A-32
Blackburn (249)....E-10
Blackwater (162)...E-11
Blairstown (97)........F-9
Bland (539)...........G-13
Blodgett (213).......J-18
Bloomfield (1,933)...............J-17
Bloomsdale (521).................G-16
Blue Eye (167).....K-10
Blue Springs (52,575)...*K-34, E-8
Blythedale (193).....A-9
Bogard (164).........D-10
Bois D'Arc..............I-10
Bolckow (187).........B-7
Bolivar (10,325)....H-10
Bonne Terre (6,864)..............H-16
Bonnots Mill.........F-13
Boonville (8,319)...E-11
Boss.....................H-14
Bosworth (305)....D-10
Bourbon (1,632)...G-14
Bowling Green (5,334).............D-14
Bradleyville............J-11
Bragg City (149)....L-17
Braggadocio..........L-17
Brandsville (161)..K-13
Branson (10,520)...J-5; (6,050) K-10
Branson West (478).................K-10
Brashear (273)......B-12
Braymer (878)........C-9
Breckenridge (383)..................C-9
Brentwood (8,055)............*D-31
Bridgeton (11,550)...........*B-31
Brighton..................I-10
Brimson (63)...........B-9
Brinktown.............G-13
Brixey....................J-12
Bronaugh (249)......H-8
Brookfield (4,542)..............C-11
Broseley................K-16
Browning (265).....B-11
Brownington (107).G-9
Brumley (91).........G-12
Bruner....................J-11
Brunswick (858)....D-11
Bucklin (467).........C-11
Bucyrus...................I-13
Buffalo (3,084)......H-11
Bunceton (354).....E-11
Bunker (407)..........I-14
Burfordville.............I-17
Burlington Junction (537)...................A-7
Butler (4,219).........G-8
Butterfield (470).......J-9
Cabool (2,146).......I-13
Cainsville (290).......A-9
Cairo (292)............D-12
Caledonia (130)....H-15
Calhoun (469).......F-10
California (4,278)..F-12
Callao (292)..........C-12
Camden (191)........D-9
Camden Point (474)..................D-7
Camdenton (3,718).............G-11
Cameron (9,933)....C-8
Campbell (1,992).K-17
Canton (2,377)......B-14
Cape Fair..............J-10
Cape Girardeau (37,941)...............I-18
Cardwell (713).......L-16
Carl Junction (7,445)..................I-8
Carrollton (3,784)..............D-10
Carthage (14,378)....I-8
Caruthersville (6,168)...............L-17
Cascade..................I-16
Cassville (3,266).....K-9
Catron (67)...........K-17
Caulfield...............K-13
Cedarcreek............K-11
Center (508).........D-14
Centertown (278).F-12
Centerview (267)....F-9
Centerville (191).....I-15
Centralia (4,027)..D-12
Chadwick...............J-11
Chaffee (2,955)......I-17
Chamois (396)......F-13
Charleston (5,947)................J-18
Cherryville............H-14
Chesterfield (47,484)..........*C-29
Chestnutridge........J-10
Chilhowee (325)......F-9
Chillicothe (9,515)..............C-10
Chula (210)..........C-10
Clarence (813)......C-12
Clark (298)...........D-12
Clarksburg (334)...F-11
Clarksdale (271).....C-8
Clarksville (442)....D-15
Clarkton (1,288)....K-17
Clayton (15,939).*C-31, F-16
Clearmont (170)......A-7
Cleveland (661)......F-8
Clever (2,139).......J-10
Clifton Hill (114)....D-11
Climax Springs (124).................G-11
Clinton (9,008).......F-9
Coatsville.............A-12
Cobalt City (226)..H-16
Coffey (166)...........B-9
Cole Camp (1,121)...............F-10
Collins (159).........H-10
Columbia (108,500).........B-17; (84,531) E-12
Commerce (67)......I-18
Conception (210)....B-8
Conception Junction (198)...................B-8
Concord (16,421)..........*E-31
Concordia (2,450)...............E-10
Conway (788).........I-11
Cooter (469)..........L-17
Corder (404).........E-10
Corning (15)...........B-6
Cosby (124)...........C-8
Cottleville (3,075).............*B-28
Couch..................K-14
Cowgill (188)..........D-9
Craig (248).............B-6
Crane (1,462)........J-10
Creighton (349)......F-9
Crestwood (11,912)..........*D-31
Creve Coeur (17,833)..........*C-30
Crocker (1,110)....G-12
Cross Timbers (216)................G-10
Cuba (3,356)........G-14
Curryville (225).....D-14
Dadeville (234).........I-9
Dalton (17)...........D-11
Danville (34)..........E-14
Darlington (121)......B-8
Davisville..............H-14
Dawn (128)...........C-10
De Kalb (220).........C-7
De Soto (6,400)...G-16
De Witt.................D-10
Dearborn (496).......D-7
Deepwater (433)....G-9
Deerfield (81).........H-8
Defiance (155)......F-15
Dellwood (5,025)............*B-32
Delta (438).............I-17
Denver (39).............A-8
Des Arc (177).........I-15
Des Peres (8,373)............*D-30
Desloge (5,054)...H-16
Devils Elbow........H-13
Dexter (7,864).......J-17
Diamond (902)........J-8
Diehlstadt (161).....J-18
Diggins (299)..........I-11
Dittmer..................G-15
Dixon (1,549).......G-13
Doe Run (915).....H-16
Doniphan (1,997).K-15
Doolittle (630).......H-13
Dora.......................J-12
Dover (103)............D-9
Downing (335)......A-12
Drexel (965)...........F-8
Duke.....................H-13
Dunnegan............H-10
Durham.................C-13
Eagle Rock (199)...K-9
Eagleville (316)......A-9
Earth City............*A-30
East Lynne (303)...F-8
East Prairie (3,176)...............J-18
Easton (234)..........C-8
Edgar Springs (208).................H-13
Edina (1,176).......B-12
Edmundson (834)...............*B-31
Edwards...............G-10
El Dorado Springs (3,593)................H-9
Eldon (4,567)........G-12
Eldridge................H-11
Elk Creek................I-13
Elkland....................I-11
Ellington (987)........I-15
Ellisville (9,133)...*D-28
Ellsinore (446).......J-15
Elmer (80).............C-11
Elmo (168).............A-7
Elsberry (1,934)....D-15
Emden..................C-13
Eminence (600)......I-14
Emma (233).........E-10
Eolia (522)...........D-15
Essex (472)...........J-17
Ethel (62).............C-11
Eugene.................F-12
Eunice......................I-13
Eureka (10,189)..*E-28
Everton (319)...........I-9
Ewing (456)..........B-13
Excello (49)..........C-12
Excelsior Springs (11,084)..............D-8
Exeter (772)...........K-9
Fair Grove (1,393).................I-10
Fair Play (475)......H-10
Fairdealing (676)..K-15
Fairfax (638)...........B-6
Fairview (383).........J-9
Falcon..................H-12
Farber (322).........D-14
Farley (269)........*G-28
Farmington (16,240)............H-16
Farrar...................H-17
Faucett....................C-7
Fayette (2,688).....E-11
Fenton (4,022).....*E-30
Ferguson (21,203)...........*B-32
Festus (11,602)....G-16
Fillmore (184).........B-7
Fisk (342).............J-16
Flemington (148)..H-10
Fletcher................G-15
Flint Hill (525).......E-15
Florence.................F-11
Florida..................D-13
Florissant (52,158)...........*A-32
Foley (161)...........E-15
Fordland (800)........I-11
Forest City (268).....B-7
Foristell (505)........E-15
Forsyth (2,255).....K-11
Fortuna..................F-11
Foster (117)...........G-8
Frankford (323).....D-14
Franklin (95).........E-11
Fredericktown (3,985)..............H-16
Freeburg (437).....G-13
Freeman (482)........F-8
Freistatt (163).........J-9
Fremont (129).......J-14
French Village......G-16
Frohna (254).........H-17
Frontenac (3,482)...........*C-30
Fulton (12,790).....E-13
Gainesville (773)..K-12
Galena (440).........J-10
Gallatin (1,786)......C-9
Galt (253).............B-10
Garden City (1,642).................F-8
Gasconade (223).F-14
Gatewood.............K-15
Gentry (72).............B-8
Gerald (1,345).......F-14
Gerster (25)..........G-10
Gibbs (107)...........B-12
Gideon (1,093)......K-17
Gilliam (197).........D-11
Gilman City (383)...B-9
Gladstone (25,410)...........*H-31
Glasgow (1,103)...D-11
Glenallen (85).........I-17
Glencoe..............*E-28
Glendale (5,925).............*D-31
Glenwood (196)....A-12
Gobler...................L-17
Golden (280)..........K-9
Golden City (765).....I-9
Goodman (1,248)....J-8
Gordonville (391)...I-17
Gorin.....................B-13
Gower (1,526)........C-8
Graff........................I-12
Granby (2,134)........J-8
Grand Pass (66)..D-10
Grandin (243)........J-15
Grandview (24,475)................E-8
Granger (34).........A-13
Grant City (859)......A-8
Gravois Mills (144)..................G-11
Gray Summit (2,701)...............F-15
Green City (657)...B-11
Green Ridge (476)..................F-10
Greencastle (275)..................B-11
Greenfield (1,371)....I-9
Greentop (442).....B-12
Greenville (511).....I-16
Greenwood (5,221).................E-8
Grover.................*D-28
Grovespring............I-12
Grubville...............G-15
Hale (419).............C-10
Halfway (173).......H-10
Hallsville (1,491)...E-12
Halltown (173)..........I-9
Hamilton (1,809)....C-9
Hannibal (17,916)...............C-14
Hardenville...........K-12
Hardin (569)...........D-9
Harris (61).............B-10
Harrisburg (266)...E-12
Harrisonville (10,019)................F-8
Hartford.................A-11
Hartsburg (103).....F-12
Hartshorn................I-13
Hartville (613)..........I-12
Harviell (106)........K-16
Harwood (47).........G-9
Hawk Point (669).E-14
Hayti (2,939).........L-17
Hayward (131)......K-17
Haywood City (206)..................J-17
Hazelwood (25,703)..........*A-31
Helena...................C-8
Hematite...............G-16
Henley..................G-12
Henrietta (369).......D-9
Herculaneum (3,468)...............G-16
Hermann (2,431)..F-14
Hermitage (467)...H-10
Higbee (568)........D-12
Higginsville (4,797)..................E-9
High Hill (195).......E-14
Highlandville (911)..................J-10
Hillsboro (2,821)..G-16
Hoberg (56).............J-9
Hogan......................I-15
Holcomb (635)......K-17
Holden (2,252)........F-9
Holland (229)........L-17
Holliday (137).......D-12
Hollister (4,426).......J-6
Holt (447)...............D-8
Holts Summit (3,247)...............F-12
Homestown (151)..................K-17
Hopkins (532).........A-7
Hornersville (663).L-17
Houston (2,081).....I-13
Houstonia (220)....E-10
Howardville (383).K-18
Huggins..................I-12
Hughesville (183)..................E-10
Humansville (1,048).............H-10
Hume (336)............G-8
Humphreys (118).B-10
Hunnewell (184)...C-13
Huntsville (1,564).............D-12
Hurdland (163)......B-12
Hurley (178)..........J-10
Iberia (736)..........G-12
Independence (113,288)...........E-8; (116,830) *J-33
Ionia (88)...............F-10
Irondale (445).......H-15
Ironton (1,460)......H-15
Isabella..................K-12
Jackson (13,758)...I-17
Jacksonville (151)...............C-12
Jadwin.....................I-14
Jameson (133)........B-9
Jamesport (524).....B-9
Jamestown (386).E-12
Jane.......................K-8
Jasper (931)..............I-8
Jefferson City (39,636)...........F-12; (43,079) D-17, F-12
Jennings (14,712)..........*B-32
Jerico Springs (228).................H-9
Jerome.................H-13
Jonesburg (768)...E-14
Joplin (45,504)........J-8; (50,150) *I-35
Kahoka (2,078).....A-13
Kaiser...................G-12
Kansas City (441,545)...........E-8; (459,787) *K-31
Kearney (8,381).....D-8
Kelso (586).............I-18
Kennett (10,932)...L-17
Kewanee...............K-18
Keytesville (471)...D-11
Kidder (323)...........C-9
Kimberling City (2,400)..............K-10
Kimmswick (157)..F-16
King City (1,013).....B-8
Kingdom City (128).................E-13
Kingston (348)........C-9
Kingsville (269).......F-9
Kirbyville (207)......K-10
Kirksville (17,505)...........B-12
Kirkwood (27,540)..........*D-31
Kissee Mills (1,109)...............K-11
Knob Lick.............H-16
Knob Noster (2,709)..............E-10
Knox City (216).....B-13
Koeltztown............G-13
Koshkonong (212).................K-13
La Belle (660).......B-13
La Grange (931)...B-14
La Monte (1,140)..E-10
La Plata (1,366)....B-12
La Russell (114).......I-9
La Tour (62)............F-9
Laclede (345).......C-10
Laddonia (513).....D-13
Ladue (8,521)......*C-31
Lake Ozark (1,586)..............G-12
Lake Spring.........H-13
Lamar (4,532)..........I-8
Lampe..................K-10
Lanagan (419)........K-8
Lancaster (728)....A-12
Laquey..................H-12
Laredo (198)..........B-10
Latham...................F-11
Lathrop (2,086)......D-8
Laurie (945)..........G-11
Lawson (2,473).......D-8
Leadwood (1,282)..............H-15
Leasburg (338).....G-14
Lebanon (14,474)............H-11
Lee's Summit (91,364)...............E-8
Leeton (566)...........F-9
Lemay (16,645)..*E-31
Lentner.................C-12
Leonard (61).........C-12
Leslie (171)...........F-14
Lesterville..............I-15
Levasy (83).............E-9
Lewistown (534)...B-13
Lexington (4,726)...D-9
Liberal (759)..........H-8
Liberty (29,149)..*H-33, D-8
Licking (3,124)........I-13
Lilbourn (1,190)....K-17
Lincoln (1,190)......F-10
Linn (1,459)..........F-13
Linn Creek (244)..G-11
Linneus (278).......C-10
Livonia (74)..........A-11
Lock Springs (57)...C-9
Lockwood (936).......I-9
Lodi.........................I-16
Lohman (163).......F-12
Lone Jack (1,050)..E-9
Lonedell...............G-15
Long Lane............H-11
Longtown (102)....H-17
Loose Creek.........F-13
Louisburg (122)....H-10
Louisiana (3,364)..............D-15
Lowndes.................I-16
Lowry City (640)....G-9
Lucerne (85).........A-10
Ludlow (137)..........C-9
Lupus (33)............E-12
Luray (99)............A-13
Macks Creek (244)..................G-11
Macomb................J-12
Macon (5,471)......C-12
Madison (554)......D-12
Maitland (343).........B-7
Malden (4,275).....K-17
Malta Bend (250)..................D-10
Manchester (18,094)..........*D-29
Mansfield (1,296)..J-12
Maplewood (8,046)............*D-31
Marble Hill (1,477)..................I-17
Marceline (2,233).C-11
Marionville (2,225)..J-9
Marquand (203).....I-16
Marshall (13,065)............E-10
Marshfield (6,633)..I-11
Marston (503).......K-17
Marthasville (1,136)...............F-15
Martinsburg (304)..................E-13
Martinsville.............B-9
Maryland Heights (27,472)............*B-30
Maryville (11,972)...B-7
Matthews (628).....J-18
Maysville (1,114)....C-8
Mayview (212)........E-9
Maywood.............C-13
McFall (93).............B-8
McGee...................J-16
McGirk...................F-12
McKittrick (61).......F-14
Meadville (462).....C-10
Mehlville (28,380)..........*E-31
Memphis (1,822)..A-12
Mendon (171).......C-11
Mercer (318).........A-10
Merwin (58)............F-8
Meta (229)............G-12
Metz (49)...............G-8
Mexico (11,543)....D-13
Miami (175)..........D-10
Middlebrook.........H-15
Middletown (167).E-14
Milan (1,960).........B-11
Milford (26)...........H-8
Mill Spring (189).................J-15
Millard (89).........B-12
Miller (699).............I-9
Millersville.............I-17
Milo (90)...............H-8
Mindenmines (365)....................I-8
Miner (984).........J-18
Mineral Point (351)...............G-15
Missouri City (267).................D-8
Moberly (13,974)..........D-12
Mokane (185).....F-13
Monett (8,873)......J-9
Monroe City (2,531)............C-13
Montgomery City (2,834)............E-14
Monticello (98)....B-13
Montier (98)........J-14
Montreal.............G-12
Montrose (384)....G-9
Moody.................K-13
Mooresville (91)...C-9
Mora....................F-10
Morehouse (973).................J-17
Morrison (139)....F-13
Morrisville (388)...I-10
Moscow Mills (2,509)............E-15
Mound City (1,159)..............B-7
Moundville (124)..H-8
Mountain Grove (4,789)............J-12
Mountain View (2,719)............J-13
Mt. Leonard (87).................E-10
Mt. Moriah (87).....B-9
Mt. Vernon (4,575)...............J-9
Murphy (8,690)...........*E-30
Myrtle...................K-14
Napoleon (222)....E-9
Naylor (632).......K-16
Neck City (186)......I-8
Neelyville (483)..K-16
Nelson (192).......E-11
Neosho (11,835)...J-8
Nevada (8,386)....H-8
New Bloomfield (669)...............F-13
New Boston........C-11
New Cambria (195)...............C-11
New Florence (769)...............E-14
New Franklin (1,089)............E-11
New Hampton (291).................B-9
New Haven (2,089)............F-14
New London (974)...............C-14
New Madrid (3,116)............K-18
New Melle (475)...............F-15
Newark (94)........B-13
Newburg (470)...H-13
Newtown (183)..B-10
Niangua (405)......I-11
Nixa (19,022)......J-10
Noel (1,832).........K-8
Norborne (708)....D-9
Normandy (5,008)...........*B-32
North Kansas City (4,208)............*I-31
Norwood...............J-12
Novelty (139)......B-12
Novinger (456)...B-11
O'Fallon (79,329)..........E-15
Oak Grove (7,795)..............E-9
Oak Ridge (243)..I-17
Oakville (36,143).........*F-32
Odessa (5,300)....E-9
Old Appleton (85)................H-17
Old Monroe (265)...............E-15
Oldfield................J-11
Olean (128).........F-12
Olivette (7,737)..........*C-31
Olney..................E-14
Oran (1,294).......J-17
Oregon (857)........B-7
Orrick (837)..........D-9
Osage Beach (4,351)............G-11
Osborn (423)........C-8
Osceola (947)......G-9
Osgood (48).......B-10
Otterville (454)....F-11
Overland (16,062).........*B-31
Owensville (2,676)...........G-14
Oxly (200)...........K-15
Ozark (17,820)....J-10
Pacific (7,002)....F-15
Palmyra (3,595)............C-14
Paris (1,220)......D-13
Park Hills (8,759)............H-16
Parkville (5,554).........*H-29
Parma (713).......K-17
Parnell (191)........A-8
Pascola (108).....L-17
Passaic (34)........G-8
Patterson..............I-16
Patton....................I-17
Pattonsburg (348)................B-9
Paynesville (77)................D-15
Peace Valley.......J-13
Peculiar (4,608)....F-8
Perkins................J-17
Perry (693).........D-13
Perryville (8,225)...........H-17
Pevely (5,484)...G-16
Philadelphia.......C-13
Phillipsburg (202)..............H-11
Pickering (160).....A-7
Piedmont (1,977)..............I-15
Pierce City (1,292)...............J-9
Pilot Grove (768)...............E-11
Pineville (791)......K-8
Pittsburg.............H-10
Plato (109)...........I-12
Platte City (4,691)..............D-7
Plattsburg (2,319)..............C-8
Pleasant Hill (8,113)...............E-8
Pleasant Hope (614).................I-10
Plevna (21).........C-13
Pocahontas (114)...................I-17
Point Lookout.......K-6
Pollock (89).........B-11
Polo (575).............D-9
Pomona (511).....J-13
Ponce de Leon...J-10
Pontiac (175)......K-12
Poplar Bluff (17,023)...........J-16
Portage Des Sioux (328)...............E-16
Portageville (3,228)............K-17
Portland..............F-13
Potosi (2,660)....G-15
Pottersville..........K-13
Powell...................K-8
Powersite............K-11
Powersville (60)................A-10
Prairie Home (280)...............E-12
Preston (223).....H-10
Princeton (1,166)............A-10
Protem...............K-11
Purcell (408)..........I-8
Purdin (190).......C-10
Purdy (1,098)........J-9
Puxico (881)........J-16
Queen City (598)...............A-12
Quincy................G-10
Quitman (45)........A-7
Qulin (458).........K-16
Racine...................J-8
Ravenwood (440).................B-8
Raymondville (363).................I-13
Raymore (19,206)............E-8
Raytown (29,526).........*K-32
Rayville (223).......D-9
Rea (50)...............B-7
Redford................I-15
Reeds (95)............J-8
Reeds Spring (913).................J-10
Renick (172).......D-12
Rensselaer (228)..............C-14
Republic (14,751)...........J-10
Revere (79)........A-13
Reynolds..............I-15
Rhineland (142).F-14
Rich Hill (1,396)...G-8
Richards (96).......H-8
Richland (1,863)...........H-12
Richmond (5,797).............D-9
Richmond Heights (8,603)..........*C-32
Richwoods.........G-15
Ridgedale..........K-10
Ridgeway (464)....A-9
Risco (346).........K-17
Riverside (2,937)............*I-30
Rives (63)...........L-17
Roach.................G-11
Robertsville.........F-15
Roby.....................I-12
Rocheport (239)...............E-12
Rock Port (1,318)..............A-6
Rockbridge..........J-12
Rockville (166).....G-9
Rocky Comfort......J-9
Rogersville (3,073).............J-11
Rolla (19,559)....H-13
Rombauer...........J-16
Roscoe (124).......G-9
Rosebud (409)...F-14
Rothville (99)......C-11
Round Spring......I-14
Rueter................K-11
Rush Hill (151)...D-13
Russellville (807)...............F-12
Rutledge (109)...B-13
Saginaw (297)....*I-35
Salem (4,950).....H-14
Salisbury (1,618)............D-11
Santa Fe............D-13
Sappington (7,580)...........*E-31
Sarcoxie (1,330)...J-9
Savannah (5,057).............C-7
Saverton............C-14
Schell City (249)..G-9
Scott City (4,565)..............I-18
Sedalia (21,387)..........F-10
Sedgewickville (173)...............H-17
Seligman (851).....K-9
Senath (1,767)....L-16
Seneca (2,336).....J-8
Seymour (1,921).I-11
Shelbina (1,704)............C-13
Shelbyville (552)...............C-13
Sheldon (543)......H-8
Shell Knob (1,379)..............K-9
Sheridan (195).....A-8
Shrewsbury (6,254)..........*D-31
Sibley (357)..........D-8
Sikeston (16,318)...........J-18
Silex (187)..........E-15
Silva.....................I-16
Slater (1,856).....D-11
Smithton (570)....F-11
Smithville (8,425)..............D-8
Solo......................I-13
South Gifford (50).................B-11
South Greenfield (90)......................I-9
South West City (970).................K-8
Spanish Lake (19,650).........*A-33
Sparta (1,756).....J-11
Spickard (254)....B-10
Spokane (177)....J-10
Springfield (151,580)........I-10; (159,498) *K-35
Squires................J-12
St. Albans...........F-15
St. Ann (13,020).........*B-31
St. Charles (60,321).........E-16; (65,794) *B-29
St. Clair (4,724)............G-15
St. Elizabeth (336)...............G-12
St. James (4,216)............G-13
St. John (6,517)...........*B-31
St. Joseph (73,990)...........C-7; (76,780) *F-35
St. Louis (319,294).....*C-32; (348,189) F-16
St. Martins (1,140)............F-12
St. Marys (360)..H-17
St. Patrick...........B-13
St. Peters (52,575).........*A-28
St. Robert (4,340)..........H-12
St. Thomas (263)..............F-12
Stanberry (1,185)............B-8
Stanton.............G-15
Stark City (139)...J-8
Ste. Genevieve (4,410)..........G-17
Steedman.........F-13
Steele (2,172)...L-17
Steelville (1,642)..........G-14
Stella (158).........J-8
Stewartsville (750)...............C-8
Stockton (1,819)............H-9
Stotesbury (18)..G-8
Stotts City (220)..J-9
Stoutland (192).............H-12
Stoutsville (36)...............D-13
Stover (1,094)...F-11
Strafford (2,358)............I-10
Strasburg (141)..E-9
Sturdivant..........J-17
Sturgeon (872).............D-12
Success.............I-13
Sullivan (7,081)..........G-14
Summersville (502)...............I-13
Sumner (102)...C-10
Sunrise Beach (431).............G-11
Sunset Hills (8,496).........*E-31
Swedeborg.......H-12
Sweet Springs (1,484)..........E-10
Syracuse (172)..............F-11
Tallapoosa (168).............K-17
Taneyville (396)..............J-11
Taos (878).........F-13
Tarkio (1,583)......A-6
Taylor................C-14
Tebbetts............F-13
Tecumseh.........K-12
Thayer (2,243).K-14
Theodosia (243)..............K-11
Thompson........D-13
Thornfield..........K-11
Tiff.....................G-15
Tiff City...............K-8
Tightwad (69)...G-10
Tina (157).........D-10
Tindall (77)........B-10
Tipton (3,262)...F-11
Town and Country (10,815).......*C-30
Treloar...............F-14
Trenton (6,001)..........B-10
Trimble (646)......D-8
Triplett (41)........D-10
Troy (10,540)....E-15
Truxton (91)......E-14
Tunas................H-11
Turners...............I-10
Turney (148).......C-8
Tuscumbia (203).............G-12
Ulman...............G-12
Union (10,204).F-15
Union Star (437)................B-8
Unionville (1,865)..........A-11
Unity Village (99)..............*L-33
University City (35,371).......*C-32
Urbana (417)....H-10
Urich (505)..........F-9
Utica (269)........C-10
Valles Mines.....G-16
Valley Park (6,942).........*E-30
Van Buren (819)..............J-15
Vandalia (3,899)..........D-14
Vandiver (71)....E-13
Vanzant.............J-12
Verona (619).......J-9
Versailles (2,482)...........F-11
Viburnum (693).............H-14
Vichy................G-13
Vienna (610)....G-13
Viola.................K-10
Vista (54)............G-9
Vulcan.................I-15
Waco (87).............I-8
Waldron...........*H-28
Walker (270).......H-8
Walnut Grove (665)...............I-10
Walnut Shade...J-10
Wappapello.......J-16
Wardell (427)....K-17
Wardsville (1,506)...........F-12
Warrensburg (18,838)..........E-9
Warrenton (7,880)..........E-14
Warsaw (2,127)..........G-10
Washburn (435).K-9
Washington (13,982)........F-15
Wasola (113).....J-12
Watson (100)......A-6
Waverly (849)...D-10
Wayland (533)..A-14
Waynesville (4,830)..........H-12
Weatherby (107)...............C-8
Weaubleau (418).............H-10
Webster Groves (22,995).......*D-31
Wellsville (1,217)..........E-14
Wentworth (147)................J-9
Wentzville (29,070).........E-15
Wesco...............H-14
West Plains (11,986).........J-13
Westboro (141)..A-6
Weston (1,641)..D-7
Westphalia (389).............F-13
Wheatland (371).............G-10
Wheaton (696)....J-9
Wheeling (271).............C-10
Whiteoak...........K-17
Whiteside (75)..D-15
Whitewater (125)...............I-17
Wildwood (35,517)........F-15
Willard (5,288)....I-10
Williamsburg.....E-13
Williamstown.....B-13
Williamsville (342).............J-16
Willow Springs (2,184)..........J-13
Wilson City (115)..............J-18
Windsor (2,901)..........F-10
Winfield (1,404)..........E-15
Winigan (44).....B-11
Winona (1,335)..........J-14
Winston (259).....C-9
Wolf Island........J-18
Woodson Terrace (4,063).........*B-31
Wooldridge (61)...............E-12
Worthington (81)...............A-11
Wright City (3,119)..........E-15
Wyaconda (227).............A-13
Wyatt (319)........J-18
Zalma (122)........I-17
Zanoni...............K-12

NA066-17

THEATERS

1 Baldknobbers Country Music Theatre .......... J-5
2 Branson Hot Hits Theatre ..... J-6
3 Branson's IMAX Entertainment Complex .......... I-4
4 God and Country Theatre ..... J-5
5 Golden Corral Showroom ...... I-4
6 Grand Country Music Hall .... J-5
7 Mickey Gilley Theatre ........... J-4
8 Presleys' Country Jubilee ..... J-5
9 RFD-TV, The Theatre ............ I-4
10 Sight & Sound Theatres ........ I-5
11 Starlite Theatre .................... J-5
12 The Oak Ridge Boys Theatre .......... I-6
13 The Shepherd of the Hills Outdoor Theatre .................... I-4
14 Welk Resort Theatre ............ K-4
15 Yakov Smirnoff Theatre ......... I-6

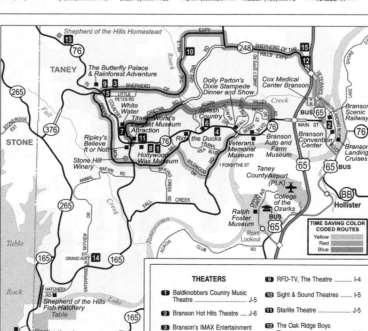

NA066-17

NA066-17

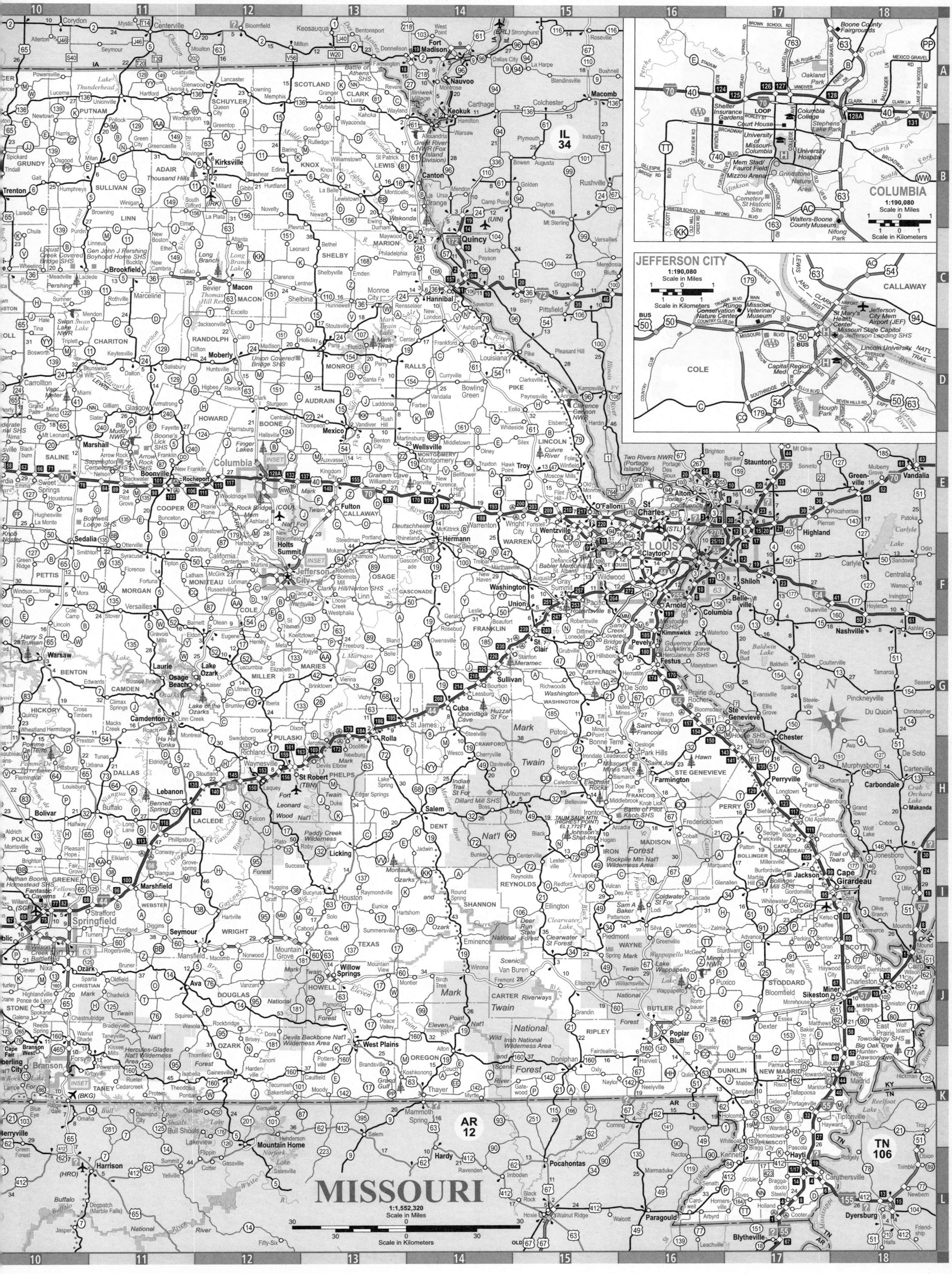

LEGEND
Interstate Highway — 95 — Wildlife Refuge
Controlled Access Hwy — Nat'l/State Park
Controlled Access Hwy Toll — National Forest

COLUMBIA
1:190,080
Scale in Miles
Scale in Kilometers

JEFFERSON CITY
1:190,080
Scale in Miles
Scale in Kilometers

**MISSOURI**
1:1,552,320
Scale in Miles
Scale in Kilometers

| Driving Distances In Miles | Billings | Bozeman | Browning | Butte | Glendive | Great Falls | Helena | Missoula |
|---|---|---|---|---|---|---|---|---|
| Billings | | 143 | 344 | 226 | 220 | 219 | 239 | 345 |
| Helena | 239 | 99 | 188 | 66 | 439 | 91 | | 115 |
| Missoula | 345 | 205 | 225 | 120 | 517 | 166 | 115 | |

See also mileage table page 2

## MONTANA

NA068-17

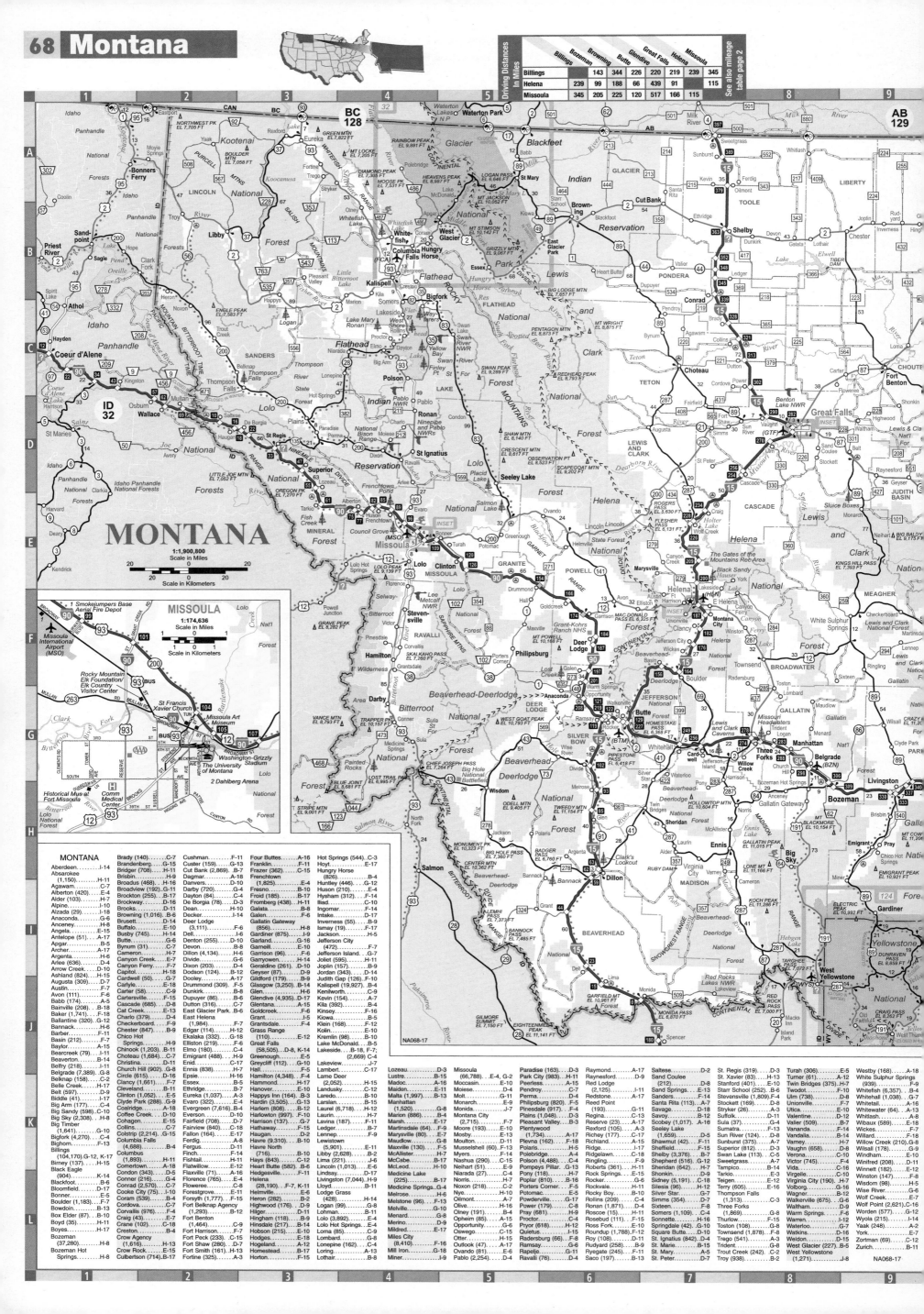

**LEGEND**

| | |
|---|---|
| Interstate Highway | Wildlife Refuge |
| Controlled Access Hwy | Nat'l/State Park |
| Controlled Access Hwy Toll | National Forest |

BILLINGS
1:174,240
Scale in Miles
Scale in Kilometers

HELENA
1:110,880
Scale in Miles
Scale in Kilometers

GREAT FALLS
1:142,560
Scale in Miles
Scale in Kilometers

INQUIRE LOCALLY FOR CURRENT CONDITIONS BEFORE DRIVING ON UNIMPROVED ROADS SHOWN ON THIS MAP

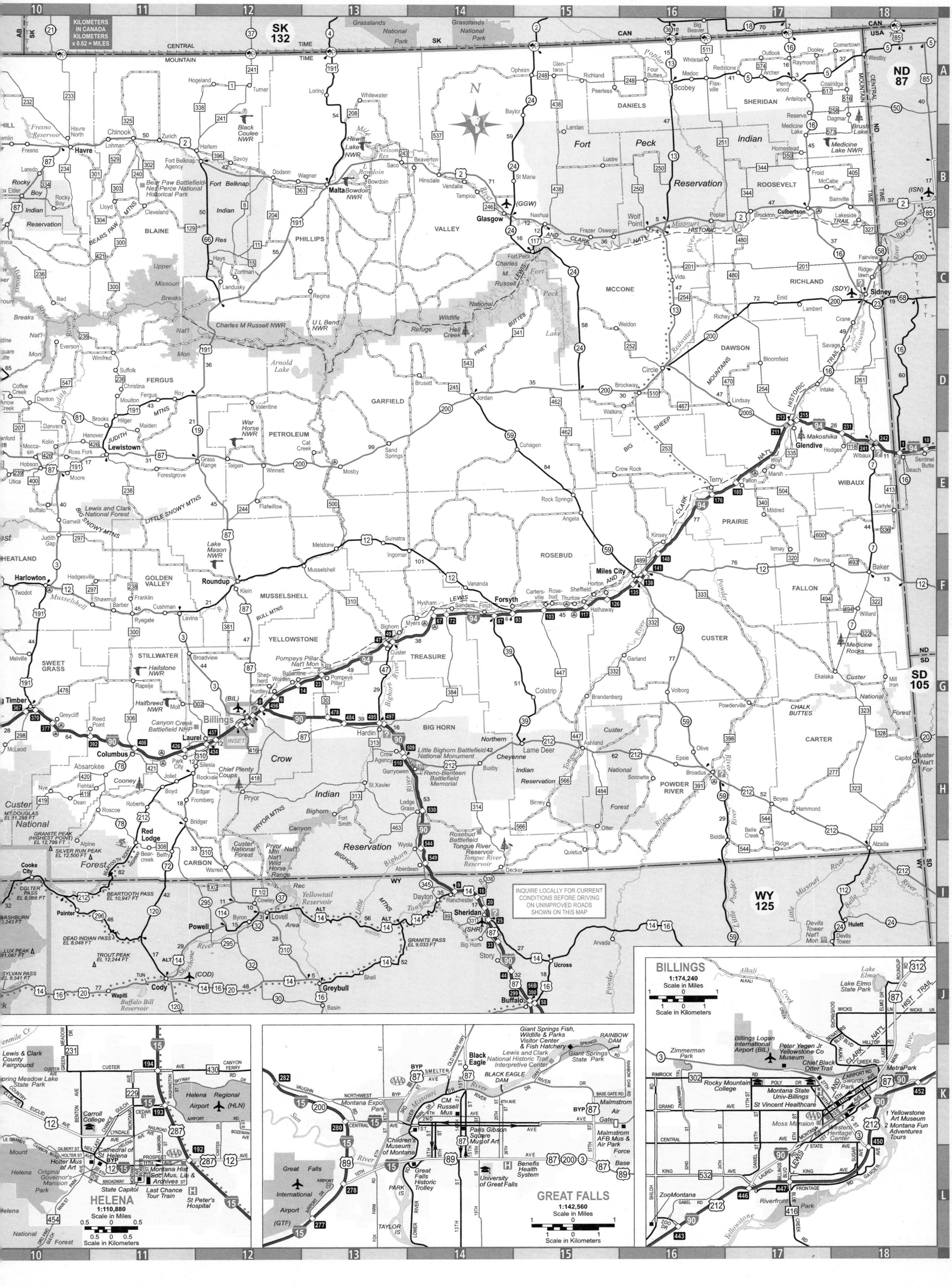

**Driving Distances In Miles**

| | Columbus | Grand Island | Lincoln | North Platte | Omaha | Scottsbluff | Sioux City, IA | Valentine |
|---|---|---|---|---|---|---|---|---|
| Lincoln | 77 | 97 | | 224 | 59 | 416 | 152 | 304 |
| North Platte | 209 | 144 | 224 | | 280 | 196 | 330 | 130 |
| Omaha | 87 | 153 | 59 | 280 | | 472 | 98 | 298 |

See also mileage table page 2

NEBRASKA

Adams (573).....K-16
Ainsworth (1,728)..F-9
Albion (1,650)...H-13
Alda (642).........J-12
Alexandria (177).K-14
Allen (377).......F-15
Alliance (8,491)...G-3
Alma (1,133).....L-10
Alvo (132)........J-16
Ames (24).......H-15
Amherst (248)...J-10
Angora............G-3
Anselmo (145)....H-9
Ansley (441).......I-10
Arapahoe (1,026)..K-9
Arcadia (311)....H-11
Arlington (1,243).........H-16
Arnold (597).........I-8
Arthur (117).......H-6
Ashby..............G-5
Ashland (2,453)..I-16
Ashton (194).......I-11
Atkinson (1,245)..F-11
Atlanta (131).....K-10
Auburn (3,460). .K-17
Aurora (4,479)...J-13
Avoca (242)......J-16
Axtell (726).......K-11
Ayr (94)...........K-12
Bancroft (495)...G-15
Barneston (116)..L-16
Bartlett (117)....G-12
Bartley (283)......L-8
Bassett (619)....F-10
Battle Creek (1,207).........G-13
Bayard (1,209)....H-2
Beatrice (12,459)........K-15
Beaver City (609)..L-9
Beaver Crossing (403)...........J-14
Beemer (678)...G-15
Belden (115)......F-14
Belgrade (126)...H-13
Bellevue (50,137)..D-17, I-17
Bellwood (435)...I-14
Belvidere (48)...K-14
Benedict (234)...J-14
Benkelman (953)..L-6
Bennet (719)......J-16
Bennington (1,458).........A-14
Bertrand (750)...K-10
Berwyn (83).......I-10
Big Springs (400)..I-5
Bingham...........G-5
Bladen (237).....K-12
Blair (7,990).....H-16
Bloomfield (1,028).........E-13
Bloomington (103)...........L-11
Blue Hill (936)...K-12
Boys Town (745)...........B-14
Bradshaw (273)..J-13
Brady (428).........J-8
Brainard (330)....I-15
Brewster (17).....G-9
Bridgeport (1,545)..........H-3
Bristow (65)......E-12
Broadwater (128)..H-3
Brock (112).......K-17
Broken Bow (3,559)..........I-10
Brownville (132)..K-17
Brule (326).........I-5
Bruning (279)....K-14
Bruno (99).........I-15
Brunswick (138)..F-13
Burchard (82)....L-16
Burr (57)..........K-16
Burton (10).......E-10
Burwell (1,210)..H-11
Bushnell (124).....I-1
Butte (326)........E-11
Byron (83).........L-13
Cairo (785)........J-12
Callaway (539).....I-9
Cambridge (1,063)...........K-9
Campbell (347)..K-11
Carleton (91)....K-13
Carroll (229).....F-14
Cedar Bluffs (610)............H-15
Cedar Rapids (382)............H-12
Center (94).......E-13
Central City (2,934)...........I-13
Ceresco (889).....I-15
Chadron (5,851)..E-3
Chalco (10,994)..C-14
Chambers (268)..F-11
Chapman (287)...I-12
Chappell (929).....I-4
Chester (232)....L-14
Clarks (369).......I-13
Clarkson (658)..H-14
Clatonia (231)...K-15
Clay Center (760)............K-13
Clearwater (419)...........G-12
Clinton (41)........E-4
Cody (154).........E-7
Coleridge (473)..F-14
Colon (110)........I-15
Columbus (22,111)........H-14
Comstock (93)...H-10
Concord (166)...F-15
Cook (321)........K-16
Cordova (137)...J-14
Cortland (482)...K-15
Cotesfield (46)....I-12
Cowles (30)......L-12
Cozad (3,977).....J-9
Crab Orchard (38)............K-16
Craig (199).......G-16
Crawford (997)....E-2
Creighton (1,154).........F-13
Creston (203)...H-14
Crete (6,960).....J-15
Crofton (726)....E-14
Crookston (69)....E-7
Culbertson (595)..L-7
Curtis (939).......K-8
Cushing (32).......I-12
Dakota City (1,919).........F-16
Dalton (315)......H-3
Danbury (101).....L-8
Dannebrog (303)..I-12
Davenport (294)..K-13
David City (2,906)...........I-14
Dawson (146)....L-17
De Witt (513)....K-15
Decatur (481)...G-16
Denton (190).....J-15
Deshler (747)....L-13
Deweese (67)...K-13
Diller (260).......L-15
Dix (255)............I-2
Dodge (612).....H-15
Doniphan (829)..J-12
Dorchester (586).J-15
DuBois (147).....L-17
Dunbar (187).....J-17
Duncan (351).....I-14
Dunning (103)....G-9
Dwight (204).......I-15
Eagle (1,024)....J-16
Eddyville (97)....J-10
Edgar (498).......K-13
Edison (133)......K-9
Elgin (661).......G-13
Elk Creek (98)...K-16
Ellsworth..........G-4
Elm Creek (901)..J-10
Elmwood (634)...J-16
Elsie (106).........J-6
Elwood (707)......K-9
Elyria (51)........H-11
Emerson (840)...F-15
Emmet (48)......F-11
Enders (42)........K-6
Endicott (132)....L-15
Ericson (92).....H-11
Eustis (401).......J-9
Ewing (387)......F-12
Exeter (591)......J-14
Fairbury (3,942)..L-14
Fairfield (387)...K-13
Fairmont (560)...J-14
Falls City (4,325).........L-18
Farnam (171)......J-8
Farwell (122)......I-12
Filley (132).......K-16
Firth (590).......K-16
Fordyce (139)...E-14
Fort Calhoun (908)...........H-17
Foster (51).......F-13
Franklin (1,000)..L-11
Fremont (26,397).......H-16
Friend (1,027)....J-14
Fullerton (1,307)..I-13
Funk (194).......K-10
Gandy (32).........H-8
Garland (216)....J-15
Geneva (2,217)..K-14
Genoa (1,003)...H-13
Gering (8,500).....G-2, L-2
Gibbon (1,833)...J-11
Gilead (39).......L-14
Giltner (352).....J-12
Glenvil (310).....K-12
Goehner (154)...J-14
Gordon (1,612)...E-5
Gothenburg (3,574)..........J-9
Grafton (126)....J-13
Grand Island (48,520)..F-17, J-12
Grant (1,165)......J-5
Greeley..........H-12
Greenwood (568)...........J-16
Gresham (223)...I-14
Gretna (4,441)....I-16
Gross (2)........E-12
Guide Rock (225)...........L-12
Gurley (214).......I-3
Hadar (293).....G-14
Haigler (158)......L-5
Halsey (76).......G-8
Hamlet (57).......K-6
Hampton (423)...J-13
Harbine (49).....L-15
Hardy (159)......L-13
Harrisburg (100)..H-2
Harrison (251)....E-1
Hartington (1,554).........E-14
Harvard (1,013)..K-13
Hastings (24,907).C-11, K-12
Hay Springs (570)............E-4
Hayes Center (214).............K-7
Hazard (70).......I-11
Heartwell (71)....K-11
Hebron (1,579)..L-14
Hemingford (803)..F-3
Henderson (991).J-13
Hendley (24)......L-9
Henry (106).......G-1
Herman (268)...H-16
Hershey (665).....I-7
Hildreth (378)....K-11
Holbrook (207)....K-9
Holdrege (5,495).........K-10
Homer (549).....F-16
Hooper (830)....H-16
Hordville (144)....I-13
Hoskins (285)...G-14
Howells (561)...H-15
Hubbard (236)...F-15
Hubbell (68)......L-14
Humboldt (877)..L-17
Humphrey (760).H-14
Huntley (44)......L-10
Hyannis (182)....G-5
Imperial (2,071)...K-6
Indianola (584)....L-8
Inman (129)......F-12
Ithaca (148).......I-16
Jackson (223)...F-15
Jansen (118).....L-15
Johnson (328)...K-17
Johnstown (64)...F-9
Juniata (755)....K-12
Kearney (30,787)..A-10, J-11
Kenesaw (880)..K-11
Kennard (361)...H-16
Keystone (59)......I-6
Kilgore (77).......E-7
Kimball (2,496)....I-2
La Vista (15,758)........C-15
Lakeside..........G-4
Laurel (964)......F-14
Lawrence (304)..K-12
Lebanon (80)......L-8
Leigh (405)......H-14
Lemoyne (82)......I-5
Lewellen (224).....I-5
Lewiston (68)....K-16
Lexington (10,230)..........J-9
Liberty (76).......L-16
Lincoln (258,379).D-13, J-15
Lindsay (255)....H-13
Linwood (88)....H-15
Lisco (64).........H-4
Litchfield (262)...I-10
Lodgepole (318)...I-4
Long Pine (305)...F-9
Loomis (382)....K-10
Lorton (41).......J-17
Louisville (1,106)..I-16
Loup City (1,029).I-11
Lyman (341)......G-1
Lynch (245)......E-12
Lyons (851)......G-16
Macy (1,023)....G-16
Madison (2,438).G-14
Madrid (231).......J-6
Magnet (57)......F-14
Malmo (120)......I-15
Manley (178).....J-16
Marquette (229)..J-13
Martinsburg (94).F-15
Maskell (76).....E-15
Mason City (171).I-10
Max (57)...........L-6
Maxwell (312)......I-8
Maywood (261)...J-8
McCook (7,698)...L-8
McCool Junction (409)...........J-14
McGrew (105)....H-2
Mead (569)........I-16
Meadow Grove (301)..........G-13
Melbeta (112).....G-2
Memphis (114)...I-16
Merna (363).......H-9
Merriman (128)...E-6
Milford (2,090)...J-15
Miller (136).......J-10
Milligan (285)....K-14
Mills..............E-10
Minatare (816)....G-2
Minden (2,923). .K-11
Mitchell (1,702)...G-2
Monowi (1).......E-12
Monroe (284)....H-14
Moorefield (32)....J-8
Morrill (921).......G-1
Mullen (509)......G-7
Murray (463).....J-17
Naper (84)........E-11
Naponee (106)...L-11
Nebraska City (7,289).........J-17
Nehawka (204)..J-17
Neligh (1,599)...G-13
Nelson (488).....L-13
Nemaha (149)...K-17
Nenzel Village (20).............E-7
Newcastle (325)..E-15
Newman Grove (721)...........H-13
Newport (97)....E-10
Nickerson (369)..H-16
Niobrara (370)...E-13
Nora (21).........L-13
Norfolk (24,210).G-14
Norman (43).....K-11
North Bend (1,177)........H-15
North Loup (297)...........H-11
North Platte (24,733)....I-7, L-3
O'Neill (3,705)...F-11
Oak (66)..........L-13
Oakdale (322)...G-13
Oakland (1,244).G-16
Obert (23)........E-15
Oconto (151).......I-9
Octavia (127).....I-15
Odell (307).......L-15
Ogallala (4,737)...I-5
Ohiowa (115)....K-14
Omaha (408,958).B-16, I-16
Ong (63).........K-13
Orchard (379)...F-12
Ord (2,112)......H-11
Orleans (386)....L-10
Osceola (880).....I-14
Oshkosh (884)....H-4
Osmond (783)...F-13
Overton (594)....J-10
Oxford (779).....L-10
Page (166)........F-12
Palisade (351)....K-7
Palmer (472)......I-12
Palmyra (545)....J-16
Panama (256)...K-16
Papillion (18,894)..D-15, I-17
Parks (23).........L-5
Pawnee City (878)...........L-16
Paxton (523).......I-6
Pender (1,002)..G-15
Peru (865).......K-17
Petersburg (333)..........G-13
Phillips (287).....J-12
Pickrell (199)....K-15
Pierce (1,767)...F-14
Pilger (352)......G-15
Plainview (1,246).........F-13
Platte Center (336)...........H-14
Plattsmouth (6,502)..........I-17
Pleasanton (341)............J-11
Plymouth (409)..K-15
Polk (322).........I-13
Ponca (961).....E-15
Potter (337)........I-2
Prague (303).....I-15
Primrose (61)....H-12
Prosser (66)......J-12
Purdum...........G-8
Ragan (38)......K-10
Ralston (5,943)..C-16
Randolph (944)..F-14
Ravenna (1,360)..J-11
Raymond (167)..J-15
Red Cloud (1,020).........L-12
Republican City (150)...........L-10
Reynolds (69)....L-14
Rising City (374)..I-14
Riverdale (182)..J-10
Riverton (89).....L-11
Rockville (106)....I-11
Rogers (95)......H-15
Rosalie (160)....G-16
Roseland (235)..K-12
Royal (63)........F-12
Rulo (172)........L-18
Rushville (890)....E-4
Ruskin (123).....L-13
Salem (112)......L-17
Santee (346)....E-13
Sargent (525)...H-10
Schuyler (6,211).H-15
Scotia (318).....H-11
Scottsbluff (15,039)...G-2, K-2
Scribner (857)...H-15
Seneca (33)......G-7
Seward (6,964)..J-15
Shelby (714)......I-14
Shelton (1,059)..J-11
Shickley (341)...K-13
Sholes (21)......F-14
Shubert (150)....K-17
Sidney (6,757).....I-3
Silver Creek (362)............I-13
Smithfield (54)....K-9
Snyder (300)....H-15
South Sioux City (13,353).......F-16
Spalding (487)...H-12
Spencer (455)...E-11
Springfield (1,529)..........I-16
Springview (242)..E-9
St. Edward (705)...........H-13
St. Helena (96)..E-14
St. Libory (264)...I-12
St. Paul (2,290)...I-12
Stamford (183)...L-10
Stanton (1,577)..G-14
Staplehurst (242).J-14
Stapleton (305)....H-8
Steinauer (75)....K-16
Sterling (476)....K-16
Stockville (25).....K-8
Strang (29).......K-14
Stratton (343)......L-6
Stromsburg (1,171)..........I-14
Stuart (590)......E-10
Sumner (236).....J-10
Superior (1,957)..L-13
Surprise (43)......I-14
Sutherland (1,286)..I-7
Sutton (1,502)....K-13
Swanton (94).....K-15
Syracuse (1,942).J-16
Table Rock (269).L-17
Tarnov (46).......H-14
Taylor (190)......H-10
Tecumseh (1,677).........K-16
Tekamah (1,736).........G-16
Terrytown (1,198)..L-2
Thedford (188)....G-8
Thurston (132)...F-15
Tilden (953)......G-13
Tobias (106)......K-14
Trenton (560)......L-7
Trumbull (205)....J-12
Tryon (157)........H-7
Uehling (230)....H-16
Ulysses (171).....I-14
Unadilla (311)....J-16
Union (233).......J-17
Upland (143).....K-11
Utica (861)........J-14
Valentine (2,737)..E-8
Valley (1,875).....I-16
Valparaiso (570)..I-15
Venango (164).....J-5
Verdel (30).......E-12
Verdigre (575)....E-13
Verdon (172).....L-17
Waco (236).......J-14
Wahoo (4,508)....I-15
Wakefield (1,451).........F-15
Wallace (366)......J-7
Walthill (780).....G-16
Walton (306)......J-16
Washington (150)...........H-16
Waterbury (73)...F-15
Waterloo (848)....I-16
Wauneta (577)....K-6
Wausa (634).....F-14
Waverly (3,277)..J-16
Wayne (5,660)...F-15
Wellfleet (78).......J-7
West Point (3,364).........G-15
Western (235)....K-14
Westerville (39)...I-10
Weston (324)......I-15
Whitman............G-6
Whitney (77).......E-3
Wilber (1,855)....K-15
Wilcox (358)......K-10
Wilsonville (93)....L-9
Winnebago (774)...........F-16
Winnetoon (68)..F-13
Winside (427)....F-14
Winslow (103)...H-16
Wisner (1,170)...G-15
Wolbach (283)....I-12
Wood Lake (63)...E-8
Wood River (1,325)..........J-12
Wymore (1,457)..L-15
Wynot (166)......E-14
York (7,766)......J-14
Yutan (1,174).....I-16

NA070-17

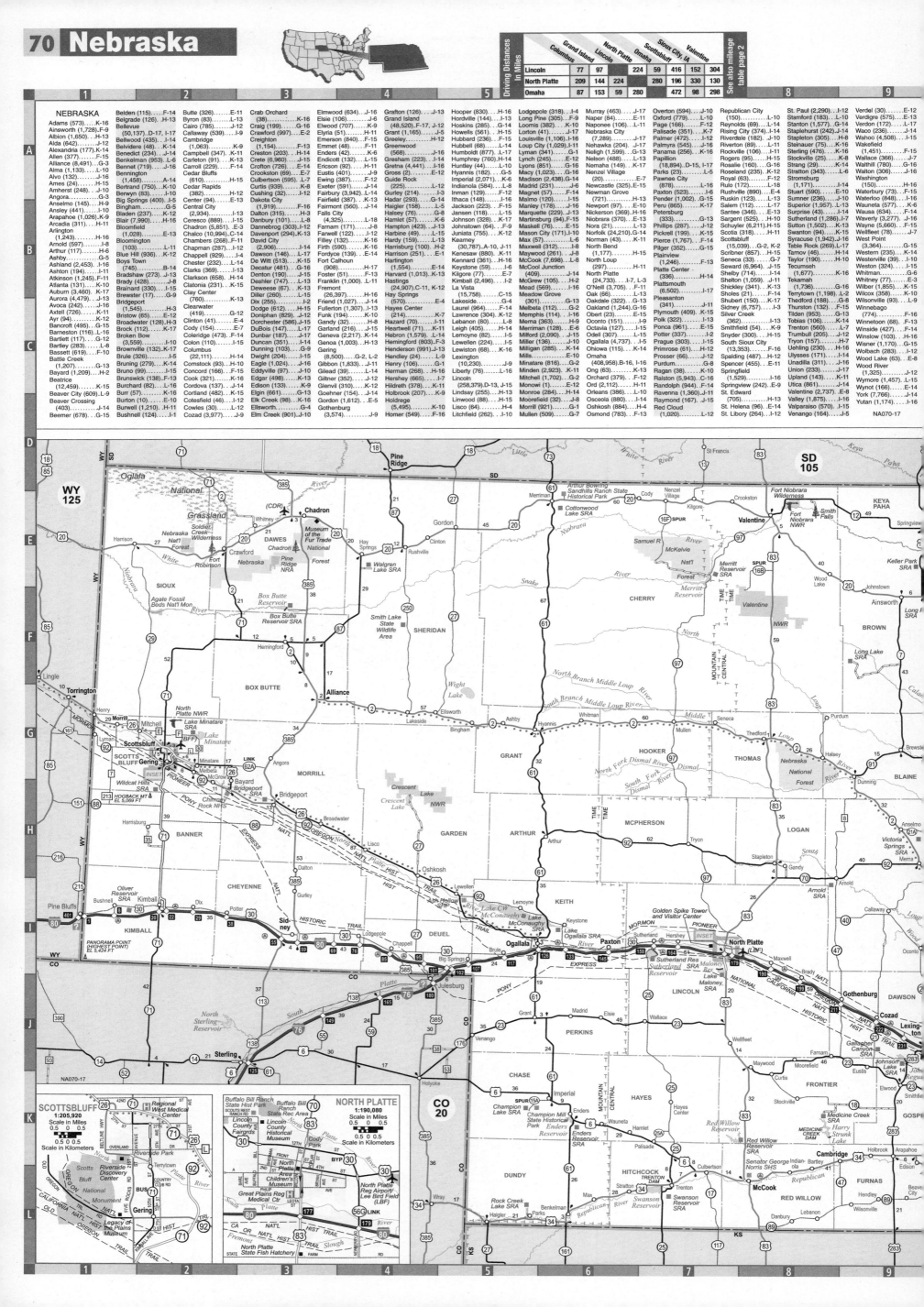

LEGEND
Interstate Highway 95
Controlled Access Hwy
Controlled Access Hwy Toll
Wildlife Refuge
Nat'l/State Park
National Forest

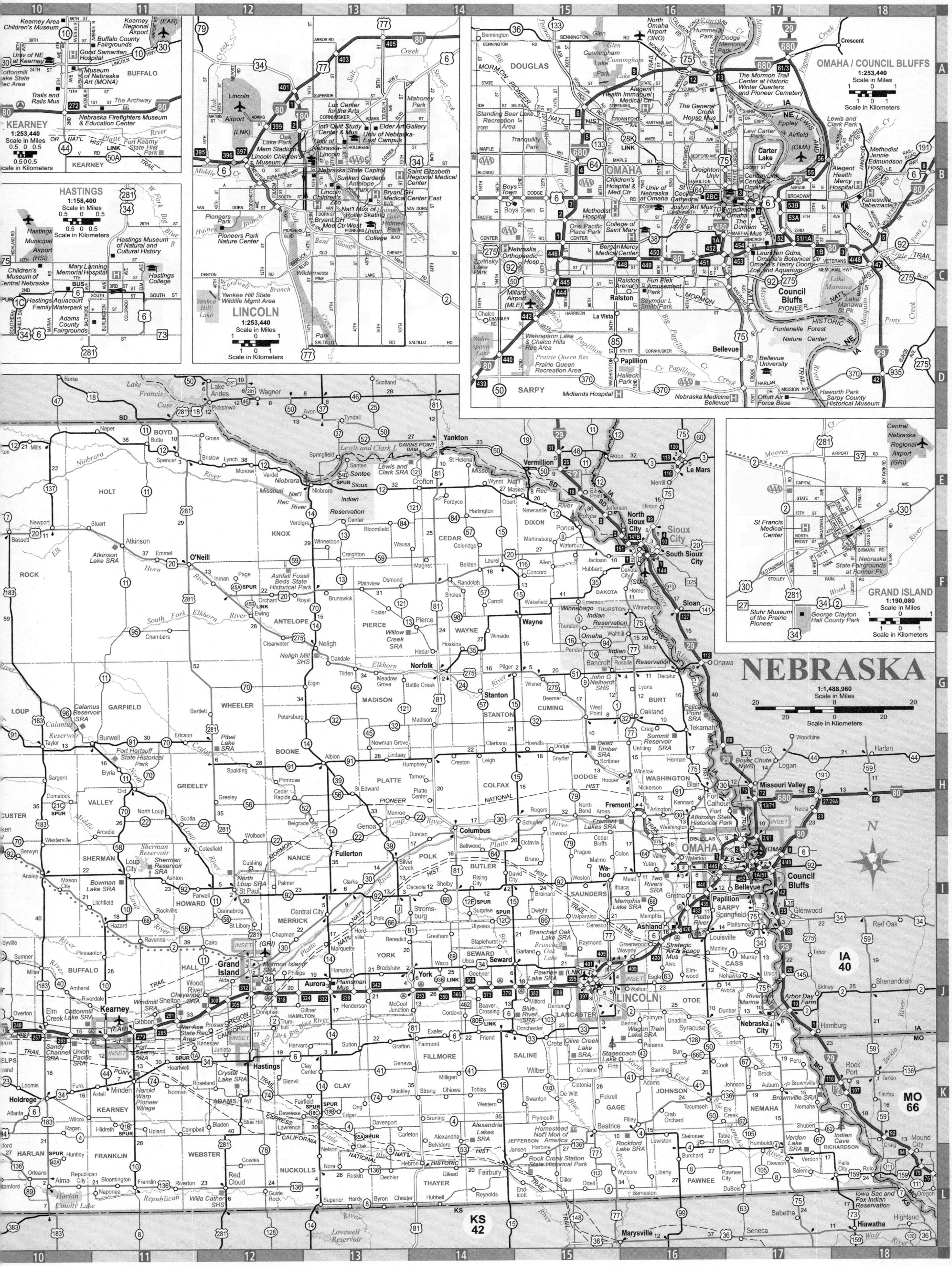

See also mileage table page 2

| Driving Distances in Miles | Austin | Boulder City | Carson City | Ely | Las Vegas | Laughlin | Reno | Tonopah | Winnemucca | Wells |
|---|---|---|---|---|---|---|---|---|---|---|
| Boulder City | 352 | | 473 | 310 | 26 | 79 | 474 | 237 | 446 | 540 |
| Carson City | 172 | 473 | | 318 | 447 | 543 | 31 | 236 | 368 | 195 |
| Las Vegas | 326 | 26 | 447 | 284 | | 97 | 448 | 211 | 419 | 514 |
| Reno | 173 | 474 | 31 | 320 | 448 | 545 | | 238 | 339 | 165 |

LAS VEGAS STRIP
1:79,200

RENO
1:142,560

LAS VEGAS
1:269,280

CARSON CITY
1:101,376

NEVADA
1:2,376,000

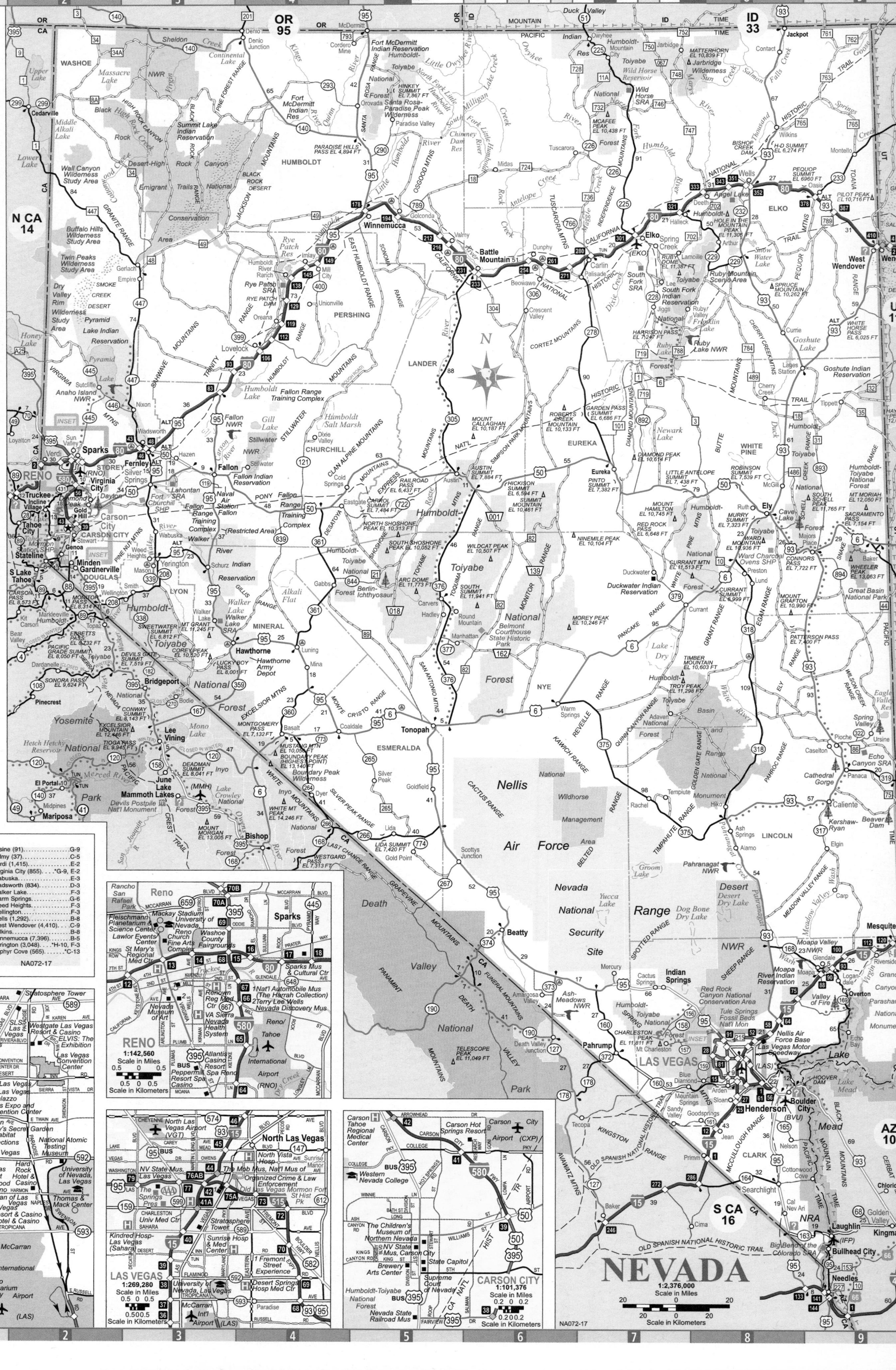

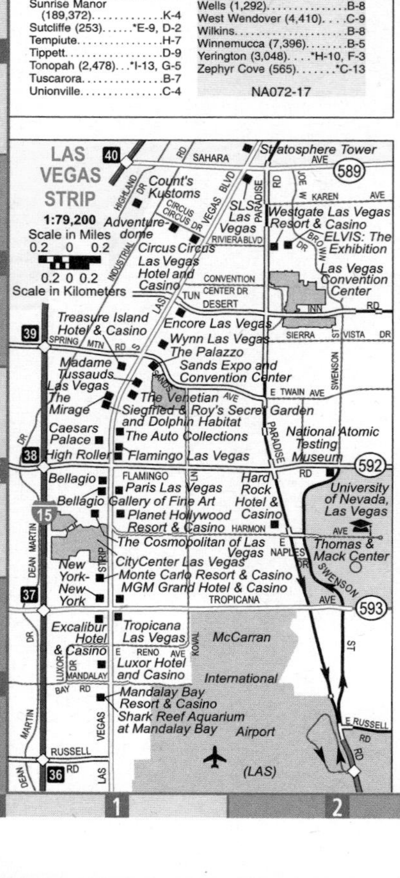

# Best Western Hotels & Resorts

**Member Discounts up to 15%!**

## Sweet Deals for AAA/CAA Members

AAA/CAA Preferred℠ Best Western Rewards®

- More than 4,100 properties in over 100 countries and territories worldwide*
- Breakfast and FREE high-speed internet**
- Earn 10 points per dollar spent plus a 10% bonus for AAA/CAA Preferred℠ Best Western Rewards®***

---

## Book your next trip at BestWestern.com/AAA and BestWestern.com/CAA

DISCOUNTS REWARDS
PREFERRED HOTELS

Rewards
PREFERRED HOTELS

---

BE THE HERO OF YOUR NEXT ADVENTURE
Make a good trip great with travel insight and personalized recommendations. Get inspector tips, editor's picks, preferred hotel offers and sightseeing suggestions — at club offices and in handy travel resources.
AAA Travel Guides
Travel Information for major cities, national parks and other destinations across North America and the Caribbean.
Where would you like to go?
We Recommend
Hyatt Regency Grand Cypress
TourBook
Tennessee
Visit AAA.com or CAA.ca
© LifeJourneys / Getty Images

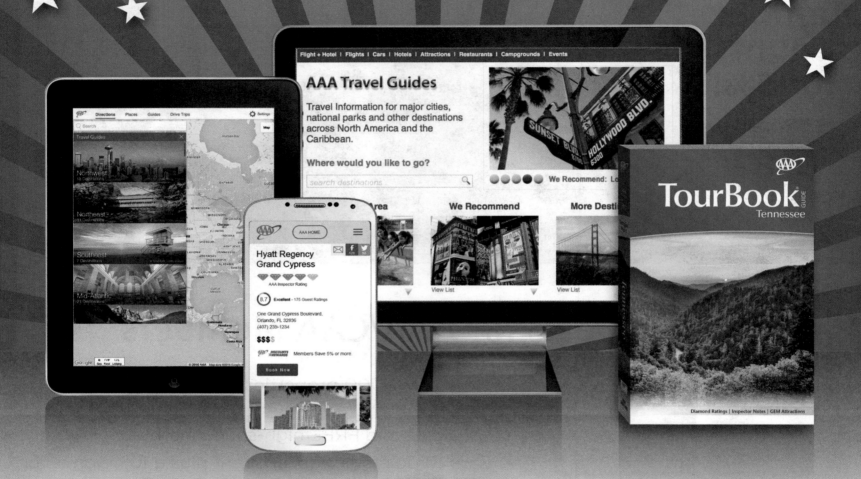

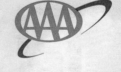

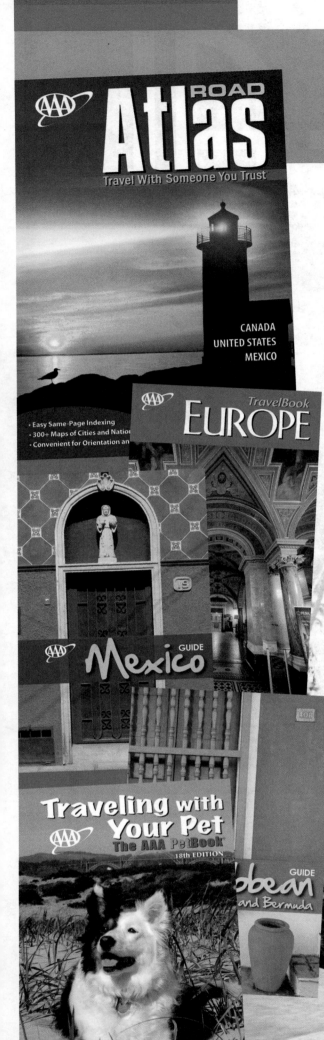

# Next Best Thing to a Personal Tour Guide

Going away? From drive trips to family getaways and world travel, your AAA/CAA office has the perfect travel guide to help with your planning and decision making — before you go and along the way.

Enjoy publications packed with vibrant maps and photos plus expert travel tips and recommendations you can trust, at discounted prices just for members.

| Driving Distances In Miles | Colebrook | Concord | Gorham | Keene | Lebanon | Manchester | Nashua | Portsmouth | Plymouth | Twin Mountain |
|---|---|---|---|---|---|---|---|---|---|---|
| Concord | 137 | | 113 | 55 | 60 | 17 | 35 | 58 | 43 | 85 |
| Manchester | 157 | 17 | 130 | 66 | 71 | | 19 | 44 | 60 | 102 |
| Nashua | 175 | 35 | 148 | 49 | 89 | 19 | | 55 | 78 | 120 |
| Portsmouth | 168 | 58 | 111 | 107 | 112 | 44 | 55 | | 101 | 117 |

See also mileage table page 2

## NEW HAMPSHIRE

NA073-17

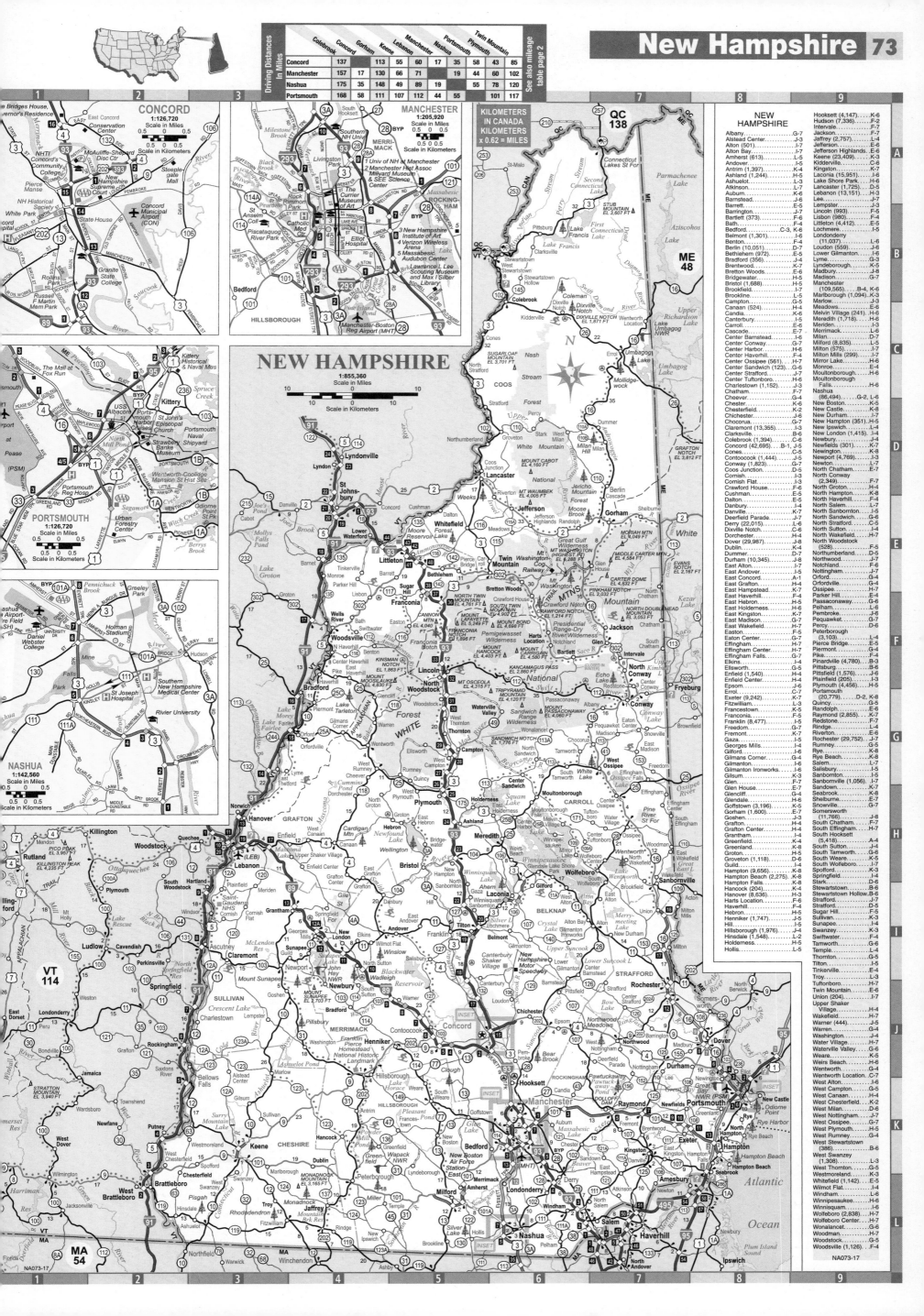

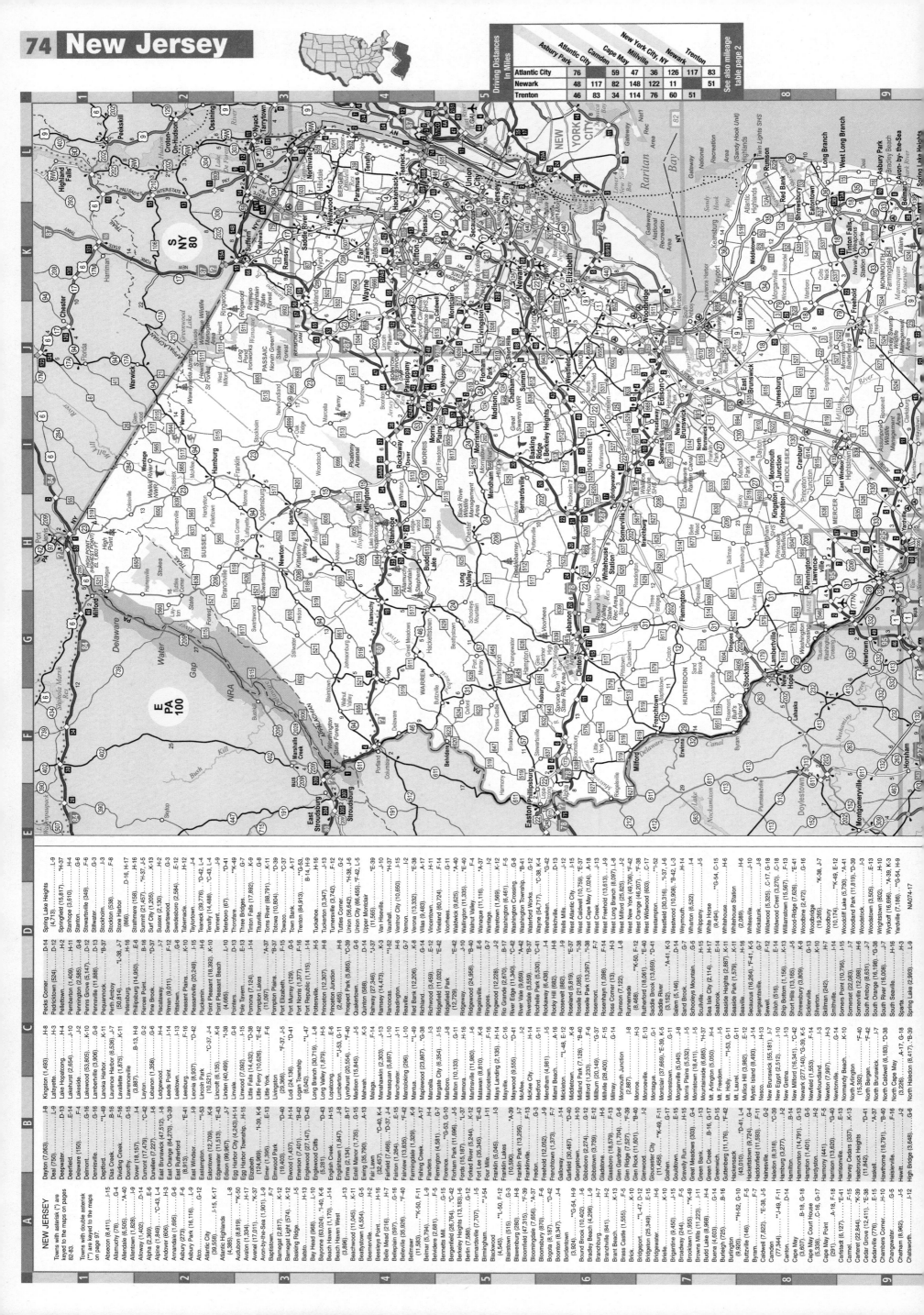

LEGEND

| Interstate Highway | 95 | Wildlife Refuge |
| Controlled Access Hwy | | Nat'l/State Park |
| Controlled Access Hwy Toll | | National Forest |

# NEW JERSEY

1:538,560
Scale in Miles
Scale in Kilometers

**CASINOS**

| | | |
|---|---|---|
| Bally's Atlantic City | Harrah's Resort | L-16 |
| Bally's Wild Wild West Casino | Resorts Casino Hotel | K-18 |
| Borgata Hotel Casino & Spa | Tropicana Casino and Resort | J-18 |
| Caesars Atlantic City | Trump Taj Mahal Casino Hotel | L-18 |
| Golden Nugget | | L-16 |

NA074-17

## ATLANTIC CITY
1:47,520
Scale in Miles
Scale in Kilometers

## CAPE MAY
1:205,920
Scale in Miles
Scale in Kilometers

## TRENTON
1:205,920
Scale in Miles
Scale in Kilometers

INSET

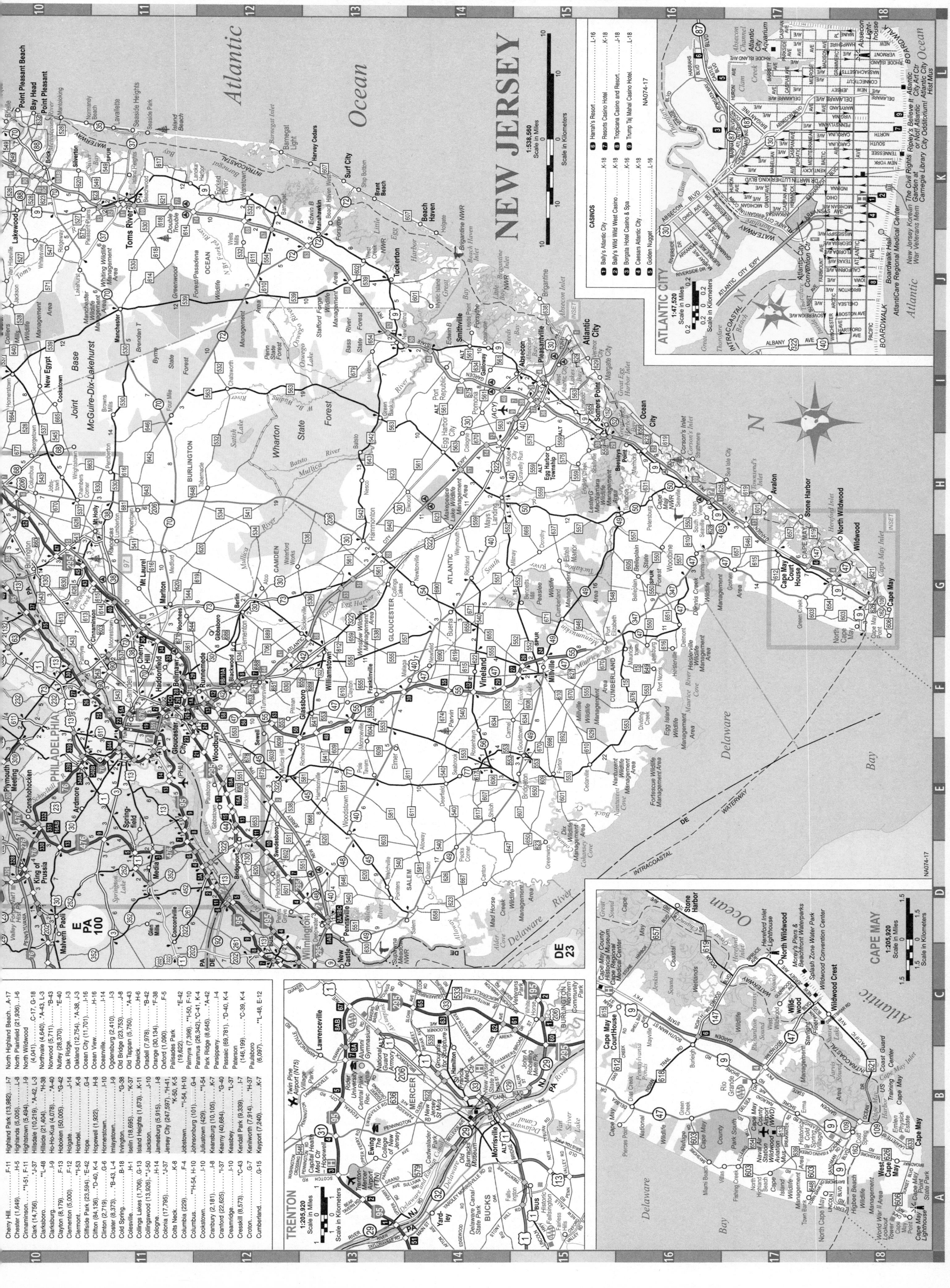

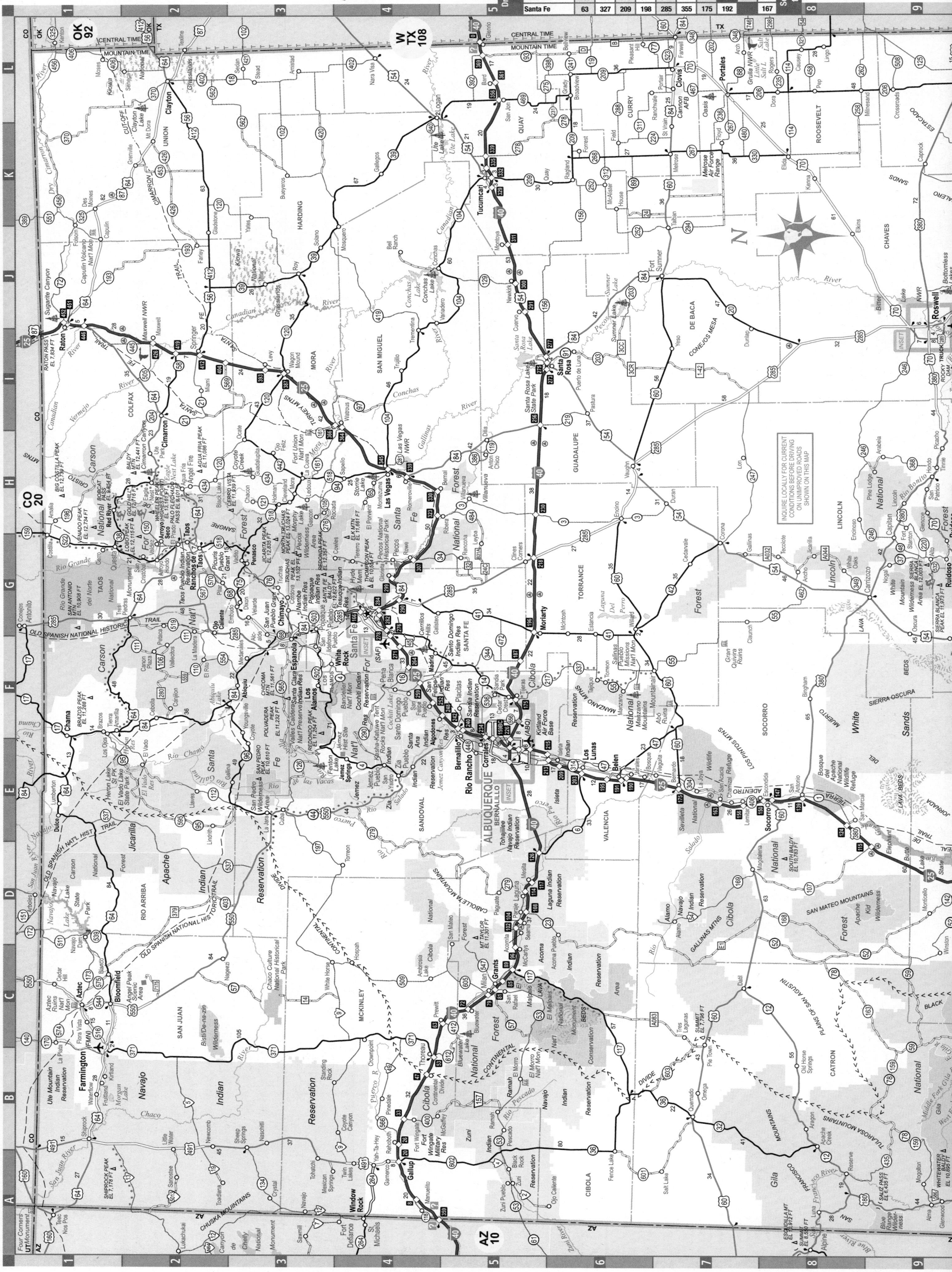

See also mileage table page 2

| Driving Distances In Miles | Albuquerque | El Paso, TX | Farmington | Gallup | Las Cruces | Lordsburg | Raton | Roswell | Santa Fe | Tucumcari |
|---|---|---|---|---|---|---|---|---|---|---|
| Albuquerque | | 265 | 183 | 138 | 222 | 293 | 230 | 200 | 63 | 176 |
| Las Cruces | 222 | 44 | 404 | 361 | | 119 | 451 | 185 | 285 | 305 |
| Roswell | 200 | 205 | 378 | 336 | 185 | 303 | 305 | | 192 | 193 |
| Santa Fe | 63 | 327 | 209 | 198 | 285 | 355 | 175 | 192 | | 167 |

**LEGEND**

| | |
|---|---|
| Interstate Highway | Wildlife Refuge |
| Controlled Access Hwy | Nat'l/State Park |
| Controlled Access Hwy Toll | National Forest |

# NEW MEXICO

Scale 1:1,647,360

Scale in Miles: 0 — 30
Scale in Kilometers: 0 — 30

MOUNTAIN TIME / CENTRAL TIME

**KILOMETERS IN MEXICO**
KILOMETERS x 0.62 = MILES

## Index

NEW MEXICO

| | | | | |
|---|---|---|---|---|
| Abiquiu (231) | F-3 | Chimayo (3,177) | F-3 | Puerto de Luna | J-6 |
| Acoma Pueblo | D-6 | Cimarron (1,021) | J-2 | Quay (141) | K-10 |
| Acomita | D-6 | Claunch | H-7 | Quemado (228) | J-7 |
| Agua Fria | F-3 | Cleveland (265) | E-11 | Questa (1,770) | E-2 |
| Alamo (1,085) | D-7 | Cliff (283) | H-3 | Radium Springs | E-11 |
| Alamogordo (30,403) | G-10 | Clines Corners | J-6 | Ramah (407) | B-9 |
| Albuquerque (448,607) | E-5 | Clovis (37,775) | K-6 | Ranchvale | K-6 |
| Alcalde (285) | F-3 | Columbus (1,664) | C-13 | Ranchos de Taos (2,518) | F-2 |

<!-- Index continues with an extensive alphabetical listing of New Mexico place names and grid coordinates -->

## City Insets

- **ALBUQUERQUE** — Scale 1:221,760
- **SANTA FE** — Scale 1:188,704
- **LAS CRUCES** — Scale 1:190,080
- **ROSWELL** — Scale 1:253,440
- **CARLSBAD CAVERNS NATIONAL PARK** — Scale 1:190,080

NA076-17

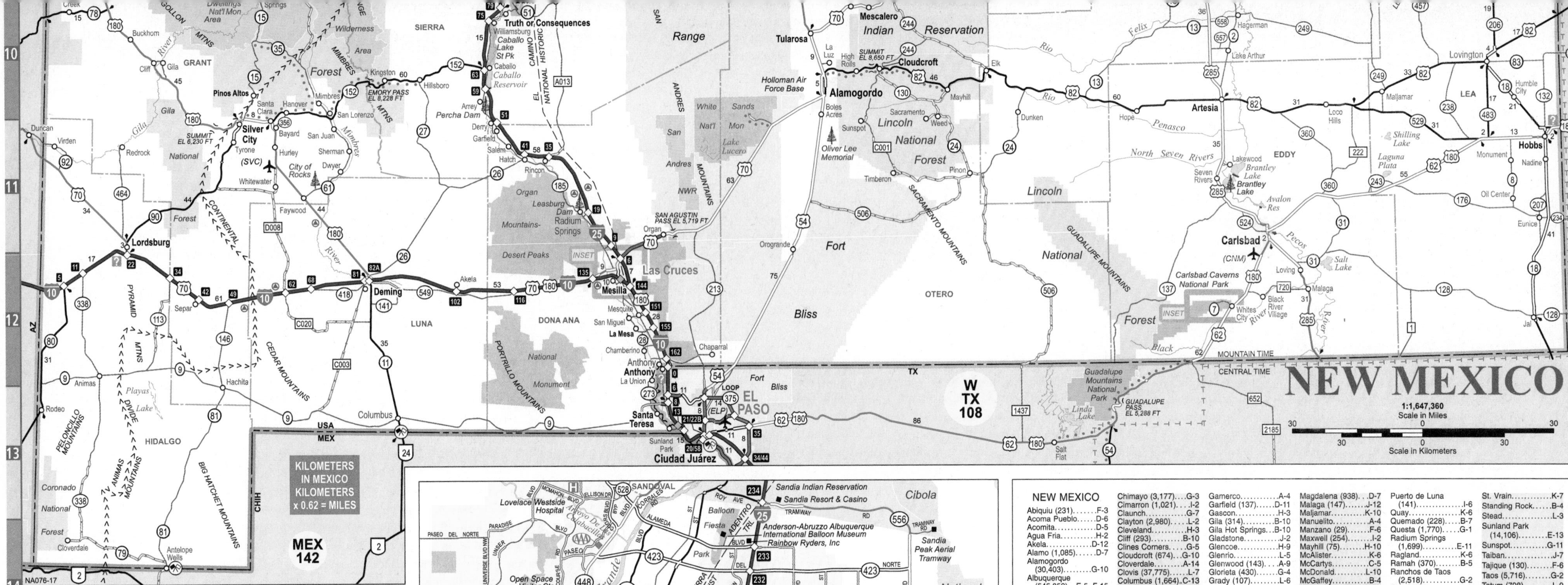

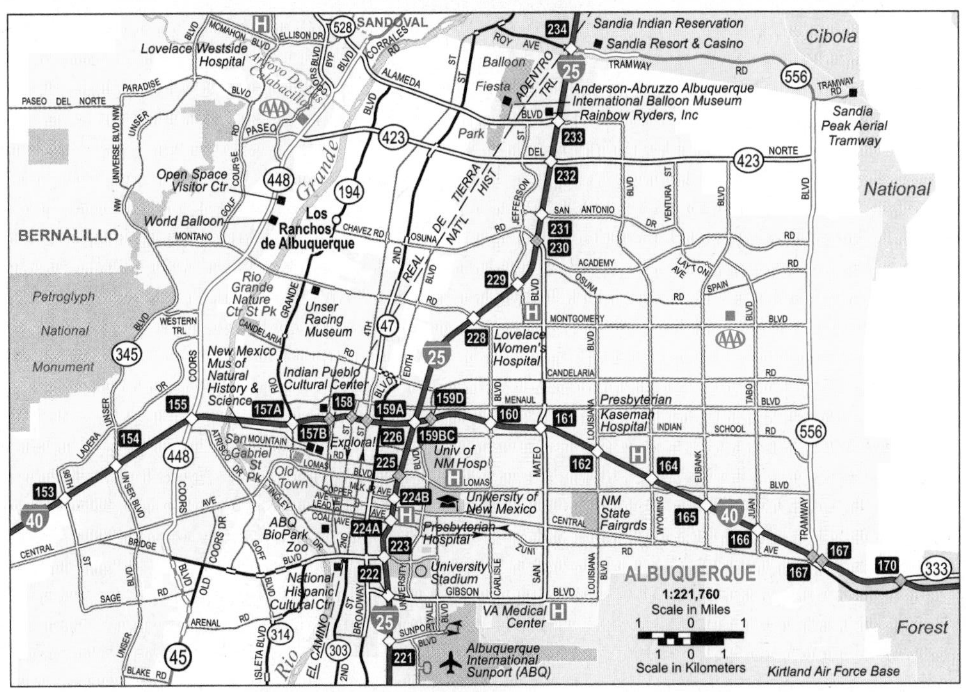

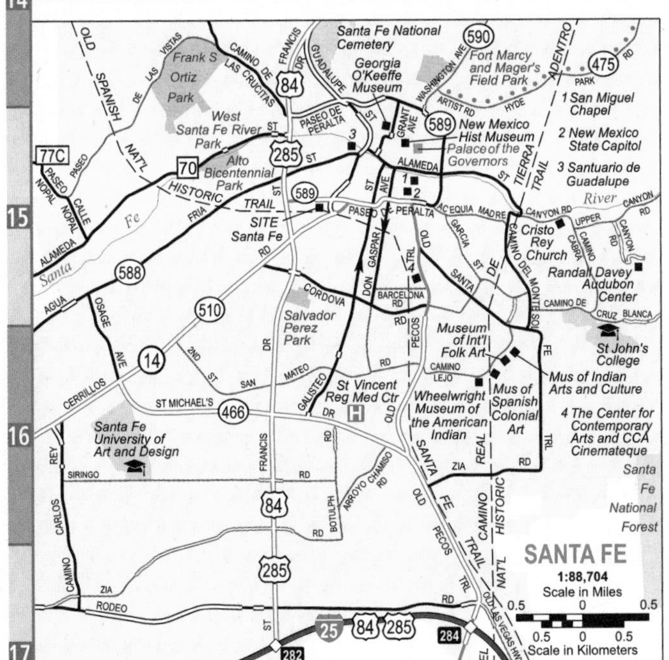

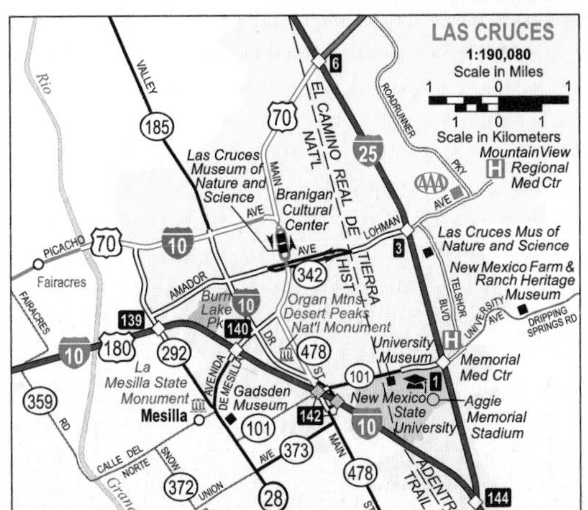

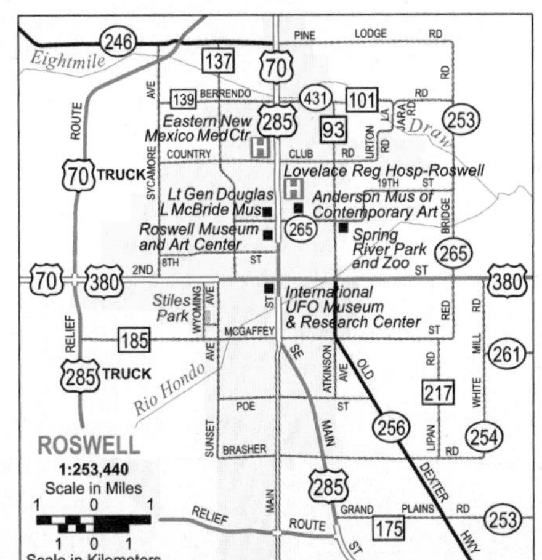

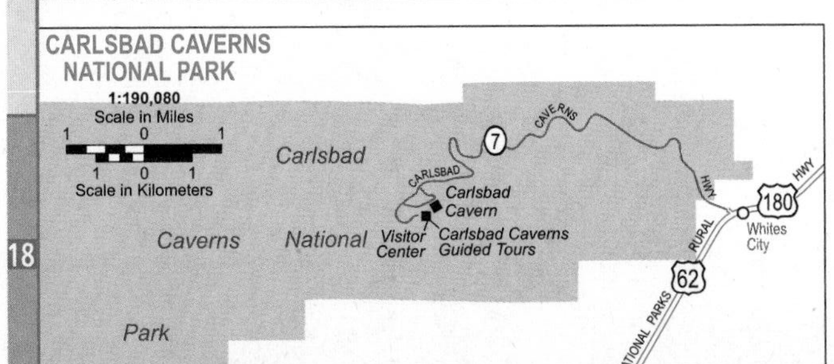

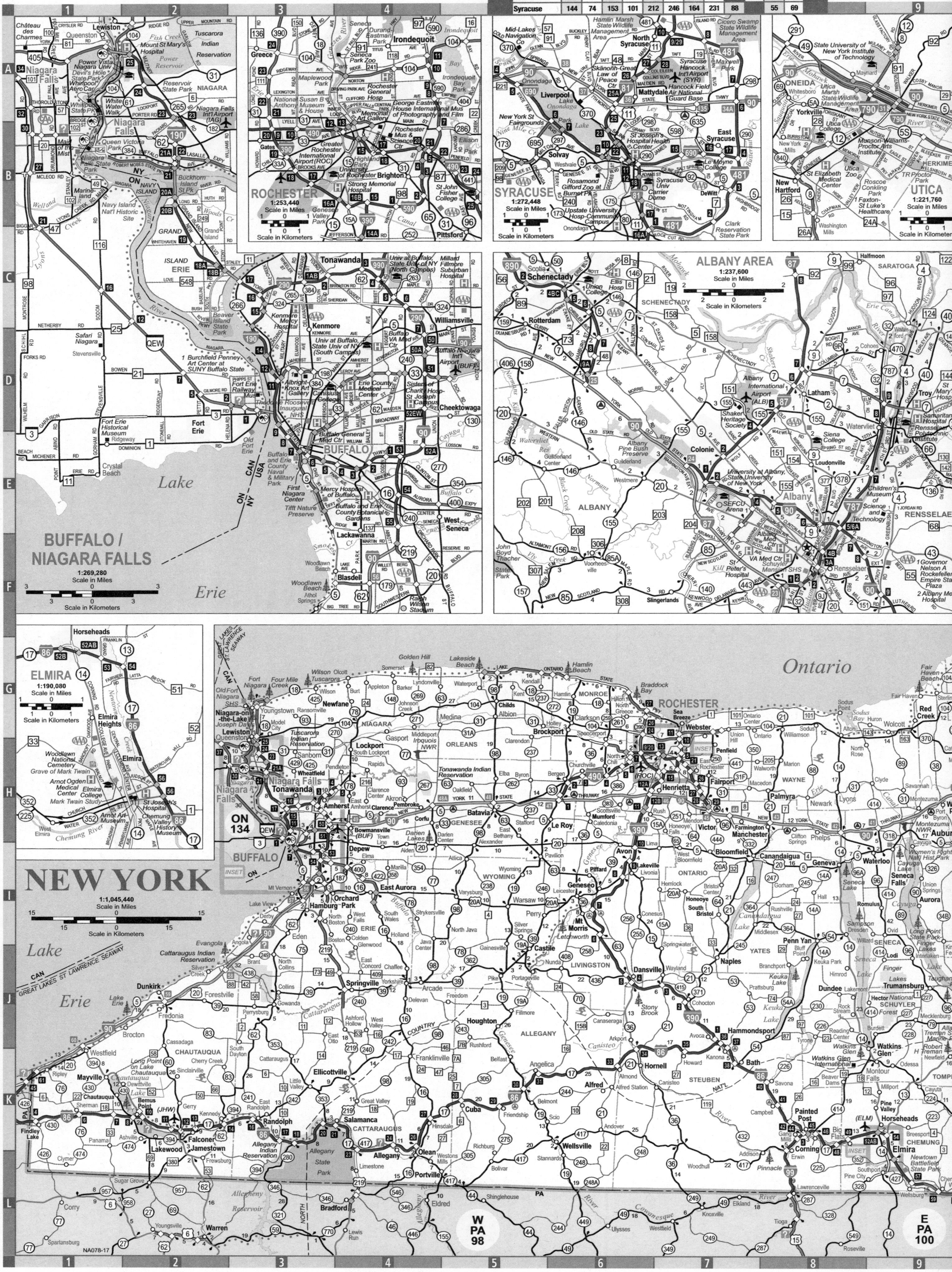

| Driving Distances in Miles | Albany | Binghamton | Buffalo | Corning | Newburgh | New York City | Niagara Falls | Plattsburgh | Rochester | Syracuse | Watertown | Utica |
|---|---|---|---|---|---|---|---|---|---|---|---|---|
| Albany | | 139 | 288 | 211 | 90 | 158 | 301 | 161 | 226 | 144 | 95 | 175 |
| Buffalo | 288 | 223 | | 125 | 338 | 373 | 21 | 383 | 74 | 153 | 88 | 215 |
| New York City | 158 | 176 | 373 | 249 | 70 | | 409 | 318 | 333 | 246 | 249 | 316 |
| Rochester | 226 | 161 | 74 | 100 | 298 | 333 | 87 | 350 | | 88 | 136 | 150 |
| Syracuse | 144 | 74 | 153 | 101 | 212 | 246 | 164 | 231 | 88 | | 55 | 69 |

See also mileage table page 2

**ROCHESTER**
1:253,440
Scale in Miles
Scale in Kilometers

**SYRACUSE**
1:272,448
Scale in Miles
Scale in Kilometers

**UTICA**
1:221,760
Scale in Miles
Scale in Kilometers

**ALBANY AREA**
1:237,600
Scale in Miles
Scale in Kilometers

**BUFFALO / NIAGARA FALLS**
1:269,280
Scale in Miles
Scale in Kilometers

**ELMIRA**
1:190,080
Scale in Miles
Scale in Kilometers

**NEW YORK**
1:1,045,440
Scale in Miles
Scale in Kilometers

Lake Erie

Lake Ontario

Ontario

NA078-17

W PA 98

E PA 100

LEGEND

Interstate Highway — 95
Controlled Access Hwy
Controlled Access Hwy Toll
Wildlife Refuge
Nat'l/State Park
National Forest

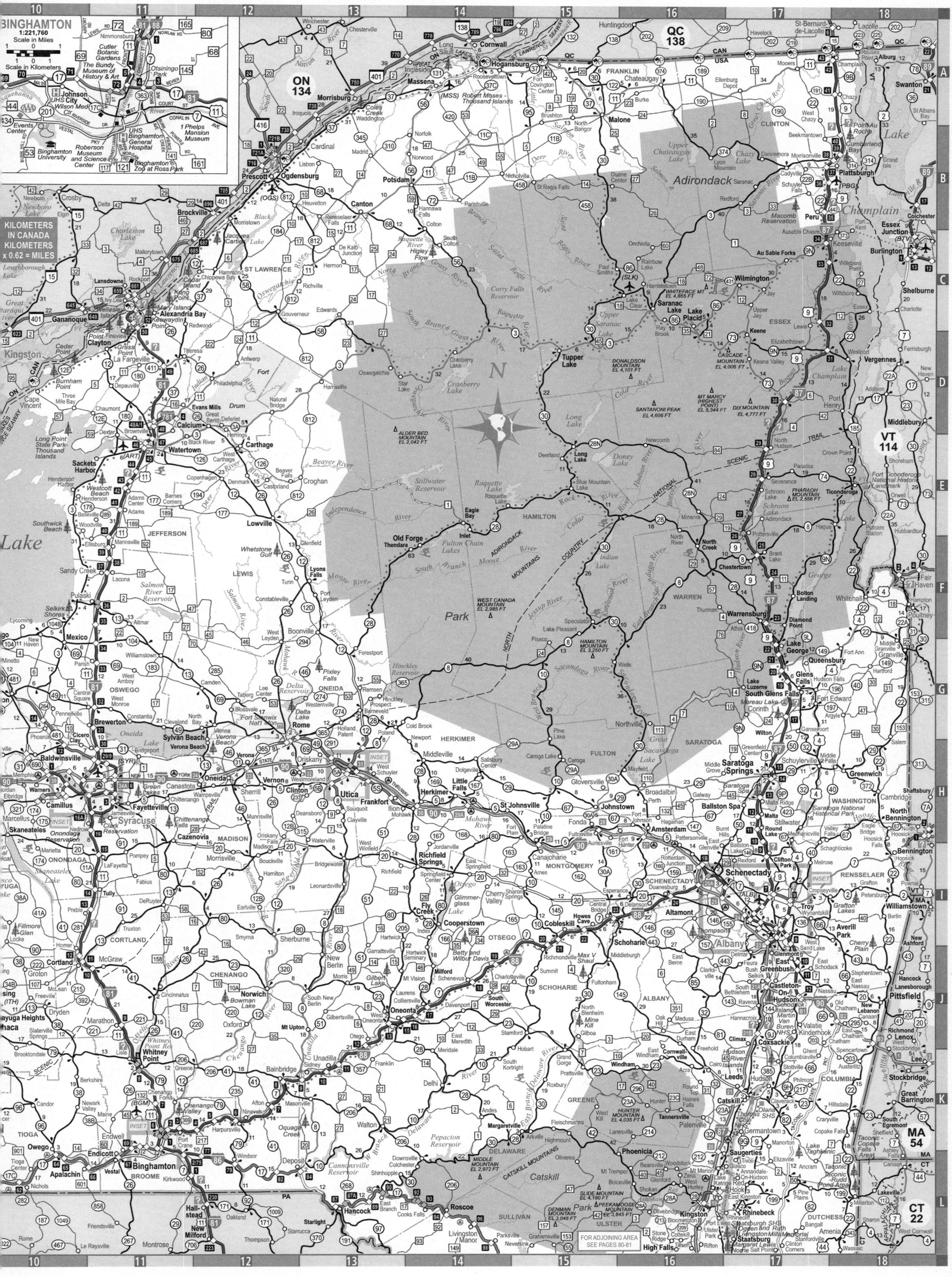

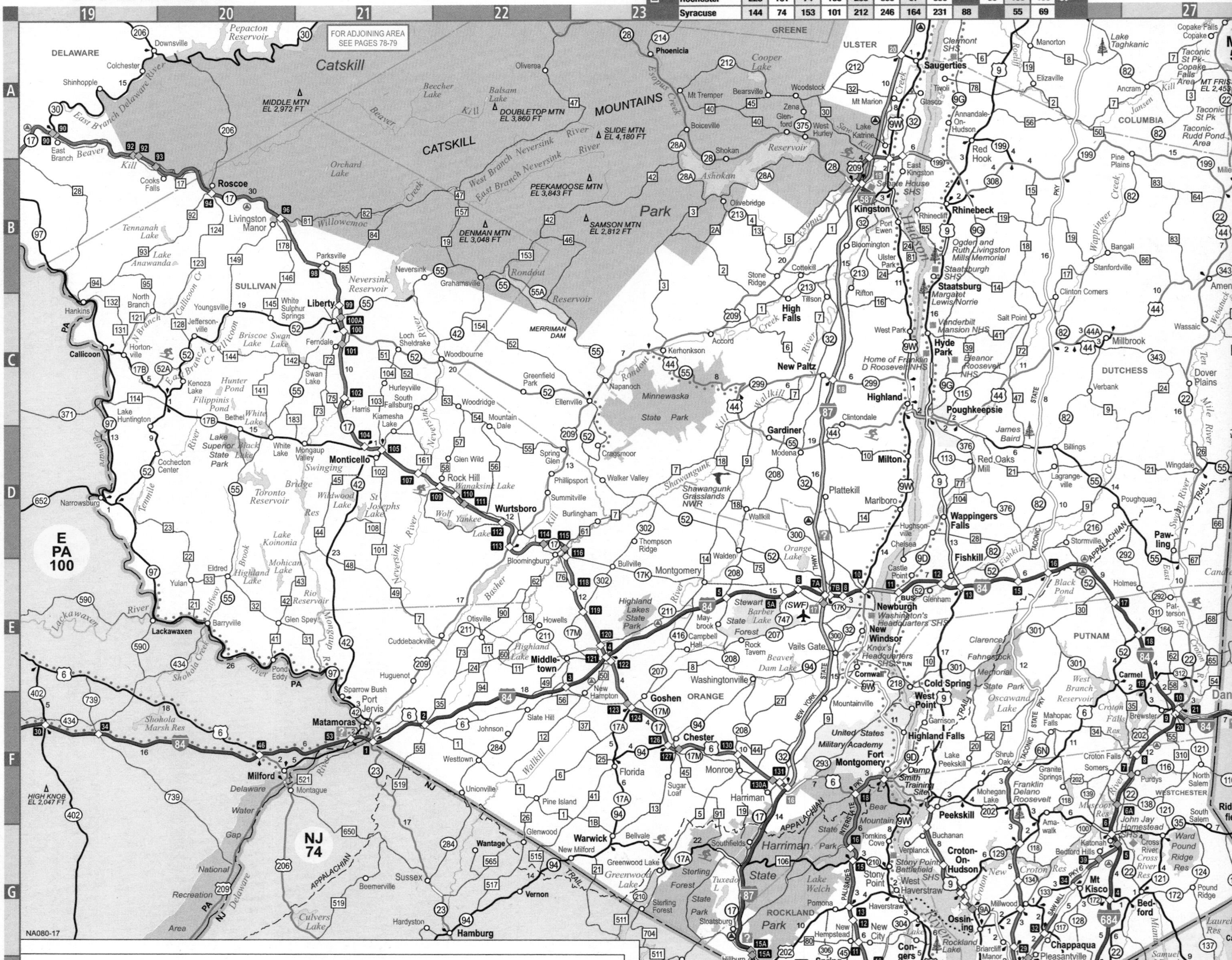

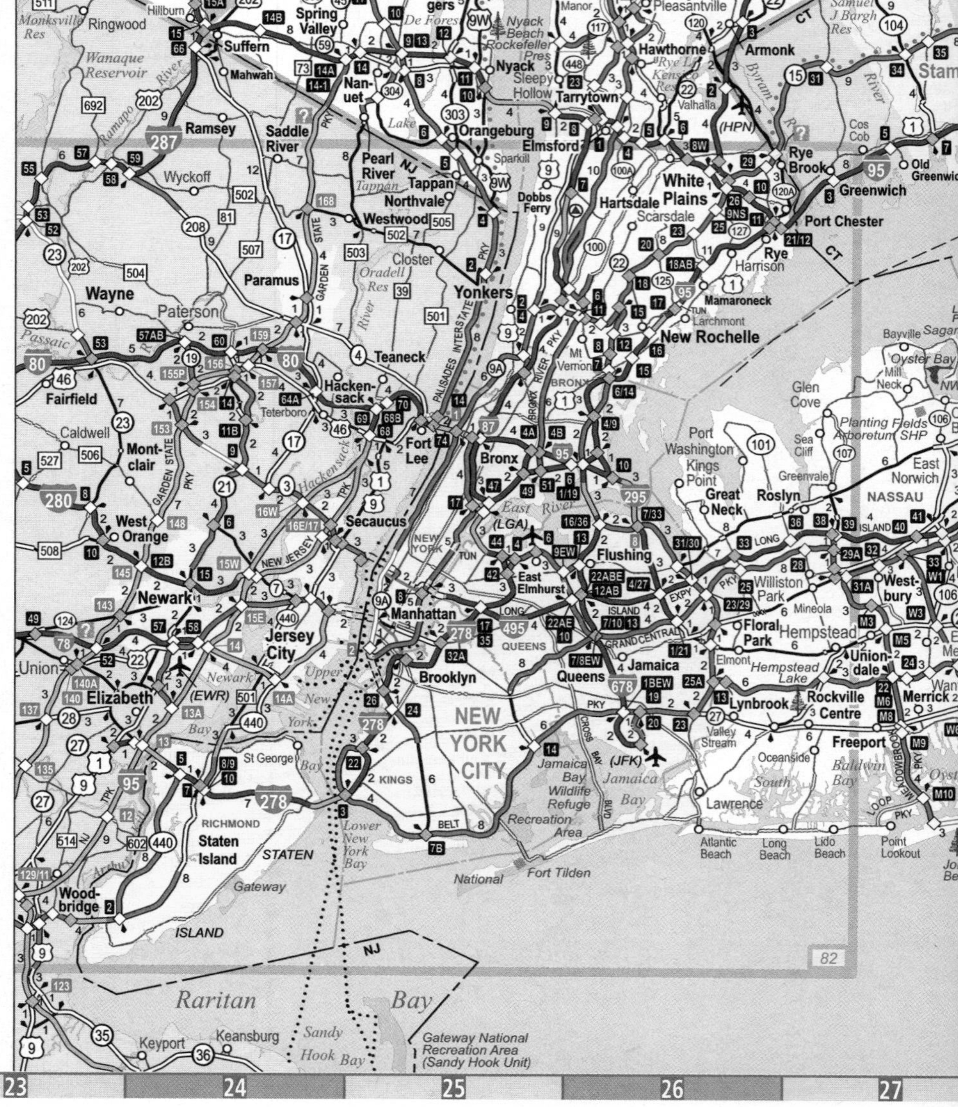

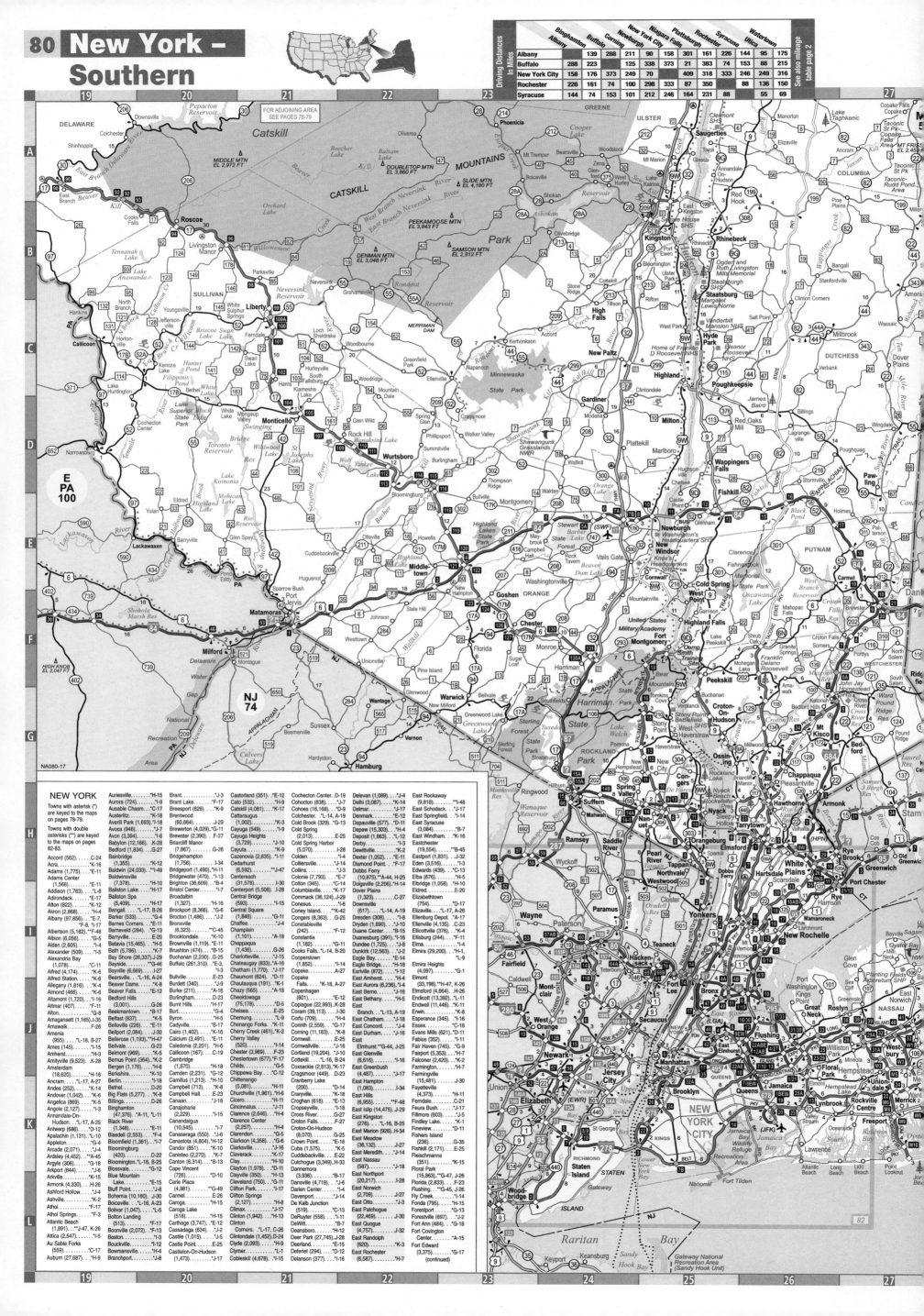

**LEGEND**

| | |
|---|---|
| Interstate Highway | 95 Wildlife Refuge |
| Controlled Access Hwy | Nat'l/State Park |
| Controlled Access Hwy Toll | National Forest |

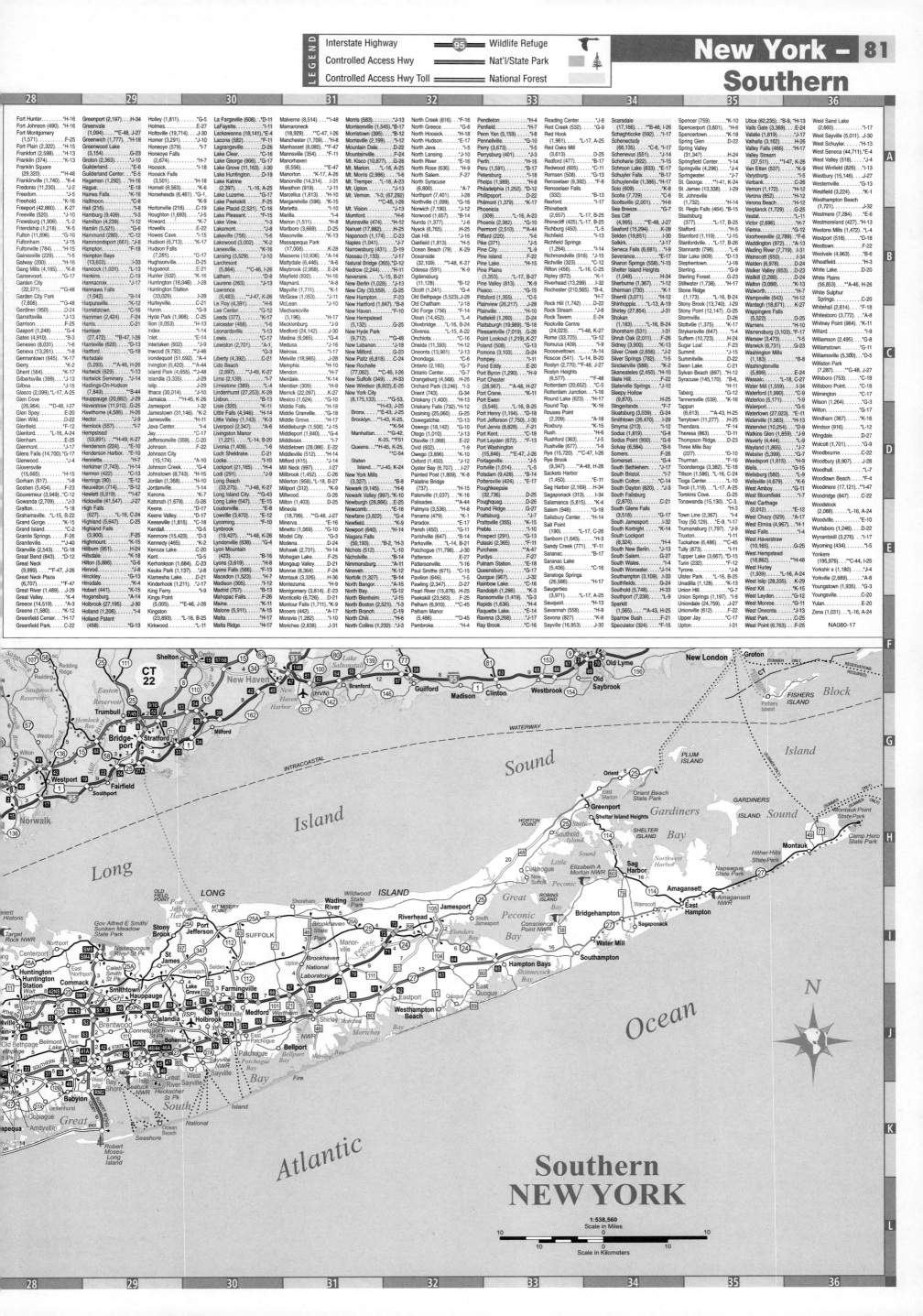

## Southern
# NEW YORK

1:538,560
Scale in Miles
Scale in Kilometers

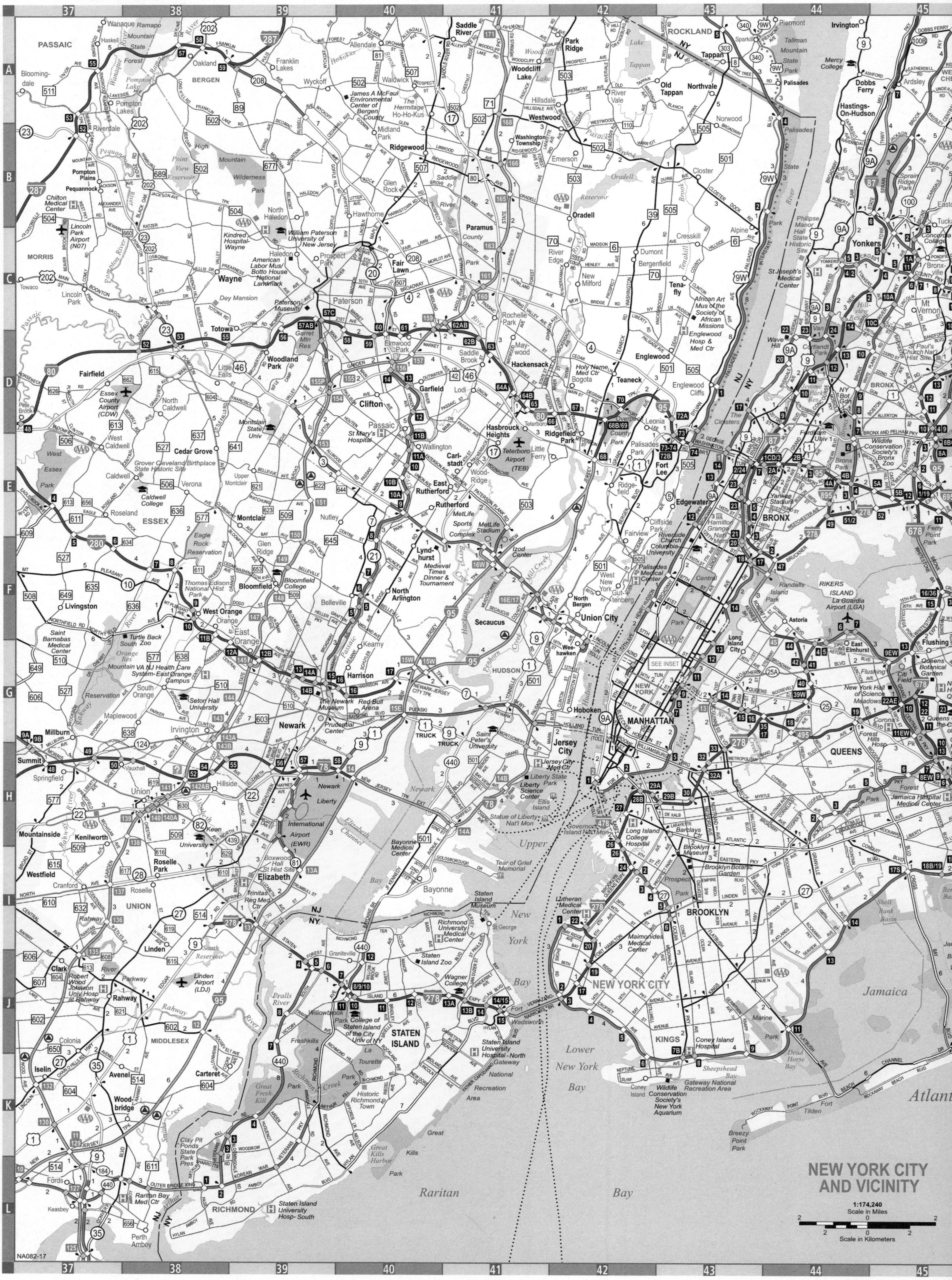

NEW YORK CITY
AND VICINITY

1:174,240
Scale in Miles

Scale in Kilometers

NA082-17

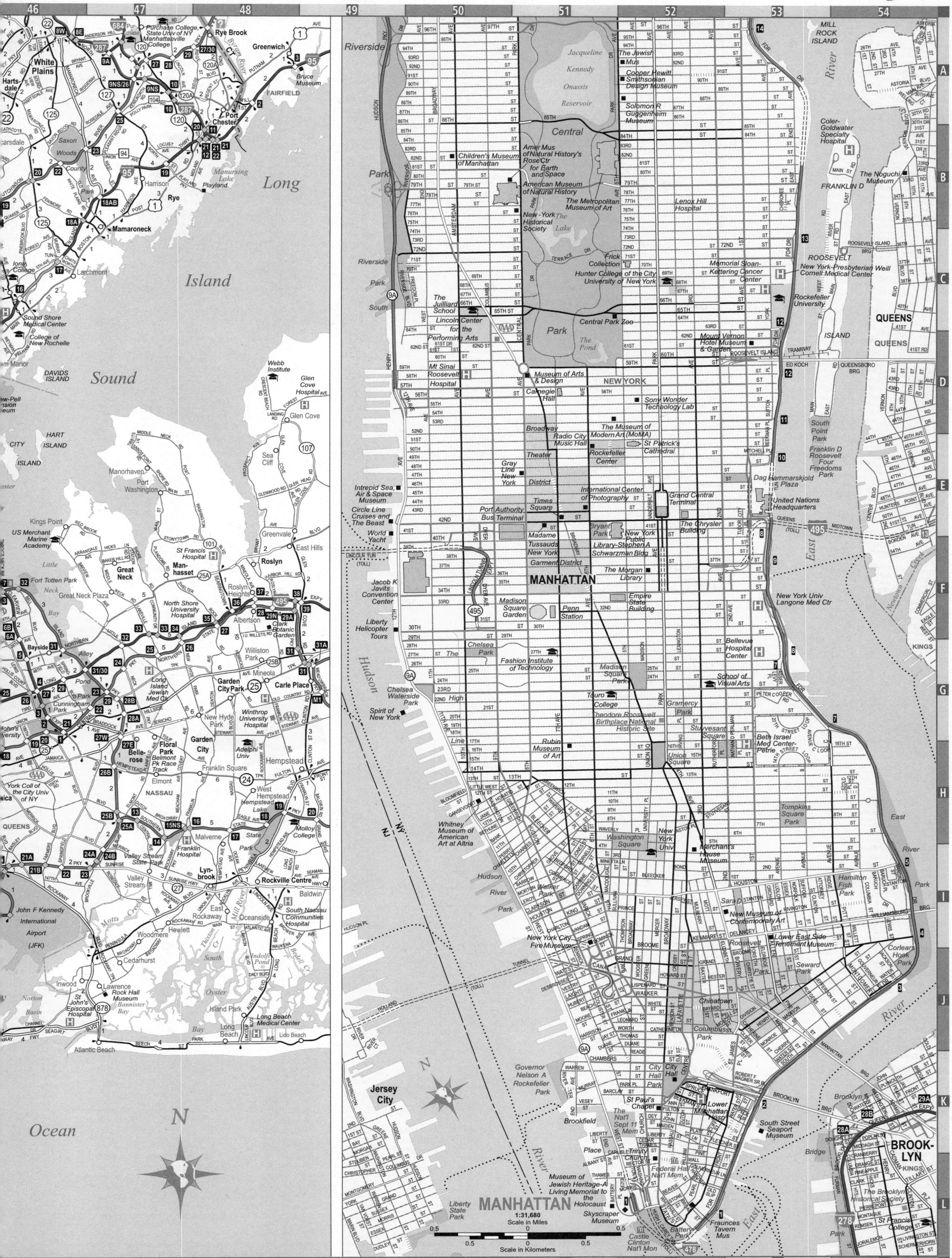

Scale in Miles
MANHATTAN
1:31,680
Scale in Kilometers

| Driving Distances In Miles | Asheville | Charlotte | Durham | Fayetteville | Greensboro | Jacksonville | Lumberton | Nags Head | Raleigh | Rocky Mount | Wilmington | Winston-Salem |
|---|---|---|---|---|---|---|---|---|---|---|---|---|
| Asheville | | 131 | 224 | 262 | 172 | 365 | 262 | 444 | 247 | 303 | 332 | 148 |
| Charlotte | 131 | | 143 | 137 | 91 | 233 | 123 | 363 | 165 | 222 | 197 | 78 |
| Greensboro | 172 | 91 | 53 | 93 | | 194 | 127 | 273 | 76 | 121 | 208 | 28 |
| Raleigh | 247 | 165 | 24 | 64 | 76 | 118 | 96 | 197 | | 56 | 131 | 105 |
| Wilmington | 332 | 197 | 156 | 90 | 208 | 51 | 79 | 242 | 131 | 141 | | 237 |

See also mileage table page 2

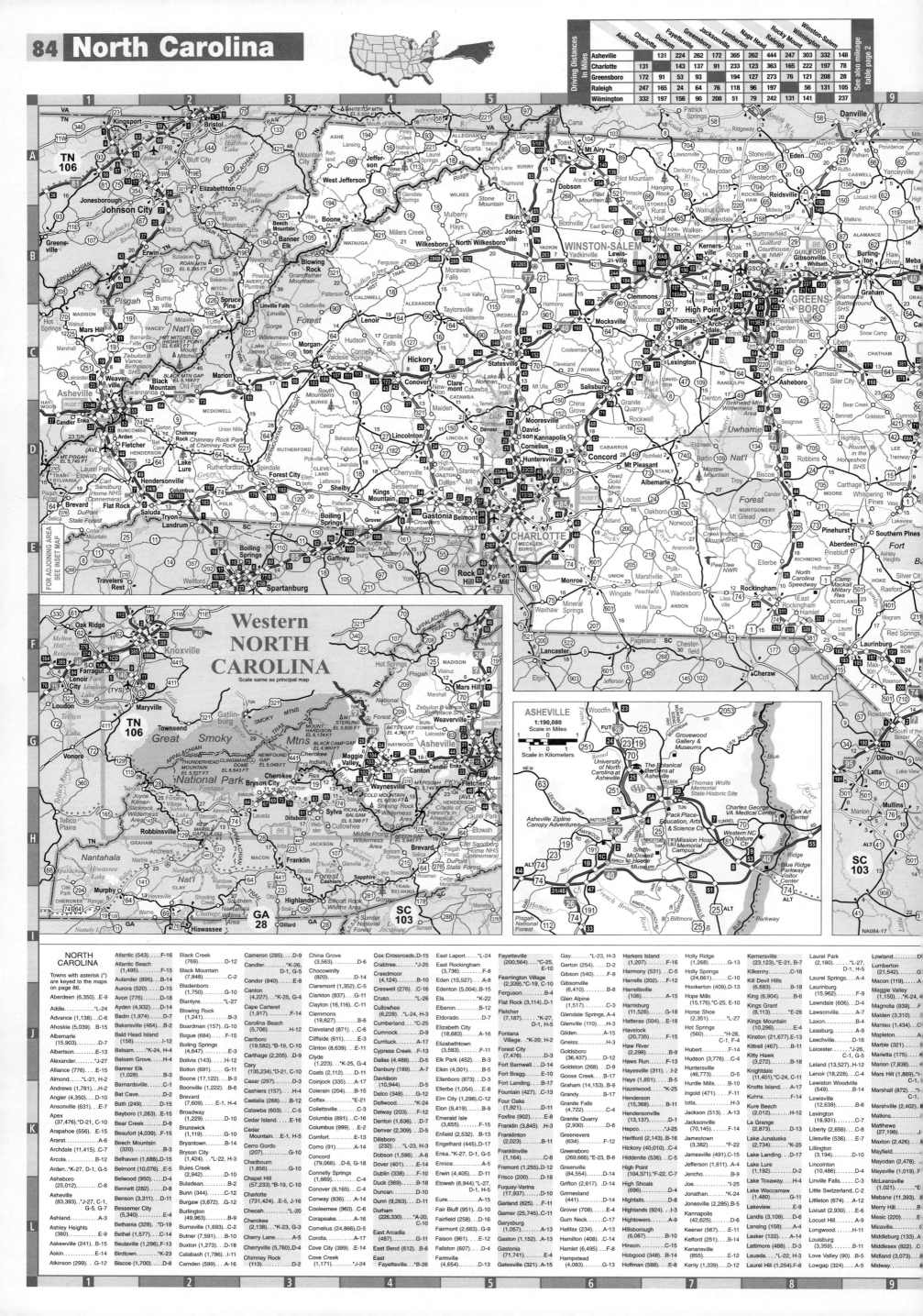

NORTH CAROLINA

Towns with asterisk (*) are keyed to the maps on page 86.

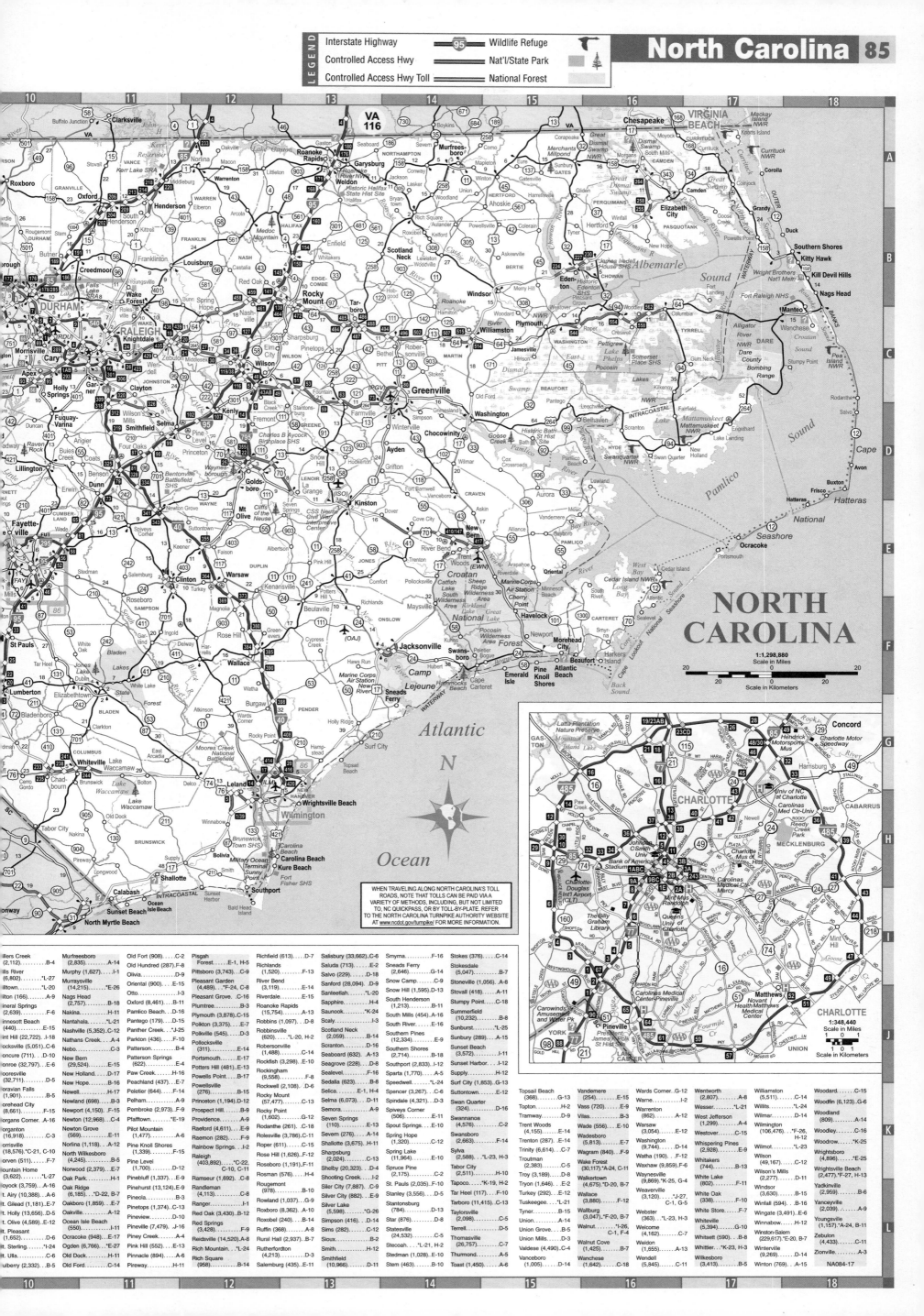

WHEN TRAVELING ALONG NORTH CAROLINA'S TOLL ROADS, NOTE THAT TOLLS CAN BE PAID VIA A VARIETY OF METHODS, INCLUDING, BUT NOT LIMITED TO, NC QUICKPASS, OR BY TOLL-BY-PLATE. REFER TO THE NORTH CAROLINA TURNPIKE AUTHORITY WEBSITE AT www.ncdot.gov/turnpike/ FOR MORE INFORMATION.

NA084-17

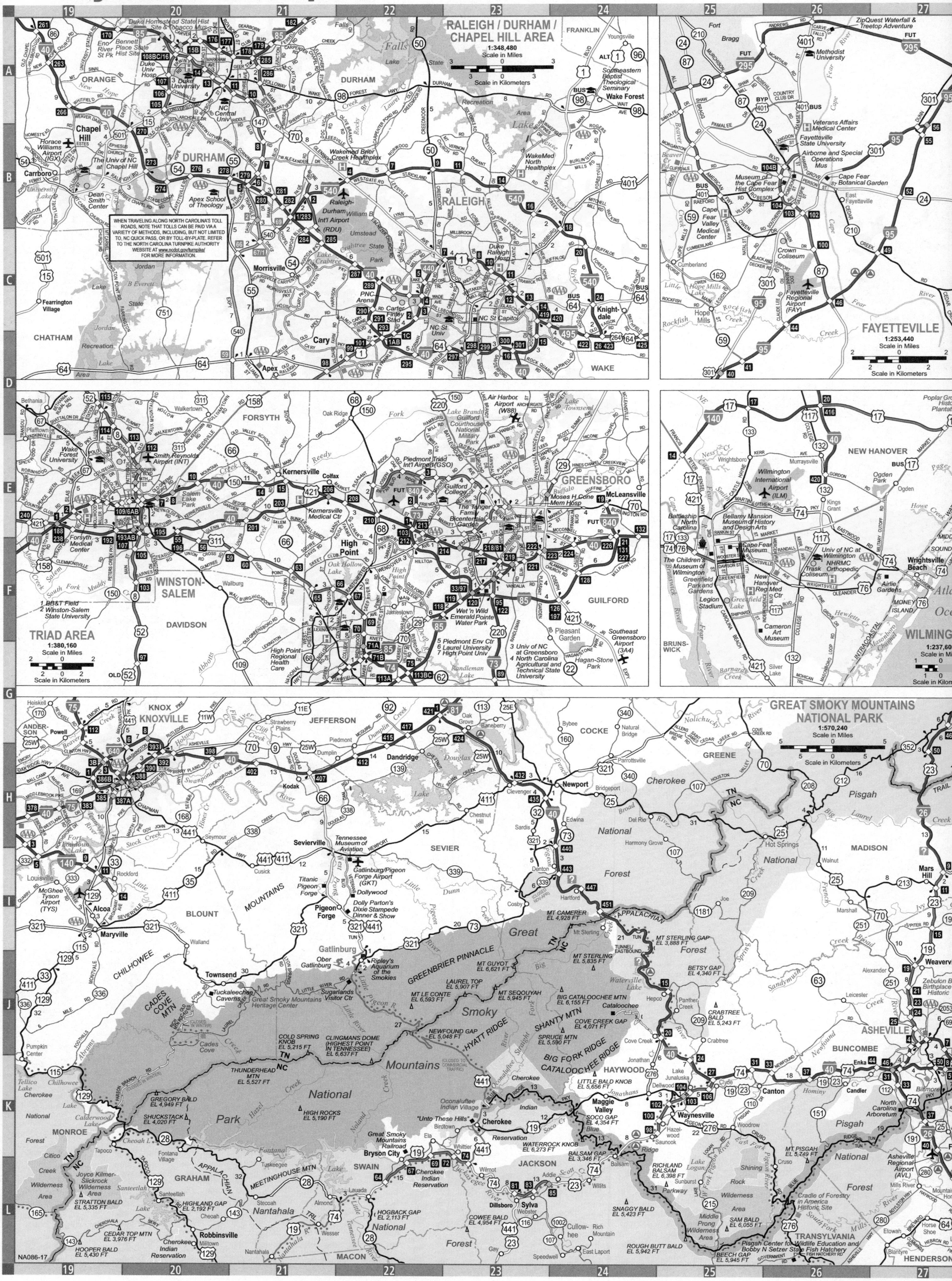

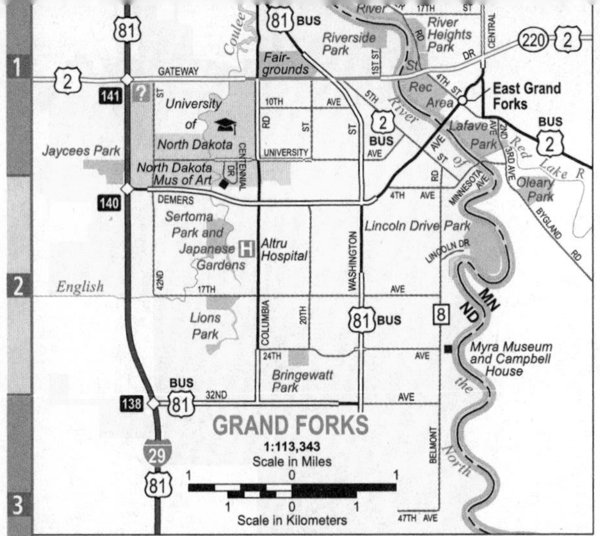

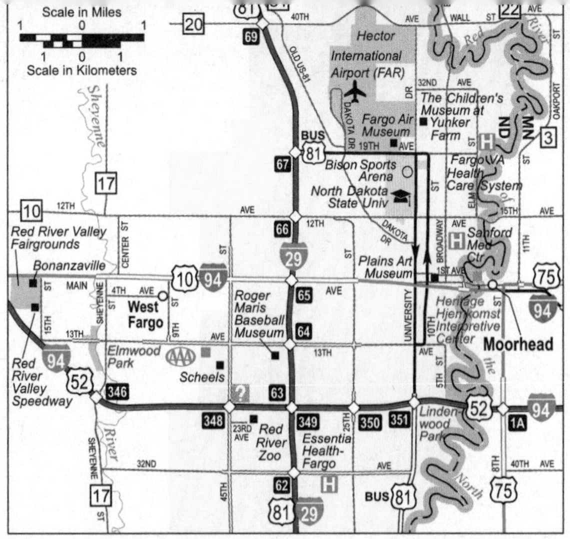

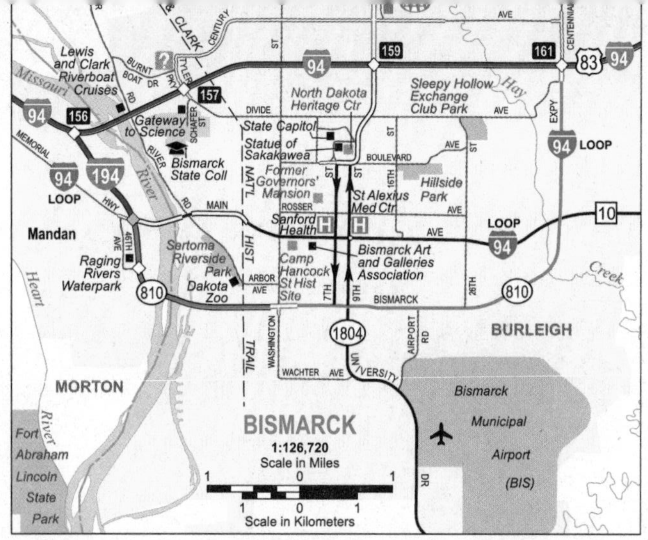

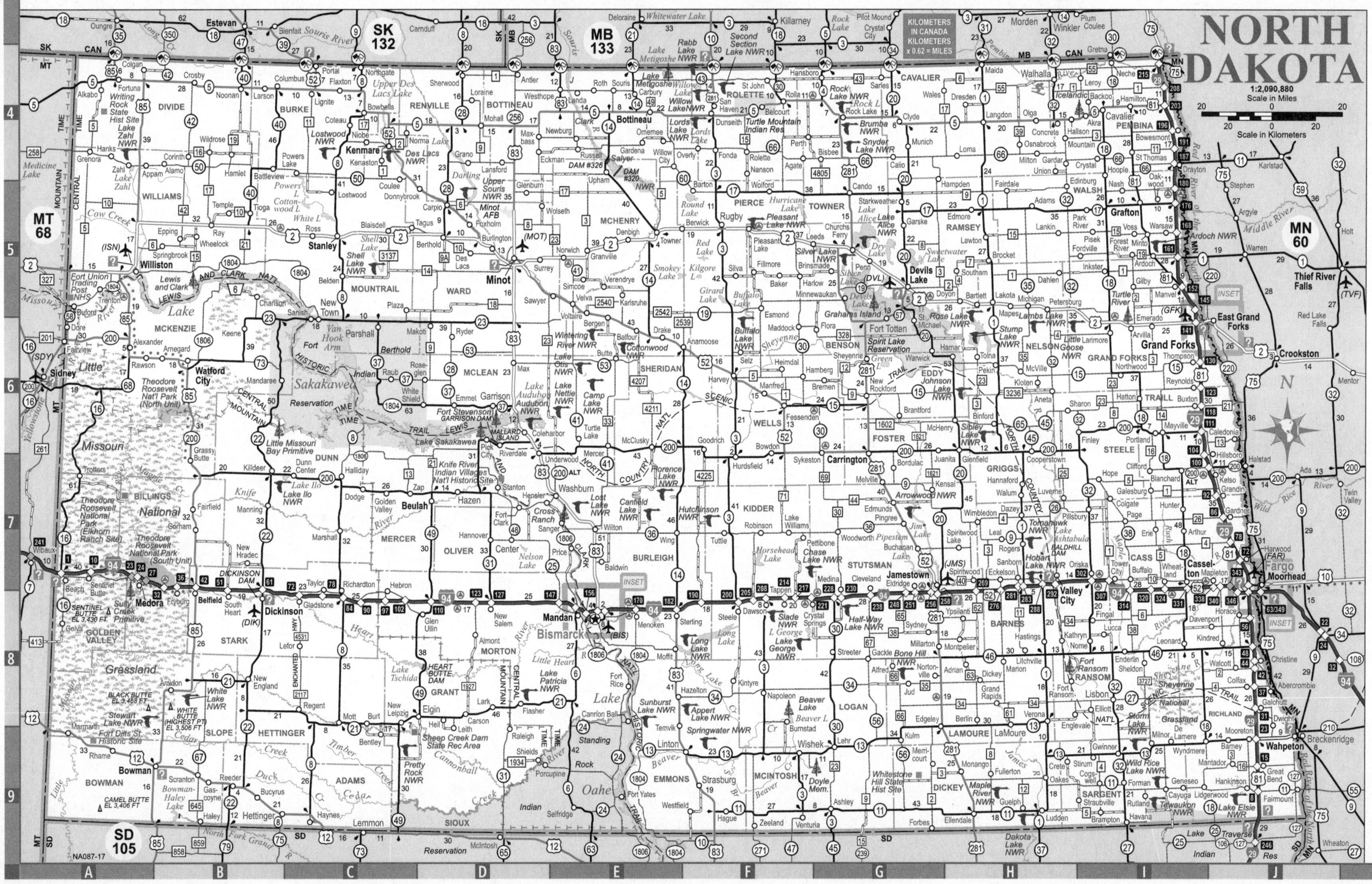

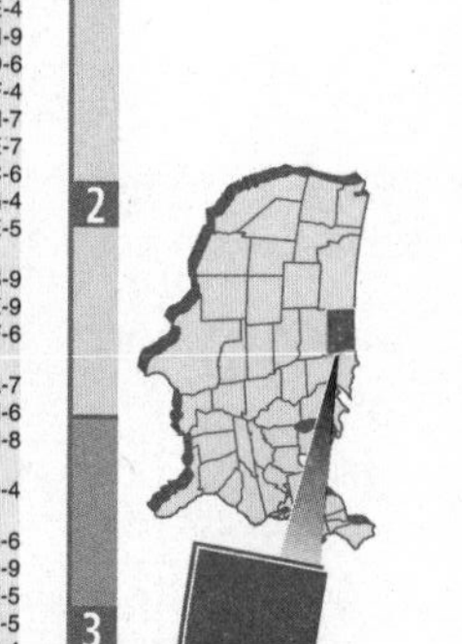

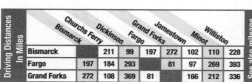

| Driving Distances In Miles | Bismarck | Churchs Ferry | Dickinson | Fargo | Grand Forks | Jamestown | Minot | Williston |
|---|---|---|---|---|---|---|---|---|
| Bismarck | | 211 | 99 | 197 | 272 | 102 | 110 | 228 |
| Fargo | 197 | 184 | 293 | | 81 | 97 | 269 | 393 |
| Grand Forks | 272 | 108 | 369 | 81 | | 166 | 212 | 336 |

See also mileage table on page 2

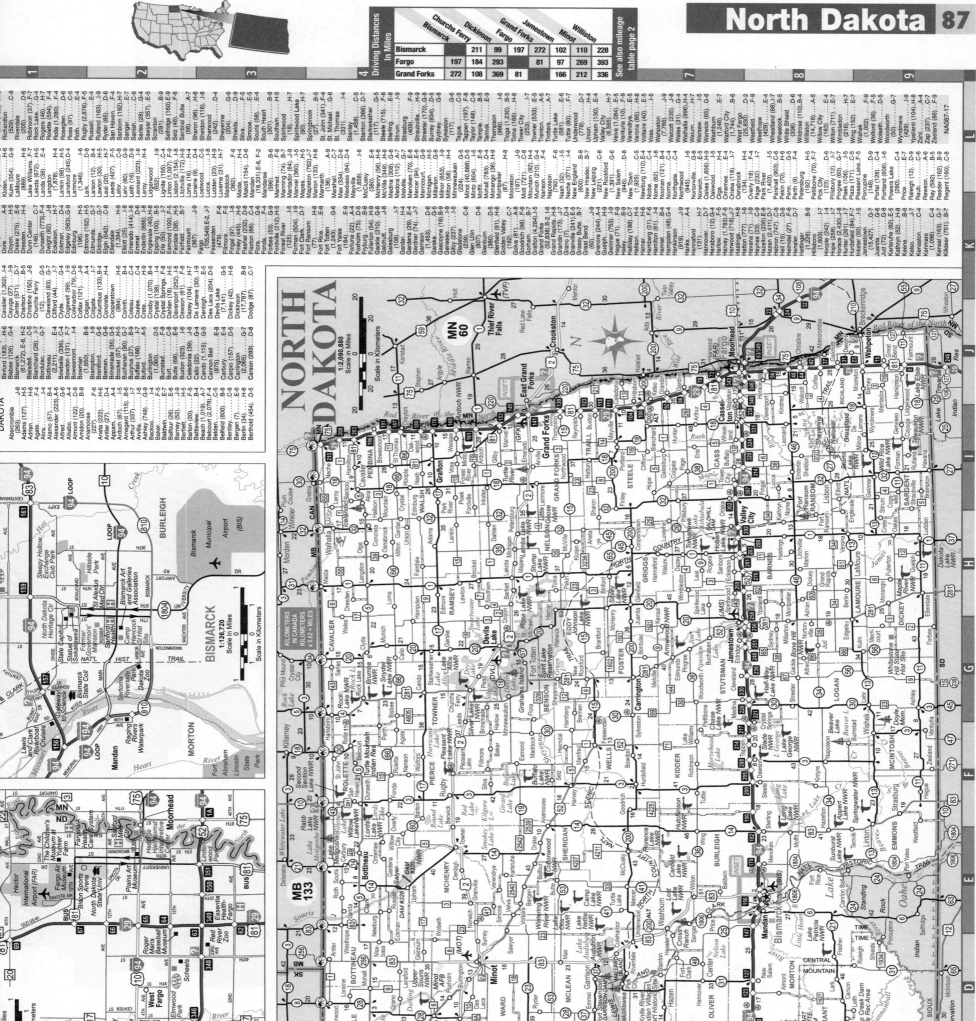

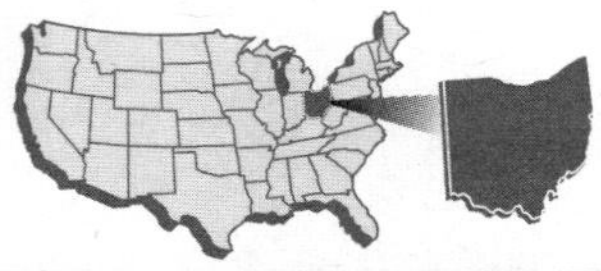

**Driving Distances In Miles** — See also mileage table page 2

| | Akron | Cambridge | Canton | Cincinnati | Cleveland | Columbus | Dayton | Lima | Mansfield | Portsmouth | Toledo | Youngstown |
|---|---|---|---|---|---|---|---|---|---|---|---|---|
| Cincinnati | 232 | 184 | 236 | | 248 | 106 | 54 | 126 | 172 | 108 | 203 | 279 |
| Cleveland | 34 | 119 | 60 | 248 | | 143 | 174 | 81 | 232 | 115 | 74 | |
| Columbus | 126 | 79 | 128 | 106 | 143 | | 71 | 103 | 66 | 90 | 143 | 173 |
| Toledo | 139 | 193 | 159 | 203 | 115 | 143 | 149 | 78 | | 118 | 234 | 172 |
| Youngstown | 49 | 121 | 58 | 279 | 74 | 173 | 243 | 204 | 112 | 263 | 172 | |

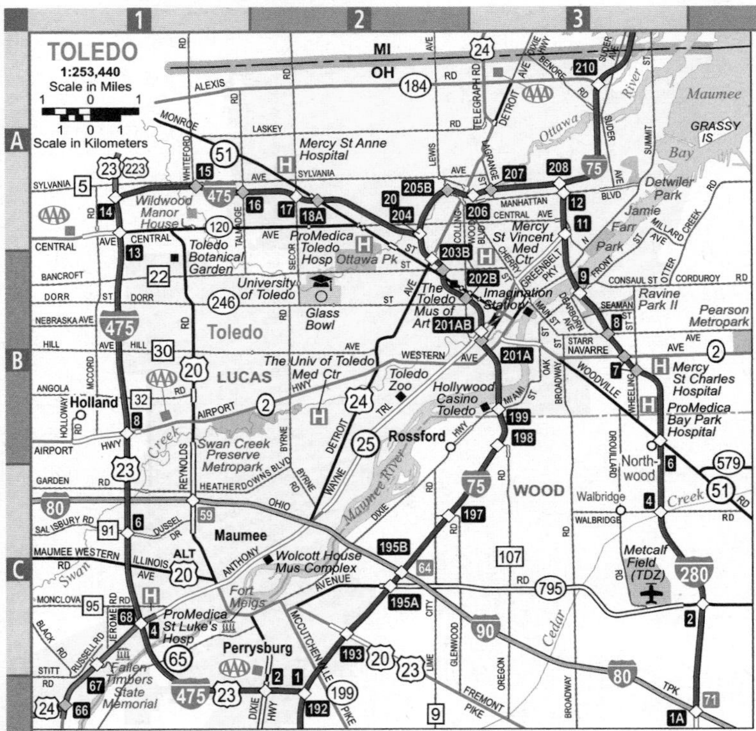

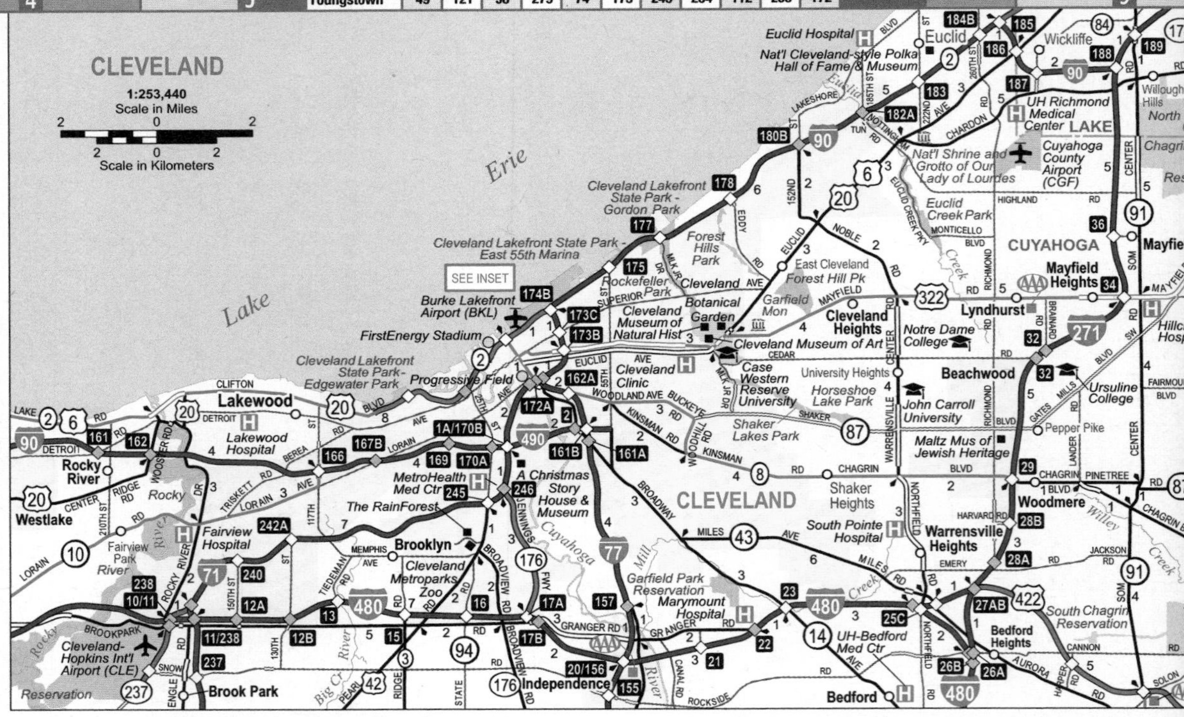

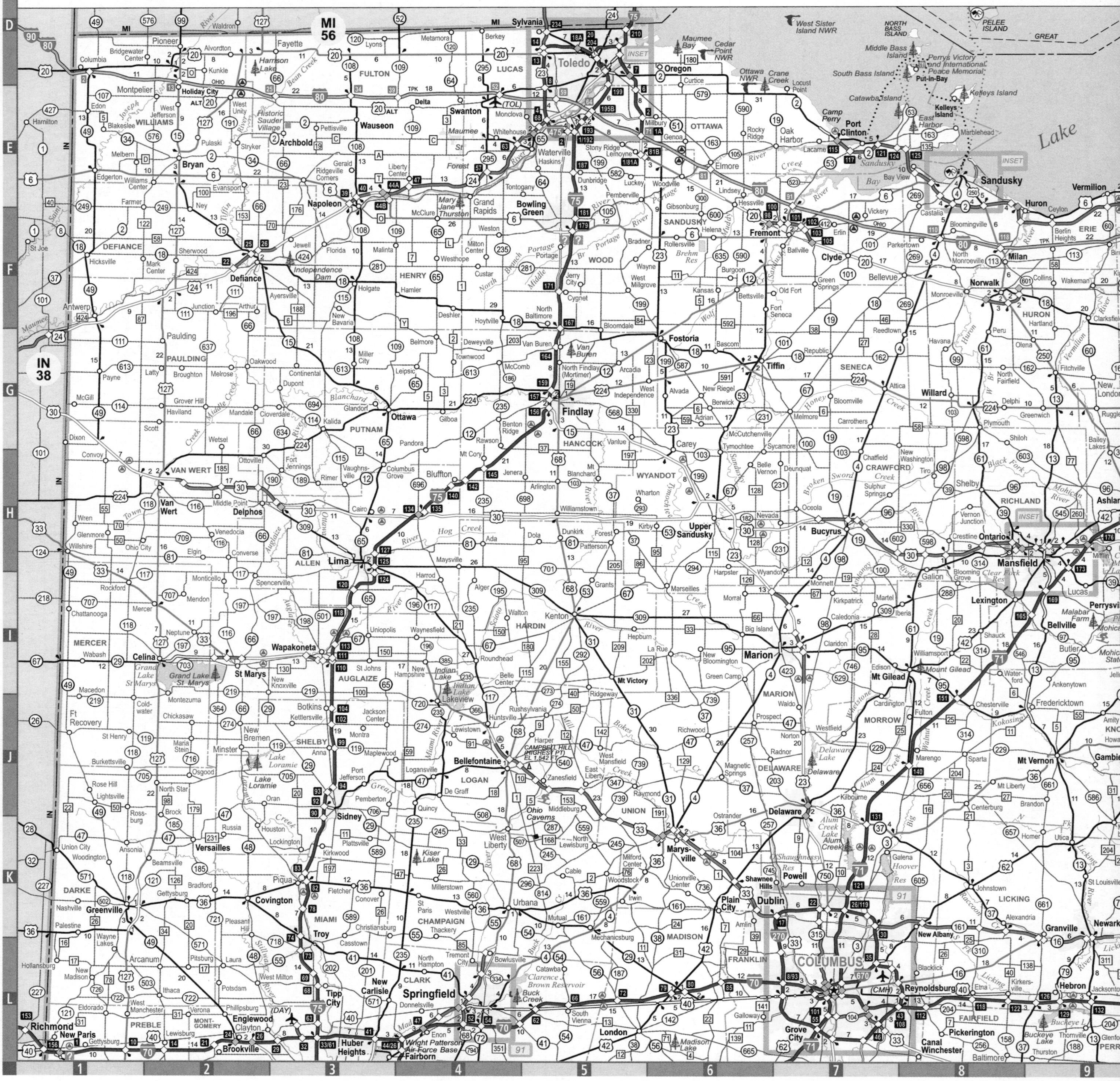

LEGEND

- Interstate Highway (95)
- Controlled Access Hwy
- Controlled Access Hwy Toll
- Wildlife Refuge
- Nat'l/State Park
- National Forest

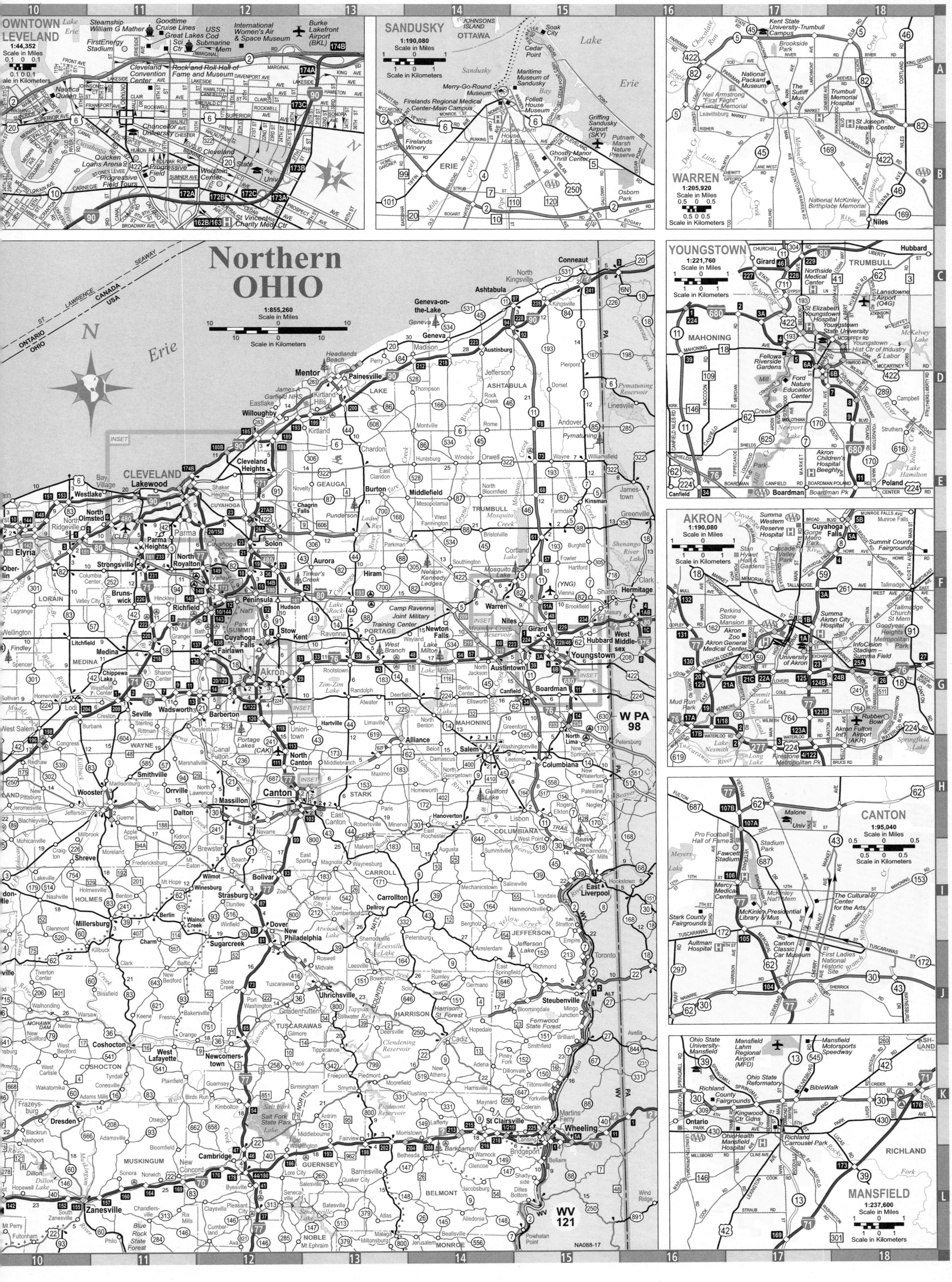

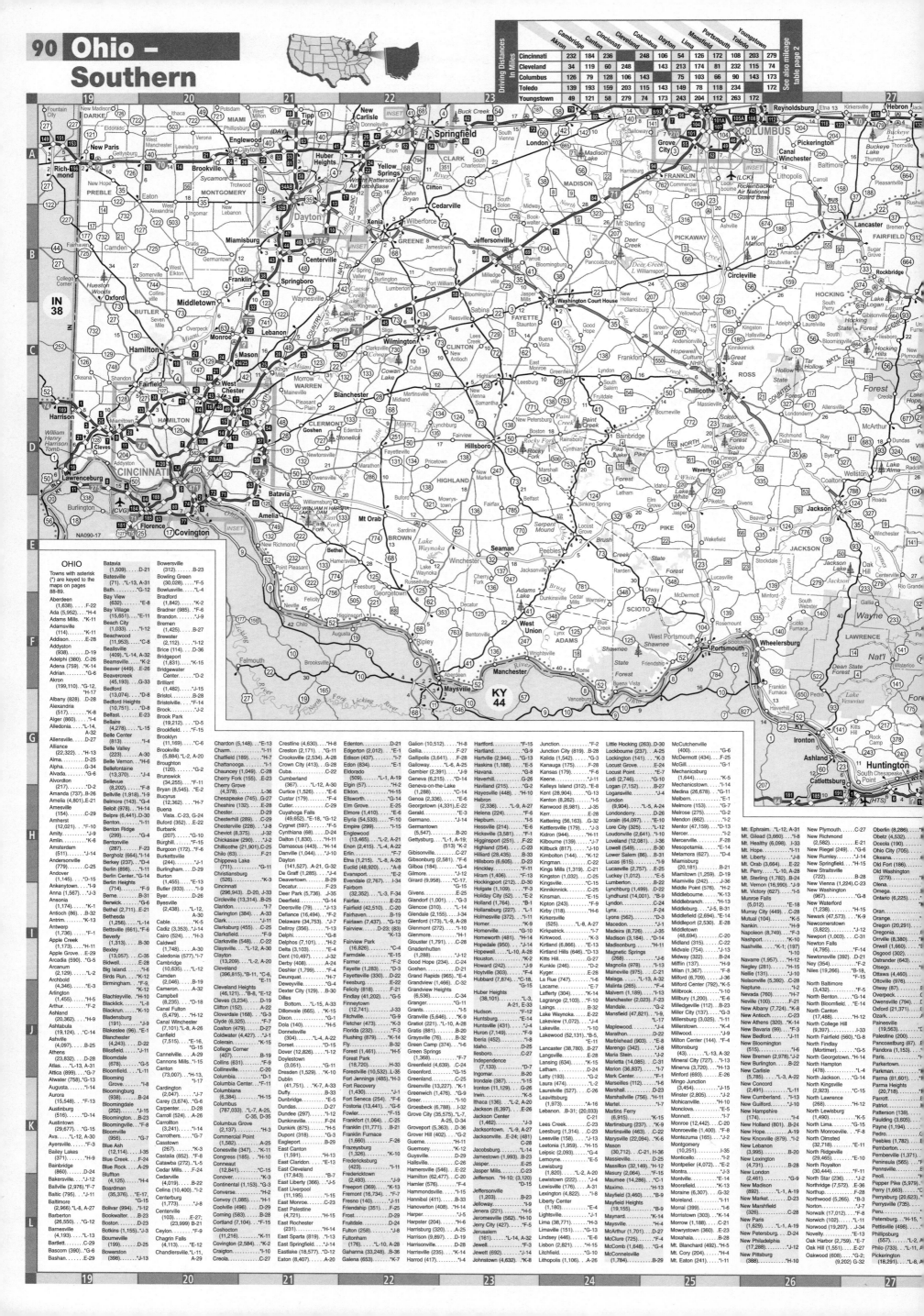

LEGEND
Interstate Highway — Wildlife Refuge
Controlled Access Hwy — Nat'l/State Park
Controlled Access Hwy Toll — National Forest

NA090-17

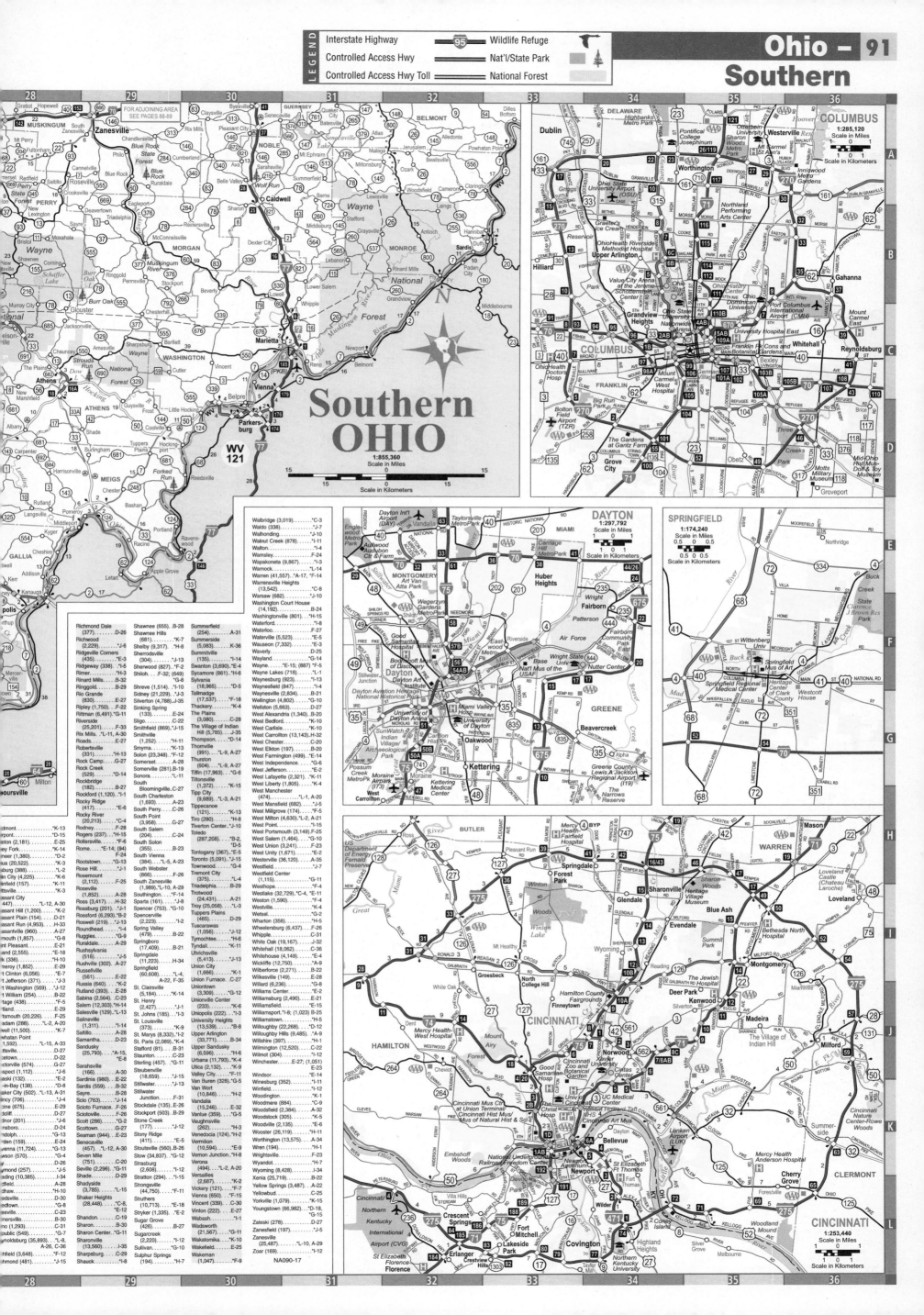

| Driving Distances In Miles | Ardmore | Enid | Fort Smith, AR | Lawton | McAlester | Muskogee | Oklahoma City | Tulsa |
|---|---|---|---|---|---|---|---|---|
| Lawton | 108 | 143 | 261 | | 209 | 218 | 86 | 190 |
| Oklahoma City | 100 | 101 | 181 | 86 | 131 | 140 | | 106 |
| Tulsa | 202 | 116 | 116 | 190 | 91 | 50 | 106 | |

See also mileage table page 2

## OKLAHOMA

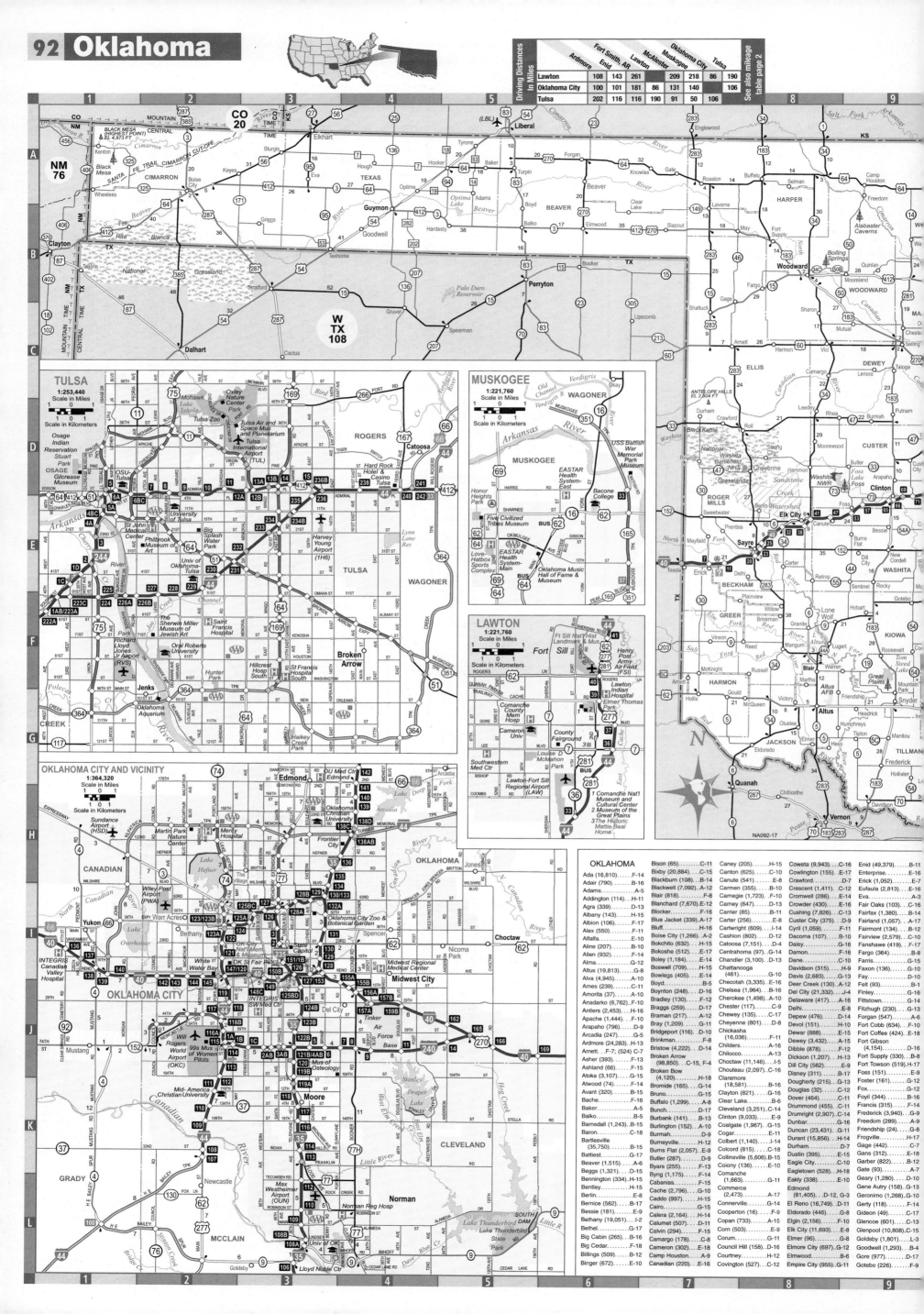

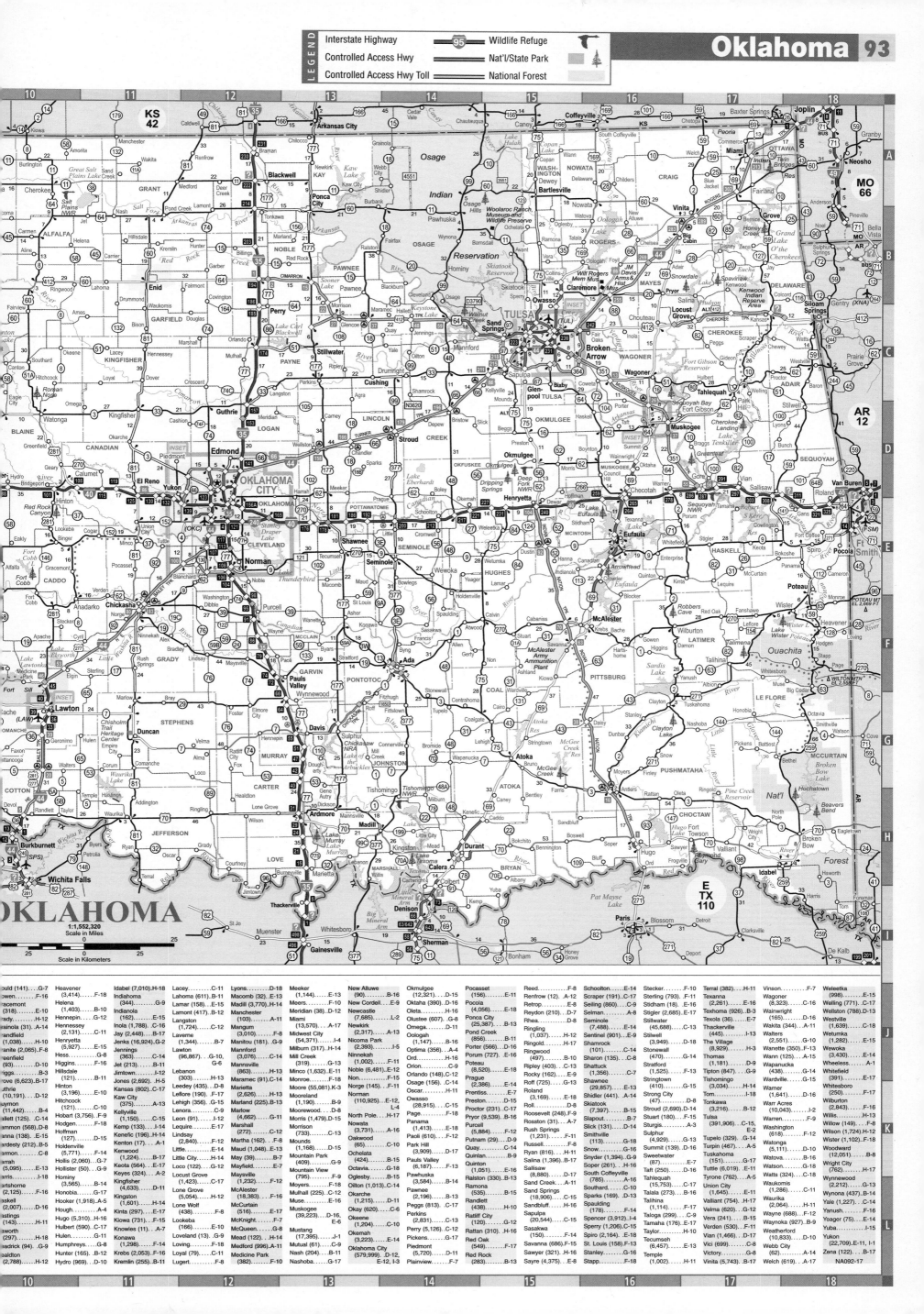

Driving Distances in Miles

| | Bend | Eugene | Grants Pass | Klamath Falls | Medford | Pendleton | Portland | Salem |
|---|---|---|---|---|---|---|---|---|
| Eugene | 116 | | 138 | 172 | 167 | 319 | 109 | 66 |
| Portland | 161 | 109 | 244 | 278 | 272 | 211 | | 46 |
| Salem | 131 | 66 | 200 | 235 | 229 | 256 | 46 | |

See also mileage table page 2

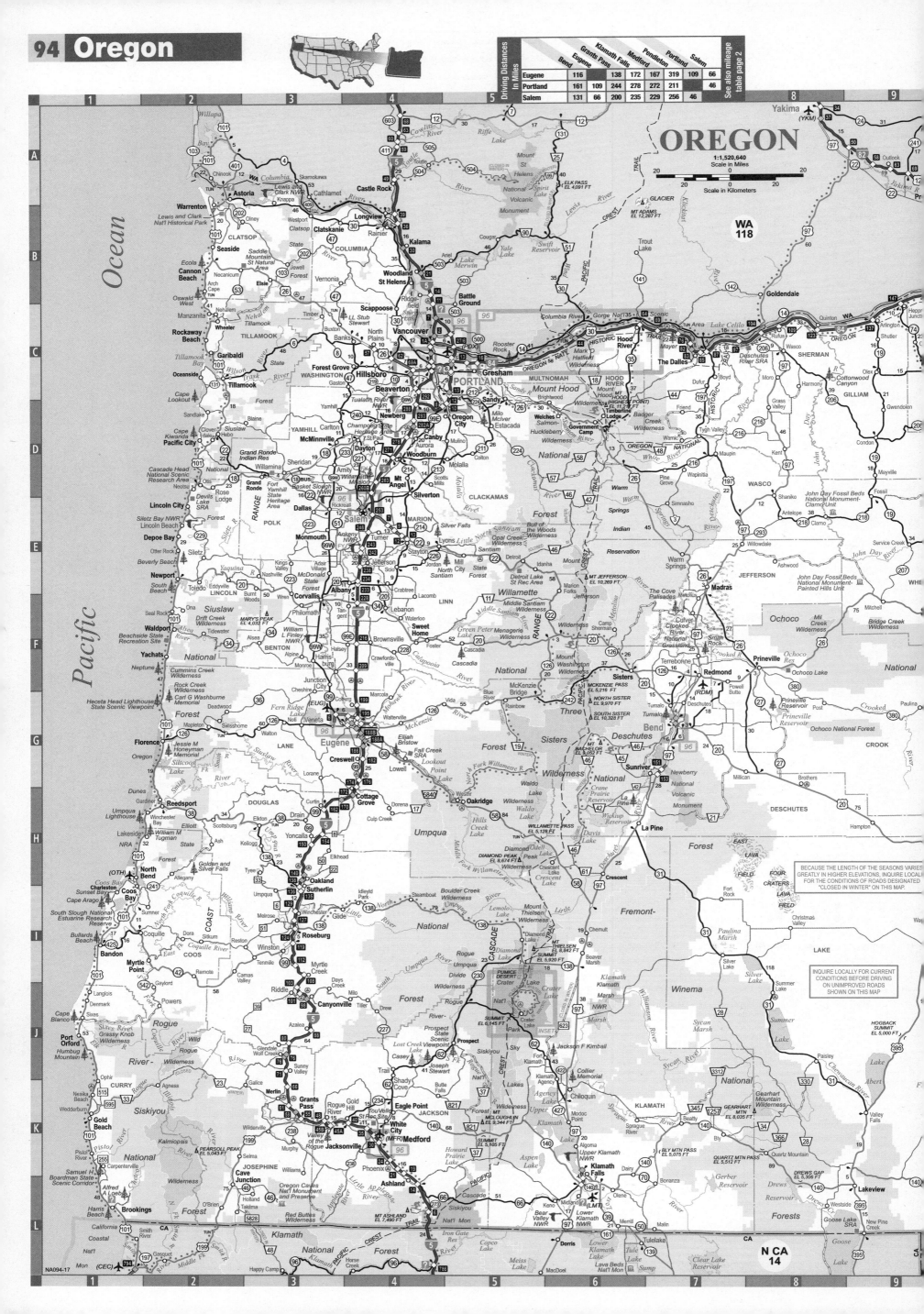

LEGEND
- Interstate Highway
- Controlled Access Hwy
- Controlled Access Hwy Toll
- Wildlife Refuge
- Nat'l/State Park
- National Forest

## OREGON

Towns with asterisk (*)are keyed to the map on page 96.

NA094-17

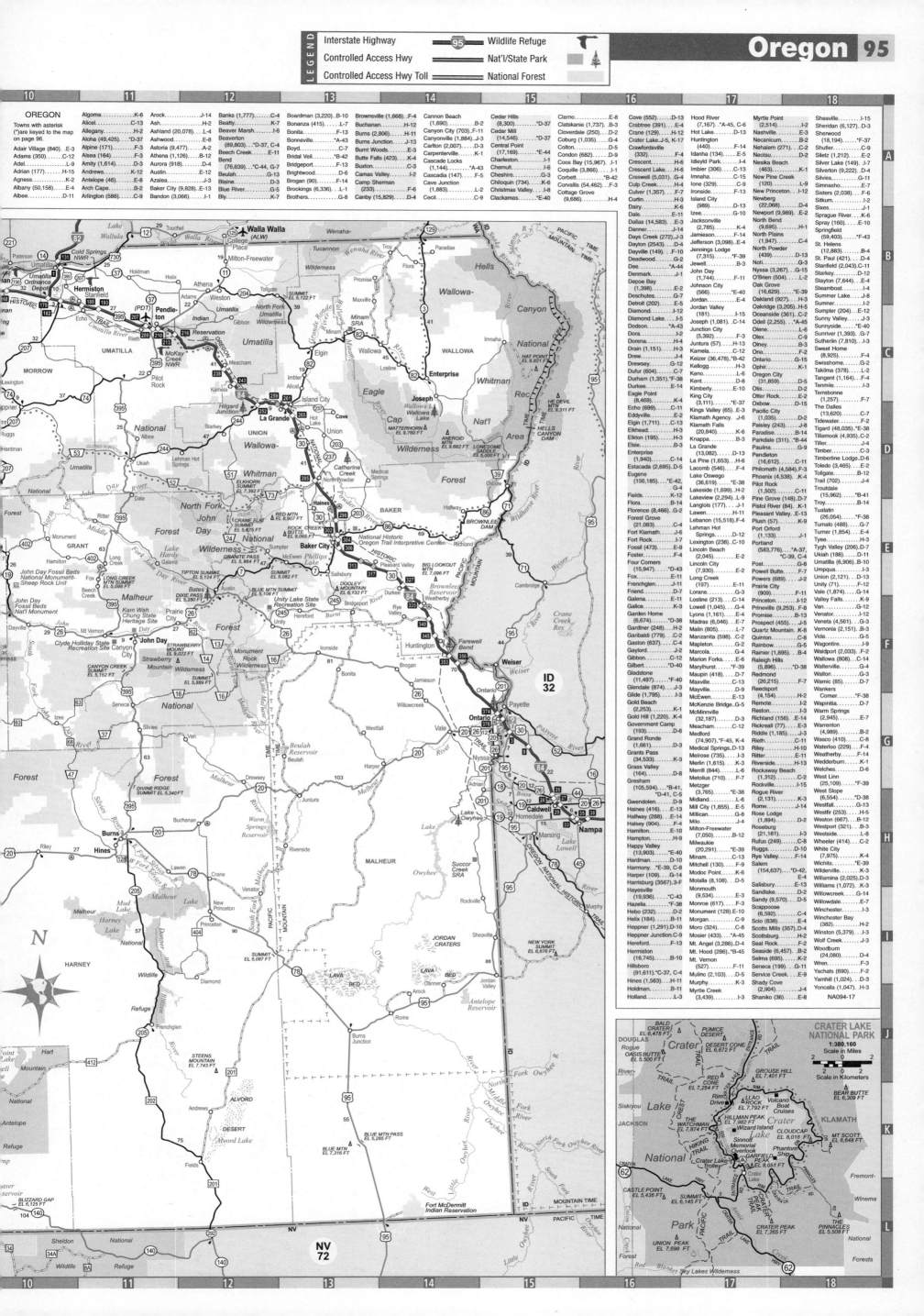

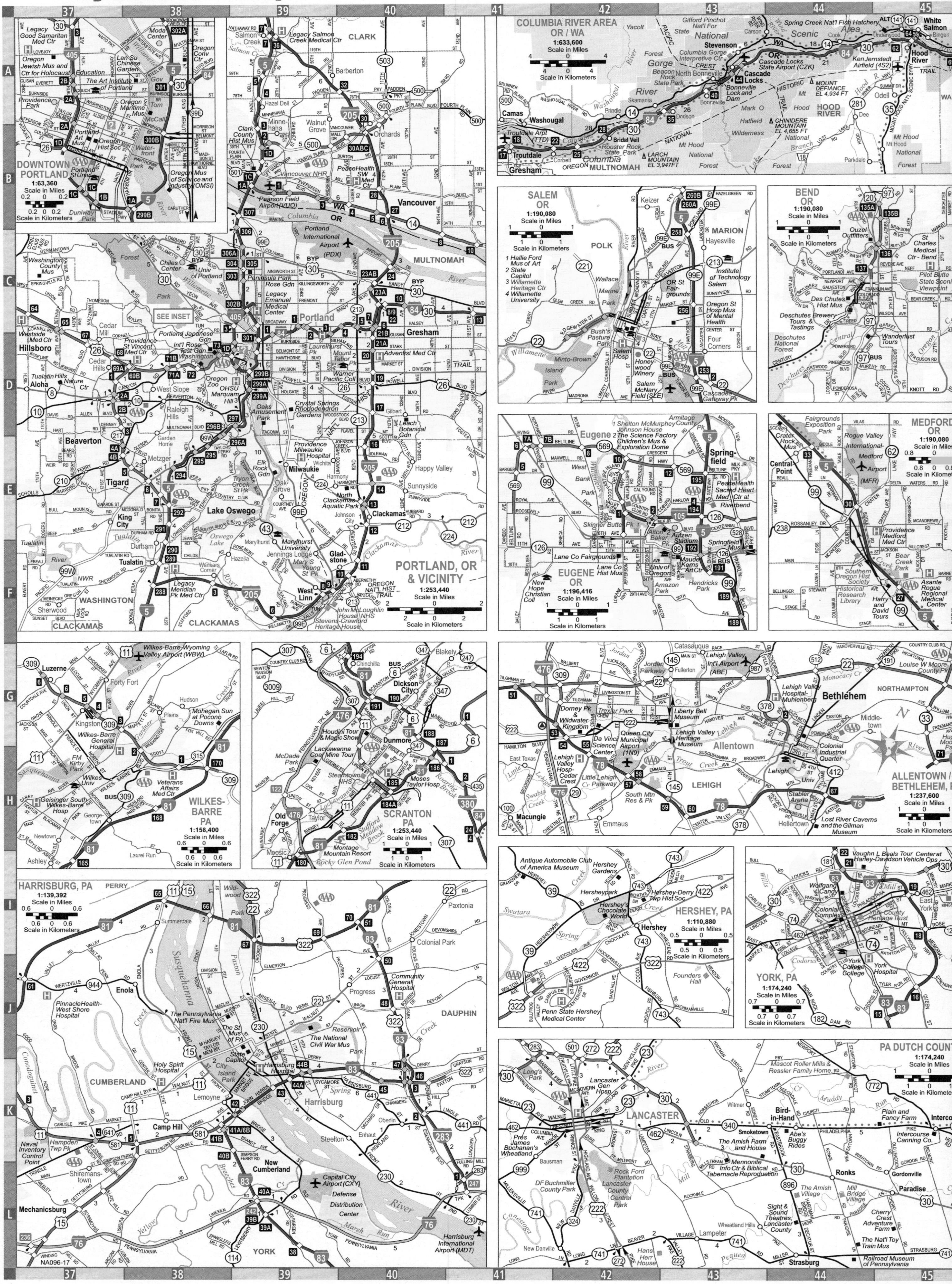

PITTSBURGH, PA
& VICINITY
1:158,400
Scale in Miles
Scale in Kilometers
DOWNTOWN
PITTSBURGH
1:30,096
Scale in Miles
Scale in Kilometers
PHILADELPHIA, PA
& VICINITY
1:269,280
Scale in Miles
Scale in Kilometers
DOWNTOWN
PHILADELPHIA
1:25,344
Scale in Miles
Scale in Kilometers
PITTSBURGH
ALLEGHENY
Sewickley
Coraopolis
Oakmont
Fox Chapel
Sharpsburg
Blawnox
Penn Hills
Monroeville
Wilkinsburg
Swissvale
Homestead
West Mifflin
McKeesport
Mt Lebanon
Bethel Park
Pleasant Hills
Carnegie
Crafton
Green Tree
North Versailles
Trafford
WEST-MORELAND
PHILADELPHIA
Camden
Horsham
Willow Grove
Levittown
Bensalem
Bristol
Bordentown
BUCKS
BURLINGTON
DELAWARE
GLOUCESTER
Chester
Media
Springfield
Bryn Mawr
Ardmore
King of Prussia
Conshohocken
Norristown
Woodbury
Runnemede
Blackwood
Gloucester City
Claymont
SALEM
Trenton

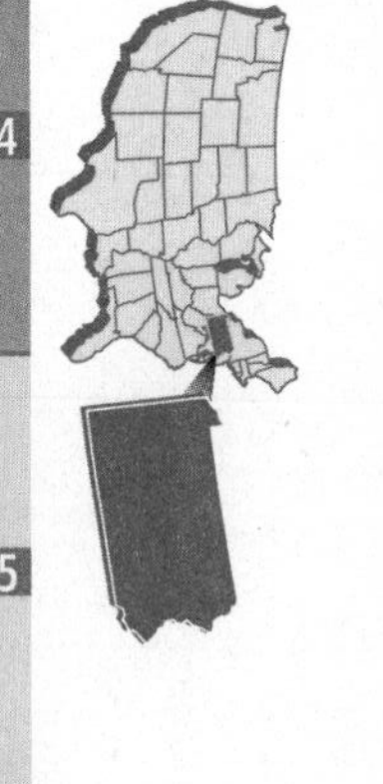

See also mileage table page 2

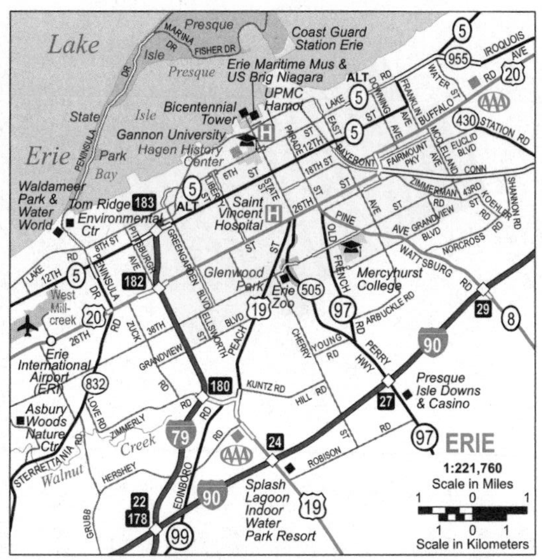

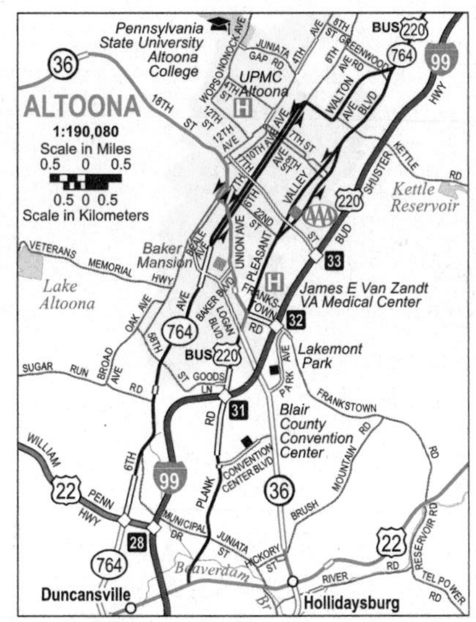

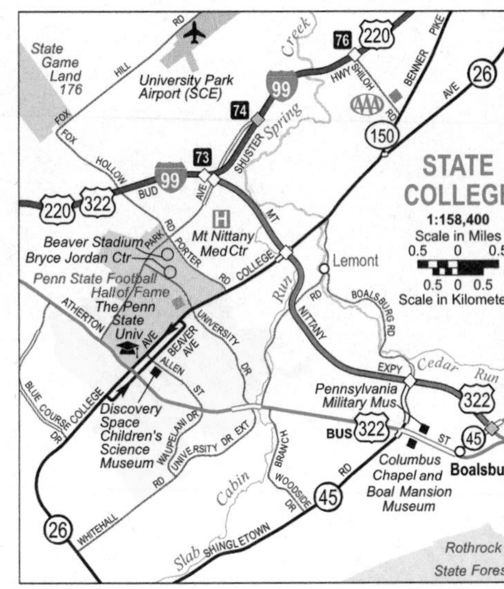

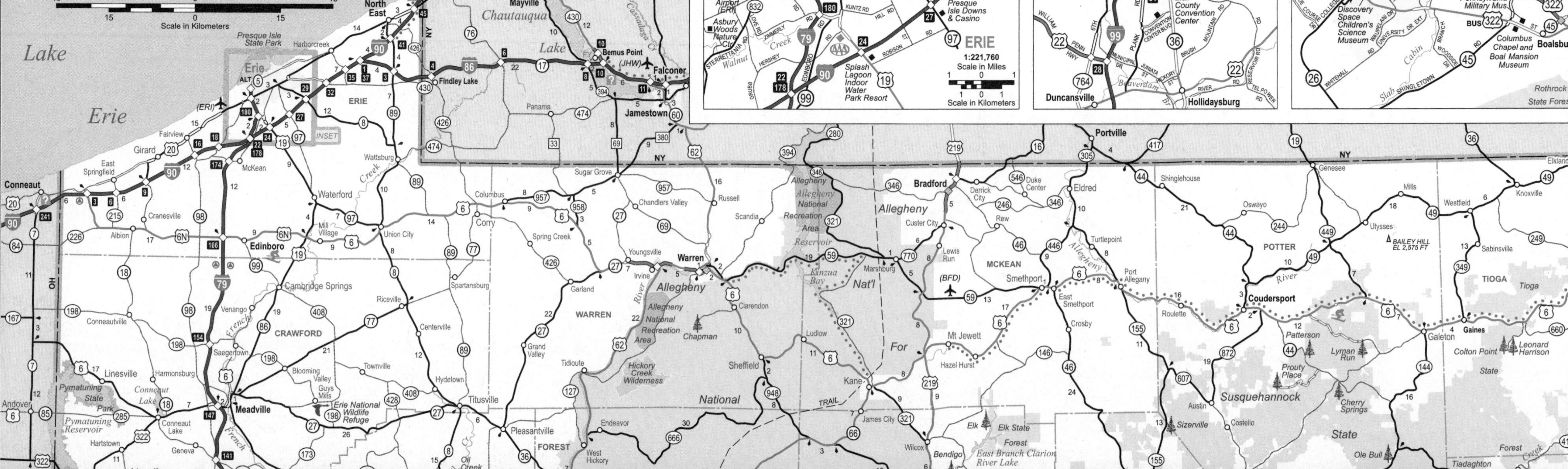

| Driving Distances In Miles | Allentown | Altoona | Gettysburg | Harrisburg | Johnstown | Lancaster | Philadelphia | Pittsburgh | Reading | Scranton | York |
|---|---|---|---|---|---|---|---|---|---|---|---|
| Erie | 372 | 205 | 307 | 297 | 178 | 335 | 420 | 128 | 353 | 322 | 327 |
| Harrisburg | 84 | 118 | 38 | | 135 | 40 | 112 | 204 | 63 | 124 | 24 |
| Philadelphia | 63 | 236 | 420 | 140 | 112 | 237 | | 71 | 305 | 59 | 125 | 102 |
| Pittsburgh | 284 | 97 | 128 | 185 | 204 | 67 | 238 | 305 | | 262 | 282 | 221 |
| Scranton | 76 | 189 | 322 | 160 | 124 | 233 | 125 | 282 | 101 | | 147 |

## STATE COLLEGE

## ALTOONA

## ERIE

## Western PENNSYLVANIA

WESTERN PENNSYLVANIA
Towns with asterisk (*) are keyed to the maps on pages 96-97.

LEGEND

| | | |
|---|---|---|
| Interstate Highway | 95 | Wildlife Refuge |
| Controlled Access Hwy | | Nat'l/State Park |
| Controlled Access Hwy Toll | | National Forest |

FOR ADJOINING AREA
SEE PAGES 100-101

N OH 88

WV 121

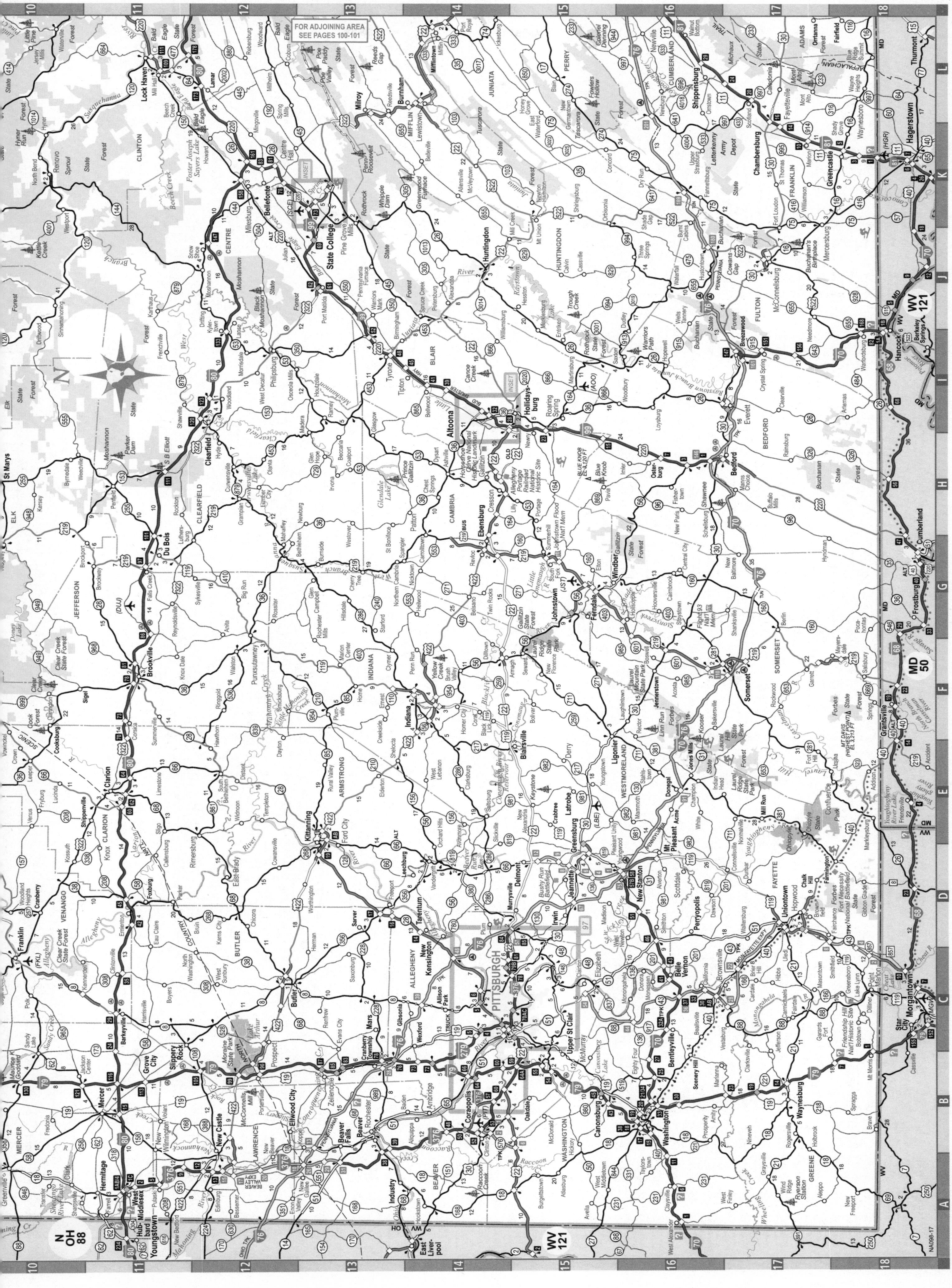

| Driving Distances In Miles | Allentown | Altoona | Erie | Gettysburg | Harrisburg | Johnstown | Lancaster | Philadelphia | Pittsburgh | Reading | Scranton | York |
|---|---|---|---|---|---|---|---|---|---|---|---|---|
| Erie | 372 | 205 | | 307 | 297 | 178 | 335 | 420 | 128 | 353 | 322 | 327 |
| Harrisburg | 84 | 135 | 297 | 38 | | 135 | 40 | 112 | 204 | 63 | 124 | 24 |
| Philadelphia | 63 | 236 | 420 | 140 | 112 | 237 | 71 | | 305 | 59 | 125 | 102 |
| Pittsburgh | 284 | 97 | 128 | 185 | 204 | 67 | 238 | 305 | | 262 | 282 | 221 |
| Scranton | 76 | 189 | 322 | 160 | 124 | 233 | 132 | 125 | 282 | 101 | | 147 |

See also mileage table page 2

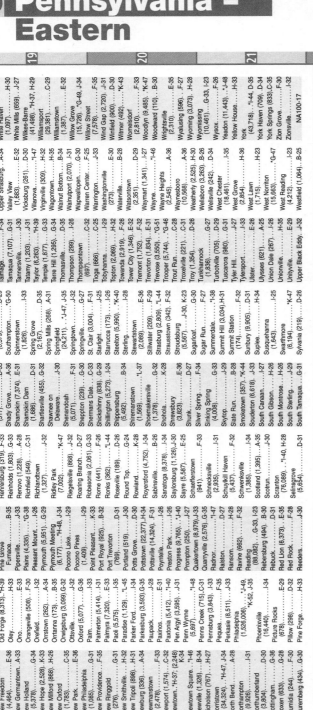

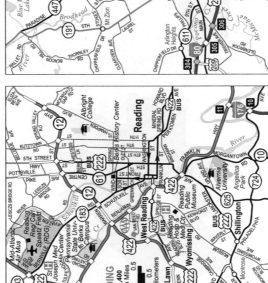

STROUDSBURG

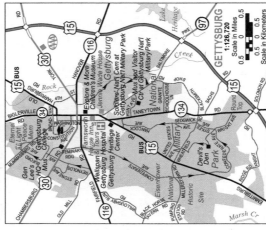

READING
1:158,400

GETTYSBURG
1:126,720

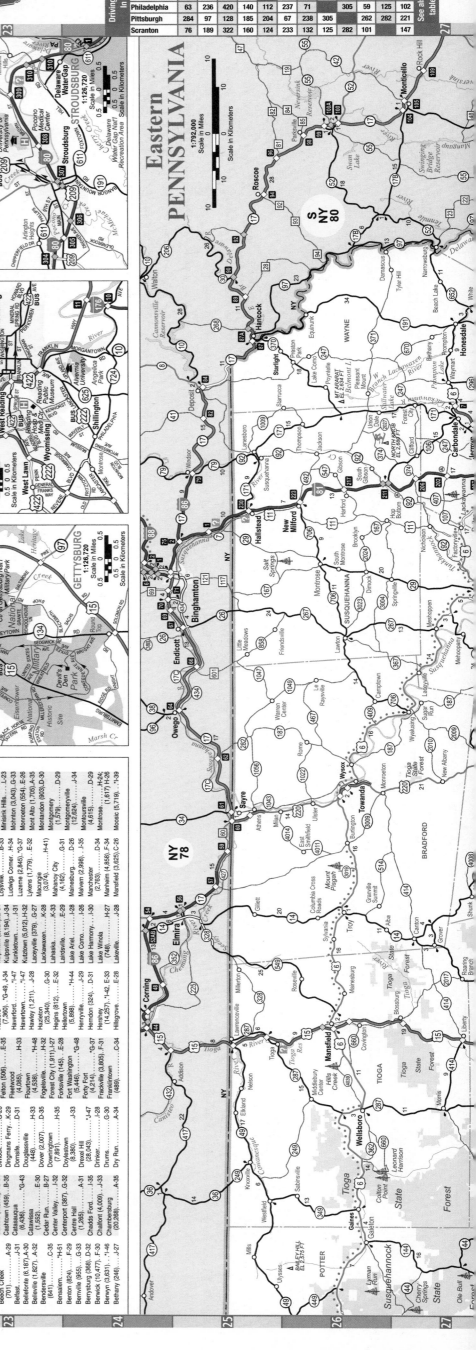

Eastern PENNSYLVANIA
1:792,000

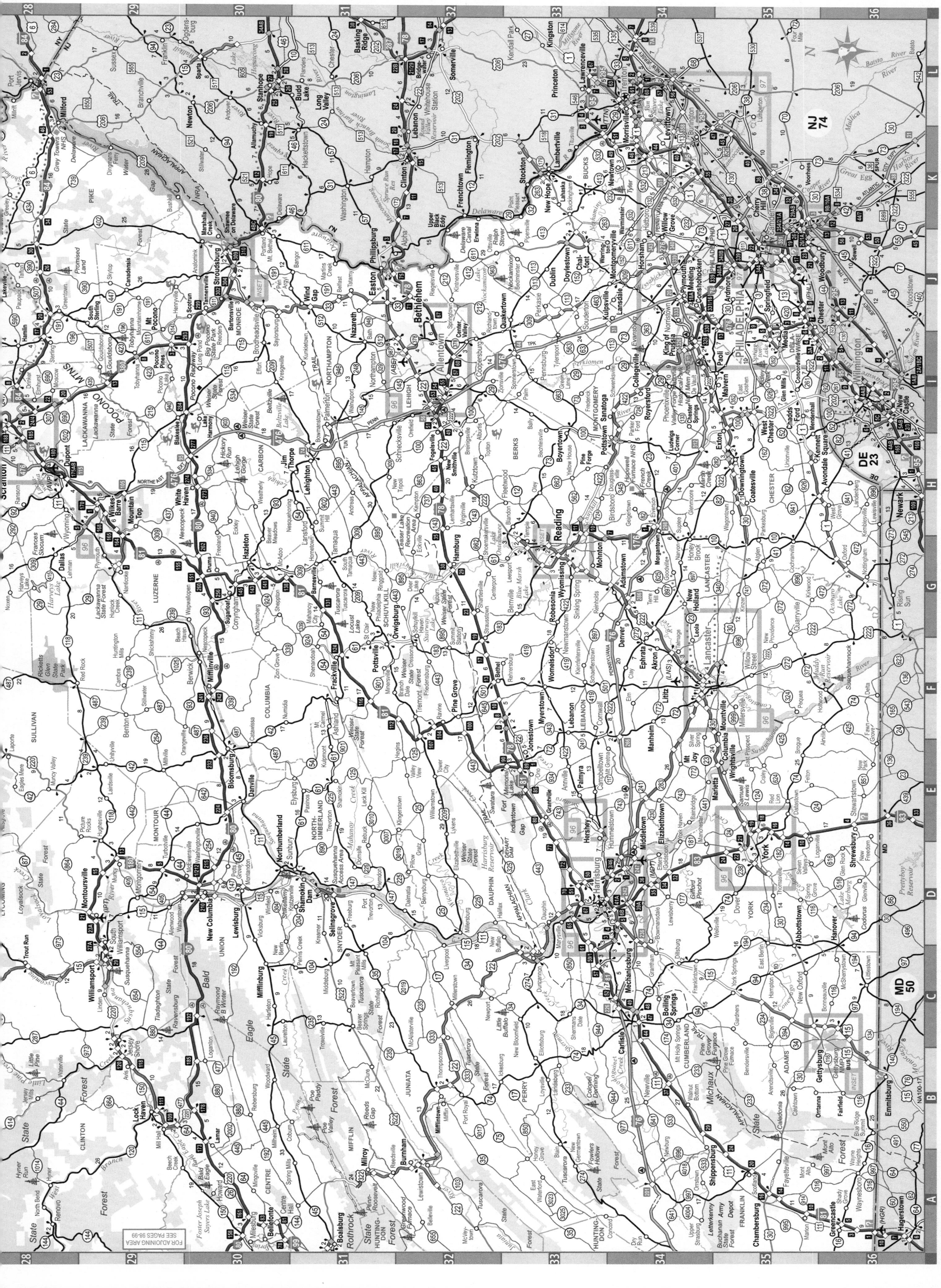

LEGEND

| | | | |
|---|---|---|---|
| Interstate Highway | 95 | Wildlife Refuge | |
| Controlled Access Hwy | | Nat'l/State Park | |
| Controlled Access Hwy Toll | | National Forest | |

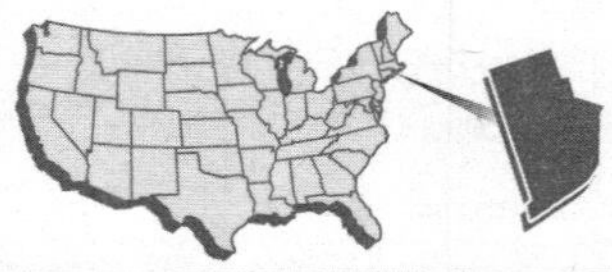

## RHODE ISLAND

1:348,480
Scale in Miles

Scale in Kilometers

NA102-17

## PROVIDENCE

1:205,920
Scale in Miles

Scale in Kilometers

## NEWPORT

1:95,040
Scale in Miles

Scale in Kilometers

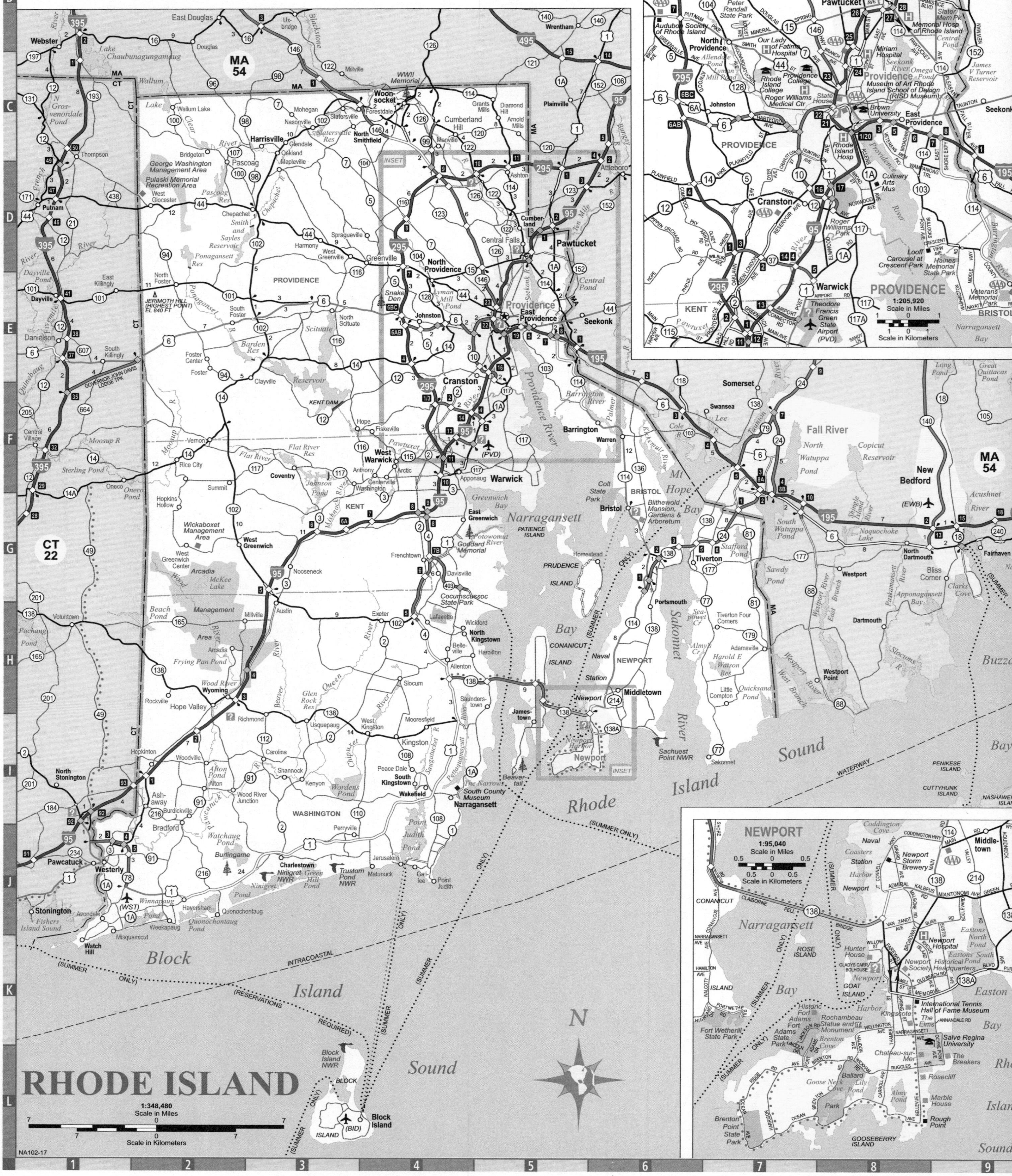

| Driving Distances In Miles | Anderson | Augusta, GA | Charleston | Charlotte, NC | Columbia | Florence | Greenville | Myrtle Beach | Orangeburg | Spartanburg |
|---|---|---|---|---|---|---|---|---|---|---|
| Charleston | 228 | 150 | | 209 | 113 | 132 | 213 | 98 | 76 | 204 |
| Columbia | 116 | 71 | 113 | 93 | | 80 | 103 | 148 | 41 | 94 |
| Greenville | 31 | 113 | 213 | 103 | 103 | 180 | | 248 | 141 | 30 |
| Myrtle Beach | 263 | 215 | 98 | 196 | 148 | 68 | 248 | | 142 | 239 |

See also mileage table page 2

Towns with asterisk (*) are keyed to the map on page 104.

NA103-17

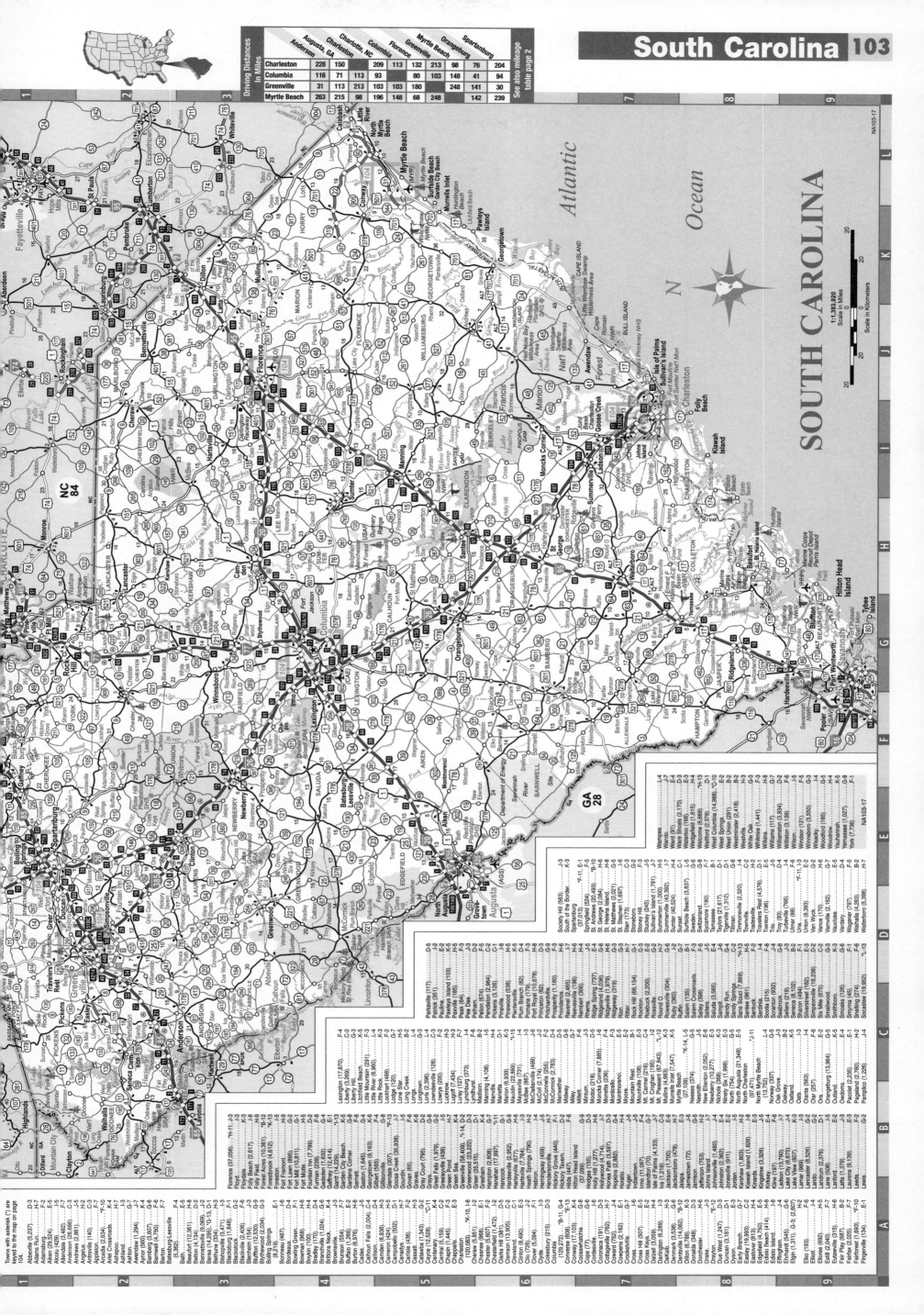

# South Carolina & South Dakota City and Area Maps

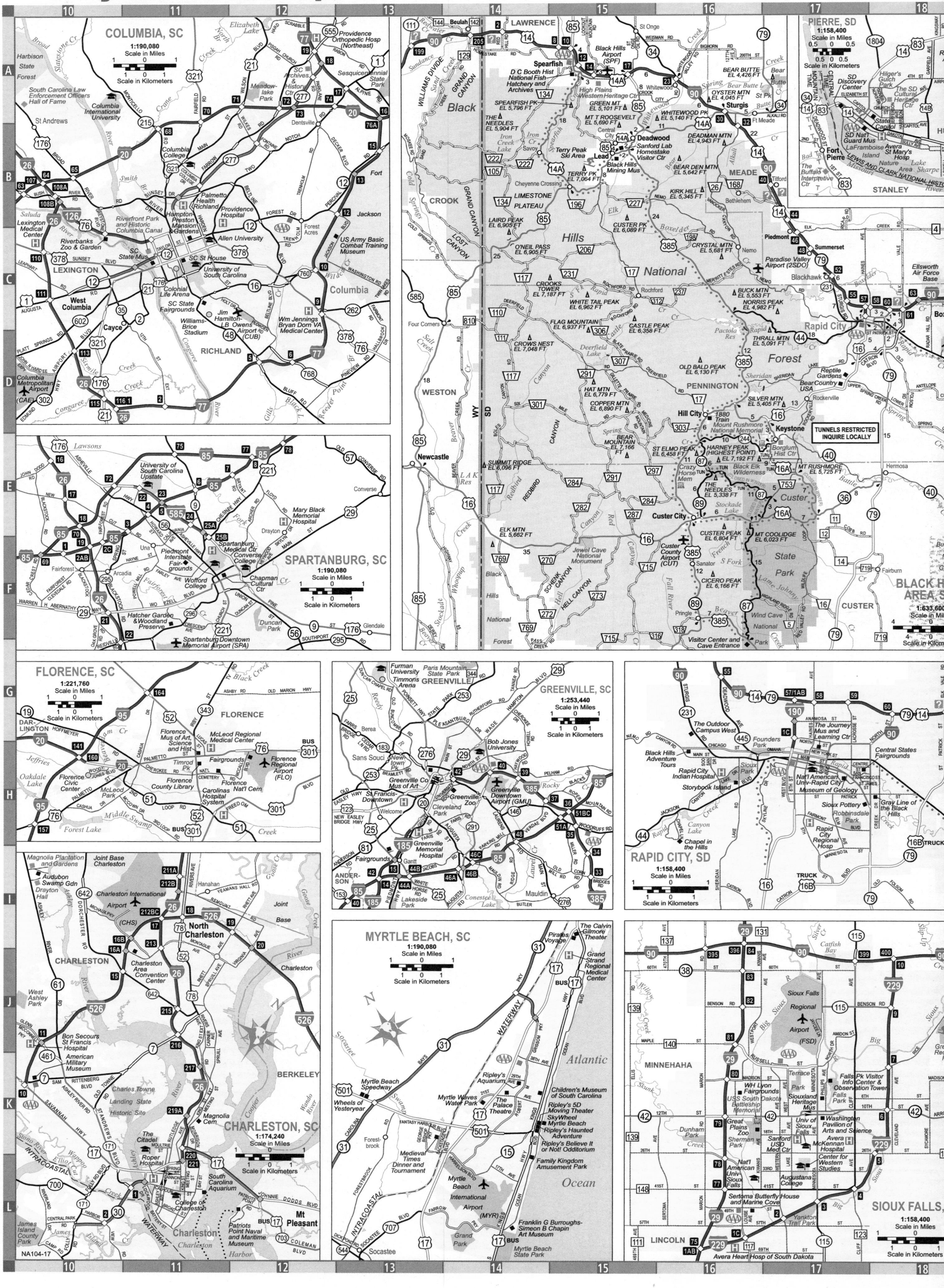

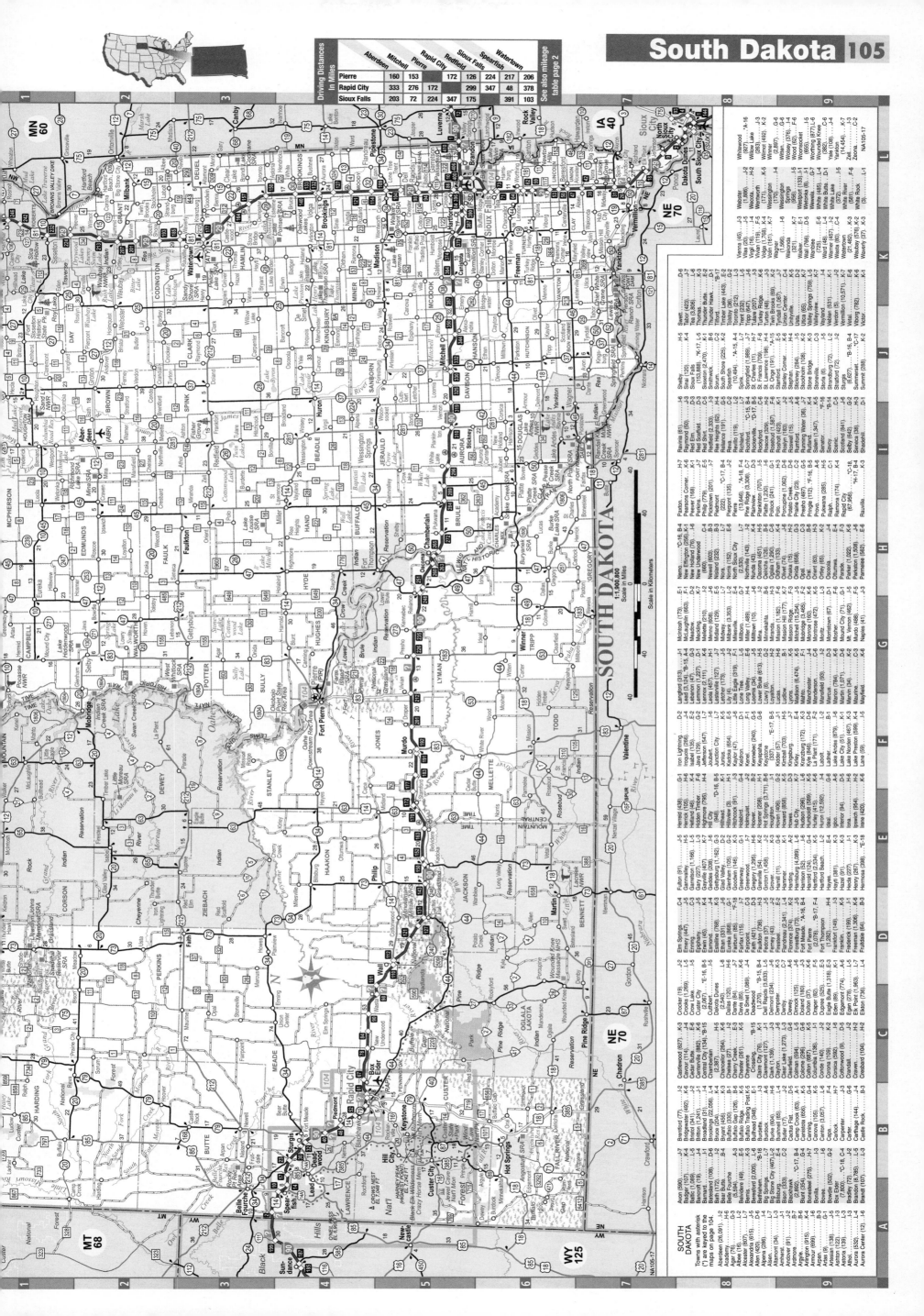

| | Aberdeen | Mitchell | Pierre | Rapid City | Redfield | Sioux Falls | Spearfish | Watertown |
|---|---|---|---|---|---|---|---|---|
| Pierre | 160 | 153 | | 172 | 126 | 224 | 217 | 206 |
| Rapid City | 333 | 276 | 172 | | 299 | 347 | 48 | 378 |
| Sioux Falls | 203 | 72 | 224 | 347 | 175 | | 391 | 103 |

Driving Distances In Miles

See also mileage table page 2

SOUTH DAKOTA

Towns with asterisk (*) are keyed to the maps on page 104.

NA105-17

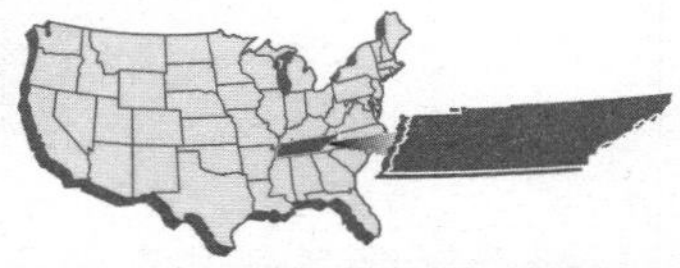

**Driving Distances In Miles**

| | Bristol | Chattanooga | Clarksville | Cleveland | Jackson | Johnson City | Kingsport | Knoxville | Memphis | Morristown | Murfreesboro | Nashville |
|---|---|---|---|---|---|---|---|---|---|---|---|---|
| Chattanooga | 222 | | 179 | 32 | 263 | 216 | 210 | 112 | 316 | 158 | 102 | 134 |
| Knoxville | 112 | 112 | 225 | 84 | 309 | 106 | 99 | | 391 | 48 | 175 | 179 |
| Memphis | 501 | 316 | 209 | 346 | 88 | 495 | 489 | 391 | | 437 | 245 | 212 |
| Nashville | 290 | 134 | 49 | 163 | 130 | 284 | 277 | 179 | 212 | 226 | 33 | |

## TENNESSEE

Acton...I-6
Adams (633)...E-9
Adamsville (2,207)...I-6
Aetna...G-8
Alamo (2,461)...G-2
Alexandria (966)...F-12
Algood (3,495)...F-11
Allardt (634)...E-15
Allens...G-4
Allons...E-13
Allred...E-14
Alpine...E-14
Altamont (1,045)...H-12
Alto...I-12
Anderson...F-10
Antioch...F-10
Apison (2,469)...I-10
Ardmore (1,213)...I-10
Arlington (11,517)...H-3
Arp...G-3
Arrington...G-10
Arthur...A-13, E-17
Ashland City (4,541)...E-9
Ashport...G-2
Athens (13,458)...H-15
Atoka (8,387)...H-2
Atwood (938)...F-5
Baileyton (431)...B-15
Bargerton...G-6
Barkertown...H-4
Bartlett (54,613)...J-4
Bath Springs...H-7
Baxter (1,365)...F-13
Bean Station (2,826)...A-14, E-18
Beardstown...G-7
Beech Bluff...G-5

Beechgrove...G-11
Beersheba Springs (477)...H-13
Belfast...H-10
Bell Buckle (500)...H-11
Belleville...I-7
Bells (2,437)...G-4
Belvidere...I-11
Benton (1,385)...I-15
Bethel Springs (718)...I-6
Bethpage (288)...E-11
Big Rock...D-8
Big Sandy (557)...F-7
Big Spring...H-15
Birchwood...H-14
Blaine (1,856)...F-17
Blanche...I-10
Blountville (3,074)...A-16
Bogota...F-3
Bolivar (5,417)...H-4
Boonshill...I-10
Boothspoint...F-3
Braden (282)...H-3
Bradford (1,048)...F-5
Bradyville...G-11
Brentwood (37,060)...F-10
Brewstertown...E-15
Brighton (2,735)...H-3
Brownsville (10,292)...G-4
Bruceton (1,478)...F-6
Brunswick...H-2
Brush Creek...F-12
Buchanan...E-6

Buena Vista...F-6
Buffalo...G-7
Buffalo Valley...F-12
Bulls Gap (738)...B-15
Bumpus Mills...D-7
Burlison (425)...G-3
Burns (1,468)...F-9
Butler...A-17
Bybee...B-15
Byrdstown (803)...E-14
Camden (3,582)...F-7
Carlisle...E-7
Caryville (2,297)...E-16
Castalian Springs (556)...E-11
Cedar Creek...H-9
Cedar Grove (314)...G-5
Cedar Hill...E-9
Celina (1,495)...E-13
Center...E-12
Centertown (243)...G-12
Centerville (3,644)...G-8
Central...F-4
Cerro Gordo...D-14
Chanute...D-14
Chapel Hill (1,445)...G-10
Chapmansboro...E-9
Charleston (651)...H-15
Charlotte (1,194)...E-9
Chattanooga (167,674)...I-14, L-14
Cherry...G-3
Chestnut Mound...F-12
Chewalla...I-5
Chic...F-3
Christiana...G-11
Church Hill (6,737)...A-16

Churchton...F-4
Clairfield...E-17
Clarkrange (575)...F-14
Clarksburg (393)...G-6
Clarksville (132,929)...E-9, K-11
Clayton...E-8
Cleveland (41,285)...I-15
Clifton (2,694)...H-7
Clifton Junction...H-7
Clinton (9,841)...F-16
Coalfield (2,463)...F-16
Coalmont (841)...H-13
Coble...G-8
Cokercreek...H-9
Coldwater...I-10
College Grove...G-10
Collierville (43,965)...I-3
Collinwood (982)...I-7
Columbia (34,681)...G-9
Como...F-5
Conasauga...I-15
Cookeville (30,435)...F-13
Cordova...H-3
Cornersville (1,194)...H-10
Corryton...F-17
Cosby...B-15
Cottage Grove (88)...E-6
Cottontown...E-10
Counce...I-6
Covington (9,038)...G-3
Cowan (1,737)...I-12

Crab Orchard (752)...G-15
Crockett Mills...G-4
Cross Plains (1,714)...E-10
Crossville (10,795)...F-14
Culleoka...H-9
Cumberland City (311)...E-8
Cumberland Furnace...E-8
Cummingsville...G-13
Cunningham...E-8
Cypress Inn...I-7
Dancyville...H-4
Dandridge (2,812)...B-14, F-18
Darden (399)...G-6
Daus...H-13
Dayton (7,191)...H-14
De Rossett...F-13
Deason...H-11
Decatur (1,598)...H-15
Decaturville (867)...H-7
Decherd (2,361)...I-12
Deerfield...H-8
Del Rio...C-15
Delano...I-15
Denmark...H-4
Dibrell...G-12
Dickson (14,538)...F-8
Dixon Springs...E-12
Doeville...A-17
Double Bridges...F-3
Dover (1,417)...E-7

Dowelltown (355)...F-12
Doyle (537)...G-13
Dresden (3,005)...E-5
Duck River...G-9
Dukedom...E-5
Dunlap (4,815)...H-13
Dyer (2,341)...F-4
Dyersburg (17,145)...F-3
Eads...I-3
Eagleville (604)...G-10
East Ridge (20,979)...L-14
Eastview (705)...I-5
Eaton...G-4
Edith...A-15
Eidson...A-15
Elbethel...H-11
Elizabethton (14,176)...A-17
Elk Valley...E-16
Elkton (578)...I-10
Elora...I-11
Englewood (1,532)...H-16
Enville (189)...H-6
Erin (1,324)...E-8
Erwin (6,097)...B-16
Estill Springs (2,055)...I-11
Ethridge (465)...H-9
Etowah (3,490)...H-15
Eva (293)...F-7
Evensville...H-14
Fairfield Glade (6,989)...F-15
Fairmount (2,825)...I-13

Fairview...B-15; (7,720)...F-9
Farner...I-16
Farragut (20,676)...G-17
Fayetteville (6,827)...I-10
Fincastle (1,618)...E-17
Finger (298)...H-5
Finley...F-3
Five Points...I-9
Flag Pond...B-16
Flat Creek...H-11
Flat Gap...A-15
Flat Woods...H-7
Fowlkes...F-3
Frankfort...F-13
Franklin (62,487)...G-10
Friendship (668)...F-4
Friendsville (913)...G-16
Frog Jump...F-4
Fulton...G-2
Gadsden (470)...G-4
Gainesboro (962)...E-13
Galen...E-12
Gallatin (30,278)...E-11
Gassaway...G-12
Gates (647)...G-3
Gatlinburg (3,944)...C-14, G-18
Germantown (38,844)...K-5
Gibson (396)...G-5
Gladeville...F-11
Gleason (1,445)...F-5
Glimp...G-2
Golddust...F-3

Goodlettsville (15,921)...E-10
Goodspring...I-9
Gordonsburg...H-8
Gordonsville...F-12
Gorman...E-10
Grand Junction (325)...I-4
Granville...F-12
Grassy Cove...G-14
Graysville (1,064)...H-14
Greenback (1,064)...G-16
Greenbrier (6,433)...E-10
Greeneville (15,062)...B-15
Greenfield (2,182)...F-5
Grimsley (1,167)...E-14
Gruetli-Laager (1,813)...H-13
Guys (466)...I-5
Habersham...E-16
Halls (2,255)...G-3
Hampshire...H-9
Hampton...B-17
Harms...I-10
Harmony...I-10
Harriman (6,350)...F-15
Harrogate (4,389)...A-13, D-18
Hartford...C-14
Hartsville (7,870)...E-11
Haysville...D-12
Heiskell...F-16
Helenwood (865)...E-16
Heloise...F-3

Henderson (6,309)...H-5
Hendersonville (51,372)...E-10
Henning (945)...G-3
Henry (464)...F-6
Hermitage...K-9
Hermitage Springs...E-12
Hickory Valley (99)...I-4
Highland...E-12, I-17
Hillham...E-13
Hillsboro (450)...H-12
Hixson...I-14
Hohenwald (3,757)...H-8
Holladay...G-7
Hoodoo...G-11
Hopewell (1,874)...I-15
Hornbeak (424)...E-4
Hornsby (303)...I-5
Houston...I-7
Howell...I-10
Humboldt (8,452)...G-5
Huntingdon (3,985)...F-6
Huntland (872)...I-11
Huntsville (1,248)...E-15
Huron...H-6
Hurricane Mills...F-7
India...I-10
Indian Mound...E-8
Iron City (328)...I-8
Isham...D-16

Jacksboro...E-16
Jacks Creek...H-6
Jackson (65,211)...G-5
Jamestown (1,959)...E-14
Jasper (3,279)...I-13
Jefferson City (8,047)...B-14, F-17
Jellico (2,355)...E-16
Johnson City (63,152)...G-16
Johnsonville...F-8
Johnsons Grove...G-4
Jones Mill...E-14
Jonesborough (5,051)...B-16
Joppa...B-13
Kelso...I-11
Kenton (1,281)...F-4
Kimball (1,395)...I-13
Kingsport (48,205)...A-16
Kingston (5,934)...G-15
Kingston Springs (2,756)...F-9
Knoxville (178,874)...F-17, L-17
Kodak...B-13, C-18
Kyles Ford...A-15
La Follette (7,456)...E-16
La Grange (133)...I-4
La Vergne (32,588)...F-10
Laconia...I-4
Lafayette (4,474)...E-12
Lake City (1,781)...E-16
Lancing...F-15
Lascassas...G-11
Latham...E-5
Laurel Bloomery...A-18

Lawrenceburg (10,428)...I-8
Leach...F-6
Leapwood...H-6
Lebanon (26,190)...F-11
Lenoir City (8,642)...G-16
Lewisburg (11,100)...H-10
Lexie Crossroads...I-4
Lexington (7,652)...G-6
Liberty (310)...F-11
Limestone...B-16
Lincoln...I-11
Linden (908)...G-7
Littleton...G-12
Livingston (4,058)...E-13
Lobelville (897)...G-8
Lone Oak (1,206)...I-13
Loretto (1,714)...I-8
Loudon (5,381)...G-16
Louisville (2,439)...G-17
Luttrell (1,074)...F-17
Lutts...I-7
Lynchburg (361)...I-11
Lynnville (287)...I-9
Macedonia...F-6
Macon...I-3
Maddox...I-5
Madison...K-8
Madisonville (4,577)...H-16
Mohawk...B-15
Monroe...E-14

Martin (11,473)...E-5
Maryville (27,465)...G-17
Mason (1,609)...H-3
Mason Hall...F-4
Maury City (674)...G-4
Mayland...F-14
Maynardville (2,413)...F-17
McBurg...I-9
McConnell...E-4
McEwen (1,750)...F-8
McKenzie (5,310)...F-6
McLemoresville (352)...F-5
McMinnville (13,605)...G-12
Meadow View...A-16
Medina (3,479)...G-5
Medon (178)...H-5
Melvine...H-14
Memphis (646,889)...I-2, K-3
Michie (591)...I-5
Middleburg...I-4
Middleton (706)...I-5
Midtown (1,360)...G-15
Midway...F-16
Milan (7,851)...F-5
Milledgeville (255)...H-6
Millington (10,176)...H-3
Milton...G-11
Minor Hill (537)...I-9
Mitchellville (189)...D-10
Manchester (10,102)...H-12

Monteagle (1,192)...I-12
Monterey (2,850)...F-14
Mooresburg...A-14
Morris Chapel...H-6
Morrison (694)...H-12
Morristown (29,137)...B-14, F-18
Moscow (556)...I-3
Mosheim (2,362)...B-15
Moss...E-13
Mountain City (2,531)...A-18
Mt. Airy...H-13
Mt. Juliet (23,671)...F-11
Mt. Pleasant (4,561)...H-9
Mulberry...I-11
Munford (5,927)...H-2
Murfreesboro (108,755)...G-11

Nashville (601,222)...F-10, K-7
Netherland...E-13
New Johnsonville (1,951)...F-7
New Market (1,334)...B-13, F-18
New River...E-15
New Tazewell (3,037)...A-13, E-18
Newbern (3,313)...F-4
Newport (6,945)...C-14
Niota (719)...H-15
Nolensville (5,861)...F-10
Norene...E-14

Normandy (141)...I-11
Norris (1,491)...F-16
North Springs
Nunnelly
Oak Hill
Oak Ridge (29,330)
Oakdale (212)
Oakland (6,623)
Obion (1,119)
Ocoee
Old Hickory
Oldfort
Olivehill
Oliver Springs (3,355)
Oneida (3,752)
Only
Ooltewah (687)
Orlinda (859)
Orysa
Ozone
Pailo
Pall Mall
Palmer (672)
Palmersville
Palmyra
Paris (10,156)
Parker Crossroads
Parrottsville
Parsons (2,373)
Peakland
Pelham (403)
Pennine
Perryville
Peters Landing
Petersburg (549)

---

# TENNESSEE

Scale 1:1,267,200
Scale in Miles
Scale in Kilometers

## MEMPHIS
Scale 1:253,440
Scale in Miles
Scale in Kilometers

## NASHVILLE
Scale 1:221,760
Scale in Miles
Scale in Kilometers

1 TriStar Centennial Med Ctr
2 Upper Room Chapel and Christian Art Museum
3 Vanderbilt University
4 Adventure Science Center
5 Country Music Hall of Fame and Museum
6 Johnny Cash Museum
7 State Capitol
8 Ryman Auditorium

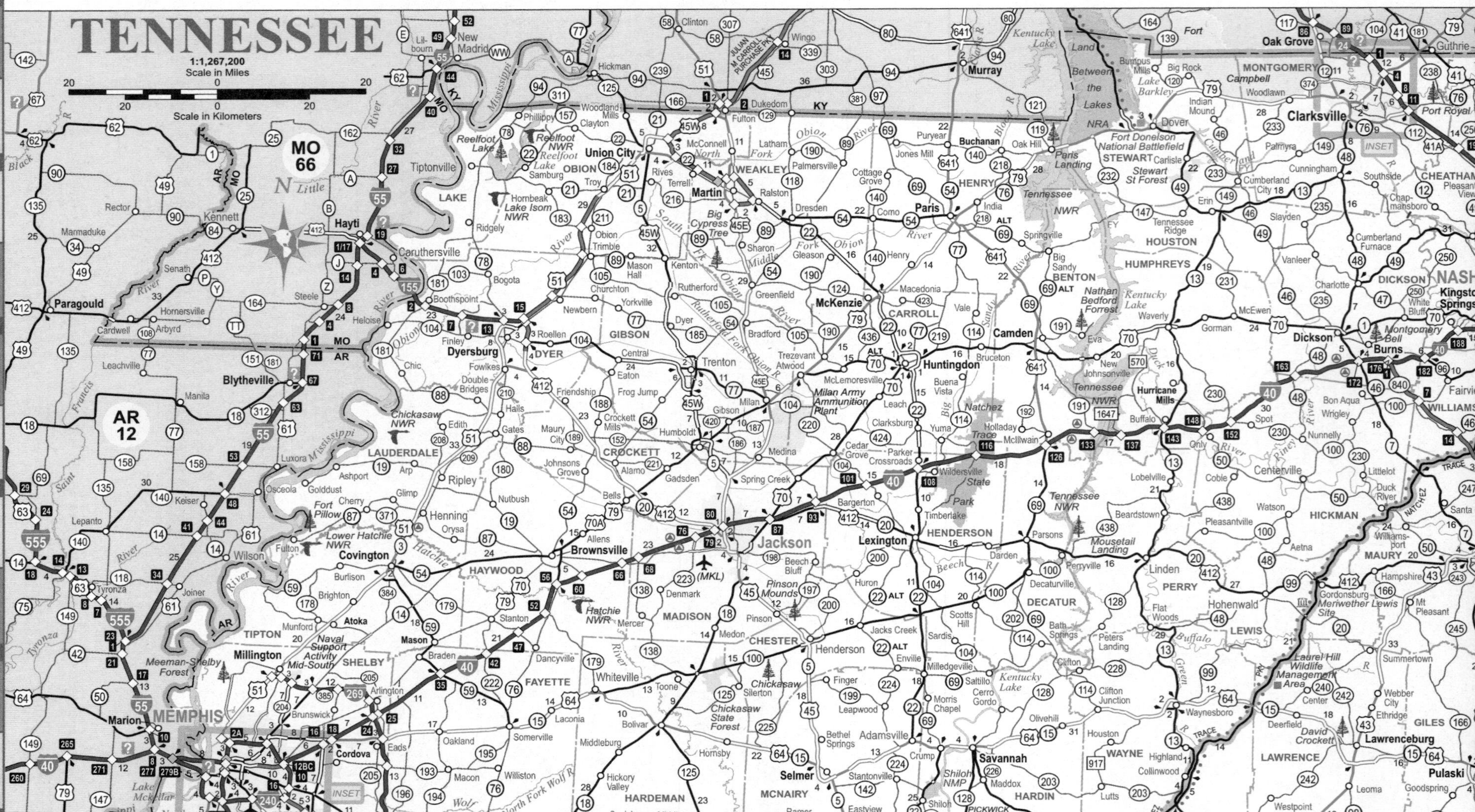

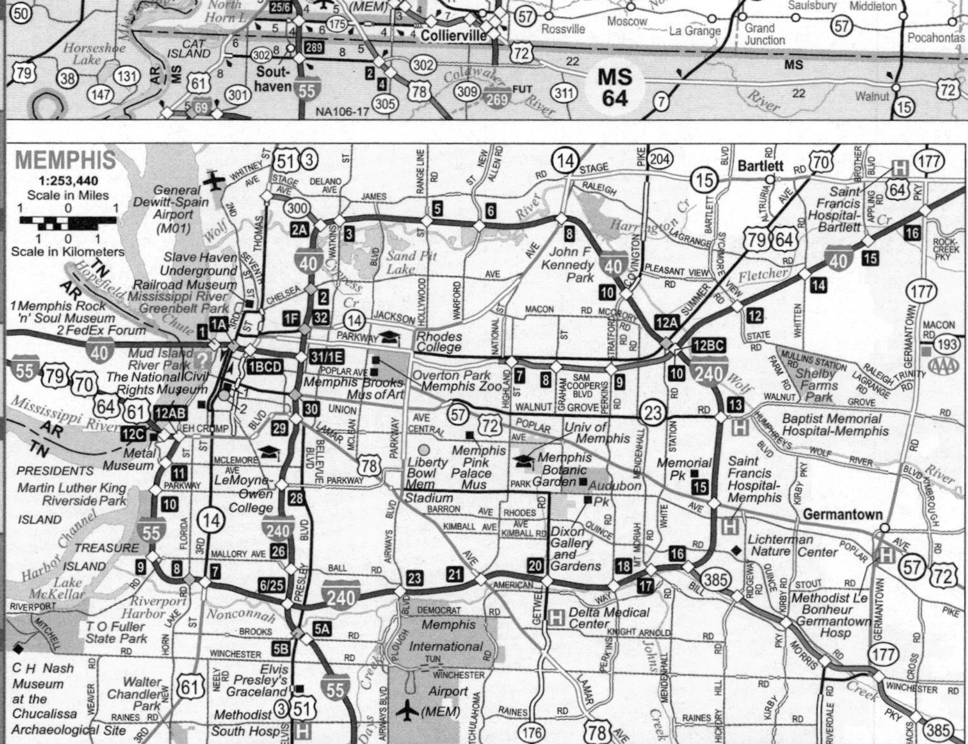

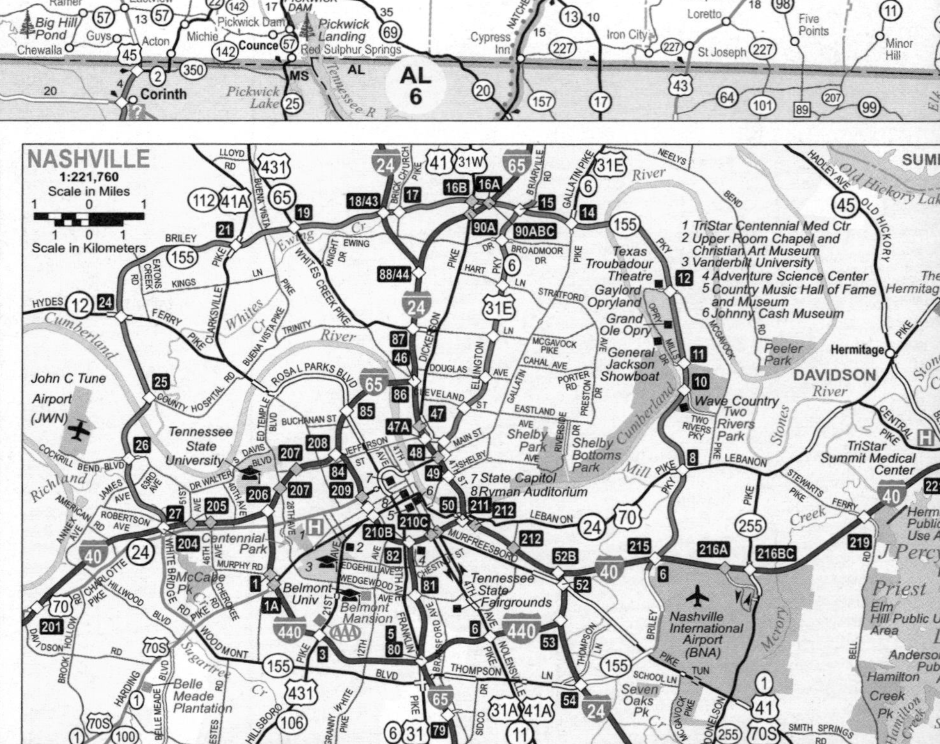

LEGEND

- Interstate Highway
- Controlled Access Hwy
- Controlled Access Hwy Toll
- Wildlife Refuge
- Nat'l/State Park
- National Forest

NA106-17

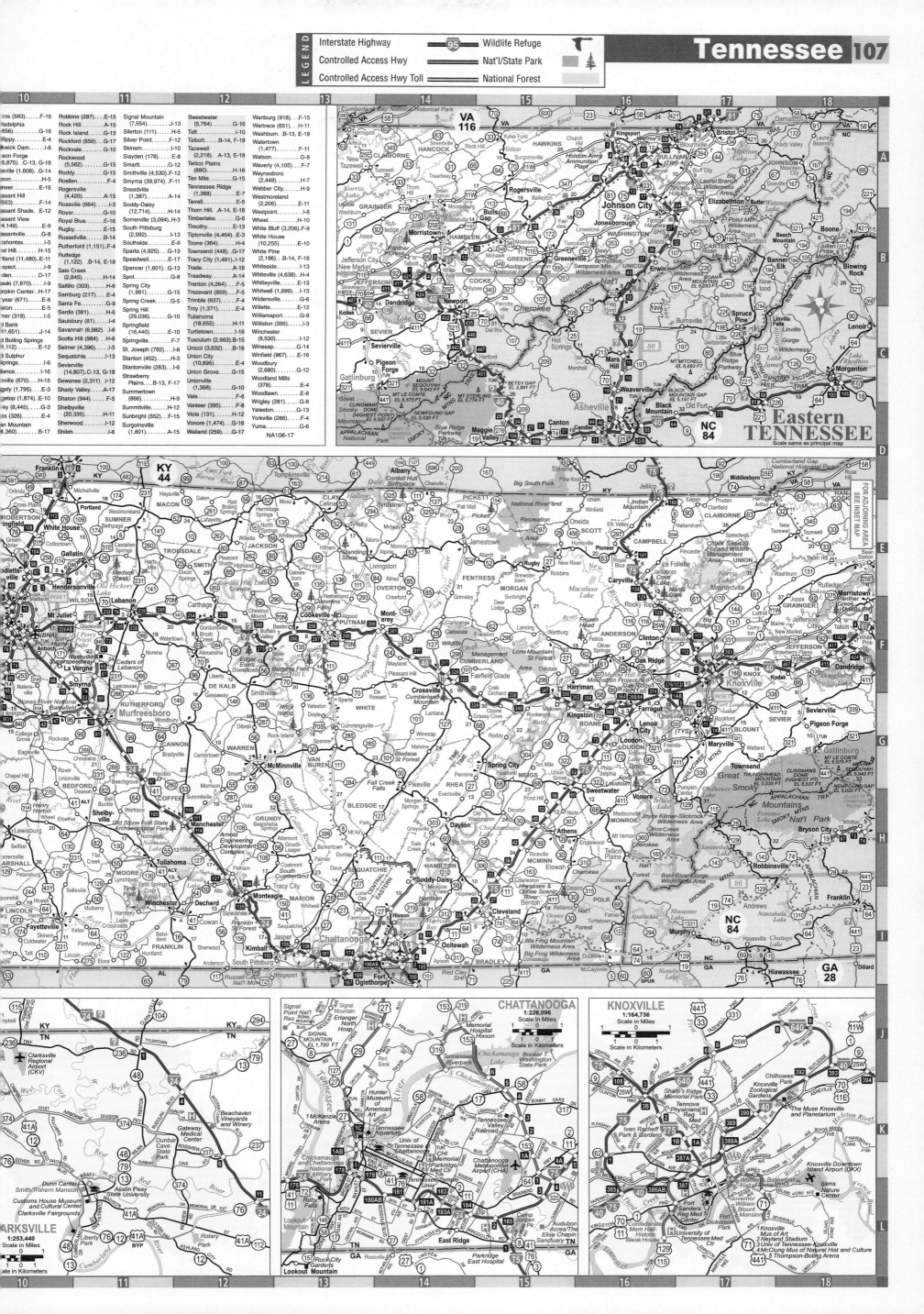

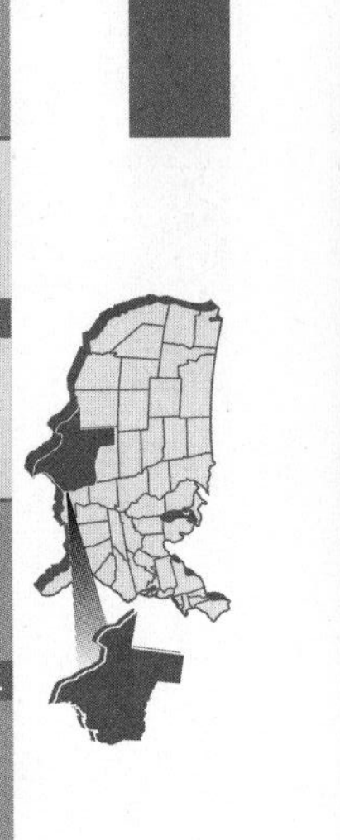

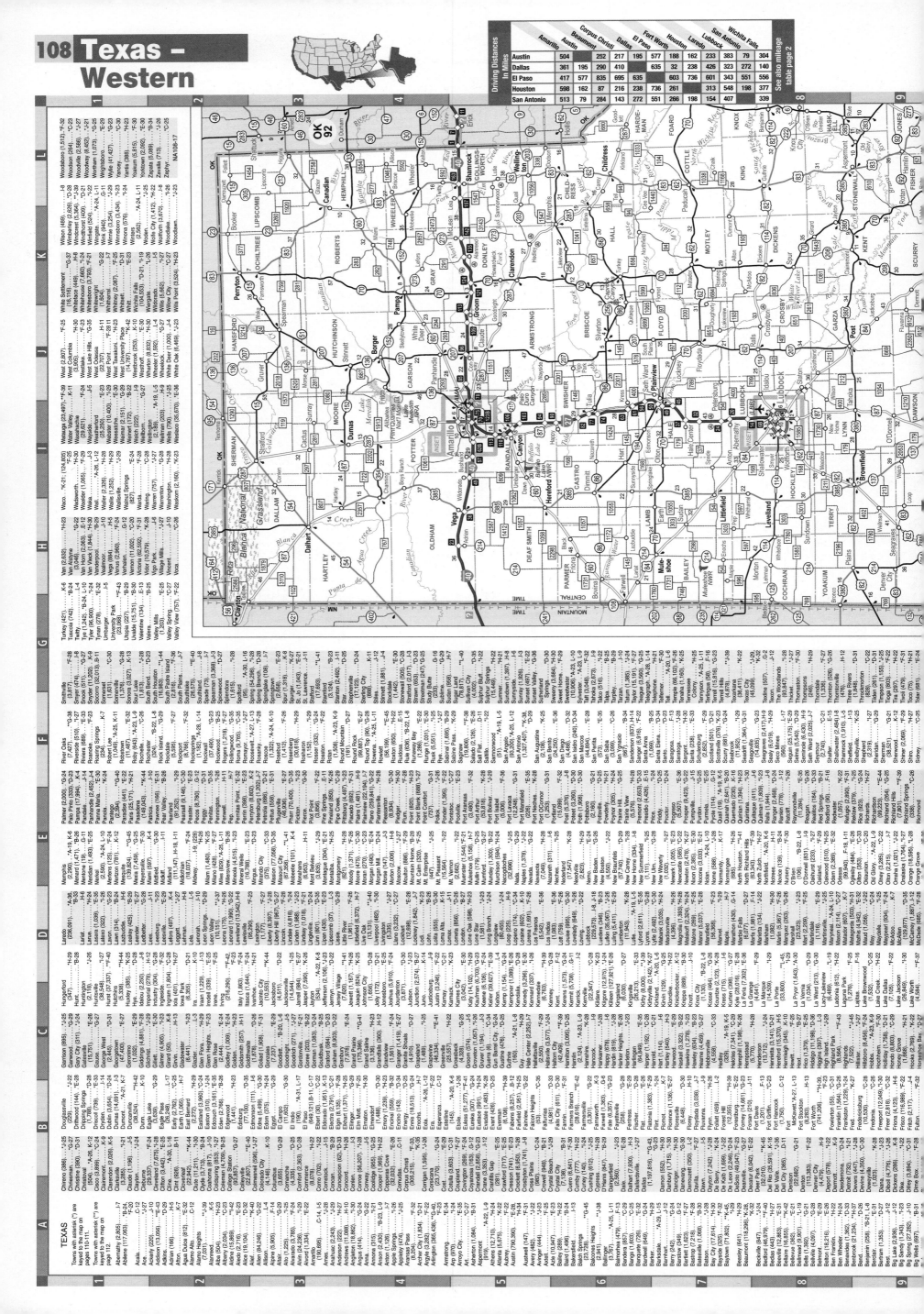

| Driving Distances in Miles | Amarillo | Austin | Beaumont | Corpus Christi | Dallas | El Paso | Fort Worth | Houston | Laredo | Lubbock | San Antonio | Wichita Falls |
|---|---|---|---|---|---|---|---|---|---|---|---|---|
| Austin | 504 | | 252 | 217 | 195 | 577 | 188 | 162 | 233 | 383 | 79 | 304 |
| Dallas | 361 | 195 | 290 | 410 | | 635 | 32 | 238 | 426 | 323 | 272 | 140 |
| El Paso | 417 | 577 | 835 | 695 | 635 | | 603 | 736 | 601 | 343 | 551 | 556 |
| Houston | 598 | 162 | 87 | 216 | 238 | 736 | 261 | | 313 | 548 | 198 | 377 |
| San Antonio | 513 | 79 | 284 | 143 | 272 | 551 | 266 | 198 | 154 | 407 | | 339 |

See also mileage table page 2

## TEXAS

Towns with asterisk (*) are keyed to the map on pages 110-111.

Towns with asterisk (**) are keyed to the map on page 112.



NA108-17

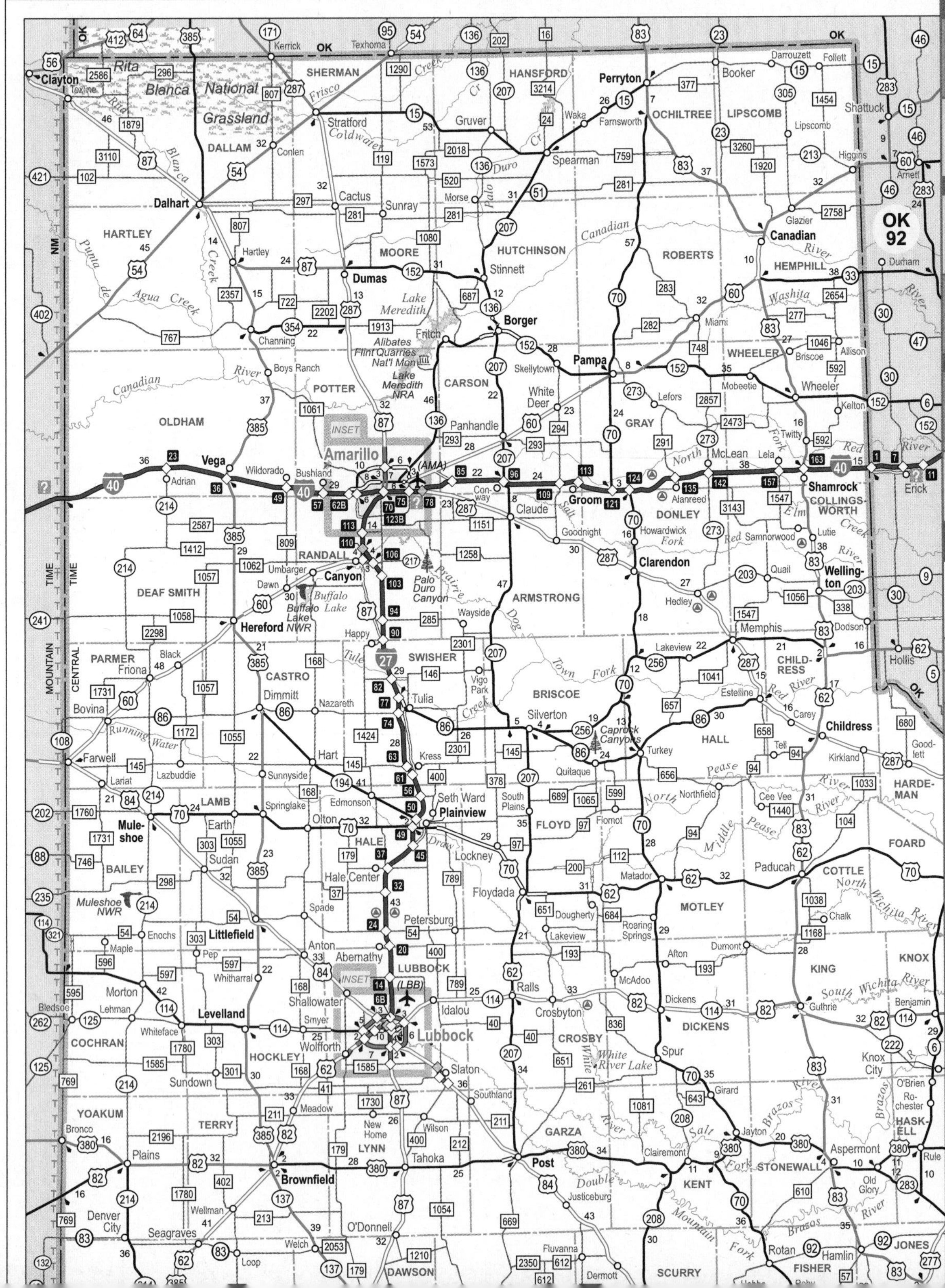

| LEGEND | | |
|---|---|---|
| Interstate Highway | 95 | Wildlife Refuge |
| Controlled Access Hwy | | Nat'l/State Park |
| Controlled Access Hwy Toll | | National Forest |

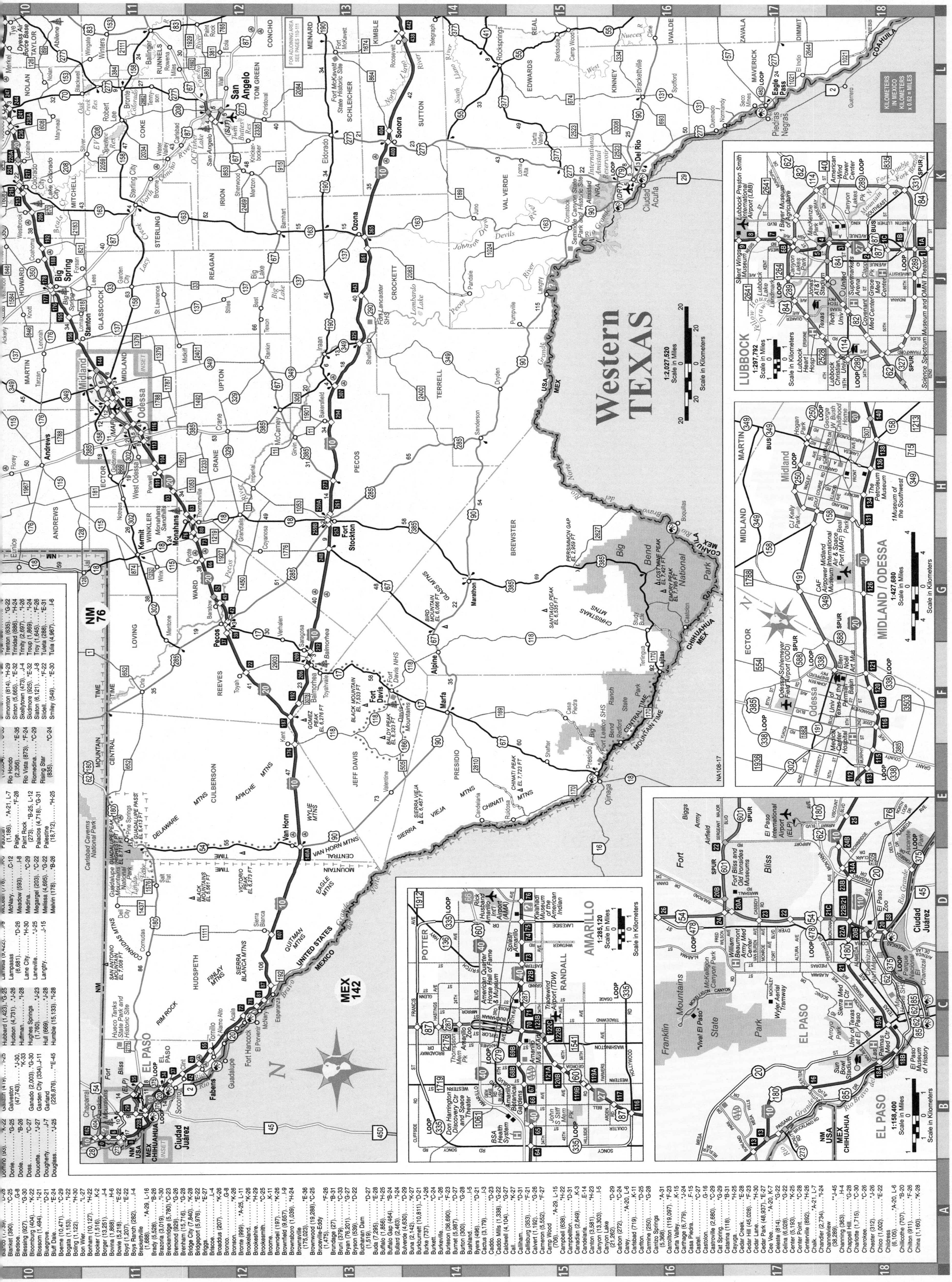

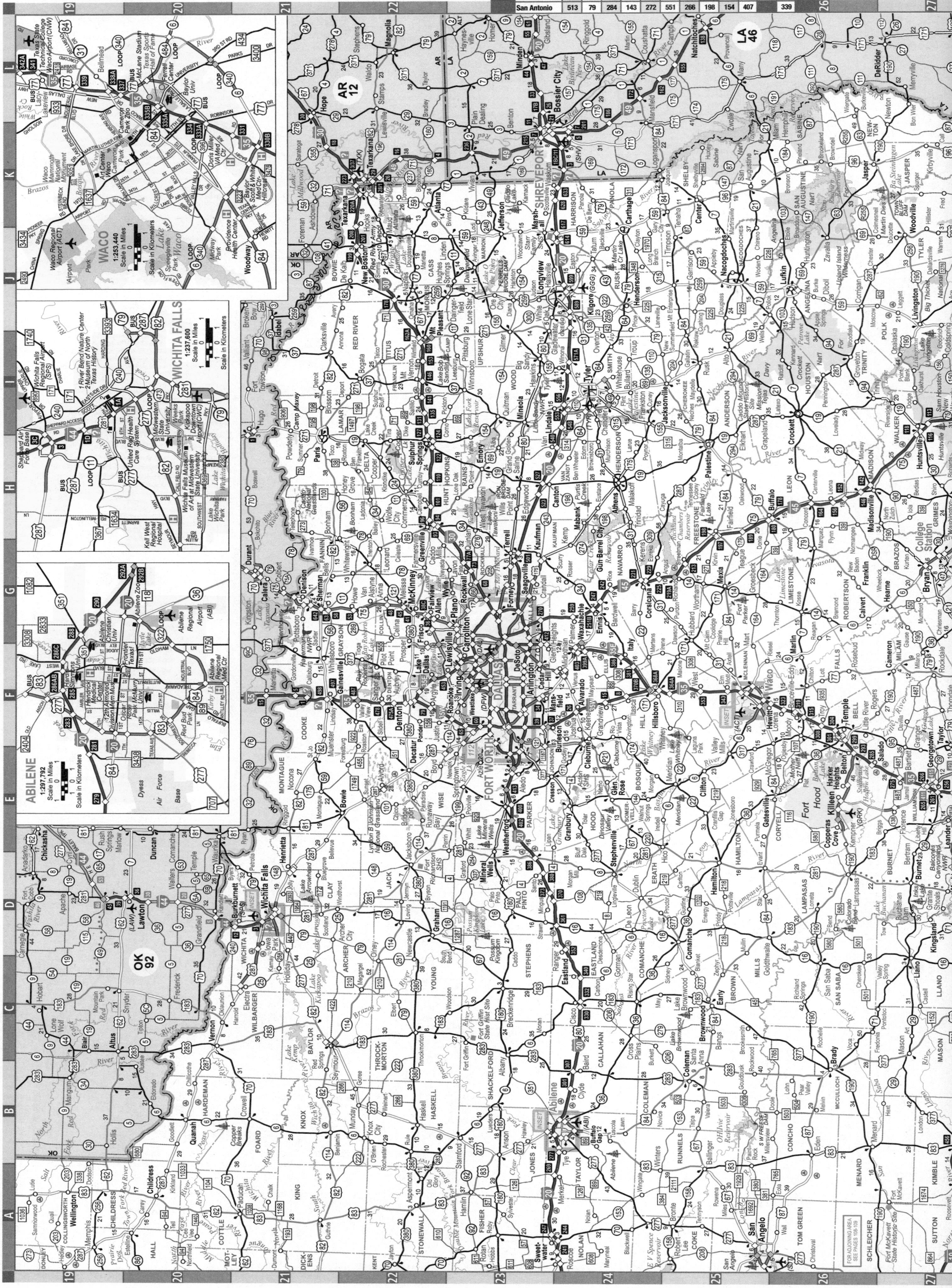

## WACO

1:253,440
Scale in Miles
Scale in Kilometers

## WICHITA FALLS

1:237,600
Scale in Miles
Scale in Kilometers
1 River Bend Nature Center
2 Museum of North Texas History

## ABILENE

1:297,792
Scale in Miles
Scale in Kilometers

LEGEND

| | | | |
|---|---|---|---|
| Interstate Highway | 95 | Wildlife Refuge | |
| Controlled Access Hwy | | Nat'l/State Park | |
| Controlled Access Hwy Toll | | National Forest | |

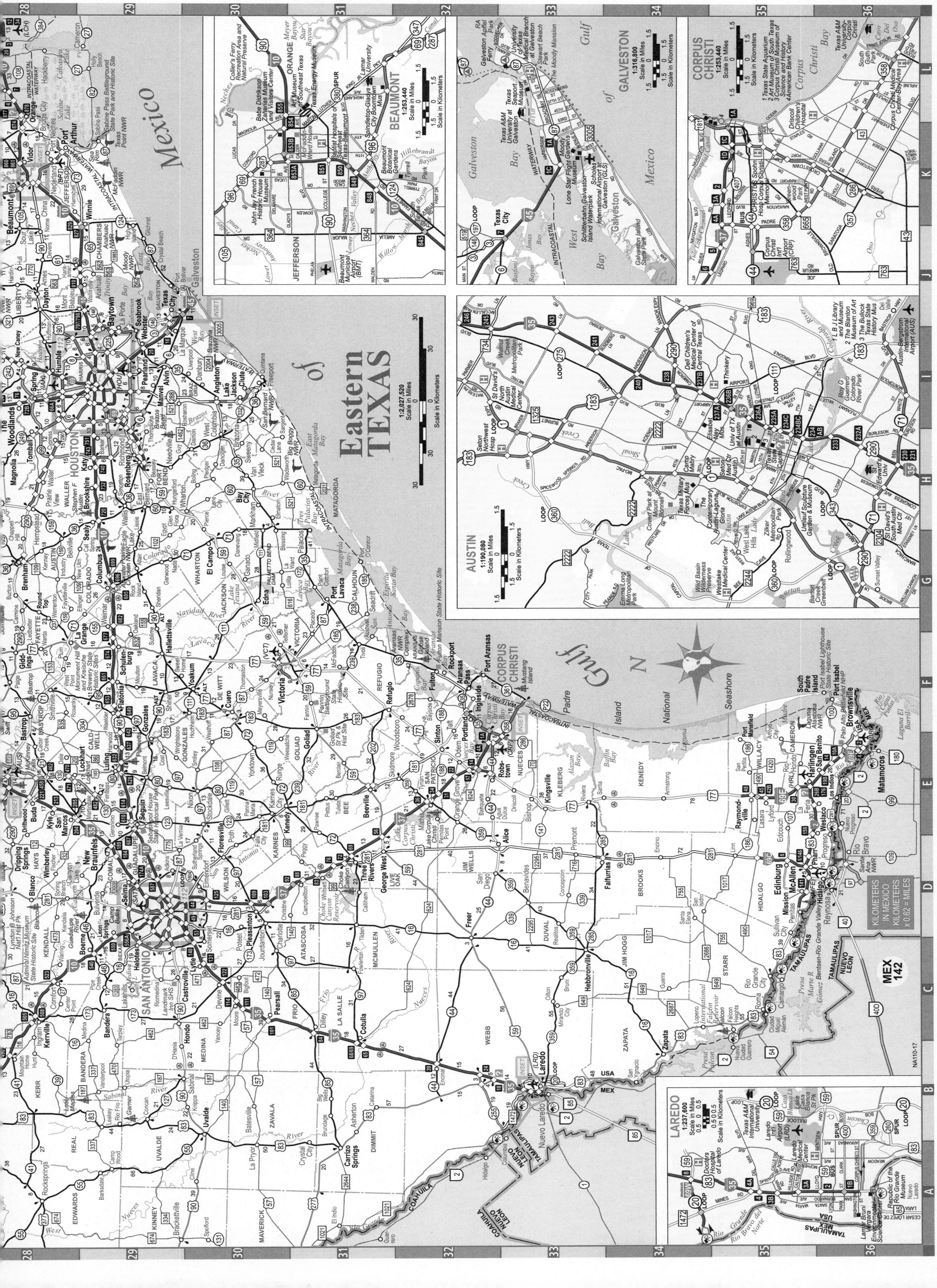

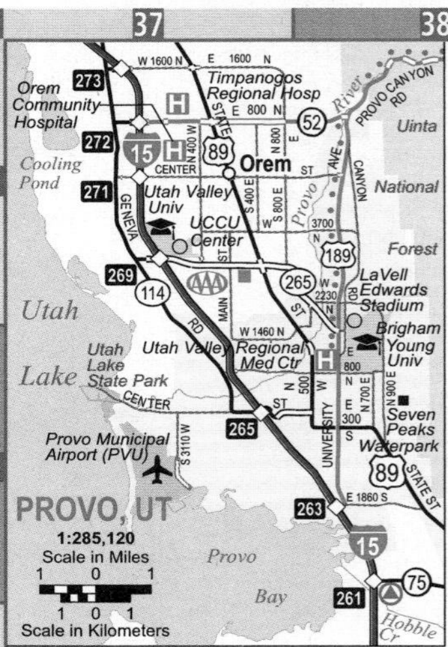

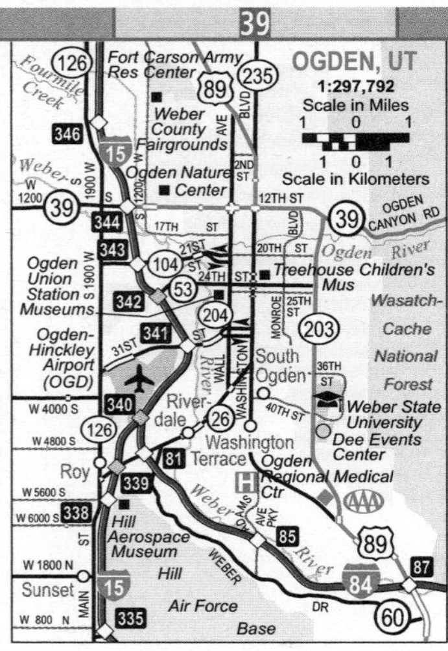

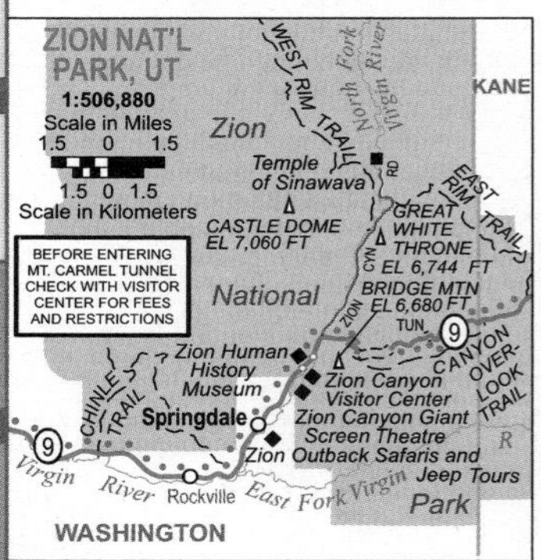

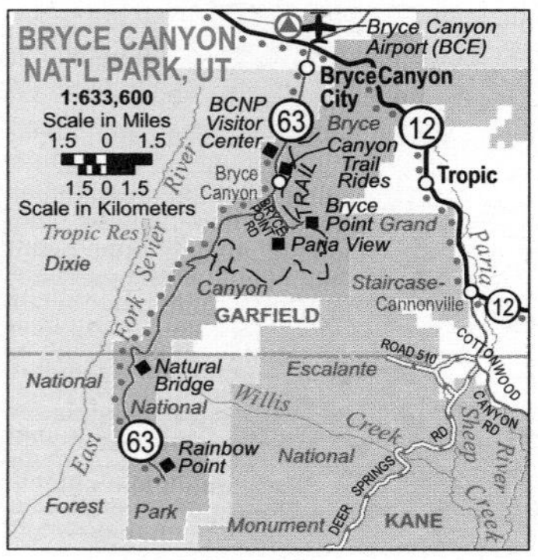

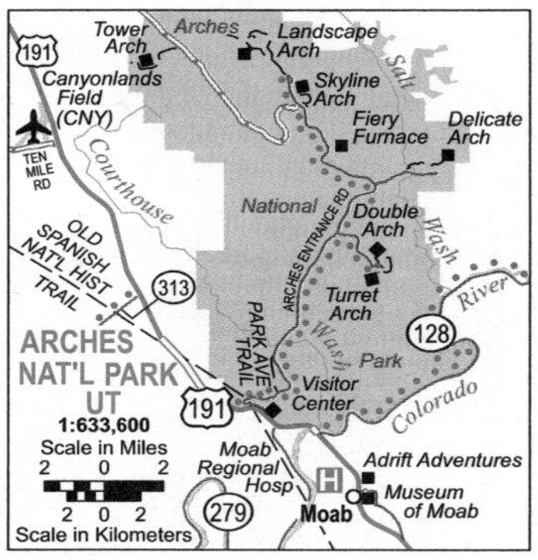

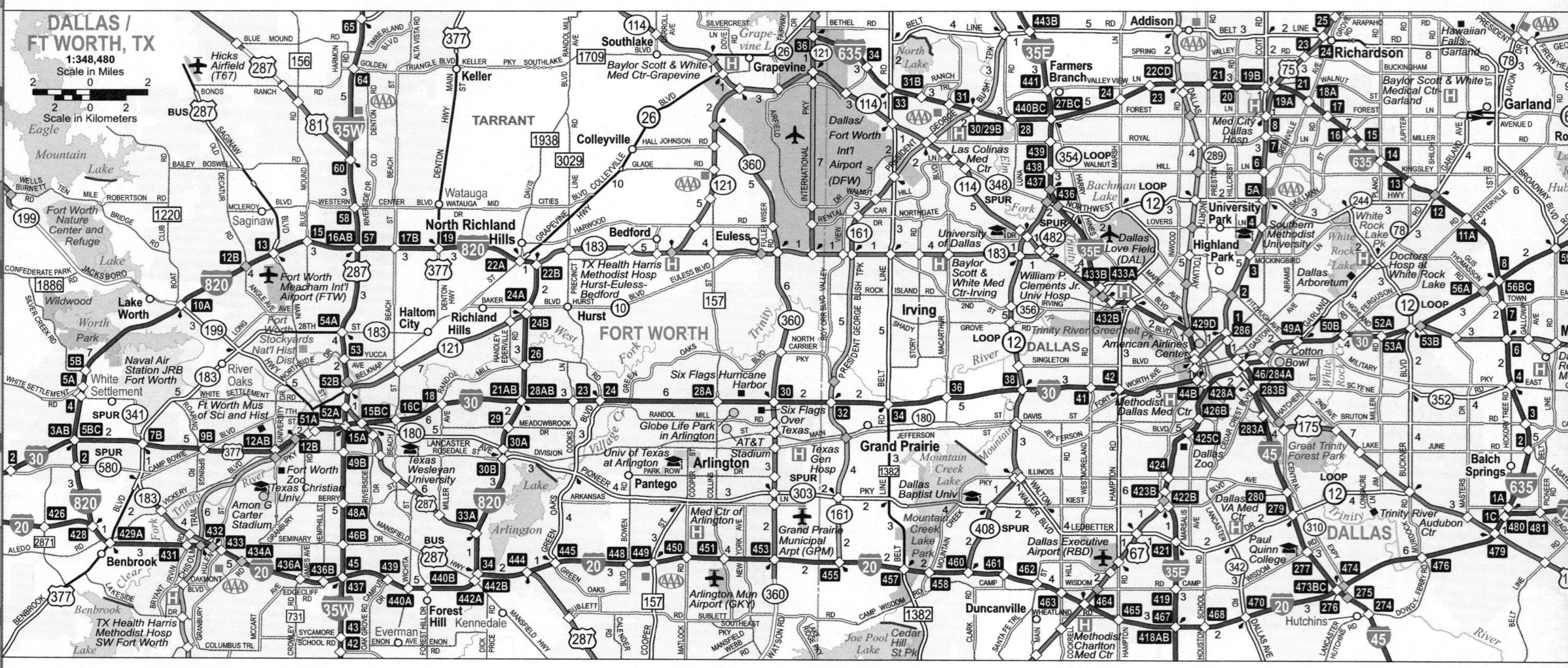

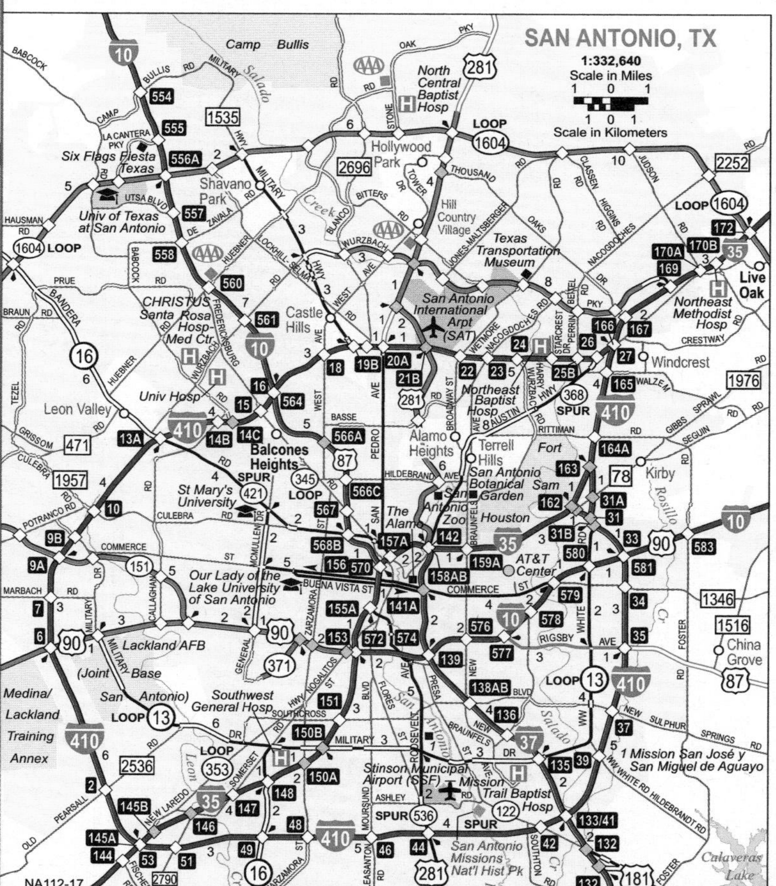

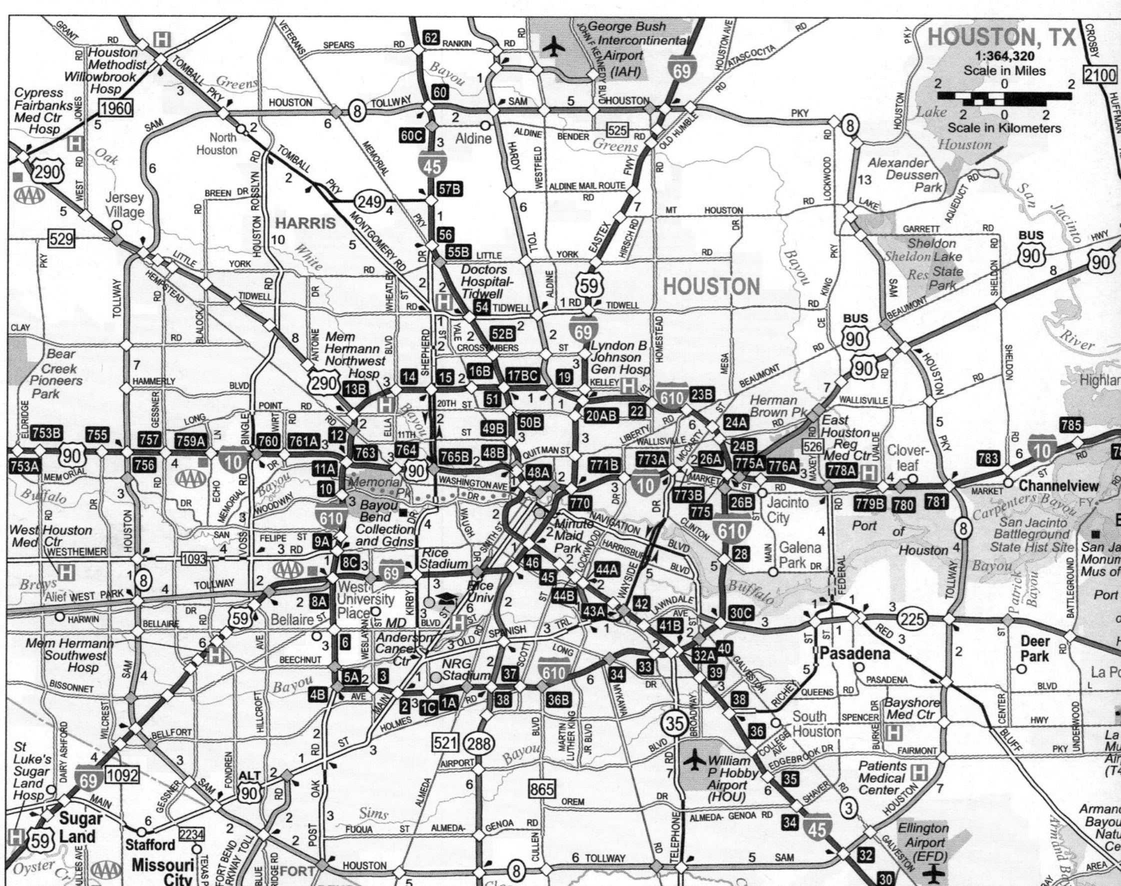

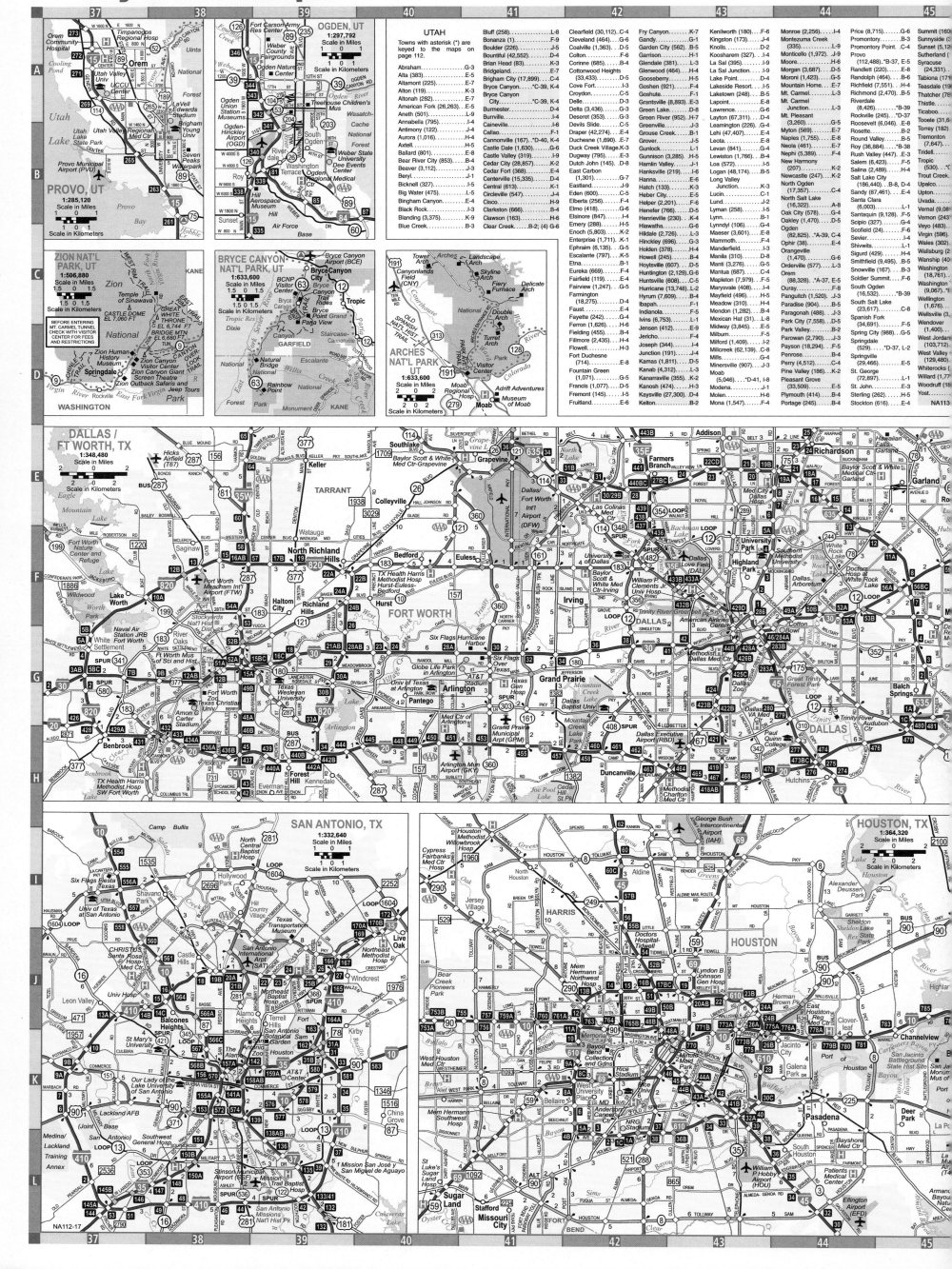

# UTAH

1:1,774,080
Scale in Miles

Scale in Kilometers

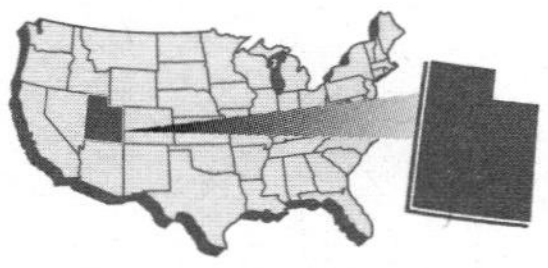

| Driving Distances in Miles | Monticello | Ogden | Provo | Salina | Salt Lake City | St George | Vernal | Wendover |
|---|---|---|---|---|---|---|---|---|
| Ogden | 323 | | 80 | 174 | 38 | 337 | 204 | 155 |
| Provo | 245 | 80 | | 97 | 44 | 259 | 154 | 163 |
| Salt Lake City | 288 | 38 | 44 | 139 | | 300 | 171 | 121 |

See also mileage table page 2

INQUIRE LOCALLY FOR CURRENT
CONDITIONS BEFORE DRIVING
ON UNIMPROVED ROADS
SHOWN ON THIS MAP

NA113-17

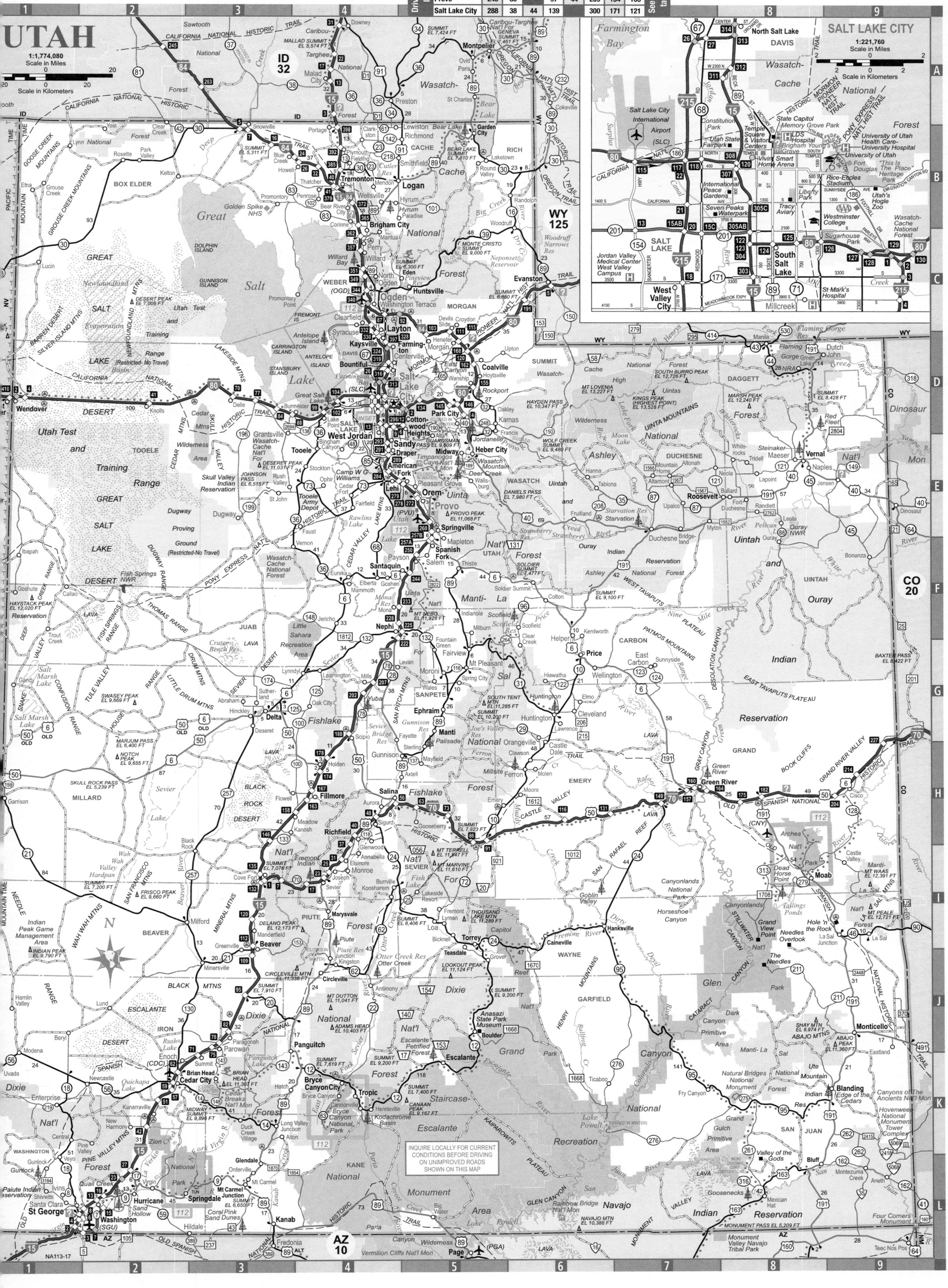

| Driving Distances In Miles | Bennington | Brattleboro | Burlington | Montpelier | Newport | Rutland | St. Johnsbury | White River Junction |
|---|---|---|---|---|---|---|---|---|
| Burlington | 122 | 152 | | 39 | 81 | 67 | 76 | 91 |
| Montpelier | 122 | 116 | 39 | | 62 | 67 | 36 | 55 |
| Rutland | 55 | 74 | 67 | 67 | 144 | | 105 | 45 |

See also mileage table page 2

VERMONT

NA114-17

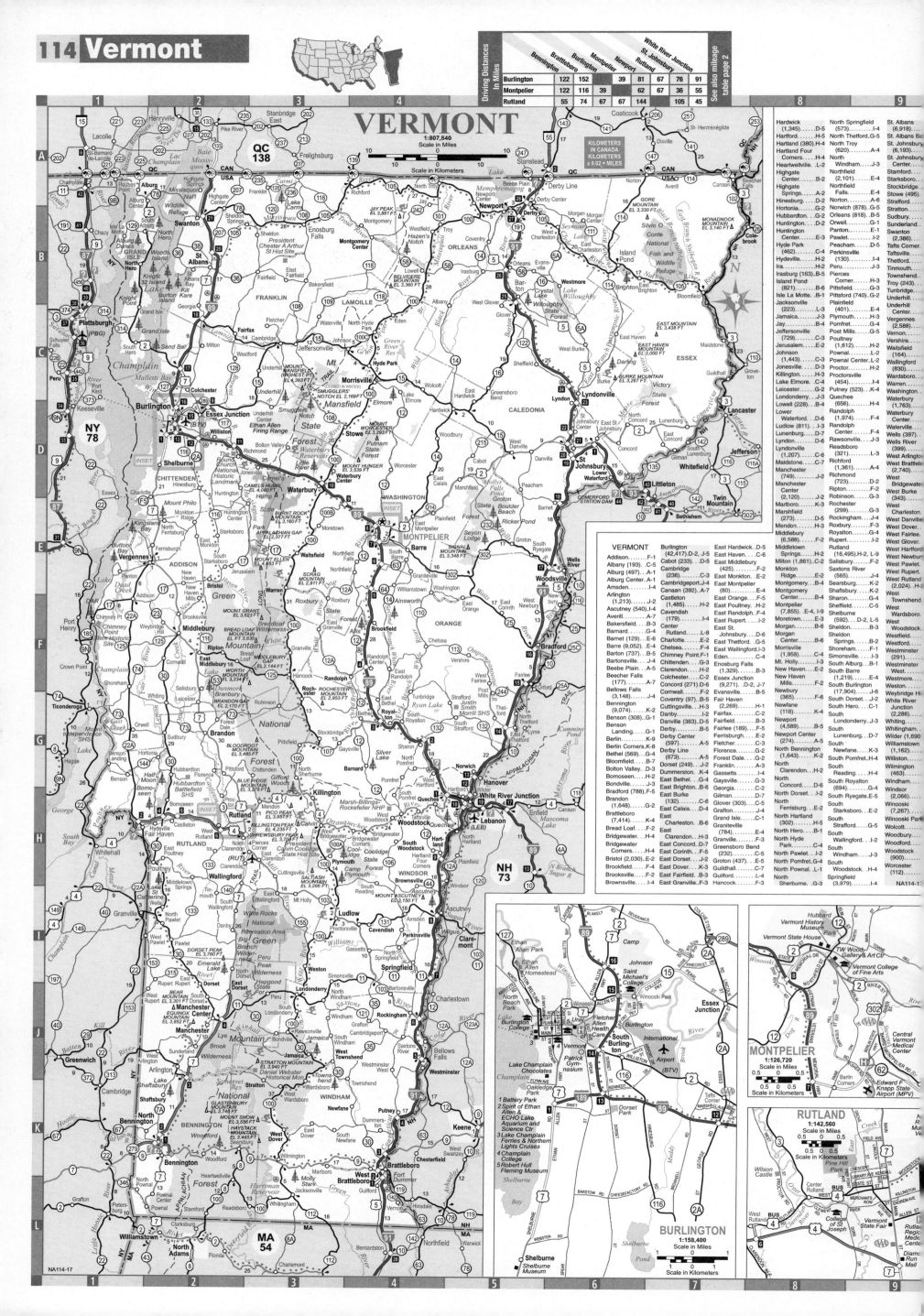

ROANOKE
1:221,760
Scale in Miles
Scale in Kilometers
VIRGINIA'S HISTORIC TRIANGLE
1:269,280
Scale in Miles
Scale in Kilometers
1 Governor's Palace
2 The Original Ghosts of Williamsburg Candlelight Tour
3 The DeWitt Wallace Decorative Arts Museum
4 College of William & Mary
RICHMOND / PETERSBURG AREA
1:269,280
Scale in Miles
Scale in Kilometers
SEE INSET
1 Virginia Mus of Fine Arts
2 Virginia Historical Society
3 Children's Mus of Richmond
DOWNTOWN RICHMOND
1:38,016
Scale in Miles
Scale in Kilometers
1 The White House of the Confederacy
2 The Museum of the Confederacy
6 Virginia Air & Space Center
7 Hampton University
8 Hampton VA Medical Center
Chesapeake
Bay
Atlantic
Ocean
HAMPTON ROADS AREA
1:253,440
Scale in Miles
Scale in Kilometers
DOWNTOWN NORFOLK
1:38,016
Scale in Miles
Scale in Kilometers
1 St Paul's Episcopal Church
2 US District Court
NORFOLK
VIRGINIA BEACH
Portsmouth
Chesapeake
Newport News
Hampton
Williamsburg
Yorktown
Petersburg
Hopewell
Colonial Heights
Chester
Chesterfield
Midlothian
Mechanicsville
Salem
Roanoke
Vinton
Cave Spring
19
20
21
22
23
24
25
26
27
A
B
C
D
E
F
G
H
I
J
K
L

| Driving Distances In Miles | Bristol | Charlottesville | Danville | Lexington | Lynchburg | Norfolk | Petersburg | Richmond | Roanoke | Strasburg | Washington, DC | Williamsburg |
|---|---|---|---|---|---|---|---|---|---|---|---|---|
| Bristol | | 256 | 192 | 190 | 203 | 416 | 315 | 325 | 149 | 296 | 377 | 375 |
| Norfolk | 416 | 164 | 195 | 229 | 192 | | 78 | 94 | 242 | 224 | 193 | 48 |
| Richmond | 325 | 70 | 146 | 137 | 114 | 94 | 23 | | 164 | 137 | 107 | 52 |
| Roanoke | 149 | 120 | 86 | 52 | 54 | 242 | 167 | 164 | | 160 | 241 | 239 |
| Washington, DC | 377 | 117 | 248 | 190 | 180 | 193 | 130 | 107 | 241 | 80 | | 151 |

See also mileage table page 2

VIRGINIA

Towns with asterisk (*) are keyed to the maps on page 115.

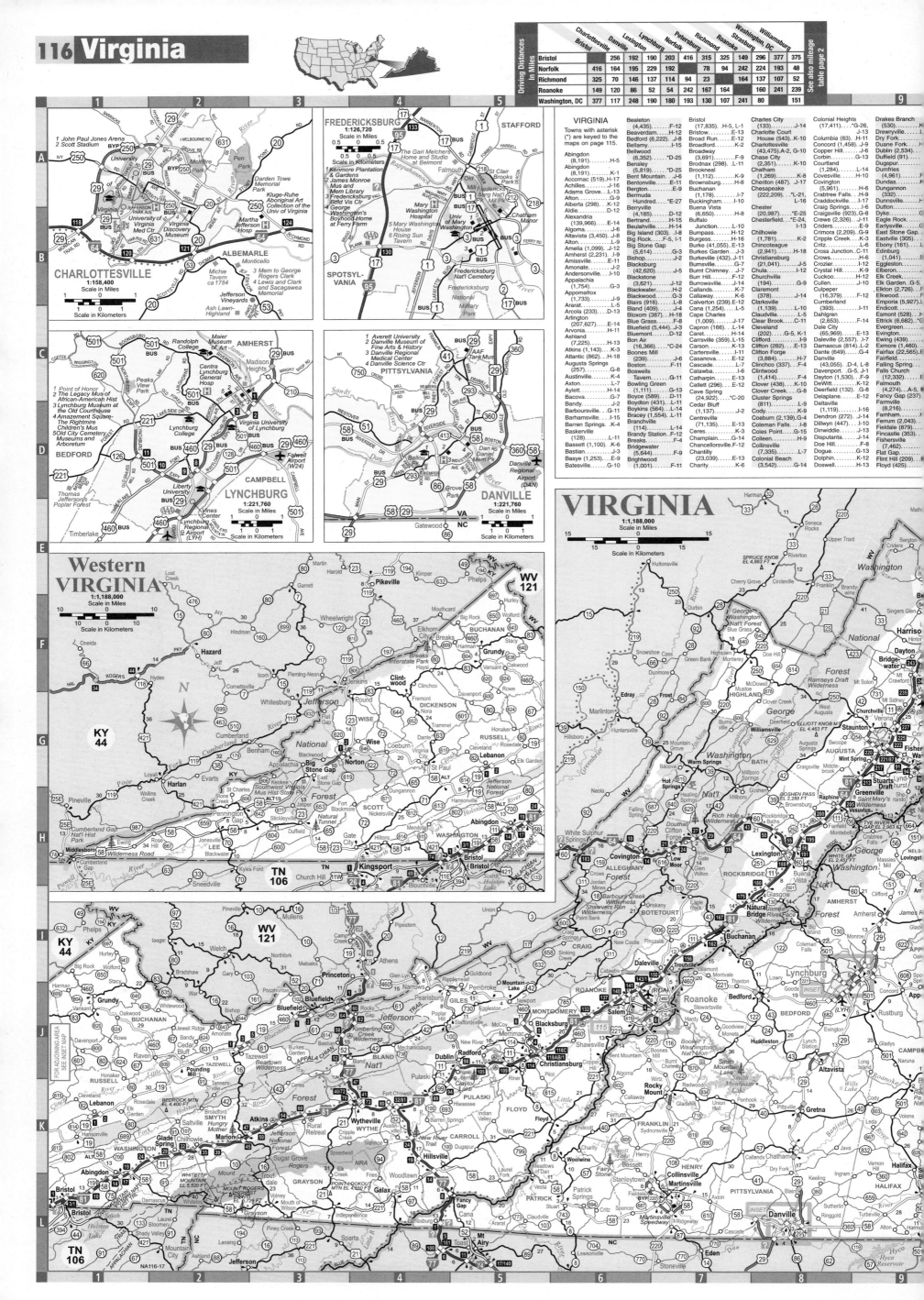

LEGEND
Interstate Highway — Wildlife Refuge
Controlled Access Hwy — Nat'l/State Park
Controlled Access Hwy Toll — National Forest

NA116-17

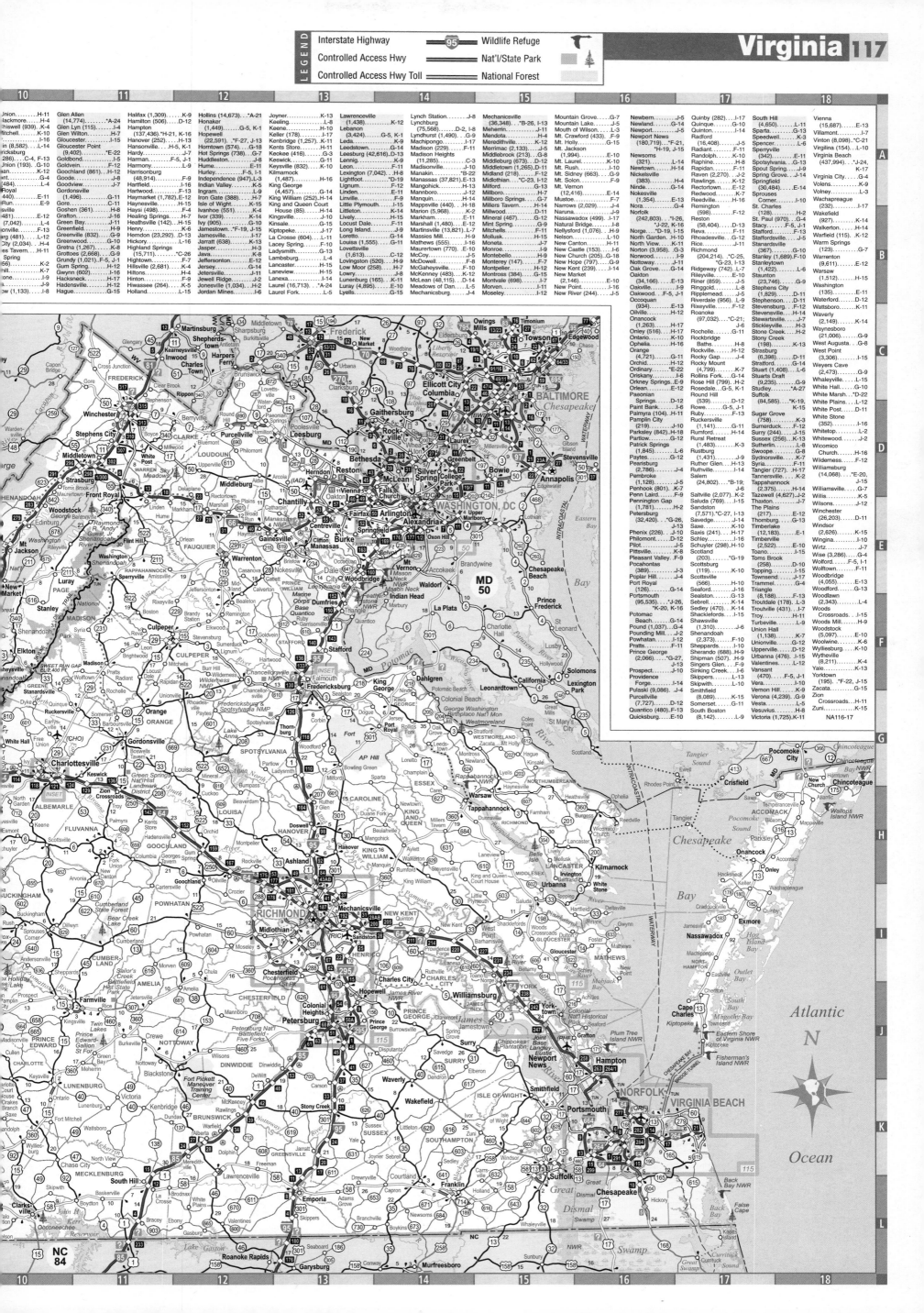

See also mileage table page 2

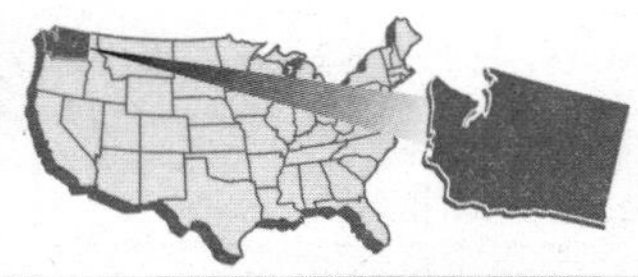

| Driving Distances In Miles | Aberdeen | Bellingham | Ellensburg | Kelso | Olympia | Omak | Port Angeles | Pasco | Seattle | Spokane | Tacoma | Yakima |
|---|---|---|---|---|---|---|---|---|---|---|---|---|
| Olympia | 50 | 149 | 148 | 66 | | 277 | 267 | 119 | 60 | 320 | 31 | 183 |
| Seattle | 109 | 89 | 107 | 126 | 60 | 237 | 227 | 82 | | 279 | 34 | 142 |
| Spokane | 369 | 362 | 173 | 366 | 320 | 140 | 136 | 397 | 279 | | 293 | 193 |
| Tacoma | 79 | 122 | 121 | 96 | 31 | 251 | 241 | 106 | 34 | 293 | | 156 |
| Yakima | 204 | 224 | 36 | 183 | 196 | 85 | 260 | 142 | 193 | 156 | | |

## WASHINGTON

Towns with asterisk (*) are keyed to the maps on page 120.

Aberdeen (16,896)..F-6
Acme (246)..F-6
Addy (268)..C-16
Aeneas..B-14
Airway Heights (6,114)..E-17
Aladdin..E-17
Albion (579)..G-18
Alderdale..I-13
Alder (403)..B-8
Algona (3,014)..*J-23
Allyn (203)..E-7
Almira (284)..D-14
Alto..H-16
Altoona (39)..H-6
Amanda Park (252)..E-6
Amboy (1,608)..I-8
Anacortes (15,778)..B-8
Anatone..I-18
Appledale..E-13
Arden..B-16
Ardenvoir..D-12
Ariel..I-8
Arlington (17,926)..C-9
Artondale (12,653)..*J-19
Ashford (217)..G-9
Asotin (1,251)..I-18
Auburn (70,180)..*J-23
Ayer..H-15
Azwell..D-13

B Z Corner..I-10
Bainbridge Island (23,025)..*D-20
Baring..D-10
Battle Ground (17,571)..J-8
Bay Center (276)..G-5
Beaux Arts Village (299)..*E-23
Beaver..C-5
Belfair (3,931)..E-7
Bellevue (122,363)..*F-24, E-9
Bellingham (80,885)..*B-26, B-8
Benge..G-16
Benton City (3,038)..H-14
Berne..D-11
Beverly..G-13
Bickleton (88)..I-12
Birch Bay (4,684)..A-8
Blaine (4,684)..A-8
Blyn (101)..D-7
Boistfort..H-7
Bonney Lake (17,374)..*K-24
Bothell (33,505)..*B-23
Boundary..A-17
Bow..B-8
Bremerton (37,729)..*E-19, E-8
Brewster (2,370)..C-13
Bridgeport (2,409)..D-13
Brier (6,087)..*B-22
Brinnon (797)..E-7
Brooklyn..G-6
Bryn Mawr..*F-23
Buckley (4,354)..F-9
Bucoda (562)..G-7
Burbank (3,291)..H-14
Burien (33,313)..*G-22
Burley (2,057)..*H-19
Burlington (8,388)..B-8

Camano..C-8
Camas (19,355)..J-8
Canby..E-16
Carbonado (610)..F-9
Carlsborg (995)..C-7
Carlson..G-9
Carlton..C-12
Carnation (1,786)..*E-9
Carson (2,279)..I-9
Cashmere (3,063)..E-12
Castle Rock (1,982)..H-7
Cathlamet (532)..H-6
Central Ferry..G-17
Centralia (16,336)..G-7
Chehalis (7,259)..G-7
Chelan (3,890)..D-13
Chelan Falls (329)..D-13
Cheney (10,590)..E-17
Chesaw..A-14
Chewelah (2,607)..C-17
Chinook (466)..H-5
Chumstick..E-11
Clallam Bay (363)..C-5
Clarkston (7,229)..H-18
Cle Elum (1,872)..F-11
Clearview (3,324)..*A-24
Clearwater..E-5
Cleveland..I-12
Cliffdell (104)..G-11
Clinton (928)..D-8
Cloverland..H-18
Clyde Hill (2,984)..*D-23
Coalfield..F-19
Colbert..D-17
Colchester..*F-20
Colfax (2,805)..G-17
College Place (8,765)..L-13
Colton (418)..G-18
Colville (4,673)..B-16
Conconully..B-13
Concrete (705)..B-9
Connell (4,209)..G-15

Cook..J-10
Copalis Beach (415)..F-5
Cosmopolis (1,649)..F-6
Cougar..I-8
Coulee City (562)..E-14
Coulee Dam (1,098)..D-14
Coupeville (1,831)..C-8
Covington (17,575)..*I-24
Creston (236)..D-15
Crystal Mountain..F-9
Curlew (118)..A-15
Cusick (207)..C-17

Dabob..B-7
Danville (34)..A-15
Darrington (1,347)..C-10
Davenport (1,734)..E-16
Dayton (2,526)..H-16
Deer Park (3,652)..D-17
Deming (353)..B-9
Des Moines (29,673)..*H-22
Desert Aire (1,626)..G-13
Diablo..B-11
Diamond Lake..C-17
Dieringer..*K-23
Discovery Bay..D-7
Dixie (197)..H-16
Dockton..*I-20
Dodge..H-17
Douglas..E-13
DuPont (8,199)..F-8
Dungeness..C-7
Dusty..G-17
Duvall (6,695)..D-9

East Wenatchee (13,190)..E-12
Eastgate (4,958)..*E-24
Easton (478)..F-11
Eastsound..A-7
Eatonville (2,758)..G-8
Edgewood (9,387)..*K-22
Edmonds (39,709)..*A-21
Elbe (29)..G-9
Eldon..E-7
Electric City (968)..D-14
Elk..C-17
Ellensburg (18,174)..F-12
Elma (3,107)..F-6
Eltopia..G-14
Elwha..D-6
Endicott (289)..F-17
Entiat (1,112)..E-12
Enumclaw (10,669)..F-9
Ephrata (7,664)..F-13
Eureka..H-15
Everett (103,019)..D-9
Everson (2,481)..A-8

Fairfield..F-17
Fairholm..C-6
Farmington (146)..F-18
Federal Way (89,306)..*J-22
Ferndale (11,415)..B-8
Fife (9,173)..*K-22
Fircrest (6,497)..*K-20
Fishtrap..E-16
Forks (3,532)..D-5
Four Lakes (512)..E-17
Freeland (2,045)..D-8
Friday Harbor (2,162)..B-7

Galvin..G-7
Garfield (597)..F-18
Geneva (2,321)..*B-27
George (501)..F-13
Gifford..D-16
Gig Harbor (7,126)..*I-19
Glacier (211)..A-9
Glen Acres..*G-21
Glenoma..H-9
Glenwood..J-10
Gold Bar (2,075)..D-10
Goldendale (3,407)..I-11
Graham (23,491)..F-8
Grand Coulee (988)..D-14
Grandview (10,862)..H-13
Granger (3,246)..*H-12
Granite Falls (3,364)..D-9
Grayland (953)..G-6

Hadley..H-16
Hansville (3,091)..D-8
Harrington (424)..E-16
Hartline (151)..E-14
Hatton (101)..G-15
Hay..H-16
Hollywood..*C-24
Hoodsport (376)..E-7
Hoquiam (8,726)..F-6
Humptulips (255)..F-5
Hunters..C-16
Hunts Point (394)..*D-23
Ilwaco (936)..H-5
Inchelium (409)..C-16
Index (178)..D-10
Ione (752)..B-17
Issaquah (30,434)..*F-24, E-9
Joyce..C-6
Kahlotus (193)..G-15
Kalaloch..E-5
Kalama (2,344)..I-7
Kamilche..F-7
Keller (234)..D-15
Kelso (11,925)..I-7
Kenmore (20,460)..*B-23

Kennewick (73,917)..H-14, L-11
Kent (92,411)..*H-23
Kettle Falls (1,595)..B-16
Kewa..C-16
Kingston (2,099)..D-8
Kirkland (48,787)..*D-23
Kittitas (1,381)..F-12
Klickitat (362)..I-10
Kooskooskie..H-16
Krupp (48)..E-14

La Center (2,800)..I-8
La Grande (109)..G-8
La Push..D-4
LaCrosse (413)..G-16
Lacey (42,393)..*C-27
Lake Forest Park (12,598)..*B-22
Lake Stevens (28,069)..C-9
Lakebay..F-8
Lakewood (58,163)..*L-20
Lamar..H-15
Lamona..E-15
Lamont (70)..F-16
Langley (1,035)..D-8
Laurier (1)..A-16
Leadpoint..A-17
Leavenworth (1,965)..E-11
Lebam (160)..G-6
Liberty..F-11
Liberty Lake (7,591)..E-18
Lilliwaup..E-7
Lind (564)..F-15
Littlerock..G-7
Long Beach (1,392)..H-5
Long Lake..E-17
Longbranch (3,784)..F-8
Longmire..G-9, L-5
Longview (36,648)..I-7
Loomis (159)..B-13
Loon Lake (783)..C-17
Lopez..B-7
Lucerne..C-11
Lummi..B-8
Lyman (438)..B-9
Lynden (11,951)..A-8
Lynnwood (35,836)..*A-22

Mabton (2,286)..H-13
Mae..F-14
Malaga..F-12
Malden (203)..F-17
Malott (487)..C-13
Maltby (10,830)..*B-24
Manchester (5,413)..*F-19
Mansfield (320)..D-13
Manson (1,468)..D-13
Maple Falls (324)..A-9
Maple Valley (22,684)..E-9
Maplewood..*E-23
Marble..A-16
Marblemount (203)..B-10
Marengo..H-17
Marietta..A-25
Markham (111)..G-5
Maryhill (58)..J-11
Marys Corner..H-7
Marysville (60,020)..D-9
Matlock..F-6
Mattawa (4,437)..G-13
Mazama..B-12
McCleary (1,653)..F-7
Mead (7,275)..D-17
Medical Lake (5,060)..E-17
Medina (2,969)..*E-23
Menlo..G-6
Mercer Island (22,699)..*E-23
Mesa (489)..G-14
Meskill..G-7
Metaline Falls (238)..A-17
Midland (8,962)..*L-21
Miles..D-16
Mill Creek (18,244)..*A-23
Milton (6,968)..*K-22
Moclips (207)..F-5
Mold..C-15
Monitor..E-12
Monroe (17,304)..D-9
Montesano (3,976)..F-6
Morgan Acres..J-17
Morton (1,126)..H-8
Moses Lake (20,366)..F-14
Mossyrock (759)..H-8
Mountlake Terrace (19,909)..*B-22
Moxee (1,821)..H-12
Mt. Vernon (31,743)..C-8
Mukilteo (20,254)..D-8

Naches (795)..G-11
Nachotta..G-5
Napavine (1,766)..G-7
Naselle (419)..H-5
Nason Creek..D-11
Neah Bay (865)..C-4
Neilton (315)..E-6
Nemah..H-6
Nespelem (236)..C-14
New London..F-5
Newaukum..*J-24
Newcastle (10,380)..*F-24
Newhalem..B-10
Newman Lake..D-18
Newport (2,126)..C-18
Nighthawk..A-13

Nordland..D-8
Normandy Park (6,335)..*G-22
North Bend (5,731)..E-9
North Bonneville (956)..A-16
Northport (295)..A-16
Oak Harbor (22,075)..C-8
Oakesdale (422)..F-18
Oakville (684)..G-7
Ocean City..F-5
Ocean Park (1,573)..H-5
Ocean Shores (5,569)..F-5
Odessa (910)..E-15
Okanogan (2,552)..C-13
Olalla..*H-19
Olympia (46,478)..*D-26, F-7
Omak (4,845)..C-13
Orcas..A-7
Orchards (19,556)..J-8
Orient (115)..A-16
Oroville (1,686)..A-13
Othello (7,364)..G-14
Outlook (292)..H-12
Oysterville..G-5
Ozette..C-4

Pacific (6,606)..*J-23
Pacific Beach (291)..F-5
Packwood (342)..G-10
Palmer..F-9
Palouse (998)..F-18
Paradise..L-5
Parkland (35,803)..*L-21
Parkwood (7,126)..*F-19
Pasco (59,781)..H-14, K-11
Pateros (667)..C-13
Paterson..I-13
Pe Ell (632)..G-7
Plain..D-11
Plymouth..I-14
Point Roberts (1,314)..A-7
Pomeroy (1,425)..H-17
Port Angeles (19,038)..C-6
Port Ludlow (2,603)..D-8
Port Orchard (11,144)..*F-19, E-8
Port Townsend (9,113)..C-8
Porter (207)..F-7
Poulsbo (9,200)..D-8
Prescott (318)..H-16
Prosser (5,714)..H-13
Pullman (29,799)..G-18
Puyallup (37,022)..*K-22

Queets (174)..E-5
Quilcene (596)..D-7
Quinault..E-6
Quincy (6,750)..F-13

Rainier (1,794)..G-8
Ralston..F-16
Randle..H-9
Ravensdale (1,101)..E-9
Raymond (2,882)..G-6
Reardan (571)..E-16
Redmond (54,144)..*D-24
Redondo..*I-22
Renton (90,927)..*G-23, E-9
Republic (1,073)..B-15
Rice..C-16
Richland (48,058)..H-14, K-10
Ridgefield (4,763)..I-8
Rimrock..G-11
Ritzville (1,673)..F-15
Riverside (280)..B-13
Roche Harbor..B-7
Rochester (2,388)..G-7
Rock Island (788)..F-12
Rockford (470)..F-18
Rockport (109)..B-10
Rollingbay..*D-20
Roosevelt (156)..J-12
Rosalia (550)..F-17
Rosburg (317)..H-6
Rose Valley..I-7
Roy (793)..F-8
Royal City (2,140)..G-13
Ruff..F-14
Ryderwood (395)..H-7

Salkum..H-8
Schrag..F-15
SeaTac (26,909)..*G-22
Seabeck (1,105)..E-8
Seahurst..*G-21
Seattle (608,660)..*B-20, E-22
Seaview..H-5
Sedro-Woolley (10,540)..B-9
Selah (6,606)..G-7
Sequim (6,606)..C-7
Shelton (9,834)..F-7
Sheridan Beach..*C-22
Shoreline (53,007)..*B-22
Silver Lake..B-24
Silverdale (19,204)..E-8
Skamania..J-9
Skamokawa..H-6
Skykomish (198)..D-10
Snohomish (9,098)..D-9
Snoqualmie Pass..E-10
Soap Lake (1,514)..E-14
Sol Duc Hot Springs..D-6

South Bend (1,637)..G-6
South Cle Elum (532)..F-11
South Prairie..*L-24
Southworth (2,185)..*F-20
Spanaway (27,227)..F-8
Spangle (278)..E-17
Spokane (208,916)..E-17, K-17
Spokane Valley (89,755)..E-17
Sprague (446)..F-16
Springdale (285)..D-17
St. John (537)..F-17
Stanwood (6,231)..C-8
Starbuck (129)..H-16
Stehekin..C-11
Steilacoom (5,985)..*L-19
Steptoe (180)..F-17
Stevenson (1,465)..J-9
Sultan (4,651)..D-9
Sumas (1,307)..A-8
Summit (7,985)..*L-22
Sumner (9,451)..*K-23
Sunnyside (15,858)..H-13
Sunrise..G-10, K-6
Tacoma (198,397)..*K-21, F-8
Tahlequah..*I-20
Taholah (840)..E-5
Tahuya..E-7
Tekoa (778)..F-18
Telma..D-11
Tenino (1,695)..G-7
Terrace Heights (6,937)..K-9
Thorp (240)..F-11
Thrall..G-12
Tieton (1,191)..G-11
Tiger..B-17
Toledo (725)..H-7
Tokeland (151)..G-6
Tonasket (1,032)..B-13
Toppenish (8,949)..H-12
Toroda..A-15
Touchet (421)..I-15
Toutle..H-8
Trinidad..F-13
Trout Lake (557)..J-10
Tukwila (19,107)..*G-22
Tumtum..D-17
Tumwater (17,371)..*D-26
Turner Corner..*B-24
Twisp (919)..C-12

Union (631)..E-7
Union Gap (6,047)..*I-9
University Place (31,144)..*K-20
Usk..C-17

Valleyford..E-17
Vancouver (161,791)..J-8
Vantage (74)..F-13
Vashon (10,624)..*G-20, E-8
Vashon Heights..*F-20
Vesta..G-6
Virden..F-11
Waitsburg (1,217)..H-16
Waldron..B-7
Walla Walla (31,731)..I-16, K-14
Wallula (179)..I-15
Wapato (4,997)..H-12
Warden (2,692)..F-14
Washougal (14,095)..J-8
Washtucna (208)..G-16
Waterville (1,138)..E-12
Wauconda..B-14
Wellpinit..D-16
Wenatchee (31,925)..E-12
Westport (2,099)..G-5

White Salmon (2,224)..J-10
White Swan (793)..H-11
Wilbur (884)..D-15
Willard..J-10
Wilson Creek (205)..E-13
Winchester..F-13
Winesap..D-12
Winlock (1,339)..H-7
Winthrop (394)..C-12
Woodinville (10,938)..*B-24
Woodland (5,509)..I-7
Woodway (1,307)..B-21
Wymer..G-12

Yacolt (1,566)..I-8
Yakima (91,067)..G-12, K-8
Yale..I-8
Yarrow Point (1,001)..*D-23
Yelm (6,848)..G-8
Zillah (2,964)..H-12

NA118-17

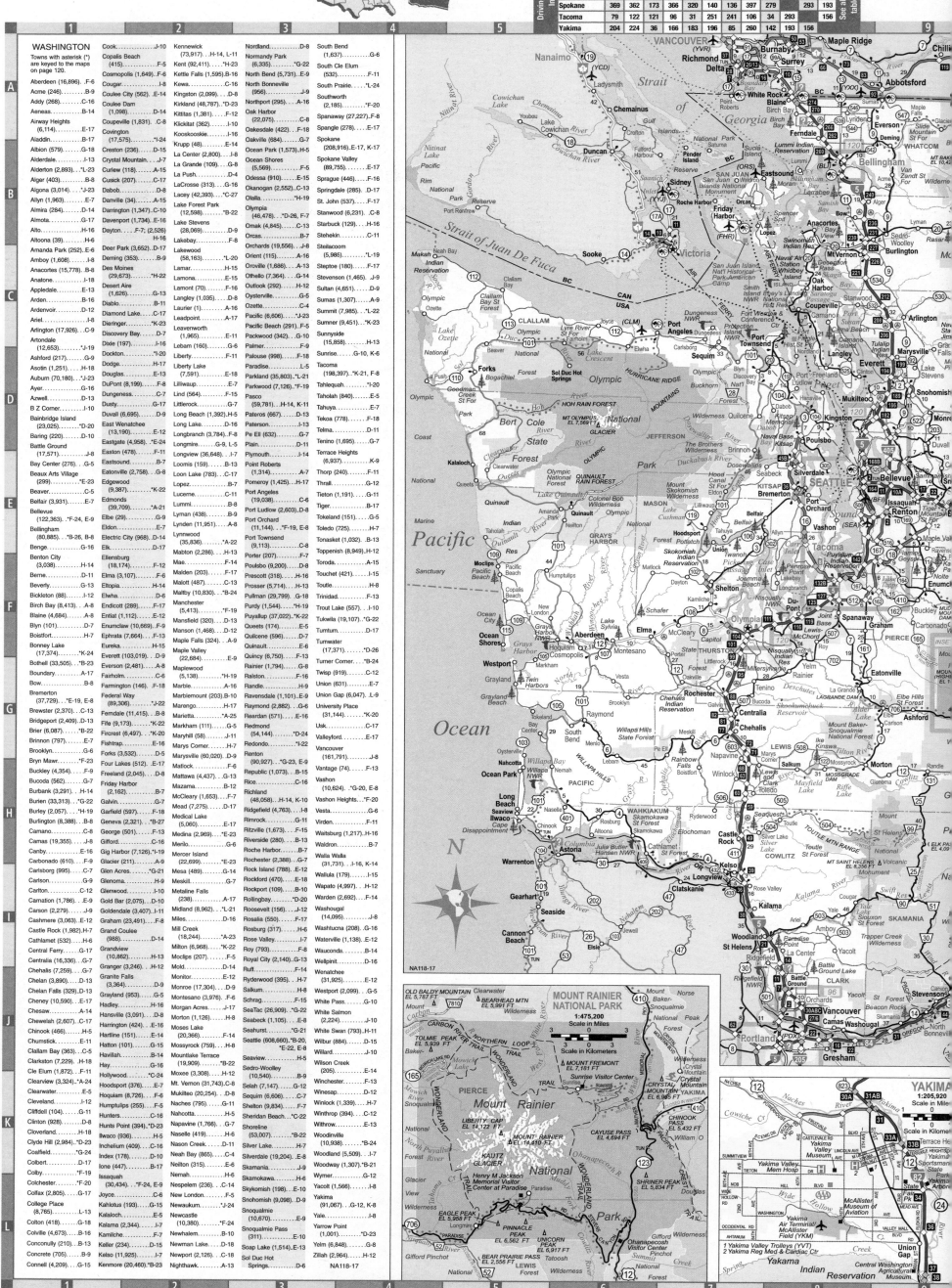

MOUNT RAINIER NATIONAL PARK
1:475,200
Scale in Miles
Scale in Kilometers

YAKIMA
1:205,920
Scale in Miles
Scale in Kilometers

1 Yakima Valley Trolleys (YVT)
2 Yakima Reg Med & Cardiac Ctr

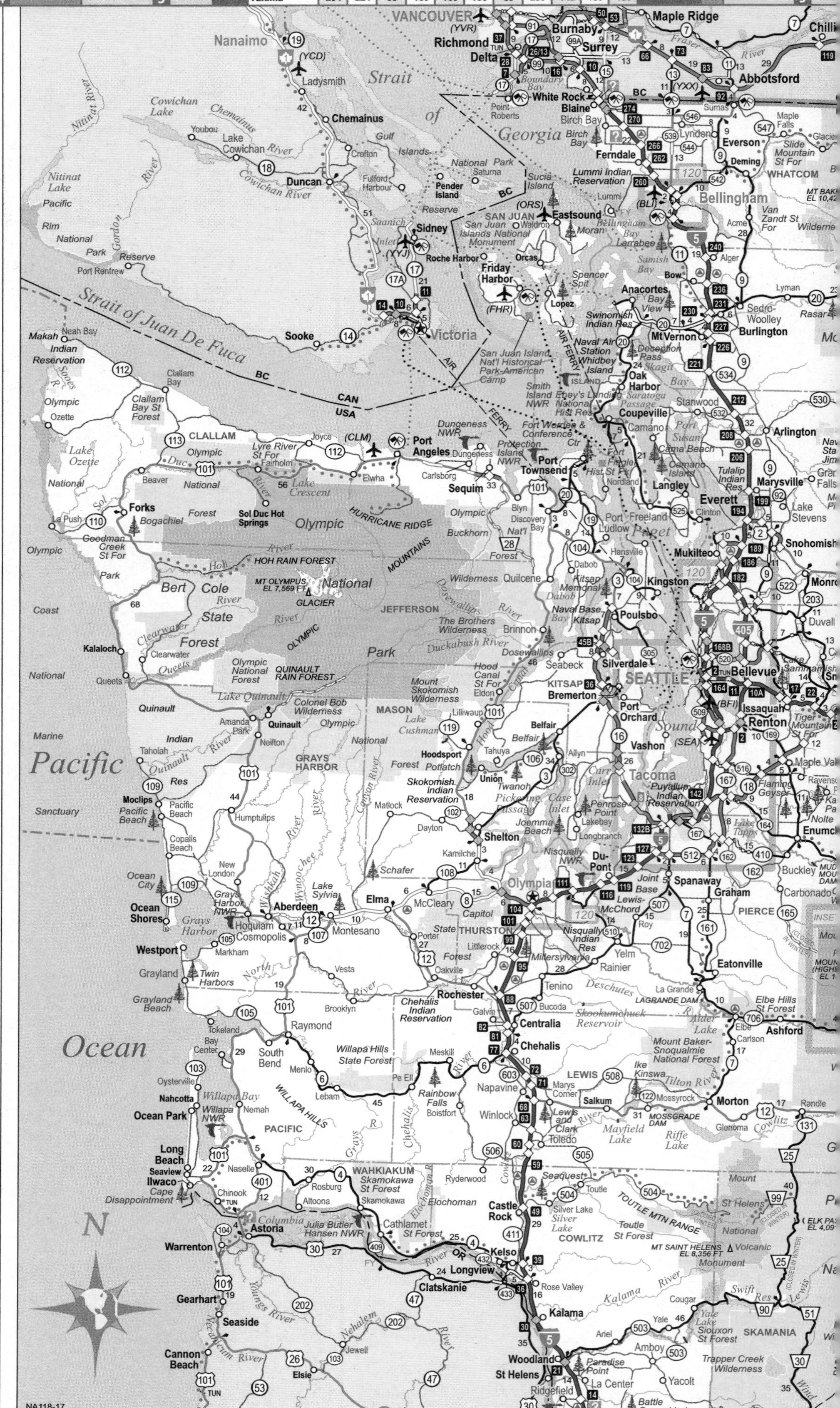

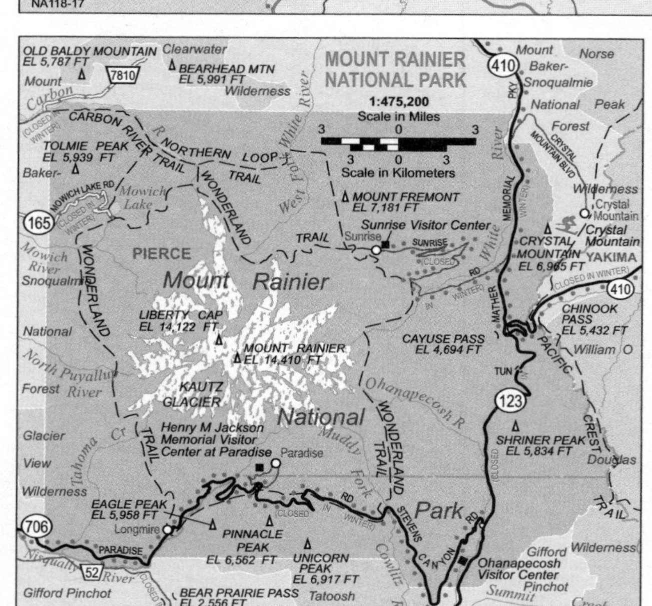

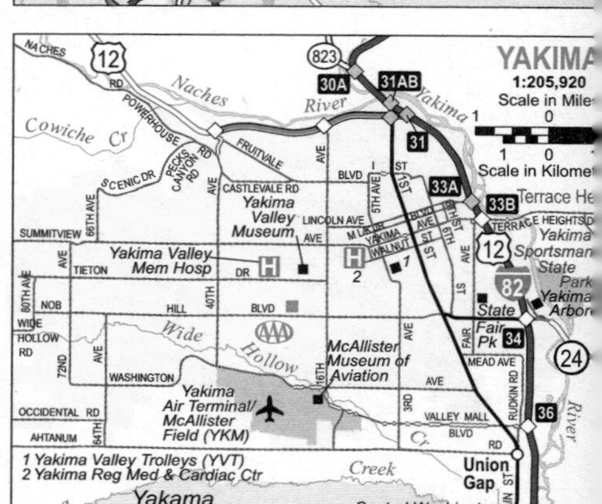

**LEGEND**

| | | |
|---|---|---|
| Interstate Highway | 95 | Wildlife Refuge |
| Controlled Access Hwy | | Nat'l/State Park |
| Controlled Access Hwy Toll | | National Forest |

KILOMETERS IN CANADA
KILOMETERS x 0.62 = MILES

BC 128

ID 32

OR 94

BECAUSE THE LENGTH OF THE SEASONS VARIES GREATLY IN HIGHER ELEVATIONS, INQUIRE LOCALLY FOR THE CONDITIONS OF ROADS DESIGNATED "CLOSED IN WINTER" ON THIS MAP.

## WASHINGTON
1:1,457,280

Scale in Miles
25    0    25

Scale in Kilometers
25    0    25

## KENNEWICK
1:253,440
Scale in Miles
0    1

## WALLA WALLA
1:158,400
Scale in Miles
1    0    1

Scale in Kilometers
1    0    1

## SPOKANE
1:190,080
Scale in Kilometers
2    0    2

1 Mobius Children's Museum
2 Mobius Science Center
3 Moore-Turner Heritage Gdns
4 Cathedral of St John the Evangelist

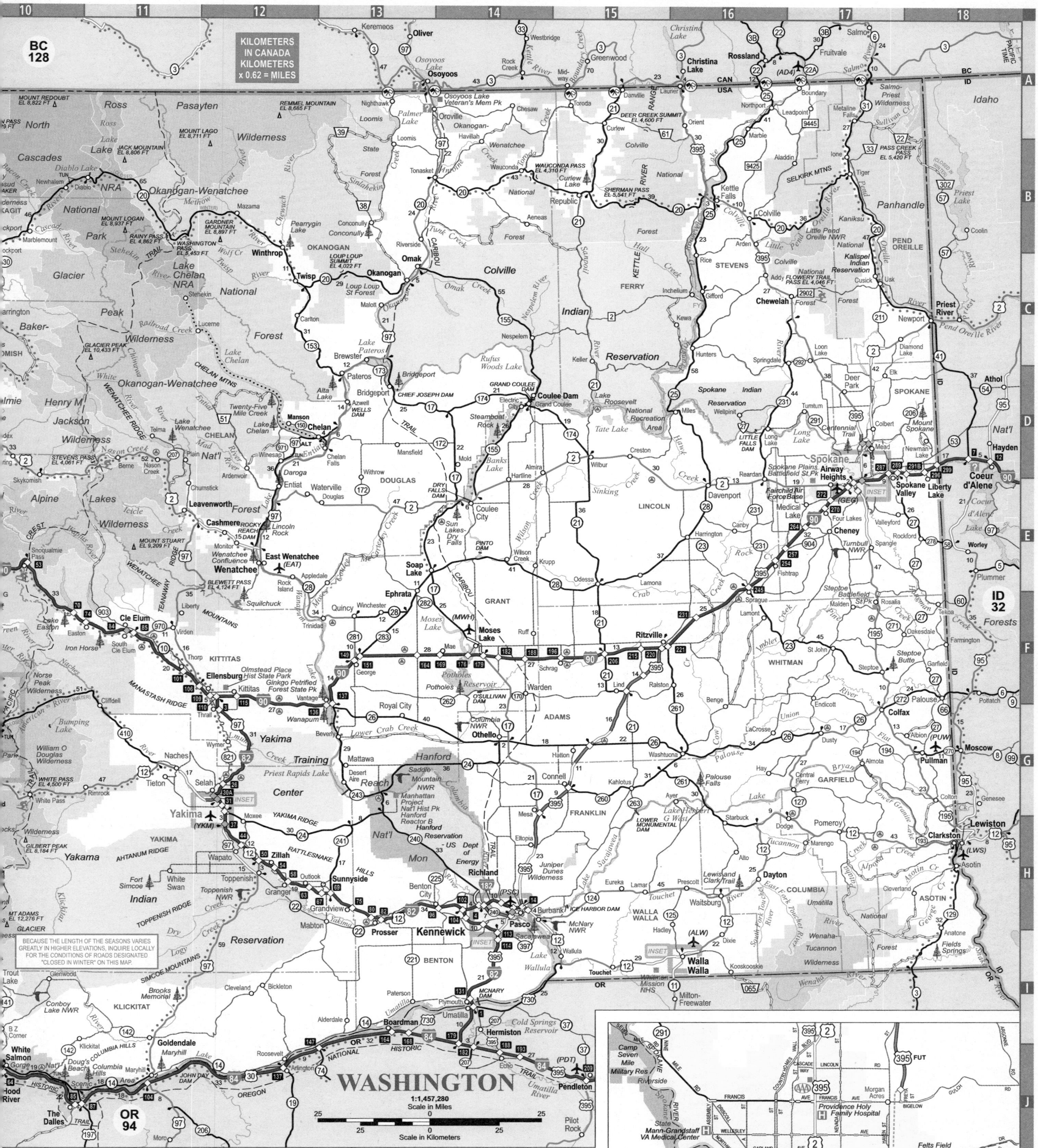

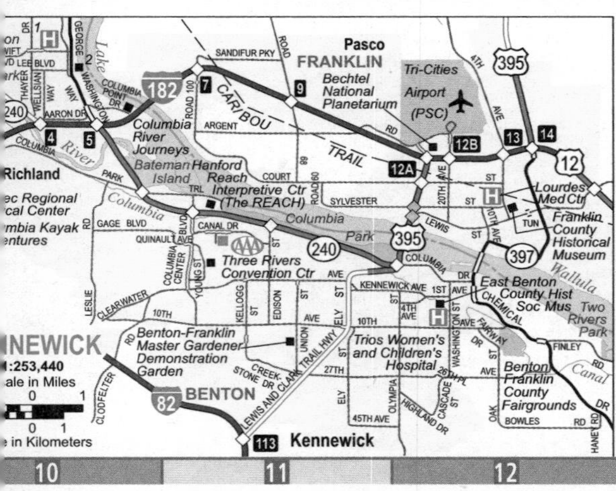

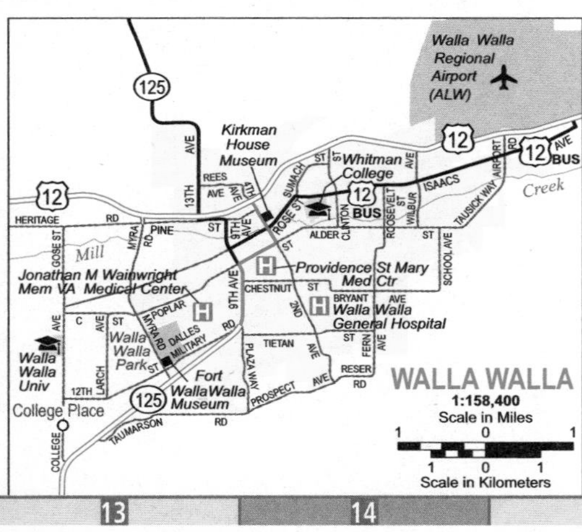

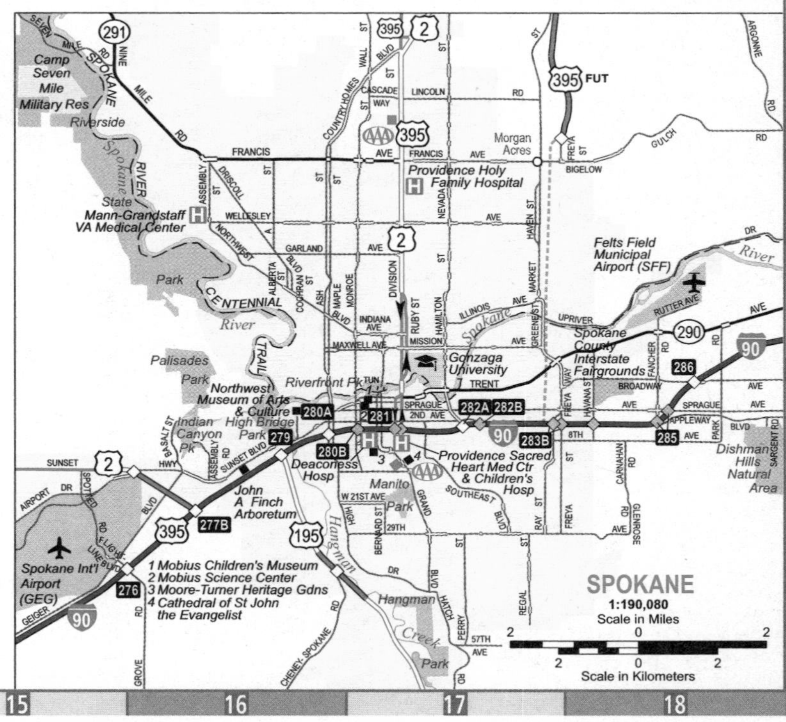

# Washington & West Virginia City Maps

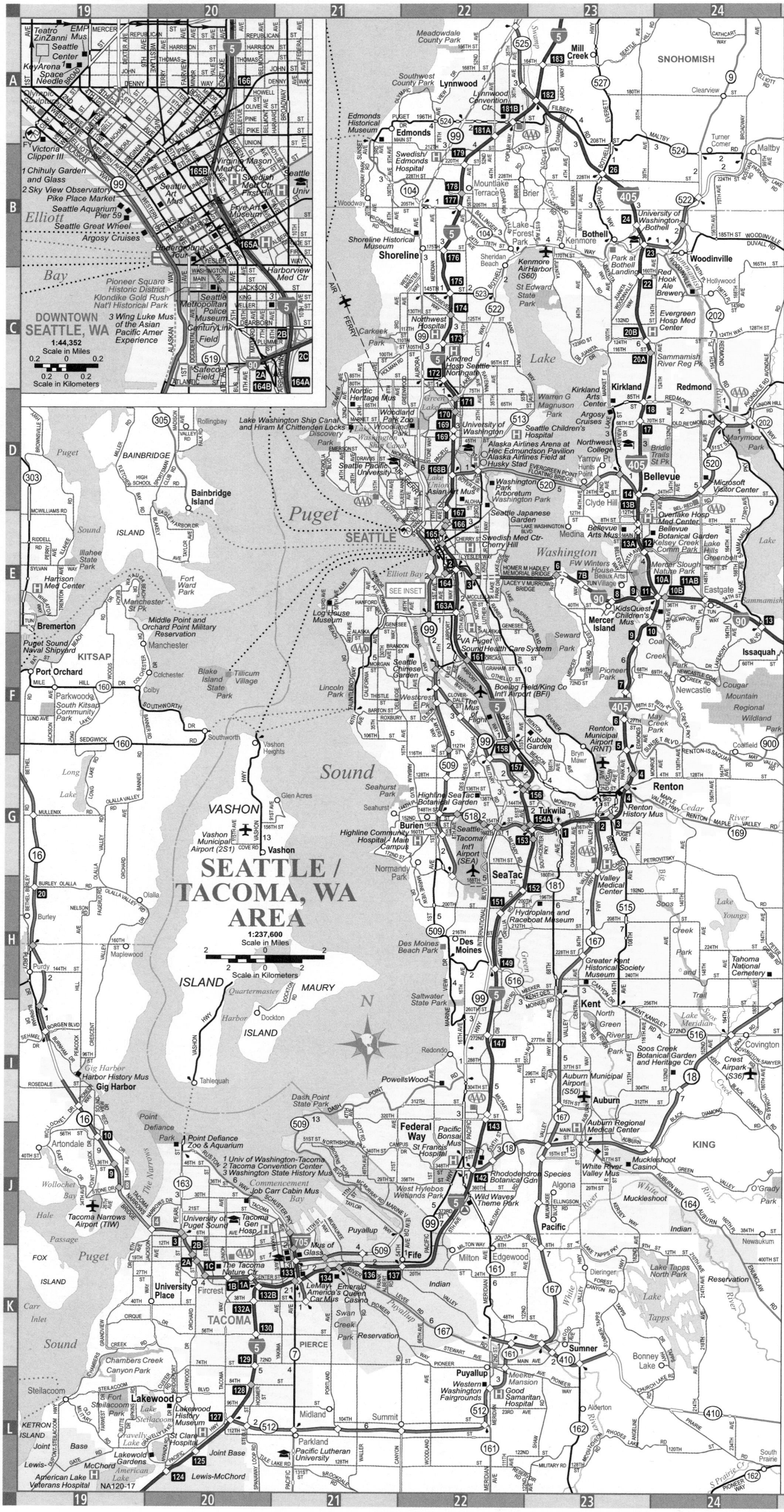

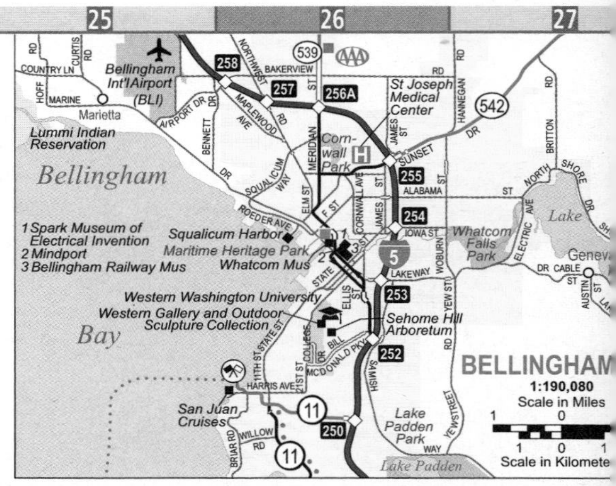

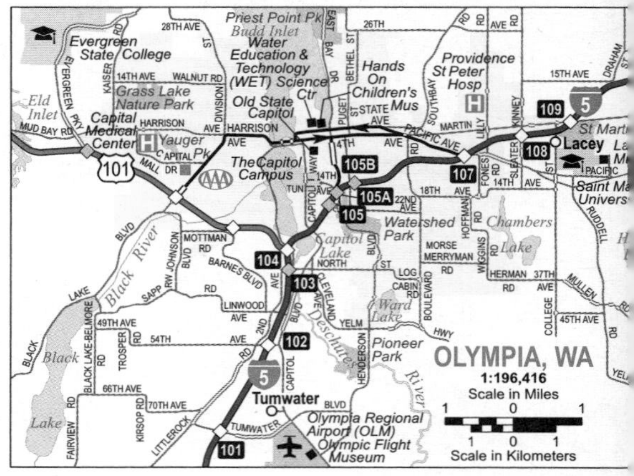

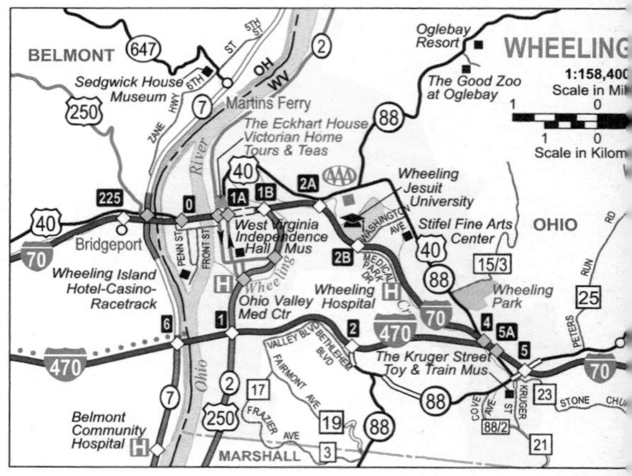

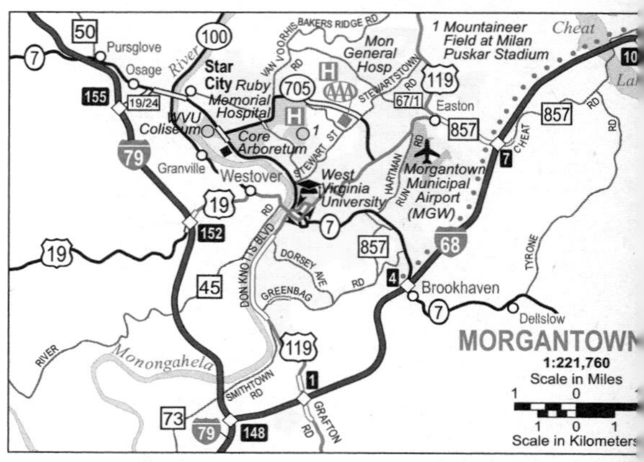

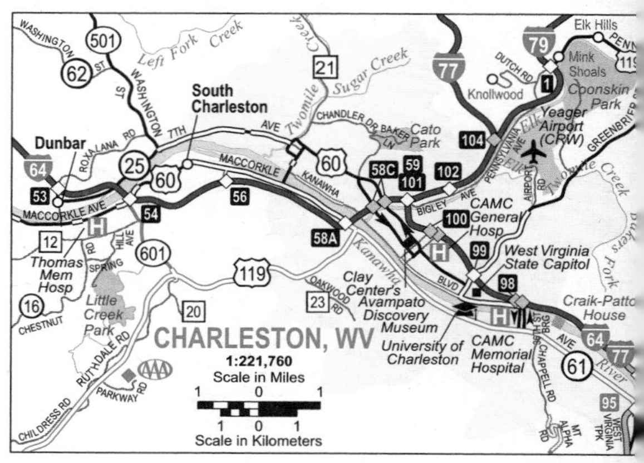

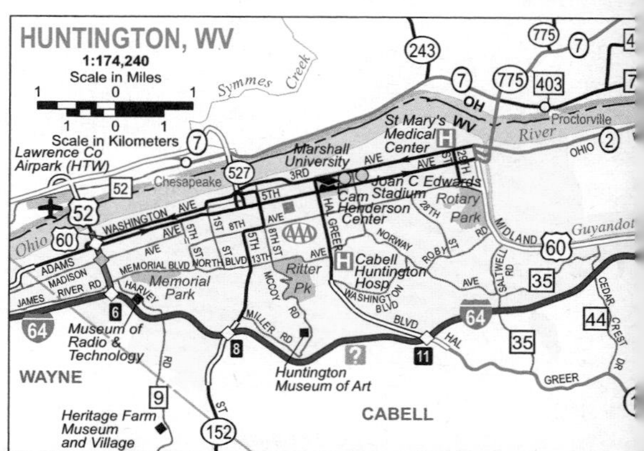

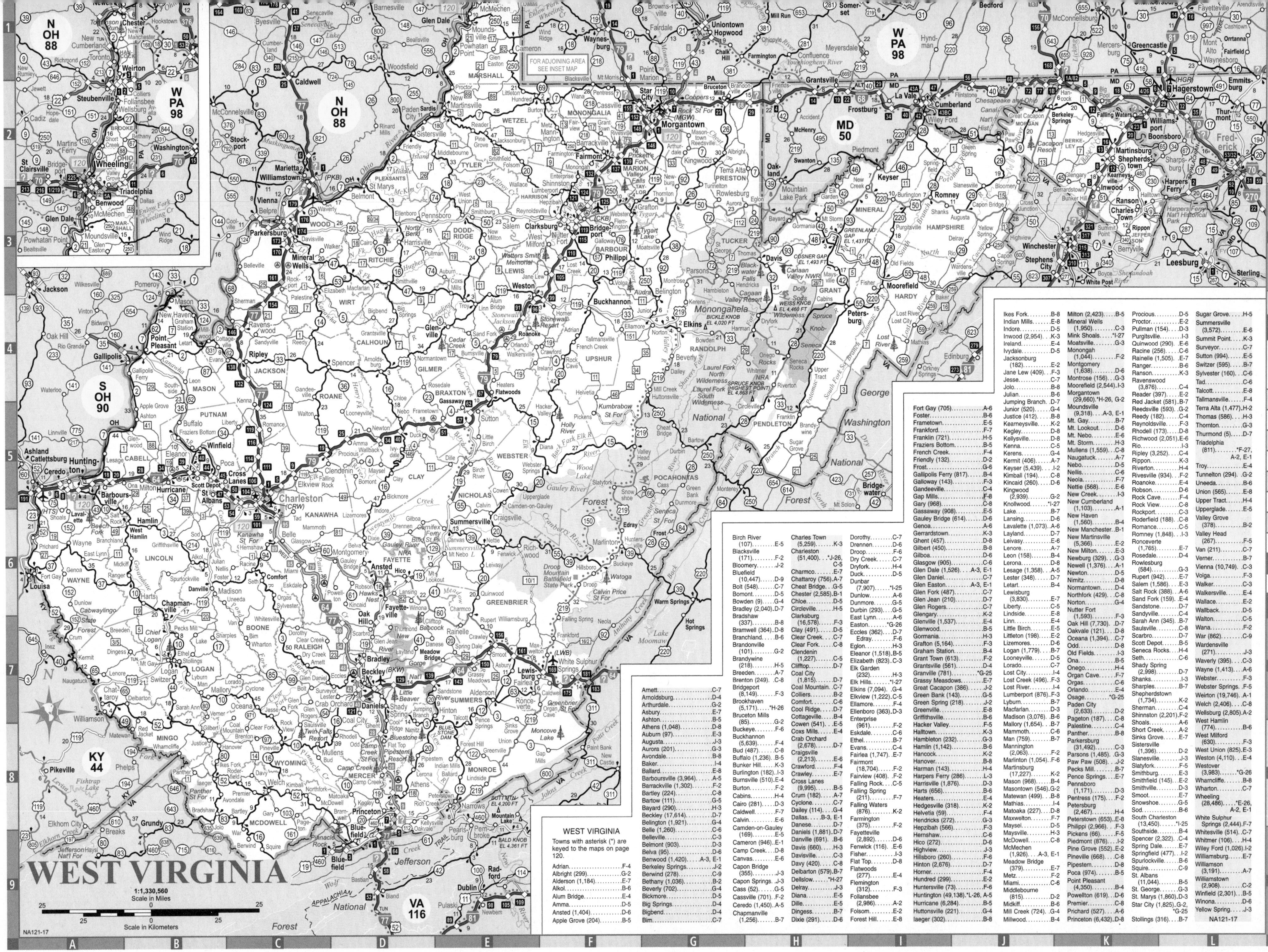

## Driving Distances In Miles

| | Beckley | Charleston | Clarksburg | Fairmont | Huntington | Morgantown | Parkersburg | Sutton | Wheeling | White Sulphur Springs |
|---|---|---|---|---|---|---|---|---|---|---|
| Charleston | 59 | | 125 | 139 | 51 | 156 | 78 | 66 | 179 | 121 |
| Huntington | 110 | 51 | 175 | 189 | | 206 | 97 | 117 | 185 | 172 |
| Parkersburg | 136 | 78 | 73 | 94 | 97 | 111 | | 109 | 106 | 197 |
| Wheeling | 237 | 179 | 93 | 95 | 185 | 79 | 106 | 169 | | 273 |

See also mileage table page 2

## WEST VIRGINIA

Towns with asterisk (*) are keyed to the maps on page 120.

WISCONSIN

Towns with asterisk (*) are keyed to the maps on page 124.

NA122-17

## Driving Distances In Miles

| | Appleton | Beloit | Eau Claire | Green Bay | Kenosha | La Crosse | Madison | Manitowoc | Milwaukee | Spooner | Tomah | Wausau |
|---|---|---|---|---|---|---|---|---|---|---|---|---|
| Eau Claire | 185 | 225 | | 193 | 280 | 90 | 178 | 232 | 246 | 82 | 81 | 101 |
| Green Bay | 31 | 182 | 193 | | 155 | 202 | 135 | 41 | 117 | 257 | 157 | 96 |
| La Crosse | 172 | 190 | 90 | 202 | 245 | | 143 | 212 | 211 | 164 | 44 | 170 |
| Madison | 105 | 54 | 178 | 135 | 113 | 143 | | 129 | 78 | 255 | 100 | 142 |
| Milwaukee | 102 | 76 | 246 | 117 | 39 | 211 | 78 | 83 | | 324 | 168 | 194 |

See also mileage table page 2

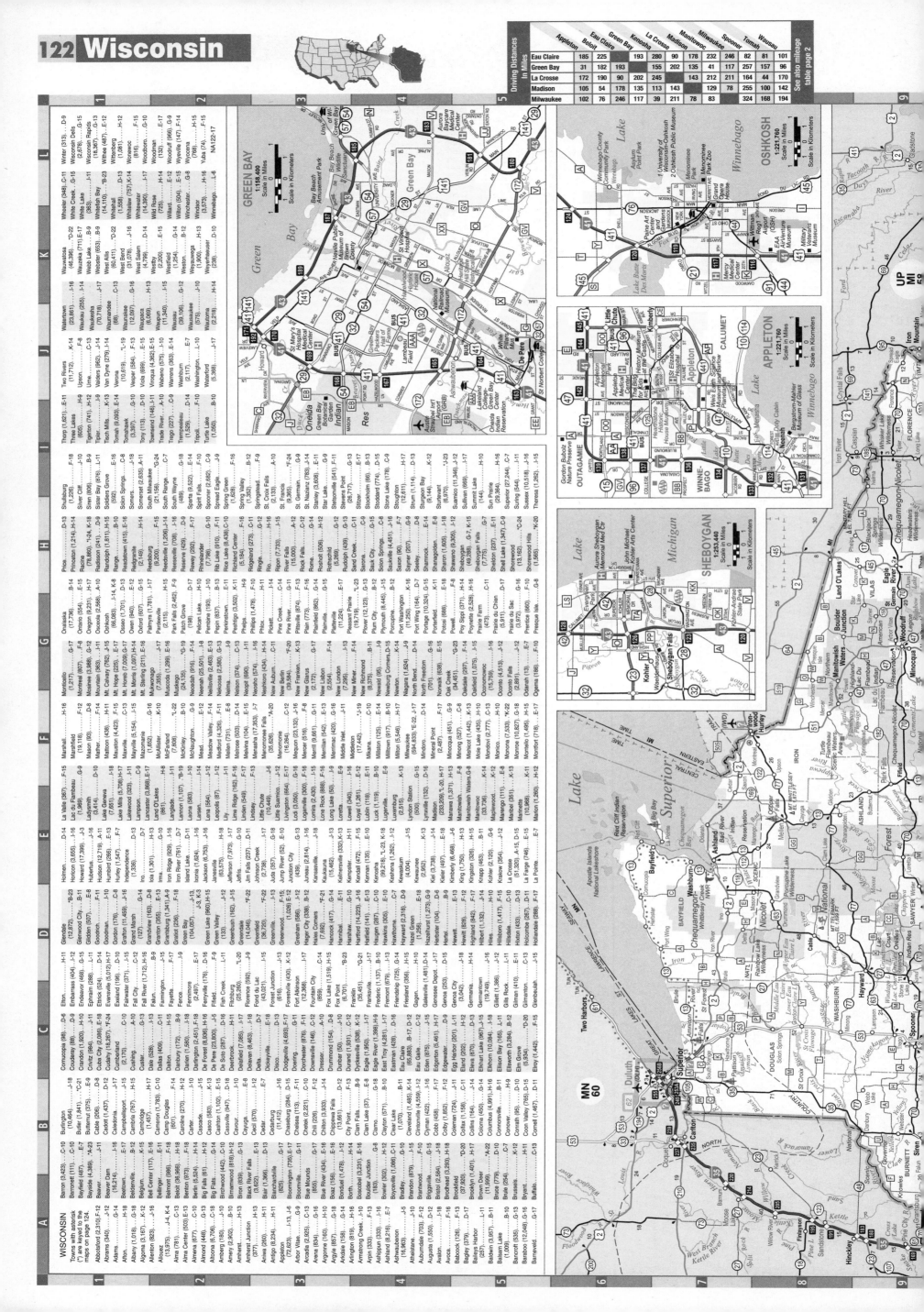

LEGEND

| | | |
|---|---|---|
| Interstate Highway | 95 | Wildlife Refuge |
| Controlled Access Hwy | | Nat'l/State Park |
| Controlled Access Hwy Toll | | National Forest |

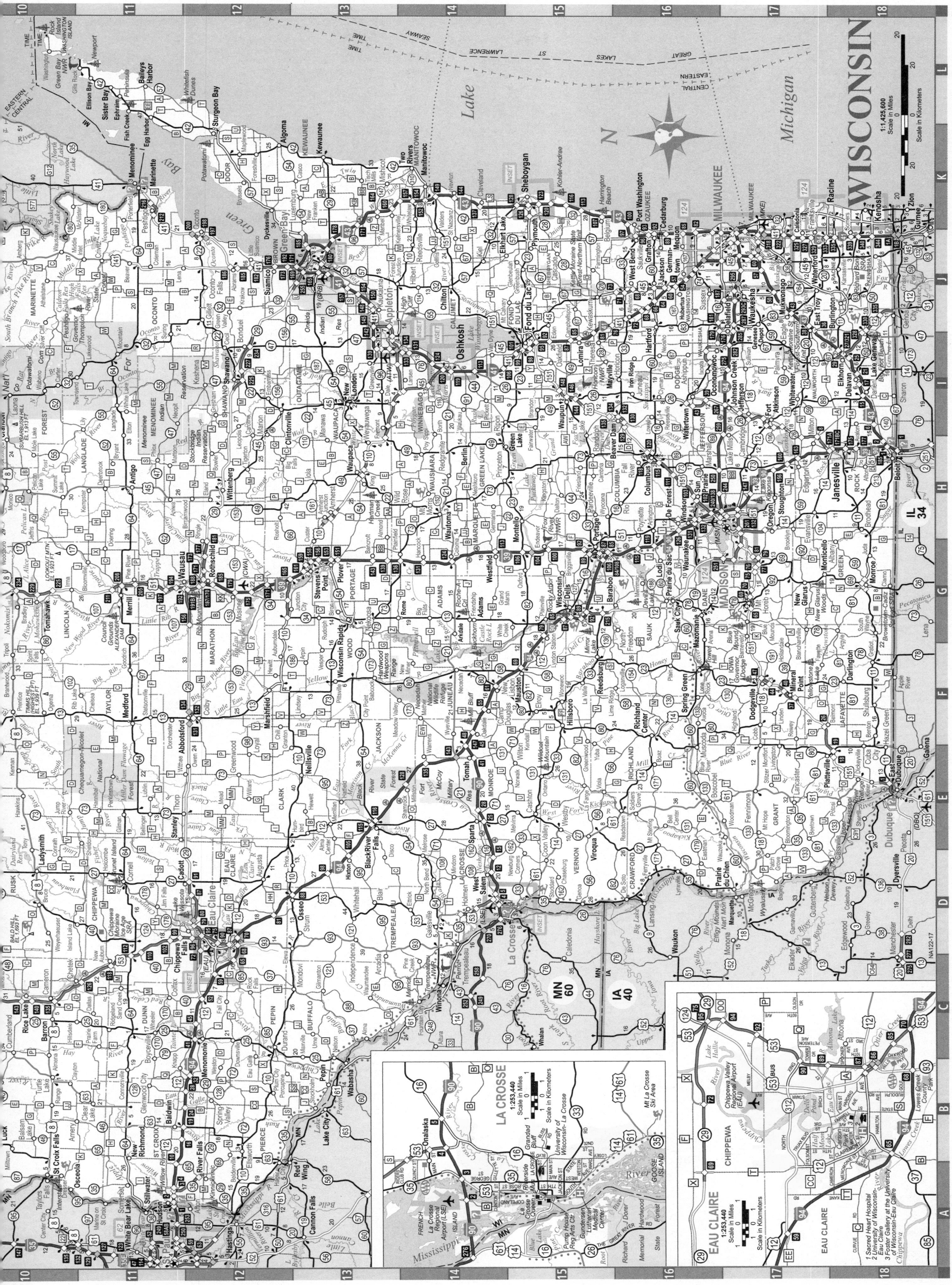

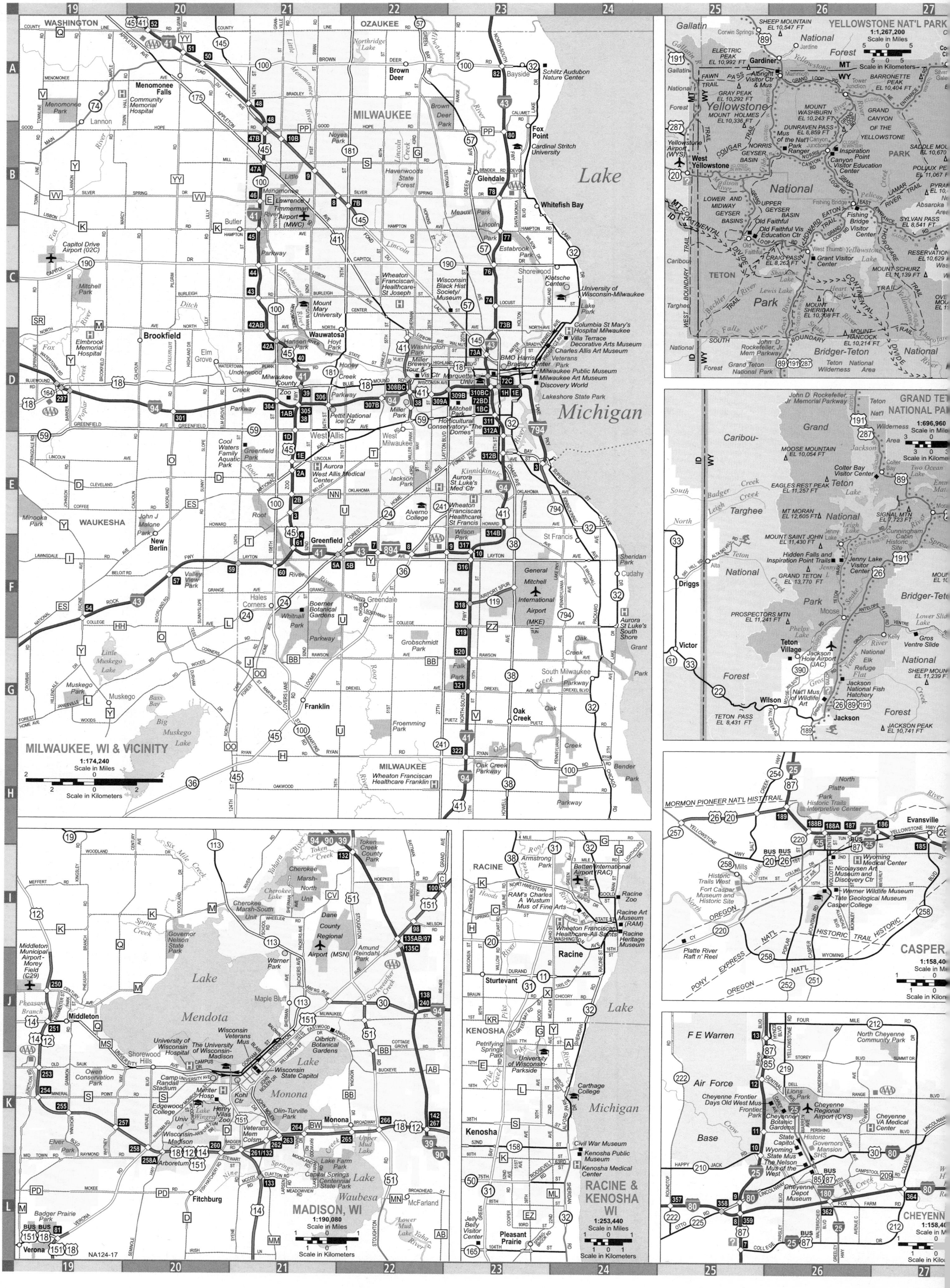

**MILWAUKEE, WI & VICINITY**
1:174,240
Scale in Miles

**MADISON, WI**
1:190,080
Scale in Miles

**RACINE & KENOSHA WI**
1:253,440
Scale in Miles

**YELLOWSTONE NAT'L PARK**
1:1,267,200
Scale in Miles

**GRAND TETON NATIONAL PARK**
1:696,960
Scale in Miles

**CASPER**
1:158,400
Scale in Miles

**CHEYENNE**
1:158,400
Scale in Miles

NA124-17

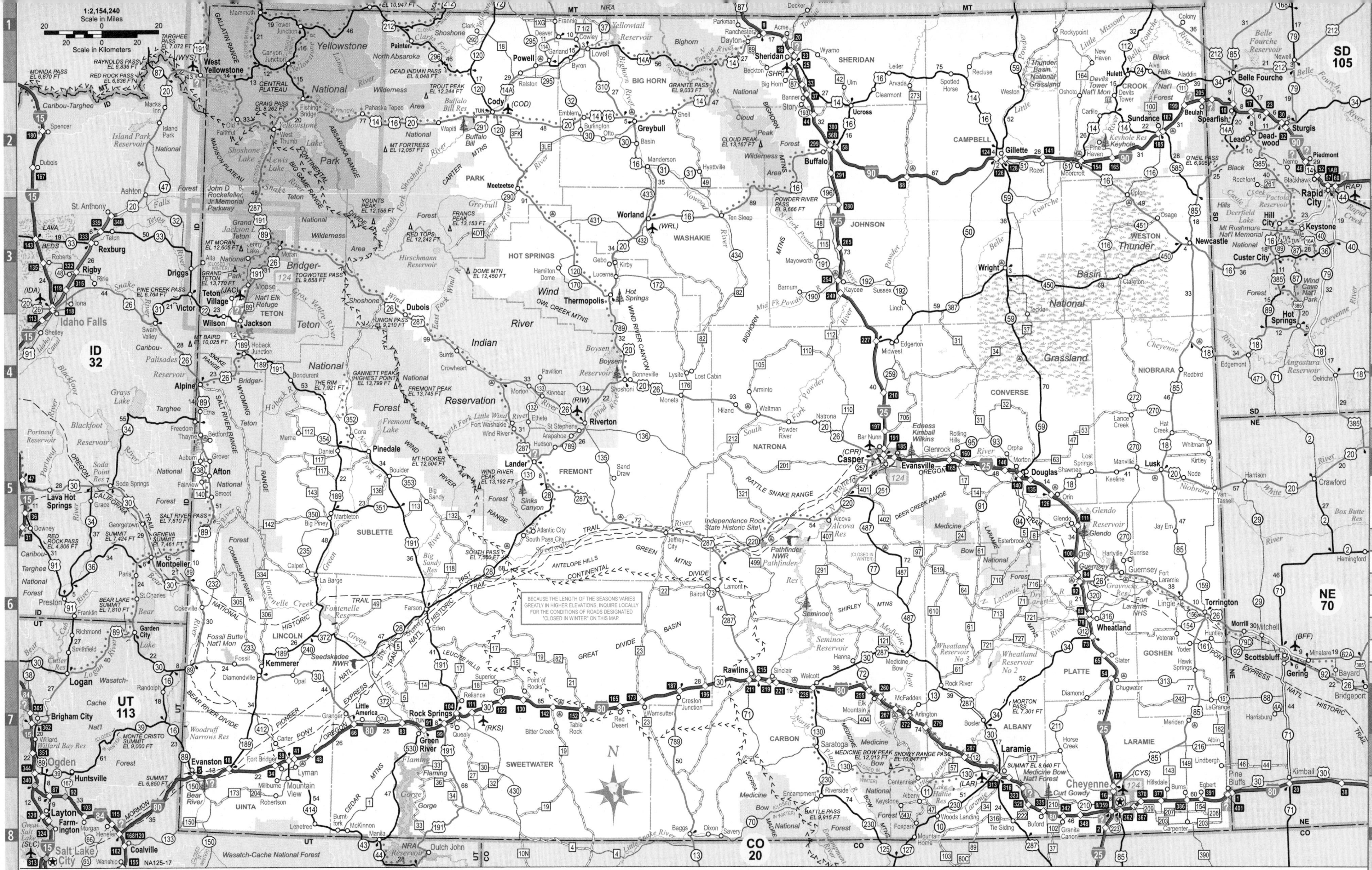

## Driving Distances In Miles

| | Buffalo | Casper | Cheyenne | Gillette | Little America | Moran | Rawlins | Sheridan |
|---|---|---|---|---|---|---|---|---|
| Casper | 112 | | 179 | 137 | 264 | 253 | 117 | 147 |
| Cheyenne | 290 | 179 | | 245 | 294 | 402 | 149 | 325 |
| Sheridan | 36 | 147 | 325 | 102 | 410 | 346 | 263 | |

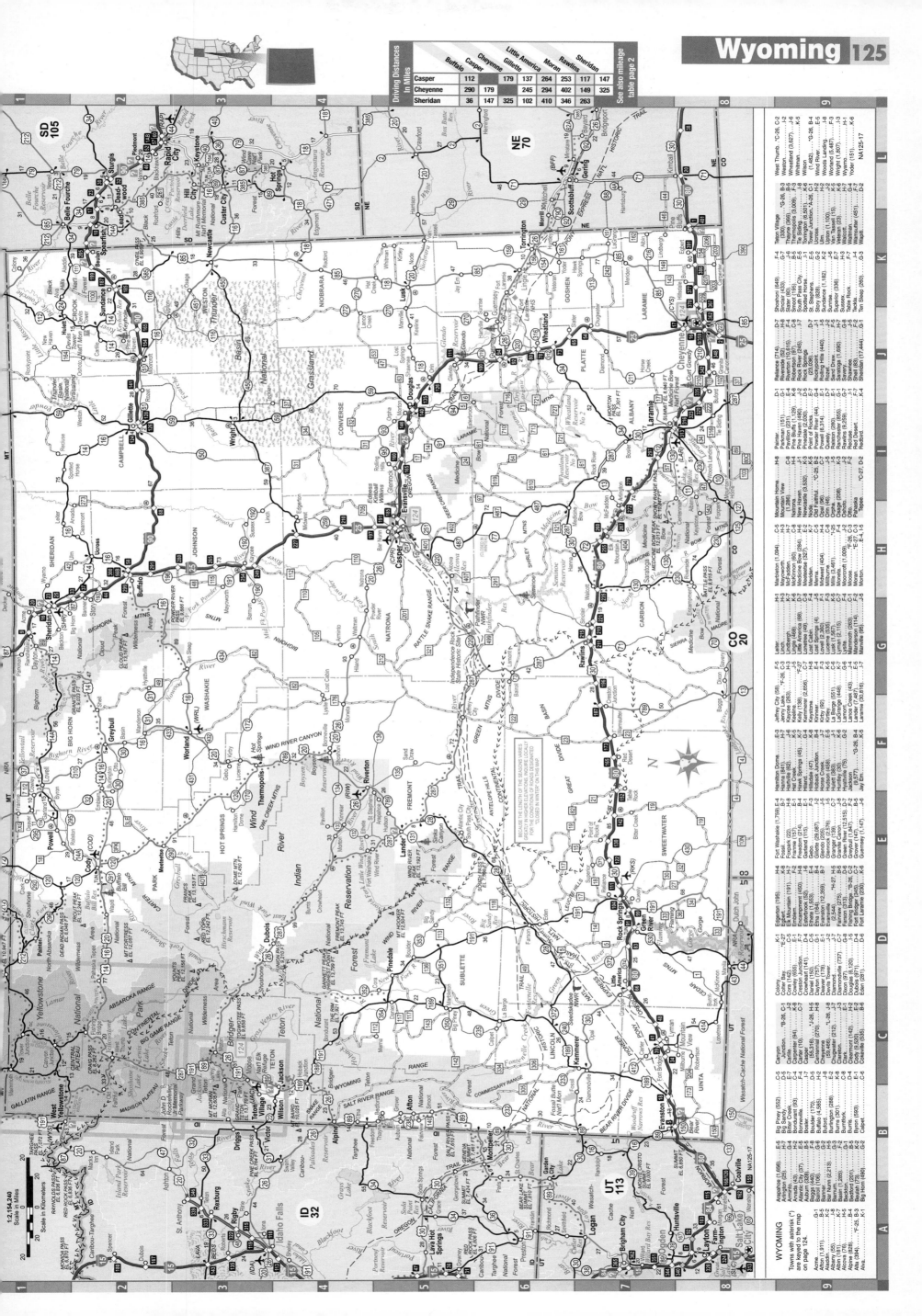

See also mileage table page 2

## WYOMING

Towns with asterisk (*) are keyed to the map on page 124.


Acme. . . . . G-1
Afton (1,911). . . . . B-5
Aladdin. . . . . K-2
Albany (55). . . . . I-8
Albin (181). . . . . K-7
Alcova (76). . . . . H-5
Alpine (828). . . . . B-4
Alta (394). . . . . *F-25, B-3
Alva. . . . . K-1
Arapahoe (1,656). . . . . E-5
Arlington (25). . . . . H-7
Arminto. . . . . G-4
Arvada (43). . . . . H-2
Atlantic City (37). . . . . E-5
Auburn (328). . . . . B-5
Baggs (440). . . . . F-8
Bairoil (106). . . . . G-6
Banner. . . . . G-2
Bar Nunn (2,213). . . . . H-5
Barnum. . . . . G-3
Basin (1,285). . . . . F-2
Beckton. . . . . G-1
Bedford (201). . . . . B-5
Beulah (73). . . . . K-2
Big Horn (490). . . . . G-2
Big Piney (552). . . . . C-5
Big Sandy. . . . . D-5
Bitter Creek. . . . . E-7
Bondurant (93). . . . . C-4
Bonneville. . . . . F-4
Bosler. . . . . I-7
Boulder (170). . . . . D-5
Buffalo (4,585). . . . . H-2
Buford. . . . . J-8
Burlington (288). . . . . E-2
Burns (301). . . . . K-8
Burntfork. . . . . C-8
Burris. . . . . D-4
Byron (593). . . . . E-1
Calpet. . . . . C-6
Canyon Junction. . . . . *B-26, C-1
Carlile. . . . . J-2
Carpenter (94). . . . . K-8
Carter (10). . . . . C-7
Casper (55,316). . . . . *J-26, H-5
Centennial (270). . . . . H-8
Cheyenne (59,466). . . . . *L-26, J-8
Chugwater (212). . . . . J-7
Clareton. . . . . J-3
Clark. . . . . E-1
Clearmont (142). . . . . H-2
Cody (9,520). . . . . E-2
Cokeville (535). . . . . B-6
Colony. . . . . K-1
Colter Bay. . . . . *E-27
Cora (142). . . . . C-5
Cowley (655). . . . . E-1
Creston Junction. . . . . F-7
Crowheart (141). . . . . D-4
Daniel (150). . . . . C-5
Dayton (757). . . . . G-1
Deaver (178). . . . . E-1
Devils Tower. . . . . J-2
Diamond. . . . . J-7
Diamondville (737). . . . . C-7
Dixon (97). . . . . G-8
Douglas (6,120). . . . . I-5
Dubois (971). . . . . D-4
Eden (281). . . . . D-6
Edgerton (195). . . . . H-4
Egbert. . . . . K-8
Elk Mountain (191). . . . . H-7
Emblem. . . . . F-2
Encampment (450). . . . . H-8
Esterbrook (52). . . . . I-6
Ethete (1,553). . . . . E-4
Etna (164). . . . . B-4
Evanston (12,359). . . . . B-7
Evansville (2,544). . . . . *H-27, H-5
Fairview (275). . . . . B-5
Farson (313). . . . . D-6
Fishing Bridge. . *B-26, C-2
Fort Bridger (345). . . . . C-7
Fort Laramie (230). . . . . K-6
Fort Washakie (1,759). E-4
Fossil. . . . . B-7
Foxpark (22). . . . . H-8
Frannie (157). . . . . E-1
Freedom (214). . . . . B-4
Garland (115). . . . . E-1
Gebo. . . . . F-3
Gillette (29,087). . . . . I-2
Glendo (205). . . . . J-5
Glenrock (2,576). . . . . I-5
Granger (139). . . . . C-7
Granite Canon. . . . . J-8
Green River (12,515). . D-7
Greybull (1,847). . . . . F-2
Grover (147). . . . . B-5
Guernsey (1,147). . . . . J-6
Hamilton Dome. . . . . E-3
Hanna (841). . . . . H-7
Hartville (62). . . . . J-6
Hat Creek. . . . . K-5
Hawk Springs (45). . . . . K-7
Hiland. . . . . G-4
Hillsdale (47). . . . . K-8
Hoback Junction. . . . . B-4
Horse Creek. . . . . J-7
Hudson (458). . . . . E-5
Hulett (383). . . . . J-1
Huntley (30). . . . . K-6
Hyattville (75). . . . . G-2
Jackson (9,577). . . . . *G-26, B-4
Jay Em. . . . . K-5
Jeffrey City (58). . . . . F-5
Jenny Lake. . . . . *F-26, C-3
Kaycee (263). . . . . H-3
Keeline. . . . . J-5
Kelly (138). . . . . *F-27
Kemmerer (2,656). . . . . C-7
Keystone. . . . . H-8
Kinnear. . . . . E-4
Kirby (92). . . . . F-3
Kirtley. . . . . K-5
La Barge (551). . . . . C-6
LaGrange (448). . . . . K-7
Lamont. . . . . G-6
Lance Creek (43). . . . . J-4
Lander (7,487). . . . . E-5
Laramie (30,816). . . . . I-7
Leiter. . . . . H-1
Linch. . . . . H-3
Lindbergh. . . . . K-7
Lingle (468). . . . . K-6
Little America (68). . . . . D-7
Lonetree (49). . . . . C-8
Lost Cabin. . . . . F-4
Lost Springs (4). . . . . J-5
Lovell (2,360). . . . . F-1
Lucerne (535). . . . . F-3
Lusk (1,567). . . . . K-5
Lyman (2,115). . . . . C-7
Lysite. . . . . F-4
Mammoth (263). . . . . C-1
Manderson (114). . . . . F-2
Manville (95). . . . . J-5
Marbleton (1,094). . . . . C-5
Mayoworth. . . . . H-3
McFadden. . . . . H-7
McKinnon (60). . . . . C-8
Medicine Bow (284). . . . . H-6
Meeteetse (327). . . . . E-2
Meriden. . . . . K-7
Merna. . . . . C-5
Midwest (404). . . . . H-4
Millburne. . . . . C-8
Mills (3,461). . . . . *I-25
Moneta. . . . . F-4
Moorcroft (1,009). . . . . J-2
Moose. . . . . *F-26, C-3
Moran. . . . . *E-27, C-3
Morton. . . . . E-4, I-5
Mountain Home. . . . . H-8
Mountain View (1,286). . . . . C-8
Natrona. . . . . H-4
New Haven. . . . . J-1
Newcastle (3,532). . . . . K-3
Node. . . . . K-5
Old Faithful. . . . . *C-25, B-2
Opal (96). . . . . C-7
Orin (46). . . . . J-5
Orpha. . . . . I-5
Osage (208). . . . . K-3
Oshoto. . . . . J-2
Otto. . . . . F-2
Pahaska Tepee. . . . . *C-27, D-2
Painter. . . . . D-1
Parkman (151). . . . . G-1
Pavillion (231). . . . . E-4
Pine Bluffs (1,129). . . . . K-8
Pine Haven (490). . . . . J-2
Pinedale (2,030). . . . . D-5
Point of Rocks. . . . . E-7
Powder River (44). . . . . G-4
Powell (6,314). . . . . E-1
Quealy. . . . . D-7
Ralston (280). . . . . E-1
Ranchester (855). . . . . G-1
Rawlins (9,259). . . . . G-7
Recluse. . . . . I-1
Red Desert. . . . . F-7
Redbird. . . . . K-4
Reliance (714). . . . . D-7
Riverside (52). . . . . H-8
Riverton (10,615). . . . . F-4
Robertson (97). . . . . C-8
Rock River (245). . . . . I-7
Rock Springs (23,036). . . . . D-7
Rockypoint. . . . . J-1
Rolling Hills (440). . . . . I-5
Rozet. . . . . J-2
Sand Draw. . . . . F-5
Saratoga (1,690). . . . . H-7
Savery. . . . . G-8
Shawnee. . . . . J-5
Shell (83). . . . . F-2
Sheridan (17,444). . . . . G-1
Shoshoni (649). . . . . F-4
Sinclair (433). . . . . G-7
Slater (80). . . . . J-6
Smoot (195). . . . . B-5
South Pass City. . . . . E-5
Spotted Horse. . . . . I-1
St. Stephens. . . . . E-5
Story (828). . . . . G-2
Sundance (1,182). . . . . K-2
Sunrise. . . . . J-6
Superior (336). . . . . E-7
Sussex. . . . . H-3
Table Rock. . . . . F-7
Teckla. . . . . I-4
Ten Sleep (260). . . . . G-3
Teton Village (330). . . . . *G-26, B-3
Thayne (366). . . . . B-5
Thermopolis (3,009). . . F-3
Tie Siding. . . . . I-8
Torrington (6,501). . . . . K-6
Tower Junction. *A-26, C-1
Ucross. . . . . H-2
Ulm. . . . . H-2
Upton (1,100). . . . . J-2
Van Tassell (15). . . . . K-5
Veteran (23). . . . . K-6
Walcott. . . . . H-7
Waltman. . . . . G-4
Wamsutter (451). . . . . F-7
Wapiti. . . . . D-2
West Thumb. . *C-26, C-2
Weston. . . . . I-2
Wheatland (3,627). . . . . J-6
Whitman. . . . . K-5
Wilson (1,482). . . . . *G-26, B-4
Wind River. . . . . E-5
Woods Landing. . . . . I-8
Worland (5,487). . . . . F-3
Wright (1,807). . . . . I-3
Wyarno. . . . . H-1
Yoder (151). . . . . K-6


NA125-17

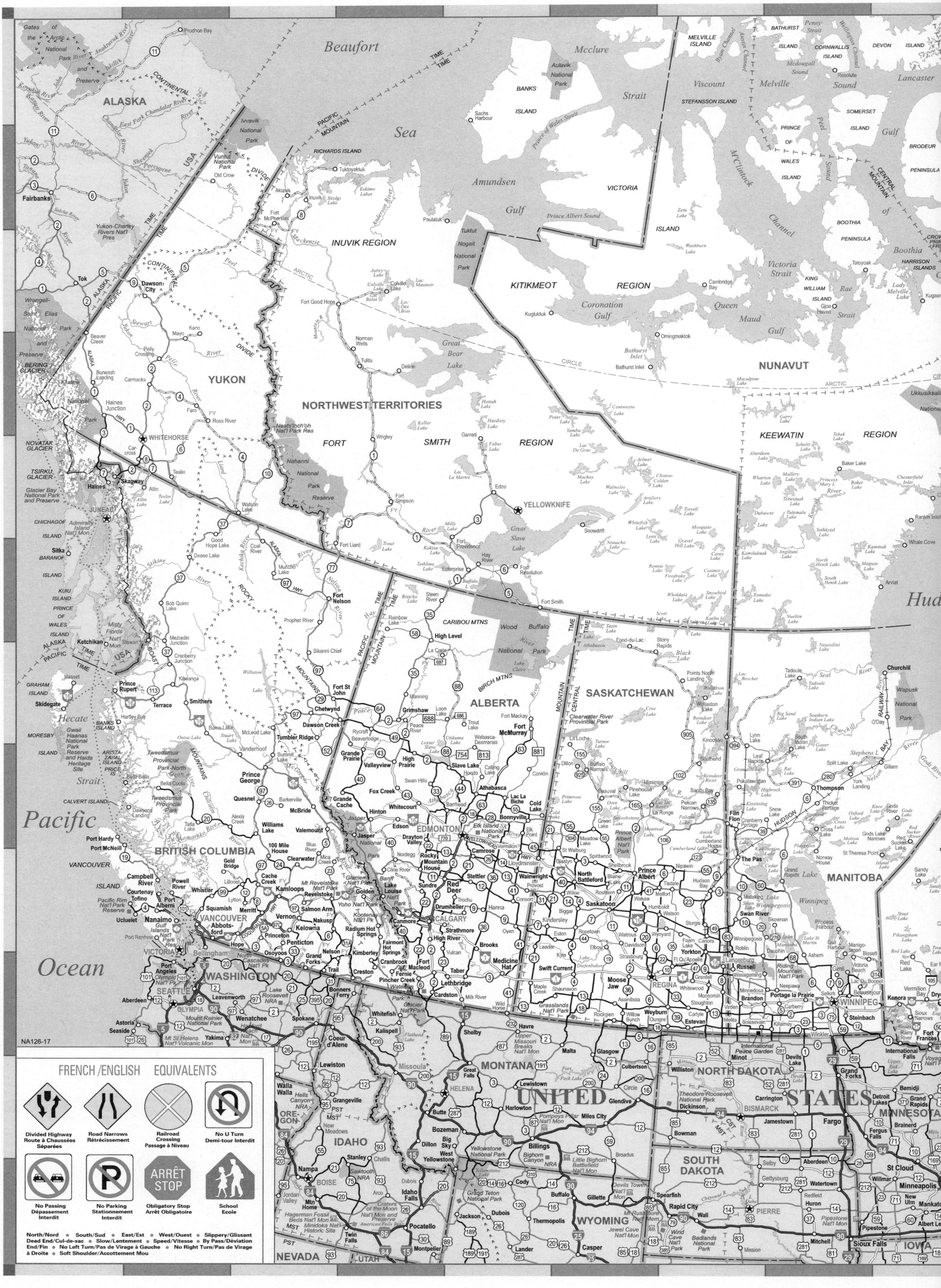

FRENCH / ENGLISH EQUIVALENTS

Divided Highway
Route à Chaussées
Séparées

Road Narrows
Rétrécissement

Railroad
Crossing
Passage à Niveau

No U Turn
Demi-tour Interdit

No Passing
Dépassement
Interdit

No Parking
Stationnement
Interdit

ARRÊT
STOP
Obligatory Stop
Arrêt Obligatoire

School
Ecole

North/Nord • South/Sud • East/Est • West/Ouest • Slippery/Glissant
Dead End/Cul-de-sac • Slow/Lentement • Speed/Vitesse • By Pass/Déviation
End/Fin • No Left Turn/Pas de Virage à Gauche • No Right Turn/Pas de Virage
à Droite • Soft Shoulder/Accottement Mou

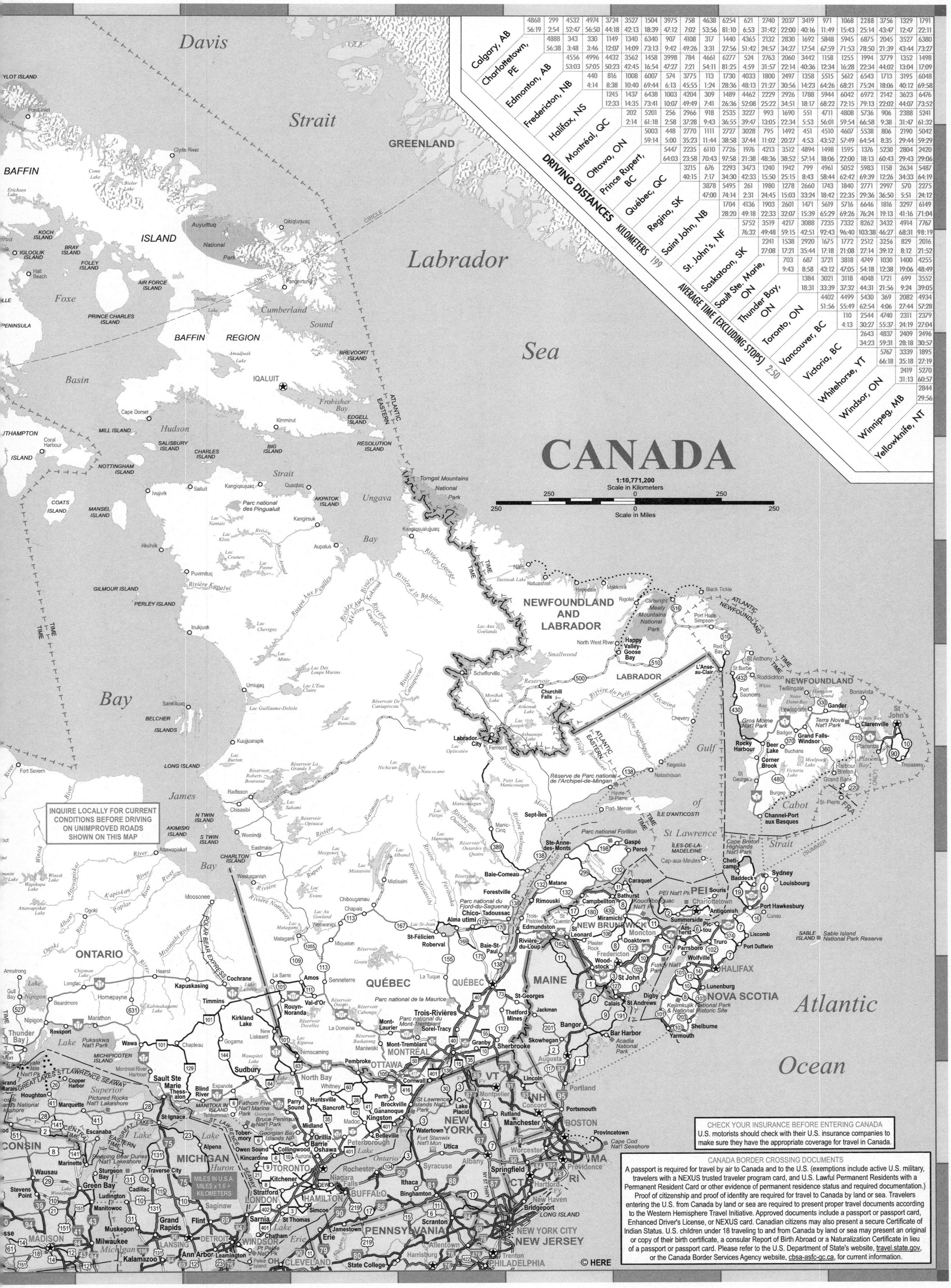

DRIVING DISTANCES — KILOMETERS (e.g. 199) / AVERAGE TIME (EXCLUDING STOPS) (e.g. 2:50)

| | Charlottetown, PE | Edmonton, AB | Fredericton, NB | Halifax, NS | Montréal, QC | Ottawa, ON | Prince Rupert, BC | Québec, QC | Regina, SK | Saint John, NB | St. John's, NF | Saskatoon, SK | Sault Ste. Marie, ON | Thunder Bay, ON | Toronto, ON | Vancouver, BC | Victoria, BC | Whitehorse, YT | Windsor, ON | Winnipeg, MB | Yellowknife, NT |
|---|---|---|---|---|---|---|---|---|---|---|---|---|---|---|---|---|---|---|---|---|---|
| Calgary, AB | 4868 56:19 | 299 2:54 | 4532 52:47 | 4974 56:50 | 3724 44:18 | 3527 42:13 | 1504 18:39 | 3975 47:12 | 758 7:02 | 4638 53:56 | 6254 81:10 | 621 6:53 | 2740 31:42 | 2037 22:00 | 3419 40:16 | 971 11:49 | 1068 15:43 | 2288 25:14 | 3756 43:47 | 1329 12:47 | 1791 22:11 |
| Charlottetown, PE | | 4888 56:38 | 343 3:48 | 330 3:46 | 1149 12:07 | 1340 14:09 | 6340 73:13 | 907 9:42 | 4108 49:26 | 317 3:31 | 1440 27:56 | 4365 51:42 | 2132 24:57 | 2830 34:27 | 1692 17:54 | 5848 67:59 | 5945 71:53 | 6875 78:50 | 2045 21:39 | 3527 43:44 | 6380 73:27 |
| Edmonton, AB | | | 4556 53:03 | 4996 57:05 | 4432 50:23 | 3562 42:45 | 1458 16:54 | 3998 47:27 | 784 7:21 | 4661 54:11 | 6277 81:25 | 524 4:59 | 2763 31:57 | 2060 22:14 | 3442 40:36 | 1158 12:34 | 1255 16:28 | 1994 22:34 | 3779 44:02 | 1352 13:04 | 1498 17:09 |
| Fredericton, NB | | | | 440 4:14 | 816 8:38 | 1008 10:40 | 6007 69:44 | 574 6:13 | 3775 45:55 | 113 1:24 | 1730 28:36 | 4033 48:13 | 1800 21:27 | 2497 30:56 | 1358 14:23 | 5515 64:26 | 5612 68:21 | 6543 75:24 | 1713 18:06 | 3195 40:12 | 6048 69:58 |
| Halifax, NS | | | | | 1245 12:33 | 1437 14:35 | 6438 73:41 | 1003 10:07 | 4204 49:49 | 309 7:41 | 1489 26:36 | 4462 52:08 | 2229 25:22 | 2926 34:51 | 1788 18:17 | 5944 68:22 | 6042 72:15 | 6972 79:13 | 2142 22:02 | 3623 44:07 | 6476 73:52 |
| Montréal, QC | | | | | | 202 2:14 | 5201 61:18 | 256 2:58 | 2966 37:28 | 918 9:43 | 2535 36:55 | 3227 39:47 | 993 13:05 | 1690 22:34 | 551 5:53 | 4711 56:01 | 4808 59:54 | 5736 66:58 | 906 9:38 | 2388 31:47 | 5241 61:32 |
| Ottawa, ON | | | | | | | 5003 59:14 | 448 5:00 | 2770 35:23 | 1111 11:44 | 2727 38:58 | 3028 37:44 | 795 11:02 | 1492 20:27 | 451 4:53 | 4510 43:52 | 4607 57:49 | 5538 64:54 | 806 8:35 | 2190 29:44 | 5042 59:29 |
| Prince Rupert, BC | | | | | | | | 5447 64:03 | 2235 23:58 | 6110 70:43 | 7726 97:58 | 1976 21:38 | 4213 48:36 | 3512 38:52 | 4894 57:14 | 1498 18:06 | 1595 22:00 | 1376 18:13 | 5230 60:43 | 2804 29:43 | 2420 29:06 |
| Québec, QC | | | | | | | | | 3215 40:15 | 676 7:17 | 2293 34:30 | 3473 42:33 | 1240 15:50 | 1942 25:15 | 799 8:43 | 4961 58:44 | 5052 62:42 | 5983 69:39 | 1158 12:26 | 2634 34:33 | 5487 64:19 |
| Regina, SK | | | | | | | | | | 3878 47:00 | 5495 74:14 | 261 2:31 | 1980 24:45 | 1278 15:03 | 2660 33:24 | 1743 18:42 | 1840 22:35 | 2771 29:36 | 2997 36:50 | 570 5:51 | 2275 24:12 |
| Saint John, NB | | | | | | | | | | | 1704 28:20 | 4136 49:18 | 1903 22:33 | 2601 32:07 | 1471 15:39 | 5619 65:29 | 5716 69:26 | 6646 76:24 | 1816 19:13 | 3297 41:16 | 6149 71:04 |
| St. John's, NF | | | | | | | | | | | | 5752 76:32 | 3519 49:48 | 4217 59:15 | 3088 42:51 | 7235 92:43 | 7332 96:40 | 8262 103:38 | 3432 46:27 | 4914 68:31 | 7767 98:19 |
| Saskatoon, SK | | | | | | | | | | | | | 2241 27:08 | 1538 17:21 | 2920 35:44 | 1675 17:18 | 1772 21:08 | 2512 27:14 | 3256 39:12 | 829 8:12 | 2016 21:52 |
| Sault Ste. Marie, ON | | | | | | | | | | | | | | 703 9:43 | 687 8:58 | 3721 43:12 | 3818 47:05 | 4749 54:18 | 1030 12:38 | 1400 19:06 | 4255 48:49 |
| Thunder Bay, ON | | | | | | | | | | | | | | | 1384 18:31 | 3021 33:39 | 3118 37:32 | 4048 44:31 | 1721 21:56 | 699 9:24 | 3552 39:05 |
| Toronto, ON | | | | | | | | | | | | | | | | 4402 51:56 | 4499 55:49 | 5430 62:54 | 369 4:06 | 2082 27:44 | 4934 57:28 |
| Vancouver, BC | | | | | | | | | | | | | | | | | 110 4:13 | 2544 30:27 | 4740 55:37 | 2311 24:19 | 2379 27:04 |
| Victoria, BC | | | | | | | | | | | | | | | | | | 2643 34:23 | 4837 59:31 | 2409 28:18 | 2496 30:57 |
| Whitehorse, YT | | | | | | | | | | | | | | | | | | | 5767 66:18 | 3339 35:18 | 1895 27:19 |
| Windsor, ON | | | | | | | | | | | | | | | | | | | | 2419 31:13 | 5270 60:57 |
| Winnipeg, MB | | | | | | | | | | | | | | | | | | | | | 2844 29:56 |

**CHECK YOUR INSURANCE BEFORE ENTERING CANADA**

U.S. motorists should check with their U.S. insurance companies to make sure they have the appropriate coverage for travel in Canada.

**CANADA BORDER CROSSING DOCUMENTS**

A passport is required for travel by air to Canada and to the U.S. (exemptions include active U.S. military, travelers with a NEXUS trusted traveler program card, and U.S. Lawful Permanent Residents with a Permanent Resident Card or other evidence of permanent residence status and required documentation.) Proof of citizenship and proof of identity are required for travel to Canada by land or sea. Travelers entering the U.S. from Canada by land or sea are required to present proper travel documents according to the Western Hemisphere Travel Initiative. Approved documents include a passport or passport card, Enhanced Driver's License, or NEXUS card. Canadian citizens may also present a secure Certificate of Indian Status. U.S. children under 18 traveling to and from Canada by land or sea may present an original or copy of their birth certificate, a consular Report of Birth Abroad or a Naturalization Certificate in lieu of a passport or passport card. Please refer to the U.S. Department of State's website, travel.state.gov, or the Canada Border Services Agency website, cbsa-asfc-gc.ca, for current information.

| Driving Distances In Kilometers | Cranbrook | Dawson Creek | Hope | Kamloops | Nanaimo | Osoyoos | Prince Rupert | Vancouver | Victoria |
|---|---|---|---|---|---|---|---|---|---|
| Kamloops | 608 | 925 | 201 | | 431 | 285 | 523 | 1237 | 349 | 446 |
| Prince George | 926 | 405 | 635 | 523 | 867 | 802 | 719 | 785 | 882 |
| Vancouver | 840 | 1187 | 150 | 349 | 85 | 396 | 785 | 1498 | 110 |
| Victoria | 938 | 1284 | 446 | 446 | 110 | 493 | 882 | 1595 | 110 |

See also mileage table page 2

## ALBERTA

Towns with asterisk (*) are keyed to the maps on pages 130-131.
Towns with double asterisk (**) are keyed to the map on page 9.

## BRITISH COLUMBIA

ALASKA · PACIFIC · Hecate Strait · Pacific Ocean

## ALBERTA BRITISH COLUMBIA

1:3,168,000
Scale in Kilometers
50    0    50
Scale in Miles
50    0    50

### ALBERTA BRITISH COLUMBIA ORIENTATION
1:15,840,000
Scale in Kilometers
100   0   100
Scale in Miles
100   0   100

HAIDA · GRAHAM ISLAND · MORESBY ISLAND · GWAII HAANAS NATIONAL PARK RESERVE AND HAIDA HERITAGE SITE · SKEENA-QUEEN CHARLOTTE · KITIMAT-STIKINE · BULKLEY-NECHAKO · Tweedsmuir Provincial Park · CARIBOO · CENTRAL COAST · COAST MOUNTAINS · STRATHCONA · POWELL RIVER · SUNSHINE COAST · SQUAMISH-LILLOOET · FRASER VALLEY · GREATER VANCOUVER · CAPITAL

Prince Rupert · Terrace · Smithers · Prince George · Quesnel · Williams Lake · Bella Coola · Port Hardy · Port McNeill · Campbell River · Courtenay · Comox · Powell River · Nanaimo · Port Alberni · Tofino · Ucluelet · Duncan · VANCOUVER · Whistler · Abbotsford · Chilliwack · Victoria · Sooke

| Driving Distances In Kilometers | Calgary | Edmonton | Fort Macleod | Jasper | Lake Louise | Medicine Hat | Peace River | Valleyview |
|---|---|---|---|---|---|---|---|---|
| Calgary | | 299 | 171 | 413 | 182 | 292 | 781 | 643 |
| Edmonton | 299 | | 465 | 365 | 470 | 577 | 487 | 349 |
| Medicine Hat | 292 | 577 | 215 | 721 | 488 | | 1062 | 921 |

See also mileage table page 2

ove
.........I-28
er (284)..E-26
on
..**G-15, J-21
mes
.........E-26
hn
)..C-28, J-21
e.......K-32
.........J-20
ke
.........E-25
2,016). .L-30
.........K-25
.........L-32
nch.......I-27
4,437). .K-26
y (395)..K-25
.**J-13, D-22
ge (10). .I-26
r
.........J-24
...I-31, L-21
pe
.**G-13, J-20
.........C-29

Grand Forks (3,985)..........L-30
Granisle (303)....D-25
Greenwood (708).L-30
Grindrod (1,453). .J-29
Groundbirch.......D-28
Hagensborg (219)..........G-24
Halfmoon Bay (396)..........K-25
Hanceville.........H-26
Harrison Hot Springs (1,468)..........K-27
Harrison Mills (405)..........K-27
Harrogate..........J-31
Hartley Bay....**K-14, E-22, K-20
Hazelton (270)...**J-14, D-24
Hedley (252)......K-28
Heriot Bay (527). .J-25
Hixon (220)........F-27
Holberg (51).......I-22
Hope (5,969)...K-27, L-21
Horsefly (137)....H-28
Horseshoe Bay. .*F-37
Houston (3,147). .E-24
Hudson's Hope (970)..........C-28
Huntingdon........L-27
Invermere (2,955). . .J-32, L-22
Iskut......**H-13, J-20
Jade City.......**G-13
Jaffray (494)......L-32
Juskatla..........E-20
Kamloops (85,678)......*D-42, J-28, L-21
Kaslo (1,026).....K-31
Kelowna (117,312).....*F-42, K-29, L-21
Kemano..........F-23
Keremeos (1,330).........L-29
Kildonan..........K-24
Kimberley (6,652).........K-32
Kingcome Inlet....I-24
Kingsgate.........L-32
Kitchener (261). . .L-31
Kitimat (8,335)..**J-14, E-23
Kitkatla..........E-21
Kitwanga.......**J-14, D-23, K-20
Kleena Kleene. . .H-25
Klemtu...........G-23
Kyuquot...........J-23
Lac la Hache (239)...........H-28
Ladysmith (7,921).........L-25
Lake Cowichan (2,974).........L-25
Langley (25,081).......*L-45
Laxgalts'ap (378).D-22
Liard River...**G-14, J-20
Likely............G-28
Lillooet (2,322)....J-27
Lions Bay (1,318).........K-26
Little Fort..........I-28
Logan Lake (2,073).........J-28
Lone Butte (316). .I-28
Longworth.........F-28
Louis Creek........I-29
Lower Nicola (1,068).........J-28
Lumby (1,731)....J-29
Lund (321).........J-25
Lytton (228).......J-27
MacKenzie (3,300).........D-27
Madeira Park.....K-25
Mahood Falls....H-28
Malahat...........L-26
Malakwa (596)....J-30
Manning Park....L-28
Manson Creek. . .D-26
Mansons Landing (149)...........J-25
Maple Ridge (76,052).......*I-45
Mara (309).........J-29
Marysville.........K-32
Masset (884)...**K-13, E-20, K-19
McBride (586)....G-29, K-21
McDame Post. .**G-13
McLeese Lake (197)...........H-27
McLeod Lake.....D-27, K-20
McLure............I-28
Meadow Creek. . .K-31
Merritt (7,113). . . .J-28
Merville (21,115)..K-25
Meziadin Junction.**I-13, J-20
Mica Creek.......H-30
Midway (674)......L-29
Minstrel Island. . . .I-24
Mirror Lake........K-31
Mission (36,426). .L-27
Moberly Lake (199)...........D-28
Monte Creek......J-29
Monte Lake.......J-29
Moricetown.......D-24
Moyie.............L-32
Mt. Currie.........J-26
Muncho Lake. . .**G-14, J-20
Nakusp (1,569). . .J-30, L-21
Namu.............H-23
Nanaimo (83,810)..K-25, L-20
Nanoose Bay (5,471).........K-25
Nelson (10,230). .K-31
Nemaiah Valley. . .I-26
New Aiyansh (758)..........**J-14
New Denver (504)...........K-31
New Hazelton (666)...........D-24
New Westminster (65,976).......*J-42
Nimpo Lake......G-25
North Vancouver (48,196)......*G-39
Oak Bay (18,015).......*B-40
Ocean Falls......G-23
Okanagan Falls. .K-29
Oliver (4,824).....L-29
Oona River.......E-22
Osoyoos (4,845). . .L-21, L-29
Oyama...........K-29
Parksville (11,977)........K-25
Parson............I-31
Pavilion...........J-27
Peachland (5,200).........K-29
Pemberton (2,369).........J-26
Pender Island. . . .L-26
Penny............F-28
Penticton (32,877)..K-29, L-21
Pitt Meadows (17,736).......*I-45
Port Alberni (17,743).......K-25
Port Alice (805). . .I-23
Port Clements (378). .**K-13, E-20
Port Coquitlam (56,342)......*H-43
Port Edward (544). .**J-13, E-22
Port Hardy (4,008). . .I-23, L-20
Port McNeill (2,505).........I-23
Port Mellon......K-26
Port Moody (32,975)......*H-43
Port Neville.......J-24
Port Renfrew (139)..........L-25
Port Simpson....D-22
Pouce Coupe (738)...........D-29
Powell River (13,165).......K-25
Prince George (71,974).....*B-42, F-27, K-21
Prince Rupert (12,508).....**J-13, D-22, K-19
Princeton (2,724)........K-28
Progress.........D-29
Prophet River....J-21
Qualicum Beach (8,687).........K-25
Quatsino (47).....I-23
Queen Charlotte (944)....E-20, K-19
Quesnel (10,007).G-27, K-21
Quilchena........J-28
Radium Hot Springs (777)...........J-32
Revelstoke (7,139).........J-30
Richmond (190,473).....*J-39
Riske Creek.....H-27
Roberts Creek (1,772)........K-26
Robson (400). . . .L-30
Rock Creek (86)..L-29
Rogers Pass......I-31
Rossland (3,556).L-30
Salmo (1,139). .L-21, L-31
Salmon Arm (17,464).......J-29
Sandspit (297). . .E-20
Savona...........J-28
Sayward (317). . .J-24
Scotch Creek (669)...........J-29
Sechelt (9,291). .K-26
Seton Portage (56)............J-27
Sewell Inlet......F-20
Shalalth..........J-27
Shelter Bay......J-30
Shuswap Falls (114)...........J-29
Sicamous (2,441).........J-29
Sidney (11,178). .L-26
Sikanni Chief.....J-21
Silverton (195). . .K-31
Simoom Sound. . .I-24
Sinclair Mills.....F-28
Sirdar............L-31
Skidegate.....**K-13, E-20
Skookumchuck. .K-32
Slocan (296).....K-30
Slocan Park.....K-30
Smith River....**G-14
Smithers (5,404). .D-24, K-20
Sointula (576)....I-23
Sooke (11,435)...L-25
Sorrento (1,255). .J-29
South Hazelton (211)..........D-24
South Slocan....K-30
Southbank (102)..E-25
Sparwood (3,667)........K-33
Spences Bridge. .J-28
Spillimacheen....J-31
Squamish (17,158).......K-26
Stewart (494)...**I-13, K-20
Sullivan Bay......I-23
Summerland (11,280).......K-29
Summit Lake....E-27, K-21
Sun Peaks.......J-29
Surrey (468,251).....*J-43
Ta Ta Creek......K-32
Tahsis (316)......J-23
Takysie Lake....F-25
Tappen (826)....J-29
Tatla Lake. . .H-25, L-20
Tatlayoko Lake..H-25
Taylor (1,373)...C-29
Telegraph Creek (5)....**H-12, J-19
Telkwa (1,350). .D-24
Terrace (11,486)....**J-14, D-23, K-20
Thornhill.........D-23
Tillicum.........*A-37
Tlell (179).......E-20
Toad River....**G-14
Tofino (1,876)...K-24
Tomslake........D-29
Topley (80)......E-25
Tulameen........K-28
Tumbler Ridge (2,710).D-28, K-21
Tête Jaune Cache........G-29
Ucluelet (1,627).K-24
Union Bay (1,156).......K-25
Upper Fraser. . .F-28
Valemount (1,020).G-29, K-21
Vancouver (603,502). . .*E-38, *I-39, K-26, L-20
Vanderhoof (4,480)..F-26, K-20
Vavenby.........I-29
Vernon (38,150).J-29, L-21
Victoria (80,017). . . .*B-38, L-20, L-26
Waglisla........G-23
Walhachin.......J-28
Wardner........K-32
Wasa...........K-32
Wells (245).....G-28
West Kelowna (30,892)......K-29
West Vancouver (42,694).....*G-38
Westbridge......L-29
Westwold........J-29
Whaletown......J-25
Whistler (9,824). .J-26, L-21
Williams Lake (10,832).....H-27, K-21
Willow River (130).........F-27
Windermere (1,019)........J-32
Winfield.........K-29
Winlaw (294). . .K-30
Winter Harbour (20)...........I-22
Wonowon.......J-21
Woss (235)......J-23
Wynndel........L-31
Yahk (140)......L-32
Yale (136)......K-27
Ymir (231)......L-31
Youbou (966). . .L-25
Zeballos (125)...J-23

NA128-17

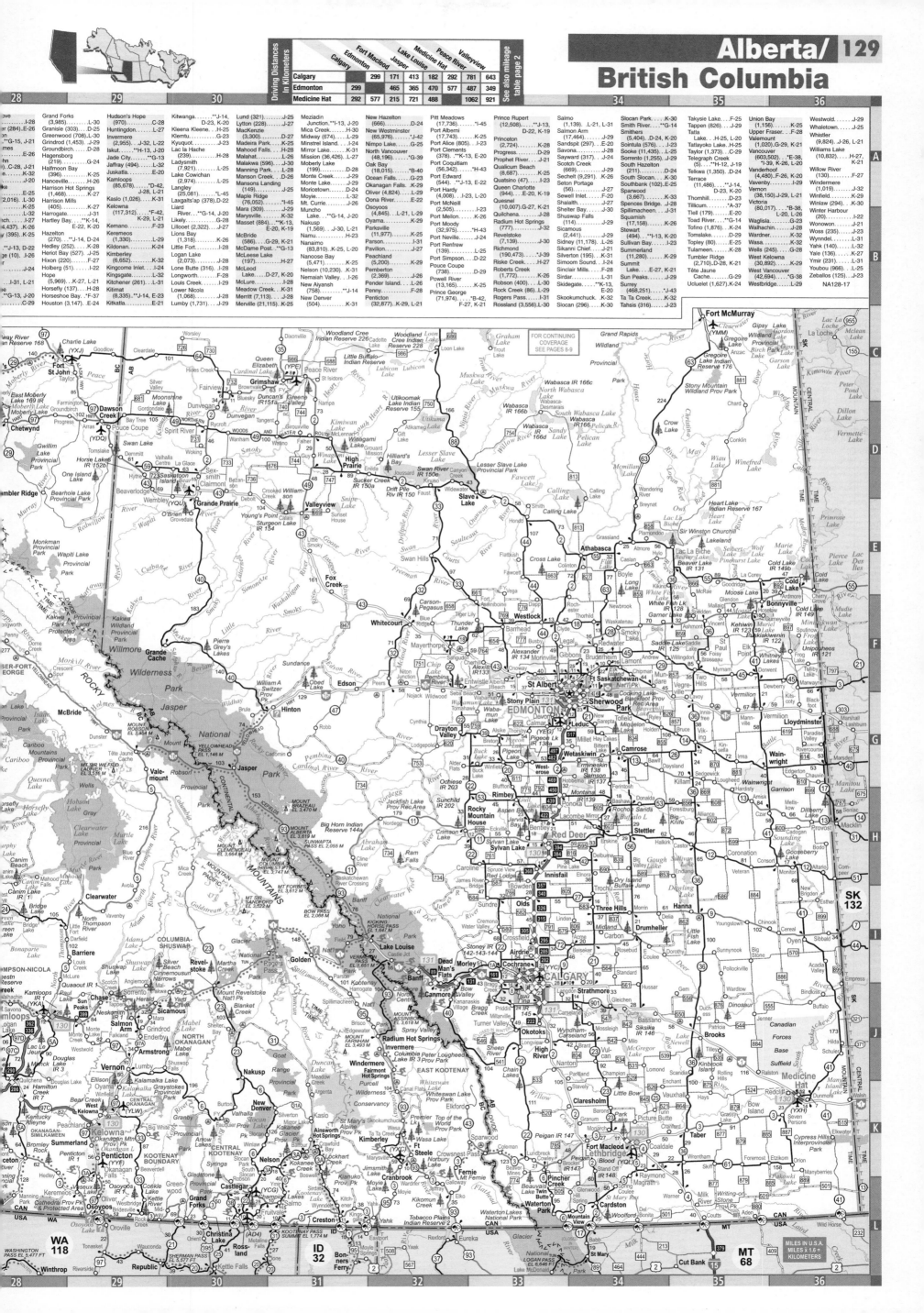

**PRINCE GEORGE, BC**
1:158,400
Scale in Kilometers
0.5   0   0.5
Scale in Miles
0.5   0   0.5

Reg Prince George Railway & Forestry Mus
McMillan Creek
Prince George Regional Hospital
Exhibition Park
The Exploration Place Museum & Science Center
Carrie Jane Gray Park
University of Northern British Columbia
Prince George Airport (YXS)

**RED DEER, AB**
1:158,400
Scale in Kilometers
0.5   0   0.5
Scale in Miles
0.5   0   0.5

Recreation Area
Cash Casino
Alberta Sports Hall of Fame & Museum
Gaetz Lakes Sanctuary
Red Deer Museum
Red Deer Regional Hosp
Red Deer College
Kin Sunnybrook Farm
Kerry Wood Nature Centre and Interpretive Canyon
St Mary's Church
Collicutt Centre
Westerner Park

**VICTORIA, BC**
1:69,696
Scale in Kilometers
0.5   0   0.5
Scale in Miles
0.5   0   0.5

Tillicum
Cedar Hill Park
Royal Jubilee Hospital
Spring Tide Whale Watching
Art Gallery of Greater Victoria
Craigdarroch Castle
Oak Bay
Miniature World
Victoria Hippo Tours
Legislative Assembly of British Columbia
Emily Carr House
The Royal BC Mus
Christ Church Cathedral
Government House and Gardens
Beacon Hill
Victoria Harbour
Strait of Juan De Fuca
Ross Bay

**DOWNTOWN VANCOUVER**
1:44,352
Scale in Kilometers
0.2   0   0.2
Scale in Miles
0.2   0   0.2

Harbour Cruises
Prince of Whales Whale Watching
DEADMAN'S ISLAND
Stanley Park
Lost Lagoon
Coal Harbour
Burrard Inlet
Vancouver Convention Centre
Canada Place
FlyOver Canada
Vancouver Lookout at Harbour Centre Tower
Christ Church Cathedral
Vancouver Art Gallery
St Paul's Hospital
Holy Rosary Cathedral
Dr Sun Yat-Sen Classical Chinese Garden
Rogers Arena
BC Place Stadium
Edgewater Casino
Science World at TELUS World of Science
English Bay
Vancouver Maritime Museum
HR MacMillan Space Centre
Vanier Park
False Creek

**KAMLOOPS, BC**
1:126,720
Scale in Kilometers
0.5   0   0.5
Scale in Miles
0.5   0   0.5

Kamloops Indian Reserve 1
McArthur Island Park
St Joseph's Church
Kamloops Art Gallery
Lake City Casino
Secwepemc Museum and Heritage Park
Thompson Rivers University
Kamloops Mus & Archives
Royal Inland Hospital
Peterson Creek Park

**MEDICINE HAT, AB**
1:110,880
Scale in Kilometers
0.5   0   0.5
Scale in Miles
0.5   0   0.5

Police Point Park
Esplanade Arts & Heritage Ctr
John's Butterfly House
Medicine Hat Regional Hospital
Medicine Hat College
Medicine Hat Municipal Airport (YXH)
Kin Coulee Park
Saamis Teepee
Persons Spec Park
Casino by Vanshaw

**KELOWNA, BC**
1:142,560
Scale in Kilometers
0.5   0   0.5
Scale in Miles
0.5   0   0.5

Bear Creek Provincial Park
Geert Maas Sculpture Gardens and Gallery
Okanagan Mountain Park
Knox Mountain Park
Lake City Casino
BC Orchard Industry Museum
Kelowna General Hospital
Kelowna Land and Orchard Co
Okanagan College
Okanagan Lake
Mission Creek Regional Park

**LETHBRIDGE, AB**
1:126,720
Scale in Kilometers
0.5   0   0.5
Scale in Miles
0.5   0   0.5

Peenaquim Park
Indian Battle Park
Galt Mus & Archives
Southern Alberta Art Gallery
Casino Lethbridge
Nikka Yuko Japanese Garden
Henderson Lake
Nicholas Sheran Lake
University of Lethbridge
Botterill Bottom Park
Chinook Regional Hospital
Henderson Lake

**VANCOUVER, BC**
1:190,080
Scale in Kilometers
3   0   3
Scale in Miles
3   0   3

Sewell's Marina
Horseshoe Bay
Cypress Provincial Park
Capilano Lake
Grouse Mountain
Lynn Headwaters Regional Park
Nelson Canyon Park
Cypress River Regional Park
Capilano Suspension Bridge & Park
Lynn Canyon Ecology Centre
Lighthouse Park
North Vancouver
Lions Gate Hosp
West Vancouver
Capilano Indian Reserve 5
North Vancouver Museum and Archives
Maplewood Farm
Burrard Inlet
Stanley Park
Vancouver Aquarium Marine Science Centre
VANCOUVER
Seymour Creek Indian Reserve 2
Pacific National Exhibition
Confederation Park
Burnaby Mountain Park
Simon Fraser Univ
Port Moody
Burrard Inlet
Belcarra Regional Park
Port Moody Station Museum
Coquitlam River Regional Park
Town Centre Park
Eagle Ridge Hosp
Minnekhada Regional Park
University Endowment Lands
Old Hastings Mill Store Museum
Jericho Beach Park
Playland Amusement Park
Deeley Motorcycle Exhibition
University of British Columbia
UBC Botanical Garden
Pacific Spirit Regional Park
Marine Drive Foreshore Park
Vancouver General Hospital
VanDusen Botanical Garden
Bloedel Conservatory
Queen Elizabeth Pk
Burnaby
Deer Lake Park
Robert Burnaby Park
British Columbia Open University
Coquitlam College
Mundy Park
Port Coquitlam
Coquitlam Indian Reserve 2
Pitt Meadows Airport (YPK)
Iona Island
Iona Beach Regional Park
Musqueam Indian Reserve 2
Musqueam Indian Reserve 4
Langara College
Central Park
Everett Crowley Park
Royal Columbian Hospital
Burnaby Fraser Foreshore Park
New Westminster
New Westminster Museum and Archives
Irving House
Queens Park
Annacis Island
Colony Farm Regional Park
Douglas Island
Barnston Island
Barnston Island Indian Reserve 3
Maple Ridge
Strait of Georgia
Sea Island
Vancouver International Airport (YVR)
River Rock Casino Resort
Mitchell Is
Lulu Island
Richmond Hospital
Richmond Nature Park
Richmond Cultural Centre
Richmond
Richmond Nature Park East
Green Timbers Urban Forest
Surrey Memorial Hospital
Surrey
Tynehead Regional Park
Fleetwood Park
Gulf of Georgia Cannery National Historic Site
London Heritage Farm
International Buddhist Temple
Deas Island Regional Park
Deas Island
Delta
Delta Museum
Delta Hospital
Westham Island
Britannia Heritage Shipyard
George C Reifel Migratory Bird Sanctuary
Bear Creek Park
Kwantlen University College–Surrey
Newton Wave Pool
Surrey Museum
Kwantlen University College
Serpentine Fen Wildlife Area
Langley
Langley Mun Flood Plain Pk
Nicomekl Flood Plain Pk
Boundary Bay Airport (ZBB)
Delta Heritage Air Park (CAK3)
Historic Stewart Farm
Mud Bay
Canoe Pass

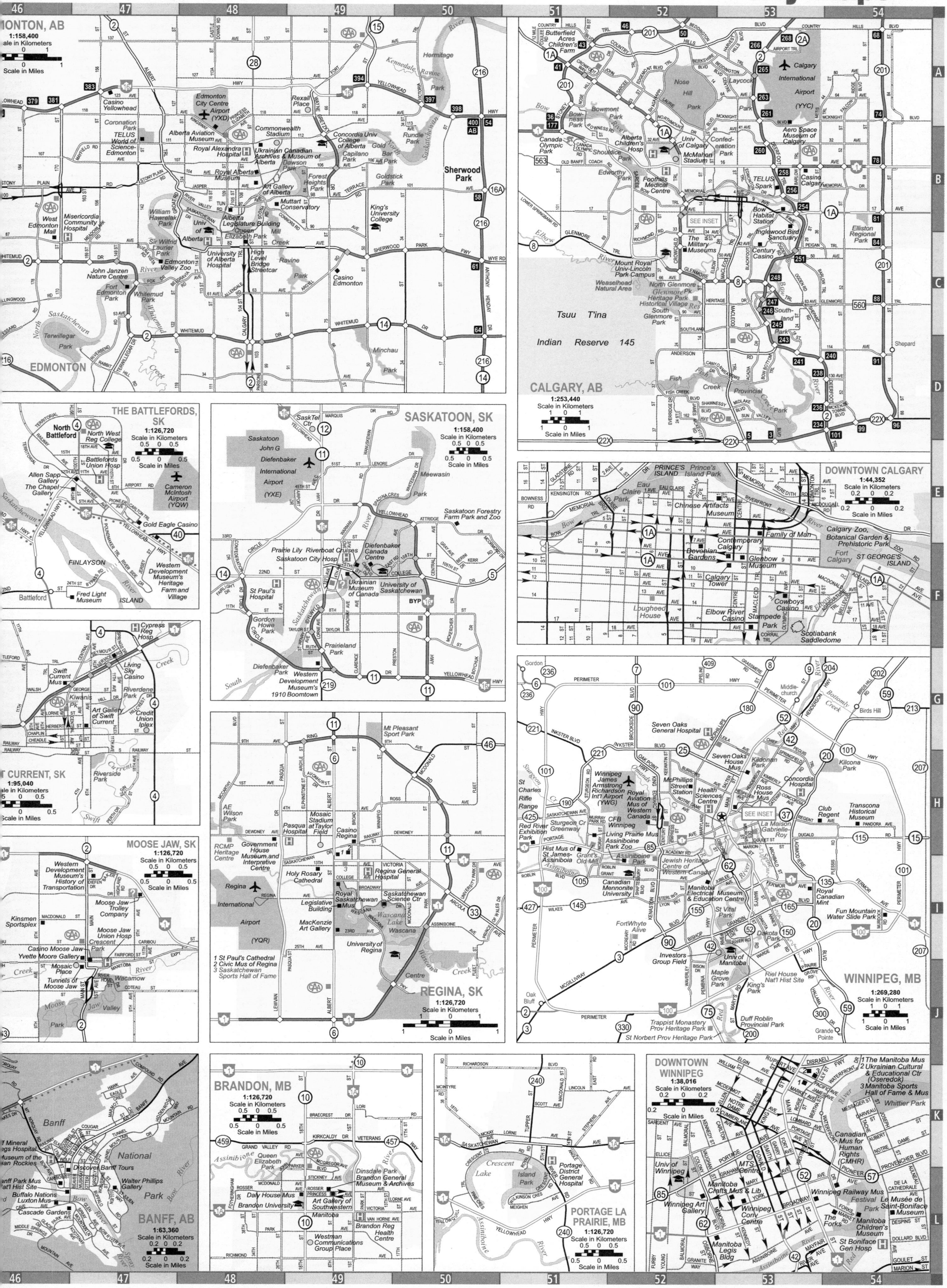

## EDMONTON, AB
1:158,400
Scale in Kilometers
Scale in Miles

Hermitage Park
Ravine Park
Rexall Place
Edmonton City Centre Airport (YXD)
Commonwealth Stadium
Concordia Univ College of Alberta
Capilano
Gold Bar
Rundle Park
Sherwood Park
Coronation Park
TELUS World of Science-Edmonton
Royal Alexandra Hospital
Ukrainian Canadian Archives & Museum of Alberta
Alberta Aviation Museum
Royal Alberta Museum
Art Gallery of Alberta
Muttart Conservatory
Goldstick Park
King's University College
Misericordia Community Hospital
West Edmonton Mall
William Hawrelak Park
Univ of Alberta
Alberta Legislature Building
Queen Elizabeth Park
Sir Wilfrid Laurier Park
John Janzen Nature Centre
University of Alberta Hospital
High Level Bridge Streetcar
Casino Edmonton
Fort Edmonton Park
Whitemud Park
Edmonton Valley Zoo
Terwillegar Park
Minchau Park
North Saskatchewan River
Sherwood Park
EDMONTON

## CALGARY, AB
1:253,440
Scale in Kilometers
Scale in Miles

Butterfield Acres Children's Farm
Calgary International Airport (YYC)
Nose Hill Park
Canada Olympic Park
Bowmont Park
Bowness Park
Alberta Children's Hosp
Univ of Calgary
Confederation Park
McMahon Stadium
Aero Space Museum of Calgary
Foothills Medical Centre
TELUS Spark
Casino Calgary
Mount Royal Univ-Lincoln Park Campus
Bow Habitat Station
Inglewood Bird Sanctuary
Elliston Regional Park
The Military Museums
SEE INSET
Century Casino
North Glenmore Park
Glenmore Athletic Park
Heritage Park Historical Village
South Glenmore Park
Weaselhead Natural Area
Tsuu T'ina Indian Reserve 145
Fish Creek Provincial Park
Elbow River

## DOWNTOWN CALGARY
1:44,352
Scale in Kilometers
Scale in Miles

Prince's Island Park
Eau Claire
Chinese Artifacts Museum
Contemporary Calgary
Family of Man
Calgary Zoo, Botanical Garden & Prehistoric Park
Devonian Gardens
Glenbow Museum
Fort Calgary
ST GEORGE'S ISLAND
Calgary Tower
Lougheed House
Cowboys Casino
Elbow River Casino
Stampede Park
Scotiabank Saddledome

## THE BATTLEFORDS, SK
1:126,720
Scale in Kilometers
Scale in Miles

North Battleford
North West Reg College
Battlefords Union Hosp
Allen Sapp Gallery
The Chapel Gallery
Gold Eagle Casino
Cameron McIntosh Airport (YQW)
Western Development Museum's Heritage Farm and Village
FINLAYSON
Fred Light Museum
Battleford
ISLAND

## SASKATOON, SK
1:158,400
Scale in Kilometers
Scale in Miles

SaskTel Ctr
Saskatoon John G Diefenbaker International Airport (YXE)
Meewasin
Saskatoon Forestry Farm Park and Zoo
Prairie Lily Riverboat Cruises
Diefenbaker Canada Centre
Saskatoon City Hosp
St Paul's Hospital
Ukrainian Museum of Canada
University of Saskatchewan
Gordon Howe Park
Prairieland Park
Diefenbaker Park
Western Development Museum's 1910 Boomtown

## SWIFT CURRENT, SK
1:95,040
Scale in Kilometers
Scale in Miles

Cypress Reg Hosp
Living Sky Casino
Swift Current Mus
Riverdene Park
Art Gallery of Swift Current
Credit Union Iplex
Kiwanis Park
Riverside Park

## MOOSE JAW, SK
1:126,720
Scale in Kilometers
Scale in Miles

Western Development Museum's History of Transportation
Moose Jaw Trolley Company
Moose Jaw Union Hosp
Kinsmen Sportsplex
Crescent Park
Casino Moose Jaw
Yvette Moore Gallery
Mosaic Place
Tunnels of Moose Jaw
Moose Jaw River

## REGINA, SK
1:126,720
Scale in Kilometers
Scale in Miles

Mt Pleasant Sport Park
AE Wilson Park
Mosaic Stadium at Taylor Field
Casino Regina
Pasqua Hospital
RCMP Heritage Centre
Government House Museum and Interpretive Centre
Holy Rosary Cathedral
Regina General Hospital
Regina International Airport (YQR)
Royal Saskatchewan Mus
Legislative Building
Saskatchewan Science Ctr
MacKenzie Art Gallery
University of Regina
Wascana Lake
Wascana Centre
1 St Paul's Cathedral
2 Civic Mus of Regina
3 Saskatchewan Sports Hall of Fame

## WINNIPEG, MB
1:269,280
Scale in Kilometers
Scale in Miles

Middlechurch
Birds Hill
Seven Oaks General Hospital
Seven Oaks House Mus
Kildonan Park
Concordia Hospital
Kilcona Park
Winnipeg James Armstrong Richardson Int'l Airport (YWG)
McPhillips Street Station
Health Sciences Centre
Ross House Mus
Transcona Historical Museum
St Charles Rifle Range
Red River Exhibition Park
CFB Winnipeg
SEE INSET
Club Regent
La Maison Gabrielle-Roy
Living Prairie Mus
Grant's Old Mill
Hist Mus of St James-Assiniboia
Assiniboine Park
Assiniboine Park Zoo
Jewish Heritage Centre of Western Canada
Canadian Mennonite University
Manitoba Electrical Museum & Education Centre
Royal Canadian Mint
Fun Mountain Water Slide Park
FortWhyte Alive
St Vital
Investors Group Field
Univ of Manitoba
Dakota Park
Maple Grove Park
Riel House Nat'l Hist Site
King's Park
Trappist Monastery Prov Heritage Park
Duff Roblin Provincial Park
St Norbert Prov Heritage Park
Grande Pointe

## BANFF, AB
1:63,360
Scale in Kilometers
Scale in Miles

Banff National Park
Banff Mineral Springs Hospital
Museum of the Canadian Rockies
Banff Park Mus Nat'l Hist Site
Buffalo Nations Luxton Mus
Cascade Gardens
Discover Banff Tours
Walter Phillips Gallery
Bow River

## BRANDON, MB
1:126,720
Scale in Kilometers
Scale in Miles

Queen Elizabeth Park
Dinsdale Park
Daly House Mus
Brandon University
Art Gallery of Southwestern Manitoba
Brandon General Museum & Archives
Brandon Reg Health Centre
Westman Communications Group Place
Assiniboine River

## PORTAGE LA PRAIRIE, MB
1:126,720
Scale in Kilometers
Scale in Miles

Crescent Lake
Island Park
Portage District General Hospital

## DOWNTOWN WINNIPEG
1:38,016
Scale in Kilometers
Scale in Miles

1 The Manitoba Mus
2 Ukrainian Cultural & Educational Ctr (Oseredok)
3 Manitoba Sports Hall of Fame & Mus
Whittier Park
Canadian Mus for Human Rights (CMHR)
Univ of Winnipeg
MTS Centre
Manitoba Crafts Mus & Lib
Winnipeg Railway Mus
Winnipeg Art Gallery
Winnipeg Conv Centre
Festival
Le Musée de Saint-Boniface Museum
Manitoba Children's Museum
Manitoba Legis Bldg
The Forks
St Boniface Gen Hosp

# Saskatchewan/ Manitoba

| | Moose Jaw | North Battleford | Prince Albert | Regina | Saskatoon | Swift Current | Whitewood | Yorkton |
|---|---|---|---|---|---|---|---|---|
| Prince Albert | 362 | 208 | | 401 | 141 | 407 | 572 | 396 |
| Regina | 76 | 398 | 401 | | 261 | 246 | 172 | 185 |
| Saskatoon | 222 | 138 | 141 | 261 | | 268 | 432 | 331 |

Driving Distances In Kilometers

See also mileage table page 2

## MANITOBA

Towns with asterisk (*) are keyed to the maps on page 131.

Alexander (2,978)...K-12
Alonsa (1,446).......I-13
Altona (3,709).......L-15
Amaranth............J-14
Angusville...........J-11
Anola...............K-16
Arborg (1,021).......I-15
Arden...............J-13
Argyle (1,073).......J-15
Ashern...............I-14
Ashville.............I-12
Aubigny.............K-15
Austin..............K-14
Bagot...............K-14
Baldur..............L-13
Barrows.............F-11
Beaconia............J-16
Beausejour (2,823)......F-17, J-16
Benito (370).........H-11
Berens River..E-17, G-15
Beulah..............J-11
Binscarth (395)......J-11
Birch River (400). . .G-11
Birds Hill...........*G-54
Birnie...............J-13
Birtle (662).........J-11
Bissett..............I-17
Boissevain (1,497)......F-17, L-12
Bowsman (315).....G-11
Brandon (41,511). .*L-49, F-17, K-13
Brochet.............D-17
Brookdale...........K-13
Brunkild.............K-15
Camp Morton.........I-15
Camperville (507)...H-12
Carberry (1,502)....K-13
Carman (2,880).....K-15
Carroll..............K-12
Cartwright (282).....L-13
Cayer................I-13
Chatfield............I-15
Churchill (923)......C-18
Clanwilliam (494)....J-13
Cormorant (334)....D-12
Coulter.............L-12
Cowan..............H-12
Cranberry Portage. .D-11
Crandall............J-12
Crane River (128). .H-13
Cromer.............K-11
Cross Lake (406)...C-14
Cypress River.......K-13
Dallas (100).........H-15
Darlingford..........L-14
Dauphin (7,906)......F-17, I-12
Decker..............J-12
Deloraine (977).....L-12
Domain.............K-15
Dominion City.......L-15
Douglas.............K-13
Duck Bay (447).....G-12
Duck Lake Post.....C-17
Dufresne............K-16
Dugald..............K-16
East Braintree......K-17
Easterville (80)......F-12
Eddystone...........I-13
Eden................J-13
Elgin................L-12
Elie.................K-15
Elkhorn (461).......K-11
Elm Creek..........K-14
Elma................K-17
Emerson (689)......L-15
Erickson (456).......J-13
Eriksdale (911).......I-14
Ethelbert (312)......H-12
Fairford.............H-14
Falcon Lake.........K-17
Fannystelle..........K-15
Fisher Branch........I-15
Flin Flon (5,836).....C-10, E-17
Fork River..........H-12
Fort Alexander......J-16
Foxwarren...........J-11
Franklin (1,768).....J-13
Fraserwood..........J-15
Garland (100).......H-12
Garson..............J-16
Gilbert Plains (760). .I-12
Gillam..............D-18
Gimli (1,891). .F-17, J-15
Gladstone (802).....J-13
Glenboro (633)......K-13
Glenella (517).......J-13
Glenora.............L-13
Gods Lake..........E-18
Gods Lake Narrows..........E-18
Goodlands..........L-12
Gordon.............*G-51
Grahamdale (1,416)............H-14
Grand Beach........J-16
Grand Marais........J-16
Grand Rapids (336).......E-17, F-13
Grande Pointe......*J-54
Grandview (839).....I-12
Great Falls..........J-16
Gretna (574)........L-15
Griswold............K-12
Gull Harbour...F-17, I-16
Gunton..............J-15
Gypsumville.........H-14
Hadashville.........K-17
Hamiota (823).......J-12
Hartney (400).......L-12
Headingley (2,726)..K-15
Hecla................I-16
Hilbre...............H-14
Hodgson.............I-15
Holland.............K-14
Inglis (200)...........I-11
Inwood..............J-15
Justice..............K-13
Kenton..............K-12
Kenville.............H-11
Killarney (2,199). . . .L-13
Komarno............J-15
La Broquerie (3,659)...........K-16
La Rivière...........L-14
Lac Brochet.........D-17
Lac Du Bonnet (1,009)...........J-16
Lake Francis........J-15
Langruth............J-14
Lauder..............L-12
Leaf Rapids.........D-17
Letellier.............L-15
Libau...............J-16
Little Grand Rapids..E-18
Lowe Farm..........L-15
Lundar (500)........J-14
Lynn Lake (714)....D-17
Macdonald (5,653). .K-14
Mafeking................G-11
Manigotagan.............I-16
Manitou (718)...........L-14
Mariapolis...............L-14
Marquette...............J-15
Matheson Island (117). .H-15
Matlock.................J-15
McAuley.................J-11
McCreary (487).........I-13
Meadow Portage (70)...H-13
Medora..................L-12
Melita (1,051)...........L-11
Miami...................L-14
Middlebro...............L-17
Middlechurch...........*G-53
Miniota (904)...........K-11
Minitonas (497).........H-11
Minnedosa (2,474).......J-13
Minto (667).............L-12
Moose Lake (205).......E-12
Moosehorn (200)........I-14
Morden (6,571)..........L-14
Morris (1,643).....F-17, L-15
Mulvihill.................I-14
Neepawa (3,298). .F-17, J-13
Nelson House...........D-17
Newdale.................J-12
Ninette..................L-13
Niverville (2,464)........K-15
North River.............C-18
Norway House (521)...........D-14, E-17
Notre Dame de Lourdes (589)..................K-14
Oak Bluff................*J-51
Oak Point...............J-14
Oakburn.................J-12
Oakville.................K-14
Onanole.................J-12
Oxford House...........E-18
Pelican Rapids (89).....F-12
Petersfield..............J-15
Pierson..................L-11
Pilot Mound (630).......L-14
Pinawa (1,450)..........J-17
Pine River..............H-12
Piney (1,755)............L-17
Pipestone (1,419).......K-11
Plum Coulee (770)......L-15
Plumas..................J-13
Pointe du Bois (100).....J-17
Poplar Point............K-14
Poplarfield...............I-15
Portage la Prairie (12,728)..*K-51, F-17, K-14
Powerview-Pine Falls (1,294).................J-16
Princess Harbour (10).............E-17, H-15
Rapid City (416).........K-12
Red Sucker Lake........E-18
Rennie (100)............K-17
Renwer..................G-12
Richer...................K-16
Riding Mountain.........J-13
Rivers (1,193)...........K-12
Riverton (537)............I-15
Roblin (1,672).............I-11
Roland (1)...............L-15
Rorketon.................I-13
Rosa.....................L-16
Roseisle.................K-14
Rosenort................K-15
Rossburn (546)..........J-12
Rossendale..............K-14
Rosser (1,364).........*G-51
Russell (1,428)....F-17, J-11
San Clara (100).........H-11
Sandy Lake..............J-12
Sanford..................K-15
Scanterbury.............J-16
Selkirk (9,515)...........J-16
Seven Sisters Falls (200)....................J-16
Shamattawa.............D-18
Shellmouth...............I-11
Shoal Lake (680)........J-12
Shortdale.................I-11
Sidney...................K-13
Sifton (796)...............I-12
Sinclair..................K-11
Skownan................H-13
Snow Lake (837)..C-12, E-17
Snowflake...............L-14
Somerset (432)..........L-14
Souris (1,772)...........K-12
South Indian Lake.......D-17
South Junction..........L-17
Split Lake...............D-17
Sprague (200)...........L-17
St Adolphe (1,048)......K-15
St Ambroise.............J-14
St Claude (588).........K-14
St Laurent (1,454).......J-14
St Malo (800)............L-16
St Martin................H-14
St-Lazare................J-11
St-Pierre-Jolys...........K-16
Starbuck.................K-15
Ste Anne (1,534)........K-16
Ste Genevieve..........K-16
Ste Rose du Lac (995)...I-13
Stead....................J-16
Steep Rock.............H-14
Steinbach (11,066).........F-17, K-16
Stonewall (4,376)........J-15
Strathclair (840).........J-12
Stuartburn (1,629).......L-16
Sundown.......L-16
Swan River (3,859).E-17, G-11
Tadoule Lake. .D-17
Teulon (1,124)..J-15
The Pas (5,589).E-11, E-17
Thompson (13,446).....D-17
Tilston..........L-11
Tolstoi..........L-16
Toutes Aides (100)........H-13
Treherne (646)........K-14
Victoria Beach (388).........I-16
Virden (3,010)..K-12
Vita............L-16
Vogar...........I-14
Waasagomach.E-18
Wanless (200)..D-11
Warren.........J-15
Wasagaming (200).........J-12
Waskada (199)........L-12
Wawanesa (535)........K-13
Wellwood......K-13
West Hawk Lake (100)........K-17
Westbourne (1,906).......J-14
Westgate......F-11
Whitemouth (1,480)......K-17
Winkler (9,106).F-17, L-15
Winnipeg (633,451). .*H-53, *J-53, *K-53, F-17, K-15
Winnipeg Beach (1,017).......J-15
Winnipegosis (628)........H-12
Woodridge.....L-16
Woodside......J-14
Zhoda..........L-16

## SASKATCHEWAN

Aberdeen (527).G-6
Abernethy (197).J-9
Admiral (30). . . .K-4
Air Ronge (1,032).......C-7
Alameda (308).L-10
Albertville (110)..E-7
Alida (106).....L-11
Allan (631)......H-7
Alsask (129). . . .H-3
Alvena (55).....G-7
Aneroid (45). . . .K-5
Annaheim (218).........G-8
Antler (40).....K-11
Arborfield (329)..F-9
Archerwill (185).G-9
Arcola (504). . .K-10
Arelee..........G-5
Arran (40). . . . .H-11
Asquith (576). . .G-5
Assiniboia (2,305)..F-16, K-6
Avonlea (381)...K-7
Aylesbury........I-7
Balcarres (598). .J-9
Baldwinton......F-4
Bankend (10). . .H-9
Bateman........K-6
Batoche.........F-7
Battleford (3,685).*F-46, F-4
Beatty (61)......F-8
Beauval (806)...C-5, D-16
Beechy (243). . . .I-5
Belle Plaine (64)...........J-7
Bengough (337).L-7
Benson..........L-9
Bethune (369)...J-7
Bienfait (748). .L-10
Big Beaver (15)..L-7
Big River (728)..E-6
Biggar (2,033). .G-5
Birch Hills (935).F-7
Birsay...........I-6
Bjorkdale (201)..G-9
Blaine Lake (472)..........F-6
Bracken (25). . . .L-4
Bredenbury (329).........I-10
Briercrest (117)..J-7
Broadview (611).........J-10
Brock (115).....H-4
Bruno (495).....G-7
Buchanan (225)........H-10
Buffalo Narrows.....D-16
Bulyea (104).....I-8
Burr.............H-7
Burstall (315)....I-3
Bushell Park....J-7
Cabri (439)......J-4
Cactus Lake....G-3
Cadillac (80)....K-5
Candiac (20)....J-9
Candle Lake (792).........E-7
Cando..........G-5
Canoe Narrows.C-5
Canora (2,013)......H-10
Canwood (337)..E-6
Carievale (241).........L-11
Carlton..........F-6
Carlyle (1,257)......K-10
Carnduff (1,012).......L-11
Caron (125).....J-7
Caronport (919)..J-7
Carrot River (941).........F-9
Central Butte (372)..........I-6
Ceylon (90).....L-8
Chamberlain (108)..........I-7
Chaplin (235). . .J-6
Chelan (45).....G-9
Chitek..........E-5
Chitek Lake (219).........E-5
Choiceland (346).........E-8
Christopher Lake (215).........E-7
Churchbridge (704).........I-11
Clair............H-8
Clavet (345). . . .H-6
Claydon.........L-3
Climax (182). . . .L-4
Cochin (208). . . .F-4
Coderre (40). . . .J-6
Cole Bay (156)..C-5
Coleville (248). .H-3
Colfax..........K-8
Colgate.........L-9
Colonsay (425)..H-7
Consul (93).....L-3
Corning (43). . . .K-9
Coronach (770)..L-7
Courval (5)......J-6
Craik (408)......I-7
Crane Valley (20)...........K-7
Craven (274). . . .J-8
Creighton (1,502)......C-10
Crooked River (57)...........F-9
Crystal Springs (23)...........F-7
Cudworth (738).G-7
Cumberland House (810). .E-10, E-17
Cupar (566)......I-8
Cut Knife (532)..F-4
Dafoe (10)......H-8
Danbury.......H-10
Davidson (958)....F-16, I-7
Debden (348)...E-6
Delisle (898)....H-5
Delmas (116). . .F-4
Demaine (20)....I-5
Denare Beach (785)........D-10
Denholm (61). . .F-5
Denzil (142). . . .G-3
Deschambault Lake.........C-9
Descharme Lake........D-16
Dilke (80)........I-7
Dinsmore (269). .I-5
Dodsland (207)..H-4
Dollard..........K-4
Domremy (124)..F-7
Dore Lake (30)..C-5
Dorintosh (127)..D-4
Drake (232).....H-8
Drinkwater (65). .J-7
Dubuc (55).....J-10
Duck Lake (610)..........F-6
Duff (30).........I-9
Dundurn (647). .H-6
Eastend (471). .K-4
Eatonia (449). . . .I-3
Ebenezer (139).I-10
Edam (399).....F-4
Edenwold (242)..J-8
Edgeley (41). . . .J-8
Elbow (294)......I-6
Elfros (110).....H-9
Elrose (453).....I-5
Elstow (91).....H-7
Endeavour (118)........G-10
Ernfold (35). . . . .J-6
Esterhazy (2,336).......J-10
Estevan (10,084).F-16, L-9
Eston (971)......I-4
Evesham.......G-3
Eyebrow (135). . .I-6
Fairlight (40). . .K-11
Fillmore (193). . .K-9
Findlater (4
Fiske (81)..
Flaxcombe
Fleming (75
Foam Lake (1,123)..
Fond-du-La
Fort Qu'App (1,919)...
Fox Valley (
Francis (14
Frenchman (64)......
Frobisher (1
Gainsborou (250)....
Gerald (124
Glaslyn (36
Glenbain...
Glenside (8
Glentworth.
Glidden....

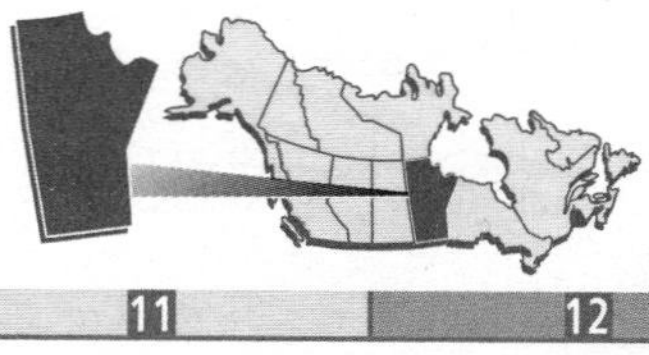

| Driving Distances In Kilometers | Brandon | Dauphin | Emerson | Flin Flon | Grand Rapids | Minnedosa | Portage la Prairie | Winnipeg |
|---|---|---|---|---|---|---|---|---|
| Brandon | | 162 | 317 | 697 | 525 | 47 | 123 | 211 |
| Dauphin | 162 | | 434 | 537 | 454 | 120 | 247 | 328 |
| Flin Flon | 317 | 434 | | | 834 | | 433 | 110 |
| Winnipeg | 211 | 328 | 110 | 834 | 433 | 217 | 85 | |

See also mileage table on page 2

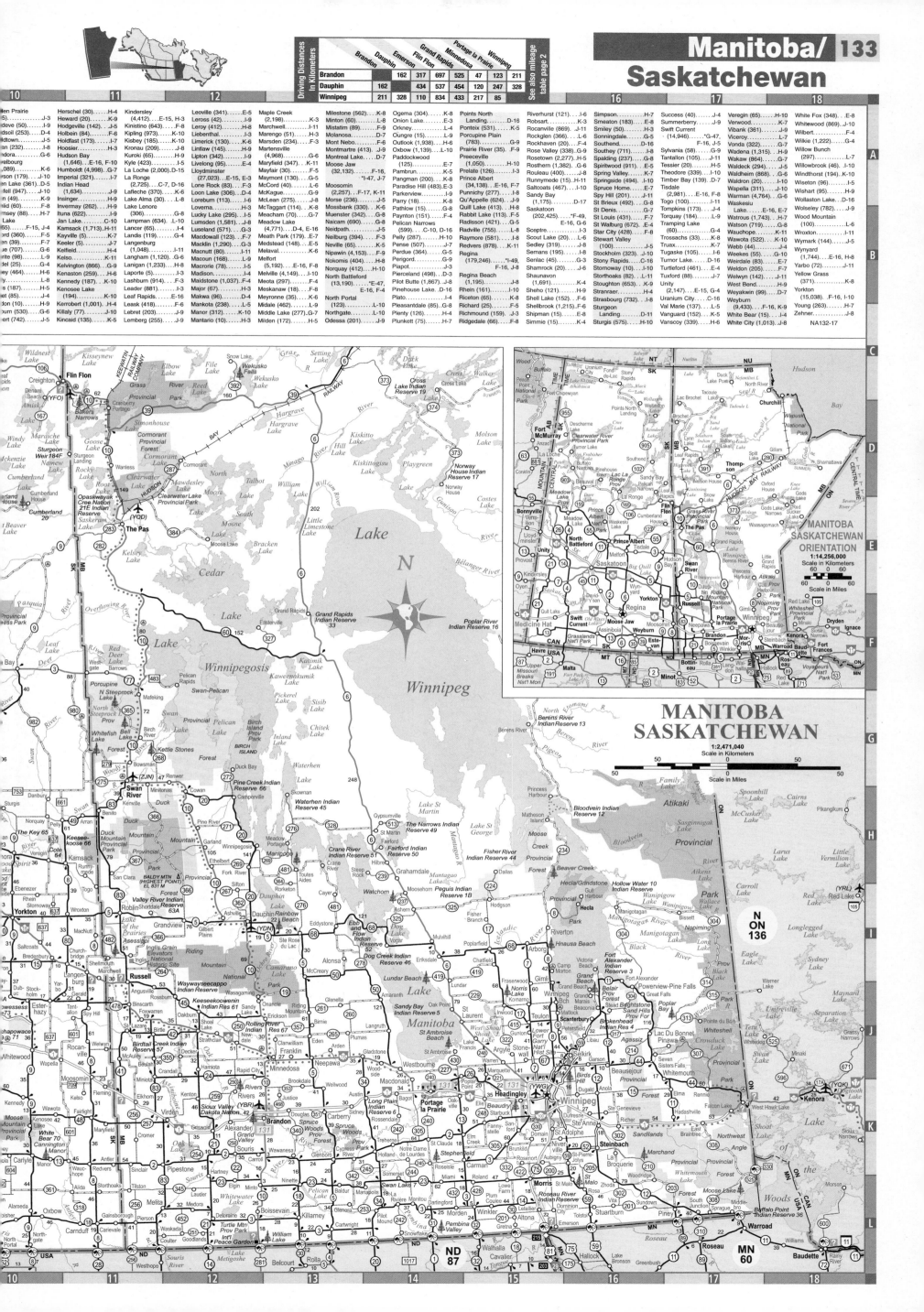

NA132-17

NA132-17

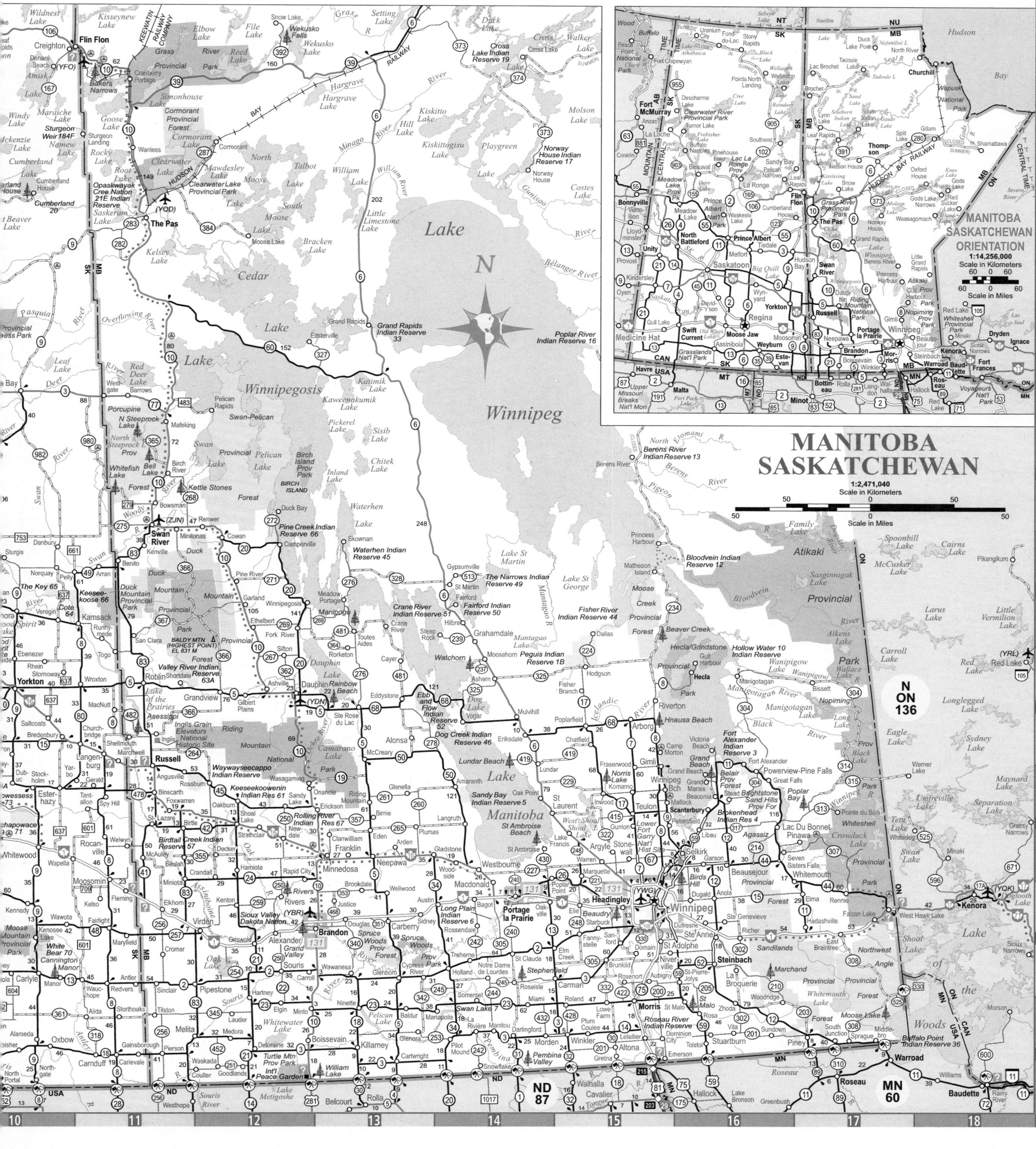

| Driving Distances In Kilometers | Hamilton | Kenora | London | Niagara Falls | North Bay | Orillia | Ottawa | Sault Ste Marie | Sudbury | Thunder Bay | Toronto | Windsor |
|---|---|---|---|---|---|---|---|---|---|---|---|---|
| London | 127 | 2038 | | 192 | 503 | 290 | 629 | 848 | 542 | 1554 | 192 | 192 |
| Ottawa | 514 | 1978 | 629 | 577 | 358 | 401 | | 789 | 490 | 1492 | 451 | 806 |
| Sudbury | 430 | 1488 | 542 | 495 | 132 | 267 | 490 | 306 | | 1004 | 382 | 718 |
| Thunder Bay | 1433 | 486 | 1554 | 1498 | 1103 | 1272 | 1492 | 702 | 1004 | | 1384 | 1721 |
| Toronto | 66 | 1868 | 192 | 128 | 342 | 131 | 451 | 687 | 382 | 1384 | | 364 |

See also mileage table page 2

ONTARIO

Towns with asterisk (*) are keyed to the maps on pages 136-137.

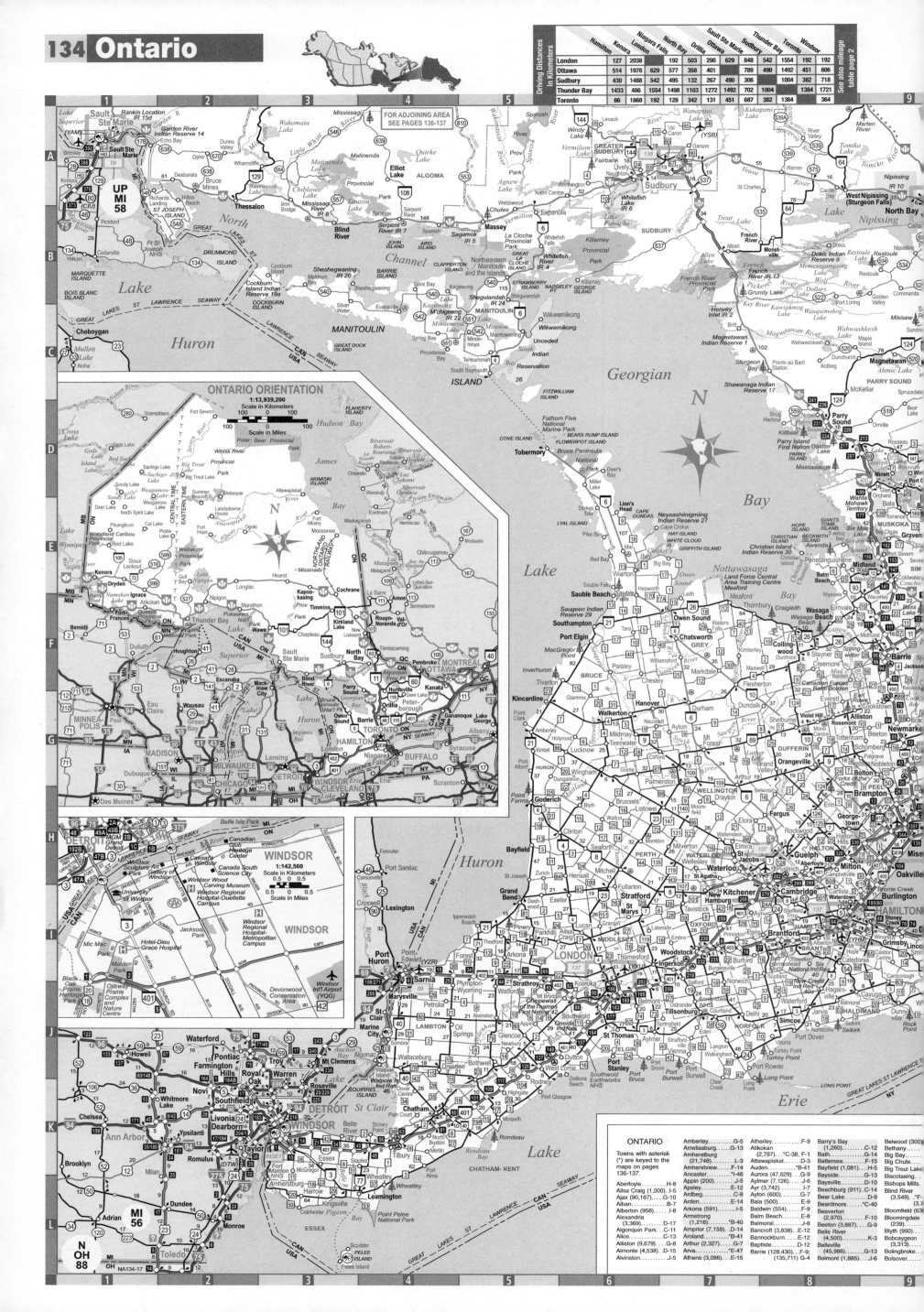

LEGEND
TransCanadian Highway — Wildlife Refuge
Controlled Access Hwy — Nat'l/Prov Park
Controlled Access Hwy Toll — National Forest

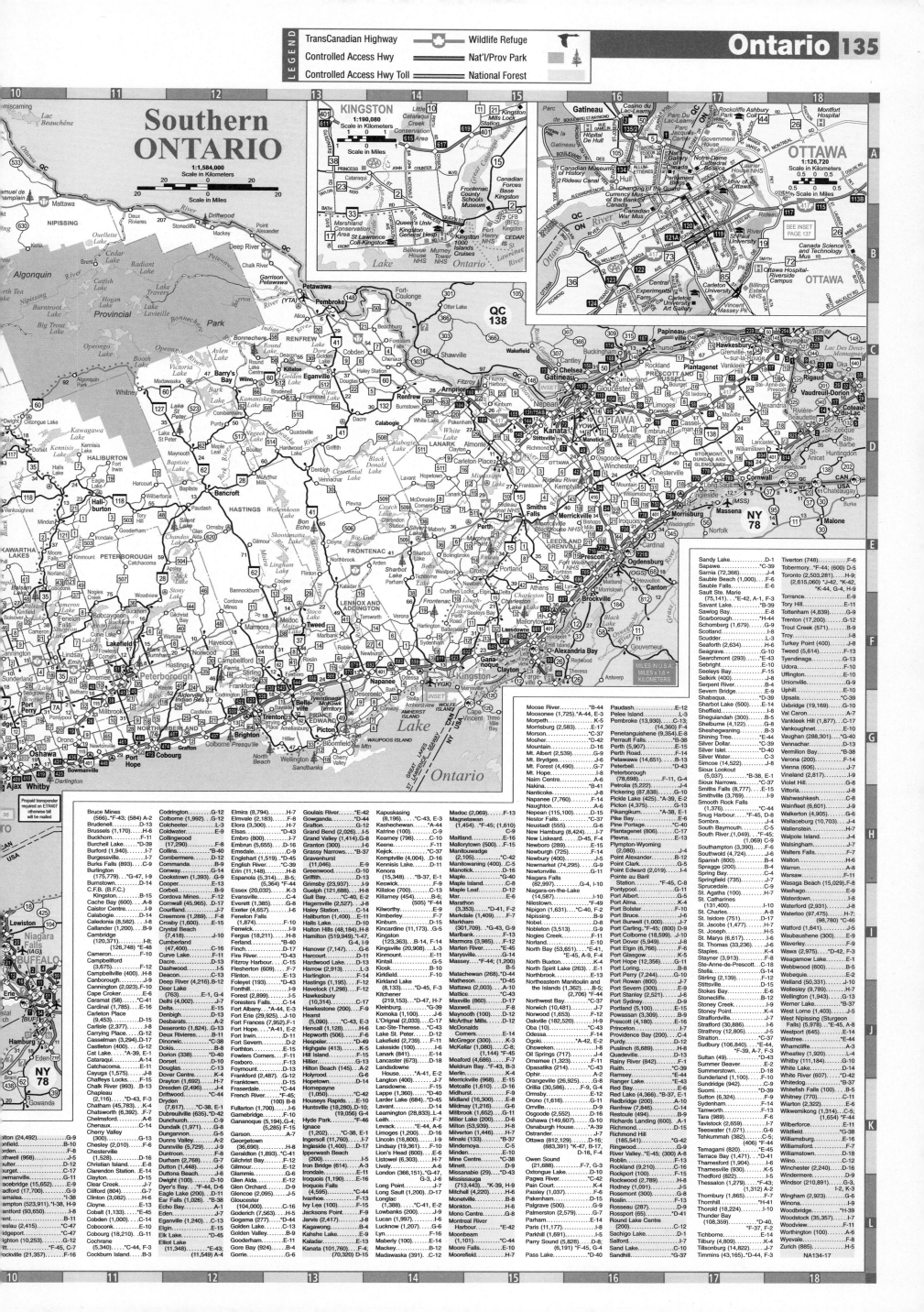

NA134-17

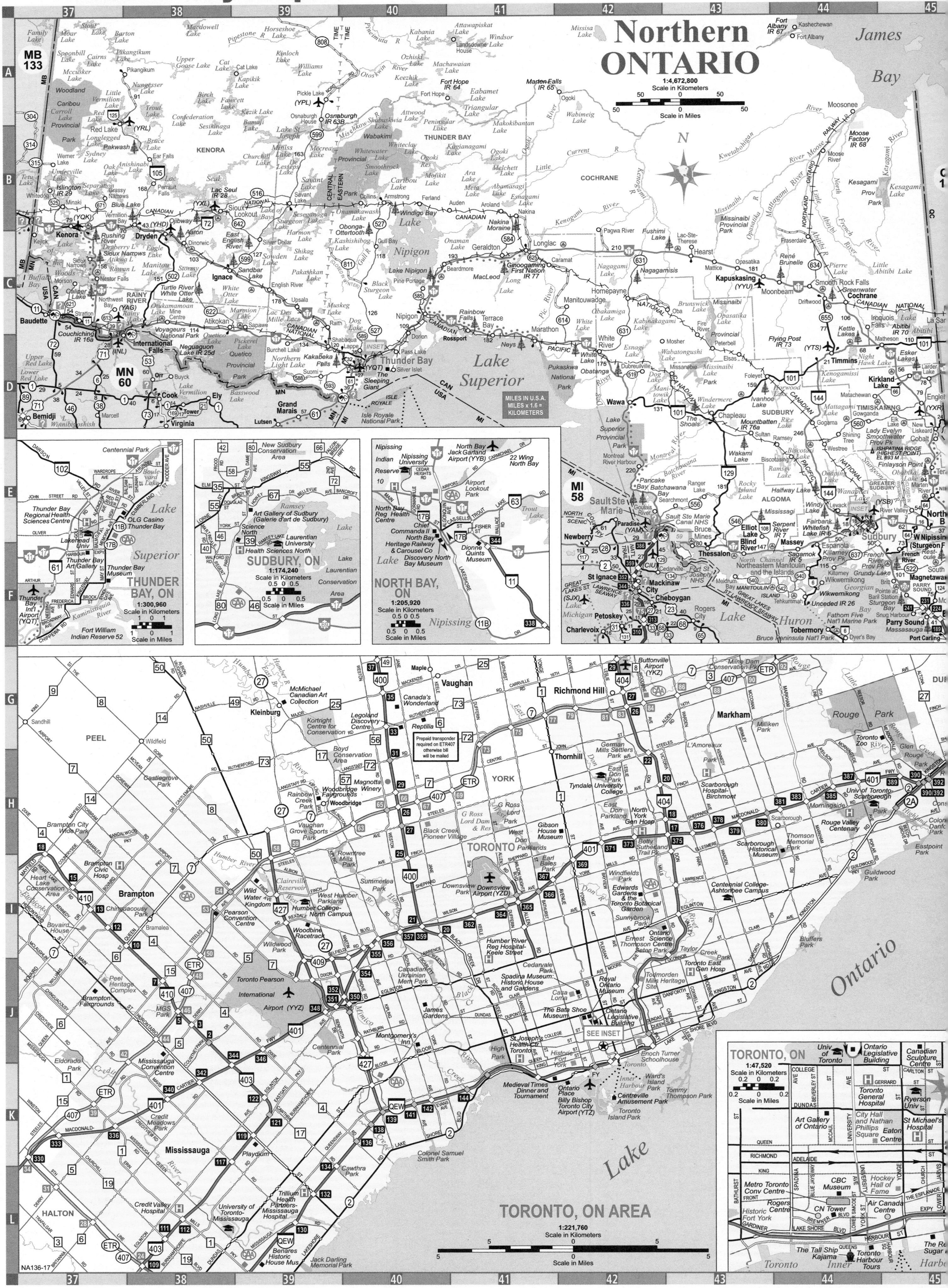

# Northern ONTARIO

1:4,672,800
Scale in Kilometers
Scale in Miles

James Bay

Lake Superior

MILES IN U.S.A.
MILES x 1.6 = KILOMETERS

## THUNDER BAY, ON
1:300,960
Scale in Kilometers
Scale in Miles

## SUDBURY, ON
1:174,240
Scale in Kilometers
Scale in Miles

## NORTH BAY, ON
1:205,920
Scale in Kilometers
Scale in Miles

# TORONTO, ON AREA
1:221,760
Scale in Kilometers
Scale in Miles

## TORONTO, ON
1:47,520
Scale in Kilometers
Scale in Miles

Lake Ontario

Lake Huron

NA136-17

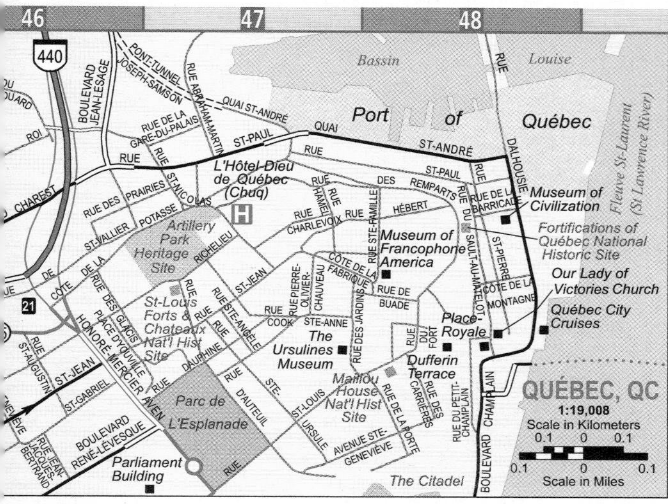

**QUÉBEC, QC** — 1:19,008 — Scale in Kilometers / Scale in Miles

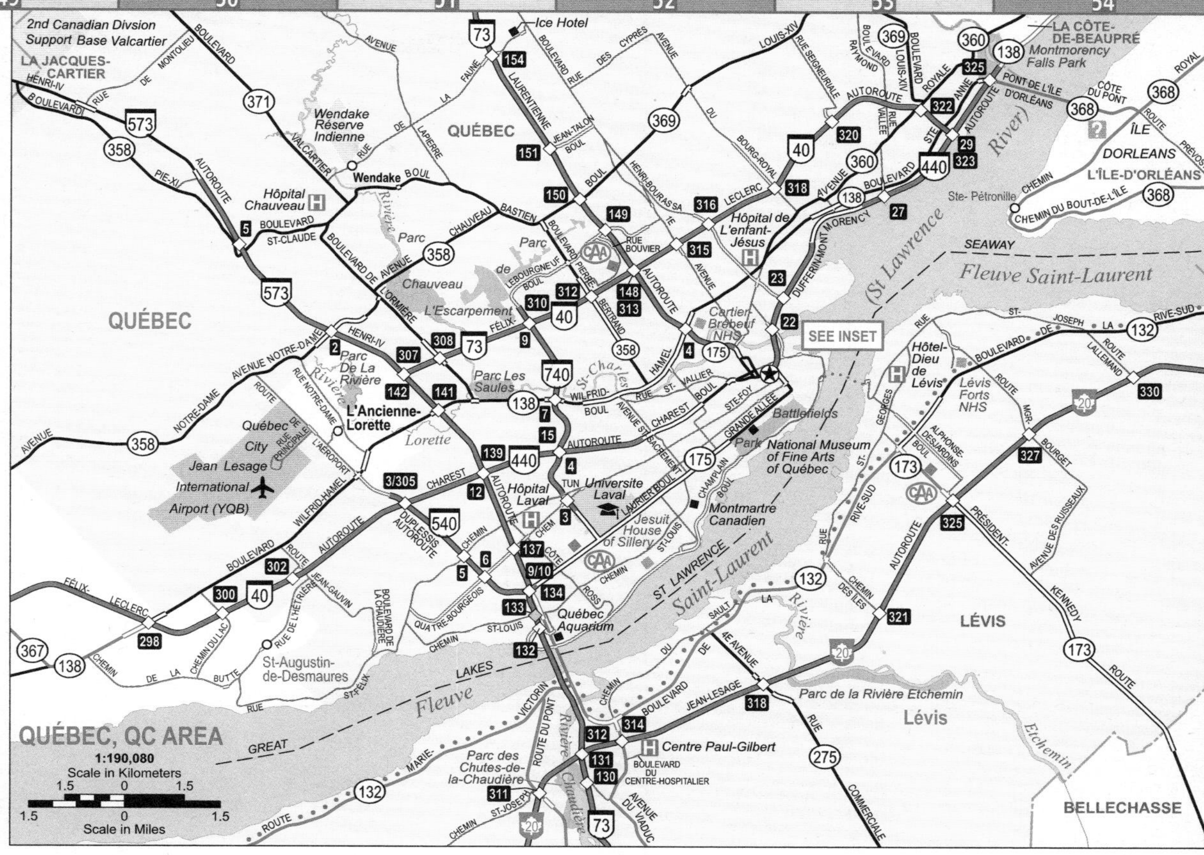

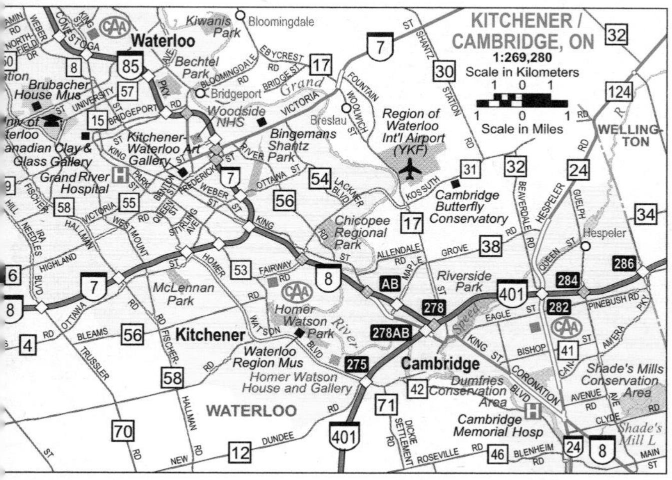

**KITCHENER / CAMBRIDGE, ON** — 1:269,280 — Scale in Kilometers / Scale in Miles

**QUÉBEC, QC AREA** — 1:190,080 — Scale in Kilometers / Scale in Miles

**LONDON, ON** — 1:53,440 — Scale in Kilometers / Scale in Miles

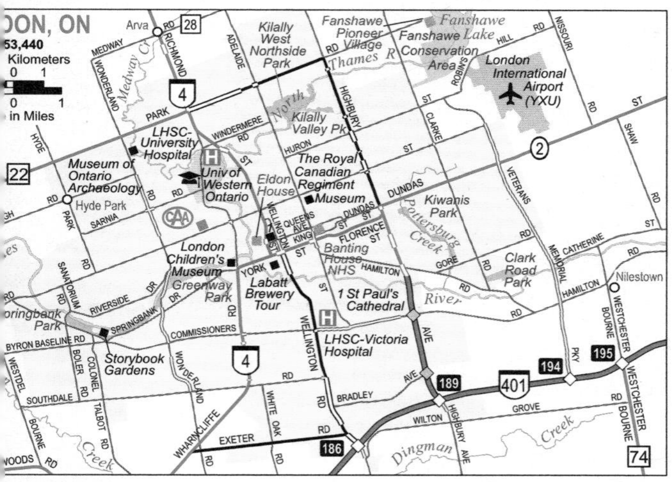

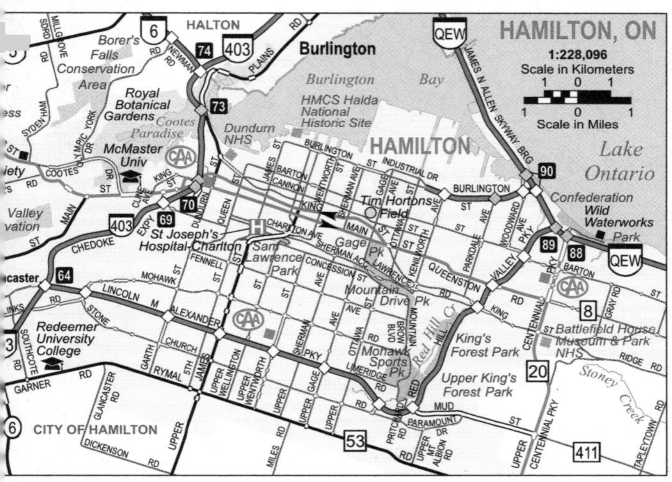

**HAMILTON, ON** — 1:228,096 — Scale in Kilometers / Scale in Miles

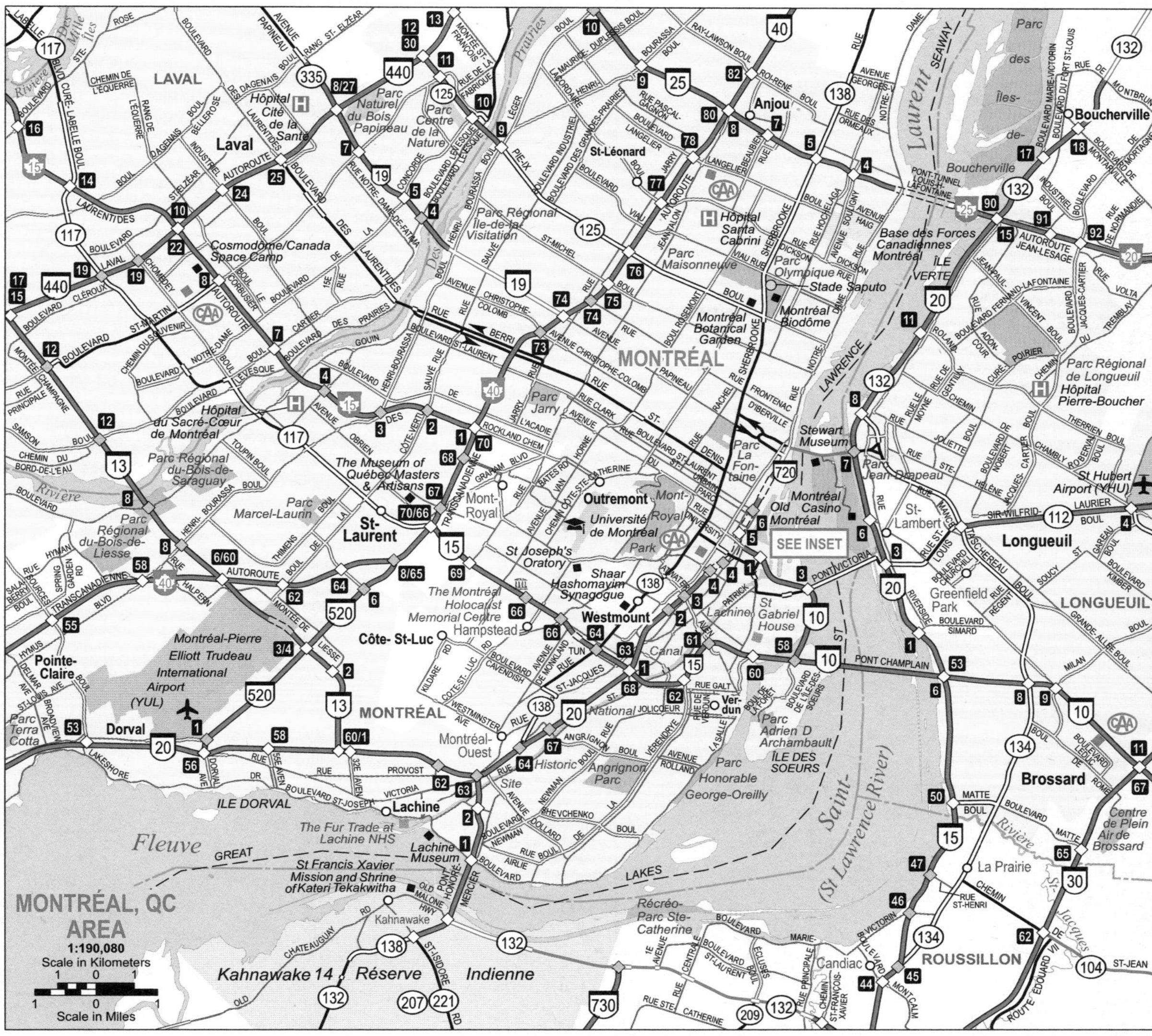

**MONTRÉAL, QC AREA** — 1:190,080 — Scale in Kilometers / Scale in Miles

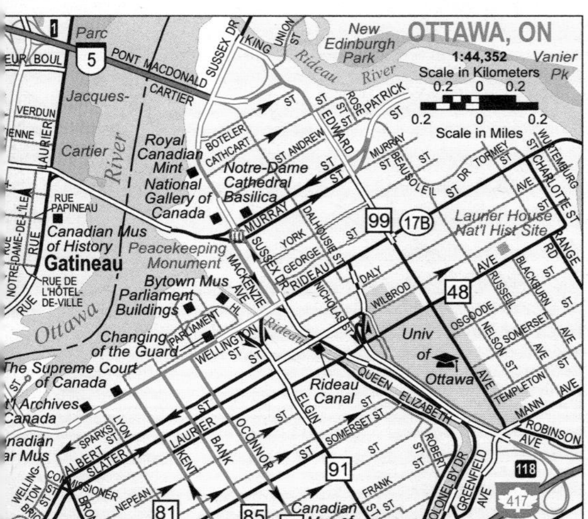

**OTTAWA, ON** — 1:44,352 — Scale in Kilometers / Scale in Miles

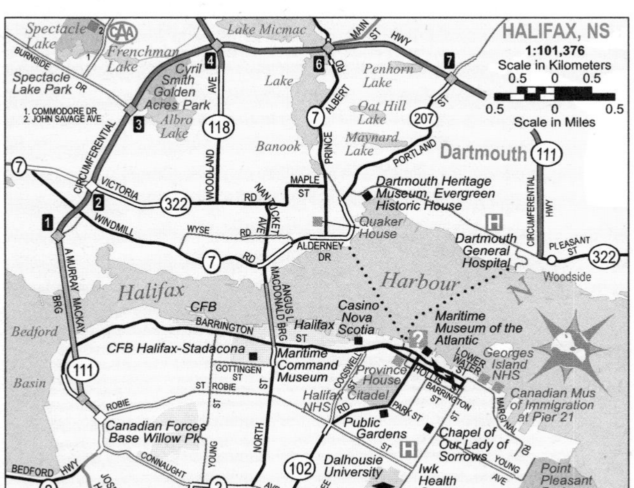

**HALIFAX, NS** — 1:101,376 — Scale in Kilometers / Scale in Miles

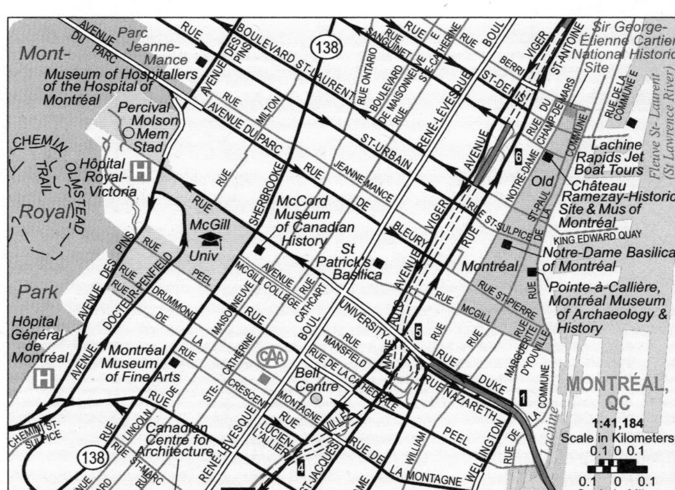

**MONTRÉAL, QC** — 1:41,184 — Scale in Kilometers / Scale in Miles

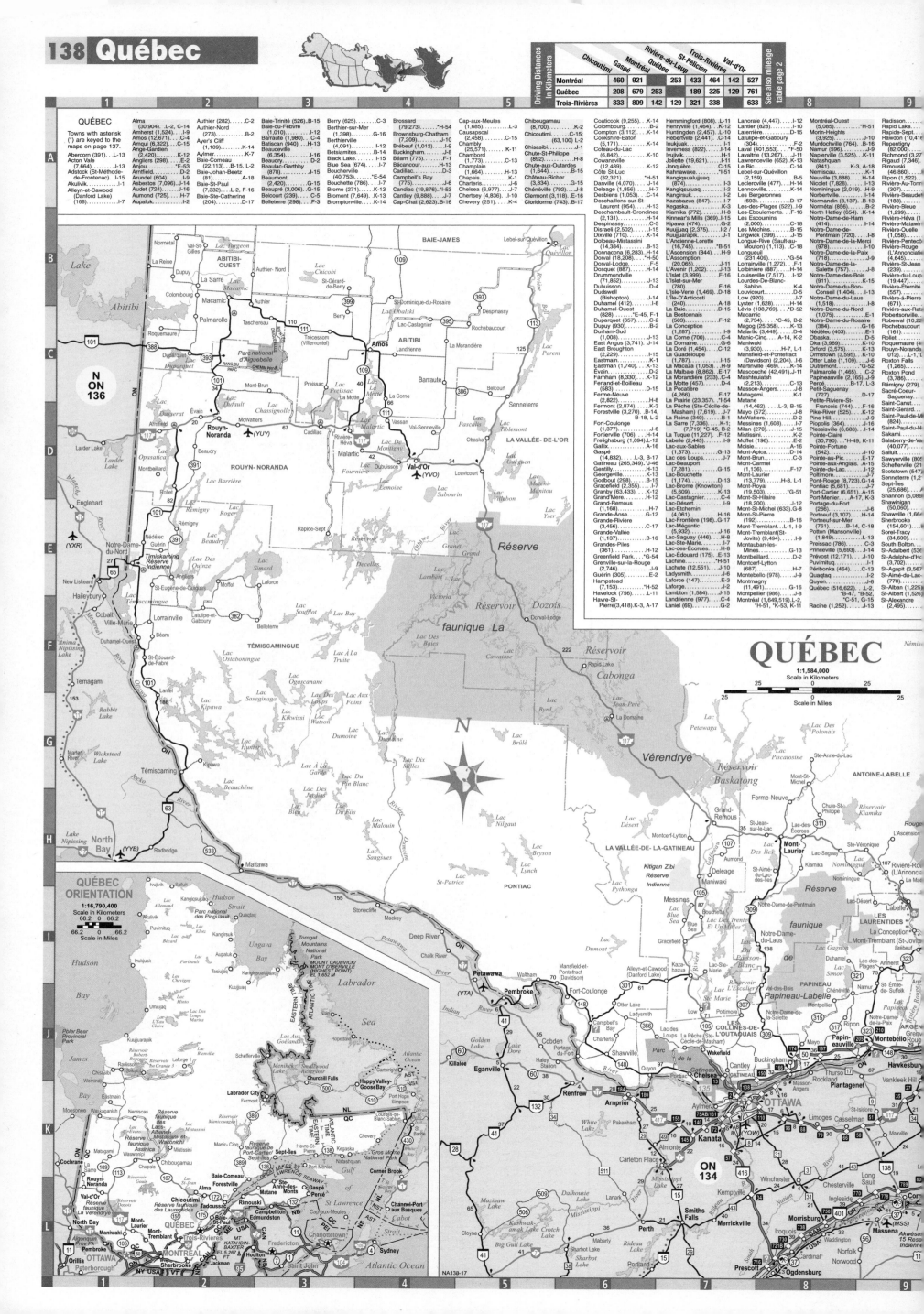

**Driving Distances In Kilometers** (See also mileage table page 2)

| | Chicoutimi | Gaspé | Montréal | Québec | Rivière-du-Loup | St-Félicien | Trois-Rivières | Val-d'Or |
|---|---|---|---|---|---|---|---|---|
| **Montréal** | 460 | 921 | | 253 | 433 | 464 | 142 | 527 |
| **Québec** | 208 | 679 | 253 | | 189 | 325 | 129 | 761 |
| **Trois-Rivières** | 333 | 809 | 142 | 129 | 321 | 338 | | 633 |

## QUÉBEC

Towns with asterisk (*) are keyed to the maps on page 137.

Abercorn (391)........L-13
Acton Vale (7,664)........J-13
Adstock (St-Méthode-de-Frontenac). (168)........I-15
Akulivik........I-1
Alleyn-et-Cawood (Danford Lake) (168)........I-7
Alma (30,904)........L-2, C-14
Amherst (1,524)........I-9
Amos (12,671)........C-14
Amqui (6,322)........G-15
Ange-Gardien (2,420)........K-12
Angliers (298)........E-2
Anjou........*E-53
Arntfield........D-2
Arundel (604)........I-9
Asbestos (7,096)........J-14
Audet (724)........I-16
Aumond (757)........H-7
Aupaluk........I-1
Authier (282)........C-2
Authier-Nord (273)........C-2
Ayer's Cliff (1,109)........K-14
Anjou........K-7
Baie-Comeau (22,113)........B-15, L-2
Baie-Johan-Beetz (81)........A-18
Baie-St-Paul (7,332)........L-2, F-16
Baie-Ste-Catherine (204)........D-17
Baie-du-Febvre (1,010)........J-12
Baie-Trinité (526)........B-15
Baliscan (940)........H-13
Beauceville (6,354)........I-16
Beaucanton........D-2
Beaulac-Garthby (878)........J-15
Beaudry........D-2
Béarn (775)........F-1
Bécancour (13,773)........H-13
Beaumont (2,420)........G-15
Beaupré (3,006)........G-15
Belcourt (239)........C-5
Belleterre (204)........D-17
Berthier-sur-Mer (1,398)........H-14
Berthierville (4,091)........J-12
Betsiamites........B-14
Black Lake........I-15
Blue Sea (674)........I-7
Boucherville (40,753)........*E-54
Berry (625)........C-3
Brossard (79,273)........*H-54
Brownsburg-Chatham (7,209)........J-10
Brébeuf (1,012)........I-9
Buckingham (8,330)........F-1
Beaudry........D-2
Beaulac-Garthby........J-15
Cadillac........D-3
Campbell's Bay (775)........J-6
Candiac (19,876)........*I-53
Cantley (9,888)........J-7
Chapais........K-1
Charteris........J-6
Château-Richer (3,834)........G-15
Chelsea (6,977)........J-7
Chertsey (4,836)........I-10
Chevery (251)........K-4
Cap-aux-Meules (1,685)........L-3
Causapscal (2,458)........G-15
Chambly (25,571)........K-11
Chambord (1,773)........C-13
Champlain (1,664)........H-13
Chapais (1,664)........K-1
Charteris (775)........J-6
Chibougamau (8,700)........K-2
Chicoutimi (63,100)........L-2
Chisasibi (892)........J-1
Chute-aux-Outardes (1,644)........B-15
Chute-St-Philippe........H-8
Clermont (3,118)........E-16
Cloridorme (743)........B-17

Coaticook (9,255)........L-14
Colombourg........B-2
Compton (3,112)........K-14
Cookshire-Eaton (5,171)........K-14
Coteau-du-Lac (6,842)........K-10
Cowansville (12,489)........K-13
Côte St-Luc (32,321)........*H-51
Danville (4,070)........J-14
Deleage (1,856)........H-7
Desbiens (1,135)........C-14
Deschaillons-sur-St-Laurent (954)........H-13
Deschambault-Grondines (2,131)........H-13
Despinassy........C-5
Disraeli (2,502)........J-15
Dixville (710)........K-14
Dolbeau-Mistassini (14,384)........C-13
Donnacona (6,283)........H-14
Dorval (18,208)........*H-50
Dorval-Lodge........F-5
Dosquet (887)........H-14
Drummondville (71,852)........J-13
Dubuisson........D-4
Dudswell (Bishopton)........J-14
Duhamel (412)........H-8
Duhamel-Ouest (828)........*E-45, F-1
Duparquet (657)........C-2
Dupuy (930)........B-2
Durham-Sud (1,287)........J-13
East Angus (3,741)........J-14
East Broughton (2,458)........I-15
Eastmain........K-1
Eastman (1,740)........K-13
Évain........D-2
Farnham (8,330)........K-12
Ferland-et-Boileau (583)........D-15
Ferme-Neuve (2,822)........H-8
Fermont (2,874)........A-17
Forestville (3,270)........B-14, B-18, L-2
Fort-Coulonge (1,377)........J-6
Fortierville (706)........H-14
Frelighsburg (1,094)........L-12
Gallix (1,373)........A-16
Gaspé (14,832)........L-3, B-17
Gatineau (265,349)........J-46
Gentilly........H-13
Georgeville........K-14
Godbout (298)........B-15
Gracefield (2,355)........I-7
Granby (63,433)........K-12
Grand'Mère........H-12
Grand-Remous (1,168)........H-7
Grande-Anse........G-12
Grande-Rivière (3,456)........C-17
Grande-Vallée (1,137)........B-16
Grandes-Piles (361)........H-12
Greenfield Park........*G-54
Grenville-sur-la-Rouge (2,746)........J-9
Guérin (305)........E-2
Hampstead (7,153)........*H-52
Havelock (756)........L-11
Havre-St-Pierre (3,418)........K-3, A-17

Hemmingford (808)........L-11
Henryville (1,464)........K-12
Huntingdon (2,457)........L-11
Hébertville (2,441)........C-14
Inukjuak........H-1
Inverness (822)........I-14
Ivujivik........H-1
Joliette (19,621)........J-11
Jonquière........C-15
Kahnawake........*I-51
Kangiqsualujjuaq (874)........J-1
Kangiqsujuaq........I-1
Kangirsuk........J-1
Kazabazua (847)........I-7
Kegaska........K-3
Kiamika (772)........H-8
Kinnear's Mills (369)........I-15
Kipawa (474)........E-2
Kuujjuaq (2,375)........I-2
Kuujjuarapik........J-1
L'Ancienne-Lorette (16,745)........*B-51
L'Ascension (844)........H-9
L'Assomption (20,065)........J-11
L'Avenir (1,202)........J-13
L'Islet (3,999)........G-16
L'Islet-sur-Mer........G-16
L'Isle-Verte (1,469)........D-18
Île-D'Anticosti (240)........A-18
La Baie........L-2
La Bostonnais (503)........F-12
La Conception (1,287)........I-9
La Corne (700)........C-4
La Doré (1,454)........C-12
La Guadeloupe (1,787)........I-15
La Macaza (1,053)........H-9
La Malbaie (8,862)........F-17
La Morandière (233)........C-4
La Motte (457)........C-4
La Pocatière (4,266)........F-17
La Prairie (23,357)........*I-54
La Pêche (Ste-Cécile-de-Masham) (7,619)........J-7
La Reine (340)........B-2
La Sarre (7,336)........B-2
La Tuque (11,227)........F-12
Labelle (2,445)........I-9
Lac-aux-Sables........H-13
Lac des Loups........J-7
Lac-Beauport (7,281)........G-15
Lac-Bouchette (1,174)........C-13
Lac-Brome (Knowlton) (5,609)........K-13
Lac-Castagnier........C-4
Lac-Désert........H-8
Lac-Etchemin (4,061)........I-16
Lac-Frontière (198)........G-17
Lac-Mégantic (5,932)........J-16
Lac-Ste-Marie (446)........I-7
Lac-des-Écorces (3,930)........H-7, L-1
Lac-Édouard (175)........E-13
Lachine (12,551)........J-10
Lachute (12,551)........J-10
Ladysmith........J-6
Laforce (147)........E-3
Laforge........J-2
Lambton (1,584)........J-15
Landrienne (977)........G-1
Laniel (69)........G-2

Lanoraie (4,447)........J-11
Lantier (428)........J-10
Laterrière........D-15
Latulipe-et-Gaboury (304)........F-1
Laval (401,553)........*F-50
Lavaltrie (13,267)........J-11
Lawrenceville (652)........K-13
Le Bic........C-18
Lebel-sur-Quévillon (2,159)........K-1
Leclercville (477)........H-14
Lennoxville........K-14
Les Bergeronnes (693)........D-17
Les-des-Plages (522)........I-9
Les-Éboulements........F-16
Les Escoumins (2,013)........C-13
Les Méchins (986)........B-16
Lingwick (399)........J-15
Longue-Five (Sault-au-Mouton) (1,113)........C-18
Longueuil (231,409)........*G-54
Lorraineville (1,272)........F-1
Lotbinière (887)........H-14
Louiseville (7,517)........I-12
Lourdes-du-Blanc-Sablon (780)........F-16
Louvicourt........D-4
Low (920)........J-7
Lyster (1,628)........H-14
Lévis (138,769)........*D-52
Lytton........E-1
Macamic (1,075)........C-2
Magog (25,358)........K-13
Malartic (3,449)........D-4
Manic-Cinq........A-14, K-2
Maniwaki (3,930)........H-7, L-1
Martinville (469)........K-14
Mashteuiatsh (2,213)........C-13
Masson-Angers........J-8
Matagami........K-1
Matane (14,462)........L-3, B-15
Mayo (572)........I-8
McWatters........D-2
Messines (1,608)........I-7
Milan (270)........J-15
Mistissini........K-2
Moffet (196)........F-2
Moisie........A-16
Mont-Apica........D-13
Mont-Brun........C-3
Mont-Carmel........F-17
Mont-Laurier (13,779)........H-8, L-1
Mont-Royal (19,503)........*G-51
Mont-St-Hilaire (18,200)........J-12
Mont-St-Michel (633)........G-8
Mont-St-Pierre (192)........B-16
Mont-Tremblant (9,494)........I-9
Mont-Tremblant (St-Jovite)........L-1, I-9
Montauban-les-Mines........H-13
Montbeillard........D-2
Montcerf-Lytton (687)........H-7
Montebello (978)........J-9
Montmagny (11,491)........G-16
Montpellier (986)........J-8
Montréal (1,649,519)........L-2, *H-51, *K-53, K-11

Montréal-Ouest (5,085)........*H-51
Morin-Heights (3,925)........J-10
Murdochville (764)........B-16
Namur (596)........J-8
Napierville (3,525)........K-11
Natashquan (841)........K-3, A-18
Nemiscau........K-1
Neuville (3,888)........H-14
Nicolet (7,828)........I-13
Nominingue (2,019)........H-9
Norbertville........I-14
Normandin (3,137)........B-13
Norméral (856)........B-2
North Hatley (752)........K-14
Notre-Dame-de-Ham (414)........I-14
Notre-Dame-de-Pontmain (720)........I-8
Notre-Dame-de-la-Paix (978)........J-8
Notre-Dame-de-la-Salette (757)........J-8
Notre-Dame-des-Bois (911)........J-16
Notre-Dame-du-Bon-Conseil (1,404)........I-13
Notre-Dame-du-Laus (1,518)........I-8
Notre-Dame-du-Nord (1,075)........E-1
Nédélec (403)........E-1
Obaska........C-4
Oka (3,575)........K-10
Orford (3,575)........K-13
Ormstown (3,595)........K-10
Otter Lake (1,109)........J-6
Outremont........*G-52
Palmarolle (1,465)........C-2
Papineauville (2,165)........J-9
Percé (3,312)........C-17
Petit-Saguenay (727)........D-17
Pike-River (525)........K-12
Pintendre........F-16
Piopolis (364)........J-16
Plessisville (6,688)........I-14
Pointe-Claire (30,790)........*H-49, K-11
Pointe-Fortune (542)........J-10
Pointe-au-Pic........F-17
Pointe-aux-Anglais........A-15
Pointe-du-Lac........I-12
Poltimore........J-7
Pont-Rouge (8,723)........G-14
Pontiac (5,681)........J-7
Port-Cartier (6,651)........A-15
Port-Menier........A-17, K-3
Portage-du-Fort (266)........J-6
Portneuf (3,107)........H-14
Portneuf-sur-Mer (761)........B-14, C-18
Potton (Mansonville) (1,849)........L-13
Preissac (786)........C-3
Princeville (5,693)........I-14
Prévost (12,171)........J-10
Quaqtaq........I-1
Quyon........J-6
Québec (516,622)........L-2, *D-52

Radisson........J-1
Rapid Lake........G-6
Rawdon (10,416)........J-11
Repentigny (82,000)........*G-55
Richmond (3,275)........J-14
Rigaud (7,346)........K-10
Rimouski (46,860)........C-18
Ripon (1,522)........J-8
Rivière-Au-Tonnerre (307)........A-17
Rivière-Beaudette (188)........K-10
Rivière-Bleue (1,299)........E-18
Rivière-Éternité (557)........D-16
Rivière-Pierre (671)........H-13
Rivière-Rouge (4,012)........I-9
Roberval (10,227)........C-14
Robertsonville (1,265)........I-15
Rollet........D-2
Roquemaure (161)........B-2
Rouyn-Noranda (41,012)........D-2
Roxton Falls (1,265)........J-13
Roxton Pond (3,786)........K-12
Sacré-Cœur-Saguenay........D-16
Saguenay (154,601)........C-15
Saint-Canut........J-10
Saint-Gérard........J-15
Saint-Paul-de-Montminy (824)........G-16
Salaberry-de-Valleyfield (40,077)........K-10
Salluit........H-1
Sawyerville (769)........K-14
Schefferville (237)........A-18
Scotstown (547)........J-15
Senneterre (2,968)........D-4
Sept-Îles (25,686)........A-16
Shannon (5,086)........G-14
Shawinigan (50,060)........H-12
Shawville (1,664)........J-6
Sorel-Tracy (154,601)........I-11
South Bolton........K-13
St-Adalbert (518)........G-16
St-Adolphe-d'Howard (3,472)........J-10
St-Agapit (3,567)........H-14
St-Aimé-du-Lac (778)........I-8
St-Alban (1,225)........H-13
St-Albert (1,526)........I-13
St-Alexandre (2,495)........K-12

## QUÉBEC

1:1,584,000
Scale in Kilometers
25 · 0 · 25
Scale in Miles

### QUÉBEC ORIENTATION

1:16,790,400
Scale in Kilometers
66.2 · 0 · 66.2
Scale in Miles
66.2 · 0 · 66.2

LEGEND

- TransCanadian Highway
- Controlled Access Hwy
- Controlled Access Hwy Toll
- Wildlife Refuge
- Nat'l/Prov Park
- National Forest

xandre-de-
nouraska
50)...........E-17
xis-des-Monts
46)...........H-12
honse
25)...........K-12
broise
46)...........C-15
broise-de-Kildare
47)...........I-11
cet (2,523). . .K-10
selme (3,458).H-15
oine-Abbé. . . .L-10
oine-de-Tilly
04)...........H-14
onin (4,027). .E-18
ène (1,253). .D-18
bert (1,409). . .F-17
gustin (478). . .C-14
gustin-de-
smaures
141).........*C-50
gustin-de-Woburn
5)...........K-16
njamin (891). . .I-16
rnard-de-Lacolle
77)...........L-11
rnard-sur-Mer..F-16
naventure
17)...........I-12
niface (4,511).H-12
no (2,636). . .C-14
mille (511).....J-14
nstant
980)..........K-11
ille-de-Wendover
89)...........I-13
estin (781). . . .I-13
saire (5,686). .K-12
me (2,198).....I-11
nis-sur-Richelieu
85)...........J-12
minique-du-
saire (434)......B-4
nat (4,130). . .H-10
ouard-de-
re..............F-1
ile-de-Suffolk. . .I-9
rem-de-
uce...........I-15
rit (1,963). . . .J-11
gène-de-Guigues
4)..............E-1
stache
154)..........J-10
bien-de-Panet
2)............H-17
ustin-Lac-Carré
85).............I-9
dinand
67)...........I-14
éle-de-Mont-
ray...........E-17
nçois-de-Sales
4)............D-13
nçois-du-Lac
57)...........I-12
gence
49)..........C-15
icien
278)..........C-13
ix-d'Otis
1)............D-16
x-de-Valois
29)............I-11
briel (2,844). . .I-11
briel-de-Valcartier
33)...........G-14
orges
173)..........I-16
orges-de-Windsor
)..............J-14
St-Germain-de-Grantham (4,551)...........J-13
St-Gervais (2,058). .G-15
St-Gilles (2,138). . . .H-15
St-Gédéon-de-Beauce (2,277)...........J-16
St-Gérard-de-Berry. .B-3
St-Henri (5,023). . . .H-15
St-Henri-de-Taillon (760).............C-14
St-Hermas..........J-10
St-Herménégilde (702).............K-14
St-Hilarion (1,181). .E-16
St-Honoré-de-Témiscouata (780).............E-18
St-Hubert-de-Rivière-du-Loup (1,235).....E-18
St-Hyacinthe (53,236)..........J-12
St-Ignace-du-Lac. . .H-11
St-Irénée (674).....E-16
St-Jacques (4,021). .I-11
St-Jean-Port-Joli. . . .F-16
St-Jean-de-Dieu (1,606)...........D-18
St-Jean-de-Matha (4,335)............I-11
St-Jean-sur-Richelieu (92,394)..........K-12
St-Jean-sur-le-Lac. . .H-8
St-Joachim-de-Montmorency. . . .G-16
St-Joseph-de-Beauce (4,722)...........H-15
St-Joseph-de-la-Rive..............F-16
St-Just-de-Bretenières (709).............H-17
St-Jérôme (68,456)..J-10
St-Lambert (21,555).........*G-53
St-Laurent.........*G-51
St-Louis-de-Blandford (903)..............I-14
St-Ludger (1,255). . .J-16
St-Léon-de-Standon (1,128)...........H-16
St-Léonard.........*E-52
St-Léonard-d'Aston (2,271)............I-13
St-Léonard-de-Portneuf (1,019)...........G-14
St-Magloire (725). . .H-16
St-Malachie (1,489)...........H-16
St-Malo (483).......K-15
St-Marc-sur-Richelieu (2,050)............J-12
St-Marcel-De-L'islet............G-17
St-Martin (2,462). . . .I-16
St-Michel-des-Saints (2,201)...........H-10
St-Nazaire (2,114). .C-14
St-Ours (1,721).....J-12
St-Pamphile (2,685)...........G-17
St-Pascal (3,490). . .E-17
St-Paulin (1,534). . .H-12
St-Philippe (5,495). .K-11
St-Philémon (742). .H-16
St-Pie (5,438).......J-12
St-Pierre-Baptiste (485)..............I-14
St-Prime (2,758). . . .C-13
St-Raphael (2,463).G-16
St-Raymond (9,615)...........G-14
St-Roch-de-Mékinac (438).............G-12
St-Roch-des-Aulnaies (967).............F-17
St-Rémi (7,265).....K-11
St-Sauveur (9,881). .J-10
St-Siméon (1,179). .E-17
St-Sylvestre (1,035)...........H-15
St-Sylvère (865).....I-13
St-Sébastien (736). .J-15
St-Théophile (743). .I-16
St-Tite..............H-13
St-Tite-des-Caps (1,506)...........F-16
St-Ubalde (1,403). .G-13
St-Urbain (1,474). . .E-16
St-Vallier (1,046). . .G-16
St-Zacharie (1,751). .I-16
St-Zotique (6,773). .K-10
St-Zénon (1,115). . .H-11
Stanbridge East (873).............K-12
Stanhope...........L-14
Stanstead (2,857). . .L-14
Ste-Adèle (12,137). .I-10
Ste-Agathe-des-Monts (10,115)...........I-10
Ste-Anne-de-Beaupré (2,803)...........G-15
Ste-Anne-de-Bellevue (5,073)...........K-10
Ste-Anne-des-Monts (6,933)......L-3, B-16
Ste-Anne-du-Lac (619)..............G-8
Ste-Barbe (1,403). .K-10
Ste-Catherine-de-la-Jacques-Cartier (6,319)...........G-14
Ste-Christine-d'Auvergne (448).............G-14
Ste-Claire (3,325). .H-15
Ste-Croix (2,352). . .H-14
Ste-Dorothée........J-11
Ste-Émélie-de-l'Énergie (1,644)............I-11
Ste-Eulalie (871). . . .I-13
Ste-Flavie (919). . . .B-15
Ste-Jeanne-d'Arc (1,089)...........B-13
Ste-Julie (30,104). . .J-11
Ste-Justine (1,845)..H-16
Ste-Justine-de-Newton (973).............K-10
Ste-Lucie-de-Beauregard (304).............G-17
Ste-Marie (12,889)..H-15
Ste-Martine (4,966)..K-11
Ste-Perpétue (1,774)...........G-17
Ste-Pétronille (1,041)..........*A-54
Ste-Rose-de-Watford (787).............H-16
Ste-Rose-du-Nord (413).............C-16
Ste-Sabine (1,120)..K-12
Ste-Thècle (2,478)..G-13
Ste-Thérèse (26,025)..........J-11
Ste-Veronique.......H-9
Stoke (2,765).......J-14
Stoneham..........G-15
Stornoway (559). . . .J-15
Sutton (3,906)......K-13
Tadoussac (813)........D-17, L-2
Taschereau (981). . . .C-3
Tasiujaq..............I-2
Terrebonne (106,322).........J-11
Thetford Mines (25,709)...........I-15
Thurso (2,455).......J-8
Tourville (633)......F-17
Tracy...............I-12
Trois-Pistoles (3,456)..........D-18
Trois-Rivières (131,338)...L-2, H-13
Trécessom (Villemontel)......C-3
Témiscaming.......G-2
Umiujaq.............J-1
Upton (2,075)......J-12
Val-David (4,450). . .I-10
Val-des-Bois (938). .J-8
Val-Senneville......D-4
Val-St-Gilles (178). .B-2
Val-d'Or (31,862).....L-1, D-4
Valcourt (2,349). . . .J-13
Vallée-Jonction. . . .H-15
Vassan..............D-4
Vaudreuil-Dorion (33,305).........K-10
Verdun............*H-52
Victoriaville (43,462).........I-14
Ville-Marie (2,595). .F-1
Villeroy (485)......H-14
Wakefield...........J-7
Waltham (384).......I-5
Warwick (4,766). . . .I-14
Waskaganish........K-1
Waswanipi..........K-1
Waterloo (4,330)...K-13
Weedon (2,683)....J-15
Weir.................I-9
Wemindji............K-1
Wendake..........*A-51
West Brome........K-13
Westmount (19,931).*G-52, *L-52
Wickham (2,470)...J-13
Windsor (5,367)....J-14
Yamaska (1,644). . .I-12

NA138-17

# Atlantic Provinces

| Driving Distances in Kilometers | Campbellton, NB | Channel-Port aux Basques, NL | Charlottetown, PE | Fredericton, NB | Halifax, NS | Moncton, NB | New Glasgow, NS | Port Hastings, NS | Saint John, NB | St. John's, NL | Sydney, NS | Yarmouth, NS |
|---|---|---|---|---|---|---|---|---|---|---|---|---|
| Charlottetown, PE | 442 | 540 | | 343 | 330 | 165 | 114 | 219 | 317 | 1440 | 355 | 536 |
| Fredericton, NB | 360 | 831 | 343 | | 440 | 179 | 404 | 510 | 113 | 1730 | 645 | 291 |
| Halifax, NS | 564 | 589 | 330 | 440 | | 261 | 158 | 266 | 405 | 1489 | 401 | 304 |
| Saint John, NB | 474 | 804 | 317 | 113 | 405 | 134 | 378 | 483 | | 1704 | 619 | 184 |
| St. John's, NL | 1855 | 904 | 1440 | 1730 | 1489 | 1554 | 1329 | 1222 | 1704 | | 1107 | 1784 |

See also mileage table page 2

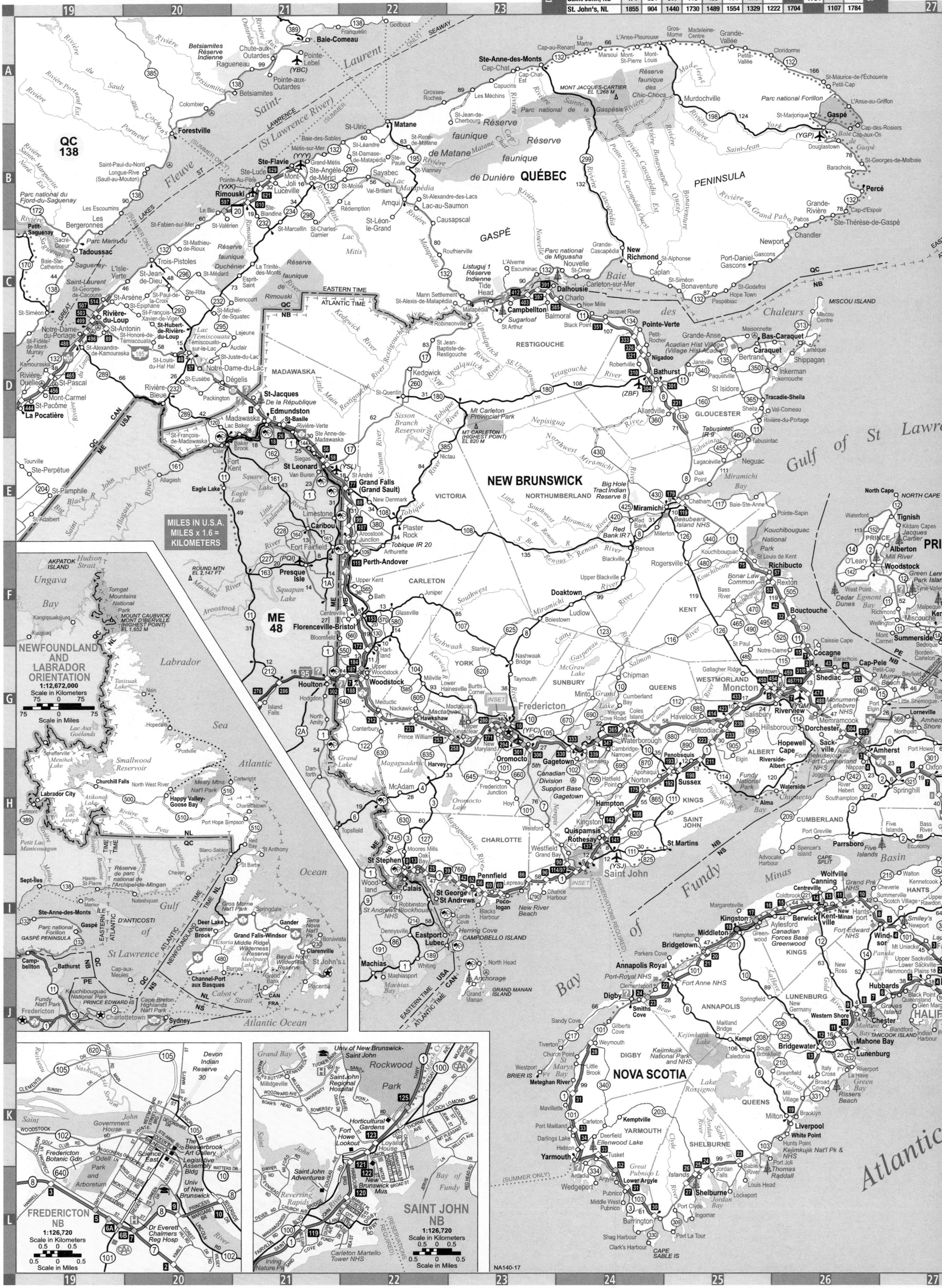

LEGEND
TransCanadian Highway — Wildlife Refuge
Controlled Access Hwy — Nat'l/Prov Park
Controlled Access Hwy Toll — National Forest

# ATLANTIC PROVINCES & GASPÉ PENINSULA

## NEW BRUNSWICK, NEWFOUNDLAND AND LABRADOR, NOVA SCOTIA, QUÉBEC, PRINCE EDWARD ISLAND

1:1,932,480
Scale in Kilometers
Scale in Miles

NA140-17

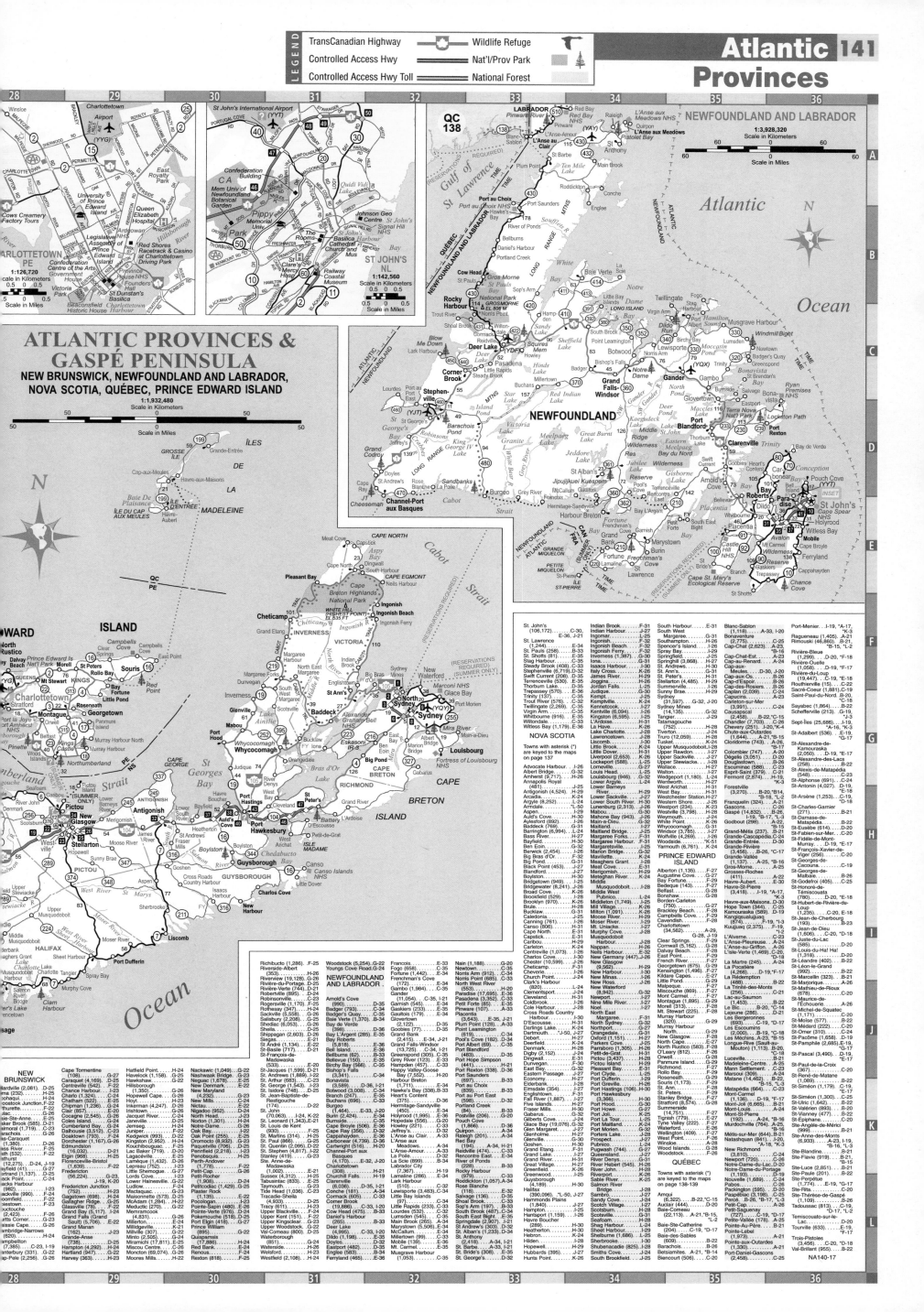

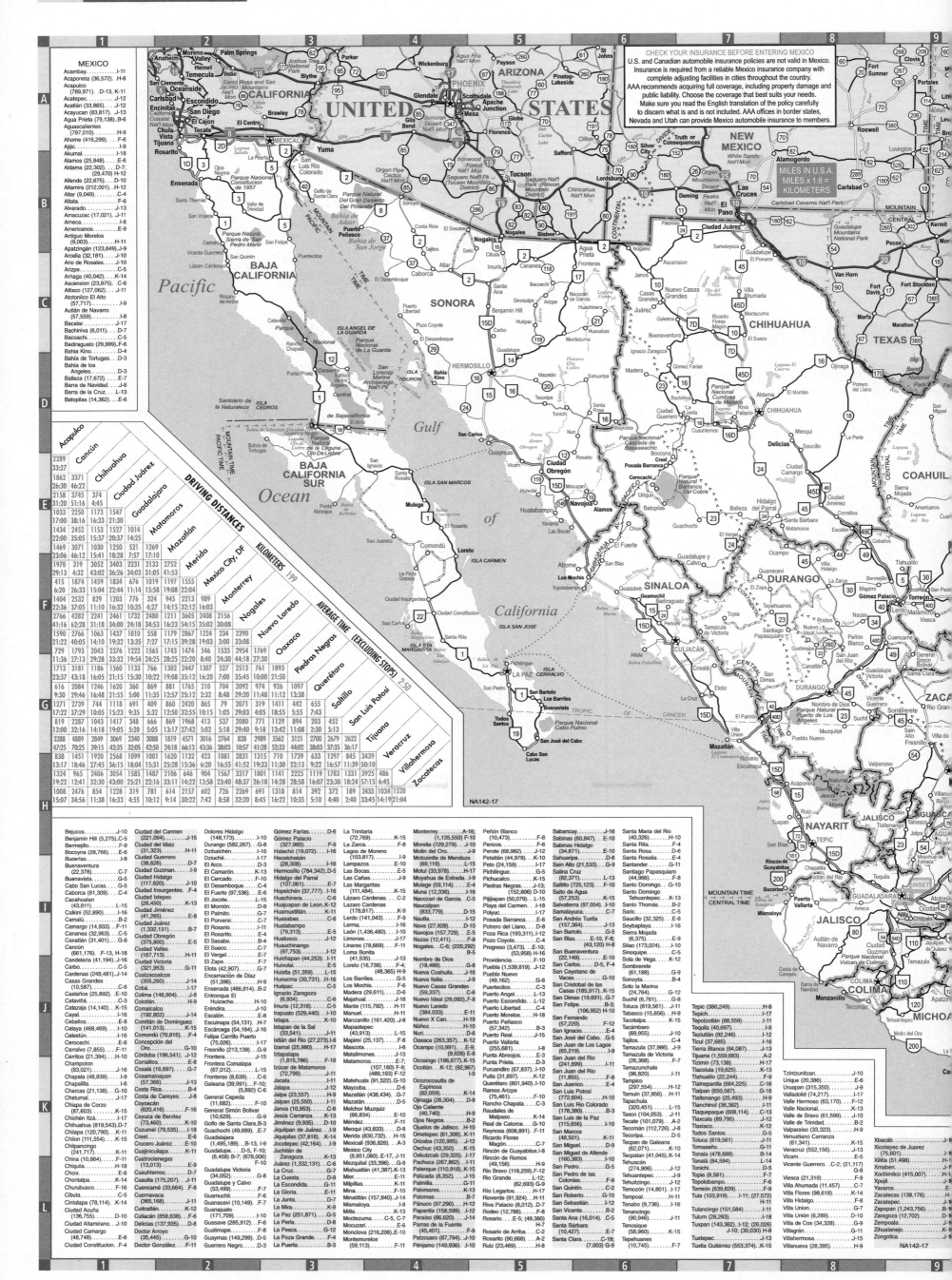

DRIVING DISTANCES

KILOMETERS 199

AVERAGE TIME (EXCLUDING STOPS) 2:50

| | Acapulco | Cancún | Chihuahua | Ciudad Juárez | Guadalajara | Matamoros | Mazatlán | Merida | Mexico City, DF | Monterrey | Nogales | Nuevo Laredo | Oaxaca | Piedras Negras | Querétaro | Saltillo | San Luis Potosí | Tijuana | Veracruz | Villahermosa |
|---|---|---|---|---|---|---|---|---|---|---|---|---|---|---|---|---|---|---|---|---|
| Cancún | 2289 33:27 | | | | | | | | | | | | | | | | | | | |
| Chihuahua | 1862 26:30 | 3371 46:22 | | | | | | | | | | | | | | | | | | |
| Ciudad Juárez | 2158 31:20 | 3745 51:16 | 374 4:45 | | | | | | | | | | | | | | | | | |
| Guadalajara | 1033 17:00 | 2250 38:16 | 1173 16:33 | 1547 21:30 | | | | | | | | | | | | | | | | |
| Matamoros | 1434 22:00 | 2452 35:05 | 1153 15:37 | 1527 20:37 | 1014 14:25 | | | | | | | | | | | | | | | |
| Mazatlán | 1469 23:06 | 3071 46:12 | 1030 15:41 | 1250 18:28 | 521 7:57 | 1269 17:10 | | | | | | | | | | | | | | |
| Merida | 1970 29:13 | 319 4:32 | 3052 43:02 | 3403 36:26 | 2231 34:03 | 2133 31:05 | 2752 41:53 | | | | | | | | | | | | | |
| Mexico City, DF | 415 6:20 | 1874 26:33 | 1459 15:04 | 1834 22:44 | 676 11:14 | 1019 15:58 | 1197 19:08 | 1555 22:04 | | | | | | | | | | | | |
| Monterrey | 1404 22:36 | 2532 37:05 | 829 11:10 | 1203 16:32 | 776 10:35 | 324 4:27 | 945 14:15 | 2213 32:12 | 989 16:03 | | | | | | | | | | | |
| Nogales | 2766 41:16 | 4282 62:28 | 2241 31:18 | 2461 34:00 | 1732 24:18 | 2480 34:53 | 1211 16:23 | 3605 54:15 | 2408 35:02 | 2156 30:08 | | | | | | | | | | |
| Nuevo Laredo | 1590 21:22 | 2766 40:05 | 1063 14:10 | 1437 19:32 | 1010 13:35 | 558 7:27 | 1179 17:15 | 2867 39:28 | 1224 19:03 | 234 3:00 | 2390 33:08 | | | | | | | | | |
| Oaxaca | 729 11:36 | 1793 27:13 | 2043 29:28 | 2376 33:32 | 1222 19:54 | 1565 24:25 | 1743 28:25 | 1474 22:20 | 546 8:40 | 1535 24:30 | 2954 44:18 | 1769 27:30 | | | | | | | | |
| Piedras Negras | 1713 23:37 | 3181 43:18 | 1186 16:05 | 1560 21:15 | 1133 15:30 | 766 10:22 | 1302 19:08 | 2447 35:12 | 1307 16:20 | 527 7:00 | 2513 35:45 | 761 10:00 | 1893 21:50 | | | | | | | |
| Querétaro | 616 9:30 | 2084 29:46 | 1246 16:48 | 1620 21:55 | 360 5:00 | 869 11:35 | 881 12:57 | 1765 25:12 | 210 2:32 | 704 8:48 | 2092 29:20 | 974 11:48 | 926 11:12 | 1097 13:38 | | | | | | |
| Saltillo | 1271 17:22 | 2739 37:29 | 744 10:05 | 1118 15:23 | 691 9:35 | 409 5:32 | 860 12:50 | 2420 32:55 | 865 10:15 | 79 1:05 | 2071 29:03 | 319 4:05 | 1411 18:55 | 442 5:55 | 655 7:43 | | | | | |
| San Luis Potosí | 819 12:00 | 2287 32:16 | 1043 14:18 | 1417 19:05 | 348 5:20 | 666 5:05 | 869 13:17 | 1968 27:42 | 413 5:02 | 537 5:18 | 2080 29:40 | 771 9:18 | 1129 13:42 | 894 11:08 | 203 2:30 | 452 5:13 | | | | |
| Tijuana | 3288 47:25 | 4889 70:25 | 2849 39:15 | 3069 42:35 | 2340 32:05 | 3088 42:50 | 1819 24:18 | 4571 66:13 | 3016 43:36 | 2764 38:03 | 828 10:57 | 2989 41:28 | 3562 52:33 | 3121 44:02 | 2700 38:03 | 2679 37:35 | 2622 36:17 | | | |
| Veracruz | 838 13:17 | 1451 18:46 | 1920 27:45 | 2568 36:15 | 1099 18:04 | 1001 15:31 | 1620 25:28 | 1132 15:36 | 423 6:20 | 1081 16:55 | 2831 41:52 | 1315 19:33 | 710 11:30 | 1739 22:13 | 633 9:22 | 1297 16:57 | 845 11:39 | 3439 50:10 | | |
| Villahermosa | 1324 19:22 | 965 12:41 | 2406 32:30 | 3054 43:00 | 1585 25:21 | 1487 22:16 | 2106 33:11 | 646 14:22 | 904 13:58 | 1567 23:40 | 3317 48:37 | 1801 26:18 | 1141 14:28 | 2225 28:58 | 1119 16:07 | 1783 23:38 | 1331 18:24 | 3925 57:15 | 486 6:45 | |
| Zacatecas | 1008 15:07 | 2476 34:56 | 854 11:38 | 1228 16:33 | 319 4:55 | 781 10:12 | 614 9:14 | 2157 30:22 | 602 7:42 | 726 8:58 | 2269 32:20 | 691 8:45 | 1318 16:22 | 814 10:35 | 392 5:10 | 372 4:40 | 189 2:40 | 2433 33:45 | 1034 14:19 | 1520 21:04 |

NA142-17

NA142-17

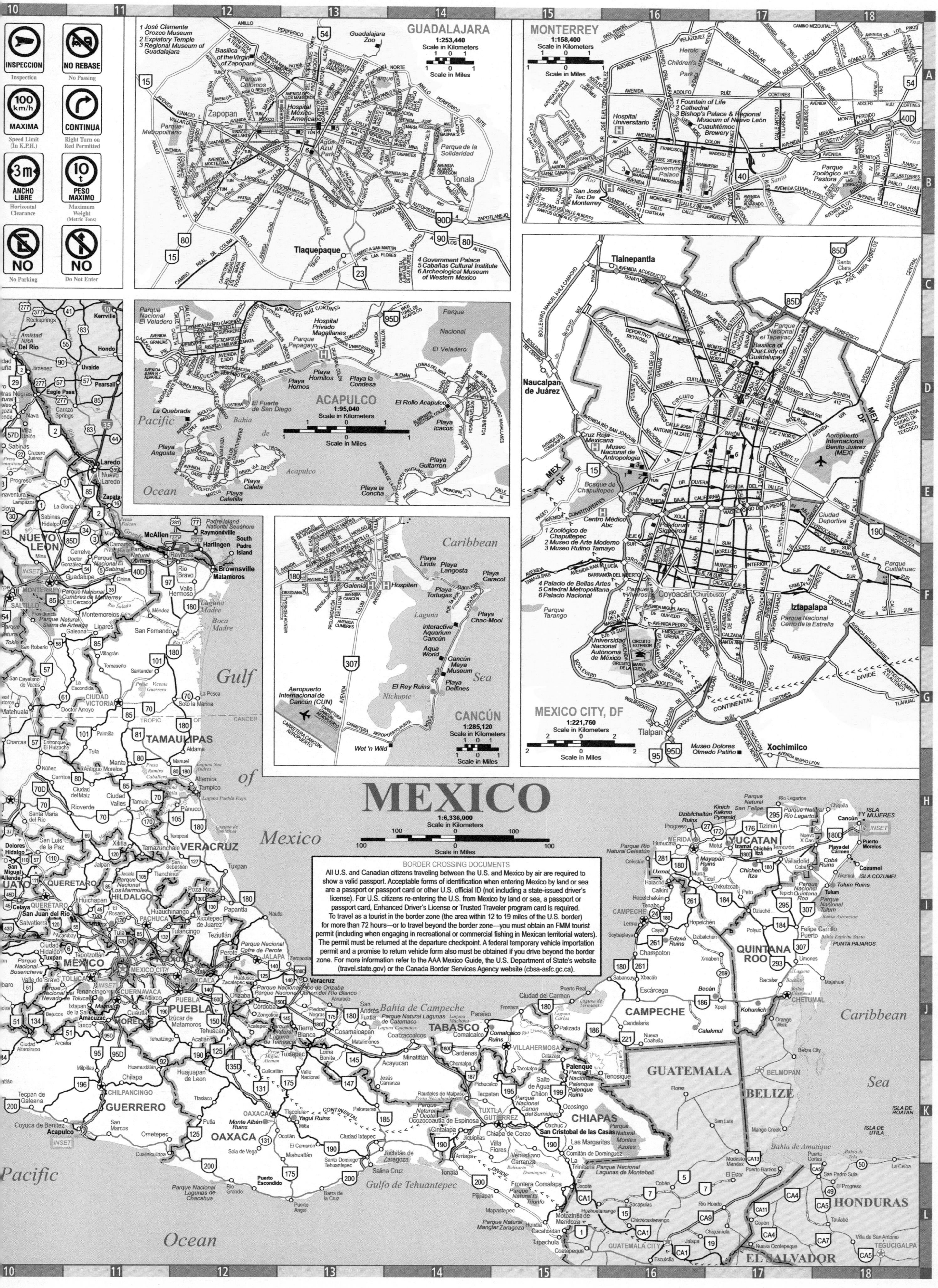
INSPECCION
Inspection
NO REBASE
No Passing
100 km/h MAXIMA
Speed Limit (In K.P.H.)
CONTINUA
Right Turn on Red Permitted
3m ANCHO LIBRE
Horizontal Clearance
10 t PESO MAXIMO
Maximum Weight (Metric Tons)
NO
No Parking
NO
Do Not Enter
GUADALAJARA
1:253,440
Scale in Kilometers
Scale in Miles
1 José Clemente Orozco Museum
2 Expiatory Temple
3 Regional Museum of Guadalajara
4 Government Palace
5 Cabañas Cultural Institute
6 Archeological Museum of Western Mexico
Zapopan
Tlaquepaque
Tonala
MONTERREY
1:158,400
Scale in Kilometers
Scale in Miles
1 Fountain of Life
2 Cathedral
3 Bishop's Palace & Regional Museum of Nuevo León
ACAPULCO
1:95,040
Scale in Kilometers
Scale in Miles
Pacific Ocean
Bahia de Acapulco
CANCÚN
1:285,120
Scale in Kilometers
Scale in Miles
Caribbean Sea
MEXICO CITY, DF
1:221,760
Scale in Kilometers
Scale in Miles
1 Zoológico de Chapultepec
2 Museo Nacional de Arte Moderno
3 Museo Rufino Tamayo
4 Palacio de Bellas Artes
5 Catedral Metropolitana
6 Palacio Nacional
Tlalnepantla
Naucalpan de Juárez
Coyoacán
Iztapalapa
Tlalpan
Xochimilco
MEXICO
1:6,336,000
Scale in Kilometers
Scale in Miles
BORDER CROSSING DOCUMENTS
All U.S. and Canadian citizens traveling between the U.S. and Mexico by air are required to show a valid passport. Acceptable forms of identification when entering Mexico by land or sea are a passport or passport card or other U.S. official ID (not including a state-issued driver's license). For U.S. citizens re-entering the U.S. from Mexico by land or sea, a passport or passport card, Enhanced Driver's License or Trusted Traveler program card is required.
To travel as a tourist in the border zone (the area within 12 to 19 miles of the U.S. border) for more than 72 hours—or to travel beyond the border zone—you must obtain an FMM tourist permit (including when engaging in recreational or commercial fishing in Mexican territorial waters). The permit must be returned at the departure checkpoint. A federal temporary vehicle importation permit and a promise to return vehicle form also must be obtained if you drive beyond the border zone. For more information refer to the AAA Mexico Guide, the U.S. Department of State's website (travel.state.gov) or the Canada Border Services Agency website (cbsa-asfc.gc.ca).
Gulf of Mexico
NUEVO LEON
TAMAULIPAS
VERACRUZ
HIDALGO
QUERETARO
MEXICO
PUEBLA
TLAXCALA
MORELOS
GUERRERO
OAXACA
CHIAPAS
TABASCO
CAMPECHE
YUCATAN
QUINTANA ROO
GUATEMALA
BELIZE
HONDURAS
EL SALVADOR
Bahia de Campeche
Gulfo de Tehuantepec
Caribbean Sea
Pacific Ocean

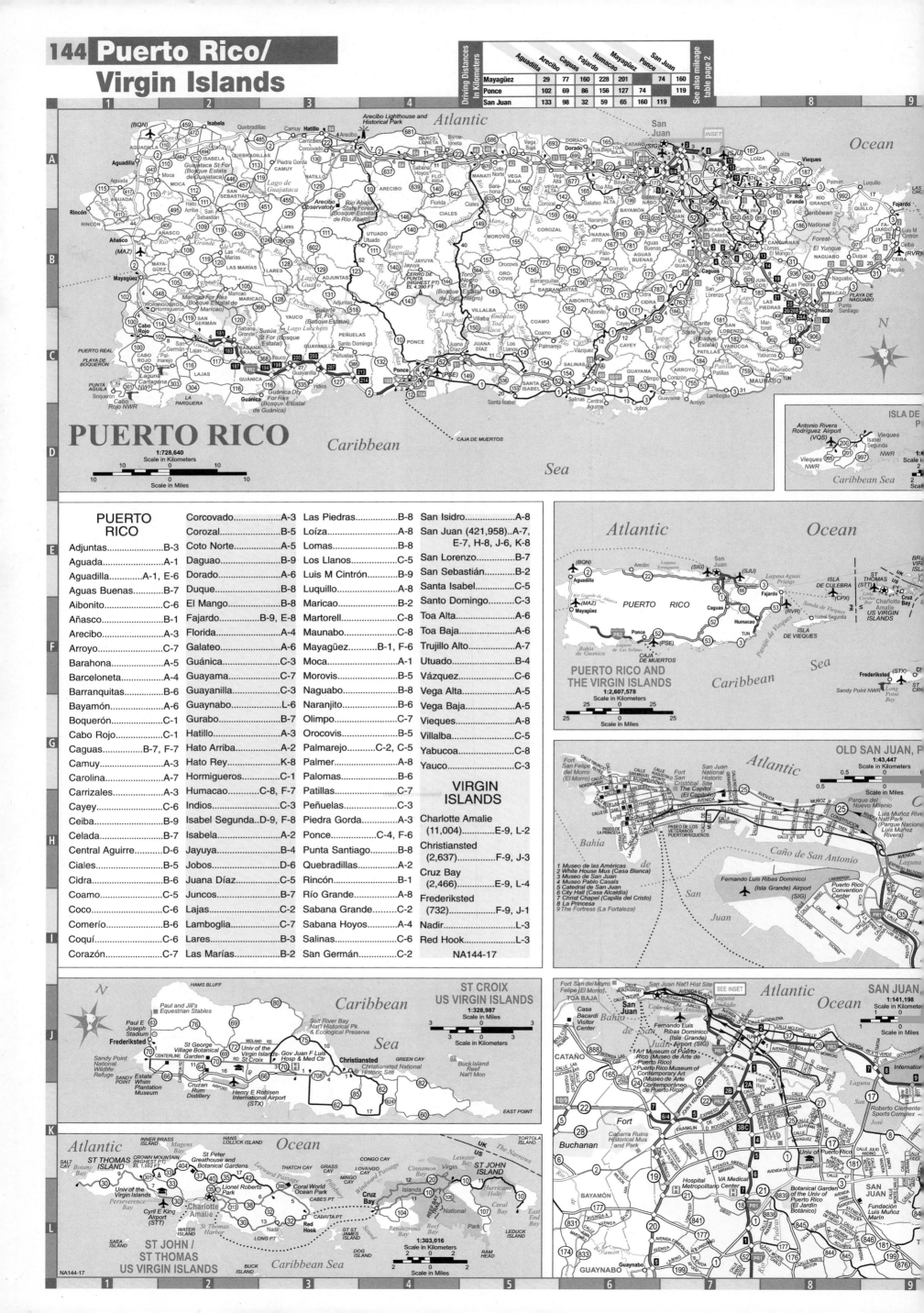

| Driving Distances in Kilometers | Aguadilla | Arecibo | Caguas | Fajardo | Humacao | Mayagüez | Ponce | San Juan |
|---|---|---|---|---|---|---|---|---|
| Mayagüez | 29 | 77 | 160 | 228 | 201 | | 74 | 160 |
| Ponce | 102 | 69 | 86 | 156 | 127 | 74 | | 119 |
| San Juan | 133 | 98 | 32 | 59 | 65 | 160 | 119 | |

See also mileage table page 2

**PUERTO RICO** — 1:728,640

**PUERTO RICO AND THE VIRGIN ISLANDS** — 1:2,607,578

**OLD SAN JUAN, P** — 1:43,447

**ST CROIX US VIRGIN ISLANDS** — 1:328,987

**SAN JUAN,** — 1:141,198

**ST JOHN / ST THOMAS US VIRGIN ISLANDS** — 1:303,016

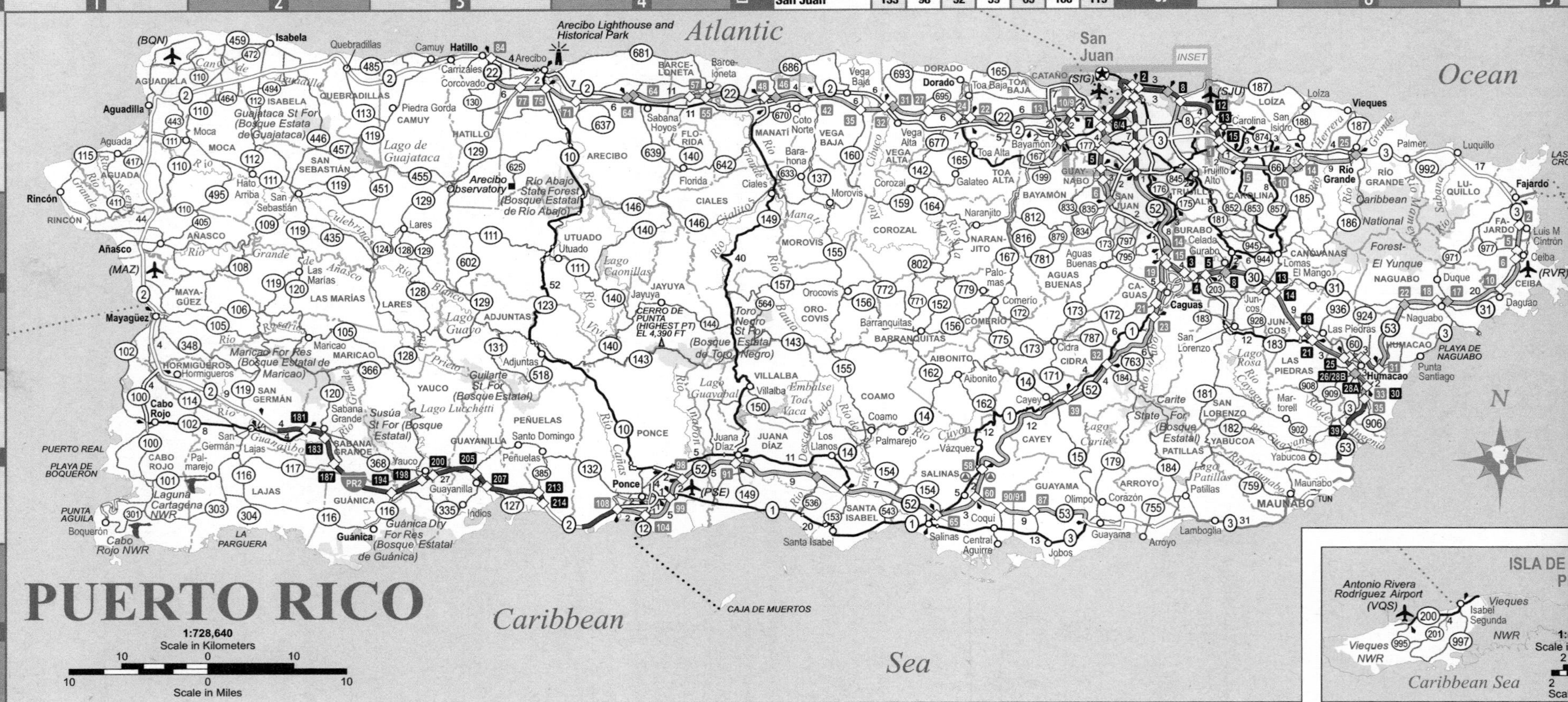

NA144-17

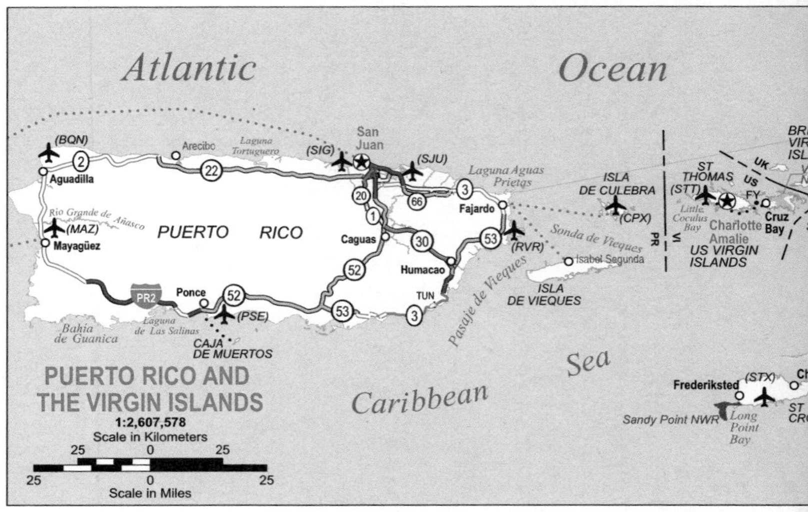

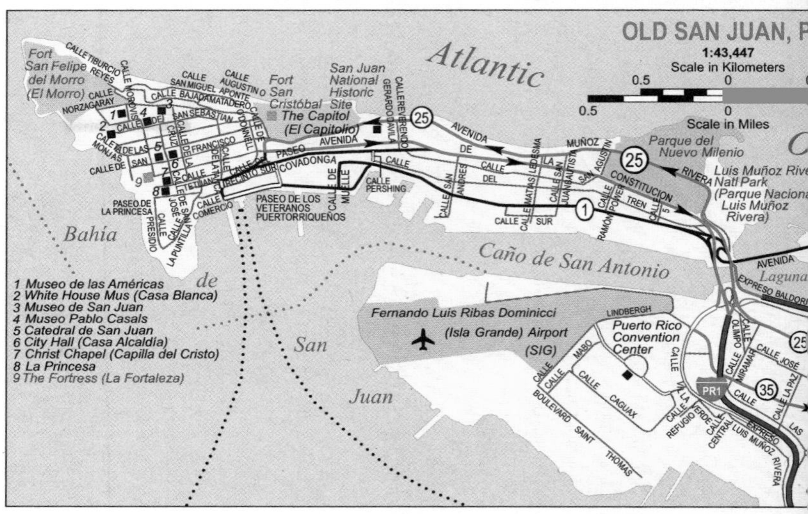

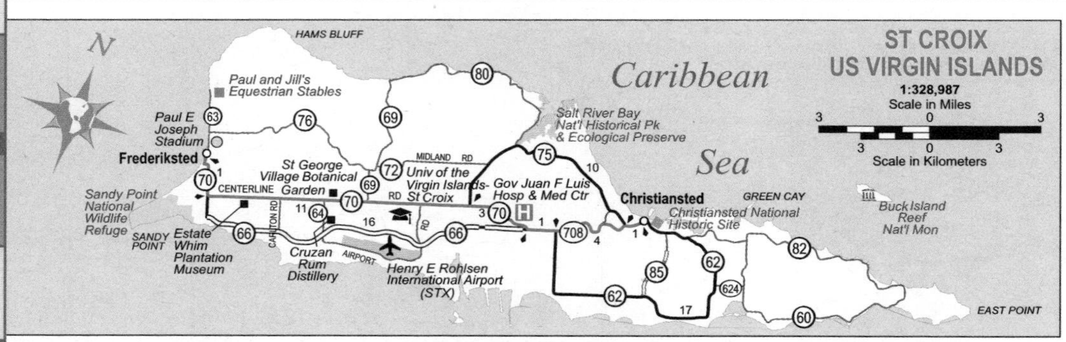

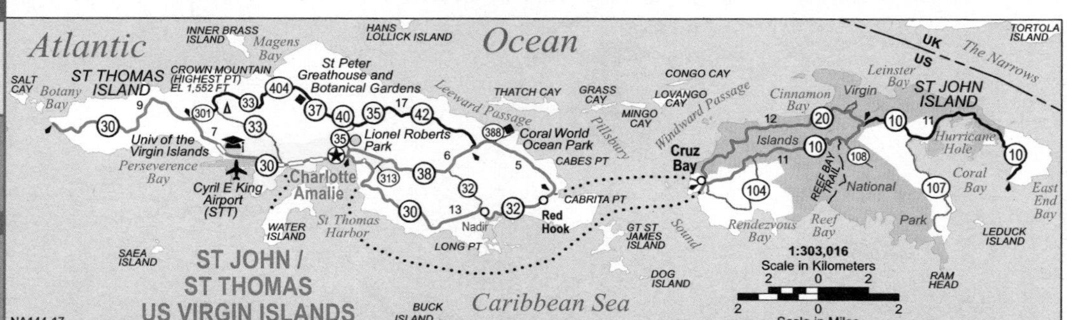

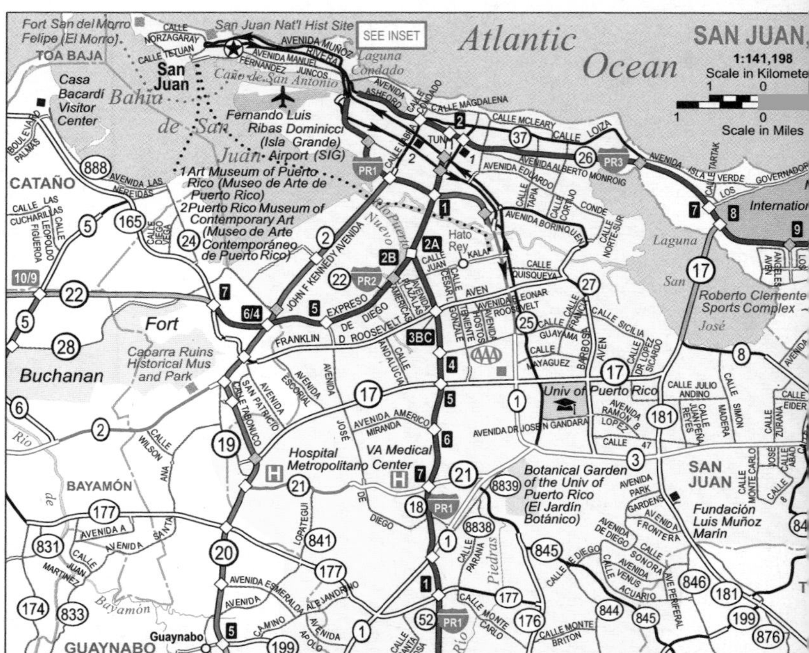